D0078942

About Island Press

Island Press is the only nonprofit organization in the United States whose principal purpose is the publication of books on environmental issues and natural resource management. We provide solutions-oriented information to professionals, public officials, business and community leaders, and concerned citizens who are shaping responses to environmental problems.

In 2004, Island Press celebrates its twentieth anniversary as the leading provider of timely and practical books that take a multidisciplinary approach to critical environmental concerns. Our growing list of titles reflects our commitment to bringing the best of an expanding body of literature to the environmental community throughout North America and the world.

Support for Island Press is provided by the Agua Fund, Brainerd Foundation, Geraldine R. Dodge Foundation, Doris Duke Charitable Foundation, Educational Foundation of America, The Ford Foundation, The George Gund Foundation, The William and Flora Hewlett Foundation, Henry Luce Foundation, The John D. and Catherine T. MacArthur Foundation, The Andrew W. Mellon Foundation, The Curtis and Edith Munson Foundation, National Environmental Trust, National Fish and Wildlife Foundation, The New-Land Foundation, Oak Foundation, The Overbrook Foundation, The David and Lucile Packard Foundation, The Pew Charitable Trusts, The Rockefeller Foundation, The Winslow Foundation, and other generous donors.

The opinions expressed in this book are those of the author(s) and do not necessarily reflect the views of these foundations.

Environmental Land Use Planning and Management

John Randolph

ISLAND PRESS
Washington · Covelo · London

Copyright © 2004 John Randolph

All rights reserved under International and Pan-American Copyright Conventions. No part of this book may be reproduced in any form or by any means without permission in writing from the publisher: Island Press, Suite 300, 1718 Connecticut Ave., NW, Washington, DC 20009.

Island Press is a trademark of The Center for Resource Economics.

Library of Congress Cataloging-in-Publication Data.

Randolph, John.
    Environmental land use planning and management / by John
Randolph.
        p. cm.
    Includes bibliographical references and index.
    ISBN 1-55963-948-2 (cloth : alk. paper)
    1. Land use—Environmental aspects. 2. Land use—
Planning. I. Title.
    HD108.3.R36 2003
    333.73—dc22   2003017156

British Cataloguing-in-Publication data available.

Design by Impressions Book and Journal Services, Inc.

Printed on recycled, acid-free paper ♲

Manufactured in the United States of America
10 9 8 7 6 5 4 3 2 1

To my father who taught me the love of work
To my late mother who taught me the love of life

Contents

List of Figures

List of Tables

List of Boxes

Preface

For thousands of years we humans have been learning how to manage our relationship with nature. Every generation creates a new set of circumstances as our population and economy grow, as our impacts on the natural environment increase, and as our knowledge of the consequences of our actions and means of controlling them advance. Every generation must adapt to those circumstances.

The human generations of the past four decades have recognized that their relationship with nature is not sustainable. We have witnessed incredible increases in human population, global economy, and environmental impact. Our patterns of agricultural and forestry production, water use, and energy and mineral consumption cannot be sustained. Our generation of wastes and air and water pollution continues to exceed nature's assimilative capacity.

Our use of the land is also not sustainable. Intensive agriculture required for our growing population and economy continues to overstress the natural land and water systems on which it depends. Land development continues to expose human settlements to natural hazards of flooding, geologic instability, coastal storms, and wildfire. Market-driven metropolitan development in the United States and other countries has spread out in sprawling patterns separating people from work, commerce, culture, and one another; creating unmanageable traffic congestion, transportation energy use, and air pollution; and converting natural and agricultural areas to impervious roads and rooftops. These land use patterns not only affect our human social fabric and the productive natural systems on which our economy depends, but they also damage natural habitats, endangering the biodiversity of desirable and unique wildlife.

Despite these challenges, the good news is that we continue to learn. As our population and impacts on nature have grown, so too have our scientific knowledge, technological capacity to mitigate impacts, and social awareness of the benefits and value of natural systems. Science has continued to improve our understanding of complex natural systems, how we change them, how we can use them for our benefit, and how we can manage them for their benefit. Our evolving social and political system has enhanced our ability to make collective decisions about the use and management of the natural environment.

This book assembles and articulates the current progress in that learning process, focusing on the relationship between human use of the land and the natural environment. What has emerged during the past decade is a diverse, comprehensive, and coordinated approach I call "environmental land use planning and management." This is the current state of an evolution of social environmental values, government policies, market forces, land use practices, development designs, and organizations that shape that relationship. The evolution is not complete. Our hope is that this learning process will continue to teach us new ways of planning and managing a sustainable relationship.

Environmental land use planning and management aims to integrate science and politics in developing effective strategies for land development and conservation. It builds on recent advances in environmental sciences, engineering, and geospatial information technologies that have enhanced understanding and analysis of the land and related hydrological, geological, and ecological systems. This book provides users with a foundation of scientific principles necessary to understand natural land systems as well as engineering approaches necessary to mitigate impacts of land use practices. It describes the use of several land analysis methods used to assess land resources and impacts.

Environmental land use planning and management also builds on the continuing environmental social movement through which increasing numbers of citizens, neighborhood groups, nonprofit organizations, government officials, landowners, planners, designers, and developers have recognized the value and benefits of natural systems. This larger and more diverse set of stakeholders has expanded the means used to improve land development and conservation. These include land use regulations that are an important foundation for effective management. While necessary, regulations are not sufficient to manage the environment effectively, especially when political leanings favor deregulation and property rights protection. They must be complemented by other means such as nonregulatory policies, acquisition of land or development rights, land trusts, environmental design, and voluntary monitoring, land stewardship, and land restoration.

In addition, environmental land use planning and management builds on enhanced democratization and collaborative decision-making processes in which a wider range of stakeholders participate in decisions about the use and protection of the land. Improved collaboration has expanded the domain of land use and environmental decision making from private markets and government approvals to include the guidance of civil society. Emerging approaches like watershed management, ecosystem management, and community-based environmental protection are based on increased stakeholder involvement in addition to improved science. Collaborative processes ensure that environmental objectives are balanced with other social and economic objectives.

This book explains environmental land use planning and management not by what could or should happen but by what *is* happening. The innovations provided by recent plans, designs, regulations, programs, and analytical approaches developed by government agencies, private designers and developers, land trusts, and nonprofit groups, not only illustrate the approaches but also demonstrate the possibilities.

The book is divided into two parts. Part I, "Environmental Land Use Management," introduces broader concepts of environmental planning and describes management approaches. These approaches include collaborative environmental management, land conservation, environmental design, government land use management, natural hazard mitigation, and ecosystem and watershed management.

Part II, "Environmental Land Use Principles and Planning Analysis," focuses on land analysis methods. These methods include geospatial data and geographic information systems (GIS); soils and slope analysis; assessment of stormwater quantity and quality; land use and groundwater protection; ecological assessment for vegetation, wetlands, and habitats; and integrated analytical techniques like land suitability analysis, carrying capacity studies, and environmental impact assessment.

The division between Part I management approaches and Part II analytical methods is not completely distinct. That is, to provide continuity of the discussion, some Part I topics describe analytical techniques, such as conservation easement procedures, environmental design methods, floodplain mapping, and watershed assessment. Likewise, some Part II topics include management approaches, including soil erosion control, stormwater management, urban forestry, wetland mitigation, coastal zone management, and habitat conservation planning.

This text provides a good introduction to environmental planning intended for advanced undergraduates, graduate students, and practitioners. However, it focuses on land use and therefore does not address other important environmental planning issues like air quality, climate change, solid and hazardous waste management, environmental health, and materials and energy conservation. In the interests of space, the book has limited coverage of some land-related issues such as environmental noise, transportation and air quality, energy and land use, public land management, and environmental justice. Users seeking comprehensive coverage of environmental planning or land use planning should complement this text with other references on these topics.

Acknowledgments

This book is the product of many years teaching and researching environmental planning. It assembles a wide range of innovations developed by practitioners in government agencies, private firms, and nonprofit organizations. It is those innovators I gratefully acknowledge. Among federal agencies, the Natural Resources Conservation Service, Environmental Protection Agency, Forest Service, Federal Emergency Management Agency, Fish and Wildlife Service, National Oceanic and Atmospheric Administration, and Geological Survey have sponsored and developed many of the techniques, methods, and information sources presented in this book.

Among state, regional, and local agencies, several innovators have developed model programs for managing land use and development, including Oregon, Maryland, California, Massachusetts, New York, and Washington; Tahoe Regional Planning Agency, San Francisco Bay Conservation and Development Commission, Twin Cities Metro Council (MN), and Pinelands Commission (NJ); Montgomery County (MD), Blacksburg (VA), Boulder (CO), King County (WA), Fairfax County (VA), and Austin (TX), among others.

Innovative developers and designers, including Michael Corbett, Peter Calthorpe, Randall Arendt, Andres Duany, and other New Urbanists, are showing that environmentally and community sensitive land development is highly marketable. Other groups and individuals have contributed consistently to the development of new knowledge and approaches, including Tom Schueler and the Center for Watershed Protection, Fritz Steiner at the University of Texas-Austin, Craig Johnson at the Utah State University, John Forester at Cornell, and others.

Nonprofit environmental groups and land trusts have increasingly complemented government and the private sector. These have been led by national organizations like The Nature Conservancy, Izaak Walton League, Trust for Public Land, and the American Farmland Trust, but the thousands of local and regional land trusts and volunteer environmental and watershed associations also provide excellent models of voluntary action and civic engagement.

This book aims to communicate the activities of these organizations as well as environmental planning concepts through both words and visuals. I gratefully acknowledge the many sources of graphic material that enhance the presentation. These include the many public domain government sources. I especially thank the holders of copyrighted material who gave their permission freely. These include private firms like ESRI, Inc., Calthorpe Associates, King Farm Associates, and Steve Price's Urban Advantage; nonprofit organizations like the Center for Watershed Protection, Fannie Mae Foundation, the Congress for New Urbanism, the Nature Conservancy, 1000 Friends of Minnesota, Northwest Environment Watch, the Chattooga Conservancy, and the Center for Rural Massachusetts; and publishers of books and journals like Elsevier, McGraw-Hill, John Wiley and Sons, W.H. Freeman, University of Wisconsin Press, and the American Planning Association.

On a personal note, I wish to thank my mentors, colleagues, and students who have pushed me to consider both the bigger picture and the detailed analyses required for effective environmental planning. I also wish to thank Heather Boyer, Cecilia González, and James Nuzum at Island Press and the staff at Impressions Book and Journal Services, Inc., who offered constructive and creative assistance in the book's development and production. My assistant Krystal Wright has always been there to help, especially with the many awkward tables in the manuscript.

Finally, I thank my boys, Jason, Watsun, and Peter, for putting up with my obsession, and especially Sandy for her love and support, without which I could never have completed this project.

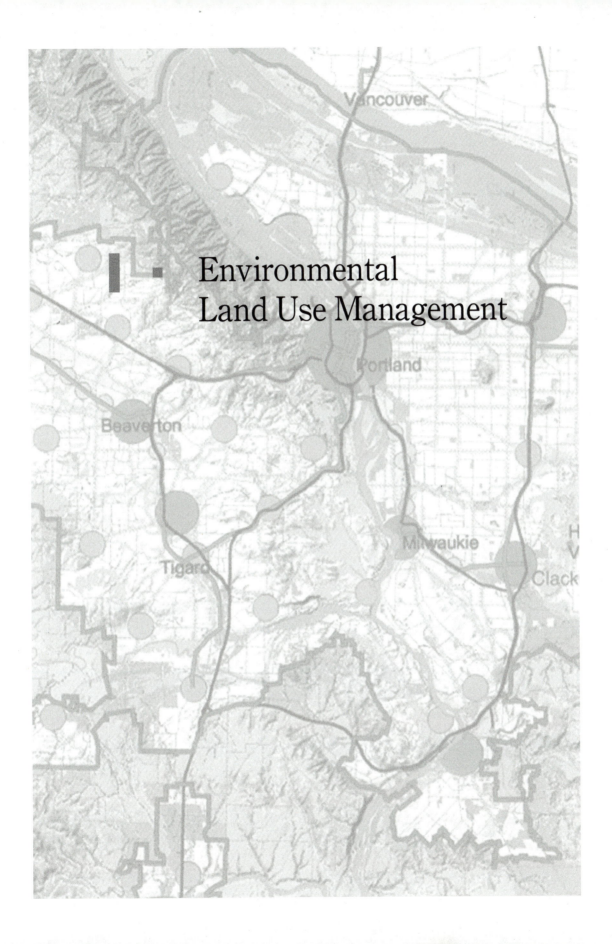

Environmental
Land Use Management

1 ▪ Managing Human-Environment Interactions

Since the dawn of their time humans have been dependent on the natural forces of the earth. As society advanced, people tried to separate themselves from the natural burdens and hazards of life common to all other living beings. Yet, like it or not, humans remain part of that natural environment, dependent on natural systems for the necessities of life—clean air and water, food, and health—as well as connected to their evolutionary heritage. And as human population and technology developed, human activity increased to affect these critical natural systems, including biogeochemical cycles, large-scale ecosystems, and atmospheric processes.

Managing their relationship with the environment has been a continuous requirement and responsibility for people and society. How society has assumed that responsibility depends on technology, human ingenuity, and the values and norms of society, which also vary across cultures and over time. Just as human beings and society have evolved, so too has their relationship with the environment and the way they manage that relationship. It is still evolving.

This chapter provides a context for this book by introducing the concepts of environmental management, the range of human values and perspectives that influences it, and emerging approaches that are part of its current evolution.

What Is Environmental Management?

Environmental management is the means of controlling or guiding human-environment interactions to protect and enhance human health and welfare and environmental quality. These interactions can affect human welfare and the environment in the following four ways:

1. The environment poses certain natural hazards to human society.
2. Society-generated pollution impacts human health through the environment.

3. Society exploits economically important natural resources at unsustainable rates.
4. Pollution and overuse undermine productive natural systems and ecosystems.

Natural hazards include flooding and other weather-related damages, geologic hazards such as earthquakes and landslides, forest and grass fires, and natural pests and disease-transmitting organisms. These hazards may be caused by natural elements, but human actions can exacerbate both the hazard and the risk by altering the natural system or locating developments in harm's way.

Human-generated pollution affects **human health.** Here the environment is a transfer medium. Contamination of air, drinking water, and food by toxic pollution can result in debilitating ailments, cancer, and genetic damage. Inadequate sanitation can foster the transmission of disease, and improper handling of dangerous materials can cause severe accidents.

Natural resources and managed natural systems are critical for human subsistence, livelihood, and quality of life. Nonrenewable resources such as fossil energy, minerals, and land are subject to depletion. Sustainable management of water resources and productive "working landscapes," like agriculture and forestry, is necessary for continued development of renewable resources, water, food, and fiber.

Human society's resource exploitation and pollution impact essential **natural systems and ecosystems.** These systems include those important to human economic productivity, like groundwater recharge, fisheries, climate regulation, and hydrologic and biogeochemical cycles. They include the many productive benefits of wetlands (e.g., flood control, water quality enhancement), vegetation (e.g., erosion and slope stability), and natural areas (e.g., aesthetic and property value).

Resource use and pollution also affect **natural ecosystems** that do not have readily measurable economic value, such as species habitats and biodiversity. However, the environmental movement has heightened public value given to these "noneconomic" natural resources. This value stems from both an anthropocentric view based on human enjoyment of these resources, now and in the future, and a perspective that natural ecosystems and the life they support have value for their own sake.

Management aims to control the interactions of people and the environment, and management itself involves the interaction of people and institutions. Although we shall see that environmental planning and management is a scientific, technical field, it is also a political one driven by the process of social and institutional interplay. Planning and management involves people interacting in a competition of ideas and values, shaping the technical, institutional, legal, and policy means of managing the environment.

Participants and Roles in Environmental Management

In the United States, a great many participants or actors in government, private markets, and civil society are involved in environmental management, as shown in figure 1.1. In our strong market economy, **private** activities (i.e., **The Market**) determine to a large extent the fate of the environment. Ultimately, the consuming public makes choices about products and designs that shape the patterns of production and development. Industrial firms, developers, and farmers play critical roles as they initiate actions that impact the environment, respond to environmental regulations and programs, and develop innovative technologies and approaches for environmental control.

For example, key private actors in land use and development are landowners, developers, and associated firms including financial institutions, realtors, and designers. Some environmental groups refer to them collectively (and not complimentarily) as the "growth machine," because their profit-motivated land use practices and development projects often impact the environment. Although they may produce a negative impact on the environment, planners and designers in this group are often responsible for innovative practices and designs that protect and preserve the environment. Examples include conservation design in land development, land use practices that reduce runoff pollution, and watershed and land stewardship. In some instances, these practices and designs have resulted from creative design or response to market forces and landowner preferences.

In other cases, the land developers have changed their practices in response to regulatory or public pressure, involving the other participants in figure 1.1. **Government** (i.e., **The State**) plays an important role using its "police power" to protect public health and welfare to regulate private activity that affects the environment. Environmental management by government has involved all three levels—federal, state, and local (in some cases, regional)—and all three branches—executive, legislative, and judicial. The legislature enacts laws establishing programs and policies; the courts interpret laws; and agencies in the executive branch (such as the federal Environmental Protection Agency [EPA] or a local planning department) develop plans and administer programs.

In the management of land use, for example, state and county and municipal local governments play the lead, although the federal government also administers a number of programs, such as wetlands permitting. State and local **growth management** aims to manage the growth machine by controlling land use and development. This involves regulatory tools, including zoning, subdivision regulations, and more innovative performance standards, to control the location and impact of development. Increasingly, state and local agencies have used nonregulatory measures such as location of infrastructure, tax policies, land acquisition, education, environmental design guidelines, and other measures to influence land use and development practices.

The third sector or category is the **public,** or **Civil Society,** which includes nongovernmental organizations, environmental and citizen groups, land trusts, property owners, and others with an interest in the activities of the market or the state. Public groups can affect activities in a number of ways: by participating in government planning and decision making; by pressuring or directly negotiating private development project proposals; or by actively preserving environmental resources through land trusts and conservation easements.

This category includes nonprofit environmental groups that engage in three areas of management: Some, like the National Wildlife Federation and the Sierra Club,

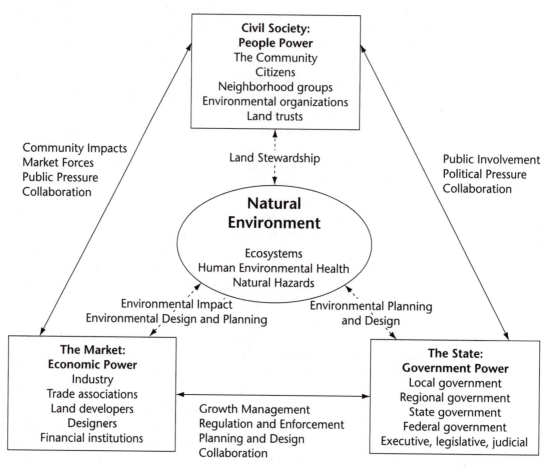

Figure 1.1   Participants and Relationships in Environmental Planning and Management

provide environmental information to the public; others, like The Nature Conservancy and hundreds of state and local land trusts, establish and protect trusts, nature preserves, and sanctuaries; still others, such as the Natural Resources Defense Council (NRDC) and Environmental Defense, use the administrative review process and the judicial courts to clarify and interpret environmental laws and policies. In this latter role, these nongovernmental organizations have been important watchdogs of environmental management in the United States and around the world.

Environmental Management: A Reflection of Social Culture, Values, and Ethics

Ultimately, how the environment is managed is based on society's culture and values. However, a complex society does not have just one set of values. Different cultures and different people within cultures have different values and ideologies about their relationship with the natural environment. These are influenced by religious belief, ethical and moral persuasion, educational and personal experience, awareness, personal security, and many other factors. Culture is not static and uniform but varies over time and across society. It is important to understand culture and values for two reasons. First, a society's approach to managing the environment is usually a reflection of its values, culture, and norms. And second, we need to understand and integrate these values in planning and decision making to manage the environment effectively.

Society's values are manifested in **ethics,** or making and defending choices based on those values. Environmental ethics has its roots deep in human history. Emergence in the United States dates back to the writings of George Perkins Marsh, Emerson, Thoreau, and Muir, among others in the mid to late nineteenth century. Aldo Leopold in his 1949 *Sand County Almanac* and Rachel Carson in her 1962 *Silent Spring* created a resurgence of environmental values related to the land and the effects of pollution on nature. In a society based largely on utilitarianism and economic efficiency, these writings struck a chord as people realized that both personal and public decisions should be based not only on utility but also on duty, responsibility, and stewardship.

Beatley (1994) suggests that natural objects have three types of value:

- instrumental value (what people can do with an object, like converting a forest to timber),
- intrinsic value (what people appreciate in an object, like seeing and experiencing the forest), and
- inherent worth (value for its own sake, irrespective of the instrumental and intrinsic value humans hold for it; e.g., the forest as a living organism) (Stone, 1974).

Instrumental and intrinsic values are anthropocentric, whereas inherent worth is nonanthropocentric.

Visions of Paradise: Contemporary Perspectives on Managing the Environment

As suggested in the last section, environmental management depends on society's culture and values. How do we characterize contemporary American values and perspectives about managing the environment? Despite libraries of scientific and technical research, universally held truths about many controversial environmental issues are elusive. People's attitudes and values about the environment filter scientific information to create an interpretation that conforms to those values. This is why technical and scientific debate continues over issues like nuclear power, global warming, and endangered species.

In the early 1970s, when I began to understand the different perspectives people had on environmental issues and the future, I wrote a short essay, "Visions of Paradise." In it I discussed the following five different points of view.

Says the "Optimist": Look how far we have come as a civilization. Imagine how far we can go. Human ingenuity and technology will continue to meet whatever challenges we face. The visions of environmental doomsayers from Malthus to Carson to Ehrlich have always been met by society's and technology's innovative solutions. There will always be advantaged and disadvantaged people, but only by advancing technology and growing the economy can we provide opportunities for the less advantaged by increasing the size of the pie. Increasing energy demand will be met by new technologies, a recovery of nuclear power, and perhaps the ultimate source, nuclear fusion. Pollution challenges will be met by improved treatment. Human-managed ecosystems will continue to benefit society. Exploiting the frontiers, technology-enhanced recovery, substituting for depleted minerals, and perhaps exploiting extraterrestrial sources will meet resource demands. For the only limits to our future are those we invent. Paradise is our destiny.

Says the "Concerned Optimist": Although we do have some major problems, we have the capability to solve them. Poverty, population, global warming, energy, species extinction, and sprawling land development pose significant challenges. However, with considerable effort and investment, technology and social adaptation will rise to the occasion. Paradise is within our grasp.

Says the "Hopeful Pessimist": The challenges we face will create serious impacts on our quality of life, ability to meet the needs of increasing numbers of the world's poor, and degrading ecosystems. Global warming and resulting climatic change and sea-level rise, ecosystem damage and species extinction, energy constraints, abject poverty, and political tensions stand in the way of a sustainable future. Environmentally benign technologies like efficient and renewable energy systems, agroforestry, and organic agriculture must be developed and implemented. Any kind of "Paradise" will require major shifts in social consciousness and economic systems, which are needed to arrest overconsumption by the rich and the false economic imperatives of material growth. This may be asking too much, but we must try, and try together.

Says the "Pessimist": Our dependence on high levels of material economic growth cannot be sustained. Major environmental problems will constrain economic advancement, widening the gap between the rich and poor. If widespread environmental catastrophes and destruction of natural ecosystems do not threaten our survival, resulting social tensions will create continuous global security problems and regional wars. Paradise Lost!

Says the "Self-Absorbed": Global problems? I've got my own problems to worry about. I have enough difficulty providing for me and mine to be concerned about global people and the planet's environment. Life is hard. I care about me, my family, my property, my job and livelihood, and my community and nation as they affect me and mine. I can't afford to worry beyond that. Let someone else worry about it. Global Paradise? Let's talk about *my* Paradise.

SIDEBAR 1.1   Others have recognized these differences. Hawken, Lovins, and Lovins (1999) describe the four colorful worldviews of the late Donella Meadows (1994):

The **Blues** are free marketers, have a positive bias, and are technological optimists. They believe conventional economic approaches are on track because they fuel the essential ingredients for positive change: individual freedom, innovation, and investment. They see economic growth as the key to increase material well-being for all and market mechanisms as the key to mitigate environmental impact.

The **Reds** hold various forms of socialism. They believe "bandit" capitalism benefits a minority at the expense of a materially and socially disadvantaged majority (witness the worldwide gap between the rich and poor). The environment is a distraction from social issues.

The **Greens** see the world in terms of ecosystems. The major threats are resource depletion, pollution damage, and population growth. Carrying capacity is a key operating concept. They are neither antitechnology nor antimarket, as they see technology and market forces as useful tools for environmental protection. They often appear less caring for people than animals. The Greens tend to be diverse, and their bold views are often splintered and self-canceling. They tend to unite enemies and divide friends, which is not a recipe for political success.

The **Whites** are synthesists who do not openly oppose or agree with any of the preceding. They are optimistic, not necessarily about technology, but about people and process, for it is "process" that will win the day. Whites often reject Blues, Reds, and Greens, because they think people who tell others what is right (or wrong) lead society astray. Therefore, they reject ideologies based solely on markets, class, or nature. They seek a middle way of integration, reform, respect, and reliance. On environment, they think all issues are local. On business, they think the fabled "level playing field" is plagued by an imperfect market, lobbying, subsidies, and capital concentration. On social issues, they believe solutions will naturally arise from place and culture, not from ideology. They want to appear like Taoist leaders, whose "subjects" feel like they succeeded by themselves.

Although it is helpful to characterize these different worldviews, it is important to understand that all people do not fit neatly into one or the other. I often debate with myself about my own worldview. Different views are not simply a matter of political ideology, and they are neither constant nor purely defined for anyone. People learn. As they do, their mind-sets, positions, perceptions, tolerance for other views, and fundamental values can also change. Learning is a key concept behind collaborative environmental planning, which is discussed later.

As these mind-sets are variable for individuals, they are also dynamic for society. Cultural and social norms, political systems, and government policies are (or should be) a reflection of a society's values. As society's views of the environment have changed over time, so have the approaches taken to manage the interactions of humans and nature.

Historical Paradigms of Environmental Management and the Evolution Toward Sustainability

Colby (1991) has characterized evolving paradigms of environmental management, including their ethical, political, economic, policy, technological, and methodological dimensions. Table 1.1 describes Colby's five paradigms: frontier economics, environmental protection, resource management, ecodevelopment, and deep ecology.

Frontier economics (FE) is characterized by an anthropocentric view that resources are limitless and progress is defined by economic growth. At the other

TABLE 1.1   **Colby's Five Paradigms of Environmental Management**

Paradigm Dimension	Frontier Economics (FE)	Environmental Protection (EP)	Resource Management (RM)	Eco-Development (ED)	Deep Ecology (DE)
Dominant Imperative	"Progress," as infinite economic growth and prosperity	"Trade-offs," as in ecology versus economic growth	"Sustainability," as necessary constraint for "green growth"	Codeveloping humans and nature; redefine "security"	"Ecotopia": Antigrowth, "constrained harmony with nature"
Human-Nature Relationship	Very strong anthropocentric	Strong anthropocentric	Modified anthropocentric	Ecocentric?	Biocentric
Dominant Threats	Hunger, poverty, disease, natural disasters	Health impacts of pollution, endangered species	Resource degradation, poverty, population growth	Ecological uncertainty Global change	Ecosystem collapse "Unnatural" disasters
Main Themes	Open access/free goods Exploitation of infinite natural resources	Remedial/ defensive "Legalize ecology" as economic externality	Global efficiency "Economize ecology" Interdependence	Generative restructuring "Ecologize economy" and Social System	Back to nature "Biospecies equality" Simple symbiosis
Prevalent Property Regimes	Privatization (neoclass) or nationalization (Marx.) of all property	Privatization dominant Some public parks set aside	Global commons law (GCL) for conservation of oceans, atmosphere, climate, biodiversity	GCL + local common and private property Regimes for intra- and intergenerational equity and Stewardship	Private, plus common property set aside for preservation
Who Pays?	Property owners (public at large; especially poor)	Income taxpayers (public at large)	"Polluter pays" (producers and consumers) (poor)	"Pollution prevention pays"; income-indexed environmental taxes	Avoid costs by forgoing development
Responsibility for Development and Management	Property owners: Individuals or state	Fragmentation: development decentralized, management centralized	Toward integration— across multiple levels of government (fed/state/local)	Private/public institutional innovations and redefinition of roles	Largely decentralized but integrated design and management

end of the ideological spectrum is **deep ecology (DE)**, the back-to-nature "bio-centric" view that reveres all nature, often at the expense of economic growth. These two worldviews have been present in U.S. society at least since the mid-1800s, and Colby argues that subsequent approaches to environmental management have evolved partly in reaction to the tension between FE and DE.

Environmental protection (EP) is characteristic of U.S. policy in the 1970s. It recognizes environmental impacts and aims to lessen them, but generally without significant sacrifice in an economic-growth objective. EP is "business

TABLE 1.1 (Continued) **Colby's Five Paradigms of Environmental Management**

Paradigm Dimension	Frontier Economics (FE)	Environmental Protection (EP)	Resource Management (RM)	Eco-Development (ED)	Deep Ecology (DE)
Environmental Management Technologies and Strategies	Industrial agriculture Fossil energy Pollution dispersal Unregulated waste disposal High population growth "Free markets"	"End-of-the Pipe" cleanup, or "business as usual, plus a treatment plant" "Command and Control" market regulation for protection of human health, environmental impact statements	Impact assessment and risk management, pollution reduction, energy efficiency, renewable resource restoration ecology, population stabilization, and technology-enhanced carrying capacity	Uncertainty (resilience) management, industrial ecology Ecotechnologies, e.g., renewable energy, agroforestry, low-input agriculture, population stabilization, and enhanced capacity	Stability management Reduced scale of market economy (inc. trade) Low technology Simple material needs Nondominating science; indigenous technology "Intrinsic values" Population reduction
Analytic/ Modeling and Planning Methodologies	Neoclassical or Marxist: Production limited by man-made factors; natural factors not accounted for Net present value maximization Cost-benefit analysis of tangible goods and services	Neoclassical plus Environmental impact assessment after design; optimum pollution levels; willingness to pay and compensation principles	Neoclassical Plus: Include natural capital Increased, freer trade Ecosystem and social health monitoring: Linkages between population, poverty, and environment	Ecological economics: Sociotechnical and ecosystem process design; integration of social, economic, and ecological criteria for technology; equity in land distribution	Grassroots bioregional planning: Multiple cultural systems; conservation of cultural and biological diversity; autonomy
Fundamental Flaws	Creative but mechanistic; no awareness of reliance on ecological balance	Defined by FE in reaction to DE; lacks vision of abundance	Downplays social factors; subtly mechanistic; doesn't handle uncertainty	May generate false security; magnitude of changes require new consciousness	Defined in reaction to FE; organic but not creative; how reduce population?

Source: Reprinted from *Ecological Economics* 3(3), Michael Colby, "Environmental Management in Development: the Evolution of Paradigms," 1991, with permission of Elsevier.

as usual plus a treatment plant" and utilizes command and control laws to control severe environmental impacts. Colby's **resource management (RM)** category is more characteristic of U.S. policy in the 1980s. It recognizes long-term sustainability as a constraint to economic growth. RM also aims to modify traditional economic accounts to include environmental values by internalizing externalities and "getting the prices right" (i.e., "economizing ecology").

Finally, **ecodevelopment (ED)** is a paradigm toward which Colby suggests we are evolving. Although Colby does not fully define it, ED is characterized by an "ecocentric" view of the world, codeveloping human society and nature, stewardship and pollution prevention, and a restructured economic system that does not simply give economic value to environmental resources but considers economic values in ecological terms ("ecologizing the economy").

Colby argues that an evolution over time toward ecodevelopment is occurring, but to a large extent all five paradigms are active today in practice and theory and in the worldviews described earlier. Shades of FE are alive and well among the Optimists, many Blues, and perhaps the Self-Absorbed. The Greens have a corner on the DE paradigm. Environmental protection and RM include some mix of Concerned Optimists, Blues, and Greens. The Whites seem anchored in RM and would argue their "process" is the key to defining ecodevelopment. The social and economic transformation implied by ED is consistent with the imperatives of the Hopeful Pessimist.

Toward Sustainable Development

Colby's ED paradigm is very similar to **sustainable development.** Borrowing from the Bruntland Commission (1988) and others, sustainable development is defined as the *paths of economic, social, environmental, and political progress that aim to meet the needs of today without compromising the ability of future generations to meet their needs.* Sustainable development aims to provide for the social and economic needs of society, while protecting environmental resources and values for the future.

Sustainability is usually characterized by the integration of "three E's," the tri-objectives of **E**conomy, **E**nvironment, and social **E**quity. I like to add two more, **E**ngagement and **E**ternity, to draw attention to necessary political participation and a future orientation. Sustainability must break from current short-term thinking and planning and adopt a long-term perspective. It can never be achieved without democratic processes that engage people in determining their own destiny.

Achieving all of these elements is no easy task, but if one is missing, true sustainability will remain elusive. Many have embraced sustainable development conceptually, but they encounter more difficulty trying to implement it operationally. There are often trade-offs between the three basic objectives (economic, environmental, social), and different groups tend to emphasize their specific interest above the others. Campbell (1996) suggests that planning for sustainability largely involves resolving conflicts among these objectives and interests: between economy and environment is the "resource conflict," between economy and social equity is the "property conflict," and between social equity and environment is the "development conflict." This conception implies trade-offs, but Campbell asserts that only by resolving these conflicts can communities become "green, profitable, and fair." Some say that sustainable development can be achieved within current economic and social systems. Others (such as Colby) suggest that because of these inherent conflicts, those systems must change before our development can become truly sustainable. Still others seek creative solutions that dissolve the conflicts and provide mutual achievement of the three primary objectives.

From Conservation to the Ecological Way

Although most would agree that we have not achieved sustainable development or ecodevelopment, there is evidence of a change over time, if not a true paradigm shift. Historians and analysts have traced the development of the environmental movement and its reflection in policy and management (Caldwell, 1970; Nash, 1990). Like Colby, Beatley (1994) suggests an evolution in recent years in which the public and public policy have extended moral horizons beyond narrow anthropocentric concerns. Whereas much of the motivation for the environmental movement has been utilitarian, it has also resulted from an expansion of the moral community to include other forms of life. Nash (1989) argues that in the United States this is part of a natural progression of the American tradition of the liberation of exploited groups—a modern-day form of abolitionism, a "rounding-out of the American Revolution." Figure 1.2 illustrates the incremental expansion of moral and legal rights over time. This expansion is not complete.

Bernard and Young (1997) describe this evolution with regard to environmental values in three waves. The first wave was the conservation movement, which emerged in the United States in the mid to late nineteenth century with philosophers like George Perkins Marsh and Henry David Thoreau, preservationists like John Muir, and utilitarianists like Gifford Pinchot, and carried through the twentieth century with Aldo Leopold and others. Many conservation organizations, like the Sierra Club and the National Wildlife Federation, and government agencies, like the National Park Service, the Fish and Wildlife Service, and the Forest Service, were established to operationalize the imperatives of the movement, to set aside natural refuges and parks for wildlife and human use, as well as manage the use and development of public natural resources.

The second wave focused on public and environmental health and protection of commonly held resources. It was born in the early-twentieth-century public health movement, which identified many relationships of environmental conditions to human health. It expanded to ecological health with Rachel Carson's *Silent Spring* (1962), which chronicled the subtle and devastating impacts of human actions on ecosystems at a time when people were witnessing firsthand major pollution problems. Garrett Hardin's "Tragedy of the Commons" (1969) surmised that individual freedom to use common resources (atmosphere, waters, ecosystems) would bring ruin to all. The movement spurred establishment of the EPA and a plethora of environmental protection laws, as well as the formation of watchdog environmental groups like the Natural Resources Defense Council and the Environmental Defense Fund.

Bernard and Young (1997) characterize the third wave as the "ecological way," borrowing from Goldsmith (1993). An extension of the first two waves, the ecological way seeks a greater integration of human habitation and use of resources with the long-term protection of natural systems. Bernard and Young offer several case examples that help describe the emergence of the ecological way. The environmental management examples are locally based, have ecosystem or watershed boundaries, and involve collaboration and partnerships of stakeholders (Prugh, Costanza, and Daly, 2000). Similar manifestations are apparent in recent emphasis on ecosystem management among federal agencies, principally

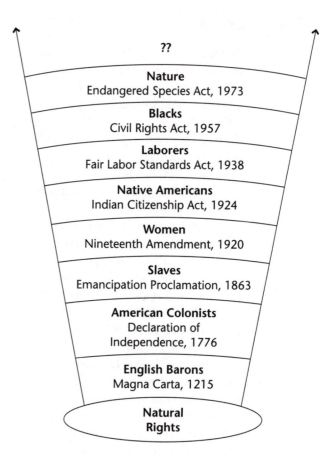

Figure 1.2 The Concept of Expanding Rights in the United States. *Source:* Nash, Roderick Frazier. The Rights of Nature: A History of Environmental Ethics. © 1989. Reprinted by permission of the University of Wisconsin Press.

the Forest Service and the Fish and Wildlife Service, in the hundreds of local watershed management programs, and in the many private landowner steward-ship programs. The Sierra Club and NRDC best represent environmental groups for the first and second waves, respectively, and The Nature Conservancy and many land trusts best illustrate the type of proactive, partnership-building organizations of the third wave.

The remainder of this book, in large part, presents the technical, political, and policy dimensions of this emerging approach, including many examples of its manifestation in the activities of communities, government, developers, landowners, and land trusts.

Summary

Environmental management is a complex field. It is complicated by the wide range of people and institutions involved and the different perspectives and values they hold on how to manage the environment. Society's perspectives on the environment ultimately determine the planning and policy framework for management, and because these perspectives change over time, so do approaches to environmental management. Some evidence indicates that more widespread environmental values and new methods of environmental analysis and evaluation are spurring new paradigms of management.

The next chapter focuses on environmental planning and how it too is evolving to better serve changing environmental needs through improved analysis, communication, and collaboration.

2 ■ Environmental Planning

Planning is a critical part of environmental management. This chapter introduces environmental planning, including a generic planning process and the multiple roles of the planner. Much of the chapter addresses the range of disciplinary perspectives involved in environmental planning.

What Is Environmental Planning?

Planning is "figuring out what needs to be done and how to do it." It is the process of "applying knowledge to action" or basic problem solving (Friedmann, 1987). It requires determining ends and means relationships. Simply, planning involves setting objectives, gathering and analyzing information, and formulating and evaluating alternative policies, projects, or designs to meet the objectives.

Table 2.1 shows that planning evolved from a design profession applied to urban form to a broader skill set applied to a range of problems and objectives, including environmental quality. In the late nineteenth and early twentieth centuries in the United States, noted urban designers laid out impressive plans for our great cities. In the 1920s to 1940s, with the growing use of zoning, urban planning became more regulatory. With the growth of federal government planning in the 1930s (e.g., the New Deal), planning became more bureaucratic, fact-finding, and analytical, in both scientific and economic terms.

The U.S. postwar housing, highway, and development boom of the 1950s and 1960s brought further physical development challenges, but the social movements of the 1960s also made planning more political. As a result, public participation grew in the 1970s, "communication" became the emphasis in the 1980s, and the 1990s saw more collaborative approaches involving stakeholders and partners "reasoning together." Many analysts today lament the loss of the earlier design emphasis of urban planning and its future orientation, and they suggest that the character of our communities has suffered (Duany, Plater-Zyberk, and

TABLE 2.1 **Evolution of Planning in the United States**

Emphasis	Era	Description
Planning as Design	1850–1950	Urban designers/planners create our cities
Planning as Regulation	1925 →	Zoning/command/control is core of government action
Planning as Applied Science	1940 →	Scientific/economic/policy analysis is problem solving
Planning as Politics	1965 →	Social movements and political action affect decisions
Planning as Communication	1975 →	Public information/participation broaden perspectives
Planning as Collaboration	1990 →	Stakeholders engaged to reason together
Planning as Integration of Policy, Science, Collaboration, Design	2000 →	Information revolution and rebirth of design innovation, informed by science, policy, and collaboration

Speck, 2000; Myers and Kitsuse, 2000; Neuman, 1998). The evolving skill set for planning in the twenty-first century includes technical and policy analysis, political communication and process, as well as innovation and creative design.

Environmental planning applies the process of planning to environmental protection and problem solving. This may entail any of the human-environment interactions discussed in chapter 1: natural hazards, human environmental health, natural resource use, productive natural systems, and ecosystems.

Environmental planning and management can be "reactive," "proactive," or "integrative." **Reactive** measures try to correct prior environmental damages, for example, remediation of old waste dumps, reclamation of abandoned mined lands, or cleanup of polluted waterways. **Proactive** measures are taken explicitly to enhance environmental quality, for example, land use controls to preserve wildlife habitats and wetlands, protect aquifer recharge areas, or restrict future floodplain development. **Integrative** environmental planning involves early and substantive consideration of environmental and social factors in the formulation of development plans and projects, like a highway or subdivision. Not only is it less costly and more effective to consider environmental factors early in the development process, but this integration is essential to achieve the tri-objectives of sustainable development.

Usually, environmental planners have specialized expertise in one or more subareas, such as land use and development, air quality, water quality, water resources, waste management, wildlife, forestry, or others. But as planners, environmental planners are also generalists, applying planning and problem-solving skills and a wide range of disciplinary perspectives (discussed later) to a variety of environmental concerns.

Approaches to Planning and the Planning Process

Although "figuring out what needs to be done and how to do it" is a simple definition of planning, it is, of course, not quite that simple. There is an extensive literature on the theory of planning, and a scholarly debate continues on the merits and needs for different planning approaches. Like environmental management, planning has and is evolving in efforts to better meet society's needs.

There are four basic approaches to planning. The **rational-comprehensive** approach is based on the scientific method and has five basic steps of objectives, information, alternatives, impact assessment, and evaluation. The **incremental approach,** or what Lindblom (1959) called the "science of muddling through," accepts limitations in human knowledge and understanding, and as a result, focuses on short-term goals and objectives and small sequential actions. Adaptive planning is a modern-day form of incrementalism (Holling, 1978). The **participatory approach** suggests that neither rational-comprehensive nor incremental approaches deal explicitly with the diverse stakeholder perspectives and conflicting values; it aims to inform and involve the public in planning and decision making. Finally, the **advocacy approach** recognizes that interested stakeholders do not speak with one voice but often line up in entrenched camps and fight for their special interests; this situation often requires some advocacy of the underrepresented and mediation to resolve differences.

Environmental planning generally requires a rational-comprehensive and participatory framework, with elements of adaptive-incremental management and advocacy planning as appropriate (Braisoulis, 1989). Box 2.1 gives a generic planning process that fits most environmental planning applications. It begins with scoping, a key first step to identify stakeholders and develop a work plan. It continues with identifying key issues and objectives, analyzing the planning situation, formulating alternatives, assessing impacts, and evaluating impacts, all of which are elements of the rational-comprehensive process, but with strong stakeholder participation. It concludes with an adaptive element: implementation, monitoring and postevaluation, and modification.

The detail of the process, the range of issues, the depth of analysis, and the comprehensiveness of the alternatives and impacts all depend on the planning context: the needs and objectives and the available data, resources, and time (Braisoulis, 1989). As discussed in the next section, environmental problems and planning issues can be very complex and involve a variety of disciplinary perspectives. In such cases, each step will involve considerable effort. On the other hand, in a focused or incremental application, all of the basic steps will occur but in an abbreviated way. Many processes start with a "rapid assessment" that takes a quick look at problems and available information and tries to move quickly to assessment and action (Sayre et al., 2000).

Although the environmental planning process appears as a sequential process, in reality it is somewhat iterative, as all steps are considered simultaneously, with changing emphasis as the process proceeds. The process is always open to new information about subsequent or previous steps at any time. Several of the planning tools highlighted in the process for participation, negotiation, assessment, and evaluation are discussed later in this chapter and in subsequent chapters.

This basic process can be applied in a simple form (see box 2.2). *Inventory* (What do we have?) includes steps 0 and 2 of box 2.1. *Needs assessment* (What are our problems, needs, objectives?) includes steps 1 and 2. *Management strategies* (What should we do?) is related to steps 3, 4, and 5. *Implementation and monitoring* (Let's do it!) includes step 6.

BOX 2.1—Process for Environmental Planning

0. Scoping

Stakeholder Issues

Identify fundamental issues, stakeholders, opportunities for participation, needs for conflict resolution, and needs for data and analysis

Draft preliminary work plan for process

Draft preliminary design for stakeholder involvement and participation

1. Identification of Issues, Opportunities, Concerns, Objectives, Criteria, Uncertainties (IOC)

Stakeholder Criteria

Identify IOC (Issues, Opportunities, Concerns), evaluative factors, including institutional, legal, technical criteria

Participation tools (advisory committees, meetings, workshops, surveys) determined by scoping

Conflict resolution and negotiation tools (advocacy) depending on degree of controversy

2. Analysis of Planning Situation

Stakeholder Local Knowledge

Scope of data gathering and analysis determined by evaluative factors

Identify data limitations and uncertainties

Participation tools (workshops, surveys)

Conflict resolution and negotiation tools (advocacy) depending on degree of controversy

3. Formulation of Alternatives

Stakeholder Alternatives

Scope of alternatives (comprehensive vs. incremental) determined by IOC, planning situation, degree of uncertainty (adaptive)

Participation tools (workshops, workbooks, surveys)

4. Assessment of Impacts

Stakeholder Assessment

Economic, environmental, and social effects

Scope of assessment (comprehensive vs. incremental) depends on evaluative factors, planning situation, and alternatives

Impact assessment tools (cost-benefit [C-B] analysis, environmental impact assessment [EIA], social impact assessment [SIA])

Organization and evaluation tools (matrices, indices, etc.)

Participation tools (workshops, surveys)

5. Evaluation and Selection of Plan

Stakeholder Evaluation

Organization and evaluation tools (matrices, etc.)

Participation tools (workshops, surveys, review and comment)

Conflict resolution and negotiation tools (advocacy) depending on degree of controversy

6. Implementation, Monitoring, Evaluation, Modification (Adaptive)

Stakeholder Implementation

Timing and extent of monitoring and modification (adaptive) determined by level of uncertainty and degree of controversy

Participation tools (citizen monitoring, workshops, annual conferences) determined by level of uncertainty and degree of controversy

BOX 2.2—Simplified Planning Process

1. Inventory (steps 0, 2)   What do we have?
2. Needs Assessment (steps 1, 2)   What are our problems, objectives, priorities?
3. Management Strategies, Plans, Programs   What should we do?
   (steps 3, 4, 5)
4. Implementation and Monitoring (step 6)   Let's do it! (and learn from it)

Interdisciplinary Considerations of Environmental Planning and Management

The complexity of environmental problems requires interdisciplinary solutions. Environmental management is an exceptionally diverse field borrowing heavily from several disciplines, including natural science and engineering, economics, law, politics, and, as discussed in chapter 1, ethics. Environmental planners may be grounded in a discipline, but as generalists, they must understand and apply a range of disciplinary perspectives to the planning process.

Environmental Science and Engineering

Though interdisciplinary, at its roots environmental planning and management is based on scientific and engineering principles. Controlling human-environment interactions to protect and enhance human health and environmental quality requires an understanding of *how natural systems work* and *how designed systems and technologies can lessen the adverse effects* of those interactions and enhance environmental quality. For example, soil erosion control requires a basic understanding of soil mechanics, available soils information, erodibility analysis, and the effectiveness of various land use practices in reducing erosion potential. Appropriate decisions concerning the management of air quality require knowledge of the effects on human health of pollutant levels, obtained from laboratory and epidemiological studies; the cost and effectiveness of various engineering treatment systems; and the relationship between levels of emissions at the stack and the quality of air people breathe.

Environmental Economics

Public policy decisions have long been based on the theory of welfare economics and economic efficiency. This largely utilitarian theory states that social welfare is improved if the total gains among those who benefit exceed the total losses by those adversely affected. The price and exchange mechanisms of the free market generally fail to allocate effectively resources according to this social welfare test of economic efficiency. Many effects of market activity occur as market **externalities;** these are goods (positive) or damages (negative) that flow from the market to individuals or firms whether they want them or not and without their paying for them or being able to avoid them by making a payment. Many environmental effects, such as pollution, wetland destruction, groundwater overdraft, and over-grazing, are negative externalities.

As a result of externalities and other market failures, public policy decisions determining natural resource use and pollution control have relied on more than the dictates of the free market. In many cases, they have been based on the explicit comparison of benefits and costs including certain nonmarket effects. Economic **cost-benefit analysis** is constrained to those costs and benefits that can be measured or estimated in dollar terms. More recent requirements, such as those set forth in the National Environmental Policy Act, broadened the objectives and definitions of costs and benefits in resources planning, but federal decisions are still based primarily on the economic efficiency test of net dollar benefits.

Cost-benefit analysis makes sense conceptually, but it is plagued with some basic problems in practice. One concerns *equity,* or the distribution of costs and benefits. The comparison of costs and benefits "to whomsoever they may accrue" does not consider who benefits and who loses. Second, many costs and benefits involve considerable *risk or uncertainty,* and these are not well considered in cost-benefit analysis. A third problem is *how effects are valued over time.* The time value of money tells us a dollar today is worth more than a dollar tomorrow since it can be invested. Future dollar effects are therefore "discounted" to a present value to be compared with today's dollars. But how do we treat environmental and human health effects? Do we discount the value of a future wilderness preserved or destroyed by today's decisions or of future cancers resulting from today's management of toxic substances?

Finally, it is difficult to place economic value on *noneconomic effects,* such as habitat destruction. In recent years, the field of **ecological economics** has emerged to improve the economic valuation of environmental resources so that they can be better accounted for in cost-benefit analysis and in planning and decision making. Environmental resource and amenity values are usually measured in terms of their **use** and **option value.** "Use" can be consumptive (e.g., cut a tree) or nonconsumptive (e.g., look at a tree). "Option" refers to the value that nonusers place on a resource as follows:

a. simply to know it exists (**existence value**),
b. for future generations (**bequest value**), or
c. for unforeseen future purposes (**insurance value,** say for a now unknown floral species that might be a cure for cancer).

However, the methods used to quantify these values have limitations, and many analysts and economists admit that some societal values cannot be put in economic terms (McAllister, 1980; Westman, 1985). The evaluation methods discussed in the next sections aim to provide a broader perspective.

Other economic issues in environmental planning include using **market mechanisms** to advance environmental protection, **cost-effectiveness** of environmental measures, and **financing** environmental projects. Despite the analytical limitations already discussed, economic market forces remain among the most important determinants of consumer and producer decisions. Market mechanisms can work in concert with regulatory approaches to protect the environment.

For example, stricter regulations on landfilling of wastes raise the cost of disposal so that recycling programs become more cost-effective.

Financing involves how to pay for environmental improvement. Private industry and land development generally must obtain private financing. Local government programs have long relied on general obligation (tax-based) or revenue (user-fee-based) bonds to finance programs such as waste management, greenways, and parks. Innovative programs such as development rights transfers and partnerships with private firms have enhanced the financial resources available for environmental preservation. Land trusts have been especially innovative in stretching their financial resources through the use of conservation easements, bargain sales, and associated landowner tax benefits.

Environmental Evaluation

Evaluation involves using objective assessment to assign values to options, compare trade-offs, resolve conflicts, and make choices. It is perhaps the most important yet most difficult element of environmental planning. Economics alone cannot provide the basis for making decisions due to analytical limitations and, more importantly, the failure of economic assessment to fully capture nonuser and nonutilitarian environmental values.

Assessing and evaluating environmental data is complicated by the frequent need to combine and compare information that is often subjective and noncommensurable. How do you determine a measure of the visual quality of a wetland, the habitat value of a woodland, or an acceptable level of risk from a hazardous waste facility? How do you compare these measures with each other and with more quantifiable factors such as economic costs and benefits to compare and select from alternative courses of action?

Evaluation uses a number of assessment methods. It is useful to distinguish between the following:

- "Partial" techniques, which aim to determine the relative importance, quality, or value of a specific environmental component, such as wildlife habitat, visual amenity, or agricultural land
- "Comprehensive" techniques, which aim to assess a wide range of economic, cultural, and environmental effects of alternatives and to compare and often combine them to rank alternatives on their relative "social worth" (Conn, 1986)

Partial Evaluation Techniques

Partial techniques may be used to evaluate changes in specific environmental conditions and thus can be used to compare the effects of alternatives on that specific factor (e.g., compare habitat condition A predicted to result from alternative A to habitat condition B predicted to result from alternative B). As such, partial techniques can be used in impact assessment and as inputs to more comprehensive methods. Alternatively, the partial evaluation techniques can be used to rank specific areas as, for

TABLE 2.2 **Hypothetical Example of Sum-of-Weighted-Factors Technique**

Factor		Unweighted Factor Values						Weighted Factor Values		
	Scale	Area 1	Area 2	Area 3		Weights		Area 1	Area 2	Area 3
Factor A	1–10	7	4	1	×	1	=	7	4	1
Factor B	1–10	3	8	5	×	3	=	9	24	15
Factor C	1–10	1	4	3	×	4	=	4	16	12
						Final Scores		20	44	28

Necessary Value Judgments: (1) Selection of factors; (2) Assignment of values under each factor; (3) Assignment of weights to each factor

example, habitats, views, agricultural land, historic buildings, or potential recreation areas, to prioritize them for protection programs or for specific uses.

Many of the partial techniques utilize a "sum-of-weighted-factors" approach to evaluate and combine environmental information into an index. See chapter 11 for a discussion of the use of indicators and indices. These methods include, for example, the Land Evaluation and Site Assessment (LESA) procedure for agricultural land evaluation (chapter 12), DRASTIC method for assessing groundwater contamination potential (chapter 15), wetland and habitat evaluation (chapters 16 and 17), land suitability analysis (chapter 18), and certain environmental impact evaluation techniques (chapter 18). Illustrated hypothetically in table 2.2, the method involves four steps:

1. selecting a number of factors deemed relevant to the assessment;
2. measuring the factors and assigning a value to that measurement on a common scale (e.g., 0–10);
3. assigning weights to each factor based on its relative importance in the assessment (e.g., 1–5); and
4. combining the products of the factor value and weight to produce a final score.

Although it is often appropriate to try to combine information to provide such a final score, or what McAllister (1980) calls a "synthesis" or "integrated view" of various impacts or factors, these aggregating techniques require distinct value judgments by the analyst. The hypothetical sum-of-weighted-factors example given in table 2.2 shows that the first three steps involve value judgments. In most cases professional planners and technical specialists can supply appropriate values, as long as the assessment is sufficiently bounded to fall within a specific area of expertise (e.g., forest habitat quality). Still, such techniques are often criticized for including arbitrary or hidden value judgments. Usually a broader range of perceptions than those of specialists should be tapped. For example, the LESA procedure includes a local committee to provide a broader community perspective in the assignment of weights and values to site assessment factors.

Comprehensive Evaluation Techniques

Whereas partial evaluation techniques are normally constrained to one or a small set of environmental components, comprehensive methods aim to consider a broad range of effects so that alternative solutions can be compared and ranked in terms of their relative overall merits or social worth. Thus, comprehensive techniques are intended to guide decision making and are used in the key step 5 of the planning process given in box 2.1. Traditional cost-benefit analysis was designed as such a method. However, because of its limitations discussed earlier, its practice is usually relegated to a partial technique.

In response, a number of other comprehensive techniques for comparing impacts have been developed. Loomis (1993) describes a number of ways to integrate evaluation criteria. The first step in evaluating alternatives to assist decision making is the selection of evaluation criteria or the factors that should determine the best choice. Like choosing factors for the sum-of-weighted-factors method, selecting criteria involves judgment. Loomis suggests five generic criteria for public lands management:

- physical and biological feasibility,
- economic efficiency,
- distributional equity,
- social and cultural acceptability, and
- administrative feasibility.

In practice, the evaluation criteria are case-specific and based on professional expertise and the planning process, especially step 1 in box 2.1. Table 2.3 illustrates the evaluation framework. The table gives a matrix of four alternatives and four criteria.

The alternative evaluation and selection process (step 5 in box 2.1) depends on the method used to integrate the criteria to provide a basis for the decision. Here are six different methods or decision rules (after Loomis, 1993):

1. *Maximize one criterion:* One criterion supersedes all others as the basis for selection.
2. *Meet minimum levels of all criteria:* Set minimum thresholds for each criterion and select the alternative(s) that meet all of these thresholds.
3. *Maximize one criterion while meeting minimum levels of others:* Select the most important criterion; set minimum thresholds for all other criteria; then select the alternative that meets all thresholds and provides the greatest contribution to the most important criterion. This approach often uses linear programming or other optimization techniques.
4. *Rank criteria and maximize from high rank to low:* Prioritize the criteria and select the alternative that provides the best combination of contributions to the most important criteria.
5. *Numerically weight each criterion, rate each alternative's contribution to each criterion, and use sum-of-weighted-factors method to score each alternative:* Produces an aggregate score or "grand index" for each alternative.

TABLE 2.3 Evaluating Alternatives Based on a Set of Criteria

Alternatives	Alternative A	Alternative B	Alternative C	Alternative D
Criteria				
Criteria 1	*	*	*	*
Criteria 2	*	*	*	*
Criteria 3	*	*	*	*
Criteria 4	*	*	*	*
Result	**	**	**	**

Source: Based on Loomis (1993).

*Boxes are filled with a description, indicator, or index score (resulting from a partial evaluation technique) of the alternative's effect on the criterion.

**Result indicates selection, ranking, or score of alternative based on decision method.

6. *Matrix approach:* Fill in matrix with the best description, indicator, or index of each alternative's contribution to or effect on each criterion, then let reviewers, stakeholders, and/or decision makers apply their own judgment to rank alternatives.

The choice of integration method depends on the planning situation and needs identified in steps 0–4 of the process (box 2.1). Methods 1–5 all require judgments setting thresholds and/or ranking or weighting criteria. If the criteria are very broad (such as Loomis's previously listed), it is difficult to come up with a universally acceptable ranking or weighting of criteria.

Method 5 aims to aggregate estimates of effects to produce a "grand index" to rank alternatives and help guide decisions. Techniques that use this approach require that effects be measured on a common scale to permit aggregation. This requires some type of sum-of-weighted-factors approach. The comprehensive techniques that aggregate factors thus encounter the same problems of value judgments and mathematical manipulations that the partial techniques do. In most cases, the problems are more substantial because the comprehensive "grand index" methods attempt to combine a far broader set of criteria than do the partial techniques. In general, the broader and more diverse are the factors or effects to be combined, the more arbitrary and judgmental do the choice, measurement, and weighting of the factors become.

Method 6 includes a broad range of factors but does not attempt to aggregate them into a grand index (e.g., the Simple Trade-Off Matrix [Westman, 1985]). Instead, the matrix approach aims to display effects and trade-offs of alternatives in a concise fashion to aid reviewers and decision makers in reaching their own conclusions based on their own values without having the judgments of analysts thrust on them. This asks more of reviewers and decision makers than the aggregation methods, but perhaps this is the way it should be. McAllister (1980) argues: "the central purpose of evaluation should be to help individuals—both citizens and public officials—reach personal judgments regarding the desirability of plans on the basis of the best obtainable information, not to compute grand index scores that seem to tell people what their attitudes ought to be. Transforming personal judgments into group decisions is a political problem that should remain within the realm of accepted democratic procedures." It is the public forum, not an analytical formula, that should decide on how best to manage the environment.

Environmental Politics

The public forum mentioned in the last sentence is the political process. Despite requisite scientific, engineering, economic, and evaluative analysis, planning and decision making end up being a competition of ideas and alternatives. Certainly, technical analysis is essential in that competition, sort of like the quality of the team "on paper" in a sports match. But how the match is actually played determines the outcome, and not always does the best team on paper win the contest. Often utilitarian values of economic growth and development win the analytical competition; for effective decisions, other values need to be represented in the political process.

Several case studies have shown that there are three ingredients for success in the political process of environmental decision making: *good technical information* provided usually by a dedicated planner, a *strong constituency* provided by an advocacy group or groups, and a *champion* provided by an elected or appointed official (Corbett and Hayden, 1981). This formula holds true in local land use decisions, environmental protection program or policy adoption, and state and federal agency decisions.

The effectiveness of the political process also depends on the "level of democracy" applied to the decision making. The spectrum of democracy ranges from nondemocratic authoritative decision making to representative democracy (often called "weak democracy") to participatory or "strong democracy." While we pride ourselves in the United States on our democratic principles, too often public decision making is more authoritative or democratically weak than democratically strong.

Participatory, strong democracy depends on an open planning process and the engagement of the public. The process depicted in box 2.1 aims to provide opportunities for engagement at each step. For effective engagement the stakeholders need to care and to believe that their political participation will affect decisions.

Participation, Collaboration, and Conflict Resolution

The democratic political process is manifested in the planning process through mechanisms for public participation. Environmental planning requires difficult public policy decisions concerning, for example, the extent to which natural resources are to be developed or preserved, at what levels and through what means pollution is to be controlled, where major facilities are to be located, and what levels of risk are acceptable. Since most of these determinations are based not only on expert judgment but also on perceptions and values, effective environmental decisions require considerable participation of interested parties.

The rationale for public participation is both philosophical and pragmatic. As discussed previously, in our participatory democracy, decisions affecting the public and public resources, like the environment, should be made in consultation with the public. More important, the implementation success of projects and programs depends on their public acceptability. Recognition of this fact has led to increasing use of collaborative decision making and public-private partnerships, which give stakeholders not only input into planning but also an active role in decisions and implementation.

The spectrum of public involvement ranges from nonparticipation or manipulation to citizen control and power, as described in Susan Arnstein's (1969) well-known ladder of citizen participation (see a variation of the ladder in figure 4.1). Although different situations may call for different levels of participation, most environmental planning cases demand higher levels of involvement. This tendency toward citizen power is what Barber (1984) refers to as "strong democracy" and King, Feltey, and O'Neill (1998) call "authentic participation."

Barber characterizes strong democracy by active participation, civility, and creative consensus, while representative or weak democracy is more passive, accountable, and contractual. King et al.'s authentic democracy (as opposed to unauthentic participation) has a collaborative (rather than conflictual) interaction style, is sought early in the process, has equal partners, has a facilitator (rather than a manager), requires interpersonal and discourse skills more than technical and managerial skills, is process more than product oriented, is proactive and design oriented rather than reactive, and produces decisions as a result of discourse rather than by administrative action.

The nature of participation has changed in the past 30 years. Just a few decades ago, participation by public agencies was characterized by "tell us what you want, and we'll go away and decide what to do." This approach did much to breed contempt and conflict between agencies and their constituents. The approach also wrongly assumed that publics speak with one voice. Planners often found themselves having to resolve conflicts among competing interests. A decade or two ago, conflict resolution stressed compromise, which often left competing interests dissatisfied.

More recent advances in collaboration and stakeholder involvement aim to go beyond traditional participation and conflict resolution. Collaborative approaches, characterized by "tell us what you want and we'll all figure out what to do together," aim to involve stakeholders in a process of collective understanding and learning and to create innovative solutions to conflicts and problems that serve multiple interests (Forester, 1999).

Box 2.1 shows stakeholder involvement occurring throughout the planning process. A number of participation techniques can be used, including public hearings, advisory committees, interactive workshops, collaborative partnerships, and Internet discussion boards, among others. These methods are discussed in chapter 4, with special attention to the elements of collaborative planning.

Although collaborative methods can resolve many conflicts, often more sophisticated alternative dispute resolution (ADR) methods, such as negotiation and mediation, are necessary for major environmental disputes. The objectives of conflict resolution are to reach an agreement efficiently, satisfy the interests of those involved, ensure the legitimacy of the process, and improve relationships.

Environmental Law

Environmental planning and management is based on technical principles and public values, but it operates through the legal system. **Environmental law** encompasses those legal principles and prescripts that have been used through the judicial system to protect human health and environmental quality. It is a composite discipline drawing from a number of legal subjects, including common law, property law, torts, constitutional law, administrative law, and the writing and interpretation of legislation (Findley and Farber, 2000).

Prior to 1970, before the plethora of substantive environmental protection legislation, environmental recourse through the courts relied primarily on the principles of common law and property law. Under **common law,** the doctrines of nuisance and public trust have served as the focus of efforts to control pollution and protect natural areas, respectively. A **nuisance** is a substantial and unreasonable interference of the use of one's property without a physical trespass and is often used to stop or seek damages from a polluting source. There are private and public nuisances, and these are addressed through state courts, which vary considerably. A private nuisance involves effects on the property of one or a small number of persons and is judged by a balancing of the interests presented. A public nuisance involves effects on the community at large, but to claim a public nuisance in court, a private claimant must show special damages beyond those borne by the general public.

The **public trust** doctrine dates from Roman and English law and holds that the government has a duty as a trustee to protect publicly owned resources. Besides specific public land holdings, these resources include navigable waters and tidelands, and it is in these areas that the doctrine has been used for environmental protection. Like nuisance, public trust is addressed in state courts, and there is high variability from state to state. To constitute a violation of the public trust, the land or resource must be transferred from public to private use, and there must be consequences that impair the public interest. In California, courts have extended the trust to lands other than tidelands by ruling that all navigable waters plus nonnavigable tributaries affecting navigable waters are subject to the trust. In the landmark 1984 public trust case, *National Audubon Society v. Superior Court,* the state was required to revoke certain previously granted water rights to Los Angeles Water and Power for withdrawal of Owens River water to the Los Angeles Aqueduct because it caused lowering of water levels in Mono Lake with resulting increases in salinity and ecological impacts. A final settlement in 1994 provided for restricted withdrawals that would return the lake to nearly historic levels (Hart, 1996).

Property law also provides a basis for environmental law. While the U.S. Constitution provides significant **property rights** to private landowners, it also provides government with the power of **eminent domain** to take or condemn property for a public purpose without the consent of the owner as long as just compensation is provided. In addition, governments also are granted **police powers** to regulate private activities, including the use of private land property, to protect public health and welfare. But due to the property rights provided by the Fifth and Fourteenth Amendments, this police power has limits. Indeed, property owners frequently file **inverse condemnation** suits against local governments alleging that land use restrictions unjustly "take" or diminish the value of their property without compensation. Based on the standard of review established by the Supreme Court in 1922 ("...while property may be regulated to a certain extent, if regulation goes too far, it will be recognized as a taking." *Penn. Coal Co. v. Mahon* [260 U.S. 393, 415]), courts have since debated at what point regulations go too far.

The **takings issue** is extremely important to environmental and land regulation, and it has affected local land use regulations and federal regulatory programs for wetlands and endangered species. Several Supreme Court cases in the 1980s and 1990s have helped to clarify the issue, although it remains a moving target and depends on the specifics of the case (see chapter 7).

A large number of judicial actions to protect the environment have used the principles of **administrative law** and **legislative interpretation,** particularly since the passage of environmental laws in the early 1970s. The Administrative Procedures Act of 1966 provides that federal agency actions are subject to judicial review except where clearly precluded by law. Using this statute, environmental groups have brought innumerable agencies to court, challenging specific decisions and, in the process, influencing judicial interpretation of several environmental statutes. For example, the National Environmental Policy Act (NEPA) has been the subject of thousands of lawsuits since its passage in 1970. The court cases have focused primarily on the administrative or procedural requirements of the Act, particularly the preparation of environmental impact statements by federal agencies.

The environmental laws of the 1970s, in addition to providing the statutory basis for judicial argument, have also enhanced the "standing" of citizens and environmental groups in court. To bring a lawsuit, the claimant or plaintiff must demonstrate specific injury or other adverse effect (which may be aesthetic, conservational, or recreational). Despite arguments made for people to represent the rights of nature in court (e.g., *Sierra Club v. Morton,* 1972; Stone, 1974), standing in court still requires human plaintiffs to show human injury in fact.

The Role of the Planner

Planners must play a variety of roles in integrating these disciplinary perspectives into planning and plan-making activity. Figure 1.1 presented environmental management as the interaction of people and institutions in the private sector, government, and civil society. Where does the planner fit into this scheme? Most environmental planners work in the government sector for local, regional, state, or federal agencies. However, professional planners are increasingly working in the private sector for development firms and consultants, and in the civil sector for land trusts and other environmental groups. The role of the planner in these contexts varies, but in all contexts it has been affected by growing democratization; increasing public value for environmental resources; an information revolution; and a movement toward more ecological, equitable, and sustainable forms of development.

Planner as Technician, as Information Source

Perhaps the most traditional and fundamental role of the planner is as a source of information. If nothing else, the planner is a technician, providing data and information that serves as a basis for decisions. Information is a source of power for planners. "A planner's source of influence includes specialized knowledge or technical expertise, a monopoly on organizationally and politically relevant information, and the role of gatekeeper of information and access" (Forester, 1989).

Information has continued to be a critical part of planning, especially as planning evolved from design to "applied science" in the 1960s and to political communication in the 1970s to 1990s. It is difficult for decision makers to ignore good information. Yet misinformation abounds, often presented by certain interests in support of their case. Planners must not only provide information but also manage misinformation that inhibits informed and participatory planning (Forester, 1989).

As a result of the "information revolution," there has been a huge increase in the quantity and quality of environmental and planning data. The Internet has provided instant access to data and information previously unavailable. The planner must convert this expansive data into information, analyze information into knowledge, and translate knowledge into intelligence to develop the best technical understanding of problems and potential solutions.

Advanced information technologies have enhanced planning to meet this challenge. Spreadsheets, statistical software, and computer models have eased data analysis and enhanced the presentation and communication of information. Geographic information systems (GIS) facilitate spatial data collection, storage, retrieval, and analysis. GIS enhances the visualization of information, alternative actions and scenarios, and impacts to nonscientific elected officials and citizens. Good information not only provides a direct basis for decisions, it also informs citizens of problems and possibilities and thus can indirectly advance decisions politically by building community support.

Planner as Facilitator of Public Involvement, Builder of Community Support, Champion of Citizen Empowerment

Although it is grounded in technical and economic information, planning, especially environmental planning, is political. Market forces, powerful development interests, even many elected officials have long been biased toward development at the expense of the environment.

Community action runs counter to this so-called growth machine, trying to compensate for the social imbalance of the market. Action by civil society has emerged as a third system of power, joining governments ("the state") and economic powers ("the market") (figure 1.1). Environmental planning needs to enlist citizen action and encourage a process of citizen empowerment. **Collaborative environmental planning** has emerged as an approach for the engagement of citizens and other stakeholders. This begins with participatory planning and joint decision making but also includes environmental education, encouragement of "counterplanning" by citizen groups, and citizen involvement in program implementation.

Planner as Regulator

Many government planners spend more time enforcing regulations, that is, permitting and approving, negotiating, or denying development proposals, than they do "planning." In this position as ministerial gatekeeper for development projects, planners have been accused of accommodating development rather than managing it. It is true that planners must react to the proposals submitted, often performing little more than ministerial review and approval. And when development plans do not conform to existing regulations, variances and rezonings are commonplace.

All enforcement officials should exercise what discretion they have in a consistent and equitable manner, to improve the quality of projects and reduce their impacts. Enforcement of regulations gives planners some authority in negotiations with resource developers. Therefore, planners need to have communicative and argumentative skills to utilize this regulatory authority to its fullest. They need to represent the interests of the community, to counter misinformation, and to foster inquiry.

Planner as Negotiator among Interests, Mediator of Conflicts

As regulators, planners must take a position in negotiations with developers. However, planners must also play a more neutral negotiation and mediation role in resolving conflicts among interests in the advocacy planning or development process. Conflict abounds in environmental decisions. The objective of negotiation and mediation is to involve disputing parties in developing agreements that benefit both sides. As citizen involvement increases, so does the need for conflict resolution.

Negotiation and mediation are necessary skills in the planner's quest for the best alternative. Some planning scholars, especially advocacy planning proponents, argue that "there is no unitary public interest and that the role of the planner is to give voice to the many 'publics' whose welfare is at stake in any public resource allocation decision." Planning can then be looked at as a competitive marketplace of ideas and alternatives (Susskind and Ozawa, 1984). In such a context, an alternative reflecting a negotiated agreement between conflicting parties stands the best chance of winning the competition for acceptance and being politically adopted and successfully implemented.

Planner as Political Adviser, as Politician

Environmental planning has become increasingly political as issues increase in controversy, as the process becomes more open, and as elected officials turn to planners for advice. "If planners ignore those in power, they insure their own powerlessness. Alternatively, if planners understand how relations of power shape the planning process, they can improve the quality of their analyses and empower citizen and community action" (Forester, 1989). To be most effective, planners must recognize the political context in which they operate and adapt their strategies accordingly.

Planner as Designer, as Visionary

It is planning's future orientation, the "vision thing," that lured most prospective planners into the field. There is a long tradition of utopianism in planning, and despite all the mundane daily activities planners must engage in, it is their potential contribution to the future that keeps them going. These day-to-day planning actions do cumulatively affect the future, but the development of community or management plans offers the best opportunity for planners to help design a community's future. Many critics of today's development patterns lament the loss of a design perspective in planning and suggest that the emphasis on rational science and political participation cannot project future scenarios necessary to create sustainable environments. However, many of the same critics see new movements in environmental design (like New Urbanism) and resource management (like ecosystem management) as a resurgence of innovation in the planning profession (Calthorpe and Fulton, 2001; Corbett and Corbett, 2000; Duany et al., 2000; Myers and Kitsuse, 2000; Neuman, 1998).

Although greater emphasis on design and visual images is needed in planning today, it cannot, perhaps should not, replicate the utopian planning of the past. Rather than designing their own creative vision for the community, planners help the community discover its vision of the future and explore means to achieve it. In this context, as Forester (1989) writes, "designing is making sense together." It is a collective process, and the vision represented by a comprehensive plan should represent the community's values.

Plan development is a participatory exercise, but this does not mean that planners are just facilitators. By providing good information, by offering creative and visual alternatives, and by clarifying opportunities, planners play a principal role in "organizing attention to possibilities" (Forester, 1989). This is no less creative a task than that of the utopian. In articulating the possibilities, there is much to draw from recent innovations in community and environmental design (see chapter 6).

Planner as Advocate

The planner should be an agent of change, working through political and participatory democratic channels to empower the community to improve society. Environmental planners' interest in promoting equitable development in harmony with nature implies an advocacy for sustainable development.

All planners can use their authority as regulators, as gatekeepers of information, as negotiators and political advisers, and as designers to promote certain programs, plans, and patterns of development or nondevelopment. However, the degree to which a planner can overtly advocate positions depends on the type of planner he or she is and the position he or she holds. For example, county and city planners, as part of local government administration, are somewhat constrained in their ability to openly promote new initiatives. Their actions need to be more discreet, working with community organizations and sympathetic elected officials. On the other hand, "citizen planners" or counterplanning community groups are the strongest advocates. However, they have less authority and their influence depends on building a constituency and using information and community support to affect decisions.

Environmental Planning in the Twenty-First Century: Toward Social and Scientific Learning through Collaborative and Adaptive Planning and Management

We used to think planning is knowing, now we realize planning is learning. A quiet revolution is under way in environmental planning and management. In response to the increasing complexity of remaining problems, protracted disputes, constrained government budgets, and recent movements toward deregulation and property rights protection, new approaches have emerged. They aim to provide more effective, more efficient, and more publicly accepted decisions in environmental management. These approaches are given different labels: "civic environmentalism," "integrated resource management," "community-based environmental protection," "ecosystem management," "watershed management," and "negotiated agreements," to name a few.

The "environmental decade" of the 1970s saw enactment of a plethora of strict "command and control" regulations, rational comprehensive planning, and costly federal environmental programs. But the 1980s brought the Reagan Republican revolution that was characterized by deregulation, reduced federal budgets, free markets, and protection of private property rights. This prompted attempts to dismantle many environmental laws, but these attempts failed, a testament to the power of environmental politics. The Reagan emphasis on economic approaches spawned the birth of ecological economics. Its imperatives were to improve economic efficiency, get the prices right, internalize externalities, and stress pocketbook decisions. Considerable attention was given to economic and pseudoeconomic approaches, such as emissions trading, wetlands mitigation banking, environmental taxes and fees, transfer of development rights, and contingent valuation to estimate use and option values. However, the results showed minor improvement in environmental quality and mostly academic economic exercises with little implementation. People were unhappy with progress in managing the environment, and they realized that regulatory, rational planning, and economic approaches are limited in their ability to protect the environment.

The 1990s brought some unthinkable thoughts to the 1970s environmentalists:

- We don't (or can't) know all (or Lindblom may have been right that we must "muddle through" without enough knowledge)!
- Environmental regulations and big government funding of environmental technologies will not solve all our environmental problems (or there may be some truth to those Reagan Republicans).
- Scientific study and economic analysis are limited and don't capture all values on which decisions about the environment should be based (or there may be something to the annoying postmodernists).

After considerable head scratching about this in the environmental literature, something interesting happened. Institutions and people who care about the environment realized that conventional tools for protecting the environment were not enough. They began trying new things. Most of this activity was experimental without clear statutory direction; much was from grassroots efforts (like local watershed associations). Their basic response was as follows:

- We don't know all, so let's learn by doing, by experiment.
- Just big government regulations and tax dollars are not enough to manage the environment effectively, so let's try decentralized community-based voluntary action.
- Science and economics don't capture all values, so let's change the decision-making formula through participation, consensus building, stakeholder involvement, and collaboration.

Thus a new approach has emerged. It has two components:

1. *Adaptive management (scientific learning)*. Rational-comprehensive approaches are insufficient. Don't just "study and do," and deny uncertainties. Rather, *adapt:* "Study and do and monitor and evaluate and learn and study and do and monitor . . ." and embrace uncertainties. Adaptive management follows the learning-by-doing process. The cyclical process involves not only planning but action, monitoring, and evaluation. Resulting learning is the basis for further planning.
2. *Collaborative environmental decision making (social learning)*. Stakeholder involvement, consensus building, conflict resolution, collaborative learning, and partnerships can build social capital (networks), intellectual capital (mutual understanding), and political capital (constituencies).

The approach aims to lead to better decisions for both the stakeholders and the environment—decisions that are more effective and efficient in managing the environment and more acceptable to the wide range of interests involved. It goes beyond traditional public participation and arbitration as it aims to foster "collaborative learning" by stakeholders so they more fully understand the perspectives of other interests. It may also lead to more creative solutions than traditional approaches, as collaborative learning uncovers new options.

Summary

Planning, especially in the public context, is a diverse and interdisciplinary field that is continuing to evolve as society changes, as democracy matures, and as methods of knowledge generation improve. This is particularly true in an environmental context that is heavily influenced by both science and human and societal values, as well as the disciplinary influences of engineering, economics, politics, communication, law, and ethics.

Making sense of it all can be fun but challenging. Planners have lightened up on their quest to know everything before making decisions by engaging in a process of learning. Although this takes the pressure off the search for the "best and only" solution, it raises different problems of process and communication. When applied to scientific learning through adaptive management, additional challenges for monitoring and evaluation are required for learning by doing.

Planning continues to evolve as we improve our capacity to make smarter decisions based on the best information available and the broadest range of public values.

3 ■ Land Use Planning for Environmental Management

This chapter turns the discussion from the concepts of environmental management to land use planning and development. The use of the land is perhaps the most significant driving force in human impact on the natural environment. Land development for human settlement and resource production poses critical impacts on the land itself, but also on water, air, and materials and energy use. The chapter first discusses historic and current land use trends and their relationship to environmental protection. After addressing some of the fundamentals of land use planning, the chapter concludes by introducing emerging approaches to environmental land use planning, including community-based environmental protection, watershed protection, and ecosystem management.

Land Use and Development

With the focus of this book on land use, it is important to understand the context of land use and development. This section traces early urban development through the advent of urban sprawl in the United States. It briefly discusses government and design responses to sprawl and comments on issues and approaches specific to rural land and community development. Finally, the section addresses land use issues on and planning for public resource lands.

Urban and Regional Development: The Evolution of and Response to Sprawl

The development and use of land has been a fundamental human activity since the dawn of agriculture and the first permanent human settlements. Hamlets, villages, towns, and cities evolved to accommodate larger populations and the developing needs of society for livelihood, security, commerce, and culture. Limits posed by pedestrian and equestrian transportation kept these settlements dense, compact, and diverse in the mix of people and land uses. The industrial revolution brought industry and rail transportation, which extended the limits of daily travel and the reaches of the city to a metropolitan context. The countryside and hinterlands continued to provide the agricultural and other resource support for the city.

European and nineteenth- and early-twentieth-century American communities followed compact and mixed patterns of urban and land development. The form of development varied. Some planned cities took a "monumental" form of enclosed and dominant landmarks, a socially and physically hierarchical spatial plan, and reliance on a grid or radial layout. A good example is L'Enfant's design for Washington, D.C. Other planned cities were more mechanistic, practical, and functional, containing autonomous parts linked to a larger whole. Company towns, speculative grid towns, or later segregated suburban land uses are examples of this type. In the "organic" or biological form, the city resembles a living thing. It has a definite boundary, an internal structure, and a symbiotic balance in the face of change. One can see this model reflected in the works of notable environmental designers of the past, such as Olmsted, Howard, Geddes, Mumford, Perry, and McHarg (Kostof 1991; Lynch, 1984).

As time progressed, the availability of convenient transportation allowed the central cities to evolve into business districts, and the outer city, then the suburb, to evolve into residential districts. Cities remained the center of business and commerce, at least for a while.

Government first played a role in commissioning urban design that guided growth. However, after the 1920s, the shape of development was directed less by grand design and more by private development projects loosely guided by government regulation. "Modernism seemed to promise that city design could take care of itself if all buildings were modern, were spaced far enough apart, and followed a few simple zoning principles" (Barnett and Hack, 2000). Zoning regulation segregated land uses initially for public health concerns; for example, keeping polluting industry away from residential areas. As zoning evolved it came to segregate a wider range of uses, including commercial from residential use, multifamily from single family residential, and large-lot from small-lot residential. This segregation of uses effectively broke the mixed-use pattern prevalent in earlier developments.

The Advent of Sprawl

After World War II, a major shift in urban development occurred in the United States: suburban growth, urban sprawl, and the development of Ex-urban and Edge Cities. **Sprawl** is land-consumptive, dispersed, auto-dependent land development made up of homogeneous segregated uses: housing subdivisions, shopping centers, office/business parks, large civic institutions, and roadways heavily dependent on collector roads.

Several forces combined in the 1950s and later to bring about sprawling patterns of land development:

- Population growth spurred by the baby boom and immigration
- Unprecedented economic prosperity
- Widespread use of the automobile
- Massive highway construction, led by the federally subsidized interstate system and other highways that created convenient access to former hinterlands
- Social decay, crime, and racial tensions of many central cities that created an exodus outward
- Urban freeway construction that disrupted many central urban neighborhoods, forcing people to look for alternatives
- Federal policies for subsidized mortgages for single-family homes (e.g., FHA, VA) that led to a construction boom as more could afford the "American dream"
- Local zoning laws that segregated uses, creating separated residential subdivisions, commercial shopping centers, and employment centers

In recent decades, Ex-urban and Edge City developments have become common. These are suburbs far from the central city that become major job and regional retail centers. *Boomburgs* is a new term given to suburban communities outside central cities that have grown to 100,000 or more, are not the largest city in their metro area, and have maintained double-digit growth rates in recent decades. The 2000 census revealed 53 Boomburgs in the United States, nearly all in the Southwest, created largely by master-planned community development and the need to create large water districts. Mesa, Arizona, one of the Phoenix metro's Boomburgs, now has a population of 396,000, more than traditional cities like Minneapolis, Miami, St. Louis, Pittsburgh, and Cincinnati. In the eastern United States, even in the Sun Belt metro areas like Atlanta, growth has been characterized by more fragmented municipalities, which have captured only a small fraction of metropolitan growth (Lang and Simmons, 2001).

The critique of sprawl has been ongoing for a quarter century or more (e.g., U.S. Council on Environmental Quality [CEQ], 1974). Sprawl's greatest triumph has been creation of the personal and family "private realm," be it home, yard, or personal car. But many argue that along with this private triumph has come a public or civic failure. Land uses have separated, and as people have become more segregated—by age, by income, by culture, by race—they have retreated from a more public life, from **communities of place,** to a more controlled life, to **communities of interest.** A landscape of isolated land uses has become a landscape of isolated kids, bored teenagers, chauffeur moms, stranded elderly, weary commuters, and immobile poor (Calthorpe and Fulton, 2001; Duany et al., 2000).

Sprawling development has spoiled the visual and cultural diversity of communities, as suburban areas in all parts of the country now look the same. Keith Charters, mayor of Traverse City, Michigan, said, "If development doesn't go somewhere, it goes everywhere. And if it goes everywhere, you look like anywhere" (quoted in Garrett, 1999).

The physical, economic, and environmental impacts of sprawl are perhaps more significant than the social ones. Land use has spread out. Development density until 1920 averaged over 6,000 people per square mile; after 1960 it was four times less dense (1,500 people per square mile). Development of houses and roads consumed an average 1/2 acre per person in the 1950s and 1960s; that grew by nearly four times (to 1.83 acres per person) by 1985 (Benfield, Raimi, and Chen, 1999).

In most sprawling development, everyone is forced to drive everywhere. Collector road designs and long commuting distances increase vehicle miles traveled, congestion, and air pollution. Sprawl consumes agricultural land, open space, and natural wildlife habitats at a rapid rate for subdivisions, shopping centers, and roads. Local governments struggle financially to provide urban infrastructure, services, and schools in response to rapidly growing, dispersed developments.

The Government Response to Sprawl—Smart Growth through Growth Management

Uncontrolled sprawl development has prompted many communities and states to adopt more aggressive growth controls to manage the impacts of development. **Growth management** is defined as those policies, plans, investments, incentives, and regulations to guide the type, amount, location, timing, and cost of development to achieve a responsible balance between the protection of the natural environment and the development to support growth, a responsible fit between development and necessary infrastructure, and quality of life. **Smart Growth** emphasizes development in areas of existing infrastructure and de-emphasizes development in areas less suitable for development. By doing so, it supports and enhances existing communities, preserves natural and agricultural resources, and saves the cost of new infrastructure.

Using an array of management tools, including innovative zoning regulations, urban growth boundaries, infrastructure investments, community planning procedures, tax policies, land acquisitions, and others, many rapidly growing localities have tried to control the pace and location of development. Where they have been unsuccessful or where individual localities have not been able to manage regional growth effectively, several states have adopted state-level guidance and requirements for growth management. Most prominent among these are Oregon, New Jersey, Florida, and Maryland. These and local and regional growth management approaches are discussed in chapters 7 and 8.

The Design Response to Sprawl—New Urbanism: Compact, Mixed-Use, and Ecological Development

The critique of sprawl prompted creative experiments with new development patterns by several designers and developers in the 1990s. These designers contend that suburban sprawl is not only ecologically but also socially destructive, and that alternative compact urban and community designs that are the most ecologically sustainable are also potentially the most socially valuable (Calthorpe and Fulton, 2001). Collectively, these efforts are called **New Urbanism,** but there are a number of variations. Some designers stress neotraditional compactness and aesthetics (e.g., Andres Duany), rural character (e.g., Randall Arendt), ecological compatibility (e.g., Michael Corbett), pedestrian and transit orientation (e.g., Peter Calthorpe), and social engagement (all of the preceding). All have become party to the Congress for New Urbanism, a movement being reflected in urban development plans in different areas of the country. Concepts of this design response to sprawl are discussed further in chapter 6.

The Regional Response to Sprawl—The Regional City

In metropolitan areas, it has become evident that sprawl development is not a local but a regional issue and that its management requires regional solutions. However, local governments have long had difficulty forging multijurisdictional solutions to regional problems because of competitive, political, parochial, and often petty differences. Clearly opportunities exist for economies of scale and efficiency in many regional solutions for water supply, wastewater treatment, air quality management, and solid waste management; and many metropolitan areas have taken advantage of them or have been required to do so by state or federal law.

Land use is another matter. Few metropolitan areas coordinate land use management efforts. However, Calthorpe and Fulton (2001) argue that the end of sprawl requires a regional approach. They envision the Regional City containing effective regional transit, affordable housing fairly distributed, environmental preserves, walkable communities, urban reinvestments, and infill development. They see the region providing social identity, economic interconnectedness, and the ecological fabric relating urban centers to bioregional habitats and protected farmlands. Regions depend on neighborhoods and vice versa. The region is the superstructure, and the neighborhood is the substructure. The region is the scale at which large metropolitan economic, ecological, and social systems operate; neighborhoods are a region's ground-level social fabric and community identity.

Bringing about their vision of the Regional City and the end of sprawl is obviously easier said than done. As architects, Calthorpe and Fulton see physical design policies as a key element using building blocks of village, town, and urban centers; districts; preserves; and corridors. They also argue for regional growth boundaries, federal transportation and open space investments, and environmental policies consistent with regional goals. Urban center reinvestment is critical to focus development within urban areas (brownfields) and away from outlying natural areas (greenfields). Still, these regional solutions require regional government or at least a high level of regional cooperation, something lacking in many metropolitan areas. A few models do exist, and they are discussed in chapter 8.

SIDEBAR 3.1   *Brownfields, Greenfields, and Other Fields*   Smart Growth, New Urbanism, and regional approaches aim to accommodate development within urbanized centers and to conserve natural environmental and agricultural lands outside developed areas. Planners have coined a number of clever labels or "fields" to characterize the appropriateness for development within this objective. The first was "brownfields," defined as vacant, potentially contaminated areas within urban centers that are difficult to develop because of suspected financial and environmental risk. Brownfields redevelopment is beneficial because it cleans up suspected contamination, improves central urban property values, and avoids development on "greenfields" outside the city.

"Greenfields" are those open, natural, or agricultural lands that provide natural amenities, wildlife habitat, natural system benefits, resource production, and community character. New development often converts greenfields to urban uses. Environmental planning and design emphasize development that minimizes impact on greenfield benefits or avoids them altogether. "In-fields," like brownfields, are vacant urban areas available for infill development and redevelopment, but they do not pose environmental risk. With existing development infrastructure and little risk of environmental impact, they are far more desirable for development than greenfields. "Greyfields" are vacant or nonprofitable older suburban commercial centers and parking lots that are prime for redevelopment. Converting such sites to community centers can bring much needed civic space to suburbs. Finally, "brightfields" describe parking lots and other large asphalt expanses available for energy production using solar photovoltaic systems that double as shading devices.

Rural Land Use and Development

The considerable attention given to urban and suburban development is appropriate because this is where most people live. However, rural and small-town land use and development are also important in environmental land use management for three reasons. First, these greenfield areas are home to important ecological, cultural, and agricultural resources. Second, inherent use of rural land for resource production of agriculture, forestry, and mineral extraction has considerable environmental impact. And third, rural places are increasingly attractive as people grow weary of the congestion and lifestyle of the city and suburbs. As a result, sprawling patterns of rural development are impacting them at an increasing rate.

The 2000 census shows that many rural counties that lost population between 1980 and 1990 rebounded with growth between 1990 and 2000. Retirees, baby boomers who retire early, and increasing numbers of telecommuters not dependent on urban jobs are choosing small-town and rural living. Many of the same environmental planning issues arise in these areas as in ex-urban areas: conversion of productive agricultural lands to nonproductive estates and subdivisions and impacts on natural habitats. An additional issue concerns impacts on the cultural heritage and social character of these communities, as residential development is followed by commercial superstores and other development that affect the economic viability of historic Main Streets.

Several environmental planning approaches specific to rural communities have been developed. Arendt (1996, 1999; Yaro, Arendt, Dodson, and Brabec, 1988) popularized conservation residential design techniques to protect rural and small-town values (see chapter 6). Sargent, Lusk, Rivera, and Varela (1991) adapted the conventional planning process to rural planning, focusing on the resource base of natural areas, agricultural lands, lakes and rivers, and cultural heritage. Other analysts have also focused recent works on rural sustainability (Audirac, 1997; Golley and Bellot, 1999).

They all agree that achieving sustainable development in rural areas is different from urban and suburban planning. It emphasizes local self-reliance and natural resource management. Watershed and ecosystem management principles are most applicable in these areas. The Nature Conservancy's (TNC's) Compatible Economic Development program was designed specifically for rural environmental, economic, and community development. The program includes rapid environmental, economic, and social assessment; engagement of local stakeholders in goal setting and alternative formulation; and fund-raising for local initiatives. TNC has applied the elements of this approach in areas where they have considerable land preserve holdings or biodiversity interests. TNC has come to realize that the effective protection and management of critical rural resources depend on local commitment and economic and community development that is compatible with those natural resources (TNC, 1999).

Public Resource Lands

Another category of land is public land, which includes federal, state, and regional forest, park, refuge, and range lands. Although public lands are not the primary focus of this book, these lands are important environmental lands, and their planning and management provide useful lessons for private land use. Federally owned land makes up about 30 percent of the total area of the United States, and 90 percent of these holdings are in resource lands administered by the Forest Service, National Park Service, Fish and Wildlife Service, and Bureau of Land Management. These lands include the premier natural lands of the nation, including prime core wildlife habitats, wilderness areas, and the natural jewels of the national parks. However, these are also productive resource lands providing timber, grazing, energy and hard minerals, and a wide range of recreational uses. The greatest planning and management challenge for the administering agencies is determining the appropriate balance among these competing multiple uses.

As society demands greater preservation of and access to wild lands and at the same time greater use of commodity resources from public lands, the challenges facing these agencies increase. They have long prepared management plans for these lands, applying the general planning process presented in box 2.1. In fact, these agencies developed some of the traditional and emerging approaches for environmental land use planning, including sustained yield and sustainability, public participation and conflict resolution, carrying capacity studies, environmental impact assessment of land uses, riparian buffers, watershed management, and ecosystem management. Their experience with many of these techniques is discussed in the chapters that follow.

Land Use and Environmental Protection

The use of land has considerable impacts on the natural and human environment. Conversion of natural and productive lands to human use, sprawling patterns and inappropriate location of development, road and building construction, and land use practices after development, all have broad impacts on human environmental health and the natural environment. Land use decisions can exacerbate natural hazards and soil erosion, alter the hydrologic balance, pollute surface and groundwater, destroy wildlife habitats, increase energy use and air pollution, and diminish community character and quality of life. This section introduces several of these effects, which are discussed in greater detail in subsequent chapters. Those chapters also address analytical, planning, engineering, and policy measures to avoid or mitigate these impacts.

Land Use and Natural Hazards

Environmental risks to humans are increased by poor location or design of land developments. Worldwide natural disasters kill 1 million people each decade and cause hundreds of billions of dollars of damage (Federal Emergency Management Agency [FEMA], 2003). (See chapter 9 for further information on natural hazards.) These do not include the millions of daily incidents of damage and injury not classified as "disasters." There is a difference between "hazard" and "risk." **Hazard** is the inherent danger associated with a potential problem; **risk** is the probability of harm caused by that hazard. People can sometimes increase the degree of hazard. For example, increasing impervious surfaces (paving, rooftops) increases downstream flood flows; undercutting steep slopes increases landslide hazard. More often, however, people increase the risk by placing themselves in harm's way by, for example, building in the floodplain or in a seismic area without proper design. Natural hazards include the following:

- *Weather-related problems* such as flooding, stormwater, snowfall, hurricane and tornado wind damage, drought and excessive heat, and lightning
  - Forty-one weather-related disasters occurred in the United States between 1988 and 2000, each of which caused a billion dollars of damage.
  - Between 1990 and 1997, U.S. *flooding* caused $4.2 billion per year in damages. In the last century, an average 100 Americans per year lost their lives in floods. The most devastating floods have come from East Coast hurricanes, such as Floyd (1999), Georges (1998), and Andrew (1992).
- *Geologic hazards,* such as landslides and avalanches, erosion, support problems, earthquakes, and volcanic activity
  - *Earthquakes* pose a severe risk in active areas of the United States, mostly in Pacific states. The 1994 Northbridge, California, quake caused approximately $30 billion in damage, and the 1989 Loma Prieta quake in northern California caused $6 billion. Although there was loss of life, effective earthquake planning kept the death toll in those quakes small compared with major quakes in less prepared parts of the world.
  - Each year, *landslides* in the United States cause about $1.5 billion in damages and 25 fatalities.
  - *Beach erosion,* measured at two to three feet per year along the East Coast, threatens 53,000 existing and 23,000 currently planned structures over the next 60 years (FEMA, 2003).

- *Ecological hazards,* including wildfire and nuisance, pestilent, and disease-carrying wildlife
  - *Wildfire* damage has increased considerably in recent years as residential development has spread to more remote areas. More than 9,000 homes have been lost to wildfires since 1985, including major fires in Oakland, California (1991), southern California (1993), and Colorado and Oregon (2002).

Planning cannot avoid all natural hazards, but intelligent location and design of structures and land uses can reduce the risks. Natural hazard mitigation requires understanding the hazard, avoiding it by appropriate location of development, reducing land use effects that increase the hazard, minimizing risk through effective design measures, and preparing for the hazard with emergency preparedness plans.

Land Use Impacts on Human Environmental Health

Land use affects human health directly and indirectly. (See chapter 15 for further information on the relationship between groundwater and human health.) **Environmental health** concerns the impacts of ambient conditions and exposures on physical and mental well-being. It refers specifically to exposure to toxic contaminants of the air, water, and food, as well as noise. It can also include quality of life and mental health issues relating to crowding, congestion, and unpleasant surroundings. Many local sustainability programs are labeled Healthy Communities. Important environmental health issues related to land use include the following:

- *Land use and active living.* Sprawling, auto-dependent land use pattterns contribute to the sedentary American lifestyle that has caused a significant increase in obesity. Health advocates are supporting compact and pedestrian oriented community design to foster more active and healthy living to reduce obesity and enhance cardiovascular activity.
- *Air quality.* The most pervasive local air pollution problem in the United States is ozone, produced by photochemical smog from mostly vehicle emissions. In 1999, 122.4 million people in the United States lived in counties with ozone concentrations exceeding the eight-hour ozone National Ambient Air Quality Standards (U.S. Environmental Protection Agency [EPA], 2000). Sprawling land use patterns increase vehicle use and air pollution.
- *Drinking water quality.* Sources of drinking water, including groundwater, rivers, and surface reservoirs, are susceptible to contamination from nonpoint source pollution from land runoff. Because groundwater is often untreated, it poses the greatest risk of health effects.
- *Fish and swimming advisories.* Water pollution from land runoff, discharge, and atmospheric deposition also affects human health through direct contact and contamination of fish. In 2000, 2,838 fish consumption advisories were issued in the United States, a 7 percent increase over 1999 and a 124 percent increase from 1993. One hundred percent of the Great Lakes and

their connecting waters and 71 percent of coastal waters of the contiguous 48 states were under advisory in 2000. Major contaminants are mercury, PCBs, chlordane, and dioxins (U.S. EPA, 2001). The Environmental Protection Agency's Beach Watch program monitors beach closings around the country. In 1999, 459 beaches (24 percent of those surveyed) were affected by at least one advisory or closing. Most advisories and closing were due to bacterial contamination (U.S. EPA, 2000).

- *Toxic and hazardous waste sites.* In the two decades of the federal Superfund program, designed to identify and clean up old waste sites posing threats to human health, 1,280 dump sites have been added to the EPA's National Priority List. By 2000, 57 percent of the sites had been cleaned up to the extent of no longer posing immediate threats to humans. However, as many as 50 sites are added to the list each year, and according to a recent study by Resources for the Future (Probst and Konisky, 2001), the program will require $14–16 billion over the next decade to keep pace with the problem.

- *Toxic pollution releases.* Although residential proximity to polluting industry is a less pervasive land use problem than in past decades, people still live close to sites that release toxic chemicals. The 1999 Toxics Release Inventory estimates that industry released 12.5 billion pounds, including 2 billion pounds of air releases, mostly from power plants and manufacturing industry, and 4.75 billion pounds of land releases, mostly from metal mining.

- *Noise, congestion, and mental well-being.* Quality of life is affected by environmental conditions. Long-term exposure to noise can cause hearing loss, but it also is a source of annoyance and depression. Likewise, congestion, crowding, and other unpleasant conditions have been shown to create abnormal responses like road rage.

Land Use Impacts on Hydrologic Systems

Land development affects the hydrologic system and pollutes surface and groundwater (see chapters 13, 14, and 15 for further information).

- *Impervious surfaces* (roads, parking lots, rooftops) associated with urban development
    - increase and speed runoff from storms, increasing downstream flooding, and
    - reduce infiltration into the ground, reducing groundwater recharge and diminishing stream low- and base-flows that are dependent on seepage of subsurface water.
- Agricultural, urban, forestry, and mining uses of the land increase erosion and sedimentation and **runoff pollution** into rivers, lakes and estuaries. Runoff pollution is now the largest source of surface water pollution in the United States.

- Land use related sources of pollution, like septic drainfields, underground storage tanks of petroleum products, and landfills and waste lagoons, are the biggest sources of **groundwater contamination.**

Land Use Impacts on Agricultural and Other Productive Land

Development converts economically productive land such as agricultural lands, forest lands, and aquifer recharge areas to urban uses (see chapter 12 for further information). The National Resources Inventory (NRI) documents land use change in the United States every five years. The latest U.S. Department of Agriculture (USDA, 2001) report covers the period 1992–1997.

- While the 98 million acres of developed land in 1997 made up only 6.6 percent of nonfederal land, development has increased dramatically. During the 1992–1997 period it increased by 2.2 million acres per year. Of the total developed land in the United States by 1997, 11 percent was developed in the previous five years and more than 25 percent in the past 15 years. At the 1992–1997 rate, developed land in the United States would double between 1997 and 2028.
- Forest land and cultivated cropland made up more than 60 percent of the acreage developed between 1982 and 1997. Between 1992 and 1997, 645,000 acres per year of prime farmland was converted to development uses. In the latest 15 years reported (1982 to 1997), 30 percent of newly developed land was converted from prime farmland.

Land Use Impacts on Ecological Resources

Land-consuming, sprawling development impacts natural ecosystems, productive wetlands, and habitats of wildlife including threatened and endangered species (see chapters 16 and 17 for further information).

- *Wetlands* loss continues, but at a much slower rate than in previous decades. The NRI estimates that half of the 100,000 acres of wetlands lost per year from 1992–97 was to land development. The Inventory estimated net loss at 33,000 acres due to wetland acres gained from restoration and creation (USDA, 2001). In most cases, new wetland acres are of less quality than lost acres.
- The latest Wetlands Status and Trends Report by the U.S. Department of the Interior (USDI; 2001) estimates annual net loss at about 58,500 acres per year over the 1986–1997 period. This does not yet conform to the federal "no-net-loss" policy, but it is a substantial improvement over estimates of loss in previous decades.
- Land conversion impacts *wildlife* by destroying and fragmenting habitat (National Wildlife Federation, 2001). The acceleration of land development in the late 1990s has had a considerable impact that has not been adequately measured. Most attention is given to the habitats of the 1,100 species listed as endangered or threatened under the Endangered Species Act. The Act pro-

vides for incidental impact of development on listed species' habitats with an approved Habitat Conservation Plan (HCP). While HCPs aim to provide habitat protection, the activity also demonstrates the increasing encroachment of development on critical wildlife habitat (USDI, FWS, 2000).

Land Use Impacts on Energy and Material Consumption

Patterns of land use and construction affect resource consumption. Energy use is increased both by inefficiency of building design and construction and by dependency on automobile transport and commuting distance. The "green building" movement has tried to address the material and energy intensiveness of buildings, while Smart Growth and transit-oriented development attempt to address transportation energy requirements through compact, infill, and transit-oriented development (see chapter 6 for further discussion).

Land Use Impacts on Cultural Heritage and Community Character

Land development, characterized by open space conversion to roads, subdivisions, and superstores and large shopping centers, can significantly change the character of communities (also see chapter 6). Although some change is inevitable, shaping that change within local context and culture can ease the impacts for local residents and preserve the social heritage. This is especially important in older rural and agricultural communities that find themselves in the path of suburban sprawl or ex-urban development.

Land Use Conflicts and Environmental Justice

Because of these many environmental impacts, conflicts over land use and development are common. Few people welcome the change and disruption they experience as a result of new land development in their neighborhoods and communities (see chapter 4 for further information). Conflicts take the form of angry residents, litigation, and civil disobedience. If a new development requires public agency approval, for example a permit or rezoning, the conflict will likely come to a public stage. When making such a decision, local planners and elected officials must consider the merits and the controversy generated by the development proposal. This is particularly true of "locally unwanted land uses," or LULUs. Examples include solid waste transfer facilities, wastewater treatment facilities, and other uses that are perceived to pose a hazard or reduction in property values.

Historically, these LULUs have been sited in areas lacking the capacity to object. Often these were poor or minority communities that were excluded from the siting process and were victims of the environmental impact. The environmental justice movement emerged in response, to ensure that all people are protected from disproportionate impacts of environmental hazards.

As discussed earlier, the planner must often play a negotiation and mediation role in trying to resolve land use disputes. The planner must also work to achieve environmental justice through inclusiveness and assessment of disproportionate impacts.

A Framework for Land Use Planning

As described in table 2.1, planning has its roots in city planning, which itself was born in the design profession. On behalf of municipal governments, great urban designers formulated the physical future development plans for many of our cities. Until about 1950, city planning focused on a physical plan reflecting an urban form. Planning was plan creation. Implementation was achieved by enforceable conformance with zoning regulations based on the plan.

However, urban economic, social, and environmental problems abounded in the 1960s, and planning shifted to address these broader issues by adapting from a design and plan-making perspective to policy analysis and problem solving. As discussed in chapter 2, it also shifted to more participatory planning, as agencies realized that they could better recognize and respond to changing conditions and needs by engaging a broader range of participants in their analysis and decision making (Neuman, 1998).

More analysis and participation strengthened planning, but the reduced emphasis on design and plan-making changed the nature of the land use plans produced. The plans gave more attention to policy elements and less attention to the physical manifestation of community futures. Despite analytical urban policy plans and zoning regulations, the form of urban development was largely left in the hands of the private development sector. The resulting patterns of development, characterized by sprawl, traffic congestion, and damage to environmental resources, have been criticized for not meeting society's needs.

The 1980s and 1990s brought a recovery of interest in urban design perspectives and a resurgence of the "master designer," such as the New Urbanism movement. Although this sense of future image and place is needed, New Urbanism has not yet fully incorporated many elements for effective urban design and planning, such as affordability, environmental sensitivity, and the discursive elements of participatory governance necessary to reflect a broad range of perspectives and needs. As table 2.1 envisions, planners are beginning to integrate analysis, collaboration, and design. More widespread use of information technology and visualization techniques, such as geographic information systems (GISs), has helped this integration by enhancing the analysis, articulating the physical dimensions of future scenarios, and presenting and formulating these scenarios through collaborative discourse.

Kaiser, Godshalk, and Chapin (1995) contend that planning is now recognized as the legitimate authority for managing land use change within the constraints of democratic governance. They characterize land use planning as a game with rules (planning and development procedures) and a number of players or actors (developers and the market, government, citizen interests, and planners). The game develops as sequential interactions among the players and results in a product—a comprehensive or land use plan and implementing mechanisms to guide future land development. Land use planning integrates population and economic forecasting, environmental and land analysis, urban and development design, engineering infrastructure, stakeholder perspectives, and growth management mechanisms.

But fundamentally, planning is done for places and people, and these vary. Plans for old central cities are different from plans for Sun Belt cities and fast-growing suburbs. To touch people and become real, plans need to focus on places within places, like neighborhoods, business districts, parks, and conservation areas. And plans vary with people, their needs, their cultures, their age, and ethnicity. Plans must be built on the context of place and people (Dalton, Hoch, and So, 2000).

The following framework for planning is synthesized from the primary literature sources, including Hoch, Dalton, and So (2000); Kaiser et al., (1995); and Anderson (1995). Preparing community plans involves six basic functions given below. These functions are performed by public agency planners performing the different roles described in chapter 2: technician (intelligence function), designer/visionary (long-range/district/functional planning functions), regulator/negotiator/politician (implementation function), and facilitator of public involvement/negotiator (building consensus function).

1. Intelligence: Background Data and Planning Analysis

General and functional planning requires a broad range of information, including census and population data, economic data, engineering data on infrastructure, environmental data, and citizen perspectives. Much of this information is obtained from primary and secondary sources, field investigation, or local knowledge of citizens. Computerized information systems such as GIS, spreadsheets, and statistical software are used to analyze, synthesize, and present information. Land use intelligence involves environmental inventorying and mapping, suitability and carrying capacity analysis, and assessment of land use perceptions (livability, attractiveness, symbolism, and quality of life). Planning intelligence is used in the process of general, functional, and district planning.

2. Long-Range General Planning

The most common community plan is the general or comprehensive plan. Although most general plans contain functional, district, and implementation plans, Anderson (1995) suggests a tiered process, in which the general plan is less voluminous, general in nature, and policy oriented. It should have about a 20- to 50-year time horizon and be reviewed every five years. The land use plan is the central element of a general plan because to a large extent land use is its physical manifestation and the determining factor for functional plans. The general land use plan is less specific than the district land use plans.

3. District Planning

District or sector plans cover a small area like a neighborhood, a central business district, a redevelopment area, or an environmental preservation area. The district plans often appear in general plans, but according to Anderson, they should be shorter range and more detailed than general plans and should be reviewed every year or two. In either case, they should be consistent with general plans.

The district plans characterize existing land use, identify critical issues, and provide a future vision represented in map and design form. The land use plan for a community comes to life in these district or neighborhood plans. The land classification plan map is the most important physical manifestation of the plan. Based on land use intelligence and public involvement, it groups land areas into appropriate uses, such as various residential, commercial, and institutional classes. It is important to include sufficient design detail at this stage to articulate future development patterns. Too often planners use "bubble" plans using "broad felt markers" to distinguish classes that lead to segregated land uses. Duany et al. (2000) suggest a "fine pencil" level of detail to represent future land use more completely and to articulate mixed use and creative design. It is quite important to engage the public in this design exercise using visioning workshops, design charrettes, and other participatory methods.

4. Functional Planning

Functional plans address single topics that cover the entire planning area, including transportation (roads, transit), infrastructure (water, sewer, stormwater, waste management), natural environment, parks and recreation, housing, and economic development, among others. Long-range plans on these topics may be included in the general plan. Short-range plans usually stand alone, are more specific, and need to be consistent with general and district plans. These functional plans usually state a vision or goal, assess the current situation including opportunities and challenges, and articulate objectives and action strategies. The development of functional plans uses the basic planning process (box 2.1) with public involvement.

5. Implementation Plans

Implementation plans and programs address the actions necessary to realize the vision, objectives, and strategies of the general, district, and functional plans. Actions include zoning and development regulations, capital improvement plans and budgets, tax policies, and other programs. Collectively, several actions may form a comprehensive growth management program including land use regulations, infrastructure investments, land acquisition, tax policies, and other mechanisms. Such a program aims to guide private land use development to achieve public objectives, including accommodation of development needs, protection of environmental and natural resources, and quality of life.

6. Building Community Consensus

Although it is listed separately here, building community consensus through stakeholder involvement and collaborative planning is part of each of the preceding five planning functions. Local knowledge of citizens and businesses contributes to planning intelligence and a variety of public input provides a foundation for effective and politically acceptable district, functional, general, and implementation plans.

Emerging Approaches for Environmental Land Use Planning and Management

Among the new approaches for environmental land use planning and management are community-based environmental protection (CBEP), watershed management, and ecosystem management. Hundreds of related projects are being developed under these labels throughout the United States. All are similar in goals and approach. They differ only in objectives and geographic scale, and many projects incorporate elements of all three. Watershed and ecosystem management are discussed in more detail in chapter 10.

Community–Based Environmental Protection

Community-based environmental protection has evolved in response to limitations of traditional government responses to environmental and land use problems dependent on centralized institutions and command-and-control regulations focused on a specific medium (e.g., air, water, or land). By thinking beyond a specific media and management approach, CBEP supplements and complements traditional approaches. It is place-based, not media or issue specific, and focuses on the health of ecosystems including people living within those ecosystems (U.S. EPA, 1997).

CBEP has six key principles:

1. Focusing on a definable geographic place, usually a community
2. Working collaboratively with a full range of stakeholders through partnerships
3. Assessing, protecting, and restoring quality of air, water, land, and living resources in the place
4. Integrating environmental, economic, health, and quality-of-life objectives
5. Integrating private actions and public regulatory and nonregulatory tools to forge effective solutions
6. Monitoring and redirecting efforts through adaptive management

The U.S. EPA monitors hundreds of CBEP projects around the country through its CBEP website (www.epa.gov/ecocommunity/).

Watershed Management

The watershed or drainage catchment has become a useful geographic boundary for managing land and water resources. **Watershed management** is not a new concept, but when coupled with new collaborative planning, it has become an effective approach to environmentally management. In 1996, EPA promoted its Watershed Protection Approach (WPA), which was based on the premise that water quality and ecosystem problems can best be addressed at the watershed level, not at the individual water body or discharger level. Managing a water body requires managing the land in its watershed (U.S. EPA, 1996).

The WPA has four basic principles:

1. Targeting priority problems
2. Promoting a high level of stakeholder involvement
3. Integrating solutions from multiple agencies and private parties
4. Measuring success through monitoring and other data gathering.

The EPA uses its watershed protection website (www.epa.gov/owow/watershed/) to network the hundreds of active local watershed management groups throughout the country.

Ecosystem Management

The management of ecosystem integrity and health has become the operating policy of federal land management agencies, like the U.S. Forest Service and the U.S. Fish and Wildlife Service. It developed in response to concerns over biodiversity and the limitations of species-specific wildlife management and commodity-based resource management to ensure resource sustainability. The ecosystem approach has been adopted by many local and regional organizations for environmental management.

Ecosystem management has five basic principles:

1. Ecological orientation: ecosystem health, biodiversity
2. Long-term time horizon and ecosystem scale
3. Scientific assessment and analysis
4. Stakeholder involvement: humans and society are part of ecosystems
5. Integrated solutions and adaptive management

Summary

Environmental land use planning and management is based on the theoretical and historical context provided in these first three chapters. It is a complex, interdisciplinary field that integrates the diverse perspectives of science, politics, policy, and design, in a process of inquiry, collaboration, and creativity. Some of the concepts are elusive (sustainability, quality of life), and some of the process elements are easier said than done (collaborative learning, conflict resolution). Yet it is worth the effort of confronting these conceptual, scientific, and procedural challenges to approach its lofty goals: mitigating effects of natural hazards, achieving more livable and environmentally friendly places to live, and protecting and enhancing natural environmental systems.

The chapters that follow provide greater detail in the quest to achieve sustainable, livable, and green communities through land analysis, planning, and policy.

4 ▪ Collaborative Environmental Management and Public Participation

A quiet revolution has been occurring over the past decade in efforts to manage the environment. Driven primarily by practice and given different labels like "civic environmentalism" and "community-based environmental protection," this evolving approach is referred to here as **collaborative environmental planning and management**. The literature is filling with articles of the concepts and case studies of this emerging practice in diverse applications, including negotiated regulations, ecosystem management, watershed management, collaborative land conservation and development, voluntary environmental monitoring, and many others. These collaborative approaches have resulted in creative partnerships of citizen groups, environmental organizations, landowners and developers, and government agencies that have forged innovative solutions to environmental problems.

As discussed in chapters 1 and 2, the process of environmental planning is by necessity participatory because of the range of values that should be considered when making land use and environmental decisions. These values include scientific and economic determinations as well as issues of social equity and environmental ethics. The aim of planning is to integrate these considerations, and the best way to do it is to engage those who care. This has been the goal of planning for decades, but a significant change occurred in the 1990s that has affected most environmental decision making. Deregulation and private property rights protection had gained political favor, and the limits of command-and-control methods for improving the environment became apparent.

Achieving the next level of environmental improvement will depend not as much on the mandates of government as on the actions of people, communities, industries, nonprofit organizations, landowners, and others, working together, often voluntarily, to protect the environment while achieving other economic and social objectives. The key to these actions is stakeholder involvement through collaborative processes. **Stakeholders** are defined simply here as those effecting change as well as those affected by it.

This chapter describes some of the basic concepts of this collaborative environmental management, including some traditional approaches to participation and collaboration. The chapter discusses the "why, what, and how" of collaborative environmental planning and gives some examples.

Shared and Social Capital

As discussed in chapter 2, the spectrum of democracy ranges from nondemocratic authoritative decision making to representative democracy (often called "weak democracy") to participatory democracy. Although we pride ourselves in the United States on our democratic principles, too often public decision making has been more authoritative or democratically weak than democratically strong. As mentioned in chapter 2, the progression toward greater collaboration and more citizen power is what Barber (1984) refers to as "strong democracy."

One of the key ingredients of a strong participatory democracy and an effective civil community is its "social capital." **Social capital** is defined as a community's stock of social trust, networks, and civic experience, upon which people draw to solve problems collectively. It is normally built on a history of formal and informal interaction, usually through community activities and in "public" spaces such as town halls, community centers, schools, and walkable town centers where people can interact. When planning issues and problems occur, people and groups can rely on their "bank" of social capital not only to help one another, but also to work together to solve problems (Drysek, 1990; Forester, 1999; Gray, 1989; Healey, 1997; Innes, 1996; Innes, Gruber, Neuman, and Thompson, 1994).

Innes et al. (1994) describe social capital as one of three components of "shared capital." In addition to social capital, successful collaboration requires "intellectual capital," or the collective knowledge of problems and potential solutions, and "political capital," or the capacity for organization and influence so necessary to achieve results in the political process. But the first of these is social capital, for without it, it is difficult to achieve collective knowledge or a common sense of purpose.

Recently scholars have lamented the deterioration of social capital and the decline in civic engagement in the United States. Putnam (1996, 2000) provides a number of indicators of this decline, including his metaphorical "bowling alone": While the number of people who bowl in the United States increased in the 1990s, the number participating in bowling leagues decreased. People are retreating from community activities to their private realms. Putnam (1996) attributes this loss of community, participation, and networking to a wide range of factors, including the following, among others:

- Suburbanization, sprawl, and dependency on the automobile, which have moved people from the public space of traditional communities to the private space of the suburbs

- Increased job mobility and changing economic structures, which have reduced the settlement and stability of local populations
- Demographic changes, including more single-person households, child-bearing later in life, two-career families, and rising divorce rates
- Advances in technology, from television to computers, which have taken people from social space to "my space"

At the same time, however, there appears to be increased public criticism of land use, transportation, and environmental decisions, and a louder cry for more input from affected parties in public and private decisions that affect neighborhoods, communities, and the environment. More groups have engaged in collective efforts to help shape better decisions, and more agencies have embraced participation and collaboration as part of their way of doing business (Daniels and Walker, 1996; John, 1994; Keuhl, 2001; London, 1995; Porter and Salvesen, 1995).

Collaborative processes can increase all three elements of shared capital. Tapping local knowledge and collaborative learning or mutual education can enhance intellectual capital. Plans and agreements forged by diverse stakeholders can increase political capital, and the process of working together for a common goal strengthens social capital.

Collaborative Environmental Planning and Decision Making

This section synthesizes much of the current literature to address three basic questions: What is collaboration and collaborative environmental planning and decision making? Why is it done and what are its objectives? How is it done?

What Is Collaborative Environmental Planning?

Table 4.1 lists four basic elements of collaborative environmental planning (CEP). The first two elements capture the balance between the political basis for decisions on the one hand and the scientific basis on the other. If either element is de-emphasized, the effort is likely to fail. The last two elements recognize the need to view environmental problems broadly, to understand the local political and technical context, and to develop appropriate creative solutions that are integrated from a range of options.

Why Collaborate?

Motivation for collaboration comes from agencies and stakeholders alike. It is based fundamentally on the failings of past planning decisions that have not engaged stakeholders effectively. These have bred pervasive mistrust, a declining sense of responsibility, and high costs of impasse and conflict. Collaboration has four desirable outcomes, all of which have motivated its application (Wondolleck and Yaffee, 2000):

TABLE 4.1   **Elements of Collaborative Environmental Planning and Decision Making**

Stakeholder Involvement	Early and extensive engagement of stakeholders in the process of planning, decision making, and implementation. Stakeholders are those effecting change in the environment and those affected by it.
Scientific Basis	Strong and sound scientific information and analysis on which to base decisions.
Holistic, Proactive Approach	Holistic understanding of environmental problems and their contexts, and proactive efforts to resolve and prevent them.
Integrated solutions	Integration of a wide range of creative solutions to problems, such as flexible regulation, economic incentives and compensation, negotiated agreements, voluntary actions, and educational programs.

- To *share information and build understanding* by educating and learning from the public and engaging in joint fact-finding
- To *make wise decisions and build support for them* by addressing common problems and resolving disputes
- To *get the work done* by mobilizing resources and sharing management responsibilities
- To *develop agencies, organizations, and communities* by building staff capacities and enhancing social capital and community

Table 4.2 gives three basic objectives of CEP. Most collaborative projects we see in practice today involve some conflicts among stakeholders, and a principal objective of CEP is to engage in a process to resolve those conflicts. As discussed later, if the process begins too late, after conflicts have become entrenched, it is difficult for the stakeholders to resolve them. If begun early, however, the group can look beyond their "positions" to find shared values (Maser, 1997). If conflict has not become entrenched, the process can productively develop a "shared vision" of the future. Perhaps most important for planning, participants in the collaborative pro-

TABLE 4.2   **Objectives of Collaborative Environmental Management**

Develop a "Shared Vision"	Some collaborative efforts intend for the stakeholders to come up with a vision or direction that they can agree to and buy into.
Resolve Conflict	Some collaborative efforts aim to engage stakeholders in a process of resolving conflicts among them through negotiation and mediation.
Formulate Creative Solutions	All collaborative efforts hope to use dialogue and group processes to develop creative solutions that may not have emerged from traditional planning exercises.

TABLE 4.3 **Critical Components in Conducting CEP**

Planning Framework	An adaptive, iterative, and open process that balances scientific information and stakeholder participation to achieve objectives:
	1. Scoping the problem and the stakeholders
	2. Gathering and analyzing scientific and other information
	3. Formulating alternatives
	4. Assessing effects of the alternatives
	5. Evaluating and selecting alternative
Stakeholder Involvement	Process of inclusive and open dialogue to resolve conflicts, develop a shared vision, and formulate creative solutions

cess can engage in a learning process to formulate creative solutions to solve problems and achieve their shared vision.

How to Collaborate?

The process and procedures for CEP must be developed to fit the situation. Table 4.3 gives two critical components: a planning framework and stakeholder involvement. Although the framework resembles a classic rational-comprehensive approach, it incorporates adaptive and participatory elements to tailor the process to the evolving planning context and balances factual information with stakeholder issues.

Stakeholder involvement is the heart of collaboration. Wondolleck and Yaffee (2000) suggest that the practice of collaboration can be enhanced through a number of procedural and substantive elements, including the following:

- *Building on common ground* associated with a sense of place or community, shared fears or aspirations, and compatible interests
- *Creating effective and enduring processes and opportunities for interaction* by sharing information; establishing structures such as advisory committees; facilitating well-managed meetings that are inclusive and representative; and using consensus decision making and early, often, and ongoing involvement
- *Focusing on the problem in new ways* by being willing to be flexible and positive; viewing the problem holistically; framing issues by problem not positions; focusing on the factual and knowledge basis of the problem; learning together through joint fact-finding and discovery; and inventing options together
- *Fostering a sense of responsibility and commitment* by transforming "them" to "us"; developing ownership of the problem, process, and decision; developing commitment to the collaborative process; and being fair
- *Understanding that partnerships are people and social interactions are essential* by focusing on individuals, not organizations; fostering understanding; building sustainable relationships by fostering trust and respect; motivating involvement by a sense of fun and hands-on experi-

TABLE 4.4 **Stakeholder Involvement: The Heart of Collaborative Environmental Planning**

Identify Stakeholders	A critical first step is to identify all stakeholders and give them an opportunity to participate; additional stakeholders may be identified during the process and should be included.
Establish Authority	To foster commitment and engagement, the stakeholder group must be given some authority for action and responsibility for implementation;
Structure the Process	Care must be taken to design a process that * gives stakeholders the opportunity to participate, * has accepted milestones and deadlines; and * divides the group into subgroups of 10–15 to achieve a working scale.
Achieve Trust	Trust is critical to the success of the effort and should be established early; trust is built on respect and understanding, and social functions can be useful to get stakeholders to know one another.
Share Authority and Assign Roles	Although stakeholders should have shared authority so that each has the opportunity to affect decisions, some "quiet leadership" is required in the form of facilitator, convenor, or negotiator, depending on the situation.
Engage in Collaborative Learning	Collaborative learning is the goal of stakeholder involvement. Through learning, stakeholders can begin to understand one another, resolve conflict, and develop shared visions and creative solutions. Possible steps in the process include: a. State issues, perceptions, and values. b. Identify hidden agendas. c. Develop shared values. d. Restate the problem. e. Seek creative solutions.

ences; embracing cultural and community differences; and acknowledging and rewarding success

▪ *Practicing a proactive and entrepreneurial approach* by enlisting community leaders and local champions; being willing to take risks; taking advantage of existing opportunities like community social networks; building on small successes; and being persistent

Some of these elements are included in table 4.4, which highlights six basic tasks involved in effective stakeholder involvement (Randolph and Bauer, 1999). The aim of inclusiveness makes the identification of stakeholders important; excluding an important stakeholder can undermine the process. Stakeholder groups lacking authority or responsibility are rarely successful. The process should be well structured with a clear schedule, explicit milestones, and the use of small working groups. Collaboration works best in small groups with a limit of about 15 people.

One of the greatest challenges of a stakeholder group is achieving trust among participants, especially with a group of diverse interests. The respect and understanding necessary for trust can be facilitated by getting to know one another through social functions (usually involving food and beverages). Collaboration is a process in which the group as a whole must be self-governing and in which all participants are equally represented in the making of joint decisions. Still, an effective leader must guide and coordinate that decision-making process.

The main goal of stakeholder involvement is **collaborative learning.** Through commitment, trust, openness, and responsibility, groups are able to rise above initial perceptions to learn from one another and develop creative solutions to problems. While different approaches are used to do this, one method of articulating perceptions and hidden agendas can lead to identification of shared values, a new problem statement, and creative solutions (Bauer and Randolph, 2000).

Implementing collaborative approaches is easier said than done. Wondolleck and Yaffee (2000) cite several challenges and barriers confronting collaborative approaches, including:

- The basic dilemma of *self-interest and competition*
- *Institutional and structural barriers,* such as conflicting goals and missions, inflexible policies and procedures, constrained resources, and lack of incentives
- *Barriers due to attitudes and perceptions,* including mistrust and misconceptions, and organizational norms and culture
- *Problems with the process of collaboration,* like lack of process skills or unfamiliarity with the process

To achieve effective collaboration, a number of conditions or prerequisites are needed to overcome these barriers. They include sufficient time, effective communication, and building understanding, relationships, trust, and reciprocity. As highlighted in table 4.5, good information is fundamental. Collaboration takes considerable time and often financial resources to support participants. More important is the commitment of participants to sustain the often lengthy process. Participants must be willing to learn, to be adaptable in their perceptions and positions. As a group they must take responsibility for their actions. They must be given sufficient authority so that they know that what they do will have an effect. That authority must be shared within the group.

Conversely, the lack of any of these conditions serves as a barrier to collaboration. Misinformation, insufficient time, lack of commitment and responsibility, entrenched positions, or uneven authority can undermine the collaborative process. In addition, if litigation or legal precedent is a goal of certain stakeholders, collaboration clearly will not work.

A critical issue for collaborative approaches to decision making is accountability (Weber, 1998). The principal concerns among critics include vested authority, exclusion, and lack of expertise. In other words, is the resulting collaborative planning decision *legitimate,* is it *fair,* and is it *wise* (Wondolleck and Yaffee, 2000)? Regarding authority, legal authority is usually vested in elected officials or delegated to agency leaders who are accountable for decisions. Although it is desirable

TABLE 4.5 **Prerequisites for and Barriers to Successful Collaborative Planning**

Prerequisites for CEP	Barriers to CEP
Good information	Missing or misleading information
Time to participate, to build trust, to learn, to resolve disputes, to create solutions	Immediate problem, no time to deliberate
Commitment of participants	Lack of commitment by participants
Willingness to learn	High level of advocacy; entrenched positions by stakeholders
Responsibility to affect and implement decision	No responsibility given to stakeholders
Shared authority	Uneven or hierarchical authority
	Litigation or precedent is the goal

to provide some authority to collaborative groups, legal authority should remain with the appropriate party. Regarding fairness, the assumption is that collaborative processes are inclusive and representative, but that is not always the case. And regarding expertise, collaborative processes must be grounded in good science so that group decision making is not based solely on perceptions and emotions.

To promote greater accountability, Wondolleck and Yaffee (2000) suggest that process reporting, performance standards, appeal procedures, independent scientific review, and monitoring and evaluation be built into the structure and procedures of collaborative processes.

From Decision Making to Action: Involving Stakeholders in Implementation

As defined in chapter 1, environmental management includes planning but also plan implementation and administration. Too often, collaborative planning efforts conclude with a decision on a plan or vision, participants congratulate one another and go home, and the plan flounders in the political process of adoption or in implementation. Margerum (1999) raises a critical issue for most collaborative planning efforts, "Getting Past Yes." This is a play on the words of the well-used books on collaboration, *Getting to Yes* (Fisher, Ury, and Patton, 1991) and *Getting Past No* (Ury, 1993), both of which deal with the important process of reaching a positive consensus decision. Margerum's useful point is that getting to a positive decision is only half the battle. Getting that decision adopted and implemented is the other half, and most scholars and practitioners fail to recognize this need to follow through.

Often planners and agency staff are left with this critical task. Collaborative efforts must tap not only social and intellectual capital to reach collective decisions, but also political capital to push the decision or plan through the political process of approval or adoption. The process doesn't end there. Stakeholder groups should also oversee implementation of plans to ensure completion and accountability. In some cases, stakeholder groups actually play a role in implementation. As discussed later in this chapter and in chapters 5, 10, and 14, volunteer groups have played an important role in implementing watershed improvement plans, water quality monitoring, stream restoration projects, habitat and trail improvements, and other environmental projects.

Considerations in Designing a Participation/ Collaboration Process

Most planning situations call for some form of public participation. Since each is unique with regard to its context, objectives, and audience, the participation program must consider these specific circumstances. Careful program design is critical for success; in fact, a poorly designed program may be worse than no participation at all (Zahm and Randolph, 1999). An effective participation program cannot be constructed unless the following key questions are answered:

- What are the motivations and objectives for participation?
- What level of participation is appropriate?
- Who should be involved?
- When should participation occur?
- What obstacles and opportunities are present?
- How should participation be evaluated?
- What tools should be employed?

What Are the Motivations and Objectives for Participation?

The motivation and objectives for participation will do much to determine the design of the process. Some are general, others more specific to the planning situation:

First, participation is a good idea. As discussed previously, participation is the foundation of a democracy, especially a "strong" democracy. Collaboration, by relying on the expertise and contributions of a wide array of organizations, agencies, and individuals, expands local know-how, makes more efficient and effective use of scarce resources, and has a greater potential for success and change than individual action.

Second, collaborative decision making is an idea that works. A carefully constructed participation program encourages an open exchange of information and ideas. This requires that planners consider an array of opinions. Together the participants establish a collective vision for the future and share responsibility for problems as well as their solutions. Collaborative problem solving generally can be accomplished with less confrontation and fewer occasions of "gridlock." Involving citizens also ensures that the solutions (including some creative or unconventional options) are tailored to local needs.

Third, public participation is often required by state statute or federal law. State planning enabling legislation often provides for public input regarding local land use and other decisions. Similarly, federal environmental laws and regulations, such as the National Environmental Policy Act (NEPA) and public lands and water resources planning rules, call for extensive public participation (Zahm and Randolph, 1999).

Fourth, the planning situation will present specific motivations and objectives for participation. The planning problem has specific needs for visioning or conflict resolution or partnership formation or other goals. These objectives must be considered in the design of the participation process, the level of participation, the participants, and other decisions.

What Level of Participation Is Appropriate?

The degree to which the public can—and will—be involved is often determined by available resources. Schedules, budgets, and staffing may place limits on the types of interactions and the number of stakeholders in the process. Even with "unlimited" time and resources, there are still trade-offs between the number of citizens that can be involved in decision making and the degree to which they actually become part of the process. As the level of interaction and involvement increases, the total number of stakeholders who are able to participate usually declines. This suggests two approaches for determining the role of citizens/stakeholders:

1. Schedule and available resources determine the degree to which citizens will be involved. The role citizens can play may also be determined by the capacity and experience of both the citizens and the planning agency in public involvement.
2. The participation goals for the program are used as the basis for resource allocations and other decisions, such as the length of the participation program, or the priority that may be placed on community capacity building—as opposed to decision making.

The array of roles that citizens may play is shown in figure 4.1. The most active form of participation, "citizen as decision maker," requires a significant commitment of time and resources by both the planner and the participating stakeholders. Toward the opposite end of the spectrum, "citizen as voter," suggests that public information is available, and that citizens are satisfied with electing decision makers who represent their views (Zahm and Randolph, 1999).

Who Should Be Involved?

The number and selection of participants will depend on the objectives of the program, budget, schedule, and level of participation. A list and profile of interested parties should be developed. This includes key decision makers, important stakeholders, and others in the community who should be involved in planning, problem solving, and decision making. Particular attention should be made to identify underrepresented stakeholders. It is important to error on the side of inclusive-

Active Participation

Citizen as Decision Maker
Citizen Control
Collaboration
Citizens have the clearest and most accurate perception of needs and priorities of their community and should make decisions themselves.

Citizen as Consultant
Delegated Power
Partnership
Citizens should be consulted to contribute their opinions during the decision-making process. When given adequate information, citizens can make educated decisions.

Citizen as Respondent
Informing
Citizens do not necessarily know what is needed or what is the best approach, but their opinions should be surveyed and used in decision making.

Passive Participation

Citizen as Constituent
Citizen as Voter
Experts and elected representatives have the right to make decisions on behalf of citizens. Citizens vote for their representatives, but public decision making is a complex pursuit and should be left to skilled experts and policymakers.

Citizens Left Out
Manipulation
Citizens are not part of the decision-making process, and elected officials are not held accountable for their actions. Citizens may be manipulated into thinking their interests are being served.

Nonparticipation

Figure 4.1 Levels of Citizen Participation. *Source:* Arnstein (1969) and Regional Environmental Center for Central and Eastern Europe (1996).

ness because groups and individuals who are excluded can raise questions about the representativeness and legitimacy of the process.

When Should Participation Occur?

Opportunities for public involvement can be identified in each phase of a program or project. This includes program planning, implementation, and evaluation. Box 2.1 shows that stakeholder involvement is appropriate at all stages of the planning process. Important milestones in the project or program represent decision points when participation or collaboration is most critical for decision making. Among other things, program design should consider what information will be needed at these key points, both by planners and by participants.

What Obstacles and Opportunities Are Present?

When planners are designing the participation process, they must consider four common factors that deter stakeholders from long-term involvement and participation in planning and decision making:

1. *No matter what you do, not everyone who needs to—or wants to—will participate,* because

- they are not identified as stakeholders and therefore are not invited to participate;
- the opportunities for input are scheduled for times and in places that are inconvenient or inaccessible;
- the information provided to participants is just too technical to be understood by the average citizen or does not consider non-English-speaking communities or other people with special needs; and/or
- some people prefer to complain!

An organized outreach program may be necessary if you are to maximize participation, at least by those important stakeholders and decision makers you are able to identify. E-mail and Internet sites can improve access to information, but they can never replace face-to-face interactions and may not reach underrepresented groups.

2. *History of past mistakes has resulted in cynicism and mistrust of government that cannot be overcome.* Regardless of the best efforts of planners, age-old biases and resentments may be impossible to define, let alone address. This problem may be exacerbated by unfriendly media coverage.

3. *The time between decision and action is too long and people give up.* Planners should consider how best to become part of the more informal and more continuous decision making that takes place within neighborhoods and communities, rather than tie decisions to government decision cycles that are often delayed. Taking some early action and showing some success helps carry the process, engage participants, and build community, civic, and social capital.

4. *The group attempts to tackle issues that are too complex.* Regardless of the scope of the problem, it may be more important to complete a small but certain task where the collaboration virtually guarantees success over the short term. Once several small successes have been achieved, the collaborators may be organized and informed enough to take on larger and more complex issues.

How Should Participation Be Evaluated?

Evaluation is an important part of participation and should be considered in the design of the process. Planners must have some way of knowing to what extent they have achieved their objectives, and participants need to know if their involvement has been successful. This assessment can be accomplished in two ways: a process evaluation, or an outcome or impact evaluation.

The *process evaluation* examines the information and other opportunities that were made available to citizens. This type of evaluation focuses on "counting," for example, the number of public hearings held and the number of citizens who attended.

An *outcomes or impact evaluation* seeks to understand how the participation process actually influenced decision making. The evaluation might attempt to determine whether stakeholders believe they played a role in decision making and how satisfied participants were with the way the process was carried out (Zahm and Randolph, 1999).

What Participation and Collaboration Tools Should Be Employed?

The results of the preceding activities will determine the tools and practices that will be employed in the participation program. These tools can be used to

- organize the community and build its capacity for problem solving;
- inform stakeholders of problems, processes, and decisions;
- involve stakeholders in planning and problem solving; and
- create new partnerships and new processes for decision making.

A review of techniques is given in the next two sections. Additional information on participation tools is given in Zahm and Randolph (1999) at http://www.uap.vt.edu/cdrom/default.htm.

Tools for Participation and Collaboration

Table 4.6 lists several techniques used in participation programs. They include traditional media announcements, public hearings, and review and comment of draft reports. Workshops, surveys, focus groups, and advisory committees tend to offer more substantive interaction. Electronic participation means are becoming more useful as a larger percentage of the public is networked. Conflict resolution includes a range of alternative dispute resolution techniques. All of these techniques are part of stakeholder collaboration and partnership building.

Most of these methods have both advantages and limitations. *Media notices and feature stories* can inform the public but are not designed to elicit feedback to involve stakeholders. *Public meetings and hearings* are usually too formal to allow a wide range of stakeholders to give meaningful input. *Review and comment on draft documents,* like hearings, are important components of "formal" participation requirements, but they are often too late in the process and are more useful for other agencies and organized groups rather than individual stakeholders. *Public brochures, surveys, and polls* can get a "pulse" of the public and can both inform

TABLE 4.6 **Public Participation Techniques, Strengths and Weaknesses**

Technique	Description	Strengths	Weaknesses
Media	Public announcements, press releases, feature stories	Efficient distribution of information: "informing"	No "involving"; can be biased
Public Meetings/Hearings	Often information meetings or formal hearings lacking substantive interaction.	Part of "formal" participation; opportunity for public to speak, if not to be heard; to vent	Tends to cater to the extremes; "loudest" tend to be heard; question of representativeness
Workshops (Brainstorming, Visioning, Charrettes)	More interactive encounters with stakeholders using exercises or games to enhance interaction and creative thinking	More interactive and two-way communication than formal hearings; very good if well designed	Representativeness and effectiveness depend on good design
Review and Comment on Draft Documents	Opportunity for external agencies, groups, and publics to review draft documents and offer comments before plans and decisions are finalized	Part of "formal" participation; opportunity for structured documented comments; good for well-organized, well-staffed groups	Too late in process to be effective; not interactive; not good for individuals or less well-organized groups; thus question of representativeness
Surveys, Brochures, Interviews, Polls	Newsletters, info brochures, mail-back surveys, polls, workbooks designed to inform interested parties and/or to generate responses, perceptions, and ideas	Can provide two-way flow of information, interviews can be interactive; can reach large and diverse population; requires less of a commitment by participants	Often not interactive; costly; response rate often low; can be misused; requires staff expertise
Advisory Committees Task Forces Study Circles	Small appointed group with representatives of different interests, which is called on throughout process to "advise" planners and decision makers	Can build constituency and provide continuity in participaton process; well-informed participants can provide technical as well as value-based info.	Question of representativeness, often elitist; requires commitment of participants
Focus Groups	Onetime meeting of a diverse "cross-section" group to get their reaction to ideas, actions, or plans	Can reach a variety of interests and can focus on issues; tend to be interactive	Question of representativeness
Electronic Networks	Use of information technology and Internet to foster communication and dialogue among participants	Can complement other methods by providing asychronous means of communicating	Not all have access to needed technology or are computer savvy—digital divide issue
Conflict Resolution Techniques	Negotiation, mediation, arbitration, "alternative dispute resolution" (ADR) techniques to achieve acceptable solutions instead of litigation and appeals.	Emerging methods can save time and legal fees in resolving conflicts; can resolve differences and develop "win-win" solutions	Often occur late in process after ineffective participation; tends to focus on compromise not consensus
Stakeholder Collaboration, Partnerships	Long-term relationship with interest groups, agencies, or firms to collaborate in plans and their implementation	Builds social capital and partnerships, builds consensus, often creates innovative solutions to problems	Not easy: needs to be started early in process; often lengthy process requiring openness and learning by participants

the public and obtain feedback. However, none of these methods are interactive or provide a forum for participants to explore issues in "give-and-take" dialogue.

Workshops and other stakeholder meetings are designed to provide discourse among participants. With less formality than the preceding methods, workshops can be flexible and creative in their exploration of issues, information, and ideas. Workshops can be used for brainstorming and visioning, assessing alternatives, or designing features through a charrette format. *Charrettes* are problem-solving sessions where participants immerse themselves in an intensive daylong or weekend experience to develop a plan or design.

Focus groups can be used to get public reaction to alternative actions or plans, but they are a snapshot in time and tend not to be fully representative of a wide range of stakeholders. *Advisory committees* are more useful to provide ongoing participation by selected stakeholders. Committees can be effective in providing technical expertise (e.g., technical advisory committee) as well as value-based information (e.g., citizen advisory committee). It is often difficult for advisory committees to be representative of all stakeholders. *Electronic networks* can enhance the work of advisory committees and study circles. The Internet can help not only disseminate information but also elicit feedback and dialogue in an "asynchronous" format where group members can log in and participate at different times. Internet-based networks can use e-mail and threaded discussions to promote discourse among committee members or stakeholder groups between meetings (Randolph and Zahm, 1998).

A number of methods are designed specifically for *resolving conflicts*. Negotiation, mediation, and alternative dispute resolution (ADR) methods are applied depending on the level of conflict. If these methods fail, conflicting parties may be forced to seek arbitration or litigation. Such extreme conflicts are beyond the assistance of participation and collaboration methods, but conflict resolution methods of facilitation, negotiation, and mediation are important elements of collaborative processes where some conflicts, misunderstandings, and preexisting disputes need to be resolved if effective collaboration is to occur.

Collaboration and stakeholder involvement employ many of the methods just described. The goal of collaboration is to provide a forum for dialogue among stakeholders so that they can learn from one another, resolve conflicts, and fashion creative solutions to problems. Collaborative stakeholder involvement must be commenced early in the planning process.

Participatory Tools for Sustainable Design

A number of tools used in conjunction with workshops and collaborative involvement can engage stakeholders in the process of community-designed futures. These include design charrettes, scenario development, impact assessment, and community surveys, among others. Participatory land use mapping, computer photo simulation, visual surveys, and scenario development use visualization to enhance community involvement.

Figure 4.2 People Involved in Participatory Mapping Exercise. *Source:* Calthorpe Associates. Used with permission.

Participatory land use mapping calls on meeting participants to formulate a future land use map. Small groups of 7–10 are given a regional or community base map and are asked to determine where and what type of land development and growth should be provided to anticipated population projections. The process is similar to a fun board game, where the base map is the board. Participants can be given icon chips to indicate existing community features to indicate the planning context based on their local knowledge. They then use color-coded pieces or chips representing different types and densities of development to show on the map their best plan to accommodate anticipated growth. The pieces are scaled to the map to show the land area covered. Figure 4.2 shows a work session and 4.3 shows some products. Participants can not only provide their perceptions and wishes about future growth but also learn about the challenge of providing growth while minimizing impacts on the community and the environment (California Local Government Commission [CLGC], 2003; Calthorpe Associates, 2000). Geographic information systems (GIS) can be used to show the results of these exercises.

Computer photo simulations alter digitized photographs to show potential visual change due to development. The change can be positive or negative. Chapters 6 and 14 give some photo simulations of development and restoration aimed to show positive effects. The aim is to bring to life the possibilities of design change.

Visual surveys are used to obtain a community response to different designs. Using slide images, participants are asked to rate each image on a positive to negative scale of +5 to −5. For example, figure 4.4 shows images used in Calthorpe Associates et al.'s (2000) *Envision Utah* study's community options workshops. Average scores given by participants indicate their preferences.

Visual surveys were popularized by Anton Nelessen Associates in the early 1990s using its Visual Preference Survey™ (see www.nelessen.org). California's Local Government Commission uses a similar technique called the Community Image Survey, using 40–60 slides, about 80 percent of which come from the local community (CLGC, 2003).

Figure 4.3 Participatory Mapping. Left map shows a community features or "social connections" map on which participants place icons to show neighborhoods, parks, civic facilities and pedestrian infrastructure. Map on right shows results of a development map on which participants place icons representing the type and density of development based on familiar existing areas. *Source:* Calthorpe Associates, Undated, I-35W Build-out Study. Used with permission of Calthorpe Associates.

Figure 4.4 Visual Survey Photos. *Source:* Calthorpe Associates et al. 2000. *Envision Utah.* Used with permission of Calthorpe Associates.

Scenario development is another useful approach to participation. It is often a product of some of the techniques discussed in the preceding. Scenarios show development options for the future and give participants a chance to register their opinions. For example, participatory scenario development was a key part of the *Envision Utah* project (Calthorpe Associates et al., 2000).

Citizen Participation in Environmental Monitoring

A major way in which citizens and groups have participated in environmental program implementation is through volunteer monitoring of environmental data. Local birding groups and lake and stream monitoring groups have long monitored and recorded information. Other applications include monitoring of well and spring water quality, land use change, wetland condition, health concerns, wildlife conditions, and pollutant releases. Recently, public agencies have recognized the value of citizen water quality monitoring and have accepted it into their databases. Citizen monitoring programs provide free labor, local knowledge, K–12 and adult education, and improved communication between agencies, the regulated community, and the public, while building a constituency for community-based environmental protection.

Water Monitoring Programs

Perhaps the best examples of citizen monitoring programs are in stream and lake water quality monitoring. The Izaak Walton League of America's Save Our Streams (SOS) program is among the oldest. Since 1969 SOS has engaged hundreds of groups in water quality monitoring, wetland protection, and watershed restoration to inspire stewardship and conservation through education and technical support. SOS focuses on monitoring benthic macroinvertebrates, which are good indicators of stream water quality and ecological health (see chapter 13). In

1993 SOS launched the Stream Doctor program, which goes beyond monitoring to help people diagnose stream problems and initiate "wellness care" for their stream (for more information, see www.iwla.org/sos/history.html).

SOS has spawned a multitude of other volunteer water programs throughout the country. By the early 1990s, 38 states had volunteer programs with over 24,000 participants monitoring 1,000 streams; 2,800 lakes, ponds, and wetlands; and four major estuaries. These programs have gained the respect of state and federal environmental agencies, which have adopted volunteer-gathered data in their water quality databases. Agencies lack the funding and staff to thoroughly monitor the nation's waters, and government monitors only 19 percent of U.S. waterways. Therefore, this citizen-generated information adds greatly to the knowledge of local water quality conditions.

For more than 10 years, the EPA has embraced citizen monitoring and established its Volunteer Water Monitoring Program (U.S. EPA, 1997). In 1999 the EPA modernized its national water and biological data storage and retrieval system (STORET) and encouraged volunteer programs to enter their data into the national centralized data server (see www.epa.gov/owow/STORET/). The following list shows a number of volunteer water quality monitoring programs (and their websites). Many of these involve local schools and students to enhance the educational objectives of the program.

Examples of Volunteer Water Quality Monitoring Programs (and Website Links)

- EPA's Volunteer Monitoring Program (http://www.epa.gov/owow/monitoring/vol.html)
- Minnesota's Citizen Lake-Monitoring Program (CLMP) (http://www.pca.state.mn.us/water/clmp.html)
- Maine Volunteer Lake Monitoring Program (http://www.state.me.us/dep/blwq/doclake/vm.htm)
- Missouri STREAM TEAM (http://www.rollanet.org/~streams/)
- Kentucky Water Watch Program (http://water.nr.state.ky.us/ww/)
- Ohio's Scenic Rivers Program Stream Quality Monitoring Project (http://www.dnr.state.oh.us/odnr/dnap/monitor/sqmproc.html)
- Kentucky River Watershed Watch (Private-Public Partnership). Simple online reporting form that reports by e-mail (KY Water Watch) (http://www.state.ky.us/agencies/nrepc/water/sip/siprepor.htm)
- Indiana Student Data Entry Form (http://www.surf-ici.com/wqdata/)

Many of these programs use online reporting of information using interactive websites. Volunteers can enter their data online and it becomes part of the database. An important issue in volunteer monitoring programs is data accuracy, and quality control of volunteer data is an important activity for volunteer organizations.

Mapping Environmental Conditions

Mapping locally monitored information helps bring it to life in visual form. Voluntary groups have become increasingly knowledgeable of GIS and Internet map-

Figure 4.5 Portion of the Green Map for Milwaukee. Some of the icons used in Green Maps. *Source:* http://www.greenmap.org. Used with permission of Wendy Brawer and Mathew Groshek.

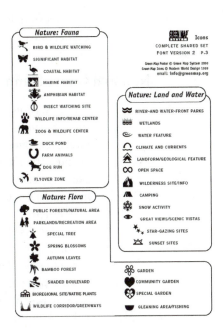

ping, and they not only produce professional maps but also post them on the Internet. Local "green mapping" has been advanced by the nonprofit organization Green Map System to improve local environmental information and education. The Green Map locates and makes visible ecologically and environmentally significant sites throughout a community. It shows the wide array of natural, built, and cultural features and the connections among them. First developed by Wendy Brawer in New York City, the Green Map System is currently being used throughout the world (see www.greenmap.org).

The system uses icons to identify locations of environmental resources and concerns. Some examples of the icons are given in figure 4.5, which shows a Green Map for central Milwaukee (part of a much larger Green Map of Milwaukee County). As of 2001, about a hundred Green Maps have been prepared in communities in 34 countries around the world. Several school systems have integrated green mapping into their curricula, enhancing the educational objective of the program.

Some Applications of Collaborative Environmental Management

Collaborative processes have become a critical part of many environmental planning applications discussed in this book. They include collaborative land conservation and development (chapter 5), brownfield redevelopment (chapter 6), comprehensive planning (chapter 7), natural hazard mitigation (chapter 9), ecosystem management (chapter 10), watershed management (chapter 10), public participation GIS (chapter 11), stream monitoring and restoration (chapters 13 and 14), urban forestry (chapter 16), habitat conservation planning (chapter 17), wetland mitigation banking and restoration (chapter 16), and environmental impact assessment and build-out analysis (chapter 18).

Two examples of collaborative approaches are given next, the first on U.S. Forest Service planning, the second on negotiated pollution control regulation.

National Forest Planning and Management in Virginia

The U.S. Forest Service improved its participatory processes significantly between the mid-1980s and the late 1990s. This change was represented in administrative directives, such as the 1992 policy statement on ecosystem management (see chapter 10) and the 1996 policy on "collaborative planning and stewardship" (see sidebar), as well as applications in land management planning. This is illustrated in Virginia's national forests.

The 1976 National Forest Management Act (NFMA) required the U.S. Forest Service to develop Land and Resource Management Plans (LRMP) for each of the national forests including Virginia's George Washington National Forest (GWNF) and Jefferson National Forest (JNF). These forests amount to 1.8 million acres or about 7 percent of the Commonwealth. As of 2002, the Forest Service is developing a revised plan for the Jefferson portion of the forest and is applying a "collaborative planning and stewardship approach."

The Forest Service turned to a collaborative approach after its planning for the Virginia forests in the 1980s taught them valuable lessons. From 1982 to 1985, the JNF developed its first Land Resource and Management Plan, relying on draft document review and comment as its principal means of public participation. This approach was not successful, as the final Plan was greeted with much criticism and several appeals. The National Forest Service headquarters granted most of the appeals, and the Plan was amended. One amendment required an annual public conference at which Forest staff would present progress on plan implementation and stakeholders could discuss Forest issues. After 10 years of annual conferences the Forest built a diverse and informed constituency and the public's issues and concerns about the Forest became well known. This has helped build social capital for its current planning effort.

If the initial planning effort for the JNF stumbled, planning for the GWNF fell flat on its face. With minimal public participation, the Forest Service completed its Final GWNF Plan in 1986. Based on the range of public outcry and appeals, the national headquarters directed the Forest supervisor to scrap the Plan and start over. To its credit, the Forest Service initiated a collaborative "negotiation" process involving a dozen diverse interest representatives, from timber production groups to local landowners to Earth First and other environmental organizations. With the help of the Institute for Environmental Negotiation at the University of Virginia, the group met over a two-year period and developed the groundwork for the 1993 GWNF Plan, which was approved without appeal. The final plan reflected many of the principles of collaborative ecosystem management (Phillips and Randolph, 1998, 2000).

SIDEBAR 4.1   *Forest Service Collaborative Planning and Stewardship*   "Most of us are familiar with top-down planning, in which the few decide for the many and change comes from the outside. Collaborative planning is different. It emerges locally—bringing together communities of place and interest. It honors a full spectrum of values, holds everyone responsible for success, and begins with educating one another and discovering common ground. There is no one leader and no one is excluded from sitting at the table. Together, the group envisions the future and creates a plan to get there. For those paralyzed by resource use conflicts, collaboration may be a way to help defuse polarization and start discussing issues in conference rooms instead of courtrooms. Collaboration works, but it is not always quick or easy. It means taking the time to reach out to people, to build trust, seek common ground and compromise, and forge integrated solutions" (USDA, Forest Service, 1996).

Merck & Co. Project XL Agreement

The second example shows how collaborative approaches are being applied to pollution regulation and environmental remediation. In the 1990s, the EPA experimented with a number of programs, such as Project XL, for pollution prevention and negotiated regulation. The objective was to achieve higher levels of pollution control by providing incentives for industry in a collaborative decision-making setting involving communities and environmental groups as well as government and industry officials.

One of the first pilot XL projects to achieve final agreement involved Merck & Co., Inc.'s, Stonewall pharmaceutical plant near Elkton, Virginia. The plant, which employs 800, agreed to invest $10 million to convert its coal-burning power to natural gas, cutting its overall emissions by 20 percent. The company will cap emissions below current actual levels, to reduce sulfur dioxide and nitrogen oxide emission to protect visibility and reduce acid deposition in nearby Shenandoah National Park.

In exchange, Merck will not need prior approval from the EPA or Virginia Department of Environmental Quality (VDEQ) for changes that cause emission increases so long as they stay below the new caps. The project involved a stakeholder team including representatives from EPA, VDEQ, the communities of Elkton and Rockingham County, the National Park Service, and regional environmental organizations. Public involvement was facilitated through newsletters; briefings for the public, national environmental groups, and Merck employees; public meetings and hearings; and a public comment period on the EPA's proposed site-specific rulemaking. The final rulemaking was published in the *Federal Register* in 1997 (Randolph and Rich, 1998).

Summary

Environmental planning in the United States has evolved to embrace participatory and collaborative approaches to enhance public acceptability, resolve conflicts, and develop creative solutions to problems. In many cases, it has improved public involvement in environmental decision making and provided increased opportunities for dialogue and discourse among stakeholders. Stakeholders include those who are creating change (e.g., developers, industry, governmental agencies), as well as those who are affected by it (e.g., citizens, neighborhoods, communities, and groups representing them and the environment).

Collaborative processes have been applied in a wide range of environmental planning endeavors, including local comprehensive and land use planning, collaborative development and design, watershed and ecosystem management, habitat conservation planning, and negotiated regulation, among others. While experience has shown potential for improved decision making and decisions, much needs to be learned about what works effectively and what does not. Collaborative approaches take time and resources, as well as the appropriate social and situational context, and often barriers stand in the way of successful application.

As a result, collaborative and participatory processes must be designed with care to limit or overcome those barriers. Processes and procedures should consider a number of factors related to who should participate when and how. Much depends on the problem situation or objectives and the political and social context. A wide array of tools is available to engage stakeholders. Some, like newsletters and public hearings, emphasize information transfer, and others, like stakeholder workshops and advisory committees, stress dialogue, involvement, and joint decision making. Although the former are important in all participation programs, the latter are essential if the process is to be truly collaborative.

The goal of collaborative planning is an acceptable, creative decision, but the objective of collaborative management also includes successful adoption and implementation. Stakeholder groups should also apply their political capital to the adoption and implementation of collaborative decisions. Stakeholders often participate in implementation through volunteer environmental improvement efforts, such as stream restoration, tree planting, and water quality monitoring.

5 ▪ Land Conservation for Working Landscapes, Open Space, and Ecological Protection

Land conservation is the permanent protection of land areas by withdrawing them from development. It is conducted by diverse public, private, and nonprofit participants, employing a number of tools for a variety of purposes. These objectives include the following:

- Protection of the natural-resource-based "working landscapes" such as agriculture, forestry, fisheries, and ecotourism
- Preservation of open space and natural character
- Provision of outdoor recreation opportunities
- Protection and restoration of ecological functions and wildlife habitat
- Mitigation of natural hazards and protection of water supplies

These purposes are not mutually exclusive but can work in concert to enhance overall benefits and justify financial investment in conservation. For example, working landscapes can be managed to minimize environmental impact and provide visual open space, rural character, and wildlife habitat. Open space and greenways provide recreation as well as habitat and ecological functions. Ecological protection provides not only wildlife habitat but also human water supply protection, high-value natural areas, scenic beauty, passive recreation, and scientific education. Mitigation of natural hazards by restricting land use in floodplains, steep slopes, and coastal dunes also provides open space, recreation, and wildlife habitat.

As a result of this broad range of objectives, a diverse set of participants is engaged in land conservation. They include all of the actors given in figure 1.1: government; land trusts, citizens, and community groups; and private landowners. There has been a continuing growth of interest in and resources for land conservation, and participants are realizing the opportunities for partnerships and collaborative programs and projects meeting multiple objectives of mutual interest.

A number of tools are used for land conservation, including land acquisition, conservation easements, collaborative conservation and development, greenway and greenspace design, private land stewardship, and enhancing the viability of working landscape uses. In most cases, a combination of tools is most effective to meet conservation objectives. Land conservation through regulation is constrained by constitutional limits protecting private property rights, but it can be used to protect human health and welfare (e.g., mitigate natural hazards, protect water supplies) and implement specific policies (e.g., wetlands protection, endangered species habitat protection). Government regulation for protection of environmentally sensitive lands is discussed in chapters 7, 8, and 9.

This chapter introduces the participants in land conservation, describes government land conservation acquisition programs, and focuses on the roles of land trusts and private landowners. It describes various tools for land conservation, including acquisition, conservation easements, greenspace planning, collaborative conservation and development, and land stewardship. Finally, it discusses the role of land conservation in Smart Growth management.

Some Dimensions of Land Conservation

Federal, state, regional, and local governments; national and local land trusts; community groups and citizens; farmers, rangers, land developers, and other property owners are involved in land conservation in the United States. Table 5.1 provides a measure of land conservation by these groups. It estimates land protected in the United States (minus Alaska) by land ownership and other means. For government, land protected is given by government-owned land. The federal government holds more than 400 million acres or 20 percent of the lower-48 state land area. State governments own about 85 million acres or 4 percent of total area. Land owned by regional and local governments is not well documented and is given by estimates of publicly owned urban and metropolitan forested lands, including parks and open space.

Land protected by land trusts includes land owned, protected by conservation easements, and purchased and transferred to public ownership. This 23-million-acre total is dominated by The Nature Conservancy (12.3 million acres), The Conservation Fund (3 million), and the Trust for Public Land (TPL; 1.3 million). More than 1,250 local and regional land trusts have protected 6.2 million acres.

Private land protection in table 5.1 includes only those lands on farmland and rangeland enrolled in the federal Conservation Reserve Program and the Wetland Reserve Program. This 36-million-acre figure grossly underestimates private land conservation, since it does not include considerable undeveloped natural acreage in private ownership that is de facto open space.

Table 5.1 indicates the relative importance of different participants in land conservation, but the numbers should be put in perspective. Federal land is managed mostly by public land agencies, the Forest Service, the Park Service, the Fish and Wildlife Service, and the Bureau of Land Management (BLM). Some lands are managed by the Departments of Defense and Energy. These federal lands are con-

TABLE 5.1 **Land Conservation by Various Parties in United States (exclusive of Alaska[1])**

Land protected by	Total acres	% total
Federal government	402 million[1]	20.6%
State government	85 million	4.3%
Local/regional government	25–50 million[2]	1.3–2.6%
Land trusts	23 million[3]	1.2%
Private land conservation	36 million[4]	1.5%

Source: Hollis and Fulton (2002).

[1]Excluding Alaska. Alaska is a special case, representing significant land conservation: federal government owns 222 million acres (44% of the state, 11% of the nation's land), state government owns 100 million (20%), native claims include 44 million acres (9%), and the Exxon Valdez trust protects 650,000 acres.

[2]From estimates of publicly owned forested land in metropolitan areas

[3]Includes lands owned, protected by easement, and transferred to public ownership/management.

[4]Includes only farmland and rangelands enrolled in Conservation Reserve Program and Wetlands Reserve Program, 2001.

centrated in the western states. Federal lands make up 50 percent of western states and less than 6 percent of midwestern and eastern states. They are managed for multiple uses, including resource production, as well as recreation, wildlife habitat, and wilderness.

State land ownership is more evenly distributed. Leading states with more than 10 percent ownership are New York, Pennsylvania, New Jersey, Michigan, Minnesota, Arizona, New Mexico, and Alaska. Most of the states' lands are managed for similar purposes as national forests and parks. Local/regional land ownership varies considerably across the country; most lands are used for human use in parks and open space. Land enrolled in federal conservation and wetland reserves is concentrated in the Midwest's farm states.

Government Land Conservation

Government land conservation includes the extensive lands owned by federal, state and local governments, as well as land conserved through government regulatory and incentive programs.

Federal Land Conservation

Federal land conservation includes management of the public lands, funding for conservation, land acquisition, and programs that affect private land conservation.

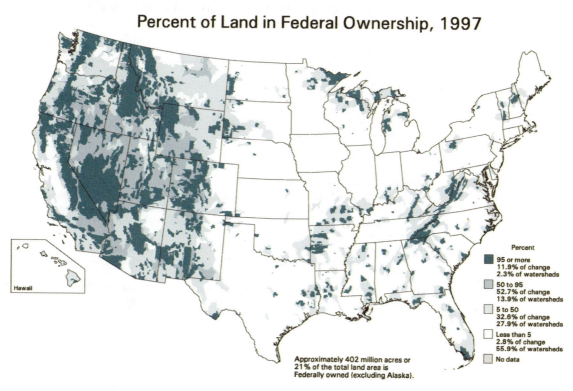

Figure 5.1 Percentage of Land in Federal Ownership, 1997. *Source:* USDA, NRCS (2001).

Public Lands

Federal public lands serve as the core of the national land conservation effort. However, as already mentioned and shown in table 5.1, most federal lands are in the western United States, with more modest holdings in the rest of the country (see figure 5.1). Also, the land management objectives vary for these lands. The national forests include prime forest- and grasslands, which are managed for multiple uses of timber and mineral production, recreation, wildlife, and wilderness. BLM lands are those federal lands not placed in national forests, parks, or refuges, and they are managed for similar multiple uses. National parks contain the nation's "natural jewels" and are managed for passive recreation and wildlife. The national wildlife refuges are managed for recreation and fish and wildlife.

There is a constant tension about the often-competing uses of these lands as agencies are confronted with diverse stakeholders representing commodity production, recreation, and preservation interests. Each agency follows planning procedures to determine the most appropriate management program within these competing uses. In recent years, agencies have worked to apply ecosystem management principles in these plans to protect the health of the resource, while providing for production and recreation use (see chapter 10).

Federal Funding for Conservation Land Acquisition

One of the principal funding sources for federal public land acquisition is the Land and Water Conservation Fund (LWCF). Established in 1965 and supported by a small portion (about 10%) of federal revenue from offshore oil and gas drilling, LWCF has provided more than $12.5 billion for land acquisition. Appropriations peaked at $800 million in 1978 and have averaged about $300 million per year since except for a onetime boost of $700 million in 1997 (Zinn, 2002a).

About 70 percent of these funds have been used for the purchase of 4.7 million acres of federal public lands, mostly national parks, such as Cape Cod and Padre Island national seashores, Voyageurs and Redwoods national parks, and Santa Monica Mountains National Recreation Area. About 20 percent of these federal land funds have purchased land in California, 10 percent in Florida, and a combined 20 percent in Washington, Texas, Oregon, Nevada, and Georgia. The Department of Interior estimates a backlog of priority federal acquisitions exceeding $10 billion (Hollis and Fulton, 2002; The Conservation Fund, undated; Zinn, 2002a).

About 30 percent of the LWCF ($3.5 billion) has been used for grants to match state and local money in support of state and local conservation projects. The grants have supported the purchase of 2.3 million acres of recreation land and development of 27,000 recreation facilities. However, most of these grants were made in the 1970s. After 10 years of low funding ($10–35 million per year) from 1986 to 1995, and four years of zero funding from 1996 to 1999, Congress appropriated $40 million for state and local grants in 2000. This will not come close to meeting the estimated needs. The $33 million appropriated in 1995 met only 5 percent of requested support (The Conservation Fund, undated).

Federal Influence on Private Land Conservation

Federal government programs affect conservation on private lands through regulations and incentives given in box 5.1. The federal government has steered away from land regulation, a domain vested in state and local government. However, certain issues of national importance such as endangered species habitats, wetlands, and mine land reclamation have prompted federal regulatory programs. These are discussed in chapters 16 and 17.

Agriculture conservation programs provide the largest federal budget outlay for private land conservation, about $3 billion a year, about 10–20 percent of the $14–28 billion agricultural support payments under the Farm Bill. The Natural Resources Conservation Service (NRCS) and the Farm Service Agency (FSA) administer these programs. Program objectives include land retirement and disincentives on environmentally sensitive areas, farmland protection, wildlife habitat enhancement, and water quality improvement. Descriptions of the following programs are taken from Congressional Research Service reports that are continually updated (Zinn, 2002c).

BOX 5.1—Federal Programs Affecting Conservation on Private Lands

Incentives

- Tax laws governing charitable contributions provide perhaps the largest incentive for private land conservation. Landowners, corporations, philanthropic organizations, and citizens can deduct the value of land donations, bargain sales, conservation easements, and financial contributions for land conservation by nonprofit land trusts.
- Agriculture conservation programs: The Conservation Reserve Program (CRP) and Wetlands Reserve Program (WRP) provide payments to farmers to take highly erodible lands and wetlands out of farm production and to manage them for conservation. As shown in table 5.1, 36 million acres are included in these programs, funded at $3 billion in 2001 (Becker and Womach, 2002) (see later section on land retirement programs).
- National Flood Insurance Program (NFIP) provides subsidized insurance for flood-prone properties, but only in localities engaging in floodplain management. This requires floodplain

zoning restricting development in floodplains, thereby providing conservation benefits. Many communities have combined this flood damage mitigation with riparian greenways for recreation and wildlife habitat (see chapter 9).

Regulations

- Endangered Species Act bans "taking" habitat of listed species. An "incidental take" is allowed with an approved Habitat Conservation Plan (HCP) showing that permanent conservation lands can provide for needs of species, while accommodating some development. More than 408 HCPs have been approved, three fourths of which have been in the southwestern and Pacific states (see chapter 17).
- Wetlands permits are required under the Clean Water Act for dredging or filling wetlands. The Corps of Engineers and EPA jointly administer the program that has been credited with slowing the conversion of wetlands to agricultural and urban uses (see chapter 16).

Land Retirement Programs

- **Conservation Reserve Program (CRP).** Established in 1985, CRP provides annual rental payments, cost-sharing for land practices, and technical assistance to farmers who retire highly erodible lands from production for at least 10 years. CRP acreage is capped at 36.4 million acres, and 35.1 million acres were enrolled in 2001. CRP expenditures of $1.5 billion per year ($43 per acre) amount to half of the agriculture conservation budget.
- **Conservation Reserve Enhancement Program (CREP).** Established in 1996, CREP targets high priority areas for higher CRP retirement rents in states that enroll and pay additional costs; 1.2 million acres in 2002.
- **Wetland Reserve Program (WRP).** Established in 1990, WRP provides annual rental payments, cost-sharing for land practices, and technical assistance to farmers who retire wetlands from farm production. As of 2001, 1.075 million acres were enrolled; 35 percent in Louisiana, Mississippi, and Arkansas. More than 90 percent of the acreage is under permanent easement, and 5 percent is under 10-year retirement.

Disincentives to Cultivate Highly Erodible Lands and Wetlands

- **Sodbuster** (1985) disqualifies from most farm program benefits farmers who cultivate highly erodible land not cultivated between 1981 and 1985.
- **Swampbuster** (1990) similarly disqualifies farmers who convert wetlands to produce crops.
- **Conservation compliance** (1985) requires all farmers to obtain an approved conservation plan to obtain farm program benefits.

Other Conservation Funding Programs

- **Environmental Quality Improvement Program (EQIP).** Established in 1996, $200 million EQIP provides cost-sharing assistance to support structural, vegetative, and land management practices for water quality and conservation improvements.
- **Farmland Protection Program (FPP).** Established in 1996, FPP provides grants to assist states and localities for agricultural conservation easements to protect farmland. The program is capped at $35 million per year.
- **Wildlife Habitat Incentives Program (WHIP).** Established in 1996, WHIP provides cost-sharing for habitat enhancements. The $50 million program is funded from CRP allocations.

Technical Assistance Programs

- **Natural Resources Conservation Service.** NRCS provides a range of technical assistance on a voluntary basis to farmers to conserve and improve natural resources and to support funding programs. Program expenditures are about $1 billion per year. Other programs include local soil and water conservation districts and cooperative extension.

State and Local Land Conservation

In addition to federal LWCF grants, 35 states and most local governments provide funds for conservation land acquisition and protection. Some of these funds are used to match LWCF grants, but most are used to purchase park and recreation lands, and in some cases, to protect working landscapes. Most open space protection is by acquisition while most working landscape protection is by conservation easement or purchase of development rights.

State Land Acquisition

Public interest in land conservation remains strong despite significant budget problems in many states. More than 82 percent of the 530 state and local open space ballot initiatives passed between 1998 and 2001. Among the funding sources are state bonds, taxes on property transfer, general funds, lottery revenues, and sales taxes. In March 2002, California voters passed a $2.6 billion parks and open space bond with 57 percent of the vote.

State Farmland Protection

Protection of working lands is a major issue in many states (Salkin, Cintron, and Fleming, 2001). Twenty-one states provide agricultural easements programs. Table 5.2 gives the farmland acreage protected, dollars spent, and dollars per acre spent for easements in the top farmland protection states. In these programs, landowners voluntarily sell development rights to the government agency. Pennsylvania and Maryland are the leading states by acreage; New Jersey and Connecticut have spent the most per acre for development rights. Conservation easements and purchase of development rights are described in detail in later sections of this chapter.

State Greenspace and Green Infrastructure Programs

Some states have begun to see open space less as an afterthought of development, and more as an integral part of the land use and development process. Open space and greenway corridors are being looked upon as **green infrastructure,** as much a part of productive and livable communities as the physical or "gray" infrastructure of roads and power, telecommunications, water, and sewer lines. Green infrastructure includes "hubs," such as large parks, preserves, and working lands, and "links," like riparian floodplains and conservation corridors, that can provide a network of land conservation to provide recreation linkages, preserve both ecological and working landscapes, and guide land development. Maryland's GreenPrint Program is described later in this chapter.

Georgia's Greenspace Program was created in 2000 and establishes a framework for high-growth counties to protect lands and receive formula grants to do so. The program is voluntary and noncompetitive. To qualify, a county must prepare and implement a greenspace plan to permanently protect at least 20 percent of the county's geographical area that meets one or more of nine conservation goals. After a county's plan and program fully complies with the program rules, grant funds for implementation are transferred from the Georgia Greenspace Trust Fund. The Fund is made up of state-appropriated, federal, and donated funds (State of Georgia, 2002).

Local Government Land Conservation

Local governments have also established land acquisition and protection programs. In addition, localities use innovative regulatory programs such as agricultural zoning, overlay zoning, open space zoning, and transfer of development rights to protect conservation lands. These regulatory programs and established land protection programs in Boulder (CO), King County (WA), and Montgomery County (MD) are discussed in chapter 7. The following are some examples of

TABLE 5.2   **Top States in Self-Funded Farmland Protection**

State	Acres Preserved	Dollars Spent	$/acre
Pennsylvania	186,321	$277 million	$1,500
Maryland	185,872	$224 million	$1,200
Vermont	88,281	$32 million	$360
New Jersey	82,889	$257 million	$3,000
Colorado	65,265	NA	NA
Delaware	60,619	$65 million	$1,000
Massachusetts	47,737	$116 million	$2,500
Connecticut	27,368	$80 million	$3,000

Note: acreage for 2001, dollars extrapolated from 2000 dollars by acreage increase between 2000 and 2001.
Sources: Daniels, 2001; Hollis and Fulton, 2002, AFT, 2002.

local land acquisition programs, typical of those established by voter approval in recent years.

- In 1998, Jefferson County, Colorado, voters overwhelmingly approved a $160 million bond to acquire open space. This funding supplemented an existing program, established with a 1972 voter-approved 1/2 cent sales tax fund that has since protected and managed 45,000 acres of land and 150 miles of trails. A local staff of 90 manages the program.
- In 1999, Phoenix voters approved by an 80/20 margin a 1/10 cent sales tax increase for open space acquisition. The fund will raise $256 million.
- In 2001, Boise, Idaho, voters approved $10 million in local property taxes to acquire open space lands in the city's foothills.

Land Trusts

A **land trust** is a nonprofit conservation organization that accepts land donations; buys conservation easements; negotiates with landowners, developers, and local governments; and manages natural areas, all in an effort to conserve natural and cultural resources and working landscapes in perpetuity. These land trusts, including national groups like The Nature Conservancy and hundreds of local land trusts, have played an increasingly important role in land preservation. They have acquired lands strategically to meet conservation objectives and worked with landowners and developers; federal, state, and local agencies; and citizens groups to bring about creative and negotiated land development that has served the interests of both land conservation and development.

TABLE 5.3 **Growth of Local and Regional Land Trusts in the United States**

Year	Number of Trusts	Acres Protected
1950	53	NA
1965	130	NA
1985	479	NA
1990	887	1.9 million
2000	1263	6.2 million

Source: Land Trust Alliance, 2003.

The Growing Role of Land Trusts

The first land trust in the United States was established in Massachusetts in 1891, but the growth of land trusts has been recent. According to the Land Trust Alliance's National Land Trust Census (LTA Census), as of 2000, there are 1,263 land trusts in the United States, a 42 percent increase over 1990 (see table 5.3). Massachusetts leads the nation with 143, followed by California (132) and Connecticut (112). California, New York, and Montana lead the nation in acreage protected by local and regional trust. As of 2000, local and regional trusts have protected 6.23 million acres of conservation lands, a 226 percent increase over the 1.9 million acres protected by 1990 (LTA, 2003).

About a dozen national land trusts are operating in the United States, led by The Nature Conservancy (12.34 million acres protected), The Conservation Fund (2.95 million acres), and the TPL (1.27 million acres). These organizations protect land in all 50 states. States with more than 1 million acres protected by all land trusts are given in table 5.4. Although these large states lead in acreage, Vermont has by far the largest percentage of the state protected by land trusts (14.7%), followed by New Hampshire, Massachusetts, Connecticut, Delaware, New Jersey, and Maryland. In all, more than 5 percent of New England acreage is protected by land trusts. This does not include the New England Forestry Foundation's purchase of development rights to 750,000 acres of Maine's North Woods in 2001 (Hollis and Fulton, 2002).

Although initial attention has been given to placing land in the trusts, an issue of growing importance for these organizations is how the land will be managed and preserved once it is in protection status. Like The Nature Conservancy, trusts often convey the property and its management to state and local governments or rely on local citizens groups to oversee the land.

National/International Land Trusts: The Nature Conservancy

Perhaps the best-known national land conservation nongovernmental organization (NGO) is **The Nature Conservancy (TNC)**. Since 1951 TNC has pro-

TABLE 5.4 **Leading States in Land Acreage Protected by Land Trusts**

State	The Nature Conservancy	Conservation Fund	Trust for Public Land	Local/Regional Trusts	Total
Nevada	1,395,202	1,136,910	11,569	12,225	2,555,906
California	989,089	12,651	181,006	1,251,782	2,431,528
New Mexico	1,207,922	15,724	104,610	271,623	1,599,879
Florida	934,242	28,126	121,956	64,456	1,148,780
New York	356,045	158,976	56,016	56,016	1,123,257
Arizona	871,900	2,838	188,539	38,175	1,101,452

Source: Hollis and Fulton, 2002.

tected over 12 million acres of natural areas throughout the country and 92 million acres around the world using outright purchases, land trades, conservation easements, and land donations. To provide revolving cash funds for additional acquisitions, the group has transferred about one third of the land it acquires to federal, state, and local governments and to other owners, usually with deed restrictions. Still, TNC manages 1,400 preserves. With more than a million members, it is the world's largest environmental organization. In 2002 it began a $1 billion campaign to save 200 of the world's Last Great Places.

As TNC has grown, its mission has become more ambitious. Once focused on protecting unique places, the Conservancy now sees a larger potential to piece those places together to preserve "the diversity of life on Earth by protecting the lands and waters" natural communities need to survive. Under its "conservation by design" policy, it aims to conserve "portfolios of functional conservation areas" within and across ecoregions. Its goal is to take direct action by 2010 to conserve 500 functional landscapes in the United States and 100 more in 35 other countries, and to leverage action to protect 2,000 more functional conservation areas in the United States and 500 abroad (TNC, 2001). (For additional information on TNC ecoregional planning, see chapter 10.)

Local/Regional Land Trusts

The explosive growth of local and regional land trusts is attributed to a growing land conservation movement fueled by people's desire to save open lands that make each community unique and to fend off the development trend that tends to make every place the same. The Land Trust Alliance (LTA) is the best source of information on this growing movement. Founded in 1982, the LTA "promotes voluntary land conservation and strengthens the land trust movement by providing the leadership, information, skills, and resources land trusts need to conserve land for the benefit of communities and natural systems" (LTA, 2003). Its website provides the most comprehensive listing and links to land trusts across the country (http://www.lta.org/findlandtrust). The LTA also chronicles land trust success stories to share lessons and network among its 1,200 member

BOX 5.2—Local Land Trust Success Stories

Montana Land Reliance: Conservation Easements, Protection of Habitat and Working Landscape

After a year of negotiations, in 2000 the Montana Land Reliance (MLR) brokered a deal to allow four neighbors to purchase 1,637 acres along seven miles of the North Fork of the Blackfoot River, recognized as one of the nation's best trout rivers and providing habitat for the endangered bull trout. As part of the deal, the neighbors donated conservation easements on the land, permanently protecting the rich fish and wildlife habitat and scenic open space, yet allowing compatible timber and agricultural management. The land had been owned by Plum Creek Timber Company. Montana Land Reliance, The Nature Conservancy, and the U.S. Fish and Wildlife Service hold 27 easements in the area, covering more than 50 miles of the river. MLR, a statewide land trust with conservation easements on more than 360,000 acres, is protecting a number of contiguous properties.

San Juan Preservation Trust, Washington: Acquisition, Habitat Protection

The San Juan Preservation Trust purchased 219 acres on Waldron Island's Disney Mountain, protecting more than a mile of shoreline as well as forested habitat for raptors and songbirds in the San Juan Islands in Puget Sound. The property was purchased for $1.2 million, raised in a 10-month capital campaign. The land, haven for stands of Garry oak, a native tree that is fast disappearing, was protected for its scenic and biological values. The parcel, which would have been sold for logging and eventual subdivision if it had not been protected, adjoins the 209-acre Bitte Baer Preserve, owned by The Nature Conservancy. Major foundation funding came from the Paul G. Allen Forest Protection Foundation, the Neukom Family Foundation, a challenge grant from The Kresge Foundation, and hundreds of individual donors. The San Juan County Land Bank purchased a conservation easement on 171 acres of the property. The San Juan Preservation Trust and The Nature Conservancy will steward the total 428 acres together. Founded in 1979, the San Juan Preservation Trust is dedicated to protecting the wildlife, scenery, and traditional way of life of the San Juan Islands in Puget Sound. The Trust now owns 32 nature preserves on 10 islands throughout the San Juans. Some of the nature preserves are open for public access for passive recreation.

Maryland Environmental Trust, Lower Shore Land Trust: Conservation Easement, Habitat Protection

The Maryland Environmental Trust and the Lower Shore Land Trust worked for about two years to place a conservation easement on 987 acres on the Chesapeake Bay in Somerset County. The land trusts, approached by a person who owned only a 5 percent interest in the property, had to locate the 15 other co-owners to consummate the deal. The natural resources value of the property—which includes eight miles bordering the Chesapeake Bay and its tributaries and an abundance of wildlife as well as a great blue heron rookery—spurred the land trusts to pursue the deal. Eventually, the land trusts found a conservation buyer for the land, an individual willing to purchase the property with its conservation easement restrictions. In this case, the easement prohibits subdivision and limits construction to a single residence. The land trusts also found the property's owners, some of whom lived as far away as Miami, Florida. The landowner who had originally offered to donate the land continued to decline payment for his share of the property.

(Land Trust Alliance, Land Trust Success Stories: http://www.lta.org)

trusts. Some recent success stories, given in box 5.2, illustrate the land deals that land trusts broker to conserve open space, habitats, and working landscapes.

Tools for Land Conservation

Land trusts and government land conservation programs employ a number of conservation tools to protect lands. Some of these are dependent on conservation objectives; others are generic to a range of programs. They include program design, tools for acquiring land and development rights, collaborative conservation and development, greenway/greenspace design, tools for protecting the working landscape, and private land stewardship.

Designing a Land Conservation Program

Land conservation programs vary according to their purpose, size, and the organization running them. Some aim to preserve ecological resources, others provide recreation, still others intend to maintain working landscapes. Some are administered by government agencies, others by nonprofit land trusts. Despite these differences, certain dimensions and procedures are common to most land conservation programs. The TPL provides technical assistance for public land conservation mostly by local government, and the LTA advises nonprofit land trusts. They have developed principles and procedures of designing and managing land conservation programs.

The TPL's key elements for local government land conservation programs are organization, community involvement, partnership building, program design and planning, financing, land acquisition, and land management. The LTA's principles for land trusts stress structure, rational decision making, and accountability (see LTA, 2003; TPL, 2002).

Acquiring Land and Development Rights

The key step in land conservation is protecting land for intended purposes. There are many means of controlling land use and development, including government land use zoning and districting, use-value tax assessment, infrastructure planning, and others discussed in chapter 7. However, these methods are only available to government agencies, and even when available, they do not provide effective permanent protection. Permanent protection requires acquisition of the land or at least the land's development rights.

Associated with each parcel of land is a bundle of rights. Like a bundle of sticks, these rights can be separated and held by different parties. For example, I may own a piece of property, but a mining company may own the subsurface mineral rights; that separation of ownership is reflected in the deed or title to the property. As a result of this bundle of rights, there are various means to acquire land or the rights associated with it. These are given in Table 5.5, along with their

TABLE 5.5 **Rights and Interests in Property That Can Be Acquired**

Method	Definition	Advantages	Disadvantages
Fee-Simple Ownership	Obtaining full ownership of the land. (Wherever possible, this should be used for larger tracts of land with a lower cost per acre.)	Gives trust or agency full control. Provides full access to the property. Guarantees permanent protection.	Expensive. Usually removes land from tax base. Ownership responsibility includes liability and maintenance.
Conservation Easement/ Development Rights	Legal agreement a property owner makes to restrict the type and amount of development that may take place on his or her property. A partial interest in the property is transferred to an appropriate nonprofit or governmental entity either by gift or purchase. As ownership changes, the land remains subject to the easement restrictions. (Well suited for preserving agricultural land and scenic areas.)	Less expensive than fee simple. Tailored to the protection requirements of the landowner and the property, and the desire of the landowner. Landowner retains ownership and property remains on the tax rolls, often at a lower rate because of restricted use. Potential income and estate tax benefits from donation. More permanent and often more restrictive than land use regulations, which often change with the political climate.	Public access may not be provided. Easement must be enforced. Restricted use may lower resale value.
Purchase of Land with Leaseback	As part of purchase contract, trust or agency agrees to lease land back to the seller, subject to restrictions.	Income through lease-back. Liability and management responsibilities assigned to lessee.	Public access may not be available. Land must be appropriate for leaseback (e.g., agricultural)
Lease	Short- or long-term rental of land.	Low cost for use of land. Landowner receives income and retains control of property.	Does not provide equity and affords only limited control of property. Temporary.
Undivided Interest	Ownership is split between different owners, each with fractional interest extending over the whole parcel. Each owner has equal rights to entire property.	Prevents one owner from acting without the consent of the others.	Several landowners can complicate property management issues, including payment of taxes.

Source: Trust for Public Land, 2002.

advantages and disadvantages. **Fee-simple purchase** provides all rights and guarantees protection but is costly since the land is bought at market value. **Conservation easements or development rights** restrict the owner from specified development uses. This provides permanent protection as the easement or development right restrictions become part of the property deed and remain intact as the land is bought and sold. **Leasing, purchase with lease-back,** and **undivided interest** are also included in the table, but they have more limited use in land conservation.

Most organizations do not have the financial capability to protect large tracts of land through fee-simple purchase. They can stretch their financial resources by acquiring easements and development rights rather than full title. The manner in which the land or rights are acquired also has financial consequences. Table 5.6 describes ways in which land or rights can be acquired by land trusts or public agencies for land conservation. **Fair market value sale** is the most costly means of acquisition. **Eminent domain** and **tax foreclosure** acquisition are restricted to government agencies.

Bargain sales and **donations** save considerable expense by the trust or agency and can provide large tax benefits to the seller to offset the lower compensation from the sale or gift. In a land or conservation easement donation either to a government agency or an IRS-registered land trust, landowners can claim the market value of the land as a charitable contribution and income tax deduction. A bargain sale is selling the land (or its development rights) at less than market value; the landowner benefits by being able to claim the difference between the purchase price and the market value as a tax deduction. The benefit depends on the owner's tax bracket and whether he or she can claim the contribution as a state as well as federal income tax deduction.

Bequest and **donation with reserved life estate** are similar in that the trust or agency does not gain use of the property until the death of the landowner. Donation with reserved life estate provides immediate tax benefits to the landowner, whereas a bequest does not. Land exchanges can be used by both land trusts and agencies to acquire conservation lands in exchange for developable lands they may have received by donation or bequest.

Conservation Easements

As discussed, the conservation easement does not involve a transfer of property ownership. A normal easement is an acquired use of someone else's land for such purposes as road access, placement of a septic drain field, or crossing the land with a transmission line. A conservation easement is a "reverse" easement in that it does not acquire a use of the land but instead restricts the use of the land by the landowner. It is defined in the following sidebar.

SIDEBAR 5.1 *Conservation Easement:* A less-than-fee-simple interest in land that is voluntarily donated or sold by a landowner to a unit of government or an IRS-recognized, nonprofit conservation organization to protect open space, recreation, ecological, agricultural, or historic resources. Most easements are granted in perpetuity. Land use restrictions are clearly defined in the deed and are negotiated between the property owner and the easement receiver based on the landowner's needs and an analysis of the property. The conveyed easement serves as a jointly held and legally binding plan for how the land will be used (Wright, 1993).

TABLE 5.6 **Techniques for Acquiring Land Title or Rights by a Land Trust or Public Agency**

Technique	Explanation	Advantages	Disadvantages
Fair Market Value Sale	Land is sold at its value at highest and best use.	Highest sales income (cash inflow) to seller.	Can be expensive.
Bargain Sale	Part donation/part sale—property is sold at less than fair market value.	Often the landowner is eligible for a tax deduction for the difference between the sale price and the fair market value because the sale is treated like a charitable contribution.	Seller must be willing to sell at less than fair market value. Can be expensive.
Outright Donation	A donation by landowner of all interest in property.	Allows for permanent protection without direct public expenditure. Tax benefits to seller since property's market value is considered a charitable contribution.	Ownership responsibility includes liability and maintenance.
Bequest	Landowner retains ownership until death.	Management responsibility usually deferred until donor's death.	Date of acquisition is uncertain. Donor does not benefit from income tax deductions. Landowner can change will.
Donation with Reserved Life Estate	Landowner donates during lifetime but has lifetime use.	Landowner retains use but receives tax benefits from donation.	Date of acquisition is uncertain.
Land Exchange	Exchange of developable land for land with high conservation value.	Low-cost technique if trade parcel is donated. Reduces capital gains tax for original owner of protected land.	Properties must be of comparable value. Complicated and time-consuming.
Eminent Domain	The right of the government to take private property for public purposes upon payment of just compensation.	Provides government with a tool to acquire desired properties if other acquisition techniques are not workable.	High acquisition costs. Can result in speculation on targeted properties. Potentially expensive and time-consuming litigation.
Tax Foreclosure	Government acquires land by tax payment default.	Limited expenditure. Land might not be appropriate for public open space but can be sold to provide funds for open space acquisition.	Cumbersome process.

Source: Trust for Public Land, 2002.

Conservation easements have several advantages over other means of land protection, and we will later compare them to other government mechanisms like purchase and transfer of development rights and zoning. Among the advantages are the following:

- They are permanent protection.
- They are less costly than outright acquisition.
- They offer compensation to landowners by payment or tax benefit.

- They stay in private ownership (reduces liability exposure, management costs; land stays on tax rolls), and
- They generally come about as a result of interest in stewardship and preservation.

The steps in developing a conservation easement include initial meetings, title search, site assessment, negotiation of easement restrictions, easement appraisal, tax benefit estimation, notification of local government, finalization of agreement, deed filing, and, finally, site stewardship. Appraisal is an important step because it will determine the payment or donation value of the easement. The property is appraised for its "highest and best use" given existing zoning and market conditions. It is then appraised with use restrictions of the conservation easement. The difference between the two appraised values is the value of the easement. Stewardship and management of the site is important to ensure that the easement is enforced.

Purchase of Development Rights

Purchase of development rights (PDR) is very similar to purchased conservation easements in that the development rights are separated from the property title, sold, and reflected in a new deed with development restrictions. Only government agencies use PDR programs, whereas both agencies and land trusts use conservation easements. Most PDR programs are used for protection of farmland and open space. Purchase of agricultural conservation easement (PACE) programs are a form of PDR for working landscapes (American Farmland Trust, 2001).

PDR programs require a funding source, usually a state or local bond. According to the American Farmland Trust, 21 states and 34 localities in 11 states have established PACE or PDR programs that protect 1 million acres of farmland. Leading states are Pennsylvania (186,300 acres), Maryland (185,900), Vermont (88,300), and New Jersey (71,000). PDR is discussed further in chapters 7 and 8.

Collaborative Conservation and Development

Collaborative conservation and development is a negotiated compromise development plan involving landowner, developer, designer, local government, and land trust in which conservation of natural and/or cultural resources and development are accommodated, generally using cluster development, conservation easements, agricultural and natural reserves, and land management and stewardship.

The 70-acre Mill Hollow Estate in Delaware County, Pennsylvania, shown in figure 5.2, offers a good example of the use of a conservation easement and land donation to a land trust as part of a comprehensive plan for site development and environmental protection. The Natural Land Trust prepared a master plan of the parcel for the landowner who wished to remain on the land but needed to realize a financial gain through subdivision and development.

The plan called for five uses shown on the map: (1) 40 acres of woodland were conveyed to the trust; (2) one acre was traded with the township; (3) five parcels (all with existing buildings) were subdivided and sold at market value; (4) the owner retained his residence and 15 acres; and (5) a stream valley conservation

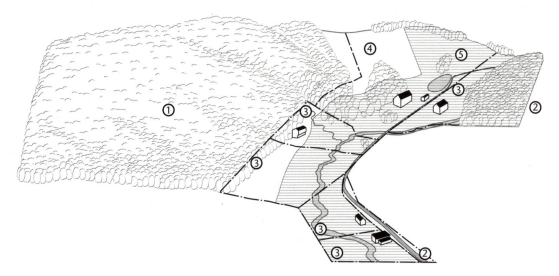

Figure 5.2 Collaborative Conservation and Development of the Mill Hollow Estate. Total area: 70 acres. (1) 40 acres convey to Trust. (2) One acre traded to town for road. (3) Five parcels subdivided, sold at market. (4) Owner retains residence and 15 acres. (5) Stream Valley Conservation Easement (hatched line area). *Source:* Metzger (1983).

easement was provided in the deeds to the subdivided lands. The Trust was also given a percentage of the sale price of each parcel to be used to manage the property. Although the direct financial return to the landowner for this transaction was less than if the entire estate were subdivided and sold, such a sale would have exposed the family to high capital gains taxes. The owner chose the master plan because it enabled the family to remain on the property and was sufficiently attractive financially since it included the tax-deductible charitable contribution of land to the Trust (Metzger, 1983).

Collaborative conservation and development is the principle behind rural cluster and conservation subdivision design popularized by Randall Arendt and discussed in chapter 6. Open space, working landscapes, historic sites, and wildlife habitats set aside in such development designs can have easements or property rights deeded to a land trust for permanent protection and stewardship. This is illustrated in figure 5.3, which shows a hypothetical rural cluster subdivision with common recreation open space held by all of the residents through the homeowner's association, non-common working landscape open space retained by the original landowner/farmer, and wildlife and passive recreation open space dedicated to a land trust or the local government. This collaborative development provides for new housing, a financial return to the original owner, a diverse mix of open space, and potential tax benefits to the developer (and reduced costs to new residents) for the land donation (Arendt, 1999).

Tools to Conserve the Working Landscape

Because of the significant conversion of agricultural land to urban development in the past several decades, states, communities, and land trusts have developed pro-

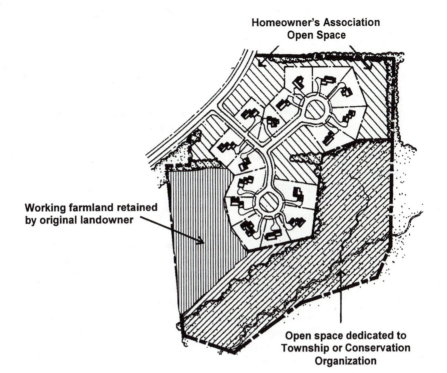

Figure 5.3 Collaborative development leads to residential use and land conservation for active and passive recreation, wildlife habitat, and working farmland. *Source:* Arendt (1999). Used by permisssion of Island Press.

grams to protect the working landscape. These programs have a number of objectives: to provide for local food production, to conserve the open space and rural character agricultural land provides, and to keep viable an agricultural economy sector (Stokes, Watson, and Mastran, 1997). More recently, certain communities have expanded these objectives to include other natural resource–based land uses, such as forestry and fisheries, and included them all under the label "working landscapes."

Tools used to conserve these lands and land uses are similar to other conservation methods discussed previously in this chapter and to growth management tools discussed in chapters 7 and 8. However, it is useful to summarize them here, along with their advantages and disadvantages for conservation of the working landscape.

Of the tools given in table 5.7, conservation easements and development rights purchase and transfer are the only methods that provide permanent protection. Zoning, even exclusive agricultural zoning, is subject to rezoning decisions. Agricultural districting, right to farm, and differential taxation help to provide a better climate for working lands, but landowners can still choose to convert their lands to other permitted uses.

Obtaining development rights keeps land out of development, but it still does not guarantee that working uses of the land will remain economically viable. A combination of measures in addition to development rights acquisition is needed. These include districting and right-to-farm, but also farming economy programs like development of farmers markets and co-ops.

TABLE 5.7 **Tools to Conserve Agricultural Land and the Working Landscape**

Tool	Description	Advantages	Disadvantages	Number of States/ *Number of Localities
Exclusive Agricultural Zoning	Regulatory zoning prohibiting nonagricultural building.	Provides strict control as long as zoning is in place.	Property rights and legal takings issues; subject to rezoning.	Localities in Oregon
Nonexclusive Agricultural Zoning	Regulatory zoning designating farming as primary use and limiting nonfarm land use by large-lot residential density.	Sets farming as primary use.	Large-lot zoning does not provide contiguous working land; may consume productive farmland at a faster rate.	Localities in 23 states
Cluster Zoning	Allows on-site density transfers or requires clustering of development to set aside open space or working land under permanent protection.	Accommodates development while permanently protecting some working land.	May not leave a critical mass of contiguous working land; may create conflicts between farms and residences.	Numerous localities
Agricultural Conservation Easements/PDR	Landowners sell or donate their right to develop their property.	Provides permanent protection of working land.	Purchasing easements or development rights is costly to government or land trusts.	14 states; localities in 13 states
Transfer of Development Rights	Allow landowners to transfer right to develop on one parcel (designated "preservation") to another (designated "development").	Provides permanent protection of working land at minor cost compared with PDR.	Requires complex administration to designate preservation and development areas, and broker development rights.	Localities in 15 states
Agricultural Districting	Farmers form special districts in which agriculture is encouraged and protected by right-to-farm, differential taxation, PDR eligibility, etc.	Can provide a critical mass of contiguous working land and benefits to farmers.	Does not provide permanent protection; farmers sign on for time period and may opt out with minor penalty.	16 states; localities in 3 states
Differential Property Taxation	Working land is taxed as use value rather than development value; "circuit breaker" programs give tax credits.	Prevents property taxes from forcing farmers to sell or develop.	Does not provide permanent protection; farmers sign on for time period and may opt out with minor penalty.	49 states

TABLE 5.7 (*Continued*) **Tools to Conserve Agricultural Land and the Working Landscape**

Tool	Description	Advantages	Disadvantages	Number of States/ *Number of Localities
Circuit Breaker Tax Relief	Working land is taxed as market value, but landowners are eligible for tax credit to offset property taxes based on income.	Prevents property taxes from forcing farmers to sell or develop.	Does not provide permanent protection; farmers sign on for time period and may opt out with minor penalty.	4 states
Right to Farm	Farmers are protected from nuisance suits; generally applied to agricultural zones or districts.	Supports farm activities.	Does not protect working land, only farming activities from lawsuits.	50 states

*Source of implementation data: American Farmland Trust, 2002.

Design and Planning Tools for Open Space, Greenways, and Green Infrastructure

Local land conservation planning and design has evolved in the past few decades (table 5.8). Although environmental designers from Olmsted and Howard to McHarg and Corbett have long relied on undeveloped natural open space, often called *greenspace,* to provide a range of social and environmental purposes, local land conservation in the United States prior to 1980 was dominated by "parks and rec" planning. This involved identifying and acquiring properties for recreation and scenic amenity, developing them according to active recreation standards, and maintaining the parks. After 1980, open space in many communities broadened planning objectives to passive recreation and protection of urban forests and outlying farmland, and tools expanded to include conservation easements. By the 1990s, there was a growing awareness of the benefits of linear greenways along stream and other corridors for passive recreation, wildlife habitat and movement, and flood damage mitigation. As a result, more communities engaged in greenway planning, design, and development.

More recently, land conservation programs have expanded in scope to integrate protected lands on a regional and state scale, not only for people's recreation and enjoyment and local wildlife habitats but also for broader scale ecological functions. In addition, as mentioned earlier, many communities and states have begun to see open space less as an afterthought of development, and more as an integral part of the land development process and growth management strategies. **Green infrastructure** planning is still a new concept, although it is being advanced by The Conservation Fund (Benedict and McMahon, 2002), the Trust for Public Land (2002), the EPA (2001), and the State of Maryland (2001). Just as plans for the built infrastructure are called blueprints, plans for green infrastructure are being referred to as "greenprints."

TABLE 5.8 **Evolving Nature of Local Government Land Conservation in the United States**

Period	Type	Conservation Tools	Primary Objectives
<1980	Parks and Recreation Planning	Land acquisition; park planning and management	Active recreation, scenic amenity
1980s	Open Space Planning	Land acquisition and easement; park planning and management	Active recreation, scenic amenity, farmland protection, urban forestry
1990s	Greenways and Open Space Planning	Land acquisition, easement, floodplain zoning; park and greenway planning and management	Active and passive recreation, scenic amenity, farmland protection, urban forestry, urban wildlife
2000	Green Infrastructure	Land acquisition, easement, flood-plain management, Smart Growth Management tools, conservation land development, partnerships with landowners, land trusts	Hubs and links for active and passive recreation, scenic amenity, farmland protection, urban forestry, urban wildlife, regional and state ecological systems, integration of conservation and growth management

Although the state-of-the-art in government land conservation is moving toward green infrastructure, it is also useful to discuss more conventional planning and design tools for open space and greenways.

Open Space and Greenway Planning and Design

The greenbelt concept was born in the English Garden City movement of the nineteenth century. Frederick Law Olmsted designed Boston's "Emerald Necklace," a series of parks and greenways from Franklin Park to the Charles River that were part of Boston's original design produced between 1878 and 1890. Greenways are open natural areas that have a linear form (Smith and Hellmund, 1993). The most successful greenspace and greenway designs are those that provide multiple objectives and are integrated into developed land uses. These objectives include recreation, transportation (bike/pedestrian), open space, conservation of wildlife corridors and riparian habitats, stream channel protection and restoration, water quality improvement, flood damage mitigation, neighborhood linkages, and education.

Open space and greenway planning is a useful mechanism to integrate a broad range of environmental planning objectives, including parks and recreation, farmland preservation, natural hazard mitigation, floodplain management, stream restoration, urban forestry, habitat conservation, and wetland protection. As a result, many communities include a chapter on open space and greenways in their comprehensive plan to address a wide range of environmental land issues and to serve as the policy basis for land conservation.

The process for developing an open space/greenway plan should be highly participatory. By engaging public stakeholders in plan development, the plan can

BOX 5.3—Open Space/Greenway Planning Process

1. Inventory (involve public)

Existing "De Facto" Open Space Greenway System

Public Open Spaces
Parks (local, state, federal)
Schools and grounds
Public buildings and grounds
Cemeteries

Private Open Spaces
Agricultural lands
Forest and woodlands
Golf courses
Railbeds ("rails to trails"), utilities

Environmental Inventory

Natural hazards
Sensitive areas (stream/riparian corridors, wetlands, habitats, shorelines)

Prime agricultural lands
Watersheds, groundwater recharge areas
Historic and visual resources

2. Evaluation, Prioritization, Objective Formulation (involve public)

Evaluate inventory
Prioritize resources and needs
Formulate objectives

3. Management Strategies (involve public)

Formulate alternatives:
  Trailway/greenway plan
  Acquisition/conservation easements
  Financing plan

4. Plan Implementation, Monitoring, and Evaluation

reflect community needs and desires and stands a greater chance of acceptance. The participation process can also serve to inform the public of the benefits of open space and environmental protection and its connection to other community goals. A process for open space/greenway planning is given in box 5.3. It is similar to our basic planning process in that it contains four basic steps: inventory, evaluation and prioritization, management strategies, and implementation and monitoring. The basic premise of the process is that all communities have a "de facto open space system." That is, the combination of public and private open spaces existing in any community forms a basic system. Open space/greenway planning should be looked upon as a means to coordinate that system and enhance it through connecting corridors and strategic additions that will serve community environmental and recreation objectives.

The Grand Forks, North Dakota, and East Grand Forks, Minnesota, project illustrates how a multipurpose greenway provides not only recreation and flood damage mitigation, but community revitalization as well. The greenway design was developed after the devastating flood of 1997 inundated 90 percent of the downtown communities. With federal and state assistance the cities relocated many buildings from the flood prone area, enhanced levies, and created a multipurpose greenway project (see Greenways, Inc: http://www.greenways.com/).

Boulder, Colorado, was one of the earliest communities to develop a comprehensive open space and greenway system to serve multiple objectives. The city purchased considerable land, made possible by revenue from a 1967 sales tax increase of 0.4% dedicated to open space acquisition. Figure 5.4a shows the greater Boulder greenbelt/greenway system proposed by the Boulder County Nature Association. Figure 5.4b zooms in on a central portion of the exisiting greenways. Boulder

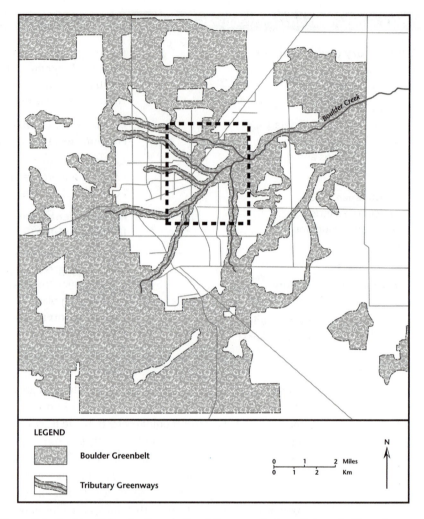

Figure 5.4a Boulder, Colorado, Greenbelt and Greenway System. *Sources:* Smith and Hellmund (1993), City of Boulder (2001). Used with permission of Paul Hellmund.

increased its open space sales tax to 0.73% in 1989 and continues to plan and upgrade its system (See also figure 7.8) (City of Boulder, 2001).

GreenPrints for Green Infrastructure

Green infrastructure (GI) is defined as an interconnected network of green space that conserves natural ecosystem values and functions and provides associated benefits to human populations. The network consists of waterways, wetlands, woodlands, wildlife habitats, and other natural areas; greenways, parks, and other conservation lands; and working farms, ranches, and forests. GI differs from conventional approaches to open space planning because, rather than looking at land conservation in isolation or in opposition to development, it aims to work in concert with land development, growth management, and built infrastructure planning. GI is "smart conservation." It is proactive not reactive, systematic not haphazard,

Figure 5.4b (continued)

holistic not piecemeal, multijurisdictional not single jurisdictional, multifunctional not single purpose, and multiscale not single scale (Benedict and McMahon, 2002).

The basic components of a GI network are

- **hubs,** such as reserves, native landscapes, working lands, regional parks, and community parks, and
- **links,** such as landscape linkages, conservation corridors, greenways, greenbelts, and riparian floodplains.

Benedict and McMahon (2002) discuss several potential benefits of the GI approach to land conservation: It recognizes the needs of people and nature; it is a mechanism to balance environmental and economic factors; it is a framework for integrating natural resources and growth management; it ensures that green space and development go where they are needed and appropriate; it identifies opportunities for restoration; and it provides predictability and certainty for both conservation and development interests.

There are several principles of GI. Localities and states should do the following:

1. Use GI as the framework for both conservation and development. Just as transportation infrastructure needs be linked to land use and development, so should green infrastructure.
2. Design and plan GI before development.
3. Provide a network of conservation rather than just islands of parks; linkage is the key.
4. Plan GI functions across multiple jurisdictions and at different scales, from the neighborhood to the region.
5. Ground GI in sound science and land use planning theories and practices.
6. Consider GI as a critical public investment, as it contributes to quality of life for people and ecosystems.
7. Involve diverse stakeholders in GI planning and design.

Perhaps the best current example of GI planning is Maryland's GreenPrint program. However, several other experiences demonstrate its potential as a new planning framework for land conservation, including the EPA's (2001) Southeastern Ecological Framework at a multistate scale; Florida's Statewide Greenways system at a state scale; Twin Cities Metro Greenways, Chicago's Wilderness Biodiversity Conservation Plan (Chicago Region Biodiversity Council, undated), and Portland's Metro Greenspace Program at the regional scale; the Kinston/Lenoir County, North Carolina, Green Infrastructure plan (UNC-CH, 2001, 2002), and several cases at the neighborhood scale.

Maryland's GreenPrint Program is a blueprint for green infrastructure. The $35 million program was established in May 2001 with the lofty objective to "preserve an extensive, intertwined network of land vital to long term survival of our native plants and wildlife and industries dependent on clean environment and abundant natural resources" (State of Maryland, 2001).

The purpose of the program is threefold:

- Identify, using state-of-the-art computer mapping techniques, the most important unprotected natural lands in the state;
- Identify linkages to connect these lands through a system of corridors; and
- Save those lands through targeted acquisitions and conservation easements.

As of 2002, the state had used satellite imaging and GIS technology to inventory the state and local green infrastructure. Hubs and links were ranked according to a GI assessment method that evaluates sites based on ecological value and vulnerability, on both local and regional scales.

The technical inventory identified the following as green hubs:

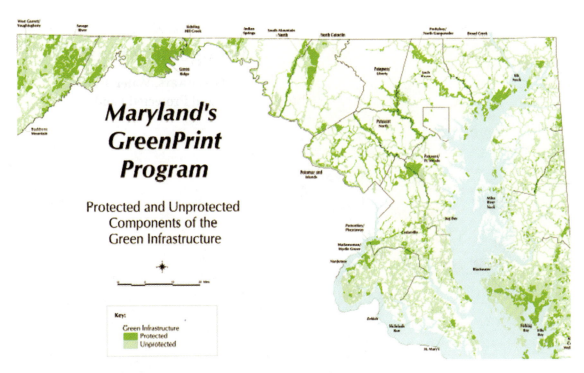

Figure 5.5 Maryland's GreenPrint Program. *Source:* State of Maryland (2001).

- Large blocks of contiguous forest, minimum of 250 acres plus 300-foot buffer
- Large wetland complexes of at least 250 acres
- Unique habitat of at least 100 acres containing rare and endangered species, unique ecological communities, or migratory bird habitats
- Relatively pristine stream and river segments of at least 100 acres including adjacent forests and wetlands having significant habitat for trout, mussels, or unique communities
- Existing protected natural resource lands

Green links included corridors along stream valleys and mountain ridges that serve as "habitat highways."

Using this approach, Maryland identified 2 million acres of ecologically significant land not yet consumed by sprawl; 1.5 million of these acres remain unprotected. These areas are shown in the *Maryland Atlas of Greenways, Water Trails, and Green Infrastructure.* The program hopes to boost protected land conservation capacity by 10,000 acres per year using state plans and funds to leverage resources from the federal government and foundations.

Figure 5.5 gives the GI for the state and distinguishes between currently protected and unprotected hubs and links. Figure 5.6 shows the detailed GI map for Montgomery County. It shows developed lands (roaded areas), state and federally

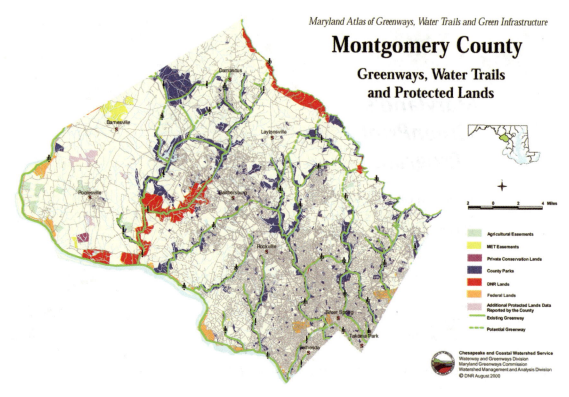

Figure 5.6 Montgomery County, Maryland, Green Infrastructure. *Source:* State of Maryland (2001).

protected lands, county parks, private conservation lands, Maryland Environmental Trust (MET) and agricultural easement lands, and existing and proposed greenways.

Private Land Stewardship

Despite the wide range of land conservation programs of government and land trusts, about 1.5 billion acres or three fourths of total land in the coterminous United States are in private ownership. This can be categorized as farmland (35%), rangeland (27%), forestland (27%), and developed land (10%) (USDA, 2001). Most of the first three categories are managed for food, fiber, and timber production, but some is in large idle blocks of private roadless land not currently in forestry or agricultural use. These idle lands provide conservation benefits, even though they are unprotected. Likewise, the developed metropolitan areas contain private open space lands in individual or common ownership. Because of the large proportion of these private lands, environmental quality depends on appropriate stewardship to reduce environmental impact and enhance ecological integrity.

The working landscape consisting of productive farmland, ranchland, and harvested forestland provides important scenic and open space benefits, but it also can create environmental impacts. These impacts include soil erosion and sedimentation, polluted runoff, riparian habitat and stream bank damage, and groundwater contamination, among others. Stewardship of these lands can not only reduce these impacts but also enhance their open space and ecological value.

Stewardship includes using best management practices (BMPs) for water quality and land protection. These include conservation tillage, vegetative buffers, nutrient management, integrated pest management, low-impact selective timber harvesting, reforestation, and set-aside of highly erodible lands, wetlands, and riparian buffers, among others.

Private lands in metropolitan areas are important because of their proximity to population and the roles they play in urban open space, environmental quality, and urban biodiversity. These include private parks, golf courses, utility rights-of-way, common areas in subdivisions, and individual land parcels. These private properties contribute to environmental degradation through impervious surfaces, polluted runoff, introduction of invasive species, removal of natural vegetation, and overuse of fertilizers and pesticides. Efforts to minimize impacts, restore environmental resources, and enhance wildlife habitats have increased in communities throughout the country. Community environmental organizations, master gardeners, neighborhood "ecoteams," and other efforts have improved scenic resources, environmental quality, and urban wildlife habitat.

The NRCS Backyard Conservation series provides information for a range of homeowner and neighborhood activities to enhance land stewardship. Guidance fact sheets are available for backyard ponds and wetlands, composting, mulching, tree planting, water conservation, and wildlife management. See http://www.nhq.nrcs.usda.gov/CCS/Backyard.html.

One of the most important categories of private land stewardship is those large blocks of roadless, natural land not currently in resource production. These are a de facto part of our nation's conservation lands, but they are not permanently protected. Many are forestland holdings whose economic value is their timber production. Ownership of these lands is typically transferred every 10 years or less, often from timber companies to holding companies. Large blocks of private roadless forestland in Virginia, for example, are now partly owned by the California public teachers pension program. Normally these lands are not managed but simply maintained in natural use, often bought and sold, waiting for the best opportunity for production. These lands are prime candidates for land conservation either by public agencies or nonprofit land trusts.

Smart Conservation and Smart Growth

For decades, land conservation has been addressed by public and nonprofit programs in isolation from and often in conflict with or reacting to land development. More recently, government programs and land trust activities have recognized that land conservation should be used in conjunction with development, either as part of growth management or an integral part of economic development. Hollis and Fulton (2002) reviewed the status of land conservation programs by government and land trusts and their role in growth management. They concluded the following:

- There has been a surge of interest in open space programs in the last ten years, especially in rapidly urbanizing areas.
- Open space is protected through a complex and decentralized system that tends to be reactive and hard to assess.
- Local land trusts tend to focus on lands that are locally significant but may not fit a larger strategic objective for metropolitan growth, while government and national land trusts may be strategic but tend to focus on significant resources and not on metropolitan growth.
- Growth management programs that establish urban growth boundaries have a significant effect on land conservation, especially protection of the working landscape outside the boundary. Still, there are few metropolitan areas with strong urban growth boundaries and their effects vary.
- The connection between open space programs and urban and metropolitan growth policy is rarely made. Federal programs focus on rural landscapes, except for Habitat Conservation Planning under the Endangered Species Act, which has affected urban growth in California and the Southwest (Zinn, 2002b). However, even these programs tend not to be coordinated with urban growth policies. States with strong growth management usually have strong land conservation programs, but they are rarely connected by policy. Two exceptions are Maryland (discussed earlier) and Florida, where communities seeking conservation funds must show that their proposals conform to their comprehensive growth management plans that are also subject to state review.
- Our understanding of the impact of land conservation programs on metropolitan growth patterns is sketchy at best. More research is needed to see how the different strategies for land conservation in different parts of the country affect urban growth.

Interest appears to be growing in connecting land conservation and urban growth management. Greenprint and GI programs aim to coordinate conservation and development. This approach is being advocated by the Trust for Public Land, The Conservation Fund, and the Sprawl Watch Clearinghouse, among others (Benedict and McMahon, 2002; Trust for Public Land, 2002). The Maryland GreenPrint program illustrates the dimensions of such programs and their potential in linking smart growth and smart conservation (State of Maryland, 2001). It will be interesting to monitor how effective this new program will be in achieving its objectives to proactively identify, prioritize, and protect ecological hubs and links, while accommodating development. It may serve as a model for other states.

Summary

Land conservation of open space, recreation lands, ecological habitats, and working landscapes has become a huge multibillion-dollar enterprise engaging all levels of government, nonprofit land trusts, local citizens groups, and major philanthropic foundations. Voters continue to support 80 percent of bond referenda and other initiatives for land acquisition and easements for open space, recreation, and protection of the working landscape. Federal and state budgets, though depleted in the recession years of 2000–2003, have still increased for land conservation. Land trusts have grown in number, in land holdings, and in influence. They number more than 1,250 in 2000, compared with less than 500 in 1985, and now protect 23 million acres in the United States.

Government and land trusts for conservation use several innovative tools. These include conservation easements, purchase and transfer of development rights, and other means of protection without outright purchase of the land. Green infrastructure is a recently coined term referring to the natural hubs and links land protection provides that create ecological functions and scenic, recreational, and cultural landscapes. Land conservation is a collaborative activity, often involving partnerships of land developers and land trusts, industry and government, property owners and neighbors. These partnerships have often created innovative solutions to land protection problems, often to the benefit of all stakeholders. Effective land protection requires all of these actors and activities.

Land conservation is now being looked at as an integral part of Smart Growth management. Greenways and greenbelts can effectively define growth areas. This green infrastructure should be planned along with grey infrastructure in the development process.

6 ▪ Design with Nature for People: Sustainable, Livable, and Smart Land Use Development

Introduction

The last half of the twentieth century saw unprecedented growth in the United States. Population increased by 86 percent from 1950's 151 million to 2000's 281 million. Massive highway construction and the rise of the automobile as the primary mode of personal transportation freed people to flee the crime and grime of the city and find personal space in the suburbs. Decades later, however, those sprawling suburbs have spread out from the city, leaving behind vacant properties and contaminated brownfields, consuming farmlands and natural areas in their wake, and isolating residents in auto-dependent developments with long, congested, and energy-intensive commutes. Some residents appear satisfied with suburban living, but many are increasingly unhappy with the dysfunctional social, environmental, and transportation problems of these land use patterns yet resign themselves to these problems as necessary evils of modern America.

Others believe there is a better way. Forward-thinking planners, developers, designers, and government officials are formulating new concepts of land use development. These concepts are characterized by several related movements, including "sustainable communities," "new urbanism," "green urbanism," "livable, walkable communities," "healthy communities," "brownfields redevelopment," and "smart growth." This chapter discusses the basic principles and practices applied under these labels and how they can advance resource efficiency and the protection and restoration of the natural environment.

Problems of Sprawl Revisited

Recall from chapter 3 that **sprawl** is land-consumptive, dispersed, and auto-dependent land development patterns made up of homogeneous, segregated land uses highly dependent on collector roads. Sprawl's greatest triumph has been creation of the personal and family "private realm," be it home, yard, or personal car. But along with this private triumph has come a public or civic failure. Land uses have separated, and as people have become more segregated, they have retreated from a more public life to a more controlled life, from experiential communities of place to communities of interest (Calthorpe and Fulton, 2001; Duany, Plater-Zyberk, and Speck, 2000). Sprawling development has spoiled the visual and cultural diversity of communities, as suburban areas in all parts of the country now look the same, dominated by activity centers of superstores, office parks, and homogeneous residential subdivisions.

Land use has spread out. Development land required per person grew by four times from the 1950s to the 1980s (Benfield, Raimi, and Chen, 1999). In most sprawling development, everyone is forced to drive everywhere. Collector road designs and long commuting distances increase vehicle miles traveled, congestion, petroleum consumption, and air pollution. Sprawl consumes agricultural land, open space, and natural wildlife habitats and creates vast water-impacting impervious surfaces for subdivisions, shopping centers, roads, and parking lots. Local governments struggle financially to provide urban infrastructure, services, and schools in response to rapidly growing dispersed developments.

Participants in Arresting Sprawl

The parties who can create new patterns of development to arrest sprawl are the same parties who created it: land developers and their investors, urban planners and designers, architects, local governments, and consumers. In addition, community groups and land trusts can play the advocate and partner in creative development plans.

The consuming public states its preferences for the location, type, and amenities of residential living through its choices and purchasing power. Consumer preference has long characterized the "American dream" as ownership of the large lot residence, usually in the suburbs. Evidence indicates that this preference is still alive and well (Audirac, 1999; Talen, 1999, 2001). However, evidence also shows that central urban residential population is on the rise, and there is a growing preference among some population segments for more dense, community-oriented living environments (Myers and Gearin, 2001; Talen, 2001). Lund (2002) conducted surveys showing that sense of community is greater in traditional and pedestrian-oriented than auto-oriented neighborhoods.

Still, consumers can only choose from among the choices they are given. The land development industry, including developers, designers, investors, and contractors, provides the supply for this demand. Even though our dysfunctional land use patterns are the result of their past efforts and these still dominate current markets, they are also our best hope for new and innovative designs that are more livable and sensitive to environmental resources.

Government is charged with managing the land development industry, but it too has failed to lead development patterns proactively. However, uncontrolled sprawl development has prompted many communities and states to adopt more aggressive growth controls to manage the impacts of development. Management

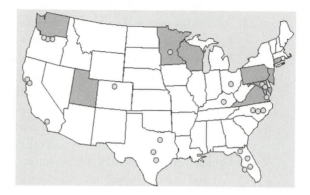

Figure 6.1 State and Local Governments Facilitating Compact, Walkable, Mixed-Use Development. *Source:* Congress for New Urbanism (2002a). Used with permission of CNU.

for "Smart Growth" emphasizes development in areas of existing infrastructure and de-emphasizes development in areas less suitable for development. By doing so, it supports and enhances existing communities, preserves natural and agricultural resources, and saves the cost of new development infrastructure. Figure 6.1 shows the states and localities that have adopted Smart Growth ordinances to facilitate the development of dense, walkable neighborhoods. Growth management for smart development is discussed in chapter 7.

Emerging Demographic and Land Development Trends

The 1990s saw increased attention to patterns of land use necessary to arrest sprawl, create livable neighborhoods and communities, and preserve natural environments, open space, and agricultural land. These actions included revitalization of existing urban and community neighborhoods that takes development pressure off ex-urban greenfield development; and new suburban developments using compact and mixed land use, public community and open space, and permanent protection of environmentally sensitive lands. Both development trends had marketing success in the late 1990s, as urban downtown populations began to grow, reversing a decades-long trend of decline, and more sustainable suburban developments were sold as quickly as they could be built.

Recent studies of the 2000 census indicate some reversing trends from the urban flight of the 1970s. Simmons and Lang (2001) looked at population trends of 36 "rust-belt" cities that all declined in population in the 1970s. More than 40 percent increased in population in the 1990s (figure 6.2).

Sohmer and Lang (2001) and Birch (2002) studied the "downtown rebound" as increasing numbers of people are choosing to live in downtown urban centers. Although the trend toward downtown living is not yet huge, Sohmer and Lang (2001, pp. 1–2) indicate it "may be a harbinger of future central-city growth. If people continue to move downtown, neighboring areas may experience spillover effects. The stronger downtown gets, the more likely it is that the surrounding central-city neighborhoods will strengthen as well." Two groups make up most of the growth. First, many "empty nesters" wish to "downsize their housing—trading in the lawn care and upkeep of a large home for the convenience of living in a

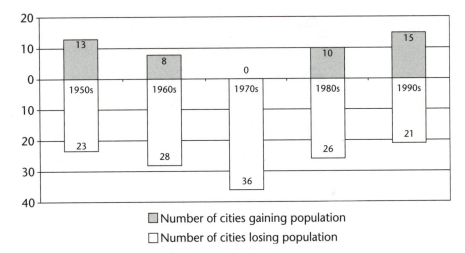

Figure 6.2 Numbers of Older Industrial Cities Gaining and Losing Population by Decade, 1950–2000. *Source:* Patrick A. Simmons and Robert E. Lang. 2001. *The Urban Turnaround: A Decade-by-Decade Report Card on Postwar Population Change in Older Industrial Cities,* Census Note 01. © 2001 Fannie Mae Foundation. Reprinted with permission.

downtown condominium" and wish to enjoy urban cultural activities, restaurants, historic character, and community life. Second, young professionals in their 20s and 30s, who have yet to have children, seek low-maintenance, urban housing convenient to work and proximate to mass transit and the amenities of urban life, like coffeehouses and nightclubs (Sohmer and Lang, 2001).

The 1990s also saw considerable redevelopment of so-called brownfields—abandoned, mostly industrial urban sites, for which there is little investment interest because of perceived environmental contamination. Federal and state programs have both eased liability concerns and provided financial incentives for brownfield redevelopment. These and other urban revitalization programs have helped bring jobs and residents back to the city.

New patterns of suburban development and small-town revitalization efforts also provide some hope of arresting sprawl. "New Urbanism" concepts of compact, walkable, mixed-use developments are being reflected in even conventional subdivisions. These developments have grown by more than 20 percent per year since 1997, 37 percent in 2001.

Based on a recent survey conducted by the National Association of Home Builders (NAHB, 2001) and 2000 census data, Myers and Gearin (2001) showed a demographic trend toward older households who have a greater preference for centrally located compact development. Combined with an expected decline in demand for new housing, they foresee a "growing market impact of home seekers who prefer compact-city alternatives" (Myers and Gearin, 2001). These forecasts are reflected in figure 6.3. They imply that market share for dense, walkable neighborhoods in new housing may grow from 15 percent in the 1990s to 30–55 percent in the current decade (Congress for the New Urbanism, 2001).

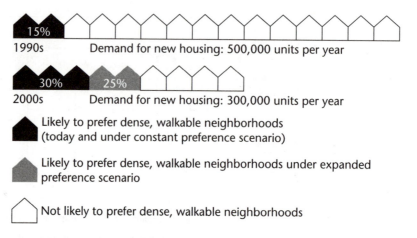

Figure 6.3 Market Share for Compact Development, 1990s and 2000s. Based on Myers and Gearin's 2001 study, market share for compact development may increase in this decade due to combined effect of growing preference for denser, walkable neighborhoods and declining demand for new housing. *Source:* Congress of New Urbanism, 2002a. Used with permission of CNU and Dowell Myers.

Basic Concepts and Early Roots of Sustainable Design

Before describing the evolving practice of sustainable and livable development design and the contemporary practitioners who are leading the movement, this section discusses the principles of these design concepts. Many of these concepts have long been alive and well in Europe (Beatley, 2000). The basic principles merge compatible objectives to protect and restore natural environment, conserve resources, and provide more livable communities for people. The compatibility of these objectives has led to a converging of contemporary social movements: New Urbanism, regionalism, livable communities, healthy communities, environmental protection/restoration, energy efficiency, brownfield redevelopment, Smart Growth, and green building, among others. The Congress for the New Urbanism (CNU) has merged the environmental and energy-efficient design principles developed in the western United States, the aesthetic and community-oriented principles emerging in the eastern United States, and new interests in regional approaches to controlling sprawl. Community revitalization, brownfield redevelopment, and urban containment are tenets of Smart Growth management. The New Urbanists' vision of walkable and transit-oriented communities is shared by those advocating energy efficiency as well as public health advocates wanting to improve air quality and promote physical activity.

Sustainable, livable, and smart land use and development begins with recognizing the natural opportunities and constraints to development. Environmentally sensitive lands are those that exhibit certain hazards to development (e.g., floodplains, unstable slopes), are vulnerable to environmental impact (e.g., highly erodible soils, soils unsuitable for septic systems), provide resource value (e.g., prime agricultural lands, aquifer recharge areas), and have aesthetic or ecological values (e.g., wetlands, wildlife habitats).

The most successful land development is that which considers the natural environment and the cultural community. The following list shows several basic features of environmentally and community sensitive design, development, and land use practices. These include preservation of natural features, the efficient use of resources (land, materials, and energy), and enhancement of community features.

Environmentally and Community-Sensitive Design, Development, and Land Use Practices

1. Preservation/Restoration of Natural Features (avoid; buffer and mitigate; restore; monitor and steward)

   Water resource protection (stormwater management, natural drainage channels, riparian lands, blueways, shorelines, aquifer recharge/wellhead areas)

   Environmental resource land protection (productive use and community character) (agricultural lands, recreation lands, open space)

   Ecologically sensitive land preservation (natural heritage, wildlife habitats, wetlands, coastal dunes)

   Protection against natural hazards (floodplains, steep slopes, seismic hazard, coastal storms)

2. Efficient Use of Resources

   Conservation of land (compact development)

   Conservation of material resources (efficient use of indigenous materials)

   Conservation of energy (energy efficient design; renewable energy; compact and mixed use; pedestrian, bicycle, and transit friendly)

3. Enhancement of Community Features

   Existing neighborhood/community revitalization and redevelopment

   Historic and cultural preservation

   Mixed land use (mixed housing [income diversity], commercial, employment, education, recreation, open space, greenways)

   Cluster development on buildable, nonsensitive areas

   Compact, discrete communities (defined community center)

   Energy-efficient, time-efficient circulation, transportation (compact scale, pedestrian/bicycle oriented inside, transit-oriented to outside)

4. Regional Context

   Neighborhoods, towns, cities fit into a regional context

   Regional growth boundaries, regional environmental policies, regional open space investments, regional transportation planning and transit

Achieving these land use practices sensitive to the human community and natural environment requires action from all of the participants discussed previously:

- Consumers must want these developments and be willing to pay for them.
- Designers and developers must provide the choice of these practices to consumers.

- Government agencies must at least be flexible to allow these land development patterns and should proactively mandate or provide incentives for these practices in land use plans and ordinances.
- Community groups must advocate such practices in the political process.
- Land trusts should provide partnering opportunities with landowners and developers to preserve sensitive lands while developing land suitable for development.

The concepts of designing land development in accord with natural systems have evolved for well over a century. In the mid to late nineteenth century, Frederick Law Olmsted, the "father of landscape architecture," developed plans as diverse as California's Yosemite Valley, New York's Central Park, the self-contained Riverside community near Chicago, and the Fens and the Riverway park plan for Boston that is based on the natural drainage system. He influenced H. W. S. Cleveland's plan for the distributive park system in the lake-rich Twin Cities (Minnesota) in 1888.

In the late nineteenth century, Ebenezer Howard popularized the British Garden City, a form of new town development that emphasized greenways and open space, especially as a ring around the central city. Garden cities are self-contained, having their own industry and surrounded by agricultural fields. Clarence Perry was instrumental in developing the concept of the neighborhood as an organizing design concept. He advocated the separation of through-transportation roads from local streets and independent pedestrian paths and vehicular roads. Some of these concepts were manifest in Clarence Stein's and Henry Wright's plan for the city of Radburn, New Jersey, in the 1920s. This plan invented the cul-de-sac, and houses were reversed so that living rooms faced the rear gardens and pedestrian paths that led to continuous park space.

In the 1920s, Benton MacKaye was one of the first to recognize the significant influence of the automobile and highway development on urban form. The strip development occurring along highways even at that early date gave rise to his notion of the "Townless Highway." His alternative was the "Highwayless Town," which separated communities from the highway and kept major traffic corridors uncluttered by commerce and development.

In the mid–twentieth century, a new breed of designers and scientists argued for land development compatible with natural systems. Aldo Leopold's *Sand County Almanac* (1949) did not specifically address community or development design, but it had a tremendous influence on designers who followed. It suggested a "land ethic," that the land itself and its intrinsic values should serve as the basis for how it is used.

By the 1960s, Ian McHarg popularized the concept of conforming development design to the opportunities and constraints provided by the land. Heavily influenced by Leopold's land ethic, McHarg's *Design with Nature* (1969) had a significant effect on subsequent environmental design and planning. As a first stage in his design process applied to scales from a site to a region, McHarg called for an environmental inventory. His 1968 inventory for the Twin Cities (Minnesota) metropolitan region served as a basis for subsequent regional planning, especially development of the regional park system. The process builds on basic environmental information to reveal areas suitable for human activities. McHarg's method of overlaying environmental data is the basis for land suitability analysis and overlay techniques used in geographic information systems (GIS) (see chapters 11 and 18).

The Evolving Practice of Sustainable and Livable Development Design

In 1972, a young builder named Michael Corbett began implementing a development concept for an intentional cooperative community that he; his wife, Judy Corbett; and some friends had been developing for several years. Corbett and his friends were heavily influenced by Howard and McHarg; "new town" developments in Reston (VA), Columbia (MD), Woodlands (TX), and elsewhere; as well as the environmental movement and emerging energy concerns. What Corbett called at the time "wholistic community design" and "design with nature for people," he applied to a 70-acre neighborhood community development, Village Homes, in Davis, California. The development has become one of the most recognized examples of "sustainable community" design. Corbett collected his design concepts in a 1981 book, *A Better Place to Live* (Corbett, 1981), and his 20-year experience of designing (and living) in Village Homes in a 2000 book, *Designing Sustainable Communities: Learning from Village Homes* (Corbett and Corbett, 2000).

Figure 6.4 gives the layout of Village Homes. The 68-acre community contains 220 single-family homes and 20 apartments, commercial and community buildings, 25 percent open space, including common recreational areas, community gardens, orchards, and vineyards (24 percent of the community's produce is grown on-site). The layout is designed around the natural drainage of the site. There is vehicle access to each house on narrow 20- to 24-foot-wide streets. However, fences and shrubs face the street, forming courtyards, while the main focus of the house is from the opposite side toward the common open space, bicycle paths and footpaths, and creekside natural drainage (figure 6.5). All buildings have south-facing solar access and incorporate passive solar heating and cooling principles. Corbett showed that incorporating solar and efficient design principles could be done with little or no added investment because of cost savings from downsized furnaces and air conditioners. The experience in Village Homes led Davis to change its energy building code, and Davis's code later became the basis for California's building code, still one of the most progressive energy building codes in the country. Studies of Village Homes compared with control neighborhoods in Davis have shown that Village Homes residents use 36 percent less energy for vehicular driving, 47 percent less electricity, and 31 percent less natural gas. Initially, Village Homes sold for the same price as others in Davis, but by the mid-1990s sold for $11 per square foot more (CESD, 2002; Corbett & Corbett, 2000).

Corbett's design concepts for Village Homes and other developments include the following:

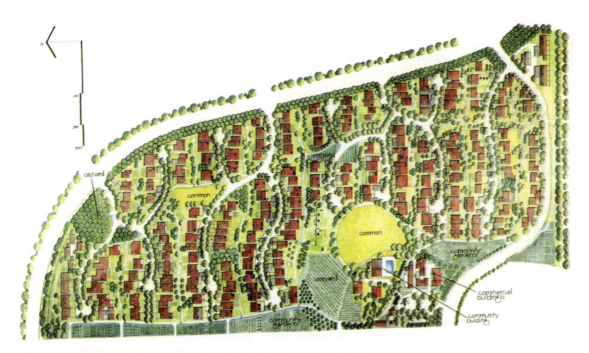

Figure 6.4 Village Homes Davis, California. *Source:* Corbett, *A Better Place to Live.* 1981. Used with permission of Michael and Judy Corbett.

Figure 6.5 Typical Village Homes Section. Street access is more like an alley and houses face common area and natural drainage. *Source:* Corbett, *A Better Place to Live.* 1981; Corbett and Corbett, 2000. Used with permission of Michael and Judy Corbett.

- Energy efficiency and natural heating and cooling
- Water resources and riparian habitat management through natural drainage systems
- Agricultural production for local consumption
- Provision of consumer services, jobs, recreation, education, and cultural opportunities within walking and cycling distance to reduce dependency on the automobile
- Orientation of development away from streets and toward pedestrian and open areas to reduce people's confrontation with vehicles
- Useful, satisfying employment within the community, including small businesses and entrepreneurial activities
- Opportunities for low-income people to get job training, to buy housing, to become part of the community

- Provision of a physical environment and fostering of a social environment that satisfies basic needs such as security, community, identity

Village Homes shows that it is possible to design very compact and attractive neighborhoods by using natural areas to provide a sense of space.

The Ahwahnee Principles and Charter for the New Urbanism

In 1991 California's Local Government Commission brought together six prominent designers to develop a set of community planning principles. These principles, which were presented to a group of 100 local elected officials at a conference at the Ahwahnee Hotel in Yosemite, came to be known as the Ahwahnee Principles (box 6.1). They later evolved into the charter of the CNU. The Ahwahnee Preamble states:

> Existing patterns of urban and suburban development seriously impair our quality of life. The symptoms are: more congestion and air pollution resulting from our increased dependence on automobiles, the loss of precious open spaces, the need for costly improvements to roads and public services, the inequitable distribution of economic resources, and the loss of a sense of community. By drawing upon the best from the past and present, we can plan communities that will more successfully serve the needs of those who live and work within them. Such planning should adhere to certain fundamental principles.

In 1999 *Newsweek* called the "New Urbanism" movement the great vision for community development in the new century. The issue featured Peter Calthorpe, a California architect and planner known for his work in sustainable communities (Van der Ryn and Calthorpe, 1984), and Andres Duany, a Florida architect known for new community designs in Seaside, Florida, and Kentlands, Maryland.

Although the reality of New Urbanism developments may have still fallen short of the rhetoric given the subject (Duany et al., 2001; Kunstler, 1993, 2001), the concepts of compact, mixed-use developments began to be applied throughout the country and were reflected in even conventional subdivisions. From an environmental perspective, the "West Coast" version of New Urbanism, characterized by regionalism, natural features, and transit, is far more attractive than the "East Coast" version's emphasis on aesthetics.

The CNU was founded in 1993 by a group of architects dedicated to creating "buildings, neighborhoods, and regions that provide a high quality of life for all residents, while protecting the natural environment" (CNU, 2002b). In 2002, CNU boasted 2,300 members in 20 countries and 49 states and claimed 400 New Urbanism developments complete or under construction in the United States. In 1996 CNU released its Charter of the New Urbanism. The following is among its proclamations:

> We stand for the restoration of existing urban centers and towns within coherent metropolitan regions, the reconfiguration of sprawling suburbs into communities of real neighborhoods and diverse districts, the conserva-

BOX 6.1—The 1991 Ahwahnee Principles*

Community Principles

1. All planning should be in the form of complete and integrated communities containing housing, shops, work places, schools, parks and civic facilities essential to the daily life of the residents.
2. Community size should be designed so that housing, jobs, daily needs and other activities are within easy walking distance of each other.
3. As many activities as possible should be located within easy walking distance of transit stops.
4. A community should contain a diversity of housing types to enable citizens from a wide range of economic levels and age groups to live within its boundaries.
5. Businesses within the community should provide a range of job types for the community's residents.
6. The location and character of the community should be consistent with a larger transit network.
7. The community should have a center focus that combines commercial, civic, cultural and recreational uses.
8. The community should contain an ample supply of specialized open space in the form of squares, greens and parks whose frequent use is encouraged through placement and design.
9. Public spaces should be designed to encourage the attention and presence of people at all hours of the day and night.
10. **Each community or cluster of communities should have a well-defined edge, such as agricultural greenbelts or wildlife corridors, permanently protected from development.**
11. Streets, pedestrian paths, and bike paths should contribute to a system of fully-connected, interesting routes to all destinations. Their design should encourage pedestrian and bicycle use by being small and spatially defined by buildings, trees,

and lighting; and by discouraging high-speed traffic.
12. **Wherever possible, the natural terrain, drainage and vegetation of the community should be preserved with superior examples contained within parks or greenbelts.**
13. **The community design should help conserve resources and minimize waste.**
14. **Communities should provide for the efficient use of water through the use of natural drainage, drought tolerant landscaping and recycling.**
15. **The street orientation, the placement of buildings and the use of shading should contribute to the energy efficiency of the community.**

Regional Principles

16. The regional land-use planning structure should be integrated within a larger transportation network built around transit rather than freeways.
17. **Regions should be bounded by and provide a continuous system of greenbelt/wildlife corridors to be determined by natural conditions.**
18. Regional institutions and services (government, stadiums, museums, etc.) should be located in the urban core.
19. Materials and methods of construction should be specific to the region, exhibiting a continuity of history and culture and compatibility with the climate to encourage the development of local character and community identity.

Implementation Principles

20. The general plan should be updated to incorporate the above principles.
21. Rather than allowing developer-initiated, piecemeal development, local governments should take charge of the planning process. General plans should designate where new growth, infill, or redevelopment will be allowed to occur.

Continued ➤

BOX 6.1—Continued

22. Prior to any development, a specific plan should be prepared based on these planning principles.
23. Plans should be developed through an open process and participants in the process should be provided visual models of all planning proposals.

** Natural environment and resource efficiency features given in **bold**.*

Authors/Editors: Peter Calthorpe, Peter Katz, Michael Corbett, Judy Corbett, Andres Duany, Steve Weissman, Elizabeth Moule, Elizabeth Plater-Zyberk, Stefanos Polyzoides

tion of natural environments, and the preservation of our built legacy. We advocate the restructuring of public policy and development practices to support the following principles: neighborhoods should be diverse in use and population; communities should be designed for the pedestrian and transit as well as the car; cities and towns should be shaped by physically defined and universally accessible public spaces and community institutions; urban places should be framed by architecture and landscape design that celebrate local history, climate, ecology, and building practice.

The Charter provides more specific principles to guide public policy, development practice, urban planning, and design at three scales: the region, metropolis, city, and town; the neighborhood, the district, and the corridor; and the block, the street, and the building. The Charter stresses social, economic, and community identity issues and is light on environmental conservation features. It includes only the following environmental planning and design principles:

For the region: the metropolitan area should gain definition from its natural boundaries, and it has a necessary and fragile relationship to its agrarian hinterland and natural landscapes.

For the neighborhood: conservation areas and open lands should be used to define and connect different neighborhoods and districts, walkable neighborhoods conserve energy and reduce air pollution.

For the block and building: natural methods of heating and cooling can be more resource-efficient than mechanical systems.

Reducing Automobile Dependence: Toward Walkable Communities and Transit Orientation

Beyond the neighborhood or subdivision scale, communities should fit together in a compact, mixed-use arrangement to foster efficient transportation, walkability, and livability. An important consideration in compact neighborhood and town design is reduced reliance on the automobile. Figure 6.6 illustrates the spatial impact of auto dependence. Circulation within discrete towns should favor pedestrian and bicycle movement over vehicle transportation. "Walkability" has become a consistent design feature of the various design approaches to community and

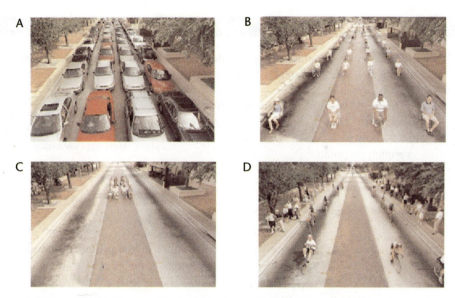

Figure 6.6 Spatial Impact of Auto Dependence. (A) shows 40 Tampa Bay residents in their cars; (B) shows them sitting where their cars were; (C) shows them if they were on a bus; (D) shows them walking and riding their bicycles. *Source:* Beamguard (1999). Used with permission of the *Tampa Tribune.*

neighborhood revitalization and is discussed further in the section on traditional neighborhoods.

Corbett's (1981) circulation schematic in figure 6.7a shows a town center more easily accessible from the neighborhoods by foot than by car. Figure 6.7b shows a similar diagram from Van der Ryn and Calthorpe's (1984) sustainable community design. Like Corbett's, their design includes mixed use, a discrete town center, and neighborhoods within a short walking radius. The town design in figure 6.7b could accommodate 5,500 people within 1/4 mile of the town center, while still providing about 20 percent in open space.

Peter Calthorpe has championed the transportation aspects of "sustainable design," first through the "pedestrian pockets," then transit connection, finally through regional integration (Calthorpe, 1993; Calthorpe and Fulton, 2001; Van der Ryn and Calthorpe, 1986). Illustrated in figure 6.8, Calthorpe's **Transit-Oriented Development** (TOD) is a mixed-use community within walking distance of a transit stop and core commercial area. Each TOD is a "pedestrian pocket," with residential and public spaces within 2,000 feet of the transit stop. Although the 2,000-foot-radius TOD is intended to be densely developed, the design aims to conserve riparian lands and other environmentally sensitive areas as shown in figure 6.8b. "Secondary areas" or those outside the central area have lower densities and accommodate agricultural uses.

TODs are linked together and to urban centers by bus or rail transit. As shown in figure 6.9, Calthorpe envisions regional development that ties a central city to

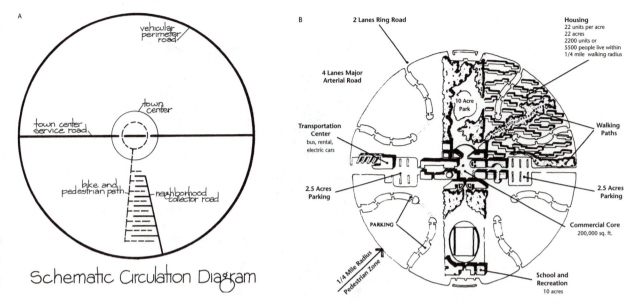

Figure 6.7 Sustainable Neighborhood Circulation. Corbett's 1981 schematic (left) favors bike and pedestrian movement over vehicles. It is similar to Van der Ryn and Calthorpe's (1986) "sustainable community" design (right). *Sources:* A: Michael Corbett, *A Better Place to Live.* 1981.Used by permission of Michael and Judy Corbett. B: From *Sustainable Communities: A New Design Synthesis for Cities, Suburbs and Towns.* © 1986 by Sim Van der Ryn and Peter Calthorpe. Reprinted by permission of Sierra Club Books.

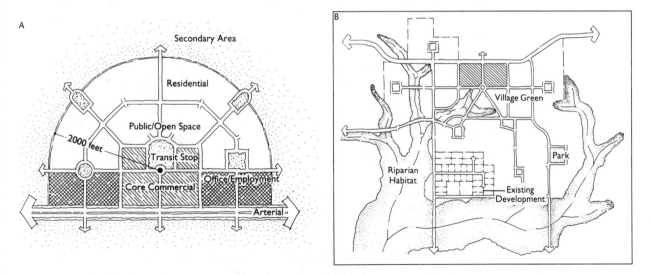

Figure 6.8 Calthorpe's Transit-Oriented Development. *Source:* Peter Calthorpe, *The Next Metropolis: Ecology and the American Dream.* © 1993 Princeton Architectural Press. Used with permission.

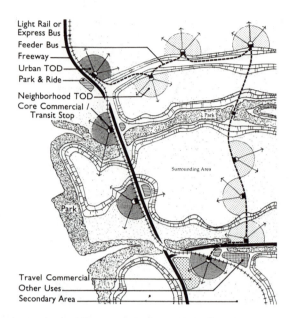

Light Rail or Express Bus
Feeder Bus
Freeway
Urban TOD
Park & Ride
Neighborhood TOD
Core Commercial / Transit Stop
Park
Surrounding Area
Park
Travel Commercial
Other Uses
Secondary Area

Figure 6.9 Regional Distribution of TODs. *Source:* Peter Calthorpe, *The Next Metropolis: Ecology and the American Dream.* © 1993 Princeton Architectural Press. Used with permission.

its surrounding bounded urban growth area made up of TODs linked by rail and bus transit (see also figure 6.17 in a later section).

Table 6.1 distinguishes three categories of communities or developments based on transportation orientation. "Walkable and/or transit-oriented" communities include villages, towns, traditional neighborhoods, and urban downtowns. Traditional neighborhoods and more contemporary "neotraditional" neighborhoods are discussed in a later section. "Auto-oriented non-land-conserving" developments include large lot subdivisions, other residential subdivisions, and large activity centers like shopping malls or industrial parks. A third category is "auto-oriented, land-conserving" development, such as rural or residential clusters. Residents of these latter developments, like subdivisions, rely on automobile transportation for travel to work, school, and commerce, but their communities are compact and provide significant community open space.

Traditional Neighborhoods, Walkability, and Community Life

Andres Duany popularized neotraditional development and coined the term *New Urbanism*. Neotraditional designs aim to replicate the dense neighborhood development patterns reminiscent of city neighborhood and town development 50 to 100 years ago. Figure 6.10 illustrates the traditional mixed-use neighborhood of Linden Hills in Minneapolis. Traditional neighborhoods are characterized by narrow rectilinear streets, small lots and shallow setbacks, front sidewalks and back alleys, mixed-use neighborhoods, and village greens and plazas.

Seaside, Florida, and the 357-acre Kentlands development near Gaithersburg, Maryland, were among Duany's first neotraditional designs using his version of

TABLE 6.1   **Three Categories of Communities and Developments Based on Transportation Orientation**

Walkable/Transit Oriented	Auto-Oriented Land-Conserving	Auto-Oriented Non-Land-Conserving
Traditional neighborhood	Rural cluster	Large-lot subdivision
Village	Residential cluster	Residential subdivision
Town		Activity center/industrial-office park
Urban downtown		

Source: After Calthorpe Associates (2000).

traditional neighborhood development (TND). His designs emphasize aesthetic design, and his early work did not explicitly aim to protect environmentally sensitive areas. Although Duany has been critical of those advocating environmental over social goals, he has recently incorporated more environmental dimensions in project design; for example, his **transect planning approach** provides design guidelines on an ecological continuum from urban centers to rural greenfields (Talen and Duany, 2002).

Most developed examples of these neotraditional developments tend to be upscale and expensive and include very restrictive design covenants intended to preserve the traditional design principles. These conditions have prompted critiques from advocates of mixed-income housing that fosters social diversity and from architects who advocate more design freedom that enhances new ideas and innovation and counters the "sameness" of many TND designs.

Despite these critiques, the compact development patterns and walkable neighborhoods of TND developments *can* lend themselves to mixed use, improved energy efficiency, and conservation open space around the dense village, *if* they are integral parts of the design. They can also be improved by providing housing for a diversity of incomes and less restrictive design covenants that still provide compact development, walkability, efficiency, mixed use, and open space. There is a growing market for these developments.

Linden Hills: *Neighborhood Retail*

Figure 6.10 Linden Hills Traditional Neighborhood in South Minneapolis. Mixed-use residential, retail, employment, and open space creates a very walkable livable community. *Source:* Calthorpe Associates, Undated, I-35W Build-out Study. Used with permission of Calthorpe Associates.

TABLE 6.2 **New Urbanism Projects by State (May 2002)**

California	56
Florida	54
Colorado	31
North Carolina	30
Virginia	25
Oregon	23
Texas	20
Maryland	17
Illinois	16
Tennessee	14
Pennsylvania	13
South Carolina	13
others	96

Source: www.cnu.com.

As of summer 2002, the CNU posted on its website (www.cnu.com) over 400 completed or planned New Urbanism projects in 35 states. They include greenfield TND neighborhoods (50%), urban infills (27%), suburban infills (16%), transit-oriented developments (5%), and some subsidized housing and greyfield redevelopments. Leading states include California (56), Florida (54), Colorado (31), North Carolina (30), Virginia (25), Oregon (23), and Texas (20) (see table 6.2).

Figure 6.11 illustrates a recent planned development marketed as a New Urbanism community, the King Farm community in Rockville, Maryland. The development is close to both the Shady Grove Metro rapid transit stop and Interstate 270. The 430-acre development includes single and multifamily residential units in two neighborhoods around a town center, parks and open space, and a commercial office activity center providing considerable local employment. Figure 6.11a and 6.11b show the town center and a typical single family neighborhood; 6.11c–f give the overall plan map and more detailed maps for the two neighborhoods and commercial office center (www.kingfarm.com). For more examples of New Urbanism developments, see the CNU (www.cnu.com) and New Urban News (www.newurbannews.com).

Community and Suburban Revitalization: Small Cities, Villages, and Neighborhoods

Smart Growth calls for concentrating growth in existing development areas where infrastructure exists. This infill and revitalization can renew and enhance economic and community development. Redevelopment in existing communities can also steer development pressure away from greenfields and environmentally sensitive natural areas. Revitalization projects should build on the community's cultural and historic character.

In a study conducted for the Twin Cities Metro Council, Calthorpe Associates (2000) focused on the revitalization potential for communities in the St. Croix

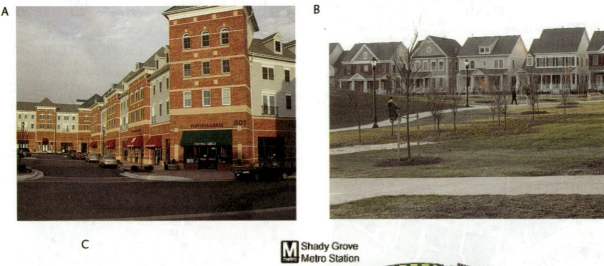

Figure 6.11 King Farm New Urbanism Development, Rockville, Maryland. Source: King Farm Associates, L.L.C., http://www.kingfarm.com. Used with permission.

Figure 6.11 *(continued)*

Figure 6.12 Simulated Photo Pairs of Redevelopment and Revitalization in Stillwater, Minnesota. The left photo shows existing conditions. The right photo simulates the same view with revitalization of the downtown building on its historic character. *Source:* Steve Price, Urban Advantage. Used with permission.

River Valley east of St. Paul, Minnesota. The study focused on four types of development opportunity:

- Downtown revitalization and streetscape enhancement
- Re-creating village character for new development
- Walkable residential development
- Rural cluster development

The study introduced prototypes of the design concepts and applied them in design plans for specific communities in the area.

Calthorpe Associates argue that a successful street accommodates different modes of movement (pedestrian, bike, auto, transit) so that different people, many of whom do not drive (seniors, disabled, children, those without cars), can still travel independently. Buildings should face the street and provide enclosures for pedestrians to encourage walking and biking. Landscaping, street furniture, and special paving can add to the character of the place.

The St. Croix study applied these concepts to several small cities in the area, including Stillwater, Minnesota, a historic riverfront community. The plan recommended construction of two mixed-use buildings, street trees, and special paving on some side streets. Figure 6.12 uses photo simulation prepared by Steve Price of Urban Advantage to illustrate the downtown revitalization plan for Stillwater. Photo simulations help residents and community groups visualize the possibilities of community revitalization.

For preserving and re-creating village character for revitalization and development, the St. Croix study used the prototype given in figure 6.13. It integrates new development (colored) with existing development and has two types of open space. The formal Village Green provides the community center. Beyond the Green, fields, forest, and wetlands are preserved for wildlife habitat. Riparian

Figure 6.13 Prototype Design for Re-creating Village Character in Small Towns. *Source:* Calthorpe Associates, 2000. *St. Croix Valley Redevelopment Study.* Used with permission of Calthorpe Associates.

areas provide a networks of pedestrian and bike ways. The mixed housing (single family, duplexes, and senior housing) and "main street" shops provide for community diversity. The walkable residential developments provide easy access to neighbors, shopping, and open space. This prototype shows how the "New Urbanism" design concepts discussed in the last section can be applied to existing communities and preserve the surrounding natural areas.

The Working Landscape, Rural Clusters, and Conservation Subdivision Design

While at the University of Massachusetts, Randall Arendt and Robert Yaro developed rural cluster design principles to preserve rural character, the working land-

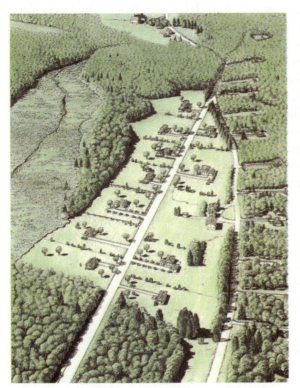

Figure 6.14 Conventional versus Conservation Development. Left: Conventional plan with new road and 26 large lots. Right: Conservation development plan with 28 clustered lots tucked in forest fringe and conservation easements on common property. *Source:* Yaro, R., R. Arendt, H. Dodson, and E. Brabec. 1988. *Dealing with Change in the Connecticut River Valley.* Courtesy, Center for Rural Massachusetts, University of Massachusetts-Amherst.

scape, and natural resources. The *working landscape* refers to productive use of the land and resources through agriculture, forestry, and other economic use of natural resources. In their design manual, *Dealing with Change in the Connecticut River Valley* (Yaro, Arendt, Dodson and Brabec, 1988), they give several examples of hypothetical developments on real sites to make their point that rural, working landscapes and views, sensitive areas, and agriculture can be preserved while accommodating development. The approach uses clustered development, generally tucked into the forest fringe, and preservation of open lands and agriculture through conservation easements or similar means.

Figure 6.14 gives one example. The 130-acre rural site contains farmland, wetlands, habitat, old-growth forest, and scenery. A proposal to subdivide the entire site into 26 large lots (figure 6.14a) with a new road met with opposition, so an alternative creative design was developed. The plan (figure 6.14b) called for 28 lots on 24 acres, preserving more than 100 acres of farmland, forest, and wetlands. Most of the lots are clustered on three locations at the forest line to preserve farmland and views. The open space area was deeded in perpetuity to a homeowner's association established to manage the common property.

Randall Arendt continued this conservation design approach in his books *Rural by Design* (1994), *Conservation Design for Subdivisions* (1996), and *Growing Greener* (1999). The design concept is simple. Instead of simply dividing up a parcel into streets and house lots, first look at the land, see what it portrays in environmental and cultural opportunities and constraints, and then use them to design a compact community.

Arendt provides numerous side-by-side examples of development plans, such as figure 6.15, to illustrate the benefits of compact development combined with sensitive land protection and community open space.

Arendt (1996) provides a useful procedure for "conservation design of subdivisions" that has two stages outlined in the following list. The *background stage* investigates contextual issues, conducts an environmental inventory of the site, and prioritizes objectives and site features into "primary" and "secondary" conservation areas. The results take the form of overlay maps of the site. The *design stage* begins with a conventional design to determine the development legally possible on the site. Putting that design aside, the alternative design begins with the overlay maps of primary and secondary conservation areas. Buildable areas are identified by avoiding these conservation areas and are used to locate house sites. Street and trail alignments are drawn to access house sites, but also are positioned to use foreground meadows to enhance views from the houses and to buffer views from main roads. See Arendt (1996, 1999) for examples of this approach.

Arendt's Design Steps in Conservation Design for Subdivisions

A. Background Stage

  1. Understanding the locational context: historical, cultural character.
  2. Mapping special features: soils, wetlands, floodplains, aquifers and recharge areas, significant wildlife habitats, slopes, woodlands, farmland, historic and cultural sites, views into/out from site.
  3. Prioritizing objectives: farmland preservation vs. mature woods vs. views vs. habitats? Specify *primary* and *secondary* conservation areas.
  4. Integrating the information layers: overlays and composites.

B. Design Stage: basic commitment to accommodate the entire amount of development that would otherwise be legally possible under conventional design.

  1. Sketch conventional design to determine legal amount of development.
  2. Identify all potential conservation areas: primary and secondary.
  3. Locate house sites (avoid, buffer conservation areas).
  4. Design street alignments and trails (use foreground meadows to enhance views from house fronts and buffer thoroughfares). Alternate steps (3) and (4) for neotraditional villages.
  5. Draw the lot lines.

Greyfield and Brownfield Redevelopment

"Greyfields" represent large shopping center activity centers in auto-oriented suburban areas that can be redeveloped into more walkable community centers.

Figure 6.15 Conventional and Conservation Development in Chester County, Pennsylvania. Arendt's alternative "neotraditional" village design (right) fits the same number of units on 60 acres leaving 100 acres of woodlands and fields for open space, recreation, and habitat. There are five internal greens or commons to enhance residential views and provide a sense of space. *Source:* Arendt, 1996. Used by permission of Island Press.

Although these centers are still primarily auto oriented, they can add needed cohesion to suburbs lacking town centers and community space. These centers can become more than simply destinations for shopping, adding multiple activities more typical of downtown or neighborhood retail centers. Table 6.3 lists 11 recent greyfield redevelopment projects in seven states that have incorporated transit and mixed use; these are documented in a 2001 CNU report, *Greyfields No More* (CNU, 2001). Figure 6.16 shows a photo simulation of a possible greyfield shopping center redevelopment in El Cerrito, California, prepared by Steve Price of Urban Advantage.

Brownfields are "abandoned, idled, or under-used industrial and commercial facilities where expansion or redevelopment is complicated by real or perceived environmental contamination" (U.S. EPA, 2001a). Redevelopment of these sites faces barriers created by two uncertainties: the level of existing contamination on the site, if any, and the responsibility for that contamination should ties to the property be established. Federal cleanup laws like the Resource Conservation and Recovery Act (RCRA) and the Superfund Act create strict standards for those responsible for contaminated property, and this has scared many potential investors away from redevelopment projects.

Brownfield redevelopment is important urban infill development with three objectives:

TABLE 6.3 **Greyfield Redevelopment Projects with Transit-Oriented Features**

Project and Location	Transit Mode	Project Description
Belmar, Lakewood, CO	Denver RTD bus	106 acres with retail, office, multifamily, for-sale residential
City Place, Long Beach, CA	LAMTA light rail	475,000 sf retail, 120 room hotel, 259 apartments, 70 condos, civic
City Center Englewood, Englewood, CO	Denver RTD light rail	City hall, library, plaza, train station, town center, 408 rental units
Crossings at Mountain View, CA	CalTrain heavy rail	Demolished mall replaced with 600 for-sale units, open space, 5000 sf neighborhood retail, new train station
Eastgate Town Center, Chattanooga, TN	CARTA bus	Plan for office, civic, and residential space; suburban town center
Mizner Park, Boca Raton, FL	Bus hub	Townhomes, apartments above grand plaza lined with small shops
New Roc City, New Rochelle, NY	Bus, rail nearby	Mixed-use multistory with retail, entertainment, office, hotel space
Paseo Cobrado, Pasadena, CA	LAMTA light rail	New mixed area on site of failed mall, retail, office, apartments
Phalen Village Center, St. Paul, MN	Metro Transit bus	City-owned redevelopment of former shopping center: housing, office
Renaissance Towne Center, Bountiful, UT	Proposed bus	On site of enclosed mall, new mixed-use town center
Winter Place Village, Winter Park, FL	Bus	32-acre mall partially replaced by retail, office, and apartments

Source: Sobel (CB Richard Ellis), CNU, 2001b.

- to remove environmental hazards from the community;
- to revitalize communities by creating productive use of abandoned land, creating jobs, and returning property to tax rolls; and
- to relieve pressure to develop pristine greenfields, open space, and farmland. EPA estimates that for every brownfield acre redeveloped into residential and commercial needs, an estimated 21.4 acres of greenfields are protected (U.S. EPA, 2001a).

Brownfields are a major environmental, real estate, community, and aesthetic problem in U.S. cities. There are an estimated half million to 1 million brownfield sites in communities across the United States. As a result, cleanup and redevelopment of brownfields has received wide-ranging community, state, and federal support. The Clinton administration spearheaded brownfield redevelopment, and it has been the major environmental initiative of the Bush administration.

The EPA's brownfields programs aim to remove barriers and provide incentives for investment in redevelopment. Brownfields remediation and redevelopment is different from traditional command-and-control cleanup. It requires cooperation and collaboration and is based more on voluntary action than strict regulation.

Figure 6.16 Greyfield shopping center can become a mixed-use town center; photo simulation shows how El Cerritos mall can be redeveloped to a mixed-use town center. *Source:* Steve Price, Urban Advantage. Used with permission.

Real estate investors and developers, community groups, and local governments, as well as state and federal agencies, are principal players in brownfield redevelopment. EPA's initiatives to promote redevelopment include tax incentives, liability relief, and funded pilot programs. In addition, most states have their own brownfield redevelopment programs; 40 states have agreements with EPA for Voluntary Clean-up Programs (VCP). The following list shows the related federal programs (U.S. EPA, 2000).

Federal Brownfield Redevelopment Programs

Brownfields Tax Incentive: $300 million annual investment leverages $3.4 billion in private investment and redevelopment of 8,000 brownfields.

Liability Relief and Brownfields Revitalization Act: May 2002 law provides liability protection from federal Superfund law for prospective purchasers and innocent landowners to facilitate brownfield redevelopment.

Voluntary Cleanup Programs: 40 states have agreements with the EPA to clean up brownfield sites faster and with less litigation than RCRA and Superfund laws by setting high cleanup standards and protecting liability of new owners of brownfield sites.

Brownfields Assessment Pilots: funding for environmental assessments and community outreach.

Brownfields Cleanup Revolving Loan Fund (BCRLF) Pilots: funding to capitalize loans that are used to clean up brownfields.

Brownfields Job Training and Development Demonstration Pilots: environmental training for residents of brownfield communities.

Resource Conservation and Recovery Act (RCRA)/Brownfields Prevention Pilots: use the inherent flexibility in RCRA regulations to prevent brownfields from forming on RCRA properties.

Clean Air/Brownfields Partnership Pilots: determine the potential air quality and other environmental and economic benefits of redeveloping urban brownfields.

Brownfields Showcase Communities: serve as national models for successful brownfields assessment, cleanup, and redevelopment.

Targeted Brownfields Assessments (TBAs): provide funding and/or technical assistance for environmental assessments at selected brownfields sites not targeted by EPA assessment pilots.

The next list gives a process for brownfield cleanup and redevelopment. It begins with preliminary scoping similar to Step 0 in our box 2.1 planning process. From the get-go, it is important to have a use of the site in mind, to begin to engage the community and key public agencies, and to understand the regulations and professional practice involved in cleanup and redevelopment. Site assessment looks at the past use of the site, prior to on-site field investigation of contamination. Cleanup options depend on the level of contamination and prospective redevelopment use. A key element is the financing plan for both cleanup and redevelopment. In most cases it is a creative finance package mixing private investment stimulated by tax incentives as well as direct funding support from federal, state, and local governments. Once the financing plan is in place, cleanup and redevelopment design and implementation can proceed.

Process for Brownfield Cleanup and Redevelopment

0. *Scoping:* plan use and redevelopment options for site, understand regulations and standard professional practice, external professional support, community involvement, government agencies

1. *Site assessment:* evaluate potential of contamination based on historical records and community involvement; determine needs for site investigation

2. *Site investigation:* if suspected contamination, conduct detailed study of cause, nature, and extent of contamination; determine goals for cleanup and acceptable and unacceptable risks for proposed end uses of site. If no contamination is found, seek approval to proceed with redevelopment

3. *Cleanup options:* evaluate technologies for capability to meet cleanup and redevelopment objectives
4. *Financial plan:* include private investment; tax incentives; and federal, state, and local government funding opportunities
5. *Cleanup design and implementation:* select appropriate and cost-effective technologies and cleanup activities
6. *Redevelopment design and implementation:* work with designers, investors, and the community to develop and implement project

Cleanup technologies for contaminated soil and water continue to improve. They include physical and chemical treatment, as well as biological means using microorganisms and vegetation to absorb or decompose contaminants.

In an effort to share lessons from its brownfield pilots, the EPA publishes descriptions of brownfield success stories (U.S. EPA, 2003). Many brownfields are converted back to industrial use, but increasingly they are used for commercial office, retail, residential, civic, and cultural facilities, and recreation and open space.

The EPA contends that using brownfields as new residential space complements a recent nationwide shift toward urban relocation. "This 'reverse suburbanization' is based on a desire for convenience as traffic problems mount in major cities" (U.S. EPA, 2002). For example:

- In Emeryville (CA) a former industrial site was transformed into 220 residential housing units, using nearly $20 million in private investment leveraged through the EPA Brownfields Pilot.
- In Somerville (MA) a contaminated former mattress factory was converted into a 97-unit, assisted-living facility.
- The Twin Cities Metro Council teamed with Habitat for Humanity to convert seven brownfield sites free of contamination into low-income housing (U.S. EPA, 2002).

Other brownfield sites have been converted to community recreation and greenspace uses (U.S. EPA, 2001b). For example:

- The City of Shreveport (LA) is redeveloping 26 acres of a 100-acre brownfields site, formerly used as a petroleum tank farm and grain operation, into a soccer field complex. Funded with city bonds, site assessments ($90,000) were completed in mid-1998, cleanup activities ($210,000) in mid-1999, and redevelopment activities ($1.2 million) in late 2000. The site now consists of a 35-acre softball/baseball complex, a 27-acre soccer complex, and 39 acres of undeveloped wooded land.
- In Tallahassee (FL) five targeted brownfields properties are being redeveloped into the two-mile Cascades Linear Greenway, which runs through Tallahassee's Gaines Street Corridor.
- The City of Denver's Northside Treatment Plant Redevelopment Project is turning most of the former 100-acre Northside Treatment Plant site,

located in a disadvantaged area, into a park, urban wildlife area, and community center.

- The Central Massachusetts Economic Development Authority (CMEDA) Pilot is creating greenspace at an abandoned mill site in the city of Worcester. The project converts a 70,000-square-foot building and its surrounding property into a visitors' and environmental training center. When completed, the site will contain bike paths and walkways that will crisscross 30 acres of restored greenspace.

Green Buildings and Green Development

"Green building" and "green development" are additional examples of emerging trends toward more sustainable design and development. *Green building* programs have proliferated throughout the country as housing consumers have voiced greater demand for more efficient, environmentally friendly, and healthier residential designs and construction. *Green development* includes these building designs and practice but extends them beyond the housing market to include commercial developments, beyond the site to include the community and cultural context, and beyond the building design and construction to include real estate finance and marketing.

"Green building" promotes new building designs that do the following:

- Provide greater energy efficiency and reduce pollution
- Provide healthier indoor air
- Reduce water usage
- Preserve natural resources through effective material usage
- Improve durability and reduce maintenance

Green building has evolved as a movement among developers, contractors, and builders in response to perceptions of the growing consumer market and their own experience that residential development can be made more efficient and environmentally friendly without substantial increases in cost. Houses in Michael Corbett's Village Homes (see figure 6.4 and accompanying discussion) still stand as a principal model of green building. Investments in energy-efficient design and construction reduced long-term operating costs and up-front costs for mechanical systems. Design with natural features in mind provided environmental protection while creating a highly marketable development that quickly appreciated in value.

Many builders' associations have teamed together to share lessons and experiences. Several local and state governments have established green building programs to educate builders and home buyers alike. These programs include training materials and rating systems. The National Association of Home Builders Research Center (NAHBRC) also provides green building research and training support to NAHB members. It sponsors an annual green building conference and issues annual awards for the year's best green building product, best project, and best program.

In 2002, the City of Austin won NAHBRC's best program award for its comprehensiveness and long-term success. The program developed "Green by Design," a guide to green building for consumers and builders. The green-by-design process includes seven steps (City of Austin, 2001):

1. Assess your needs.
2. Form a team: designer, builder, lender, building officials, etc.
3. Design for your conditions: climate, site, community.
4. Choose "green" materials: Is the material effective in your conditions, healthy and safe, durable and easily maintained, used efficiently, available and workable, cost-effective, aesthetically satisfying?
5. Choose the right mechanical systems: energy-efficient heating/cooling, lighting, and appliances; choose solar and other renewable energy applications as appropriate.
6. Get the maximum benefit from your site and landscape: design with natural features, minimize runoff, minimize landscape maintenance.
7. Evaluate and maintain the green building after occupancy.

Colorado's state "Green Built" program is also notable. Begun in 1995 by the Home Builders' Association (HBA) of Denver, the governor's office, the nonprofit E-Star Colorado, and a private firm, it is now the largest green building program in the nation with more than 100 builder members, 45 sponsor members, and a 10-member Built Green Industry Leaders Group. The program has addressed one of the critical questions in any green marketing program, defining "green." To be labeled "Built Green," buildings must achieve a minimum score from a Built Green Checklist. The rating system has several criteria, including energy rating and energy use, materials, water use, and waste management. Although scores are self-reported, a random sample of labeled homes is inspected by certified inspectors from the independent agency E-Star Colorado (Green Built Colorado).

"Green development" is very similar to "green building," but it expands the client base from builders and consumers to real estate investors, lending institutions, and large-scale developers, and it includes commercial, office, retail, and institutional buildings in addition to residential development. Popularized by the Rocky Mountain Institute's 1998 book, *Green Development,* the concept aims to integrate two, often conflicting values—ecology and real estate.

Green development emphasizes four process elements: whole system thinking, front-loaded design, end-use/least-cost considerations, and teamwork including community involvement. It aims to provide both

- environmental benefits (environmental responsiveness, resource efficiency, community and cultural sensitivity), and
- economic benefits (reduced capital cost, reduced operating costs, marketing benefits, valuation premiums, streamlined approvals, reduced liability, health and productivity, staying ahead of regulations, new business opportunities).

In principle, green development starts with land use, aiming to work with what is already there. In other words, adaptive reuse, renovation, infill and brownfield

TABLE 6.4   **Examples of Green Development Projects**

Name	Location	Size	Units
Residential/Mixed Use			
Dewees Island	South Carolina	1200 (420) acres	78 lots
Prarie Crossing	Grayslake, Illinois	667 (207) acres	317 SF homes
Spring Island	South Carolina	3,000 acres	500 homes
Village Homes	Davis, CA	70 (32) acres	240 units
Civano	Tucson, AZ	1,145 (916) acres	2,600 units
Eco-Village	Loudon County, VA		
Eagle Lake	Orcas Island, WA	300 acres	
Armory Park del Sol	Tucson, AZ		99 sf homes
Commercial Office			
The Way Station	Frederick, MD	30,000 sq. ft.	
AAAS building	Washington	22,110 sq. ft.	
Audubon House	New York	98,000 sq. ft.	
Real Goods Solar	Hopland, CA	12 acres	

Sources: CESD, 2002; Rocky Mountain Institute, 1998.

development, and restoring damaged sites have priority over greenfield develop-ment. If greenfields are part of the development, ecological design principles should be used, such as cluster/open space development, compact neotraditional designs, and corporate campuses.

Site design should include water-conserving, low-maintenance native land-scaping, and natural drainage and low-impact stormwater management. Building should incorporate green design principles, as well as fit the site, foster commu-nity, and be adaptive and durable.

The Center of Excellence for Sustainable Development (www.sustainable. doe.gov/greendev) provides several resources for green development and chroni-cles the many green development success stories occurring across the country. Table 6.4 lists several developments and some of their features.

It will be interesting to observe the further evolution of green development and whether it grows beyond its current small, mostly upscale market niche. Rocky Mountain Institute (1998) authors foresee green developers moving from pioneer to mainstream markets over time, but that will require continued educational development of designers, developers, investors, and the public; cities' establish-ing an institutional and regulatory framework for green development; and improved marketing.

The Regional Context

The previous sections have emphasized the importance of development strategies in communities and rural areas. However, if land use development is to be managed to arrest sprawl and effectively protect and restore the environment, local strategies alone are not sufficient. Calthorpe and Fulton (2001) take the concepts of sustainable and livable development to the regional level, arguing that only a metropolitan and

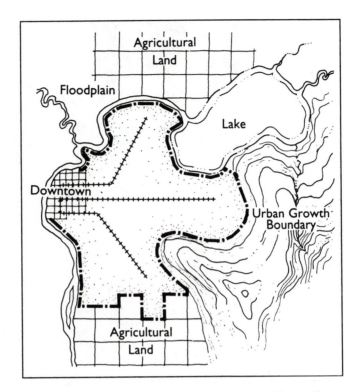

Figure 6.17 Urban Growth Boundary. *Source:* Peter Calthorpe, *The Next Metropolis: Ecology and the American Dream.* © 1993 Princeton Architectural Press. Used with permission.

regional approach can manage sprawl. They use neighborhood, town, and urban design principles as the basic building blocks for redesigning the "regional city," but they argue that regional policies for urban growth boundaries, transit and transportation, education balancing, and revenue sharing are critical to build regional awareness. In addition, regional investments in environmental programs for pollution control and open-space protection, in transportation and transit, and in urban and town revitalization are essential. These can come from federal and state sources or from regional agreements of local governments. Some examples of regional cooperation to manage growth and the environment are discussed in chapter 8.

The **urban growth boundary** (Figure 6.17) is an effective means to bound development, promote infill, and protect greenfields and agricultural lands. Development is accommodated and encouraged within the boundary, and discouraged outside through regulation or reduced urban services or infrastructure investment. The use of urban growth boundaries as a Smart Growth management tool is discussed in chapters 7 and 8.

Calthorpe Associates has recently applied the tools of regional development planning in several metropolitan areas including Portland (OR), Twin Cities (MN), and Salt Lake City (UT). These are described in Calthorpe and Fulton (2001) and in several project reports (Calthorpe Associates, 2000; Calthorpe Associates et al., 2000). Key elements of these plans include discrete development centers (cities, towns, villages), transit corridors, regional greenways and open space,

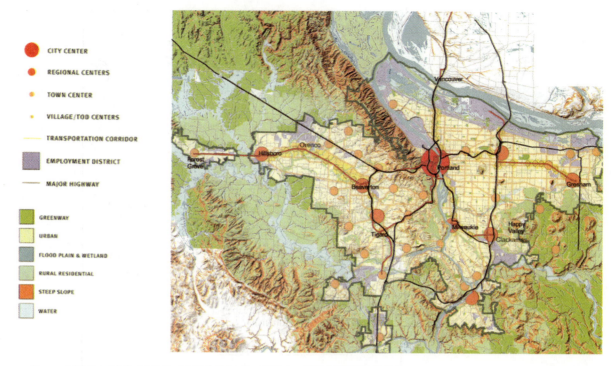

CITY CENTER

REGIONAL CENTERS

TOWN CENTER

VILLAGE/TOD CENTERS

TRANSPORTATION CORRIDOR

EMPLOYMENT DISTRICT

MAJOR HIGHWAY

GREENWAY

URBAN

FLOOD PLAIN & WETLAND

RURAL RESIDENTIAL

STEEP SLOPE

WATER

Figure 6.18 Portland's 2040 Framework Plan. The Plan shows open space elements, urban growth boundary, and metro centers, districts, and transit corridors. *Source:* Calthorpe and Fulton (2001). Used by permission of Island Press.

and urban growth boundaries. Figure 6.18 shows Portland's 2040 Framework Plan.

Process for Sustainable Land Use Design

The process for developing sustainable and livable land use designs is technical, creative, and participatory. It combines

- land analysis to understand the land's natural features and development opportunities and constraints;
- creative design that incorporates features of land protection, community aesthetics, and livability; and
- stakeholder involvement, including community groups, local government, land conservation organizations, existing residents, and potential consumers, to provide local knowledge, perceptions, and cultural context.

Chapter 2 introduced the renewed need for design in planning today. It should not replicate the utopian planning of the past, where the designer created his own creative vision for the community. Today "designing is making sense together." It is a collective process. The planner helps the community discover its vision of the future and explore means to achieve it. Still, planners and designers are more than just facilitators. By providing good information, by offering creative and visual alternatives, and by clarifying opportunities, planners play a principal role in "organizing attention to possibilities" (Forester, 1989).

Pragmatic developers have long recognized the need to know what consumers want to market their products. Increasingly, they are realizing that successful developments also depend on community acceptability to generate support and relieve potential conflict. This is important for both new developments and especially revitalization and redevelopment projects.

Chapter 4 described several tools for participation in the design process, including participatory mapping, photo simulations, visual surveys, and scenario development. Some excellent applications of these approaches are provided in Calthorpe Associates' projects in the Twin Cities and in Utah's Wasatch Basin (Calthorpe Associates, 2000; Calthorpe Associates et al., 2000). Photo simulations by Steve Price at Urban Advantage are illustrated in figures 6.11 and 6.16. A large number of other examples are given on the Urban Advantage website. It's worth a look: www.urbanadvantage.com.

Summary

Since 1950 land development patterns in the United States have been dominated by urban flight, suburban consumption of agricultural and natural areas, auto dependency, and growing transportation gridlock from congestion. In the last 10 years, architects and planners have responded with new, more sustainable models of development intended to protect natural areas, relieve auto dependency, and at the same time create more livable neighborhoods and communities. These models are land-conserving, compact, walkable, and often transit oriented; have mixed-income residential and commercial uses; and set aside greenspace for recreation and environmental protection. They also focus on revitalization of existing communities through infill, brownfield, greyfield, and downtown redevelopment to create more livable neighborhoods and town and city centers and relieve development pressure on greenfield working landscapes and natural areas.

These sustainable models have grabbed the attention of government officials, builders, and consumers alike. Government officials call it Smart Growth. Builders and realtors call it green building and development. Designers call it New Urbanism. Consumers call it livable communities.

The movement appears poised to take off. Projects carrying these various labels are increasing exponentially. New Urbanism development projects have grown from a handful five years ago to more than 400 according to the inventory kept by the CNU. People are returning to live in center cities and towns. Studies show a growing market for compact and walkable neighborhoods as many empty nesters and young families are choosing the walkable community and cultural life of cities and towns over the car-dependent private isolation of the suburbs.

The key elements of this movement include: regional integration, conservation design of rural and greenfield development, suburban revitalization, village and small-town development, and urban infill and brownfield redevelopment.

Regional integration (think regional): The many New Urbanism projects are site specific, but solutions to sprawl require a regional perspective. The region is the scale at which large metropolitan economic, ecological, and social systems operate. Although the task of coordinating many, often competing jurisdictions is a daunting one, it is critical for metropolitan areas to achieve a regional identity and develop a regional growth plan that includes growth centers and protection of environmental and working landscapes. Calthorpe's experience in the Twin Cities; Utah's Wasatch Basin; Portland, Oregon; and other areas shows that not only is such a plan possible, but it can be formulated through a participatory planning process.

Neighborhood features (act local): Calthorpe and Fulton see the region as the superstructure of human communities and neighborhoods as the substructure. Neighborhoods are a region's ground-level social fabric and community identity. The focus on the neighborhood scale is perhaps the greatest contribution of the new design orientation—compactness, walkability, mixed use, open space, natural drainage, community space.

Urban infill and brownfield redevelopment: A key to Smart Growth is taking advantage of development opportunities in existing urban areas through infill and brownfield redevelopment. The EPA estimates that development of an acre of brownfields prevents development of 21 acres of greenfields. In addition, the contamination and aesthetic blight of brownfields and other vacant properties detract from the integrity of communities, preventing other investments. Redevelopment not only heals the sores of the city but also acts to cure other social and economic ailments by spurring medicinal investment in surrounding properties.

Village and small-town development and revitalization: A region's villages and small towns serve as critical nodes for revitalization and development, building on existing culture and physical infrastructure. Like urban infill, small-town revitalization relieves development pressure on greenfields.

Suburban revitalization: Suburbs can become more livable communities through revitalization projects, such as shopping center greyfield redevelopment, infill with traditional neighborhoods, mixed use, and transit connections.

Rural and greenfield development: Despite existing community revitalization, development of some greenfield areas is necessary. Arendt and others have shown that rural development can occur while protecting working and natural landscapes. This requires cluster housing and permanent protection and management of agricultural, forestry, wetlands, and other sensitive lands.

7 ▪ Local Government Smart Growth Management for Environmental Land Use

Local governments are in a strategic position to plan and manage land use, development, and conservation. Although we shall see in the next chapter that a few states and regional areas have retained some authority for land use management, local governments have the bulk of the responsibility for guiding and regulating land use development. They are the closest governmental unit to community life, the primary planning agent for the community's future, and the first "line of defense" for solving community problems.

This chapter discusses the role of local government in environmental land planning and management in the United States. This takes the form of an array of land use planning and growth management approaches and tools. The chapter begins by defining Smart Growth management and describes a number of planning, regulatory, and nonregulatory tools to control development and protect and restore environmentally sensitive areas. The chapter uses a number of innovative local government environmental land use planning and management programs to illustrate the tools, including those in Boulder (CO), Davis (CA), King County (WA), Austin (TX), Blacksburg (VA), and Montgomery County (MD).

> **Growth management** is defined as those government policies, plans, investments, incentives, and regulations to guide the type, amount, location, timing, and cost of development to achieve a responsible balance between the protection of the natural environment and the development to support growth, a responsible fit between development and necessary infrastructure, and enhanced quality of community life.
>
> **Smart Growth** emphasizes compact and mixed development in areas of existing infrastructure and de-emphasizes development in areas less suitable for development. Smart Growth is the result of effective growth management; growth management is the set governmental tools needed to achieve Smart Growth.

Using an array of management tools, including innovative zoning regulations, urban growth boundaries, infrastructure investments, community planning procedures, tax policies, land acquisitions, and others, many rapidly growing localities have tried to control the pace and location of development (Benfield, Terris, and Vorsanger, 2001; Nelson and Duncan, 1995).

But growth management is not without its critics or controversy. In some places, there is a general opposition to land use regulation or any government "tampering" with how landowners wish to use their property. In some slow-growth or economically disadvantaged communities, the desire for more development overshadows that need to control it. Some argue that growth controls can constrain development, cause escalating housing costs, and reduce affordability.

For example, after years of successful growth management, Boulder, Colorado, realized that one of its primary community concerns was housing availability and affordability. In 2000 its ratio of jobs to population rose to nearly 0.92:1 and was projected to hit 1.21:1 by 2020 if trends continue. A balanced ratio is 0.65:1. This is one of three key issues of the latest revision to Boulder Valley's Comprehensive Plan (Boulder Valley Comprehensive Plan, 1996; City of Boulder, 2001).

Recognizing this issue, the Fannie Mae Foundation has promoted the concept of **Fair Growth**, which is Smart Growth that accommodates affordable housing. Whereas Smart Growth aims to reconcile economic and environmental goals, Fair Growth adds social equity, completing the tri-objectives of sustainable development (Arigoni, 2001; Fannie Mae Foundation, 2000).

Despite these critiques, citizens in communities with high levels of growth and development have witnessed land abuse or rapid disruptive change. They have called out for greater local control of growth and development. Some of the tools they have used in managing land use and the environment are described next.

Tools for Smart Growth Management and Land Use Control

Box 7.1 lists several tools that are available for growth management. This chapter addresses local growth management, but the same tools are used in state and regional growth management programs discussed in chapter 8. The tools are divided among three categories: planning, regulatory tools, and nonregulatory tools. **Planning** provides the technical, political, and policy framework for growth management implementation programs that are regulatory or nonregulatory in nature. **Regulatory tools** include controls on the type, location, and timing of development. Because of the limitations of conventional land use regulations like zoning and subdivision ordinances, a number of more innovative regulatory mechanisms have been developed to manage development and its impacts on the environment. **Nonregulatory tools** include land acquisition, tax policies, and using infrastructure development to guide the timing and location of development. Most effective growth management programs use a combination of tools.

BOX 7.1—Growth Management Tools

Planning

- Technical (including environmental) and political basis for land use management
- The comprehensive or general plan
- Functional plans; for example, capital improvement plan, stormwater management plan, open space/greenway plan, greenprint plan

Regulatory Tools

- Conventional Land Use Regulations
  - Zoning ordinance: Use and density restrictions
  - Subdivision regulations: Rules for land division
- Innovative Land Use Regulations
  - Variations on use and density restrictions; for example, agricultural zoning, cluster/conservation zoning
  - Overlay districts: Environmental zoning

  - Performance/flexible zoning: Performance criteria
  - Transfer of development rights (TDR)
  - Phased development: Timing of development
- Development/Design/Construction Standards and Plan Review: EIA, Smart Growth scorecard, Green building scorecard
- Environmental Ordinances (e.g., Green Building Codes, Stormwater, Tree Preservation)

Nonregulatory Tools

- Land acquisition, conservation easements, purchase of development rights
- Infrastructure development: Roads and sewers determine location of development
- Differential development impact fees
- Tax policies: Use-value taxation, level-of-service areas

Comprehensive/General Planning

Prior to 1900, most urban planning was conducted by designers commissioned by city government. The concept of community-based land use planning was born in the early 1900s. Hartford established the first city planning commission in 1907, and Milwaukee and Chicago followed in 1908 and 1909. In 1913, Massachusetts required all cities of more than 10,000 people to have planning boards. The principal planning tool was land use zoning, which divides the city into districts where certain land uses are allowed. New York City adopted the first zoning ordinances in 1916, and by the time the U.S. Supreme Court upheld the constitutionality of zoning in 1926, over 500 cities had zoning regulations (Morris, 1982). But regulation is not planning, and the incremental actions of zoning boards tended to fragment cities into haphazard sections defined by the whims of board members and the influence of individual landowners.

The U.S. Department of Commerce issued a Standard State Zoning Enabling Act in 1926 to assist states desiring to grant localities the authority to zone. Although the model Act provided that zoning regulations must be made "in accordance with a comprehensive plan," it provided no guidance on what a comprehensive plan was. Generally, courts viewed the zoning map itself as the comprehensive plan (NRDC, 1977).

The need for a more comprehensive view of city planning was not recognized until the late 1930s and later. In 1954, federal financial assistance for local comprehensive planning became available through section 701 of the Housing Act. This "701" program grew through the 1960s and 1970s, established the

BOX 7.2—Six Elements of Community Planning

1. Intelligence: Background Data and Planning Analysis

Land use intelligence involves environmental inventorying and mapping, suitability and carrying capacity analysis, and assessment of land use perceptions (livability, attractiveness, symbolism, and quality of life). Planning intelligence is used in the process of general, functional, and district planning.

2. Long-Range Comprehensive or General Planning

Most general plans contain functional, district, and implementation plans.

3. District Planning

District or sector plans cover a small area like a neighborhood, a central business district, a redevelopment area, or an environmental preservation area. The district plans characterize existing land use, identify critical issues, and provide a future vision represented in map and design form. The land use plan for a community comes to life in these district or neighborhood plans.

4. Functional Planning

Functional plans address single topics that cover the entire planning area, including transportation, infrastructure, natural environment, greenspace/greenways, parks and recreation, housing, and economic development, among others.

5. Implementation Plans

Implementation plans and programs address the actions necessary to realize the vision, objectives, and strategies of the general, district, and functional plans. Actions include zoning and development regulations, capital improvement plans and budgets, tax policies, and other programs.

6. Building Community Consensus

Although listed separately here, building community consensus through stakeholder involvement and collaborative planning is part of each of the five planning functions.

framework for comprehensive planning, and provided considerable experience in the field. The Department of Housing and Urban Development (HUD) 701 program was terminated by the Housing and Community Development Amendments of 1981. However, the program requirements for planning established the model for a comprehensive plan.

The **comprehensive plan,** first and foremost, is a vision of the future community developed and accepted by the community and adopted by its elected officials. The plan is a set of policies, goals, objectives, and strategies dealing with various aspects of the community—land use, housing, transportation, natural environment, economic development—that can guide the community's physical development. The policies are to be based on an evaluation of the area's needs and to serve as the basis for the formulation of specific plans and programs to meet those needs.

The Housing and Community Development Act of 1974 further required that comprehensive plans funded by HUD contain a housing element and a land use element. The land use element was to serve as a community guide for all matters relating to the use of the land, including air and water quality, protection of coastal areas, open space, agricultural land, environmental conservation, energy consumption, and land development. HUD guidance also required localities to prepare an environmental assessment of their plans and policies. Although the land use element and land use plan are not the only parts of the comprehensive plan, they have come to be viewed as the plan's key components.

BOX 7.3—The Local Comprehensive or General Plan

The comprehensive plan provides a vision adopted by the community and the technical and political basis for growth management and local government programs. Prepared every 4–10 years, the plan has a 10- to 50-year time horizon.

- Vision of the Community
- Statement of Community Policies
- Strategic Plan: Goals, Objectives, Strategies
- Functional Plans or Communitywide Topical Chapters: Natural Environment, Land Use, Parks and Recreation, Utilities, Transportation, Housing, Public Safety
- District or Sector Plans: Neighborhood Plans

As discussed in chapter 3, comprehensive planning is part of a community planning process made up of the six elements given in box 7.2. All comprehensive plans contain the "long-range general plan," and most also include "district" and "functional" plans. In other cases these latter plans are separate and updated more frequently. Planning "intelligence" includes the background inventories, analyses, and public participation that serve as the foundation of the planning effort.

Box 7.3 gives a simple definition of the comprehensive plan and some of its basic components: a vision statement, policy statements, communitywide topics or elements, and district or neighborhood plans. Maps and graphical materials are important visual components to illustrate the plan and the future it portends.

The following list gives the table of contents of the 2001 Comprehensive Plan for Blacksburg, Virginia, a college town of 40,000 (Town of Blacksburg, 2001). The plan is revised every five years and has a 50-year time horizon. The plan presents the community vision as "portraits" of the town in 50 years. Part II provides chapters on plan elements of communitywide topical areas; they are presented in strategic plan format: goals, objectives, and strategies. Part III presents district or neighborhood plans. After the 1996 plan, the zoning ordinance was totally rewritten to reflect the plan.

Components of the Town of Blacksburg (VA) 2001 Comprehensive Plan

Introduction
Part I   The Town as a Whole
          Community Values and Mission
          Background Data and Planning
          Elements Expected to Shape Future
          Land Use Trends
          Portraits of Blacksburg
              Today, 1996
              Tomorrow, 2046
          Plan goals
Part II   Townwide Topics (Elements)
          Community Design

Natural Environment and Open Space
Parks and Recreation
Greenways
Historic Preservation
Economic Development
Information Technology
Utility Services
Transportation
Community Facilities/Human Services
Public Safety
Part III   Sectors (Neighborhood Planning)
Overall Land Use Policies
Sectors (Neighborhoods)

The strategic plan format of goals, objectives, and strategies is a key part of the plan because it articulates the community's direction and vision and serves as the basis for implementing regulations and programs. Figure 7.1 shows townwide land use in 2046 according to the plan. Using the interactive WebGIS, residents can zero in on their neighborhood and see what land use changes are called for in the plan.

King County, Washington, is the size of Delaware (2,130 square miles), and, among the nation's counties, it contains some of the most beautiful scenery, diverse ecosystems, productive farmland, and vibrant economies. Its 1.7 million people are concentrated in 39 cities, including Seattle. The 2000 comprehensive plan focuses on the county's unincorporated (noncity) land, which is 82 percent of its area and holds 21 percent of its population (360,000). The plan is heavily influenced by the 1994 Washington State Growth Management Act, which required 13 planning goals of all local comprehensive plans, including the establishment of urban growth boundaries. Among its nine chapters are Regional Planning, Rural Legacy and Natural Resource Lands, Environment, and Preserving and Enriching Our Communities. Figure 7.2 shows land use for most of the county and delineates urban growth areas and rural areas (separated by an urban growth boundary), as well as protected open space and agricultural and forest production districts (King County, 2000).

Regulatory Tools for Growth Management

States have the constitutional authority to regulate private activities including development, and most states have delegated the responsibility for land use control to local governments. The degree to which state governments have delegated land use control to localities varies considerably from state to state. States can be divided into "Dillon's Rule" and "Home Rule" states. In Dillon's Rule states, communities only have those powers vested to them by specific state legislation.[1] In Home Rule states, communities are free to exercise powers, *unless* specifically prohibited by the state. In some of these Home Rule states, the state government

---

1. This is named for Judge John Foster Dillon, who in 1868 (*City of Clinton v. Cedar Rapids and Missouri Railroad Co.,* 24 Iowa 455) formulated the doctrine that municipalities only have those powers "expressly granted" to them by the state.

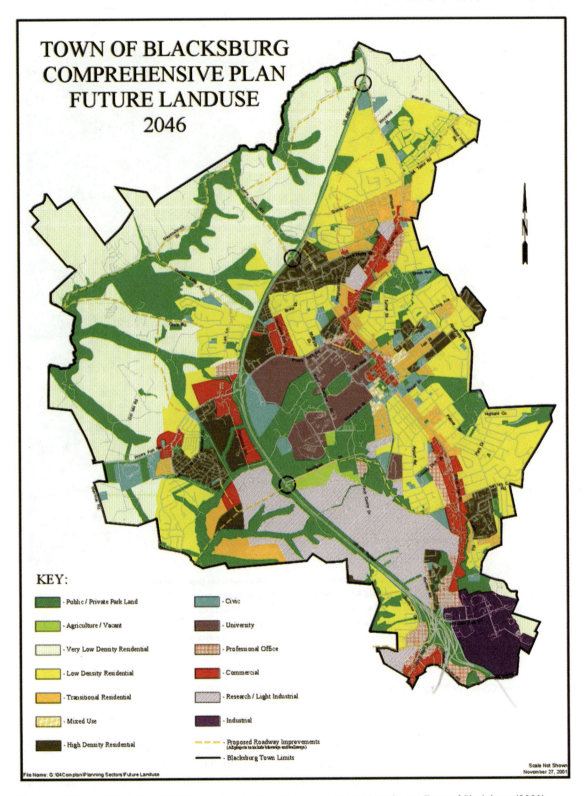

Figure 7.1 Town of Blacksburg (VA) Comprehensive Plan: Future Land Use 2046. *Source:* Town of Blacksburg (2001).

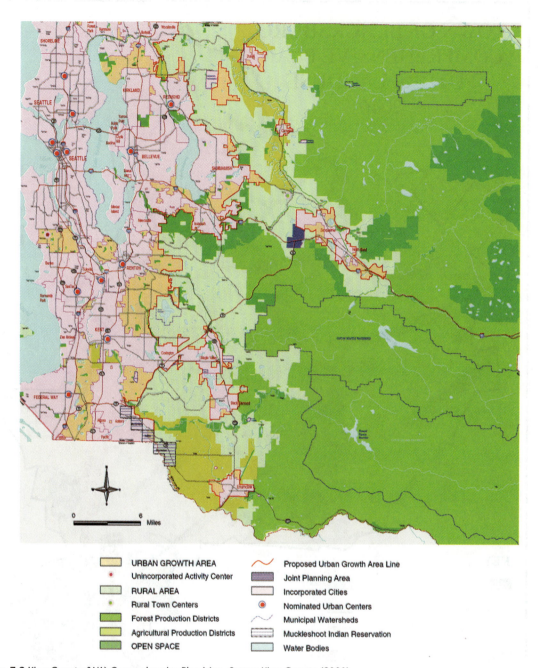

Figure 7.2 King County (WA) Comprehensive Plan Map. *Source:* King County (2001).

is actually precluded from imposing laws on local jurisdictions. Dillon's Rule is still effective to varying degrees in 37 states (Richardson, 2002).

This constitutional variation among the states affects the constraints and opportunities available to both state and local governments in their efforts to control land use. What works for one state may not be available to another; what has been successful in one community may not be legal for a locality with similar problems in another state. In all communities, the "police" or regulatory powers that local governments can employ to control land use are constrained by the rights of personal property provided by the U.S. Constitution.

Property Rights and Legal Constraints on Environmental Land Use Regulation

As shown in box 7.1, land use regulation is the principal mechanism that local government uses to manage growth. Although communities are granted the police power by the state to control land development to protect public health, safety, and welfare, that authority is not boundless. Community regulatory authority is constrained by the protection of property rights contained in the Fifth and Fourteenth Amendments to the Constitution, which bar government from "taking" private property for public use without just compensation. "Takings" occur when government regulations go "too far" in restricting private property use, and courts can enjoin the regulations and/or order compensation. However, the definition of "too far" is not always clear, and local governments must consider potential takings litigation when designing regulatory programs to manage growth and protect the environment.

In the 1970s, courts tended to view the public welfare quite broadly and ruled in favor of a broad range of community regulatory devices, especially when they addressed health and safety issues and were based on technical analysis and a publicly adopted comprehensive plan. In the 1980s and 1990s, legal advocates for property rights argued successfully for their interests in several cases, and even though takings law continues to evolve, some legal clarity has emerged. The Supreme Court decided three major takings-issue cases[2] in 1987, two more in the early 1990s,[3] and one in 2002,[4] which all helped establish a judicial "taking equation" consisting of a three-level inquiry. Some of the key issues are discussed in box 7.4.

The first inquiry involves whether the purpose of the regulatory action is a "legitimate state interest" and if the means used to achieve the objective "substantially advance" that purpose. The legitimacy of the state interest is clear for the protection of public safety, such as for floodplain zoning, but is less clear for protecting environmental resources, such as agricultural lands or nonendangered wildlife habitat.

The second inquiry concerns whether a "reasonable use" of the property by the landowner remains after the regulation. If the government acquires title to the

---

2. *Keystone Bituminous Coal Association v. DeBenedictis*, 107 S. Ct. 1232 (1987); *First English Evangelical Lutheran Church v. County of Los Angeles*, 107 S. Ct., 2378 (1987); *Nollan v. California Coastal Commission*, 107 S. Ct. 3141 (1987).

3. *Lucas v. South Carolina Coastal Council* (1992), *Dolan v. City of Tigard* (1994). The Lucas case is discussed and illustrated in the coastal zone management section of chapter 9.

4. *Tahoe Sierra Preservation Council, Inc. v. Tahoe Regional Planning Agency* (2002). Called the "most definitive win for good planning in over a decade," the decision validated development moratoria, emphasizing the value of a community's taking time to "develop a citizen-based plan for conserving its treasured resources" (Lucero and Soule, 2002). Planning for Lake Tahoe is discussed in chapters 8 and 18.

BOX 7.4—Property Law and the "Takings" Issue

- Tenth Amendment to Constitution grants government **police power** to protect public health and welfare. The Fourteenth Amendment extends this power to state and local government.
- Fifth Amendment protects **private property**; the "takings clause" requires "just compensation when government affects a taking of property." This does not prohibit condemning private property for the public good through eminent domain.

Key issues in determining if regulations are an appropriate use of the police power

- The regulation must **substantially advance legitimate state interests.** The "legitimate state interests" must be based on the prevention of public harm rather than the provision of public benefit.
- The regulation involves a **connection (nexus)** between the potential private action and achieving the state interest. Regulation cannot impose a requirement that is not closely related to the state interest or the public impact.
- The regulation does not deny an owner **"reasonable use"** of his or her property. Reasonable use often involves a balancing test of state interests versus economic impact on the owner.

---

property or physically invades the land, the regulation will generally be a taking. If the landowner retains the land but is left with no reasonable use, the burden is on the government to demonstrate that any use of the land would significantly impact the interest of the state.

If some use of the property remains after the regulation, the third inquiry involves a balancing test of economic impact. The court would decide whether the public interest is outweighed by the economic or other burden on the landowner. The inquiry will look at the "reasonableness" of remaining use and the diminution in value caused by the regulation.

Land Use Regulations

The following list outlines and describes a number of land use regulations that are used to control growth and protect the environment.

Land Use Regulations for Growth Management and Environmental Protection

Conventional Zoning: Use and density restrictions, often some design standards, for example, setbacks. For environmental objectives, large-lot zoning is sometimes used.

Subdivision Ordinance: Requirements for layout of streets, drainage, water, sewer, and so on, to achieve "orderly development" at the land subdivision stage.

Agricultural Zoning:

    a. Exclusive: Prohibits construction of nonfarm buildings. Possible "takings" conflicts, but often supported in courts when part of comprehensive planning and when development areas are specified.

b. Nonexclusive: allows limited amount of nonfarm development
   1. *Large-lot zoning: May actually convert farmland to development at a faster rate.*
   2. *Sliding-scale zoning: Number of units per acre decreases as parcel size increases; also, maximum acreage per development unit (e.g., 2 acres).*

Overlay Zoning: Aims to protect environmental resources or safeguard in natural hazard areas. "Overlay district" is determined by boundaries of environmental resource or hazard and are placed on top of existing zoning. In overlay district special additional land use restrictions apply, such as restricted development, extra standards, or extra documentation. Used for floodplain zones, seismic hazards, wellhead protection areas, watersheds, habitat zones, riparian zones.

Conservation, Open Space or Cluster Zoning: Provides density transfers on-site to enable clustering/concentrating development on buildable areas while leaving permanently undisturbed open space on sensitive areas.

Conditional Zoning: Although zoned for a specific use (e.g., high-density residential, large-scale commercial, industrial), this zone requires "special-use permit" before approval. Special-use permit may require exactions or impact fees and gives local officials negotiating leverage. Proffers or voluntary design features or development fees are often used with conditional zoning.

Performance Zoning: Requires meeting certain performance criteria rather than prescriptive standards.

Flexible Zoning: Provides for "planned" developments or negotiated development based on performance criteria or negotiation. Allows for creativity in development design.

Urban Growth Boundaries: Contains development within a set boundary separating urban and rural uses.

Transfer of Development Rights: Enables transfer of development rights from a "preservation zone" to a "development zone." Landowners in preservation zone are compensated from payments made by landowners in the development zone.

Phased Development: Controls not the location but the rate of development or the number of units per year to keep pace with the provision of public services.

Concurrency: Development plans can be approved only if they are "concurrent" with plans for infrastructure and/or other public services.

Zoning has long been the principal land use regulation used by localities. Conventional zoning specifies the location of different types of land use (e.g., residential, commercial, industrial, agricultural, conservation) by dividing the community into specific land use zones. Different residential, agricultural, and conservation zones are distinguished by development density or the maximum number of dwelling units

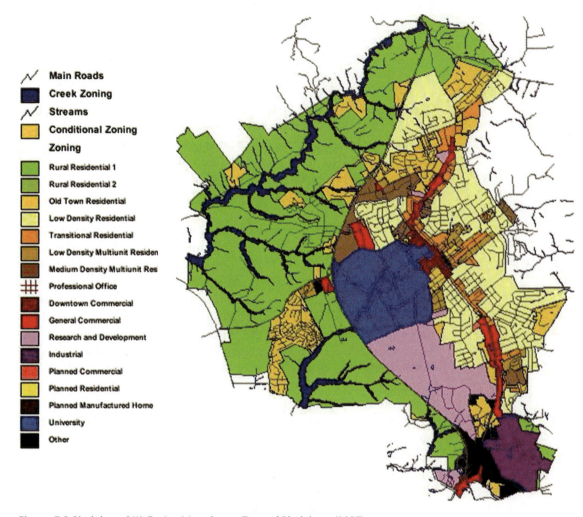

Figure 7.3 Blacksburg (VA) Zoning Map. *Source:* Town of Blacksburg (1997)

allowed per acre. In addition, zoning regulations define other development parameters including maximum building height, lot size, maximum percent of lot covered, minimum setbacks from property lines, and so on. Figure 7.3 gives the zoning map for the Town of Blacksburg.

Subdivision ordinances, which set requirements for layout of streets, drainage, water and wastewater, and so on, are another traditional measure to achieve "orderly development" at the land subdivision stage. Although conventional zoning and subdivision ordinances have done much to separate incompatible land uses and standardize subdivision practices, they have not met all the land use control needs of many communities.

One critique of conventional zoning is that it assumes use and density restrictions can protect environmental and community values. These restrictions are not sufficient because they assume all land is the same (i.e., there are not environmentally sensitive lands). Large-lot zoning (e.g., 1 unit per 5 acres or 1 unit per 20 acres) can reduce some of the impacts associated with dense development but

TABLE 7.1 **Sliding Scale Zoning Development Right Allocation for Different Parcel Size Classes, Clarke County, Virginia**

Size Class (Acres)	Average Parcel	Number Development Rights	Nonfarm Acres/ Average parcel*	Farm Acres/ Average parcel*	Percentage of site in Agriculure
0–14.9	4.2 acres	1	2	0	0
15–39.9	23.6 acres	2	4	20	83
40–79.9	51.6 acres	3	6	46	88
80–129.9	102.7 acres	4	8	95	92
400–499.9	418.7 acres	10	20	399	95
860–1029.9	930.0 acres	14	38	902	97

* 2-acre lot maximum
Source: Coughlin, 1991

may cause others. For example, this practice consumes more land per dwelling unit, can be socially exclusionary (i.e., only the rich can afford such large lots), and can lead to greater sprawl. In many cases, when local governments have "down-zoned" property (e.g., from 1 unit per acre to 1 unit per 5 acres) to protect open space or environmental resources, property owners have sued, arguing a "taking" of property without due compensation.

The "Land Use Regulations for Growth Management and Environmental Protection" list at the beginning of this section shows several innovations in land use regulations that have responded to the critique of conventional zoning and aimed to protect environmental resources more effectively. **Agricultural zoning** aims to preserve agricultural land use, production, and rural character. Exclusive agricultural zoning prohibits construction of non-farm-related buildings. Some communities have been successful with exclusive agricultural zoning (see Oregon state program discussed in chapter 8), but because of potential takings conflicts, most communities have opted for nonexclusive agricultural zoning, which allows a limited amount of nonfarm development. This has been done primarily with large-lot zoning, but as already discussed, it has often accelerated the conversion of productive agricultural lands to nonagricultural uses.

One innovation is **sliding scale zoning.** It is similar to large-lot zoning, but it provides for different densities depending on the property size. It can also limit the acreage of lots that are developed. One of the best-known examples of sliding scale zoning is in Clarke County, Virginia. Table 7.1 lists the development right allocation system for 6 of the 14 parcel-size classes. The rights per acre decrease with increased parcel size. For example, a 10-acre parcel has 1 development right (1 per 10 acres), while a 120-acre site has 4 rights (1 per 30 acres), and a 480-acre property has 10 rights (1 per 48 acres). Subdivision of land is limited by the allocated development rights, and development parcels are limited to 2 acres each. Table 7.1 shows how this system preserves farmland. Column 4 gives the acreage in development for an average size parcel under each size class. Columns 5 and 6 show what acreage and percentage of land would be left in agriculture for an average parcel. If the county were "built out" under the sliding scale zoning program,

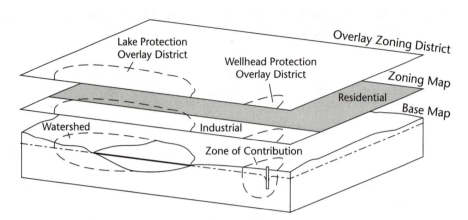

Figure 7.4 Overlay Zoning for Wellhead and Lake Watershed Protection. *Source:* Jon Witten and Scott Horsley. 1995. *A Guide to Wellhead Protection.* Planning Advisory Service Report 457/458. Used with permission of the American Planning Association.

76,000 of the county's 83,000 acres of agricultural land would be left in agriculture (Coughlin, 1991).

Perhaps the most used and useful innovation in zoning for environmental protection is **overlay zoning,** which acts to protect environmental resources or safeguard land use in natural hazard areas. The "overlay" district is applied on top of existing zoning requirements, so its conditions apply to different conventional zones, for example, low-density residential, commercial, and so on. The "overlay" district boundaries are determined by an environmental inventory or land analysis that shows the location of a resource or hazard. Within the overlay district special additional land use restrictions apply. These may include restricted development, extra standards, or extra documentation. Overlay zoning is used for floodplains, watersheds, wellhead protection areas, habitats, slope instability, seismic hazards, fire hazards, etc. (see figure 7.4).

Figure 7.5 shows a portion of the City of Austin's (TX) Desired Development Zone map, which contains overlay zones for drinking water aquifer protection, creek buffer, and Balcones Canyon habitat protection (BCCP), as well as development zones (see chapter 17 and table 17.2 for more on BCCP) (City of Austin, undated [a], [b]).

Environmental zoning can use overlays or simply establish special requirements for designated areas. A good example is the Environmental Quality Corridor (EQC) System adopted by Fairfax County, Virginia, in 1990. As shown in figure 7.6, the EQC includes 100-year floodplains; areas of 15 percent or greater slope adjacent to floodplains or 50 feet from streams; all wetlands connected to stream valleys; all land measured from the streambank 50 feet plus 4 feet per percent slope. To provide habitat, wildlife corridors, pollution reduction, and aesthetic benefits, development of EQC land is prohibited. The policy provides for on-site density transfers, allowing for sites containing EQC to be developed to their overall gross density, but with development concentrated on non-EQC land (Fairfax County, 1991).

Based on the Fairfax EQC model, Blacksburg (VA) adopted its Creek Overlay District in 1997. The District (Creek Zoning) is shown in the zoning map in figure

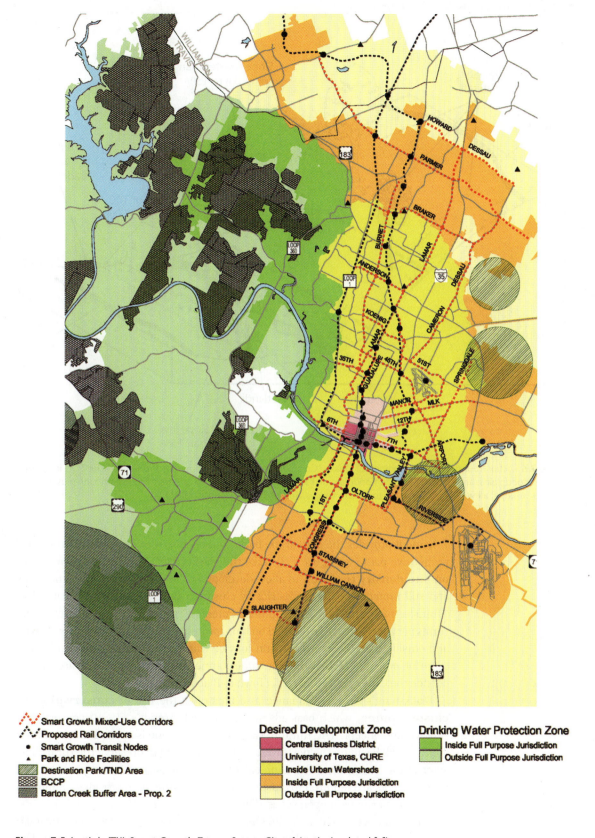

Figure 7.5 Austin's (TX) Smart Growth Zones. *Source:* City of Austin (undated [a])

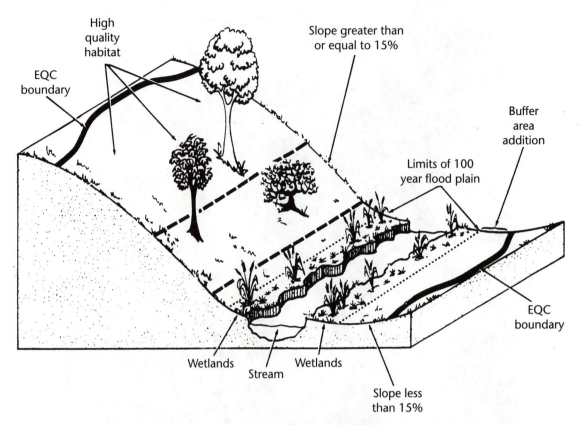

Figure 7.6 Fairfax County's (VA) Environmental Quality Corridor in Which Development Is Prohibited. The EQC includes 100-year floodplains; areas adjacent to the floodplain of 15% or greater slope; land 50 feet from streambank plus 4 feet per each % slope; all wetlands connected to stream valleys. *Source:* Fairfax County (1991).

7.3, and it provides the core of the parks and open space component of the comprehensive plan (see figure 7.2). Like the Fairfax EQC, the District provides an **on-site density transfer,** to allow development to achieve development rights and still protect the Creek District by clustered development on the site. The "Transfer of Residential Development Potential" states: "Development density (units per acre) otherwise allowed on land located within the Creek Valley District and outside the 100 year floodplain may be transferred to those portions of the same lot, or to other lots within the same planned development, which are located outside the Creek Valley District" (Town of Blacksburg, 1997).

Blacksburg's zoning ordinance also illustrates the use of **conservation or cluster zoning,** which basically applies Randall Arendt's (1999) conservation subdivision concept. The Rural Residential (RR-1) zone is applied to most of the Tom's Creek Basin on the northwest section. Intended to preserve the rural character of the Basin, the RR-1 zone calls for gross density of 1 unit per acre, but developments are required to cluster development on-site to provide a minimum 50 percent permanent open space. The text of the RR-1 is given in box 7.5.

The ordinance also includes an Open Space Design Overlay District (OSDOD) to encourage open space within most residential zoning districts of the Town. The

BOX 7.5—Blacksburg's Rural Residential Zoning Ordinance

The purpose of the **Rural Residential** (RR-1) district is to provide for residential development at a scale intended to conserve the rural character of the Tom's Creek Basin. Development within the Rural Residential district is intended to promote the following goals and objectives. Development proposals shall be evaluated for their adherence to these goals:

(a) Conservation of agricultural and forestal lands, including farm fields and pastures.

(b) Conservation of natural resources including wetlands, flood plains, natural drainage ways, aquifer recharge areas, existing tree cover, steep slopes, ridge lines, hilltops, wildlife habitats, deer wintering areas, stream valleys, locations comprising scenic views or scenic view corridors, and other outstanding natural topography.

(c) Conservation of a unified open space area, which is preserved with a permanent conservation easement.

(d) Creation of residential developments on a rural scale, with small villages surrounded by agricultural, forestal, or open space.

(e) Flexibility/creativity in design of residential subdivisions, less suburban-style sprawl, less consumption of open land.

These measures will prevent soil erosion by permitting development according to the nature of the terrain, provide larger open areas with greater utility for rest and recreation, and encourage the development of more attractive and economic site design. They will create a convenient, attractive, and harmonious community, and facilitate the provision of parks, forests, playgrounds, and other recreational facilities. These goals are intended to preserve existing agricultural, forestal, and other lands of significance for the protection of the natural environment.

Development Standards

Each residential lot shall be of a size and shape to provide a building site which shall be in harmony with the natural terrain and other features of the land. Residential lots shall be designed in such a way as to promote the purposes of this chapter. The following minimum standards shall apply.

(a) Density: Maximum density shall be one dwelling unit per acre, excluding acreage within the 100 year floodplain.

(b) Minimum Lot Requirements: No minimum lot size; 20 feet minimum frontage on a publicly owned and maintained street

(c) Minimum Setback Requirements: Front yard: 8–13 feet on minor streets; 35–60 feet of collector road; Rear: 20 ft; Side: 10 ft

(d) Minimum Building Separation: front-front: 80–90 feet; side-side 20–30 feet; back-back 40–60 feet;

(e) Maximum Floor Area Ratio: Maximum floor area ratio shall be 0.30, except townhouse 0.50.

(f) Maximum Height of Structures, except church spires, chimneys, flues, flagpoles, television antennae: 35 feet

(g) Maximum Dwelling Unit Occupancy: a family plus two persons unrelated; or no more than three unrelated persons.

(h) All utility lines, electric, telephone, cable television lines, etc, shall be placed underground.

Minimum Open Space

A minimum of 50 percent of the total area shall be designated as permanent open space, not to be further subdivided, and protected through a conservation or open space easement held by the Town, the Virginia Outdoors Foundation, or by a recognized land trust or conservancy. All undivided open space shall be restricted from further subdivision through a permanent conservation or open space easement, in a form acceptable to the Town, and recorded in the Montgomery County Circuit Court Clerk's office.

underlying district prescribes the gross density, but if a minimum of 30 percent of the site is designated as permanent open space protected by conservation easement, that density can be clustered on the remaining 70 percent of the site.

Blacksburg's RR-2 zone is an example of **incentive zoning,** which provides a **density bonus** from 1 to 2 units per acre if the landowner "proffers" or voluntarily incorporates one or more of 14 specified features that are in the town's interest. These include: additional open space, recreational facilities, land dedication to town park or greenway, visual buffers, affordable housing, among others. The Ashland, Oregon, 1980 zoning ordinance, for example, provides the following density bonuses (to a maximum 60%) for planned unit developments (PUDs) (Randolph, 1981):

Energy-efficient housing	up to 40% bonus
Solar hot water	up to 5%
Common open space	up to 15%
Recreational facilities	up to 10%
Low-cost housing	up to 10%
Good design features	up to 10%

Figure 7.7 illustrates the incentive zoning concept. In Isle of Wight County, Virginia, developers have options for open space design in a zone with a permitted density of 1 unit per 10 acres and a requirement for 50 percent permanent open space. The first option (7.7A) is an on-site density transfer that provides the 50 percent open space and 10 five-acre lots. The second option provides 70 percent open space and gives a density bonus of 100 percent, allowing 20 lots of 1.5 acres each (7.7B).

Conditional zoning aims to manage impacts of specific developments, such as industrial plants or large subdivisions. While an area is zoned for a particular use, say residential or industrial, the conditional zone requires a **special-use permit** that may require meeting certain conditions, such as **exactions** or **impact fees** to offset impacts of the development or to cover public services required by the project. The special-use permit gives local officials negotiating leverage about the design of the development. **Proffers** are voluntary modifications, design features, or development fees added to the development proposal to enhance the prospects of obtaining a special-use permit. Conditional zoning is often applied to natural hazard overlay zones. For example, a conditional zone might be established for a steep slope; development will be allowed only if the development plan is approved by a licensed engineer for slope safety.

Performance zoning varies from conventional zoning by providing performance criteria or standards rather than prescriptive requirements for developments. For example, instead of specifying a specific size detention basin to mitigate storm discharges, a performance approach might simply specify a zero net increase and let the developer decide and demonstrate how the requirement will be met. Generally, performance criteria allow for more creativity in development design but require more documentation in the development proposal to show how the criteria will be met. Some performance-based zoning specifies land coverage or open space percentages or ratios that must be met for certain environmentally sensitive areas. On-site density transfers are usually provided. Burks County, Pennsylvania, was one of the first localities to use this approach. Its criteria and that of Maryland's Queen Anne County are given in table 7.2. Based on a site land

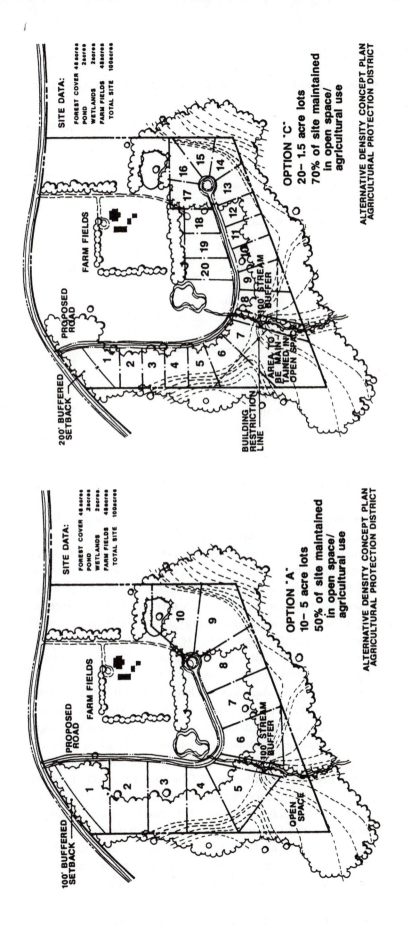

Figure 7.7 Density Bonus Options in Isle of Wight County, Virginia. Base zoning (A) provides 1 unit per 10 acres and requires 50% open space. Increasing open space to 70% (B) gives a 100% density bonus. *Source:* Reprinted with permission from Randall Arendt, *Rural by Design,* copyright 1994 by the American Planning Association, Suite 1600, 122 South Michigan Ave, Chicago, IL 60603-6107.

TABLE 7.2 **Performance Criteria Used in Burks County (PA) and Queen Anne's County (MD)**

Burks Co. Protection Performance Zoning		Queen Anne's Resource Protection Standards			
			Open Space Ratios		
Resource	% Open	Resource	Coast	Upland	Agriculture
100-year floodplains	100%	Wetlands			
Alluvial soils	100	Tidal	1.0	—	—
Wetlands	100	Nontidal	1.0	1.0	0.8
Natural retention areas	90	Drainageways	0.5	0.3	0.8
Lake and pond shores	70–80	Woodlands			
Forests	60–80	Mature hardwood	0.8	0.7	0.5
Steep slopes over 25%	85	Mature Evergreen	0.8	0.6	0.5
Steep slopes 15–25%	70	Young	0.8	0.3	0.2
Steep slopes 8–15%	60	Old Field Succession	0.3	0.0	0.85
Class I agricultural soils	95	Farm Fields	0.0	0.0	0.85
Class II agricultural soils	85	Erosion Hazard Area	1.0	—	—
Class III agricultural soils	80	Beach	1.0	—	—
Class IV agricultural soils	60	Bluffs	1.0	—	—
		Shore Buffer	1.0	—	—

cover inventory, the performance criteria require leaving open a certain percentage or ratio of the land in resource areas.

Flexible zoning includes planned unit developments, cluster zoning, and floating zones, which are all designed to reduce the rigid standards imposed by conventional zoning. **Planned unit developments (PUD)** do not rely on specific regulations but rather on a process of administrative review of proposed development plans and negotiation between the developer and planning agency. Such developments can incorporate creative designs not allowed by conventional zoning. **Floating zones** simply identify a zone and its requirements, but not its location; they are often used for PUDs. Flexible zoning allows for creativity and innovation in development design but requires a fairly sophisticated planning staff and is enhanced by public involvement.

Communities have also enacted a long list of other codes and ordinances with specific requirements for developers. Los Angeles's grading ordinance has helped to limit land and landslide damages. Building codes are applied in nearly all communities. Erosion and sedimentation control ordinances and tree removal and planting ordinances are also examples of environmental controls.

Urban growth boundaries (UGBs) are a method of containing development within a set boundary separating urban and rural land uses (see figure 6.17). UGBs were first used in Oregon's Land Conservation and Development program established in 1973. Oregon's UGBs are shown in figure 8.9, and Portland's (OR) UGB is shown in figure 6.18. They have become an important tool to achieve Smart Growth's objective to emphasize development in areas with existing infrastructure and de-emphasize development in greenfields. UGBs are usually intended to accommodate growth for a specified period of time; 15 to 20 years is common.

Other states and localities have adopted UGBs. Washington's 1994 Growth Management Act requires a UGB for the state's cities and urban counties. Figure 7.2 shows King County's (WA) UGB. The Twin Cities Metro Council established a UGB called the Metro Utility Service Area (MUSA) (see chapter 8). Maryland has attempted to establish UGBs without regulation. The state will provide financial support for development infrastructure in Priority Funding Areas, essentially UGBs identified by localities (see figure 8.12).

Boulder Valley's (CO) growth management program depends significantly on a UGB that is divided into planning areas. Boulder has adjusted the UGB over time to accommodate development needs. Figure 7.8 shows the boundaries for the various growth areas:

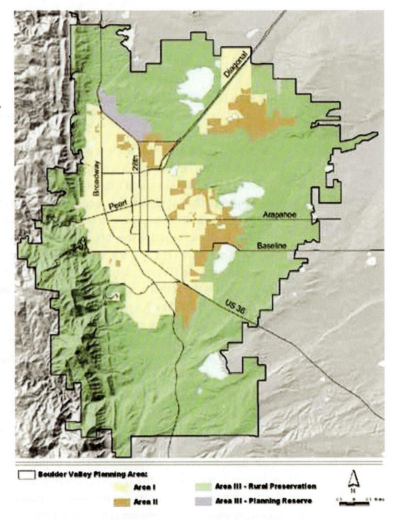

Figure 7.8 Boulder Valley Planning Areas. Area I and II are available for development within the planning period (15 years). Area III includes preservation lands as well as a planning reserve for development beyond the planning period. *Source:* City of Boulder (2001).

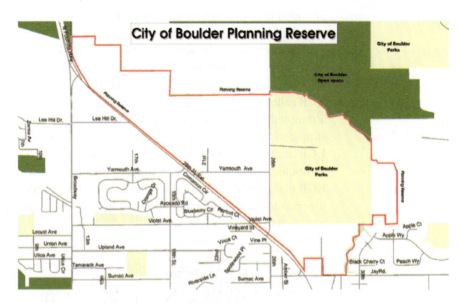

Figure 7.8 (*Continued*)

- Area I is that area within the city of Boulder that has adequate urban facilities and services and is expected to continue to accommodate urban development.
- Area II is the area now under county jurisdiction, where annexation to the city can be considered consistent with comprehensive plan policies. New urban development may only occur coincident with the availability of adequate facilities and services and not otherwise. Departmental master plans project the provision of services to this area within the planning period. Area IIA is the area of immediate focus within the first three years, and Area IIB is available to accommodate development within the balance of the 15-year planning period.
- Area III is the remaining area in the Boulder Valley, generally under county jurisdiction. Area III is divided into the Area III-Rural Preservation Area, where the city and county intend to preserve existing rural land use and character and the Area III-Planning Reserve Area, where the city and county intend to maintain the option of expanded urban development in the city beyond the time frame of the 15-year planning period (City of Boulder, 2001).

Transfer of development rights (TDR) is similar to purchase of development rights (see chapter 5). Instead of buying development rights, TDR transfers rights from areas the community wishes to protect to areas that are more appropriate for development. Such a program requires the designation of a "preservation" or sending area from which rights are transferred and a "development" or receiving area where those development rights are applied. The advantage of TDR to the community is that the costs of development right purchase are borne by private landowners in the receiving area, not the local government. However, the pro-

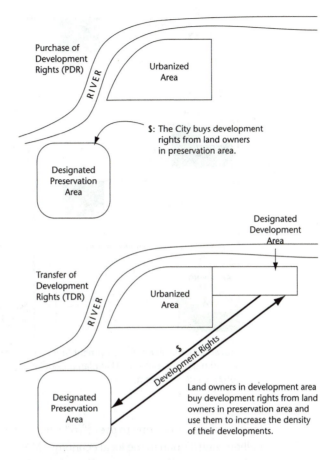

Figure 7.9 Comparing Purchase and Transfer of Development Rights. In PDR, preservation area landowners receive compensation for development rights from the city, and in TDR, they receive it from landowners in the development area who can increase their development density.

gram is more complex than PDR—it requires a buyer of rights, not just a seller, and a mechanism to get these parties together to transfer the rights or to bank or broker the rights. Figure 7.9 illustrates the difference between TDR and PDR. Figure 7.10 shows how TDR can lead to Smart Growth by focusing development in existing communities and protecting rural areas and greenfields.

Hollis and Fulton (2002) found that 24 states permit localities to use TDR programs. Pruetz (2003) identified 124 local and regional TDR programs designed to protect working landscapes, open space, resource lands, and historic districts. Regional growth management programs for the Lake Tahoe and the Pinelands, New Jersey, areas discussed in the next chapter include a TDR component.

Montgomery County, Maryland, has one of the most successful TDR programs, which has operated since 1980. As of 2002, the TDR program has protected more than 41,000 acres of farmland. Other local easement and trust programs protect another 12,000 acres. The programs have helped maintain an agricultural industry

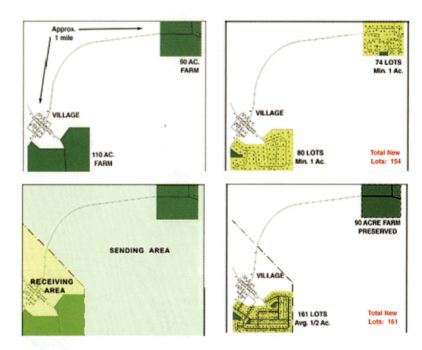

Figure 7.10 Transfer of Development Rights and Smart Growth. Top: existing land use and build out. Bottom: TDR plan and build out. *Source:* 1000 Friends of Minnesota (2002). Used with permission.

in the county, amounting to over 875 farms and enterprises, 10,000 jobs, and $350 million contribution to the local economy (Montgomery County, 2002; 2003).

King County, Washington, adopted two TDR program in the late 1990s. One provides up to 150 percent of baseline zoning in receiving areas in existing residential and commercial zones in the unincorporated parts of the county. The other provides transfers from rural parts of the county to incorporated cities (Pruetz, 2003; Northwest Environment Watch, 2002; Taus, 2002).

Although regulations may specify the location and type of land use, many communities need to control the rate at which development takes place. Rapidly growing communities have been confronted by their "infrastructure carrying capacity"; they have had difficulty providing public services such as water, sewage treatment capacity, school facilities, police and fire protection to meet the needs of an expanding population. In the 1970s, Petaluma, California, and Ramapo, New York, established programs to **phase development** by capping the number of development permits per year. After Petaluma's program was upheld by the Supreme Court in 1972, other communities established similar programs, including Boulder and Fort Collins, Colorado, and the Lake Tahoe Region (see chapter 8).

Concurrency policies attempt to achieve the same objectives of phased development by requiring that development plans are "concurrent" with plans for infrastructure, such as water and sewer service, roads, and other public services. This approach became part of Florida's statewide growth management (see chapter 8) and has been adopted by other localities across the country.

Development/Design Standards and Plan Review

In addition to land use zoning, localities use plan design standards and plan review criteria to achieve community objectives and enhance the quality of development. A few states and several localities require environmental impact assessments for development proposals. State-led programs, like Washington's SEPA (State Environmental Policy Act) requirements are discussed in the next chapter, and EIA (environmental impact assessment) procedures are presented in chapter 18. More recently, localities have developed design criteria and review standards to address Smart Growth and green building objectives.

Green building criteria were discussed in chapter 6. Most of these are voluntary and marketing programs. Some localities, like Boulder, require a minimum number of "green points" for new development or renovation projects. These green points go beyond minimum building codes. For example, new construction must document a minimum number of points (e.g., 65 for a new 2,000-square-foot house) drawn from a list of design enhancements, such as use of recycled materials, xeriscape landscaping, water conservation, lumber from sustainable forestry, energy efficiency, solar energy, and indoor air quality measures.

Fleissig and Jacobsen (2002) advocate the use of a Smart Growth index or "scorecard" to assess development projects in the project review stage. Such an assessment tool could be used for regulatory purposes (like Boulder's green points), marketing (like other green building programs), or education. They suggest a set of scoring criteria including availability of infrastructure, mixed land uses, compactness, walkability, site design, environmental quality, redevelopment, housing and social diversity, and collaborative process. When using such an assessment tool, communities should develop their own criteria and weights. Austin, Texas, uses a variation, its Smart Growth Matrix, not in regulatory review but as a basis to waive development fees.

Nonregulatory Tools

Regulations alone are necessary but not sufficient for effective Smart Growth management. **Nonregulatory** tools can complement regulations and help to move growth management beyond the legal and political limits posed by regulations. There are four basic nonregulatory tools often used in growth management: acquisition of land or development rights, selective provision of urban services and infrastructure, financial incentives and disincentives including development fees and exemptions, and tax policies.

Land Acquisition, Conservation Easements, Purchase of Development Rights

Permanent protection of environmentally sensitive lands is difficult to achieve through regulation. Parcels are often rezoned in response to economic and political pressure. As discussed in chapter 5, perhaps the best way to protect sensitive environmental lands is to buy them, and many state and local governments and local land trusts have established funds to do so.

Boulder, Colorado, has an extensive land acquisition program for parks, open space, and greenbelts. In 1967, city voters passed a measure to levy a 0.4 percent sales tax to fund land acquisition; this was increased to 0.73 percent in 1989. The program has acquired about 41,000 acres of protected lands. Boulder's greenbelt system is described in chapter 5 (see figure 5.4).

However, limits on local finances constrain the land area that can be acquired for parks, open space, and natural area protection. **Purchase of development rights (PDR)** and **conservation easements** have become common methods for protecting agricultural lands and natural areas without fee-simple purchase of the property. As discussed in chapter 5, associated with a parcel of land is a bundle of distinct rights, one of which is the right to develop the land. Without purchasing the land itself, the development rights can be acquired at a far lower cost than the land itself. This easement is reflected in the title to the land and remains there when the land is sold.

As discussed in chapter 5, several local communities have passed bond measures for purchase of land and easements for parks, open space, and farmland protection. Since the mid-1990s, voters have approved about 80 percent of these local bond measures, which are usually passed by a large margin.

Several localities have developed their own PDR programs. King County's (WA) PDR program ran from 1979 to 1987 after the voters overwhelmingly approved a $50 million bond to purchase the development rights of 10,000–15,000 acres of farmland. Although the program permanently protected 13,000 acres, it may have done more to protect open space than in maintaining a viable farming economy. Following a recommendation in its 1989 General Plan, Sonoma County, California, started a similar program in 1990 when voters approved a 1/4 cent sales tax increase for land acquisition. This produced a revenue stream of about $12 million per year. The Open Space District protected about 27,000 acres at a cost of $50 million between 1990 and 2000. Only 11 percent of the 80 land transactions were fee-simple acquisition and 80 percent were conservation easements for farmland or open space (Hollis and Fulton, 2002).

Provision of Urban Services and Infrastructure

Where infrastructure goes, so goes development. "Build it, they will come." Conversely, "Don't build it, and they can't come." Public services and infrastructure necessary for development—roads, sewers, water lines—affect the location and amount of development that will occur. Thus, one way to guide development according to the community land use plan is to link that plan to the capital improvement plan for its infrastructure. Development densities in environmentally sensitive areas can be kept low simply by not planning or providing the services that large-scale or dense development requires.

Many have used their authority to decide where services will go and linked this to the development process through "concurrency" requirements. As discussed in the next chapter, the Twin Cities Metropolitan Council has used effectively the provision of sewer extensions to guide metropolitan development. Maryland's Smart Growth program identifies growth areas as "priority funding areas" (PFAs) that are eligible for state funds for infrastructure; areas outside PFAs can be developed, but state funds will not be provided. Florida's growth management program aims to restrict development that does not have "concurrent" plans and financing for necessary infrastructure and services.

In the mid-1950s, Boulder, Colorado, witnessed considerable development pressure on higher elevations overlooking the city. The city did not favor sprawling development up the mountainside and also realized that the cost of extending city services, especially water supply, to higher elevations would be cost prohibitive. In 1958, the city established a "blue line" at 400-feet elevation above the city center, above which no city services would be made available. Since well water was nearly unattainable in the area, this policy essentially halted this development trend.

Development Impact Fees

Development impact fees are fees charged to developers for the impacts of their projects. Some communities use these fees as an incentive or disincentive to help steer development toward desirable and away from undesirable locations. Albuquerque's (NM) recent comprehensive plan and development policies use impact fees to establish a graduated urban development boundary. The fee schedule is based on the local government costs of services necessary to support development. Impact fees are zero for developments within the area of existing infrastructure, but they are considerable for development outside the boundary and increase quickly for development farther away. Thus, developers have a strong incentive to locate developments within a growth boundary, and a disincentive to locate outside.

Austin uses its Smart Growth Matrix scoring system as a basis for waiving development and other fees. The Matrix provides a quantitative measure of how well a development project accomplishes the city's Smart Growth goals. It incorporates scores on 10 factors that reflect the city's three Smart Growth goals: determining the appropriate location of development, enhancing quality of life, and increasing the tax base. The maximum score is 705. Incentives begin at 251 points and increase at different point thresholds. These include waiving of application and especially development fees, savings on infrastructure costs, and property tax incentives (City of Austin, 2001).

The incentives have proven very attractive to the development community. Developers have contacted the city to score their projects on the matrix early in the process to increase their chances of achieving a certain threshold and fee reductions and other benefits. If they are close to the next threshold, they often make changes needed to increase their score (Fleissig and Jacobsen, 2002).

Tax Policies and Voluntary Practices

As discussed in chapter 5, 49 states provide for differential taxing of farmland and/or forestland by local governments (see table 5.7). Landowners who participate in the program have their property assessed based on their use value as farmland, forestland, or open space, not on their development value. In exchange, landowners agree to keep their land in that use for a period of time.

Agricultural and forestal districting, used in 16 states, offers use-value taxation as well as right-to-farm protection to those landowners who voluntarily enroll in the program. Participating landowners can pay a penalty and back out of the program, so these measures do not provide permanent land protection. However, they can assist farmers in retaining their land in productive agricultural use.

Integrating Tools for Smart Growth Management and Environmental Protection

The most successful local growth management and land conservation programs are those that integrate several regulatory and nonregulatory tools into a comprehensive program. For example, Austin uses a strong comprehensive plan, environmental overlays to protect water supplies and threatened habitat, Smart Growth zones, rail infrastructure, a green building program, and incentives tied to a Smart Growth scorecard. All of these measures work together for a common objective— better development. Together they also send a message to citizens, developers, and landowners that Smart Growth is the city's policy.

Programs need to be integrated across jurisdictional boundaries. One locality may have very effective growth management, only to transfer haphazard development to a neighboring community. Boulder and Austin are good examples of cities that have partnered with their surrounding counties and neighboring jurisdictions. Portland, Oregon, and the Twin Cities in Minnesota also have developed excellent interjurisdictional programs with the assistance of state or regional guidance. Their programs are discussed in chapter 8.

Summary

This chapter illustrated local growth management to conserve environmental lands and arrest sprawl using several examples of successful communities. A wide range of regulatory and nonregulatory tools are available and the effective programs are those that are tailored to the needs, resources, and political climate of the community. The foundation of any local program is a comprehensive plan based on sound technical information, including an environmental inventory and other studies, as well as extensive public involvement.

Innovative regulatory tools such as overlay environmental zones, flexible and performance zoning, conservation cluster zoning, and urban growth boundaries can steer development toward appropriate areas and away from environmentally sensitive ones. Design standards and incentives have helped advance mixed-use, compact, and transit-oriented development. In some cases, compensation is required to achieve environmental objectives, and land acquisition, conservation easements, or purchase or transfer of development rights are appropriate. The location of development infrastructure is a useful tool to steer development to growth centers and to reduce sprawl.

In many cases, local government action is not enough to manage growth and development effectively. In some cases, the state has stepped in with regional or statewide programs to complement or guide local action. Several examples of these regional and state growth and environmental management programs are discussed in the next chapter.

8 ■ Regional, State, and Federal Management of Environmentally Sensitive Lands

Local governments are not alone in Smart Growth management and environmental land protection. Indeed, effective programs for environmental land use planning and management require coordination, guidance, resources, and sometimes mandates from higher levels of government. Regional, state, and federal agencies have played important roles in land conservation and land development design. This chapter addresses the additional roles these governmental levels have and can play in improving the effectiveness of Smart Growth management and environmental land protection.

Most growth and land use management in the United States still falls to local governments. However, regional, state, even federal programs have stepped in to provide assistance or take control when localities have failed to provide sufficient land use controls or if growth problems are beyond their management capabilities. Such programs, especially at the regional and state level, have provided models for effective environmental management, and others are using these models to design proactive environmental and land use programs.

This chapter discusses some of these model programs. First, it describes some innovative substate regional programs for environmental land protection and growth management. Although most regional approaches to land use management lack sufficient authority, agencies in the Lake Tahoe area, the Twin Cities in Minnesota, the New Jersey Pinelands, and Adirondack Park in New York demonstrate the advantages of regional authority.

Second, several state approaches to Smart Growth management are presented. About half the states have adopted statewide programs of varying types and authority to manage growth or protect critical environmental areas. Finally, the chapter discusses federal programs that affect private land use. Although the federal government has in most cases steered away from direct regulatory land use controls, it has provided a range of incentives and assistance for state and local land use planning and management and to landowners to conserve environmental lands and working landscapes.

Regional Programs for Smart Growth Management and Environmental Land Protection

A regional approach to managing the environment has long been proposed in the United States, but there were few applications through the mid-1960s. The Tennessee Valley Authority, established in 1933, used water and power development in the Tennessee River Basin as a vehicle for economic development. The Delaware River Basin Commission, established in 1961, had broad responsibilities for water pollution control and water resources development. Most other river basin regional organizations had limited authority. The river basin approach appeared dead until the plethora of grassroots, cross-jurisdictional watershed management associations took hold in the 1990s. The broader scale Chesapeake Bay Program and Great Lakes Joint Commission have also had some success. But even these programs have been limited to planning and technical and financial assistance of local governments and groups.

Most metropolitan areas engage in some sort of regional planning or coordination. Single-mission regional agencies dealing with transportation, sewage and water, air pollution control, or other activities are common. Regional planning districts, councils of governments (COGs), and metropolitan planning organizations (MPOs) have been established in nearly all rural and metropolitan areas in response to requirements for regional review of federal grant applications. These regional organizations are generally made up of representatives of local jurisdictions, but they have limited authority, especially over control of land use activities.

The need for regional approaches has never been more apparent. Metropolitan sprawl is clearly a regional problem that individual localities cannot manage alone. As discussed earlier, Calthorpe and Fulton (2001) argue that the end of sprawl requires a regional approach. They envision the "regional city" containing effective regional transit, affordable housing fairly distributed, environmental preserves, walkable communities, urban reinvestments, and infill development. They see the region providing social identity, economic interconnectedness, and the ecological fabric relating urban centers to bioregional habitats and protected farmlands. They also argue for regional growth boundaries, federal transportation and open space investments, and environmental policies consistent with regional goals. Urban center reinvestment is critical to focus development within urban areas and away from outlying natural areas.

Around the country, a few regional agencies established in the late 1960s to early 1970s have been effective in managing growth for large multijurisdictional areas. Despite their success, few comparable agencies have emerged elsewhere. The five agencies discussed next all experienced environmental land use problems that were not being adequately addressed by local governments. In response, the states involved (and in two cases with federal legislation) established regional governing

Figure 8.1 Depiction of 1960s Filling Rate of San Francisco Bay. *Source:* San Francisco BCDC (1998).

bodies to deal with the problems. The experiences of regional agencies in five areas—Adirondack Park (NY), Twin Cities (MN), San Francisco Bay (CA), Lake Tahoe Basin (CA, NV), and the Pinelands (NJ)—provide examples of the opportunities and problems of the regional approach to environmental land management.

San Francisco Bay Conservation and Development Commission (BCDC)

By the early 1960s, development along the shores of San Francisco Bay had resulted in the filling of one-third of the Bay's saltwater marshes. When, in 1961, the U.S. Army Corps of Engineers produced a long-term plan for the Bay depicting it as the "San Francisco River" (see figure 8.1), local citizens' groups called for action to avert the alarming trend of filling in the Bay. Some look back on this outcry as the beginning of the modern national environmental movement. In 1965, the state legislature established the San Francisco Bay Conservation and Development Commission (BCDC) to develop a plan for the Bay. Upon the completion of the plan in 1969, the legislature made BCDC a permanent agency to implement its plan. The Bay Plan has been updated, most recently in 1998. Figure 8.2 shows a sample map from the latest Plan; policies for specific locations are given by number and described in the document (San Francisco BCDC, 1998). Figure 8.3 gives an inventory map showing ecological and scenic values.

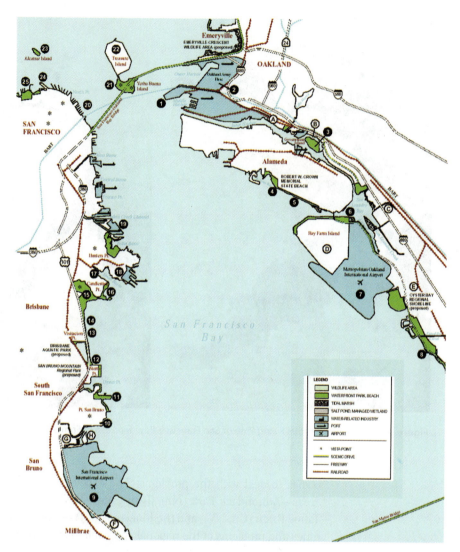

Figure 8.2 1998 BCDC Plan for Central Bay. Numbers indicate specific BCDC plan policies. *Source:* San Francisco BCDC (1998).

A permit from BCDC is required for all development in the Bay and in a shoreline area extending 100 feet inland from high tide. Permits are granted if the developments are consistent with the San Francisco Bay Plan or they are necessary for the health, safety, or welfare of the people in the area. Although the Commission was initially criticized by some environmental groups as being too accommodating to developers, in its first 10 years it succeeded in essentially halting filling of the Bay (Natural Resources Defense Council, 1977). BCDC served as a model for the regional coastal commissions established by the California Coastal Zone program in 1972.

Twin Cities Metropolitan Council

The postwar housing boom in the suburban areas of Minneapolis and St. Paul, Minnesota, led to a serious public health problem: In 1959 it was discovered that

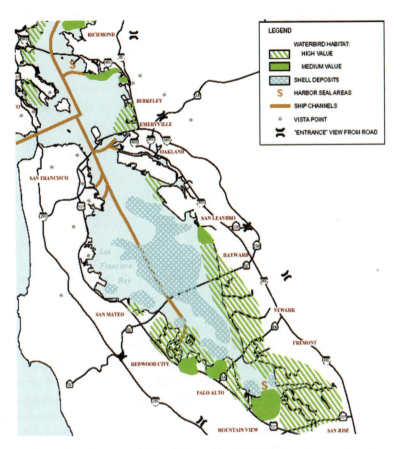

Figure 8.3 Ecological and Scenic Values of Central and Southern San Francisco Bay. *Source:* San Francisco BCDC (1998).

nearly half of the individual home wells of the area were being contaminated by effluent from septic tanks. In attempting to respond to this crisis, it became evident that the fragmented control of local jurisdictions was not leading to orderly growth of the area, and that the regional Metropolitan Planning Commission did not have sufficient authority to rectify the situation. In response, the state legislature established the Twin Cities Metropolitan Council in 1967 to oversee development in the 3,000-square-mile region, which included seven counties and several cities and towns.

The authority of the Council grew incrementally in the years that followed. Initially, it had the authority to prepare Development Guides for the region, to review and approve plans for a number of regional functional agencies, and to review plans of local jurisdictions. At first, the strongest authority of the Council was its "sewer power." One of the functional agencies under its control was the Metropolitan Sewer Board, later changed to the Metropolitan Waste Commission. Due to the water and sewer problems of the area, septic systems were severely restricted, and the location of sewer lines did much to regulate growth in the region. In its review and approval of the Waste Commission's sewerage plans, the Council was able to steer sewer lines, and thus development potential, according to its Development Guides.

TABLE 8.1 **Smart Growth in Twin Cities Metro: New Housing Units 2000 to 2030**

Percentage	Location	Development/Land Type
30	In central cities, in developed and developing suburbs, and in rural and regional growth centers	On redeveloped land or infill
45%	Within 2020 MUSA and rural growth centers	On new land *inside* current 2020 MUSA
20%	In expanded MUSA (2030)	On new land *outside* current 2020 MUSA
< 5%	In the rural area	Using on-site systems outside MUSA cities and rural growth centers

In 1974, the Metropolitan Council was authorized by the state legislature to spend $40 million to acquire parkland and thus establish a true regional park system. The Council used the 1968 ecological study prepared by Wallace, McHarg, Wallace, and Todd to develop its protection and recreation open space plans. By 2000, the regional open space system included 50,000 acres in parks and trails, and the 2001 Regional Recreation Open Space Policy Plan called for additions of 5,000 acres (Metropolitan Council, 2002).

In 1976, the Council was given added authority over local jurisdictions; local comprehensive plans were not only to be reviewed by the Council, but also to be approved to ensure compliance with the Development Guides. One of the keys to the success of this regional approach was that a tax-revenue-sharing scheme provided that all jurisdictions shared in tax-revenue benefits of the region's growth. This reduced typical jurisdictional competition and bred more cooperation.

By the 1990s, the Metro Council had matured into an effective regional government with considerable authority over regional infrastructure and open space, and approval authority over local comprehensive plans. The Council developed a Smart Growth program and retained Calthorpe Associates to provide design and planning assistance. The Smart Growth program established urban growth boundaries, called metropolitan urban service areas (MUSAs). The Smart Growth Blueprint 2030 plan, developed in 2002, anticipates 461,000 new households in the Metro area by 2030. Table 8.1 shows that 30 percent will be located in central cities, 45 percent in established MUSA and rural growth centers, and 20 percent in expanded MUSA. At most, 5 percent of new housing units will be in rural areas. Chapter 6 describes Calthorpe Associates' Metro Council design study for the St. Croix corridor, and chapter 4 highlights the regional participation process that was applied in the region (Calthorpe Associates, 2000).

Adirondack Park Agency

The 6-million-acre Adirondack Park (see figure 8.4) was established by the New York state legislature in 1892, and although 3.5 million acres of the area are still in private holdings, it remained largely pristine and undeveloped through the 1960s. With the completion of Interstate 87 between New York City and Montreal in 1968, it became apparent that some type of regional land use control would be necessary to avert large-scale second-home development in the park area. In

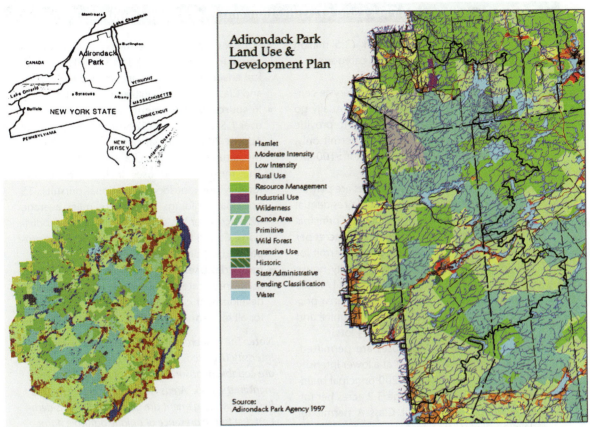

Figure 8.4 Adirondack Park Land Use and Development Plan. *Source:* APA (2001).

1971, the legislature passed a law establishing the Adirondack Park Agency (APA), despite opposition from Adirondack area legislators and residents. The APA was to develop a master plan for all state-owned lands (which was completed in 1972) and a land use plan for privately owned land. The second plan was far more controversial, and after a series of 15 public hearings, it was approved in May 1973. Subsequent laws added requirements for shorelines, wetlands, and wild and scenic rivers. The plan for privately owned land was last updated in 1996; the plan for state lands was last updated in 2001.

The plan classifies the privately owned lands into six categories (described in box 8.1) and specifies for each a maximum development level given in number of principal buildings per square mile and average acres per lot. State-owned land is classified into eight categories. The APA is given permitting responsibility for significant private projects having a regional impact, whereas less disruptive projects are controlled by local governments once their land use control programs are approved by the APA. Box 8.1 gives overall intensity guidelines and permitting requirements for different land uses in different land use zones. Regional permits are class A (most scrutiny), class B, and class IC-B (incompatible use). Figure 8.4 shows the parkwide land classification and zooms in on Oswegachie/Black River Watershed at the western boundary of the park (Adirondack Park Agency, 2001).

BOX 8.1—Adirondack Park Land Classification and Permitting Requirements

All private lands in the park (3.5 million acres) are classified into six categories:

- **Hamlet:** These are the growth and service centers of the park. Hamlet boundaries usually go well beyond established settlements to provide room for future expansion. Local permit only, except APA regional Class A permit if >100 lots or units.
- **Moderate-Intensity Use:** Most uses are permitted, but relatively concentrated residential development is most appropriate: 500 principal buildings per square mile, average 1.3 acres per lot. Local permit only, except Class A permit for development (Class B for single family house [SFH]) near critical environmental area (1/4 mile from river, 1/8 mile from wilderness area or > 2,500 feet elevation) or for > 74 lots/units, and Class B permit if multifamily or > 14 lots.
- **Low-Intensity Use:** Most uses are permitted, but residential development at a lower intensity than above is appropriate: 200 principal buildings per square mile, average 3.2 acres per lot. Local permit only, except Class A permit for development (Class B for SFH) near critical environmental area and for > 34 lots/units, and Class B permit if multifamily or > 9 lots.
- **Rural Use:** Most uses are permitted, but rural uses and lower-intensity development is most suitable: 75 principal buildings per square mile, average 9.5 acres per lot. Local permit only, except Class A permit for development (Class B for SFH) near critical environmental area and for > 19 lots/units, and Class B permit if multifamily or > 4 lots.
- **Resource Management:** These areas include over 1.5 million acres (52% of private lands as of August 2000). Special care is taken to protect the natural open space character of these lands. The most suitable uses include agriculture, forestry and outdoor recreational pursuits. 15 principal buildings per square mile, average 42.7 acres per lot. Class A permit for all subdivisions, Class B for all SFH, and Class IC-B (incompatible use) permit for multifamily.
- **Industrial Use:** This is where existing industrial uses are located and where future industrial development can be located. Class IC-B permit for all residential land use.

Note: The Moderate-Intensity Use and the Low-Intensity Use areas are intended to provide for and are capable of absorbing most of the new development in the park. Areas classified as Rural Use and Resource Management are given special consideration due to the presence of unique natural characteristics, terrain, or proximity to public lands.

State-owned lands (2.5 million acres) are classified into eight categories: Wilderness, Canoe Area, Primitive, Wild Forest, Intensive Use, Historic, State Administrative, and Pending Classification.

New Jersey Pinelands Commission

The New Jersey Pinelands is a 1.1-million-acre region in southern New Jersey, which has a colorful history and significant ecological values. Although the area is sparsely settled, the development of Atlantic City as a major gambling center in the 1970s exposed the region to increasing development pressures. In response, the federal and state governments took steps in 1978 to protect the area's environmental values. The 1978 National Parks and Recreation Act created the Pinelands National Reserve, offering federal cooperation to the state in developing a comprehensive management plan for the area. In 1979, New Jersey enacted the State Pinelands Protection Act establishing the Pinelands Commission to develop the plan and oversee its implementation.

The Commission approved the Pinelands Comprehensive Management Plan in late 1980 and amended it on occasion since. It called for a mix of land manage-

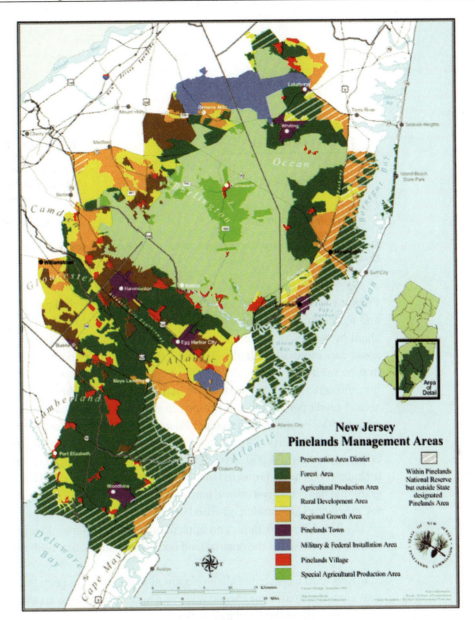

Figure 8.5 New Jersey Pinelands Management Areas. *Source:* New Jersey Pinelands (2002).

ment devices including acquisition, regulation, and transfer of development rights (TDR). The regulatory component involves a regional land use plan and implementing local plans and programs. The Commission's land plan divides the region into management areas, each with specified development densities. Figure 8.5 shows the management areas as of 1999. Local jurisdictions are required to develop local plans and ordinances conforming to the Commission's plan; the Commission regulated development until the local plans were approved.

The land protection provisions are considerable. Since 1980 more than 150,000 acres have been protected, and 40 percent of the Pinelands is now considered to be permanently protected. The Pinelands Development Credits (PDC)

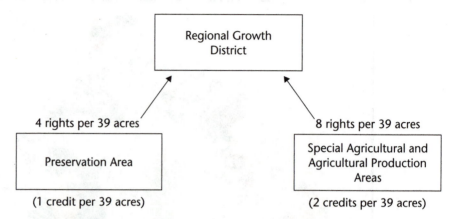

Figure 8.6 Pinelands Transfer of Development Rights Program. *Source:* New Jersey Pinelands Commission (undated).

Program, a TDR program, compensates landowners in designated preservation and agricultural production areas for the reduced value of their land brought about by the restriction on development. Owners of land in the regional growth areas can increase their development density (to a maximum of 12 dwelling units/acre) by purchasing development credits from landowners in the preservation and agricultural areas. As shown in figure 8.6, the credits vary with protection area, 1 credit per 39 acres in preservation and 2 per 39 areas for agricultural; in addition, 0.2 credits are offered per 39 acres for wetlands. Each protection credit per 39 acres converts to 4 rights or 4 units per acre in the regional growth area. By 2002, more than 34,000 acres had been protected by the PDC program. This includes 6,000 acres protected in 2001 through a special state PDC purchase program that has preserved critical land at an average cost of $850 per acre (New Jersey Pinelands Commission, undated).

The Third Progress Report on implementation (New Jersey Pinelands Commission, 2002) states that the original land use strategy adopted in 1980 remains intact:

- Less than 6 percent of all development in 20 years has been located in areas designated for conservation and agriculture; these areas amount to 70 percent of the Pinelands region.
- Since 1980 more than 150,000 acres have been protected through purchase, easement, or development right transfer.
- By 2001, under PDC, 8,300 development rights had been allocated; 3,300 had been severed; and 3,000 sold by "sending area" property owners. "Receiving area" landowners purchased 2,600 rights. The average purchase price in 2002 was $7,500–$9,000 per right, up from $7,000 in 2001 and $3,500 in 1991.
- The Infrastructure Trust Fund has financed sewer service for tens of thousands of new homes in designated growth areas.
- Watershed protection programs and private forestry regulations have protected water resources.

> ▪ Localities have taken the lead in land use regulation and development proposal review; the Commission has intervened in less than 7 percent of projects and overturned only 0.5 percent.

Tahoe Regional Planning Agency

The Lake Tahoe Basin (shown in figure 8.7) is one of the most naturally beautiful, as well as one of the most studied and planned areas of the country. After 30 years of planning, the region has adopted an innovative and effective program to protect the Basin's natural resources and accommodate additional development.

Tahoe's problems began in the 1950s when the area of only 3,000 permanent residents was discovered for second-home and recreational development. The pristine lake, the second-deepest in the world, surrounded by 10,000-foot peaks, offered outstanding potential for lake-related summer sports, skiing in the winter, and gambling in Nevada-side casinos. By 1978, the permanent population ballooned to 60,000 with 150,000 visitors on a peak summer day; there were 12 casinos, 22 improved public beaches, and numerous hotels.

The victim of this growth was the lake and the Basin's overall environmental quality. Planning to control land use in the Basin began in 1958. However, due to the institutional complexity of the region, with two states, five counties, and several municipalities, little was achieved until the 1969 formation of a bistate planning compact and the Tahoe Regional Planning Agency (TRPA) by the legislatures of both states and the U.S. Congress.

TRPA's first 10 years were controversial as the agency's 10 members (5 from each state) time and again split over decisions on development proposals: California representatives took a proenvironmental stance, Nevada representatives voted prodevelopment. The 1969 compact provided that tie votes would be considered approval. In response, California strengthened the California TRPA, which acted to slow development on the California side but had no effect in Nevada. California then withdrew funds from the bistate TRPA in 1978 and 1979.

However, the state legislatures and Congress adopted a new compact in 1980 that changed the complexion of the TRPA. The membership of the agency was increased to 14 (7 from each state) and tie votes were no longer considered sufficient—development proposals required an affirmative vote for approval. The compact required TRPA to establish environmental thresholds characterizing the region's carrying capacity and to adopt a regional plan by August 1983 to achieve these thresholds.

The overall environmental management process is given in box 8.2. It involved three main components: threshold development, plan development, and implementation. The development of the threshold standards is discussed in chapter 18. Based on the thresholds, three alternative planning strategies were developed and labeled—maximum regulation, development with mitigation, and redirection of development (two other strategies, no action and maxi-

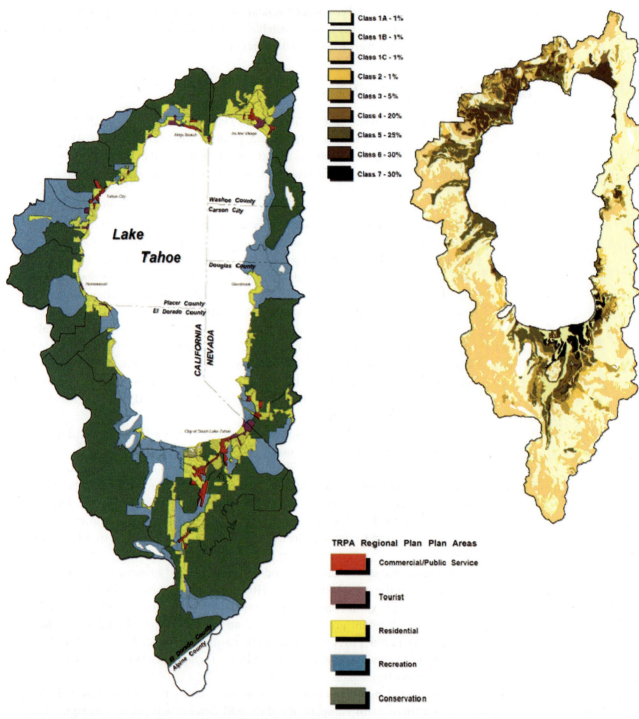

Legend (top right):

- Class 1A - 1%
- Class 1B - 1%
- Class 1C - 1%
- Class 2 - 1%
- Class 3 - 5%
- Class 4 - 20%
- Class 5 - 25%
- Class 6 - 30%
- Class 7 - 30%

Map labels:

Lake Tahoe

Tahoe City

Washoe County
Carson City

Douglas County

Glenbrook

Placer County
El Dorado County

CALIFORNIA
NEVADA

City of South Lake Tahoe

El Dorado County
Alpine County

TRPA Regional Plan Plan Areas

- Commercial/Public Service
- Tourist
- Residential
- Recreation
- Conservation

Figure 8.7 Tahoe Regional Planning Agency (TRPA) Regional Plan Planning Areas and Land Capabilty Classes with maximum impervious surface percentages. *Source:* TRPA (1986).

BOX 8.2—The Environmental Management Process of the Tahoe Regional Planning Agency

Threshold Development

1. Identify issues and environmental components.
2. Identify the variables that affect the environmental components.
3. Evaluate relationships between variables and select best variables for use as thresholds.
4. Develop thresholds for selected variables.
5. Adopt the thresholds.

Plan Development

1. Develop goals and policies based on thresholds.
2. Formulate five alternative planning strategies.
3. Prepare EIS on five alternative planning strategies.
4. Adopt regional plan and the plan area statements.

Implementation

1. Develop and adopt necessary ordinances.
2. Adopt single-family residence evaluation system.
3. Implement development management system for residential and commercial developments.
4. Coordinate capital improvements with local jurisdictions.

mum development were eliminated). After nine months of public hearings, a final plan was developed and adopted in April 1984.

The plan includes a wide range of implementation programs designed to achieve the thresholds. These are summarized in box 8.3. "Plan area statements" provided specific direction to 175 planning areas in the region. Each area was given one of five land use designations (conservation, recreation, residential, commercial and public service, tourist) and one of the three management strategies. "Maximum regulation" was applied to four large wilderness areas. "Redirection" was applied to most developed and partly developed areas to encourage infill and redevelopment. "Development with mitigation" was the predominant designation; it allows development as long as all on- and off-site impacts are mitigated.

The development management system puts upper limits on the amount of new residential and commercial development. Residential permit applications are evaluated on a point system. All development must meet the requirements of the land capability system (designated maximum coverage of lots) and mitigation (e.g., offset 150% of water quality impacts). A TDR system allows development right transfer from environmentally sensitive areas to suitable development areas in an effort to "retire" some 70,000 in these sensitive areas. The Environmental Improvement Program (EIP) targets specific areas for ecological restoration and has grown to $58 million per year, but it has identified almost $1.5 billion in needed projects.

TRPA has monitored progress and revised its program accordingly. Table 8.2 summarizes the 2001 Threshold Evaluation, showing 15 of the 36 threshold indicators. Of the 36 threshold indicators, only 8 were in "attainment" in 2001, 25 were in

BOX 8.3—Implementation Programs for TRPA Regional Plan

Plan Area Statement for 175 Planning Areas

One of the following three general strategies is applied to each of 175 planning areas:

1. Development with mitigation (most common strategy)
2. Redirection of development (restoration, relocation)
3. Maximum regulation (applied to sensitive areas)

Development Management System: Phased Development

- Maximum of 1,800 residential permits allowed over 3 years
- Maximum 10 major commercial permits per year (major => 1000 sq. ft.); maximum 65,000 sq. ft. major and minor commercial each year.

Residential Evaluation System

Point system based on environmental constraints, service access, site design, and mitigation measures.

Land Capability Classification

Maximum land coverage for different size capability districts: (see inset in figure 8.7 showing districts)

District	1A	1B	1C	2	3	4	5	6	7
Max. Impervious Cover	1%	1%	1%	1%	5%	20%	20%	30%	30%
Acreage, % of basin		76%			6%	4%	8%	6%	

Mitigation Requirements

- All residential, commercial, and public projects must offset **150 percent** of water quality impacts, which can be accomplished by providing off-site erosion and runoff control measures or contributing to an implementation fund for such projects
- All minor residential and commercial projects must pay an air pollution offset fee; all major projects must file an environmental impact and integration statement.

Transfer of Development Rights

Allows transfer of development rights from residential lots in environmentally sensitive areas, which cannot be developed, to areas able to support development.

Financing

Sources of funds: government jurisdictions, mitigation fund, property transfer tax, and various user fees and taxes.

Environmental Improvement Program

Target specific projects for restoration that will improve progress toward achievement of thresholds.

Monitoring and Evaluation

- Progress toward achieving thresholds monitored every five years.
- If necessary adjustments will be made to thresholds and programs.

Source: TRPA, 1986, 2002.

TABLE 8.2   **Tahoe Basin Environmental Threshold Compliance Status for 15 of 36 Indicators**

	Threshold	1991	1996	2001	Trend
I.	Air Quality				
	AQ-4 Visibility	**Attainment**	Nonattainment	Nonattainment	▼
	AQ-7 Vehicle Miles Traveled	Nonattainment	Nonattainment	Nonattainment	▼
II.	Water Quality				
	WQ-1 Turbidity (Shallow)	**Attainment**	**Attainment**	**Attainment**	---
	WQ-2 Clarity, Winter	Nonattainment	Nonattainment	Nonattainment	▲
	WQ-3 Phytoplankton Primary Production	Nonattainment	Nonattainment	Nonattainment	▼
III.	Soil Conservation				
	SC-1 Impervious Coverage	Nonattainment	Nonattainment	Nonattainment	▼
IV.	Vegetation				
	V-1 Relative Abundance and Pattern	Nonattainment	Nonattainment	Nonattainment	▲
	V-2 Uncommon Plant Communities	**Attainment**	**Attainment**	**Attainment**	▲
V.	Fisheries				
	F-1 Lake Habitat	Nonattainment	Nonattainment	Nonattainment	▲
	F-4 Lahontan Cutthroat Trout (New)			**Attainment**	▲
VI.	Wildlife				
	W-2 Habitats of Special Significance	**Attainment**	Nonattainment	Nonattainment	▲
VII.	Scenic Resources				
	SR-2 Scenic Quality Ratings	Nonattainment	Nonattainment	Nonattainment	▼
	SR-4 Community Design	Unknown	Nonattainment	Nonattainment	▲
VIII.	Noise				
	N-3 Community Noise	Nonattainment	Nonattainment	Nonattainment	---
IX.	Recreation				
	R-1 High Quality Recreational Exper.	Unknown	Unknown	Nonattainment	▲

Positive Trend ▲   Negative Trend ▼   No Trend ---
Source: TRPA 2002.

"nonattainment," and three were unknown. However, 19 showed a positive trend, while 7 showed a negative trend, and 10 showed no trend (TRPA, 2002). The evaluation concluded that many elements of the 20-year-old standards require study for recalibration or amendment. TRPA plans to complete and update all thresholds by 2004 and use this as the platform to construct the 2007–2027 regional plan.

State Growth Management Programs: Toward Smart Growth

Localities obtain their authority and requirements for planning from the states. As discussed in chapter 7, about three-fourths of the states have adopted some version of the Dillon's Rule, meaning localities have only those powers vested to them by the state. The remainder are primarily Home Rule states, in which localities are free to implement programs that the state does not explicitly restrict.

In recent years, several states have recognized that local control of growth and development has been insufficient to arrest sprawl and create livable communi-

PLANNING REFORM ACTIVITY

Implementing moderate to substantial statewide reforms

Pursuing first major statewide reforms

Pursuing additional statewide, regional or local reforms

Not pursuing statewide reforms

Figure 8.8 State Planning Reform Activity. *Source:* Reprinted with permission from *Planning for Smart Growth, 2002 State of the States*, published by the American Planning Association, February 2002.

ties. They have developed statewide programs to foster better local planning or to create state planning. State planning legislation varies considerably from state to state. In recent reviews of state land use planning programs, the American Planning Association (1999, 2002) concluded the following:

- About one-quarter of the states have moderate to substantial statewide planning reforms.
- About half of the states are using dated planning enabling legislation dating back to the Standard City Planning Enabling Act from the 1920s.
- The vast majority of states make local comprehensive planning optional.
- In 2002, about one-third of the states were pursuing their first land use planning reforms.
- The most modernized state planning laws are in states on the East and West Coasts where urbanization and growth are significant (see figure 8.8).
- Six states have taken major initiatives in reforming planning legislation. They include Maryland, New Jersey, Oregon, Rhode Island, Tennessee, and Washington.

- As many as 12 other states, not in figure 8.8, are studying or proposing planning legislation updates.
- There are different approaches to state land use planning programs.

Most states have simply left land use regulation to localities. States that have developed a state growth management program have taken different approaches outlined in the following list. Some states have formulated comprehensive statewide land use programs (referred to here as Type 1). Others have focused their programs on certain "critical areas," such as coastal areas, wetlands or farmlands, or large development projects (Type 2). Those with statewide programs have taken one of four basic approaches: 1A, statewide planning and guidelines, with state approval of local plans and implementation; 1B, statewide economic incentives for Smart Growth; 1C, environmental impact assessment; and 1D, statewide planning and permitting.

State Approaches to Growth Management

Type 1. Statewide Approaches

    1A. *Statewide planning, state criteria and guidelines with local plans and implementation; state approval of local plans and implementing programs.* Initiated by Oregon in 1973, this approach has become the model for state growth management. Florida adopted it in 1985; New Jersey in 1987; Vermont, Maine, and Rhode Island in 1988; Georgia in 1989; Washington in 1991.

    1B. *Economic incentives for development within designated urban growth boundaries and for resource conservation outside of such boundaries.* Maryland's Smart Growth program includes Priority Funding Areas and Rural Legacy program (1996–97) and Green-Print Program (2000). Tennessee adopted a similar program in 1999.

    1C. *Environmental Impact Assessment (EIA) for new development.* Washington (since 1971) requires an EIA for discretionary approval of private projects. A few other states (e.g., New York, California) require EIA for local government plans and decisions.

    1D. *Statewide plan and state permitting for selected types of development.* Initiated by Hawaii in 1960 and adopted by Vermont and Maine in 1970, Colorado in 1973, and Rhode Island in 1978, this approach has essentially been abandoned by all except Hawaii.

Type 2. State Critical Area Approach

    State program focus on critical resources (e.g., coastal areas, wetlands, agricultural land) or geographic area; certain restrictions or permit requirements are applied to these critical areas with State agency or local implementation. Many states apply this approach to coastal development (e.g., Washington [1971], California [1972], Maryland [1986], Virginia [1988]), wetlands (Massachusetts [1972], Michigan [1979], Minnesota [1979]), and agricultural lands (nonregulatory programs in Maryland, Massachusetts, New Jersey).

Table 8.3 summarizes the features of six innovative state growth management programs highlighted by the American Planning Association (1999). The table compares the state laws or programs on their requirements for local planning, coordination with environmental programs, farmland and open space protection, historic and cultural preservation, economic development, transit planning, and affordable housing.

Statewide Land Use Programs (Type 1)

There are many variations in state growth management programs, and other sources provide a comprehensive comparison of their approaches and effectiveness (American Planning Association, 1999, 2002; National Governors Association, 2001). It is useful here to profile a few programs to understand the role of the states and the effectiveness of their programs. This section describes some Type 1 statewide programs. The next section highlights some Type 2 critical areas programs.

Oregon's Land Conservation and Development Act (Type 1A)

Many consider Oregon to have the most advanced state-administered, land use planning system in the country (American Planning Association, 1999). Oregon's approach to land use control uses a structured relationship between state and local governments and established the 1A model that has become the standard for state growth management programs. The planning framework was initiated by the Land Conservation and Development Act of 1973, which established the Land Conservation and Development Commission (LCDC) to promulgate state land use goals and guidelines. Local governments were then to develop comprehensive land use plans in compliance with the 19 LCDC goals, which range from farmland and forest land protection to energy conservation and low-income housing. The goals are given in the following list. Not only are the comprehensive plans to be reviewed and approved by the LCDC, but the Commission also reviews the implementing mechanisms such as zoning ordinances, to ensure compliance with the plans. Other states require local governments to produce comprehensive plans, but this requirement for implementation and enforcement placed Oregon apart.

Oregon's 19 Statewide Planning Goals

1. **Citizen Involvement:** To develop a citizen involvement program that ensures the opportunity for citizens to be involved in all phases of the planning process.
2. **Land Use Planning:** To establish a land use planning process and policy framework as a basis for all decisions and actions related to use of land and to ensure an adequate factual base for such decisions and actions.
3. **Agricultural Lands.** To preserve and maintain agricultural lands.
4. **Forest Lands.** To conserve forest lands by maintaining the forest land base and to protect the state's forest economy by making possible economically efficient forest practices that ensure the continuous growing and harvesting of forest tree species as the leading use on for-

TABLE 8.3 **Innovative State Growth Management Programs Profiled by the American Planning Association**

State	Year Enacted	Local Planning	Environment Protection	Farmland Open Space	Historic Cultural	Economic Development	Transit Planning	Affordable Housing
Maryland	1992/1997	Smart Growth optional	Chesapeake Bay	200,000 acre goal by 2011	Optional under local plan	Incentives for Smart development	Emphasis on multimodal	Optional under local plan
New Jersey	1992	Grants for multijurisdiction	Pinelands, Meadowlands	$1 billion, 10-year bond	State bond support	Compact development encouraged	Transport/economic linked	State oversight of local efforts
Oregon	1973	UGB required	Salmon, other species	16 million acres protected	Must be addressed in local plan	Strong emphasis on Smart development	Coordinated with land use plan	Addressed in local plan
Rhode Island	1988	21 of 39 have plan approved	Narragansett Bay, others	$15 million bond program	In two elements of state plan	Incentives for Smart development	Emphasis on multimodal	Mandatory element of local plan
Tennessee	1998	Consistent w/county plan	Consistent w/ Natural Areas Act	Must identify rural areas for protection	Required under local plan	Incentive for growth management	May be addressed in county plans	Must be addressed in growth plans
Washington	1990–91	CompPlan requires growth measures	Salmon	Local plans must identify agricultural lands	Addressed in Growth Mgmt Act	For land use, transportation, capital improvements	Consistent with regional transportation goals	Locals laws must identify land for affordable housing

Source: American Planning Association (1999).

est land consistent with sound management of soil, air, water, and fish and wildlife resources, and to provide for recreational opportunities and agriculture.

5. **Open Spaces, Scenic and Historic Areas, and Natural Resources.** To protect natural resources and conserve scenic and historic areas and open spaces.

6. **Air, Water, and Land Resources Quality.** To maintain and improve the quality of the air, water, and land resources of the state.

7. **Areas Subject to Natural Disasters and Hazards.** To protect life and property from natural disasters and hazards.

8. **Recreational Needs.** To satisfy the recreational needs of the citizens of the state and visitors and, where appropriate, to provide for the siting of necessary recreational facilities including destination resorts.

9. **Economic Development.** To provide adequate opportunities throughout the state for a variety of economic activities vital to the health, welfare, and prosperity of Oregon's citizens.

10. **Housing.** To provide for the housing needs of citizens of the state.

11. **Public Facilities and Services.** To plan and develop a timely, orderly, and efficient arrangement of public facilities and services to serve as a framework for urban and rural development.

12. **Transportation.** To provide and encourage a safe, convenient, and economic transportation system.

13. **Energy Conservation.** To conserve energy.

14. **Urbanization.** To provide for an orderly and efficient transition from rural to urban land use.

15. **Willamette River Greenway.** To protect, conserve, enhance, and maintain the natural, scenic, historical, agricultural, economic, and recreational qualities of lands along the Willamette River as the Willamette River Greenway.

16. **Estuarine Resources.** To recognize and protect the unique environmental, economic, and social values of each estuary and associated wetlands; and to protect, maintain, where appropriate develop, and where appropriate restore the long-term environmental, economic, and social values, diversity, and benefits of Oregon's estuaries.

17. **Coastal Shorelands.** To conserve, protect, where appropriate develop, and where appropriate restore the resources and benefits of all coastal shorelands, recognizing their value for protection and maintenance of water quality, wildlife habitat, water-dependent uses, economic resources, and recreation and aesthetics.

18. **Beaches and Dunes.** To conserve, protect, where appropriate develop, and where appropriate restore the resources and benefits of coastal beach and dune areas; and to reduce the hazard to human life and property from natural or human-induced actions associated with these areas.

19. **Ocean Resources.** To conserve marine resources and ecological functions for the purpose of providing long-term ecological, economic, and social value and benefits to future generations.

The main concern that prompted passage of the 1973 Act was agricultural land conversion, particularly in the fertile Willamette Valley. Thus the program's strongest requirements relate to farmland protection. In their plans, communities are required to delineate **urban growth boundaries (UGBs).** Figure 8.9 shows the current UGBs statewide; figure 6.18 shows the Portland UGB. The UGBs are defined as areas adequate to provide 20 years of growth. "Exception areas" are those lands outside UGBs determined to be committed by past development patterns or policies to rural residential uses. Areas outside of these boundaries which have soil capabilities (see box 12.2) qualifying as farmland (classes I-IV soils in western Oregon, classes I-VI in eastern Oregon) must be placed in Exclusive Farm Use (EFU). Fifteen million acres have been so placed in these agricultural zones. An early 1980s case study of Salem showed that once the boundary was set, it was treated as a given; land speculation slowed and farmers proceeded to invest in their land with reduced fear of suburban encroachment (Leonard, 1982).

The Oregon program has a strong emphasis on land conservation, but its success has depended on how it accommodates urban development. Although in the

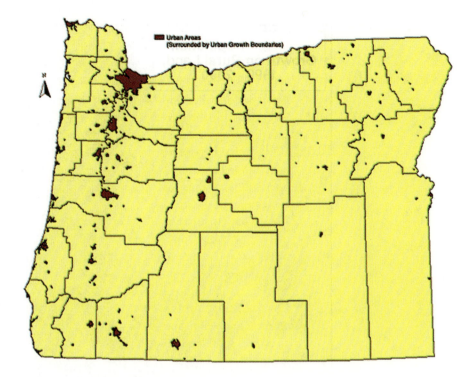

Figure 8.9 State of Oregon Urban Growth Boundaries. *Source:* Oregon Department Land Conservation and Development. Retrieved from http://www.lcd.state.or.us/fastpdfs/UGBmap_large.jpg.

1970s state voters twice defeated efforts to repeal the law, political pressure to balance conservation and development still remains. In perhaps the program's biggest challenge, the voters passed Measure 7 in 2000 by a 53–47 percent margin. The measure would require compensation when government regulation reduces the value of property. However, in February 2001, an Oregon district court and, in October 2002, the Oregon Supreme Court ruled the measure unconstitutional (1000 Friends of Oregon, 2003).

Figure 8.10 shows the results of a recent study by Northwest Environment Watch (2002) of the growth trends in the Portland metropolitan area, including Clark County and the city of Vancouver, Washington, across the Columbia River. Clark County is subject to similar development pressures but not to Oregon's growth management program. Between 1990 and 2000, low-density development outside the city boundaries has been far more prevalent on the Washington side than in Oregon, and Portland has a greater concentration of development within the city than Vancouver. Portland has the density to support rail transit and walkability, while Vancouver does not. Per capita, Clark County converted about 40 percent more land from rural to suburban population densities than did the comparable Oregon counties.

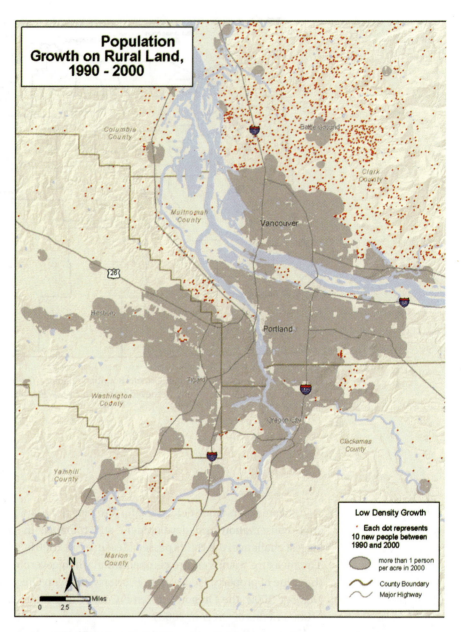

Figure 8.10 Relative Population Growth in Vancouver (WA) and Portland (OR). Each red dot represents 10 new people 1990–2000, showing urban sprawl is far greater on the Washington side than the Oregon side. *Source:* Northwest Environment Watch. 2002. *Sprawl and Smart Growth in Metropolitan Portland.* Produced by CommEn Space in Seattle (http:/www. commenspace.org). Used with permission.

The Oregon dedication to land use planning and growth management has spurred local and regional planning efforts. The Willamette Valley is home to 70 percent of the state's population and 50 percent of the state's agricultural sales. The citizen-based Willamette Restoration Initiative (WRI) is a watershed management program and the Willamette Alternative Futures Project is developing scenarios of future growth in the region (ECONorthwest, 2000).

Maryland's Smart Growth and Neighborhood Conservation Initiative (Type 1B)

Maryland's Governor Glendening popularized the term *Smart Growth* and developed the Type 1B multifaceted, incentive-based approach to growth management, resource conservation, and economic development. The program responded to the realization that Maryland's growth pattern was consuming rural land at an alarming rate. Figure 8.11 shows the dramatic change in growth patterns before 1960 and after. Before 1960 development was concentrated in urban centers; after 1960 the flight from the city began in earnest and consumed rural land in its wake.

Maryland's Smart Growth Program includes five component programs that aim to direct growth to areas where infrastructure is already in place (or is planned). In so doing, Smart Growth aims to revitalize existing communities and reuse older industrial sites and to conserve agricultural and open space resources critical to the state's economy and its quality of life. Whereas many other state programs are regulatory, Maryland's is based on economic incentives, not regulations. However, to gain access to state financial resources for infrastructure, especially roads, water, and sewer; for rural land protection; and for redevelopment, localities must abide by the state rules for location of these projects. The five components include the following (Frece, 1997):

1. **Smart Growth Areas** or **Priority Funding Areas** (PFA). One of the most powerful elements in the initiative steers the resources of the state's $15 billion budget to older towns and cities or other areas specifically designated by local governments for growth. Baltimore and all other municipalities in Maryland, as well as the heavily developed areas inside the Baltimore and Washington beltways, are automatically designated as Smart Growth areas or priority funding areas (PFAs) eligible for state assistance. PFAs are defined as those areas with approved water and sewer plans and other features. Figure 8.12 shows the PFA boundaries.

2. **Rural Legacy Areas.** Maryland earmarked up to $140 million over five years to protect its rural legacy areas (RLAs)—farmland, forests, and open spaces threatened by development. Under this program, local governments and private land trusts may apply for funds to buy the land outright, or to acquire easements to preserve it from development. Figure 8.12 shows the RLAs as of 2000.

3. **Brownfields Cleanup and Redevelopment Program.** Industrial redevelopment incentives are provided through the Brownfields Cleanup and Redevelopment Program, which provides for cleanup of previously developed and contaminated industrial sites. Fear of liability has driven potential developers to build elsewhere, too often on farmland or other open spaces where expensive new infrastructure is required. The program aims to help revitalize older urban areas, increase local government revenues, create jobs, and clean up contaminated land.

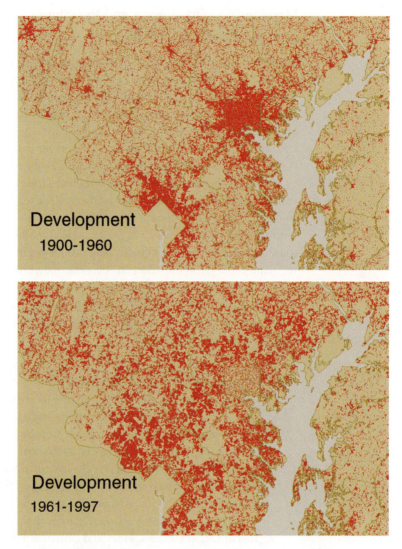

Figure 8.11 Patterns of Development in Washington-Baltimore Corridor 1900–1997. Until 1960, development was concentrated in the cities and suburban fringe. From 1961 to 1997 almost all development was outside the cities in what was rural areas. *Source:* Frece (2000).

4. **Job Creation Tax Credit.** This tax credit encourages development and expansion of small businesses within locally designated Smart Growth areas. It lowers from 60 to 25 the number of new jobs a business must create to qualify for a onetime income tax credit.

5. **Live Near Your Work** matching grant program. Under this program, the state, local jurisdictions, and individual employers form a partnership to provide at least $1,000 each to individual home buyers who agree to purchase homes near their work. This program strengthens neighborhoods by increasing homeownership; promotes linkages between employers and nearby communities; increases land values and revenue to local government; reduces commuting costs; reduces

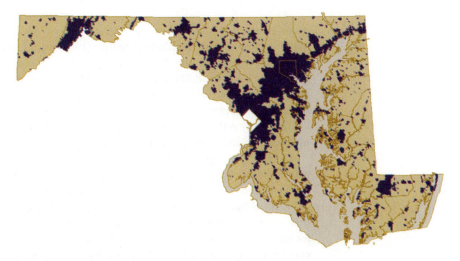

Figure 8.12 Maryland's Priority Funding Areas (blue) and Rural Legacy Areas (green) as of 2000. *Source:* Frece (2000).

air pollution; reduces employee turnover, training, and recruitment costs; and makes Maryland a more attractive place for business to locate and expand.

6. **GreenPrint Program.** GreenPrint is the newest component of Maryland's Smart Growth program, adopted in 2001, and is discussed in chapter 5. It aims to identify and conserve a statewide "green infrastructure" made up of hubs and links. Maryland identified 2 million acres of ecologically significant land not yet consumed by sprawl; 1.5 million of these acres remain unprotected (see figure 5.5). The program hopes to boost protected land conservation capacity by 10,000 acres per year using state plans and funds to leverage resources from the federal government and foundations.

Since it relies on incentives rather than regulations, Maryland's program does not preclude sprawling development, it just makes it more costly to achieve compared with development within PFAs.

SIDEBAR 8.1

Florida. In 1972, Florida enacted the Environmental Land and Water Management Act. The next decade showed this approach to be inadequate to manage growth and protect the environment under Florida's intense development pressures. The State and Regional Planning Act, passed in 1985, substantially changed the program.

Under the 1972 Act, the Division of State Planning was to recommend to the governor, and he was to designate, "critical areas of state concern." These areas could involve (a) environmental or cultural resources of regional or state importance, (b) sites of existing or proposed major public facilities, or (c) sites with major development potential. The Act limited the areas so designated to only 5 percent of the land in the state. Within six months of the designation of the areas, local governments were to prepare development regulations following state guidelines to protect the areas. In addition, the Act established a procedure for regional and state review of proposals for "developments of regional impact" (DRI) such as an airport, stadium, power plant, transmission line, large industrial facility, large shopping center, and so on. Although a state permit was not required for such projects, state and regional officials could influence the approval process.

The 1985 Act repealed the earlier program and established a Type 1A program with the dual aim of preventing urban and suburban sprawl, protecting the environment, and coordinating infrastructure construction and land development. The Act defined "sprawl" as "scattered, untimely, poorly planned urban development that occurs in urban fringe and rural areas and frequently invades lands important for environmental and natural resource protection." The program established the concept of "**concurrency**" or requiring that "public facilities and services needed to support development shall be available concurrent with development." These services included transportation, schools, water, sewer, solid waste collection and disposal, parks and recreation, and stormwater management. This "pay-as-you-grow" approach meant that before permits could be issued to developments, plans and funding for these services had to be in place. The program also had an objective of fostering compact development and fostering urban growth boundaries, but the approach gave localities more flexibility than Oregon's program and appears to have been less effective at containing growth within boundaries.

State Environmental Impact Requirements (Type 1C): Washington and California

Over half of the states have passed legislation, similar to the National Environmental Policy Act, establishing a state environmental policy and some type of environmental impact statement (EIS) requirement. Most of the states simply require state agencies to prepare an environmental assessment of major actions. Only four states—California, Massachusetts, New York and Washington—and Puerto Rico impose certain requirements on both state and local public agencies. Massachusetts provides a form of impact assessment, build-out analysis, for all of its localities. Chapter 18 describes procedures for both EIS and build-out analysis.

All five jurisdictions apply EIS requirements to public projects, but only California and Washington apply them to local planning and permitting decisions. In New York, permitting decisions have been interpreted to be "ministerial," that is, if codes and regulations are met, agencies have little or no discretion in granting approval. However, in California and Washington, permitting has been viewed as a discretionary act; that is, even though codes are met, public agencies are to look upon the impacts of the proposal and decide if the policies of the state environmental act are being met.

This interpretation has given local jurisdictions added responsibility and discretionary power in permit approvals. The guidelines to implement Washington's State Environmental Policy Act (SEPA) establish the procedures agencies and developers must follow as well as the types of projects that are exempt (State of Washington, 1998). The procedure has increased the quality of developments, mostly through the negotiation process. The SEPA procedure includes the following decision points at which local planners have an opportunity to negotiate with the developer:

1. the "threshold determination" of whether or not an EIS is required ("Gee, if you made these changes to your proposal, you probably would not have to prepare a costly EIS"),
2. when the draft EIS is circulated for review ("You know, we will have to decide on your project, and we'd really like to see these changes."), and
3. at the approval decision.

State "Critical Area" Protection Programs (Type 2)

Several states have taken action to control specific developments or development in specific "critical areas," such as coastal areas, wetlands, and farmlands. Several of these state programs are discussed in other chapters, including: state farmland protection programs (see table 5.7), coastal zone management and wetland protection (see chapter 16 for discussion on wetlands and coastal programs and a profile of the California Coastal Commission).

Virginia, Maryland, and Pennsylvania were signatories to the 1983 interstate Chesapeake Bay Agreement. Virginia's most notable effort to comply with the Agreement came in the Chesapeake Bay Preservation Act of 1988. In passing the Act, the General Assembly realized that only through effective and widespread land use controls to reduce nonpoint source pollution could the goals and objectives of the Agreement be achieved; it also realized that local governments must play the leading role in implementing those controls.

To assist local governments in this task, the Act established the Chesapeake Bay Local Assistance Board (CBLAB), with staff support from a new Chesapeake Bay Local Assistance Department (CBLAD). The Board was made responsible for formulating, adopting, and updating criteria and regulations for (a) local delineation of Chesapeake Bay preservation areas (CBPAs), and (b) management of land use and development within the designated areas to prevent further damage to the quality of the Bay and its tributaries, yet accommodate development. Matching grants have been provided to localities to implement the regulations. All 84 localities in Tidewater, Virginia, are required to comply with the regulations. These localities were included under the Act for two reasons: First, as part of the Coastal Basin, they were nearest the Bay and had the greatest effect on water quality; and second, the vast majority of growth projected to occur in Virginia's part of the watershed was in this region. Other local governments not in Tidewater are authorized to use the criteria and conform their ordinances on a voluntary basis to protect the quality of state waters.

The Chesapeake Bay Preservation Act Regulations became effective in October 1989. Tidewater localities were given a year from that date to adopt the criteria and two years to fully integrate them into their local governments' plans and ordinances. The regulations have three basic elements:

1. specific local requirements and adoption deadlines for water-sensitive plans and zoning ordinances,
2. criteria for designating local CBPAs, and
3. performance criteria for land use and development in CBPA.

The CBPAs are divided into resource protection areas (RPAs), which have special water quality value (e.g., tidal wetlands, tidal shores), and resource management areas (RMAs), which are less sensitive than RPAs but still may impact water quality (see figure 11.19d for example of RPAs). Areas outside of designated RPAs and RMAs are not subject to the regulations. Areas within RPAs and RMAs having existing development are designated as intensively developed areas (IDAs); these may be redeveloped so long as the applicable performance criteria are met. Other non-IDAs that have existing development may also be redeveloped.

Federal Programs for Environmental Land Use Planning and Management

Historically in the United States, the federal government's activities in land use have focused on management of federally owned public lands. Control of private land use has been left to state and local governments. However, many activities of federal agencies—from highway funding to issuing flood insurance—have a significant influence on environmentally sensitive lands, and many private land use decisions impact federally managed resources, such as air and water quality. As a result, several federal programs have been enacted that influence private land use.

Federal Programs Affecting Private Land Use

Several federal government programs influence private land use on environmental grounds. Since the federal government is still reluctant to directly regulate private land use, the controls used are often subtle. The programs involve six different approaches:

1. **Financial assistance for land acquisition, land conservation.** For example:
   - The Land and Waters Conservation Fund that provides grants to states and localities for land acquisition (see chapter 5)
   - The Conservation Reserve Program, Wetlands Reserve Program, and related programs providing funding for farmer stewardship of highly erodible lands and wetlands (see chapter 5)
   - Agricultural Conservation Program providing cost-share funds for soil and water conservation
   - Other federal grants for community-based environmental programs
2. **Technical assistance to private landowners.** For example:
   - Natural Resources Conservation Service technical assistance programs to farmers

- Other agencies educational programs for private land stewardship

3. **Funding for state or local environmental planning.** For example:
   - Coastal Zone Management program grants for state and local planning (see chapter 16)
   - Clean Water Act funds (sec. 319) for nonpoint source pollution control grants (see chapter 14)

4. **Withdrawal of federal funds from development or use in certain areas.** This approach is similar to Maryland's Smart Growth program approach 1B. Examples include:
   - Sodbuster and swampbuster programs cutting farm subsidies to farmers cultivating highly erodible land or wetlands (see chapter 5)
   - Coastal Barriers Resources Act of 1982 that withdraws all federal assistance for development in specified Barrier Resources Protection area

5. **Threatened withdrawal of federal funding.** Examples include:
   - National Flood Insurance Program: Communities must implement floodplain management or residents cannot get subsidized flood insurance and communities cannot get federal assistance, including disaster relief, for any project in flood-prone areas. As a result, all 19,000 flood-prone communities have enacted floodplain management and zoning (see chapter 9).

6. **Direct regulation.** Although rare, federal regulation of private land use occurs in special cases, including:
   - Wetlands permitting under the Clean Water Act (see chapter 16)
   - Habitat Conservation Planning under the Endangered Species Act (see chapter 17)
   - Surface mine reclamation under the Surface Mining Control and Reclamation Act. All surface mine operations must be permitted and develop and implement a postmining reclamation plan.

Policies Guiding the Activities of Federal Agencies

In the 1970s, a number of laws and executive orders provided specific guidance to federal agencies concerning environmentally sensitive lands. The most universal directive came in the **National Environmental Policy Act (NEPA)** of 1969. Since NEPA a number of more specific policies have been established concerning federal agency impacts on floodplains, wetlands, habitats of endangered species, and agricultural lands. Federal agencies planning and managing the nation's public lands and water resources have had to respond to yet another set of statutory directives.

NEPA (PL 91–190) was signed into law on January 1, 1970, at the height of the environmental movement in the United States. It established an environmental policy for the federal government and aimed to implement that policy through an action forcing provision, the EIS. The statement was to address potential impacts on not only environmentally sensitive lands but also pollution discharges and other aspects of the human environment. The Act's policy statement establishes an environmental priority yet balances it with other national objectives: "it is the continuing policy of the Federal government…to create and maintain conditions under which man and nature can exist in productive harmony, and fulfill the social, economic, and other requirements of present and future generations of Americans" (sec. 101(a)).

Section 102 contains several provisions which aim to implement the policy. Section 102(2)(a) directs federal agencies to utilize a "systematic, interdisciplinary approach" to ensure the use of scientific information and environmental design techniques in planning and decision making. The Act's most specific and forceful provision, contained in section 102(2)(c), requires agencies to prepare a detailed statement on the environmental impacts of and alternatives to "major Federal actions significantly affecting the quality of the human environment." The EIS must be made available for review by all interested parties, including the public.

Public Land Management

The public lands contain nearly one-third of the U.S. land area and are administered primarily by the Forest Service, the Bureau of Land Management (BLM), the National Park Service, and the Fish and Wildlife Service (see figure 5.1). In addition, the federal government has primary responsibility over the nation's navigable waters, and several agencies—including the Corps of Engineers, the Soil Conservation Service, the Bureau of Reclamation, and the Tennessee Valley Authority—actively plan, design, and construct water development projects for navigation, flood control, irrigation, water supply, power generation, and other purposes. For all of these agencies administering federal natural resources, a number of planning and management principles and procedures have been developed to ensure environmental considerations in management and development decisions. The public land agencies all operate under directives requiring management planning.

Policies concerning the environmental resources of public lands involve two principles: **multiple use** and **withdrawal** of certain lands from development. The national parks, refuges, and wilderness areas are examples of withdrawal programs; however, even these programs are managed to balance recreation and resource protection. The BLM (330 million acres) and the Forest Service (190 million acres) manage the majority of the public lands. The Multiple Use and Sustained Yield Act of 1960 established for the Forest Service a set of appropriate uses for Forest Service lands, including timber production, grazing, recreation, watershed protection, fish and wildlife management, and mineral development. The Resources Planning Act of 1974 and the National Forest Management Act of 1976 required the Forest Service to develop management plans for each national forest. Multiple-use areas designated for timber production must be managed to protect water quality and fish and wildlife.

BLM is guided by the Classification and Multiple Use Act of 1964, which established grazing, recreation, mineral development, and fish and wildlife as BLM's multiple uses. Like the Forest Service, BLM was charged with specific planning and management responsibilities by the Federal Lands Policy and Management Act (FLPMA) of 1976 and the Public Rangelands Improvement Act (PRIA) of

1978. In their current planning, BLM, the Forest Service, and the Park Service are applying more holistic "ecosystem management" (see chapter 10) (Randolph, 1987; Phillips and Randolph, 1998).

Summary

In the 1970s, the Council on Environmental Quality wrote about the "quiet revolution" in land use control (U.S. Council on Environmental Quality, 1974). That revolution fell silent in the early 1980s but resounded in the mid-1990s with an increasing number of state programs to promote Smart Growth in response to the problems of sprawl development. Oregon and Maryland are two states that have led the way with different programs: Oregon's regulatory program relies heavily on local implementation; Maryland's, too, relies on locals but uses incentives rather that regulations. Both use the concept of defined development areas or urban growth boundaries and defined conservation areas. Some other states have followed suit.

Regional authorities for land use control established in the 1960s and 1970s continue to be very active and show signs of effectiveness 30 years later, creatively using the full array of growth management tools available. Still, few regional metropolitan areas have developed the degree of cooperation and especially authority needed to take a regional approach to Smart Growth management. The federal government has some influence on private use of specific environmental lands, but almost all authority remains with state and local government.

9 ■ Natural Hazard Mitigation

Throughout human history, people have combated the elements of nature, seeking security from the hazards of flooding, hurricanes, tornadoes, extreme heat and cold, earthquakes, volcanoes, landslides, avalanches, wildfire, pestilence, and environmentally transmitted disease. These natural hazards continue to pose significant risk to human populations—an estimated 1 million people still die each decade from natural disasters (FEMA, 2000a). Although natural hazards will always concern us, approaches are emerging in land use planning and the use of engineering and nonstructural means to help mitigate hazards and the risks they pose. This chapter first discusses approaches to natural hazard mitigation and then describes responses to specific hazards of flooding; coastal erosion and storms; geologic seismic, slope, and support problems; and wildfire.

Natural Hazard Mitigation

Through the millennia, people and their institutions have tried to lessen or mitigate the effects of natural hazards that threaten human health, safety and welfare. The estimates of worldwide natural disasters' death and damage toll of 1 million deaths and hundreds of billions of dollars each decade do not include the millions of daily incidents of natural hazard damage and injury not classified as "disasters," such as localized flooding and landslides. From 1990 to 2002, federal disaster assistance totaled $39 billion, five times the previous 12-year period (General Accounting Office, 2002). This section introduces natural hazard mitigation and describes emerging approaches to reduce damage, injury, and death.

Hazard, Exposure, Vulnerability, and Risk

As introduced in chapter 3, there is difference between hazard, exposure, vulnerability, and risk (figure 9.1).

Figure 9.1 Hazard, Exposure, Vulnerability, and Risk. Risk is where a hazard, exposure, and vulnerability overlap.

- **Hazard** is the inherent danger associated with a potential problem, such as an earthquake or avalanche. It includes regional susceptibility as well as relative hazard of specific areas within that region. For example, San Francisco Bay Area is an earthquake-prone region, yet within the region, areas underlain by soft materials have a groundshaking hazard much greater than other areas.
- **Exposure** is the human population, ecological resource, or property exposed to the hazard.
- **Vulnerability** is the unprotected nature of the exposure. Vulnerability can be reduced by engineering design (e.g., floodproofing, earthquake resistant design, heating and air conditioning systems to temper extreme heat and cold).
- **Risk** is the probable degree of injury and damage likely to occur from exposure of people and property to the hazard over a specific time period. Risk analysis involves combining (or overlaying as maps) assessment of relative hazard, exposure, and vulnerability, as well as analyzing the probability of occurrence. This statistical assessment relies on inventory, historical, and scientific data. For example, flood hazard probability relies on historical hydrologic data, and earthquake probability is based on subsurface geologic data.

People can sometimes increase the degree of hazard. For example, undercutting steep slopes increases landslide hazard, and paving parking lots and roads increases impervious surface that exacerbates flooding downstream. More often, however, people increase their exposure and vulnerability by placing themselves in harm's way and doing so without necessary protection. For example, they build in a seismic or flood-prone area without proper design. Environmental risks to humans are increased by poor location and poor design of land developments.

Hazard Mitigation

In the United States, a number of agencies are charged with managing natural hazards. The U.S. Geological Survey (USGS) (geologic hazards), the National Oceanic and Atmospheric Administration (NOAA) (weather-related hazards), the U.S. Army Corps of Engineers (flooding and disaster response), the Centers for Disease Control (environmental disease), the U.S. Forest Service (wildfires), and the Environmental Protection Agency (contaminants) all have responsibility for specific hazards. The **Federal Emergency Management Agency (FEMA)** has broad responsibilities for disasters and relief. FEMA is also charged with administering the National Flood Insurance Program (NFIP) and the natural hazard mitigation program. The NFIP is discussed in detail later in this chapter.

Hazard mitigation is defined as the long-term reduction of the effects of natural hazard events. The term *mitigation* is applied to many aspects of environmental planning and management. As discussed in subsequent chapters, mitigation is an important issue in wetlands management and environmental impact assessment. In general, mitigation strategies aim to lessen impacts, and they follow a clear hierarchy given in the following list: Avoid the impact, lessen the impact by location, lessen the impact by design, offset the impact.

Hierarchy of Environmental Impact Mitigation Strategies

1. Avoid the impact (move away altogether).
2. Lessen the impact by modifying location on site (move away to lesser impact area).
3. Lessen the impact by modifying design (apply engineering or design features).
4. Offset the impact (compensate for the impact by monetary relief, reconstruction, or re-creation).

The federal Natural Hazard Mitigation Program was initiated by the 1988 Robert T. Stafford Disaster Emergency Assistance Act, last amended in 2000. The program was prompted by the growing perception that the nation was not dealing effectively with natural hazards. Indeed, despite ever-increasing federal funds for damage mitigation, emergency preparedness, forecasting, and disaster response, damages from natural hazards continue to rise. The nation seemed locked in a disaster-relief-rebuild-disaster syndrome (figure 9.2). Following natural hazard damage or disaster, the government provides needed monetary and humanitarian relief, including funds to clean up and rebuild. Rebuilding often occurs in the same location, only to be followed by subsequent disasters with potentially greater damage and more relief. The fundamental hazard, exposure, vulnerability, and risk are not adequately addressed.

Some federal programs have tried to address this syndrome. The NFIP stipulates that for a community's residents to obtain subsidized federal flood insurance (the only flood insurance available), the community must implement floodplain zoning, that is, restricting new development, or significant rebuilding after a flood, in the floodway. This applies to hurricane flooding as well. However, inadequate

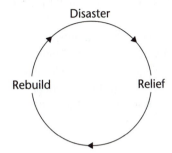

Figure 9.2 The Disaster-Relief-Rebuild-Disaster Syndrome

enforcement of these provisions has limited their effectiveness (Godshalk, Beatley, Berke, Brower, and Kaiser, 1999).

The 1988 Stafford Act aimed to break this syndrome by creating further requirements for disaster relief applicable to all natural hazards. Under section 409, the provision of disaster relief requires a state to have a natural hazard mitigation plan certified by FEMA (the so-called 409 Plan). The Act also provides grants for "mitigation" projects under section 404. A study by Godshalk et al. (1999) traced the implementation of the Act in the 1990s and showed the program had limited effectiveness in addressing the syndrome, and in fact, in many respects, had exacerbated it.

Their findings included the following:

- Mitigation plans were reactive rather than proactive. 409 Plans were often prepared in response to a disaster so that the state could receive relief funds. To become eligible as soon as possible, the plans were often hurried and inadequate, more a "hoop to jump through" than a carefully prepared, implementable plan.
- Section 404 grants were mostly directed to rebuilding projects, not mitigation programs, and there was little implementation connection between the 409 plans and the 404 projects. The contribution of 404 projects to long-term risk reduction was not evident.

Godshalk et al. (1999) recommend that plans become more proactive and preventative, that they be prepared with care before disasters occur, that they be revised and improved after each hazard event, and that they deal with multiple hazards rather than different plans on single hazards. Mitigation grants should focus on risk reduction programs rather than recovery projects. Programs can go beyond temporary relief of hardship to long-term avoidance of risk, such as buyout and relocation programs and improved building and land use regulations to lessen exposure and vulnerability.

Section 322 of the Stafford Act, as amended in 2000,

1. improves upon the 409 planning process. Section 322 requires a state mitigation plan as a condition for receiving hazard mitigation grants program (HMGP) funds.

2. provides additional funds for states that adopt "enhanced state mitigation plans."
3. requires local mitigation plans.
4. authorizes up to 7 percent of HMGP funds for mitigation planning.
5. requires state and local governments to develop and adopt hazard mitigation plans by November 2004 to qualify for HMGP funding after that date (Belo, 2003; FEMA, 2002a, 2002b).

Natural Hazard Mitigation Planning

Natural hazard mitigation planning follows the basic planning process (see box 2.1). As shown in box 9.1, fundamental objectives are to avoid, prevent, and reduce the impacts from natural hazards. Mitigation planning can be used iteratively to break the disaster-relief-rebuild-disaster syndrome and reduce the degree of impact and the cost of relief from subsequent natural hazard events. Preventative mitigation is a continual adaptive process that responds to successive disaster events. Mitigation planning should learn from each event so that mitigation investments can be targeted to progressively reduce the damages and relief costs of the next disaster.

Plans should address multiple hazards, although specific assessments and alternatives depend on the hazards involved. **Hazard and risk assessment** involves three steps:

1. **Hazard identification** is usually found in the comprehensive plan. It provides descriptions and inventory maps of hazards, including history, generalized hazard boundaries, and critical facilities.
2. **Hazard exposure and vulnerability assessment** combines the information from hazard identification with an inventory of the existing (or planned) property and population exposed to a hazard and predicts how a hazard will affect different properties and population groups.
3. **Risk analysis** estimates the communitywide or site-specific damage, injuries, and costs likely to be experienced in an area over a period of time. Risk includes the magnitude of the harm that may result, and the probability of the harm occurring (Oregon Department of Land Conservation and Development, 2000).

Natural hazard mitigation plans should be part of a community's comprehensive plan, and implementation mechanisms include land use zoning, building codes, public works structural measures, education programs, and evacuation procedures. (For more information on comprehensive planning and land use controls, see chapter 7.) The Institute for Business and Home Safety (IBHS) developed a Community Land Use Evaluation (CLUE) questionnaire to assess a community's comprehensive plan for natural hazards (IBHS, 2001). The following list gives the categories and samples of the 71 questions in CLUE. The plan is graded on positive answers to the questions, where an "A" grade is given for 52 or more affirmative answers. The full questionnaire is given at www.ibhs.org.

BOX 9.1—Natural Hazard Mitigation Planning

Identify objectives: Avoid, prevent, and reduce impacts from natural hazard events.

Assess situation: Hazard and risk assessment.

Hazard assessment: Assess degree of hazard by location.

Exposure assessment: Assess population location in relation to hazards.

Vulnerability assessment: Assess building and land use standards.

Risk assessment: Assess impact probability, based on hazard, exposure and vulnerability.

Develop mitigation alternatives:

Education (exposure and vulnerability reduction): Raise awareness of hazard, risk, and mitigation.

Avoidance (exposure reduction), e.g., land use controls and zoning, evacuation plans.

Lessen by location (exposure reduction), e.g., land use controls.

Lessen by design (hazard and vulnerability reduction), e.g., structural public works, building and land use engineering and design, building codes.

Offset (vulnerability and risk reduction), e.g., emergency response, relief.

Assess options and formulate natural hazard mitigation plan:

Assess the effectiveness and economic, social, and environmental effects of mitigation options.

Select an array of appropriate mitigation options in a natural hazard mitigation plan.

Implement the natural hazard mitigation plan.

Implement preventative measures and response actions.

Evaluate the mitigation plan during and after each natural hazard event.

Monitor the effectiveness of mitigation measures and modify plan accordingly.

Community Land Use Evaluation (CLUE) for Natural Hazards: Survey Categories and Sample Questions

1. *Basics:* 1.3 Does the plan contain an overall statement summarizing the broad goals and guidelines of the community to address natural hazards and to mitigate their effects?

2. *Quality of Data:* 2.4 Does the plan include maps that identify hazardous areas?

3. *Identification of Issues:* 3.3 Does the plan identify development alternatives within or outside of hazard areas?

4. *Community Support:* 4.3 Were citizens given information about natural hazards during the plan preparation process?

5. *Policies:* 5.5 Does the plan have a policy to steer capital improvements away from the areas most vulnerable to natural hazards?

6. *Coordination:* 6.2 Is the plan consistent with statewide guidelines or principles for hazard-prone areas?

7. *Implementation:* 7.1 Are plan goals and objectives tied to specific actions, rather than to general intentions?

In a study of the effect of natural hazard planning on damages in the 1994 Northridge earthquake in southern California, Nelson and French (2002) provided useful conclusions about natural hazard mitigation generally. First, they argue that building codes are important but limited in mitigating natural hazard risk. Although codes reduce hazard vulnerability to a certain magnitude, disasters exceeding this magnitude can be catastrophic. Codes thus can lead to a false sense of security, resulting in more development in the vicinity of hazard areas and increasing exposure and risk.

Second, comprehensive plans are critical but often lack strong factual information about hazards, effective policies based on facts, or both. Plans are often less restrictive of development in hazard areas than they should be because local governments fear strict standards will reduce the fiscal benefits of growth, and they realize that federal government relief will bail them out if a disaster occurs.

Nelson and French's study concludes that the most effective strategies for hazard mitigation include retrofitting older homes to current standards, quality comprehensive plans, and effective implementation, including land use controls and building codes. They argue that without state and regional mandates and/or enforcement, local governments are usually ineffective in mitigating natural hazards as well as preserving natural resources, containing sprawl, and improving infrastructure delivery. California's state requirements for earthquake hazard mitigation are diminished by weak enforcement of local implementation (Nelson and French, 2002). For more information on regional and state mandates, see chapter 8.

FEMA developed "Project Impact" to enhance local hazard mitigation planning and build disaster-resistant communities. The program has four aims: (1) to build community partnerships of local governments, civic groups, and businesses to work together; (2) to assess risks and improve planning; (3) to prioritize needs and actions to reduce vulnerability and risk; and (4) to build support and communication about hazard mitigation within the community. FEMA began the program with seven pilot communities in the mid-1990s, and by 2000, there were more than 250 Project Impact communities and 2,500 business partners (FEMA, 2000b). To assist in awareness, education, and rapid assessment, FEMA has partnered with the consulting firm Environmental Systems Research Institute (ESRI) to provide online hazard mapping (FEMA and ESRI, 2001; http://www.esri.com/hazards).

The remainder of this chapter explores specific hazards and the application of these mitigation concepts. These natural hazards include flooding, coastal hazards, geologic hazards, and wildfire.

Flooding and Flood Hazard Mitigation

When stormwater flows exceed channel capacity, water will overtop channel banks and spread out as floods. Analysis of stormwater flow and channel capacity is discussed in chapters 13 and 14. Flood damage mitigation is discussed here because of its importance in natural hazard mitigation. Between 1990 and 1997, U.S. flooding caused $4.2 billion per year in damages. In the last century, an average 100 Americans per year lost their lives in floods (FEMA, 2000a). Although

Figure 9.3 Flooding of East Grand Forks, Minnesota, April 1997. *Source:* Photo by David Saville/FEMA News Photo.

damages continue to increase, loss of life has decreased in this country as a result of better flood warning systems. Figure 9.3 shows downtown East Grand Forks, Minnesota, during the 1997 flood.

Approaches to Flood Hazard Mitigation

Several approaches can be taken to mitigate flood hazards and reduce damages. Box 9.2 distinguishes between structural and nonstructural measures. In its efforts to mitigate flood damages, prior to 1973 the U.S. federal government focused on structural measures built by the U.S. Army Corps of Engineers and other agencies. These measures were euphemistically referred to as "flood control," but after an investment of more than $11 billion in such measures while flood damages continued to rise, it became clear that structures alone would not solve the problem. Increasingly, federal and local planners have turned to nonstructural measures, such as floodplain management, land acquisition, and relocation of structures, to avoid future damages. Other measures such as insurance and disaster relief aim to manage the financial risk and hardship associated with flood damages.

Table 9.1 highlights the structural measures. More than 260 large flood control **dams** and **reservoirs** have been built on rivers in the United States. Essentially large detention basins, they can detain runoff to reduce peak flows downstream, but they also permanently flood large areas of riparian lands and free-flowing channels within the reservoir pool. Some 6,000 miles of **levees, dikes,** and **floodwalls** across the country protect specific areas by artificially raising the channel bank. This

---

BOX 9.2—Approaches to Flood Hazard Mitigation

Structural Measures

- Guide flood waters by building levees, flood walls, channel enlargement (flood protection).
- Lessen flood waters (peak discharge) through upland runoff control measures including detention (dams and reservoirs) (flood abatement).
- Adjust site characteristics by elevating sites with fill material.
- Adjust building characteristics by elevating and floodproofing structures and related infrastructure.

Nonstructural Measures

- Do nothing.
- Provide emergency preparedness measures such as flood warnings.
- Provide relief through private and federal disaster assistance.
- Provide affordable insurance for flood damages.
- Provide information, such as maps of floodplains and general information about flood risks and safe floodplain building practices.
- Adjust future land use by floodplain planning, vacant land acquisition, and regulatory zoning.
- Adjust existing land use by acquiring and relocating buildings.

---

prevents floods from spilling to their accustomed floodplains, but the water must go somewhere, so it often rises higher and floods areas not normally prone to flooding.

Channelization is the modification of streams, often by straightening, widening or deepening, to increase channel capacity and speed water drainage. Although such modifications can benefit those living near them, they can increase the volume and velocity of water carried by the stream and thus cause greater peak flows downstream. Channelization can also destroy natural channels, their aesthetic qualities, and their ability to support aquatic and riparian life. Recent designs, such as the bench channel shown in figure 9.4, can preserve the natural channel and one side of the riparian lands while increasing capacity.

These structural flood control measures have prevented considerable damages. The Corps of Engineers estimated in 1975 that the $10 billion spent by federal agencies on control measures since 1936 prevented $60 billion in flood damages. However, as noted, total damages and deaths due to flooding have actually increased over time. The major reasons for this include increased property values and increased human occupancy of floodplains. This further encroachment of development on the floodplain has been due in some cases to ignorance of the flood hazard and in others to a false sense of security provided by the presence of flood "control" measures. Flood control structures never give absolute protection; they merely make a devastating event less frequent.

Table 9.1 also lists "innovative" structural measures, including on-site detention and infiltration, which help diminish increases in flood flows due to urbanization. These measures are discussed at length in chapter 14. However, these on-site measures will not reduce flooding in naturally occurring flood-prone areas. These areas require special attention. Experience has shown that floodplain man-

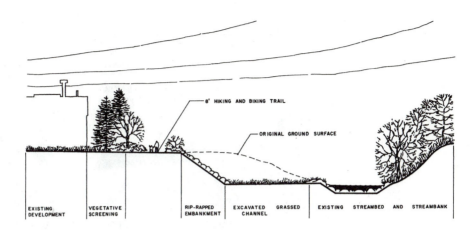

TYPICAL CHANNEL SECTION

Figure 9.4 Bench Channel Method of Improving Capacity of Stream. *Source:* U.S. Army Corps of Engineers (1984).

TABLE 9.1 **Structural Flood Mitigation Measures**

Measure	*Effects*	*Problems*
Traditional "Flood Control"		
Dams and Reservoirs	Retains stormwaters	Transfers flooding; false sense of security
Channel modification (widening, straightening, lining)	Increases capacity, speed of drainage	Destroys natural channels; increases flood flow downstream
Levees, floodwalls	Protects one side	Water surge may flood other side and areas previously not flooded
Innovative Stormwater Management		
Upstream detention and infiltration on-site or after preliminary concentration (see chapter 14)		

agement is far more effective in reducing damages over time than localized structures like channel modification and floodwalls.

Floodplain Management

As the effectiveness of structural measures has been questioned, greater attention has been given to managing floodplain development as an alternative approach for mitigating flood damages. Floodplain management may involve a number of measures directed at new and existing development. Encroachment of new development onto the floodplain not only can expose new occupants to flood damage but also can cause a surcharge in flood level due to cutting and filling. Figure 9.5 illus-

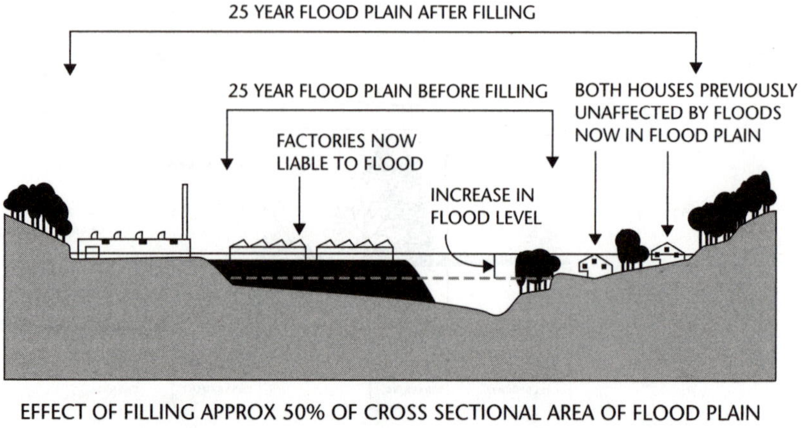

25 YEAR FLOOD PLAIN AFTER FILLING

25 YEAR FLOOD PLAIN BEFORE FILLING | BOTH HOUSES PREVIOUSLY UNAFFECTED BY FLOODS NOW IN FLOOD PLAIN

FACTORIES NOW LIABLE TO FLOOD

INCREASE IN FLOOD LEVEL

EFFECT OF FILLING APPROX 50% OF CROSS SECTIONAL AREA OF FLOOD PLAIN

Figure 9.5 Effect of Floodplain Encroachment on Flood Elevation

trates the effects of floodplain encroachment. As a result of land filling, the 25-year floodplain will be much wider than before.

The most straightforward way to control encroachment is by restricting land use in the floodplain to uses that are compatible with periodic flooding, such as recreation and agriculture. In response to certain requirements of the NFIP, nearly all of the 19,000 flood-prone communities in the United States have implemented floodplain management, including **floodplain zoning.** Readers unfamiliar with zoning fundamentals should consult chapter 7. Floodplain zoning prohibits development in the "floodway" and allows development with floodproofing in the 100-year floodway fringe. A 100-year event has a 1 percent chance of occurring in any year. Floodproofing usually involves elevating structures or portions of structures prone to damage above the 100-year flood elevation plus the one-foot surcharge. The floodway and floodway fringe are defined in figure 9.6 as:

- The **floodway** is a fairly narrow area close to the stream that must remain open so that flood waters can pass through.
- The **floodway fringe** is the area within the 100-year floodplain that can be subject to encroachment or filling without causing more than a one-foot surcharge in the height of the 100-year flood carried by the floodway.

Homeowners can only obtain flood insurance through the NFIP. Private insurers participating in NFIP actually provide the policies under subsidized rates. However, homeowners can obtain this insurance only if their local government is implementing floodplain management and zoning. In addition, if localities do not have floodplain zoning in accord with the preceding conditions, they cannot receive any other federal financial aid, including disaster relief for flood damages or assistance for projects in the floodway fringe. FEMA provides enforcement of this provision.

Figure 9.7 shows how floodplain zoning can affect floodplain development. Appropriate uses of the floodplain include open space, recreation, and agriculture. The FEMA rules for floodplain management are limited. Although they may be

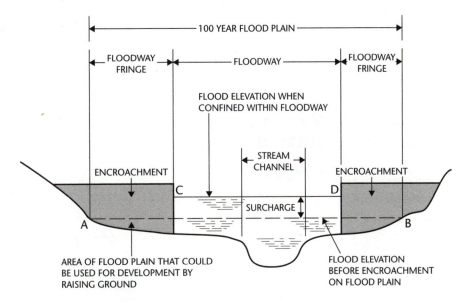

Figure 9.6 The Floodway and the Floodway Fringe. *Source:* FEMA (1979).

effective in preventing development in the floodway (if enforced), they have been criticized for actually encouraging development of the floodway fringe. Such development may be safe from the 100-year flood, but a larger event will cause more damage than if this development did not occur. In addition, the floodway fringe may contain riparian vegetation that provides aesthetic benefits and wildlife habitat. By encouraging floodway fringe development, floodplain management impacts riparian and stream corridor values. Some communities prohibit development in the entire 100-year floodplain.

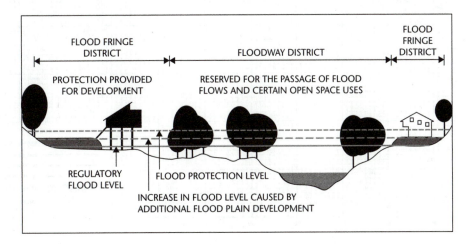

Figure 9.7 Floodplain Zoning Using Floodway and Floodway Fringe Districts

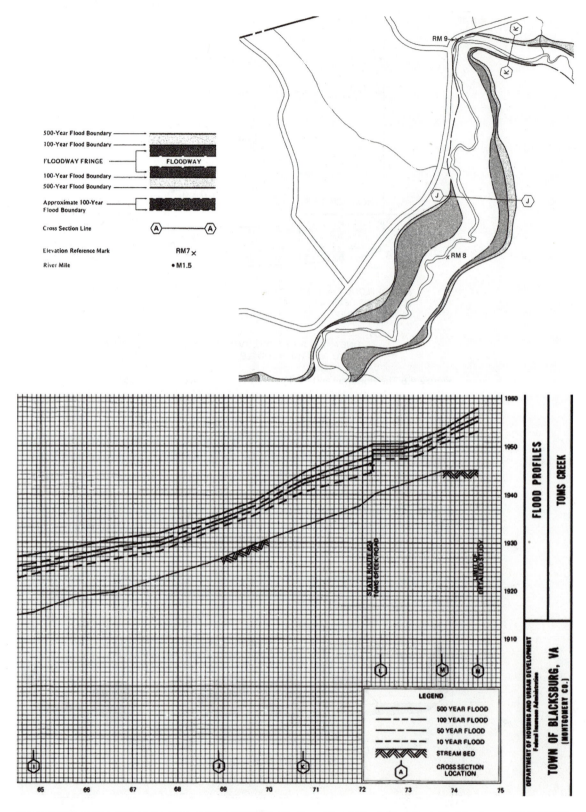

Figure 9.8 Flood Hazard Boundary Map and Flood Profile for Section of Tom's Creek, Blacksburg, Virginia. *Source:* FEMA (1979).

Floodplain Maps and Flood Profiles

The first step in managing floodplains is to identify them. Fortunately, **floodplain maps** are available for nearly all flood-prone areas through FEMA and its implementation of the NFIP. Through the program, FEMA identifies flood-prone areas on flood hazard boundary maps (FHBM). If a community enrolls in the program, a more detailed flood insurance rate map (FIRM) is produced.

An example of the hazard boundary maps is shown in figure 9.8. The basis for the maps is a set of **flood profile** charts produced in the Flood Insurance Study, which accompanies the maps. A hypothetical flood profile is given in figure 9.9. For the length of the stream, the profile charts the water elevations for floods of various recurrence frequencies: 10-year, 50-year, 100-year, and 500-year events. For example, in figure 9.9, the elevation of the 100-year flood at point A along the stream is 1,100 feet above sea level. Floodplains for these floods can then be drawn by elevation on a topographic map. The FEMA maps identify the floodway, the flood fringe, as well as the 100-year and 500-year floodplains. They are keyed to the profiles by a series of cross sections, labeled by letter, shown on both the maps and profiles. In addition, a table of floodway elevations for each cross section is provided so that landowners can determine the regulatory floodway elevation below which building or filling is not allowed.

For example, if you have a building site near a stream, you will need to survey the site to determine its elevation above sea level. This is fairly easy if there is a nearby elevation benchmark. To determine if you can get a building permit for the site, the local planner or building inspector will identify the site on the flood profile and floodplain map (including "working" maps used by FEMA to prepare the official boundary maps). If the site elevation is above the 100-year flood elevation, the site passes the test. If not, the site elevation must be compared with the regulatory elevation to see if it is within the floodway.

Figure 9.10 shows a portion of a FIRM, based on the FHBM. The legend reveals the categories of insurance rates based on the relative hazard. Zone A is within the

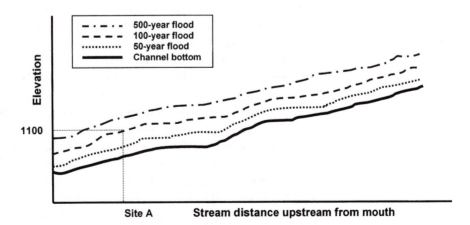

Figure 9.9 Hypothetical Flood Profile.

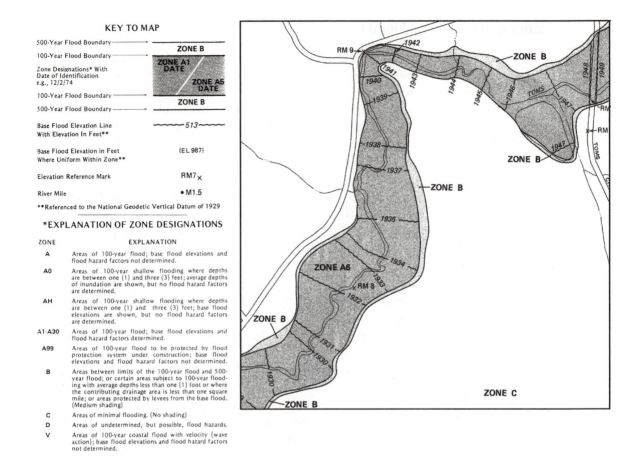

KEY TO MAP

500-Year Flood Boundary

100-Year Flood Boundary

Zone Designations* With
Date of Identification
e.g., 12/2/74

100-Year Flood Boundary

500-Year Flood Boundary

ZONE B
ZONE A1
DATE
ZONE A5
DATE
ZONE B

Base Flood Elevation Line
With Elevation In Feet**   ———513———

Base Flood Elevation in Feet
Where Uniform Within Zone**   (EL 987)

Elevation Reference Mark   RM7×

River Mile   ●M1.5

**Referenced to the National Geodetic Vertical Datum of 1929

---

*EXPLANATION OF ZONE DESIGNATIONS

ZONE	EXPLANATION
A	Areas of 100-year flood; base flood elevations and flood hazard factors not determined.
A0	Areas of 100-year shallow flooding where depths are between one (1) and three (3) feet; average depths of inundation are shown, but no flood hazard factors are determined.
AH	Areas of 100-year shallow flooding where depths are between one (1) and three (3) feet; base flood elevations are shown, but no flood hazard factors are determined.
A1-A30	Areas of 100-year flood; base flood elevations and flood hazard factors determined.
A99	Areas of 100-year flood to be protected by flood protection system under construction; base flood elevations and flood hazard factors not determined.
B	Areas between limits of the 100-year flood and 500-year flood; or certain areas subject to 100-year flooding with average depths less than one (1) foot or where the contributing drainage area is less than one square mile; or areas protected by levees from the base flood. (Medium shading)
C	Areas of minimal flooding. (No shading)
D	Areas of undetermined, but possible, flood hazards.
V	Areas of 100-year coastal flood with velocity (wave action); base flood elevations and flood hazard factors not determined.

Figure 9.10 Flood Insurance Rate Map (FIRM) Showing Rate Zones. *Source:* FEMA (1979).

100-year floodplain, Zone B is between the 100-year and 500-year flood boundary, Zone C is outside the 500-year boundary, and Zone D is undetermined. Subcategories of Zone A are possible if specific flood hazards are determined. Zone V applies to coastal flooding wave surges (see the section on coastal flooding).

FEMA has recently made floodplain maps available on the Internet. The agency has scanned as .tif files the FHBMs and FIRMs, as well as flood insurance studies that contain flood profiles. They are searchable by location at FEMA's Flood Map Store. The maps can be ordered (paper copies) or viewed online. Images can be viewed and manipulated using F-MIT software, which enables users to zoom in and out and produce "FIRMettes" or "FHBMettes" that zoom in on the location of their interest. Maps can be saved as .pdf files, or printed in letter, legal, or 11″×17″ sizes. In addition, the Flood Map Store offers digital flood data for use in GIS. For more information and to retrieve floodplain maps and data of your choice, see http://store.msc.fema.gov/webapp/wcs/stores/servlet/StoreCatalogDisplay?storeId=10001&catalogId=10001&langId=-1&userType=G.

Floodplain management focuses on new development and does not manage flood damages to existing structures. As already mentioned, in some cases, acquisition and relocation of structures and/or occupants has proven more economical than providing structural flood control or sustaining periodic inundation. More often, emergency measures such as flood forecasting, warning systems, evacuation, and remedial controls such as sandbagging are provided for developments in flood prone areas. FEMA and the Army Corps of Engineers have placed increased emphasis on property buyouts and relocation of structures and whole communities in some cases (FEMA, 1998).

Coastal Zone Hazards

Coastal areas exhibit significant dynamic physical hazards and intense human exposure, combining into major risk. Coastal processes involve the erosion and deposition of sand and sediment by water and wind and intense storm hazards. Figure 9.11 shows coastal places of concern in a barrier island context, typical of the Atlantic and Gulf coasts. They include the **beachfront,** the **dunelands,** the **barrier flats** including grassland and forest, **saltwater wetlands** and marsh, the **backbay** or coastal basin, and finally the landward **backbay shoreline.** The beach and dunelands are those areas most prone to the ocean's dynamic forces from normal wave action and violent storms, while the coastal basins, estuaries, and saltwater wetlands are ecologically productive. Beach and bluff erosion processes are more typical of the West Coast.

The constant action of waves on the beach is the prime force against the highly erodible sand. Wave action at an angle to the beach will produce a littoral current down the beach causing a **littoral drift** of eroded sand. If a barrier such as a **groin** or breakwater is erected on the beach, it will slow the flow of water causing the deposition of sand and a broadening of the beach; but the down-flow side of the groin will experience continued erosion with no deposition, and there the beach will be narrowed. This littoral drift depends on the wave intensity and direction, which in turn depend on the shape of the underwater shelf and the season. Headlands not only experience waves first, but those waves have more energy. Wave direction often varies with the season, so that the direction of the littoral drift and the shape of the beach may change throughout the year.

Beach erosion is a continuous process, and storm waves exacerbate the process. The higher water associated with storms takes higher, more eroding waves further inland. This eroding force can undermine beach dunes, which provide the primary defense against the storms. These waves can also undermine seawalls designed to protect structures built too close to the beach.

Figure 9.11 also shows the development of a dune system on a barrier beach. The primary force is the ocean wind that erodes beach sands and carries them inland until wind barriers (initially a poorly developed dune) reduce velocity and cause deposition. As the deposition grows a distinct dune, it provides increased protection from wind and storm waves. Vegetation can then prolifer-

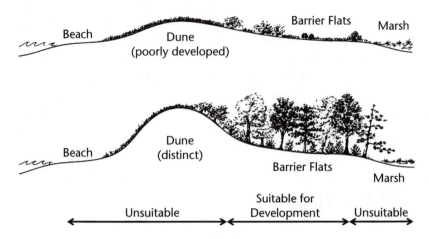

Figure 9.11 Dune Development and Its Effect on Barrier Flat Vegetation. The dune system creates suitability zones for development. *Source:* Clark, J., J. Banta, and J. Zinn. 1980. Based on drawing from M. Mow from S. Leatherman, Barrier Island Handbook, National Park Cooperative Research Unit, Univ. Massachusetts-Amherst.

ate behind the dune, adding more stability to highly erodible sandy soils. The vegetation on the dune itself is essential to its formation and stability. Dune grasses begin to halt the advance of sand, arresting erosion and contributing to deposition. If this dune vegetation is disturbed by construction or intensive recreation use, wind and storm waves are more likely to erode the dunes, reducing the storm protection they provide for the barrier flats. A cardinal rule of coastal management is to control development in storm-damage-prone beach areas as well as on protective dunes.

Coastal Storm Hazards

Natural hazards affecting coastal areas are caused by hurricanes and other coastal storms. Hazards include coastal flooding, high winds, wave and tidal surges, and beach erosion and bluff failure. Offshore earthquake-driven tsunamis are also relatively prevalent on the Pacific coast of the United States, especially Hawaii and Alaska, and in other coastal regions of the world. In the eastern United States tropical storms and hurricanes are the greatest problem. Figure 9.12 shows the most prevalent sources of coastal flooding in the United States. South Florida, southeast Texas, and North Carolina have been the hardest hit and are the most susceptible to land falling hurricanes.

Coastal storm hazards include severe wind, storm surge flooding, upland flooding, and tornadoes. Hurricanes are rated on the Saffir-Simpson 1–5 scale. Table 9.2 gives

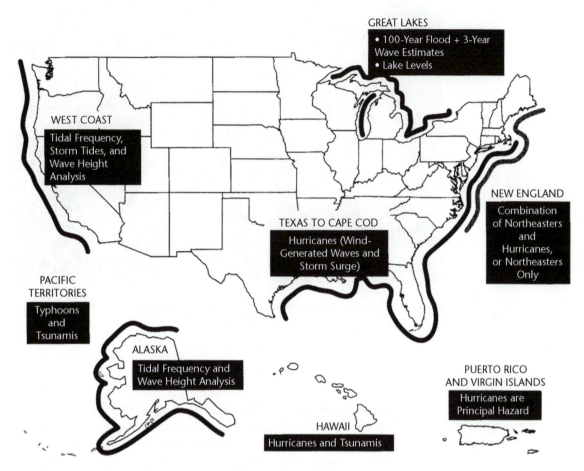

Figure 9.12 U.S. Coastal Storm Hazards. *Source:* FEMA (2000c).

TABLE 9.2 **Saffir-Simpson Hurricane Scale and Recent Examples in United States**

Category	Wind Speed	Surge Height	Coastal Damage	Recent Examples
1	74–95 mph	4–5 feet	Minimal	Agnes (1972—Florida, Northeast U.S.)
2	96–110 mph	6–8 feet	Moderate	Marilyn (1995—Virgin Islands)
3	111–130 mph	9–12 feet	Extensive	Fran (1996—North Carolina)
4	131–15 mph	13–18 feet	Extreme	Andrew (1992—Florida)
5	>155 mph	>18 feet	Catastrophic	Camille (1969—Mississippi)

Figure 9.13 Hurricane Damage from Hurricane Andrew, August 24, 1992. One million people were evacuated and 54 died in this hurricane. *Source:* FEMA News Photo.

that scale and also some of the most destructive hurricanes of the past few decades in the United States. Figure 9.13 gives examples of hurricane damage.

Damages from coastal flooding result from hydrodynamic forces of wave action and tidal surge, hydrostatic forces of high water, sediment overwash, and beach and bluff erosion. In addition, heavy rains cause upland flooding well inland, including dangerous flash flooding in higher elevations. For example, Category 1 hurricanes Agnes (1972) and Floyd (1999) caused little coastal damage, but their rains dumped 20–30 inches of rain inland and caused billions of dollars of flood damage.

Coastal damage also results from high winds. The American Society of Civil Engineers (1998) has developed minimum design loads and wind speeds for buildings that range from 85 mph on the West Coast to 120 mph in New England to 150 mph in south Florida.

Because of storm surges, high winds, and highly mobile sandy soils, coastal areas are extremely vulnerable to erosion. The dynamic forces in the beach, dune, and bluff environment require careful consideration in siting and designing coastal residential and other development. Shoreline segments that lose more sediment than they gain are subject to *erosion;* segments that gain more than they lose are subject to *accretion;* and segments that balance gains and losses are said to be *stable.*

Shoreline erosion is measured by linear retreat (e.g., feet of recession per year) or volumetric loss (e.g., cubic yards of eroded sediment per foot of shoreline per year). Erosion rates are usually given as long-term average annual rates, but they are not uniform in time or location on the shoreline. Figure 9.14, from a study by Douglas, Crowell, and Leatherman (1998), illustrates the difference between medium-term and long-term shoreline dynamics.

Storm-induced erosion is rapid and dynamic, but longer-term erosion is caused by natural changes (e.g., littoral transport, tidal inlets) and human activities (e.g., dredging, damming rivers, alteration of vegetation or dunes). Storm-induced erosion can cause the equivalent shoreline change of several decades of long-term erosion. Large dunes can be eroded as much as 75 feet and small dunes can be destroyed.

Mitigating Coastal Hazards through Smart Land Development Practices

Coastal storms and hurricanes pose one of the most damaging and dangerous natural hazards. Damages are exacerbated by poor location of development and construction practices. In an effort to foster smarter development practices, the federal government has assisted the states to improve planning and management through the Coastal Zone Management program. This is discussed at length in chapter 16. In addition, FEMA has developed land use regulations in conjunction with the NFIP as well as technical guidance for states and localities. As discussed in the section on flood hazard mitigation, the NFIP provides subsidized flood insurance only in those communities that implement zoning to restrict development in flood prone areas. FEMA's *Coastal Construction Manual* provides the most comprehensive source to date for planning, siting, designing, constructing, and maintaining buildings in coastal areas (FEMA, 2000c).

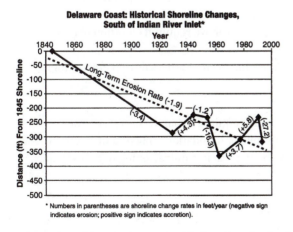

Figure 9.14 (A) Long-Term versus Medium-Term Erosion Rates and Erosion Vulnerability. *Source:* FEMA (2000c). (B) Short-Term Erosion at Melbourne Beach, Florida, 1999. *Source:* Photo by Ty Harrington/FEMA News Photo.

Principles of Coastal Zone Planning, Siting, Design, Construction, and Maintenance (FEMA, 2000c)

Hazard Identification

- Flood damage results from both short- and long-term increases in water levels, wave action, and erosion.
- Long-term erosion increases flood hazards over time.
- Flood hazards mapped as "A" zones on coastal flood insurance rate maps (FIRMs) can have greater hazard than riverine "A" zones because of wave height and changing site conditions (e.g., erosion, dune loss).
- Slope stability hazards and landslides are exacerbated in coastal bluff areas due to effects of drainage changes, removal of vegetation, and site development.

Siting

- Building close to the shoreline is vulnerable and removes any margin of safety against hazards.
- Because of erosion and shifting shoreline, even elevated buildings close to the shoreline may find themselves standing on active beach.
- Building close to other structures and to protective structures can redirect and concentrate storm forces.
- Siting buildings on top of erodible dunes and bluffs renders them vulnerable to serious damage.
- Buildings near unstabilized tidal inlets are subject to large-scale shoreline fluctuations; even stabilized tidal inlets have high erosion rates.

Design

- Shallow spread footing and slab foundations and continuous perimeter wall foundations may be subject to collapse in areas subject to wave action or erosion.
- Designs should incorporate freeboard above required elevation of the lowest floor.
- Corrosion-resistant materials are important in this salt-rich environment.

Construction

- Special construction practices are required in harsh coastal environments: structural connections, pile or foundation embedment, properly installed utility system components, bracing and fastening roofs and wall, proper inspection.

Maintenance

- Inspection, repair, and replacement of structural elements and connectors and maintenance of erosion and coastal flood protection measures are very important in the dynamic coastal environment.

Coastal Hazard Zones

Figures 9.15 and 9.16 illustrate the NFIP categories for FIRMs and coastal land use zoning. There are three hazard zones:

"**V**" **Zone:** Coastal high hazard area (HHA) in the special flood hazard area (SFHA) extending from offshore to the inland limit of a primary frontal dune or any area subject to high velocity wave action greater than 3 feet.

"**A**" **Zone:** Area of the SFHA within 100-year flood zone, subject to wave heights less than three feet, not within HHA.

"**X**" **Zone:** Shaded X (zone B) is in 500-year flood zone. Unshaded X (zone C) is above 500-year zone.

The dynamics of the coastal zone and the difficulty managing them are apparent in the well-known Lucas case in Isle of Palms, South Carolina. David Lucas bought two beachfront lots in the late 1980s and was restricted by a state law from building on the property due to erosion hazards. He took the case all the way to the U.S. Supreme Court and won a landmark decision that the restriction constituted a "taking" of his property. As a result, the state law was overturned and the state bought the properties, which were sold and developed. The top photo in figure 9.17 shows the property had a large beachfront in 1989, but the erosive forces changed the shoreline considerably by 1997 and undermined the new house built on the property. Figure 9.17 also shows the changing shoreline between 1949 and 1997.

Site planning can reduce the coastal wind, erosion, and flooding hazards by placing buildings outside of the V zone. Figure 9.18 shows that a modified layout places homes on the landward portion of the lot. Better yet, a cluster layout can provide community open space and coordinated open space management.

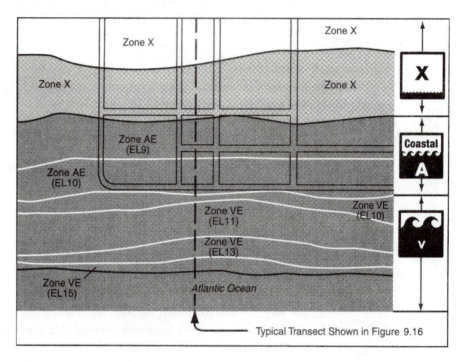

Figure 9.15 Plan View of Coastal Flood Zones: V, A, and X. *Source:* FEMA (2000c).

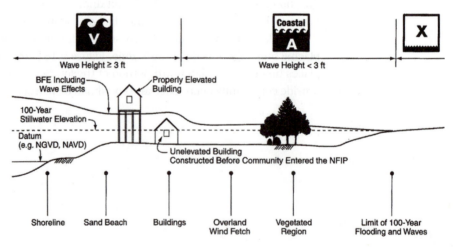

Figure 9.16 Elevation View of Coastal Flood Zones: V, A, and X. *Source:* FEMA (2000c).

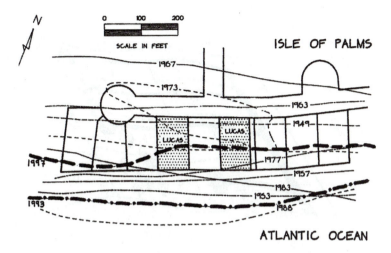

ISLE OF PALMS

SCALE IN FEET

0   100   200

1967

1973

1963

1949

LUCAS

LUCAS

1997

1977

1957

1983

1953

1993

1988

ATLANTIC OCEAN

Historical Vegetation Lines Superimposed on Lucas Lots

Figure 9.17 Shifting Shoreline on Lucas Property in Isle of Palms, South Carolina. Photos show site in 1989 and eroded shoreline in 1997. *Source:* FEMA (2000c).

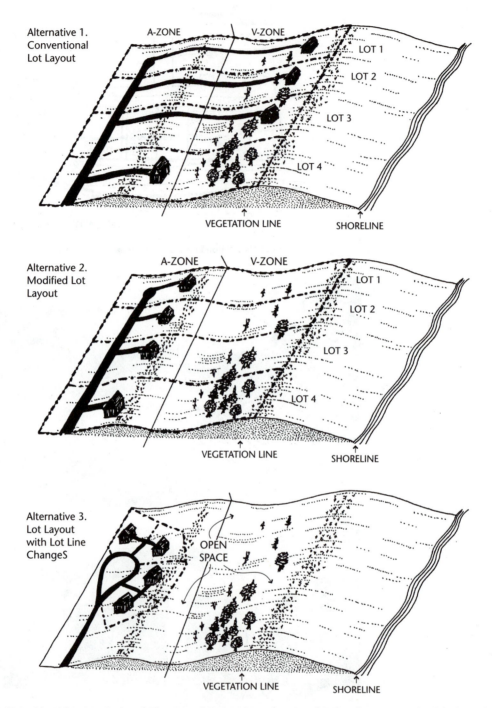

Figure 9.18 Residential Layout Options in the Coastal Zone. Alternatives 2 and 3 place homes outside of the hazardous V zone and allow the dynamic forces of the beach and dune area to act without causing damage or danger to people and property. *Source:* FEMA (2000c). Original graphic by Thomas Bartik, in Marya Morris, "Subdivision Design in Flood Hazard Areas." FEMA and American Planning Association, Planning Advisory Service Report 473. 1997.

Mitigating Geologic Hazards

Geologic hazards include localized slope problems (e.g., landslides), support problems (e.g., subsidence), and wider-scale seismic hazards (e.g., earthquakes, volcanic activity). These geologic hazards pose problems for building and development and must be considered in land use planning and management.

Applying hazard mitigation planning to geologic hazards involves the key steps of *assessing and mapping the hazard,* as well as exposure and vulnerability; *formulating measures to reduce exposure and vulnerability;* and *implementing these measures.* Most hazards pose relative risks depending on location, and it is important to understand the relative risk spatially and apply mitigation measures accordingly.

For example, an entire region may be susceptible to earthquake risk, but certain areas have a greater groundshaking and damage risk due to underlying geology. Some steep slope areas have a higher risk than others due to underlying materials. These relatively higher risk areas must be identified, and measures to reduce exposure (restricting all development) and vulnerability (requiring strict building standards) must be applied.

Perhaps the best source of geologic information is the USGS geologic map. A portion of a geologic map is given in figure 9.19 (for the full map see http://pubs.usgs.gov/mf/2003/mf-2412/mf-2412.pdf). It provides a map of surficial geology at the scale of the USGS quadrangle series (1:24,000), as well as several cross sections. Unfortunately, these maps are not available for the entire United States. For a complete description of geologic maps and map symbols see http://www.aqd.nps.gov/grd/usgsnps/gmap/gmap1.html.

Where available, they identify bedrock formations, the degree of consolidation of materials, and the locations of areas of geologic interest including mines and landfills, faults, sinkholes, and karst. The discussion accompanying the map provides geologic history and mineral resource potential of the area, as well as the geologic factors affecting land development.

Slope Stability

Each year, landslides, debris flow, and avalanches in the United States cause about $1.5 billion in damages and 25 fatalities (FEMA, 2000a). Slope failure occurs when the gravitational force of slope materials exceeds the resisting forces of friction, strength, and cohesion of the supporting materials. Certain properties of sloped terrain (such as steepness, layering or fracturing of materials, and absence of vegetation) can make them inherently susceptible to failure, and superimposing factors (such as additional moisture, overloading, and undercutting) can make matters worse (box 9.3). These factors can occur naturally or can be induced by humans' activities. Box 9.4 describes various types of slope failure and some of the nomenclature used in the field.

The hazards of slope failure or landsliding are obviously most prevalent in mountainous regions, although localized hazards may occur in other areas as well. The challenge to a local community concerned about landslide hazards involves

BOX 9.3—Factors Affecting Slope Failure: Gravity versus Resistance

Inherent Factors

- Slope
- Properties of underlying materials
  Slippage potential
  Layering
  Fracturing
  Unconsolidated materials
- Vegetation
- Moisture

Superimposed Factors

- Deterioration of materials
- Increased moisture
- Overloading
- Undercutting
- Earthquakes or other shocks

BOX 9.4—Types of Slope Failure

Slope failure can be distinguished by five types: **falls; slides; slumps; flows;** and **lateral spreads** that may occur on flat or gently sloping land due to liquefaction of underlying materials.

Fall—masses of rock and/or other material that move downslope by falling or bouncing

Slump—coherent or intact mass or rock and/or other material that moves downslope by rotational slip on surfaces that underlie and penetrate the landslide

Slide--incoherent or broken masses of rock and/or other material that have moved down-slope by sliding on a surface

Flow—masses of soil and other colluvial material that have moved downslope is a manner similar to the movement of a viscous fluid

Fall—masses of rock and/or other material that moves downslope by falling or bouncing

Slide—incoherent or broken masses of rock and/or other material that has moved downslope by sliding on a surface

Slump—coherent or intact mass or rock and/or other material that moves downslope by rotational slip on surfaces that underlie and penetrate the landslide

Flow—masses of soil and other colluvial material that have moved downslope in a manner similar to the movement of a viscous fluid

Flows can be characterized by the speed of movement and by the materials involved. In flows, materials actually take on the characteristics of a fluid. Air and water generally accompany the material making it more fluid by reducing friction. Slow flows are generally laminar where materials move without pulling apart, and rapid flows generally become turbulent where materials are churned. Exceptionally rapid flows of soil, rock and water, snow, and/or ice on very steep slopes are called **debris avalanches.** These are triggered by heavy rain or snow, melting snow, added weight, or shocks from earthquakes or other causes. Slower flows of solid materials, air, and water are called **debris flows.** If more than half of the solid material is smaller than sand, it is referred to as a **mudflow.** Soils subject to liquefaction may be subject to spontaneous flows. Very slow downslope flow of soils is called **creep.** The average flow rate of materials can range from a fraction of an inch per year to 4 or 5 inches per week. Most slope failures occur not as strictly falls, slides, slumps, or flows but as combinations called slide-flow combinations or **landslides.**

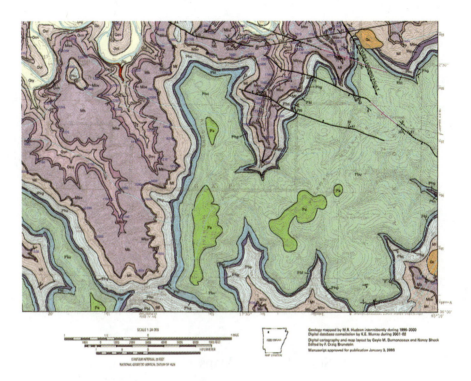

Figure 9.19 Portion of a USGS Geologic Quadrangle Map. Produced in 1997, the surface geology map is complemented by two sections. The lengthy text of the map (not shown here) describes in detail the geologic history, structure, stratigraphy, materials, mineral resources, and land use constraints. *Source:* Hudson and Murray (2003). For full map, see http://pubs. usgs.gov/mf/2003/mf-2412/mf-2412.pdf.

first identifying and mapping potential landslide areas. Based on this information, the community can then assess the degree of hazard and develop policies and controls to mitigate the hazard

Inventorying and Mapping Landslide Hazards

In mapping landslide hazards, the USGS suggests a sequence of progressively more detailed steps so that a general distribution of hazardous areas emerges early, and further study provides refinement. The first level of investigation, coincident with our rapid assessment, involves preparing a **slope map** and a **landslide inventory.** Slope mapping is described in chapter 12. The inventory identifies areas where landslides have occurred. Simple inventories can be done by carefully reviewing aerial photographs for landslide deposits and scars. More detailed inventories involve some field investigation in addition to photo analysis and may distinguish active from old slides, the type and depth of the slide, and the kind of geologic materials involved. Figure 9.20 gives an example of a landslide inventory map.

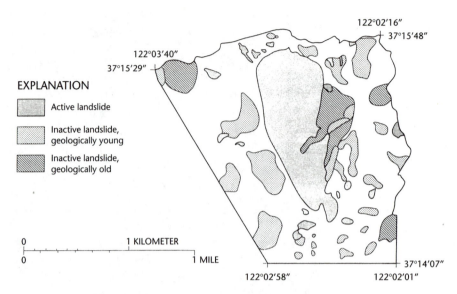

Figure 9.20 Landslide Inventory. *Source:* U.S. Geological Survey (1982).

Slope-Stability Maps

These maps distinguish the relative potential of different areas for landsliding. As discussed, many factors influence an area's susceptibility to slope failure. Including all of these factors in an analysis of slope stability is impractical. USGS has employed a fairly simple procedure that is reasonably well accepted. It is based on three parameters—the underlying bedrock material, steepness, and the presence or absence of earlier landslide deposits. Landslide deposits are identified by landslide inventories, and steepness is represented in slope maps. (Chapter 12 describes how to map slope steepness using topographic maps.)

Underlying geologic materials that are poorly consolidated contribute to landslide susceptibility. These include bedrock units with extensive shearing or jointing, or with structurally weak components such as breccia, and surficial deposits such as alluvial, colluvial, terrace, and talus deposits and artificial fill. The location of such materials can be interpreted from geologic maps. A simple method of identifying geologic units that may be susceptible to sliding is to overlay a landslide inventory map onto the geologic map. The types of geologic units where landslides have occurred are probably those most likely to fail.

Given the locational information on the three variables—slope, geologic materials, and landslide deposits—a composite map can be produced to rate areas on slope stability. In the slope-stability mapping of the San Francisco Bay region the following five slope stability categories were developed based on the three parameters (Nilsen, Wright, Vlasic, and Spangle, 1976):

1. **Stable:** Areas of 0–5% slope that are not underlain by landslide deposits.

2. **Generally Stable:** Areas of 5–15% slope that are not underlain by landslide deposits.
3. **Generally Stable to Marginally Stable:** Areas of greater than 15% slope that are not underlain by landslide deposits or bedrock units susceptible to landsliding.
4. **Moderately Unstable:** Areas of greater than 15% slope that are underlain by bedrock units susceptible to landsliding but not underlain by landslide deposits.
5. **Unstable:** Areas of any slope that are underlain by or immediately adjacent to landslide deposits.

Figure 9.21 shows an example of a landslide susceptibility map for the Congress Springs area of Santa Clara County, California. To produce the map, several factors were considered: steepness of slope, type of rock or surficial deposit, and locations of bedrock faults, springs, and former marshes. Note the "Yes-No-Maybe" approach (green light, red light, yellow light) for recommended land use. "Maybe" areas are those shown as Yes* and No* in figure 9.21. This type of overlay environmental zoning recognizes that some areas clearly are not hazardous and should be appropriate for construction and some areas are very hazardous and inappropriate for development. However, there are areas on the margin where moderate problems can be addressed with engineering design or construction practices, or where there is uncertainty. For these areas, a caution flag is raised by requiring an engineering site assessment before a building permit will be granted.

Support Problems

In addition to slope problems, ground failure can also result from support problems caused by the lowering of the ground surface due to **settlement** or **subsidence.** Settlement, which is discussed under soil properties in chapter 12, results from construction on compressible soils of low strength (table 12.1 in chapter 12 classifies soil strength). In the ground stability study of the San Francisco area cited earlier (Nilsen, Wright, Vlasic, and Spangle, 1976) a sixth category unrelated to slope was included:

Unstable Due to Settlement: Areas of 0–5% slope that include tidelands, marshlands, and swamplands that are underlain by moist unconsolidated muds.

Subsidence

Subsidence is most commonly caused by the removal of underground fluids (groundwater, oil, or natural gas), which play a role in supporting ground surfaces by filling the pores and layers of unconsolidated soils. Removal of these fluids causes the underlying materials to sink, and the ground surface drops. Groundwater withdrawals have caused considerable lowering of land surfaces in Mexico City where portions of the city have dropped over 30 feet, in the San Joaquin Valley

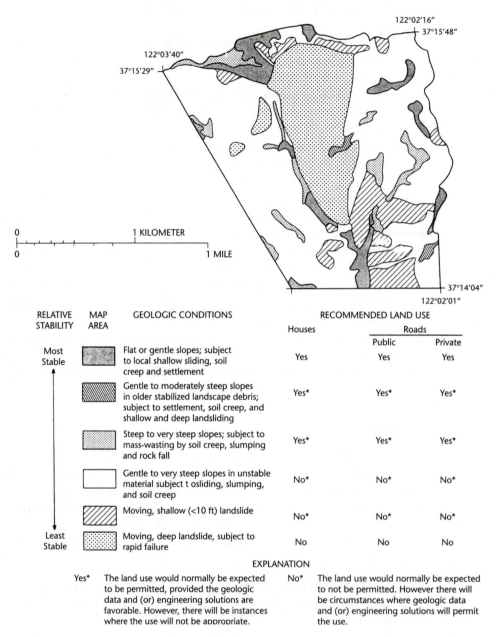

Figure 9.21 Potential Ground Movement and Recommended Land Use Policies. Compare to the landslide inventory map, figure 9.20. *Source:* U.S. Geological Survey (1982).

in California (26 feet at one location), and in the Houston-Galveston area of Texas (9 feet) (Griggs and Gilchrist, 1983). The Houston-Galveston subsidence has caused active surface faulting and has necessitated the construction of costly levees and other measures to protect subsided areas from flooding. Figure 9.22 shows the subsidence in the San Joaquin Valley from 1925 to 1977.

Figure 9.22 Ground Level Drop Due to Subsidence from Groundwater Withdrawal in San Joaquin Valley, California, Near Mendota. Approximate altitude of land surface based on research efforts of Joseph F. Poland (pictured). *Source:* U.S. Geological Survey (2000c).

Although subsidence caused by fluid extraction is usually irreversible, the process can be arrested by stopping the withdrawal or by injecting other fluids to replace those withdrawn. Other common causes of subsidence are the dewatering of wetlands, full-extraction underground mining methods, and underground solution in limestone terrain. Subsidence from underground mining has been a problem in central Appalachia, where mining occurs in populated areas and companies own subsurface rights and landowners own surface rights (Roth, Randolph, and Zipper, 1991; Zipper, Balfour, and Randolph, 1997).

Karst

Areas underlain by limestone or dolomite may develop **karst** or pocked topography. Acidic groundwater dissolves the carbonate or evaporative rocks and produces underground cavities into which surface materials can fall causing **sinkholes.** Figure 9.23 shows that the carbonate karst problem is common in Florida, Missouri, Texas, and most of Appalachia. Solution weathering of limestone and other carbonate or soluble rock creates pocked landscape, sinkholes and caves (figure

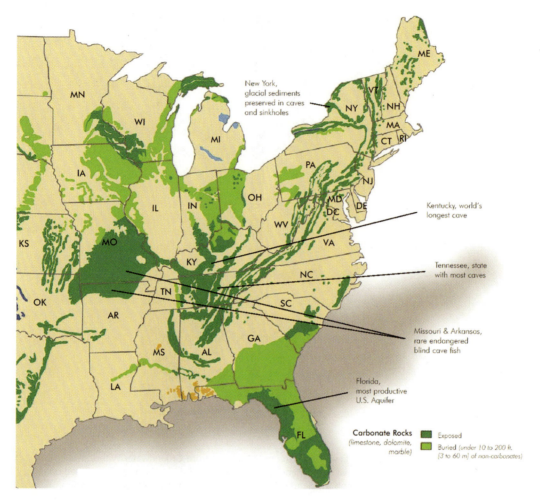

Figure 9.23 Karst (Sinkhole) Terrains of the Eastern United States That Are Underlain by Soluble Rock. *Source:* George Veni. 2002. "Revising the Karst Map of the United States." *Journal of Cave and Karst Studies* 64(1): p.49. Copyright National Speleological Society, used with permission.

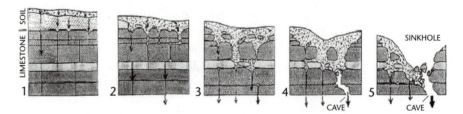

Figure 9.24 Solution Weathering of Limestone Creates Karst.

9.24). Figure 9.25 shows a sinkhole collapse risk map, based on geologic investigation of surface, subsurface, and drainage characteristics. Not only do karst sinkholes cause serious support problems, but also they provide direct avenues for groundwater contamination, particularly with the common practice of filling them with waste materials (see chapter 15). They are also subject to flooding when

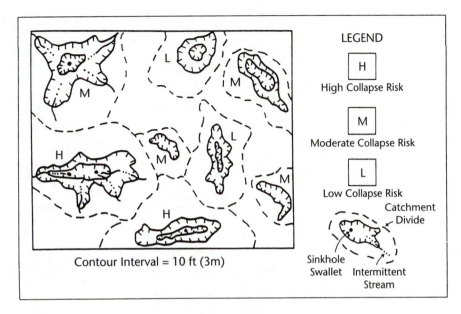

Figure 9.25 Sinkhole Collapse Risk Map. *Source:* Phillip Kemmerly, 1993, "Sinkhole Hazards and Risk Assessment in a Planning Context." *Journal of the American Planning Association* 58(2): 227. Reprinted by permission.

runoff exceeds the drainage capacity of the sinkhole. The natural process of sinkhole development can be accelerated by human activities including water withdrawal and ground vibrations.

Construction of structures and waste disposal systems like sewage lagoons and landfills should obviously avoid areas of potential sinkhole activity. These areas can be identified from USGS 7.5-minute quadrangle maps, which show existing sinkholes, and from geologic maps, which indicate sinkholes, abandoned mines, karst areas, and limestone deposits susceptible to karst activity. An increasing number of communities are developing overlay zoning in karst areas to protect groundwater, sensitive caves, and property values (Belo, 2003).

Seismic and Volcanic Hazards

Earthquakes pose a severe risk in active areas of the United States, mostly in the Pacific states. The 1994 Northridge, California, quake caused approximately $30 billion in damage, and the 1989 Loma Prieta quake in northern California caused $6 billion (FEMA, 2000a). Although there was loss of life, effective earthquake hazard mitigation planning kept the death toll in those quakes small compared with major quakes in less prepared parts of the world. The lesser magnitude 1985 Mexico City quake killed more than 5,000 people.

Most earthquakes are caused by the tectonic movement of the earth's major crustal plates, shown in figure 9.26, that float on more fluid interior materials. Figure 9.27 shows that nearly all of the earthquake history of the United States is at those plate interactions. Stress is generated on these plates by convection currents in the fluid materials and is released by slippage along weaknesses or faults in the

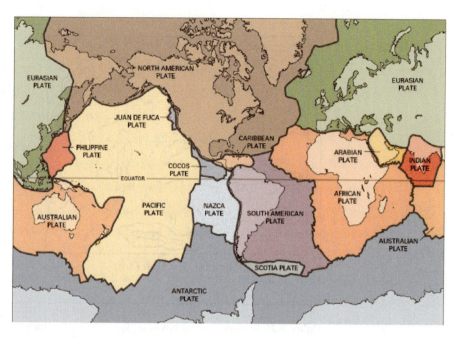

Figure 9.26 Tectonic Plates. As these plates move, strain accumulates, faults slip, and earthquakes occur. *Source:* U.S. Geological Survey, http://geology.er.usgs.gov/eastern/plates.html.

crust. Over time, plate movement builds up pressure that must be relieved periodically. If fault surfaces are smooth, plates may move "aseismically" without building pressure. However, if movement along faults sticks, compresses, or bends, pressure will build up, ultimately to be relieved "seismically" by a sudden dramatic movement or earthquake.

Faults occur throughout the tectonic plates, and major intraplate fissures can result in significant quakes. The famous New Madrid, Missouri, quakes of 1811–12, were caused by major intraplate rifts near the middle of the North American plate. However, most major faults occur where two tectonic plates interact. More than 95 percent of earthquake epicenters are located along the plate boundaries shown in figure 9.26. The 1985 Mexican earthquake that was measured at a magnitude of 7.8 on the Richter scale[1] and killed more than 5,000 was centered where the Cocos plate intersects the North American plate.

Earthquake Hazards

Earthquakes pose a number of hazards for human developments as a result of fault displacement, groundshaking, ground failure, flooding, and indirect effects such as fire, fuel or water line rupture, and damage to critical facilities. Seismic or

---

1. Earthquake magnitude is a measure of the strain energy released by an earthquake as calculated from the record made by the event on a seismograph. In 1935, Charles Richter defined local magnitude, or Richter magnitude, as the logarithm (base 10) of the amplitude in micrometers of the maximum amplitude of seismic waves that would be observed on a standard torsion seismograph of a distance of about 60 miles from the epicenter.

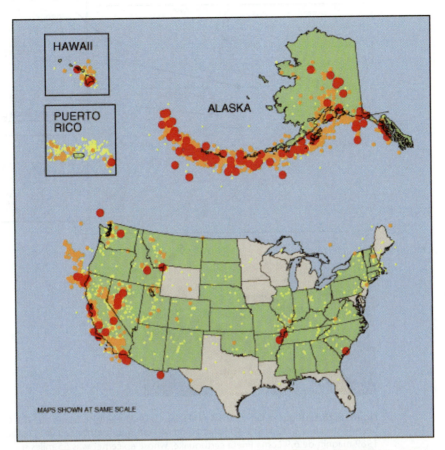

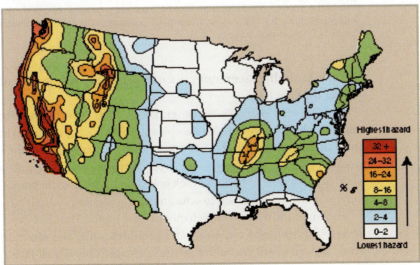

Figure 9.27 History of Major Earthquakes and Hazard Risk Map of the United States. *Source:* U.S. Geological Survey (2003a).

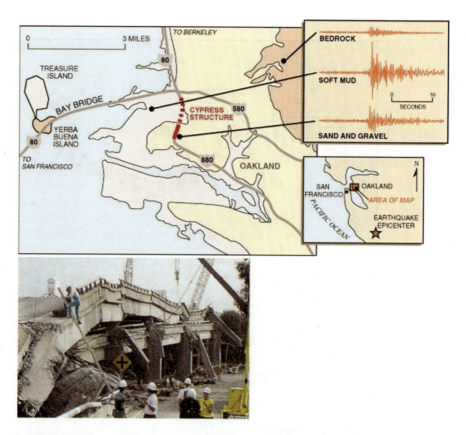

Figure 9.28 Earthquake Groundshaking Depends on Underlying Materials. The Cypress freeway structure in Oakland (CA) that stood on soft mud (dashed red line) collapsed in the 1989 magnitude 6.9 Loma Prieta earthquake, whose epicenter was 55 miles south. Adjacent parts of the freeway (solid red) that were built on firmer ground remained standing. Seisograms show that the shaking was especially severe in the soft mud. Photo: Lloyd S. Cluff. *Source:* U.S. Geological Survey (2001).

aseismic **fault displacement** can cause significant damage to structures built on or near the fault line.

Most seismic damages, however, result from **groundshaking,** which can extend far beyond the earthquake epicenter. Although groundshaking in the vicinity of an earthquake will obviously depend on the magnitude of the quake and the distance from the epicenter, it also depends on the underlying soils and geology. As shock waves travel from dense rock to less dense rock to unconsolidated material such as alluvium and finally to saturated materials like muds, they tend to increase in amplitude and decrease in velocity. Ground motion thus lasts longer and is more severe in unconsolidated and water-saturated soils, and structures located on these materials will encounter greater damage. This is well illustrated in figure 9.28. It describes the groundshaking from the 1989 San Francisco Bay area earthquake that caused the collapse of the Oakland I-880 freeway. Groundshaking grew in magnitude as the shock waves encountered the soft bay muds.

Potential damage due to groundshaking also depends on the structures themselves. Wood frame houses tend to be about the safest, while old, unreinforced masonry structures are the most dangerous. Newer reinforced concrete buildings may allow some deformation without fracturing and thus be able to absorb some groundshaking; and modern steel-frame buildings generally are flexible enough to absorb shock, although the movement will likely damage glass and other rigid components (Jaffe, Butler, and Thurow, 1981). As the relationship between damage, groundshaking, and underlying geologic materials has been better understood, land use and building codes have reflected this understanding. Figure 9.30 shows that building strength codes not only have become more stringent in California but also have distinguished underlying materials, with higher standards required for construction on soft soil as compared with hard rock.

Ground failure due to landslides, liquefaction, subsidence, and settlement can be triggered by earthquakes. In assessing earthquake hazards it is important to locate areas susceptible to these slope and support problems. Flooding of low-lying areas can also be a potential hazard as a result of earthquake-induced dam failure or tsunamis (the "tidal waves" caused by earthquakes in the bottom of the sea or bay).

In the 1906 San Francisco earthquake, most of the damage came not from the groundshaking and failure but from the fires caused by them; furthermore, ruptured water lines impeded the effort to control the fires. These and other **indirect earthquake hazards** should be considered in a comprehensive earthquake risk assessment and mitigating effort. Of particular importance are potential damages to "critical facilities." These may include facilities required to maintain health and safety such as hospitals and fire stations; large population centers such as sports arenas; and facilities that could pose special dangers if damaged, such as nuclear power plants, chemical plants, hazardous waste storage sites, and so on.

Assessing Seismic Hazards

A first step in assessing seismic hazards is to gauge the earthquake potential of the area to see what community concern and response is warranted. Figure 9.27 gives a map of earthquake intensity based on historical seismic activity in the United States. Intensity is based on expected earthquake damage.[2] Much of California is shown in the most hazardous zone as expected, but so are several other areas of the country that have experienced intraplate quakes.

Based on historic information, if hazard mitigation is warranted, an inventory and mapping of earthquake hazards should be conducted. These maps may include the following:

- A map showing unconsolidated and water-saturated soils can indicate where groundshaking is likely to be most severe. For example, figure 9.29

---

2. Magnitude measures the amplitude of the shock waves of a quake; intensity indicates the potential observed effects of an earthquake of an expected magnitude at a particular place. A 12-grade Modified Mercalli Intensity Scale is used today ranging from I ("Not felt except by a very few") to V ("Felt by nearly everyone; some dishes broken; pendulum clocks may stop") to XII ("Damage total; waves seen on ground; objects thrown upward into the air").

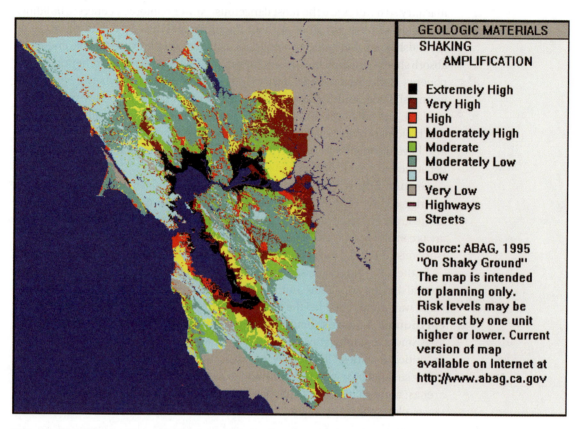

Figure 9.29 Earthquake Groundshaking Potential in San Francisco Bay Area. Low shaking areas are on bedrock; high shaking areas are on soft materials. Figure at right zooms in on area at south end of the Bay. *Source:* Association of Bay Area Government (1995).

shows two maps prepared by the Association of (San Francisco) Bay Area Governments (ABAG), showing the risk of earthquake groundshaking in Bay Area communities. The small-scale map shows the entire region, and the large-scale map zooms in on a portion of Santa Clara County at the south end of the Bay on the regional map.

- Maps showing unstable slopes and dam failure and tsunami inundation areas can indicate areas susceptible to earthquake-induced landsliding and flooding. The differentiation of risk zones is the first step in land use planning for seismic hazard mitigation.
- A map showing critical facilities can locate important and hazardous facilities.

California's Seismic Hazard Mapping Act of 1990 mandated the California Department of Conservation (CDC) to identify and map the state's most prominent earthquake hazards. The department's Seismic Hazard Zone Mapping Program maps California's areas prone to liquefaction (failure of water-saturated soil) and earthquake-induced landslides. Cities and counties use the maps to regulate development. They can withhold development permits until geologic or soils inves-

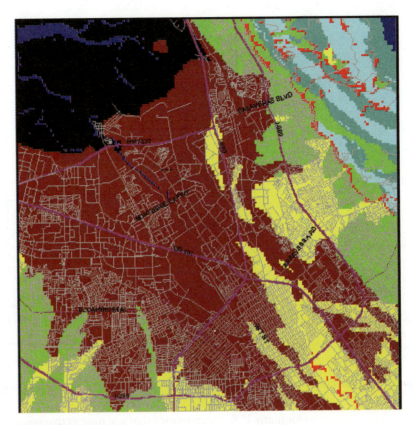

Figure 9.29 (Continued)

tigations are conducted for specific sites and mitigation measures are incorporated into development plans. Sellers of property use the maps to determine if their sites are in a hazard area; if so, they must disclose this to the buyer. The CDC produced the first maps in 1996 and continues to prepare them in 2003 (CDC, 2003).

All of these maps can provide the spatial or locational basis for developing safety policies and controls to mitigate seismic hazards, such as land use zoning and building codes. Figure 9.30 illustrates how California building codes have become increasingly more stringent in seismic safety between the 1950s and the 1980s. As discussed earlier in this chapter, Nelson and French's (2002) study of the 1994 Northridge earthquake argued that effective earthquake hazard mitigation must go beyond building codes to include retrofitting older buildings to current standards, quality comprehensive plans, and effective implementation of land use controls and codes.

Volcanic Hazards

Another related geologic hazard comes from active volcanoes. Only few areas of the world are subject to these hazards, but for those that are, the hazard is potentially catastrophic. The eruption of Mount St. Helens in 1980 was a wake-up call

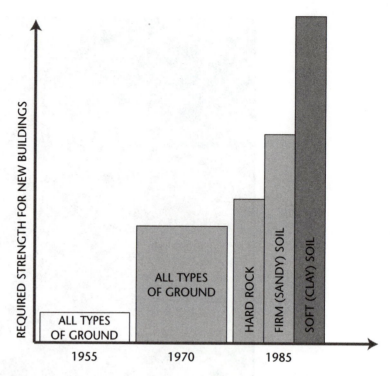

Figure 9.30 California Earthquake Building Codes for New Construction. *Source:* U.S. Geological Survey (2001).

for many U.S. communities that are near active volcanoes. The hazards of volcanoes are generally four:

1. **Lava flows:** Molten rock or magma that pours or oozes onto the earth's surface.
2. **Pyroclastic flows:** Hot avalanches of lava fragments and volcanic gas formed by the collapse of lava flows or eruption clouds.
3. **Tephra:** Fragments of rock blasted high into the air. Large fragments fall close to the volcano. Small fragments or ash can travel hundreds of miles.
4. **Lahars:** Fast-moving slurries of rock, mud, and water that look and behave like flowing wet concrete. Pyroclastic flows can generate lahars by melting snow and ice.

Whereas tephra and the earthquakes accompanying volcanic eruptions affect large areas adjacent to the volcano, the other hazards follow topographic characteristics of surrounding land and thus can be mapped. Figure 9.31 shows a hazard zone map for lahars and pyroclastic flows for Glacier Peak in the Cascade Mountains east of Bellingham, Washington. Identifying areas that are at risk can inform both land use plans and emergency preparedness plans. USGS has conducted volcanic hazard assessment reports and maps for most volcanoes in the Pacific Northwest (U.S. Geological Survey, 2003b).

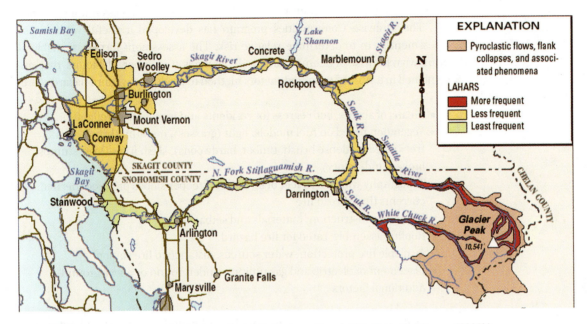

Figure 9.31 Volcanic Hazard Map for Glacier Peak, Washington. *Source:* U.S. Geological Survey (2000b).

Wildfire Hazards

Wildfires have always been a hazard to forestland, but suburban and ex-urban residential development has brought that hazard to America's backyard. Wildfires in 2002 in Colorado and Oregon demonstrated once again the hazard and risk to communities. As early as 1985, when 1,400 homes were destroyed by wildfire in California and Florida, it became apparent that a concerted effort was necessary to mitigate wildfire hazards.

As a result, the U.S. Forest Service, the National Fire Protection Association, and other organizations established the National Wildland/Urban Interface Fire Program. That program initiated the Firewise Communities program to mitigate wildfire hazards by education and technical assistance to community firefighters, urban planners, landscape architects, building designers, and contractors (Firewise, 2001).

Like most natural hazards, wildfire is plagued by the disaster-relief-rebuild-disaster cycle discussed earlier. People tend to ignore a hazard until a disaster occurs, then reach out for help, only to rebuild in the hazardous area and subject themselves (and others) to future disasters. After Oakland lost 3,500 homes to wildfire in 1991, many rebuilt in the same area without vegetative cleanup or improved construction practices. Though they thought such a wildfire would never return, history showed that disastrous fires had struck in 1923 and 1970. Memories are short.

Wildfire hazard mitigation planning follows the same process outlined in box 9.1. The Firewise Communities program has developed a useful wildfire risk assessment form to determine relative risk. The assessment form is available at http://www.firewise.org/communities/. It includes a number of factors that are combined in a sum-of-weighted-factors method to produce a wildfire hazard score:

- Means of access, both egress for residents and ingress for firefighters
- Vegetation based on fuel models: light (grasses), medium (brush, small trees), heavy (dense brush, timber, hardwoods), slash fuels (logs, stumps, broken understory)
- Topography within 300 feet of structure: steeper slopes produce thermal currents that spread fire
- Building construction: materials and setbacks
- Roofing assembly: rated for fire hazard
- Available fire protection: water sources, distance to fire station
- Placement of electric and gas utilities: underground or above ground
- Additional factors

Specific measures to reduce wildfire hazard include fire-resistant landscaping and construction materials, maintenance of wild vegetation that serves as fuel, and improved fire protection and response.

Other Natural Hazards

Most other natural hazards, like flooding and coastal storms, are weather related. Tornadoes, lightning storms, and winter storms create damage and death throughout the United States every year. Different from geologic, flooding, and coastal hazards, these weather hazards are more pervasive. Certain regions are more susceptible to tornadoes ("tornado alley" of the Midwest—Oklahoma, Kansas, Nebraska, Missouri, Texas, and surrounding states) and to winter storms (northern states) and they need to mitigate these hazards with building codes and emergency response.

Although we think of major storms as the main weather-related hazards, and they are in terms of property damage, extreme heat is the biggest killer. About 175 people die each year from extreme heat, mostly in urban areas. These do not include air-pollution-related deaths. Urban air pollution episodes are often coincident and exacerbated by extreme heat. Drought and heat impacts water supplies, air quality, natural and introduced vegetation, and aquatic life. Smart land use reflects an understanding of these hazards and impacts and incorporates measures to mitigate them. These include use of drought-resistant and native landscaping, contingency water supplies, and conserving natural vegetative buffers at the land-water interface.

The National Drought Mitigation Center at the University of Nebraska provides drought information, forecasts, and a daily drought index. The index combines information used in a number of drought indices relying on rainfall, snowpack, streamflow, temperature, soil moisture, and vegetation condition. The index ranges from D0 (abnormally dry) to D4 (exceptional drought) (see http://enso. unl.edu/monitor/monitor.html).

Summary

This chapter introduced the important topic of natural hazard mitigation and discussed its application to flooding, coastal, geologic, wildfire, and other hazards. Effective hazard mitigation requires understanding the hazard, mapping relative hazard based on that understanding, and formulating and implementing enforceable measures to mitigate exposure and vulnerability. These measures include land use and building regulations that preclude development in high hazard areas and require stringent standards in moderate hazard areas; property acquisition and relocation in high hazard areas; education; and emergency preparedness. Natural hazard mitigation plans should address multiple hazards, be prepared in anticipation rather than after a natural disaster, and be reevaluated and modified as necessary after each hazard event.

Inland flooding hazard mitigation requires quality mapping and land use controls. Through FEMA, the U.S. NFIP has made flood hazard boundary maps available to all flood-prone communities. In addition, the availability of flood insurance is conditional on local floodplain management, including restrictive zoning in the 100-year floodplain. These standards provide a baseline of protection for new development, but many communities have gone beyond these requirements to protect more flood-prone and riparian areas and have addressed existing exposed developments through relocation.

Coastal hazards result from the dynamic nature of beach, dune, and bluff processes and exposure to coastal storms including hurricanes. Restricting development in hazard areas and preserving natural protection mechanisms like dune systems are important elements of coastal hazard mitigation.

Slope-stability hazards are a function of slope steepness and underlying materials. Mapping these features as well as evidence of past landslides can give a good spatial representation of slope stability and provide information on which to base land use regulation to reduce exposure and vulnerability.

Likewise, support problems like karst and sinkholes can be assessed, mapped, and controlled. Subsidence problems are usually caused by human activities like groundwater, oil, or natural gas pumping and subsurface mining. Hazard mitigation requires understanding the processes involved and controlling the activities to reduce the hazard, exposure, and vulnerability.

Unlike slope and support problems, earthquake hazards affect entire regions. More pervasive hazards from earthquake groundshaking require more widespread controls, like building standards for all new development. Still, there are areas within earthquake regions that are more susceptible to groundshaking hazards than others due to underlying materials such an unconsolidated materials, clays, and muds. Effective mitigation requires identifying and mapping these areas of higher relative hazard and applying more stringent mitigation measures.

10 ■ Ecosystem and Watershed Management

Ecosystem management (EM) and watershed management (WSM) have emerged as holistic approaches to integrate the wide range of objectives and perspectives in environmental land planning and management. These two approaches share some common themes. They both aim to

- integrate science and politics;
- consider variable scales, telescoping to larger landscapes and zooming in to smaller sites (see figure 10.1);
- have a long-term time perspective, in terms of both process and outcomes;
- be scientifically based, using both initial "best science" assessment and long-term scientific learning;
- focus on ecological integrity and incorporate social and economic objectives;
- consider a wide range of regulatory and nonregulatory solutions and integrate them into a comprehensive strategy;
- engage stakeholders to tap scientific and local knowledge, perceptions, and values; and
- use monitoring and adaptive management to learn from implementation and fine-tune strategies.

This chapter first describes the basic principles of ecosystem management and watershed protection, including scientific assessments and integrating strategies and programs. The chapter then explores institutional arrangements for ecosystem and watershed management, and finally, presents recent applications of EM and WSM.

Principles of Ecosystem Management

Historically, we have managed environmental resources with a singular, reductionist approach. In nature, however, these resources are inextricably linked not only to each other but also to human activities. It makes sense to look at them as a

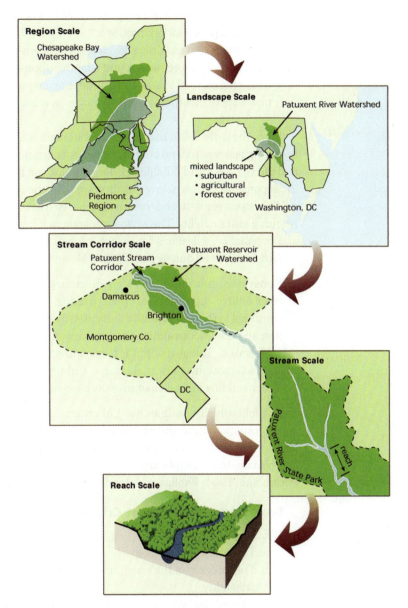

Figure 10.1 Ecosystem and Watershed Management Act across a Hierarchy of Scales. *Source:* FIWSCR (1998).

whole, to manage them as ecosystems. Ecosystems can be studied at a variety of scales, from an isolated tidal pool to a continent (figure 10.1). Human society is an important component and must be viewed as part of the ecosystem to be managed.

The current movement toward EM was prompted in the late 1980s by a number of converging factors, including the following:

▪ Heightened recognition of the "biodiversity crisis" of habitat destruction and species extinction

- Limited success of piecemeal environmental laws and programs in meeting the expectations of a range of stakeholders, including both development and preservation interests
- Theoretical and empirical developments in environmental management that called for more holistic and adaptive approaches
- Changing societal values and attitudes about natural systems, requiring new ways of incorporating those values in management

Since the early 1990s managing ecosystem integrity and health has become the operating policy of federal land management agencies, like the U.S. Forest Service and the U.S. Fish and Wildlife Service (Phillips and Randolph, 1998). It developed in response to concerns over biodiversity and the limitations of species-specific wildlife management and commodity-based resource management to ensure resource sustainability. The ecosystem approach has been adopted by many local and regional organizations for environmental management (Yaffee et al., 1996). As it has evolved during the 1990s, EM can be defined as follows:

> **Ecosystem management** is an integrative, interdisciplinary, adaptive, and collaborative approach to policymaking, planning, and management, grounded in the best scientific information available, recognizing uncertainties, and the understanding that human activity and ecosystems are inextricably linked. The goal of EM is to sustain and/or restore ecosystem integrity and biological diversity at all spatial and temporal scales through scientific understanding and collaborative decision making.

The following list outlines five EM criteria. They include an ecological orientation; appropriate time and spatial scales; scientific data collection and analysis; a distinct role of humans in ecosystems and in planning and management; and appropriate interdisciplinary, interagency, and adaptive management actions (Grumbine, 1994; Phillips and Randolph, 2000; Smith, 1995).

Ecosystem Management Criteria

1. Ecological Orientation
   a. The ecosystem dictates use and management strategies.
   b. The integrity of the ecosystem is to be preserved in ways to seek sustainability.
   c. Natural biodiversity is to be maintained, focusing on how the biologic community functions as a whole within the ecosystem.
2. Time and Spatial Scale
   a. Long-term time horizon, looking at future generations of species including people.
   b. Boundaries are set by the ecosystem, not by jurisdictional borders.
   c. Hierarchy of ecosystem scales allows addressing larger landscape interconnections through site-scale actions.
3. Scientific Basis, Data Collection, and Analysis
   a. Acquire as complete a knowledge base as possible within technological, scientific, and budgetary limits.

b. Use adaptive approaches to experiment and acquire new information to fill gaps in knowledge.

4. Role of Humans and Society

a. Humans are part of ecosystems: Social, cultural, and economic values of humans must be considered in management of land and ecosystems;

b. Humans have damaged the environment: Practice restoration.

c. Humans will change the environment: Minimize and mitigate impact.

d. Collaborative planning and decision making requires stakeholder involvement.

5. Management Actions

a. Integrate management within agencies and between agencies.

b. Integrate interdisciplinary practices into management strategies.

c. Monitor management practices for effectiveness.

d. Practice adaptive management: Learn from monitoring and modify practices as necessary.

The experience and experimentation in EM has been widespread. The approach has many well-accepted concepts. However, putting them into practice has proven difficult. Early experiments, such as the Greater Yellowstone Ecosystem program proved too complex to overcome political and interagency conflicts (Goldstein, 1992). The federal agencies have had problems institutionalizing the concepts of EM in their planning and management (Fitzsimmons, 1999). In addition, the principles have been applied in literally thousands of ecological and watershed restoration projects on private and public lands with mixed success.

Ecosystem Management on Public Lands

Ecosystem management did not enter the federal government vernacular until the early 1990s, but its roots go back much further. The organic acts of the national forest system (1891) and the national park system (1916) contain some of the principles of the "Ecosystem Management Criteria" list. The multiple use and sustained yield concepts of the 1950s and 1960s related to time and spatial scale and scientific analysis but were largely interpreted by the agencies to be a basis of commodity production rather than ecosystem integrity. However, the passage of the National Environmental Policy Act (NEPA) in 1970 and public lands planning legislation in the late 1970s, forced agencies to incorporate broader issues into their planning. Still, most efforts were procedural. It became clear that it is difficult to teach "old agency dogs" new tricks. It took some time before EM principles began to replace commodity production objectives in the Forest Service and the Bureau of Land Management and recreation interests in the Park Service. But, the agencies have been moving away from expert-driven, commodity/recreation-based, rational-comprehensive planning and decision making to more participatory, ecosystem/integrity-based, adaptive planning, although most analysts agree that the transformation is not complete.

By the late 1980s, many of the "old dogs" were retiring and were replaced by a new generation of natural resources managers, many fresh out of progressive academic programs. They began to transform the agencies. In professional forestry associations and in the Forest Service, for example, a new movement called New Perspectives, then New Forestry, began to rethink forest management in response to concerns over diminishing public support, declining biodiversity, and long-term ecosystem health that would ultimately determine resource sustainability. By the early 1990s, this movement evolved to EM, which Forest Service chief Dale Robertson declared in 1992 would be the policy for the national forest system.

However, efforts to institutionalize this policy in Forest Service planning regulations in 1995 met with political opposition from commodities interests who feared diminished production from the national forests and from some policy analysts who questioned the ability to systematically manage the resources on an ecological rather than an economic basis (Flick and King, 1995). The proposed rules were withdrawn, and attention was refocused on "forest health" (a "Mom and apple pie" issue no one could oppose) rather than EM. By late 2000, however, the National Forest Service did approve revised planning rules, incorporating many of the principles of EM, as shown in box 10.1 (USDA, USFS, 2000). But the Forest Service had been practicing EM for many years under the 1992 administrative policy, and forest management plans began reflecting the principles long before the change in rules (Phillips and Randolph, 1998). Some of these cases are presented in the last section of this chapter.

Ecosystem Management on Private Lands

Many skeptics thought that EM would be limited to public land and resource applications because of the complexities involved. They assumed that single ownership of large blocks of natural landscapes was necessary to achieve ecosystem functions and objectives. However, in April 1993 Secretary of Interior Bruce Babbitt described three habitat conservation plans (HCPs) on private land under the Endangered Species Act (ESA) as examples of "ecosystem management." Responding studies of HCP projects conducted at that time showed that they fell short of the EM criteria given in the "Ecosystem Management Criteria" list (Smith 1995). Still, his statement begged the question of whether or not EM could be practiced on private lands.

Land conservation efforts across the country during the 1990s indicated that EM principles could be used in managing ecosystem integrity and biodiversity at a variety of scales and ownerships by federal, state, and local agencies; property owners; and nonprofit groups. These efforts are chronicled in different sources, including Yaffe et al.'s (1996) "Ecosystem Management in the United States: An Assessment of Current Experience." These inventories list hundreds of examples of mostly community-based activities in ecological restoration, landowner stewardship, land trusts for habitats and biodiversity, and other programs and projects. Although these projects are labeled "ecosystem management," most of them used watersheds as the defining boundaries for planning and management. With private lands, it is often difficult to distinguish between EM and WSM, especially when watershed protection and restoration programs aim to protect habitats and other ecological resources.

BOX 10.1—Forest Service Planning Rules Reflecting Ecosystem Management Principles

Framework for Planning

1. Identification and consideration of issues
2. Information development and interpretation
3. Proposed actions (plus NEPA requirements)
4. Plan decisions, amendments, revisions
5. Site specific decisions
6. Monitoring and evaluation for adaptive management

Key Principles

- Collaborative planning for sustainability
- Ecological, social and economic sustainability
- Contribution of Science
- Special considerations
- Planning documentation

(National Forest System Land Resource Management Planning: Final Rule, November 2000)

Ecosystem Management, TNC-Style: "Conservation by Design"

Among the groups and agencies throughout the world engaged in some version of EM, The Nature Conservancy (TNC) is a good example. TNC is now the world's largest environmental organization with over 1 million members. As a land trust, the Conservancy has protected 12 million acres in the United States and 92 million acres around the world. As TNC has grown, its mission has become more ambitious. Once focused on protecting unique sites ("the Last Great Places"), the Conservancy now sees a larger potential to piece those places together to preserve "the diversity of life on Earth by protecting the lands and waters" natural communities need to survive. Under its "conservation by design" policy, it aims to conserve "portfolios of functional conservation areas" within and across ecoregions (TNC, 2001).

TNC's approach to "ecoregional planning and management" is characterized as comprehensive, scientific, collaborative, and community-based. TNC has realized that to protect functioning ecosystems, it must look scientifically beyond individual properties to larger ecological mosaics. The following four basic steps, given along with key terms, are used in the conservation-by-design ecoregional planning process:

1. ***Set priorities through ecoregional planning.*** The Conservancy is using the best available science to analyze each of the country's 63 ecoregions, rate the most significant natural areas, and identify the suite of sites (portfolio) that must be conserved within each ecoregion to sustain its ecological processes and diversity.

   - **Ecoregion:** Relatively large geographic areas of land and water delineated by climate, vegetation, geology, and other patterns (see figure 10.2).
   - **Portfolio:** The suite of conservation areas within an ecoregion selected to represent and conserve the conservation targets and their genetic and ecological variation.

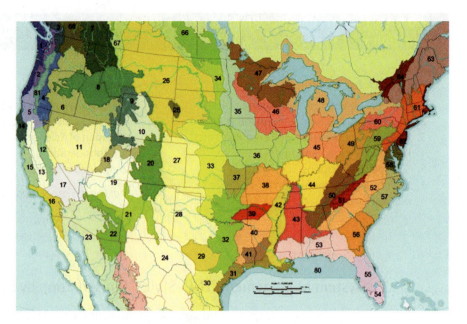

Figure 10.2 63 Ecoregions of the United States. *Source:* Dan Dorfman, The Nature Conservancy, (2001). Used with permission.

- ▪ **Conservation targets:** Specific components of biodiversity used to design ecoregional portfolios and develop and prioritize conservation strategies: ecological systems, natural communities, species (see figure 10.3 of Sonora Desert).

2. ***Develop conservation strategies.*** Identify conservation targets and evaluate methods of abating threats by analyzing stresses (e.g., inappropriate development, ditching/draining wetlands, fire suppression, habitat fragmentation, degradation of waterways, invasive species).

- ▪ **Platform sites:** Placed to showcase effective threat abatement and ecosystem protection by collaborating with key agencies, organizations, and individuals whose partnerships are essential to achieve tangible, lasting conservation at an effective scale.

- ▪ **Functional landscapes:** Intended to conserve all biodiversity and are large in scale (>20,000 acres).

3. ***Take direct conservation action.*** TNC often tries to identify unroaded natural areas that may serve as functional landscapes that may be available for protection. Figure 11.20 shows a GIS inventory map produced from data layers on vegetation and roads that shows such forested blocks >15,000 acres. TNC can then target these areas for acquisition or conservation easements.

- ▪ **Conserve:** Area is conserved or functional when its biodiversity health score has achieved a rank of good or very good, and its threat is low or medium.

- ▪ **Functional conservation area:** Geographic area needed to maintain conservation targets and supporting ecological processes within acceptable ranges of variability over the long term.

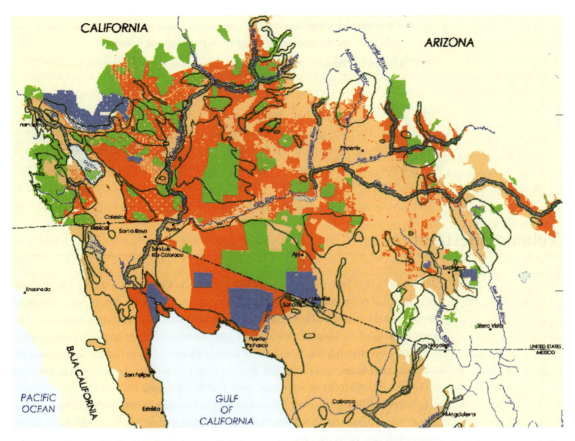

1

An area having permanent protection from conversion of natural land cover and a mandated management plan in operation to maintain a natural state within which disturbance events (of natural type, frequency, intensity, and legacy) are allowed to proceed without interference or are mimicked through management.

1.3 Million Acres within Ecoregion   **1.3 Million Acres within Conservation Sites**

2

An area having permanent protection from conversion of natural land cover and a mandated management plan in operation to maintain a primarily natural state, but which may receive uses or management practices that degrade the quality of existing natural communities, including suppression of natural disturbance.

4.8 Million Acres within Ecoregion   **3.2 Million Acres within Conservation Sites**

3

An area having permanent protection from conversion of natural land cover for the majority of the area, but subject to extractive uses of either a broad, low-intensity type (e.g., logging) or localized intense type (e.g., mining). It also confers protection to federally listed endangered and threatened species throughout the area.

12.1 Million Acres within Ecoregion   **5.9 Million Acres within Conservation Sites**

4

There are no known public or private institutional mandates or legally recognized easements or deed restrictions held by the managing entity to prevent conversion of natural habitat types to anthropogenic habitat types. The area generally allows conversion to unnatural land cover throughout.

37.0 Million Acres within Ecoregion   **12.9 Million Acres within Conservation Sites**

Figure 10.3 GAP Analysis of Sonoran Desert Ecoregion Showing Conservation Sites and GAP Status Codes (1–4). *Source:* Rob Marshall, The Nature Conservancy, 1999. Used with permission.

- **Functional sites:** Intended to conserve a small set of conservation targets, such as one species with limited spatial requirements.
4. ***Measure conservation success.*** After conservation action is taken, monitor biodiversity and ecological health.

For example, Virginia has six distinct ecoregions and TNC has applied its conservation by design approach in six portfolio areas (Virginia Coast Reserve, Green Sea, Chesapeake Rivers, the Piedmont, Warm Springs Mountain, and Clinch Valley Reserve). In each area, TNC staff work with local communities on platform programs to conserve sites and ecological functions.

Ecological Restoration

Ecosystem management usually focuses on protection and conservation of existing ecological resources. However, in many cases, human impacts have damaged resources and ecological functions to the extent that restoration is required. The growing field of ecological restoration has developed in response to challenges posed by overgrazing, surface-mined land, clear-cut forests, damaged wetlands, contaminated soils, and degraded surface and groundwater. Nature has amazing resiliency and restorative capacity. Left alone, damaged ecosystems have shown an inherent ability to recover. However, recovery takes considerable time and may not occur at all if the threats or causes of degradation are not removed. Active restoration practices can remove threats and accelerate recovery.

Some define ecological restoration as the return of an ecosystem to a close approximation of its condition prior to disturbance (National Research Council [NRC], 1992). However, because of constraints on knowledge of preexisting conditions and costs, this ideal is often impractical. As a result, the Society for Ecological Restoration (SER) provides this definition:

> Ecological restoration is the process of assisting the recovery of an ecosystem that has been degraded, damaged or destroyed. It involves restoring and managing ecological integrity, which includes a critical range of variability in biodiversity, ecological processes and structures, regional and historical context, and sustainable cultural practices. (SER, 2002)

Several terms used in the restoration literature have subtle but important differences (SER, 2002):

- **Restoration** aims to reestablish preexisting biotic integrity in terms of species composition and community structure.
- **Rehabilitation** emphasizes reparation of ecosystem processes and services (e.g., reforestation).
- **Reclamation** provides stabilization of terrain, public safety, aesthetic improvement, and return of the land to productive use (e.g., mined land reclamation).

- **Mitigation** lessens or compensates environmental damage (e.g., rehabilitating a wetland to compensate for filling a wetland).
- **Creation** is the establishment of a different kind of ecosystem from what occurred historically (e.g., created wetlands).
- **Ecological or bio-engineering** manipulates natural materials and living organisms to solve problems (e.g., streambank stabilization).

Restoration potential depends on the degree of disturbance of both the site and its surrounding landscape, but the site's condition is more important (NRC, 1992). An important consideration in ecological restoration is the reference ecosystem or conditions that serve as the model for planning and evaluating a project. References are usually given as a composite description of conditions and processes taken from multiple sites.

The SER provides guidelines for developing and managing restoration projects (Clewell, Rieger, and Munro, 2000):

- *Conceptual planning* delineates the site, the type of restoration project, restoration goals, and interventions needed.
- *Preliminary tasks* include organizing and staffing, gathering baseline data, setting objectives, and engaging the public and other stakeholders.
- *Installation planning* provides more detailed plans, performance standards and monitoring procedures, and procurement of materials, prior to the actual *installation actions*.
- *Postinstallation tasks* include site protection, maintenance, monitoring, and adaptive management as recommended by *evaluation*.

Principles and Process of Watershed Protection

Water resources engineers have long recognized the need to manage watersheds to maintain yields and quality of water supply reservoirs. At a larger scale, river basin commissions were established in the 1960s to provide a broader approach to water management. Some of these commissions, like the Delaware River Basin Commission, were successful at improving water conditions, but others became mired in interjurisdictional conflicts across state boundaries.

In the 1990s, the U.S. EPA and other agencies recognized the limitations of point discharge controls and other conventional approaches to water quality and quantity management. It became clear that managing a water body requires managing the land that drains to it. The watershed or drainage catchment became a useful geographic boundary for managing land and water resources. Based on many experimental local programs, the EPA developed guidance for what emerged as the watershed protection approach. Watershed management was not a new concept, but when coupled with new collaborative planning, it has become an effective approach to environmental management.

The Watershed Protection Approach

In 1996, the EPA promoted its watershed protection approach (WPA), which was based on the premise that water quality and ecosystem problems can best be addressed at the watershed level, not at the individual water body or discharge level (U.S. EPA, 1996). There are now an estimated 3,500 active watershed groups in the United States implementing variations of this approach. Many states have adopted WSM as an organizing approach for their water quality management programs. EPA embraced the watershed approach in its Clean Water Action Plan of 1998, but the approach is still not formally part of the Clean Water Act, which has not been reauthorized since 1987. Although it was born in the Clinton administration, the WPA is nonpartisan, as demonstrated in the January 2002 announcement of the George W. Bush administration's initiative for renewed federal support for community-based watershed protection (U.S. EPA, 2002).

The WPA has four basic principles:

1. Targeting priority problems and applying good science to understand them
2. Promoting a high level of collaboration through stakeholder involvement
3. Integrating multiple solutions from multiple agencies and private parties
4. Measuring success through monitoring and other data gathering

The following list outlines three components of a typical WSM program: inventory, planning, and implementation. The inventory is a key first step. Subsequent chapters describe several methods of assessing the watershed and its lands and waters.

Three Components of a Watershed Management Program (*Source:* Commonwealth of Virginia, 1999)

A. Inventory
  1. Define the *watershed boundary*.
  2. *Identify the stakeholders* responsible for developing, implementing, and updating the plan to ensure long-term accountability. Engage the stakeholders in inventory, planning, and implementation.
  3. Conduct a *watershed inventory* of natural resource features (wetlands, floodplains, stream corridors, greenways, rare and endangered species, steep slopes, erodible soils, karst bedrock areas, sensitive habitats, fish and wildlife resources, recreational areas, sources of water supply).
  4. Conduct a *stream inventory* (size, order, water and habitat quality, flow regime).
  5. Identify significant *environmental features* in neighboring watersheds (large pollution sources, wildlife refuges, sources of water supply).
  6. Identify and quantify *existing sources* of point and nonpoint source pollution.

7. Model the *existing hydrology* and hydraulics of the watershed (understand the impact of land use, conveyances, land cover, stormwater management facilities, stream cross sections, roadway crossings, flooding, and drainage problems).

B. Planning
   1. *Define the goals* of the WSM plan (what is envisioned for the watershed and who is going to lead the implementation efforts).
   2. Identify and quantify *future sources* of point and nonpoint source pollution.
   3. Model the *future hydrology* and hydraulics of the watershed.
   4. *Develop and evaluate alternatives* to meet the goals and manage water quality (point and nonpoint source pollution) and quantity (hydrology and hydraulics).
   5. Identify *opportunities to restore* natural resources.
   6. *Develop the WSM plan* (include specific recommendations on development and land use evaluation, selection of structural and nonstructural BMPs, public education needs, regulatory requirements, and funding).

C. Implementation
   1. Define the *implementation costs* (capital costs and annual administrative, operations and maintenance costs) and who will pay for the implementation of the WSM plan (provide incentives and secure commitments).
   2. Establish an implementation schedule.
   3. Develop a watershed monitoring program.
   4. Develop an evaluation and revision process for the WSM plan.

EPA uses its watershed protection website (www.epa.gov/owow/watershed/) to network the hundreds of active local watershed management groups throughout the country. The agency continues to provide useful guidance based primarily on local experience (U.S. EPA, 1995, 1997, 2000a, 2000b, 2001).

Other organizations have advanced the cause and practice of watershed protection. The nonprofit Center for Watershed Protection, founded and directed by Tom Schueler in Ellicott City, Maryland, is one of the best sources of practical and technical information on watershed planning and restoration (see www.cwp.org, www.stormwater.org).

Center for Watershed Protection's Basic Concepts in Watershed Planning

The following list shows some basic concepts in watershed planning taken from Schueler (2000). These are based on Tom Schueler's considerable experience including his work at the Metropolitan Washington Council of Governments (e.g., Schueler, 1987), numerous case studies of projects throughout the country, and recent innovative guidance for watershed and stormwater management prepared by the Center for Watershed Protection (Commonwealth of Virginia, 1999; State of New York, 2001) (see chapter 14).

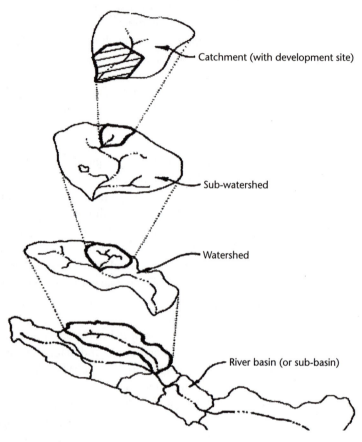

Figure 10.4 Nested Watersheds. *Source:* Adapted from Schueler (2000).

Basic Concepts in Watershed Planning (after Schueler, 1997, 2000)

1. The Tiered Approach: Nest your watersheds—think globally (basin), act locally (catchment).
2. Classify your subwatershed.
3. Take care of precious headwaters.
4. Employ eight WSM tools: land use planning, land conservation, aquatic buffers, cluster and low-impact site design, erosion and sediment control, stormwater treatment, control of septic system and other discharges, and watershed stewardship and monitoring.
5. Focus on impervious cover in urban watersheds.
6. Make technical choices about mapping, modeling, monitoring, and management measures.
7. Reach broad consensus among stakeholders.
8. Focus on action: Implement your watershed plan.

The **tiered approach** or watershed nesting relates to **scale.** Watersheds are defined by a point on a stream or river and include the land area draining to that point. Chapter 13 describes a method to delineate watersheds. Watershed size can range from very large basins to very small catchments (see figure 10.4). Table 10.1 describes the characteristics of each. As you move from larger basins to smaller catchments, the effect of impervious cover on watershed health increases and management measures converge from basinwide planning to on-site design and management practices.

- Catchment: area that drains development sites to their first intersection with stream
- Subwatershed: 1–10 square miles: second-order streams
- Watershed: 10–100 square miles
- Subbasin: 100–1000 square miles
- Basin: 1000–10,000 square miles

Watershed units in the United States are defined by **hydrologic unit code** (HUC) using a system developed by USGS. The hierarchy is described in table 10.2, which shows an example from South Carolina. HUCs are based on a classification system that divides the United States into progressively smaller hydrologic units. Each unit is identified by a unique HUC consisting of two to eight digits based on the four classification levels. NRCS and other agencies have further delineated fifth- and sixth-level watersheds in many states. HUCs for these additional watershed levels consist of 11 and 14 digits, respectively, and represent a scale from a few hundred down to tens of square miles. Fifth- and sixth-level HUCs are generally a good scale for watershed projects (U.S. EPA, 2000a).

TABLE 10.1 **Characteristics of Five Watershed Management Units**

Watershed Management Unit	Typical Area (square miles)	Influence of Impervious Cover	Sample Management
Catchment	0.05 to 0.50	Very strong	Practices and site design
Subwatershed	1 to 10	Strong	Stream classification and management
Watershed	10 to 100	Moderate	Watershed-based zoning
Subbasin	100 to 1,000	Weak	Basin planning
Basin	1,000 to 10,000	Very weak	Basin planning

TABLE 10.2 **Example of Hydrologic Unit Codes (HUCs) from South Carolina**

HU Level	Hydrologic Unit	Hydrologic Unit Name	Hydrologic Unit Area (mi²)	HUC
1st	Region	South Atlantic Gulf	—	03
2nd	Subregion	Edisto-Santee	23,600	0305
3rd	Basin (Accounting Unit)	Santee	15,300	030501
4th	Subbasin (Cataloging Unit)	Enoree	731	03050108
5th	Watershed	Unnamed	82	03050108040
6th	Subwatershed	Unnamed	41	03050108040010

Source: Bower, Lowery, Lowery, and Hurley, 1999.

Most effective watershed planning is guided by larger issues of the basin but focuses on smaller scale subwatersheds and catchments for action. Guidance, policies, and financial and technical assistance may be basinwide, but specific plans and implementation occur in subwatersheds. The **subwatershed** is a critical scale for management: It is small enough to be within one or a few jurisdictions, there is a strong influence of land use and impervious surface, there are few compounding pollutant sources, it is small enough for monitoring and mapping at a workable yet detailed scale, and stakeholders have a close connection to the issues and are manageable in number.

Watershed classification helps focus on planning objectives. Table 10.3 gives eight categories of subwatersheds based on their condition, location, and beneficial use. "Sensitive," "impacted," and "nonsupporting" categories reflect the degree of impairment depending on habitat and water quality. "Restorable" are those impacted or nonsupporting streams that have a high potential for restoration. "Urban lakes" and "coastal-estuarine waters" indicate location and sensitivity. "Water supply reservoir" and "aquifer protection" trigger a public health objective.

Watershed and Ecosystem Assessment

Scientific and technical assessment plays a critical role in EM and WSM. Scientific inventory and analysis are used to evaluate ecosystem/watershed conditions and problems, guide the choice of protection and restoration measures, and monitor progress in adaptive management.

Assessment in EM depends on management objectives and can be complex. In recent years, we have gained considerable knowledge about ecosystem functions and dynamics from conservation biology and landscape ecology. We continue to improve our understanding of natural systems. However, we often need to make decisions about resources without perfect knowledge of the systems involved. The goal of adaptive management is to learn from these decisions by taking limited action and monitoring results. In most cases this is an appropriate means of managing resources and adding to our understanding of ecosystems. But in some cases it is a risky business if the action taken causes irreversible change to sensitive or endangered species before we have a chance to monitor the effects.

Watershed assessment is normally more straightforward. The hydrologic and water quality systems are more predictable than ecological systems. However, ecological components of watershed assessment often encounter the same uncertainties as ecosystem assessment. Watershed assessment usually focuses on the stream channel, the riparian zone, and upland areas. In urban watersheds, special attention is given to impervious surface relationships and effects.

Assessments should make good use of visual and mapping tools. Maps can show subwatershed and catchment boundaries; land use and land cover; ecosystem and watershed resources and conditions; and location of floodplains, stream buffers, wetlands, land conservation areas, stormwater practices, strategic monitoring stations, and many other features. Geographic information systems (GIS) can inte-

TABLE 10.3 **Categories of Subwatersheds**

Subwatershed Category	Description
Sensitive Stream	Less than 10% impervious cover
	High habitat/water quality rating
Impacted Stream	10% to 25% impervious cover
	Some decline in habitat and water quality
Nonsupporting Stream	Watershed has greater than 25% impervious cover
	Not a candidate for stream restoration
Restorable Stream	Classified as Impacted or nonsupporting
	High retrofit or stream restoration potential
Urban Lake	Subwatershed drains to a lake that is subject to degradation
Water Supply Reservoir	Reservoir managed to protect drinking water supply
Coastal/Estuarine Waters	Subwatershed drains to an estuary or near-shore ocean
Aquifer Protection	Surface water has a strong interaction with groundwater
	Groundwater is a primary source of potable water

Source: Schueler (2000).

grate existing maps and digital data, as well as remote sensing information like aerial photos and digital images, into assessment product maps (see chapter 11).

The rapid-intermediate-advanced assessment approach is often applied to watershed and ecosystem studies. Rapid assessment relies primarily on existing information such as natural resource maps and past environmental reports. Although it is somewhat broad-based and qualitative, rapid assessment can reveal important insights about watershed functions and interactions. Some limited action may be taken based on the results of rapid assessment.

In intermediate and advanced assessment, experienced analysts utilize more data collection, quantitative assessment tools, field surveys, and computer-based models to provide a higher level of certainty or confidence in the assessment results. This requires more time and resources than rapid assessment but is often necessary when rapid results are indeterminate.

Subsequent chapters present a wide range of methods that are used in watershed and ecosystem assessment. Rapid assessment relies primarily on existing information, much of which is available in local agency offices and on the Internet. EPA's EnviroMapper Storefront (http://www.epa.gov/enviro/enviromapper) and Fish and Wildlife Service's Interactive wetland mapping tool (http://wetlands.fws.gove/mapper_tool.htm) are especially useful. For rapid watershed assessment, a first step is EPA's Surf Your Watershed site (http://www.epa.gov/surf), which allows selection of watersheds down to HUC level 4 (subbasin). A wide range of information is available for these watersheds, including location of impaired waters from EPA's database, locations of toxic releases and superfund sites, and registered stream restoration efforts. The interactive site allows users to add information to the database. There is a link to EPA's Index of Watershed Indicators, which gives a wide array of water quality, ecological, and demographic data for the subbasin. Box 10.2 lists those indicators and also provides links to the EPA's website describing them.

BOX 10.2—Index of Watershed Indicators (IWI) Developed by the EPA

1. Population Served By Community Drinking Water Systems Violating Health-Based Requirements (01)
2. Population Served By Unfiltered Surface Water Systems at Risk from Microbiological Contamination (02)
3. Population Served By Community Drinking Water Systems Exceeding Lead Action Levels (03)
4. Source Water Protection (04)
5. Fish Consumption Advisories (05)
6. Shellfish Growing Water Classification (06)
7. Biological Integrity (07)
8. Species at Risk (08)
9. Wetland Acreage (09)
10. Drinking Water Supply (10a)
11. Fish and Shellfish Consumption (10b)
12. Recreation (10c)
13. Aquatic Life Designated Use (10d)
14. Ground Water Pollutants: Nitrate (11)

15. Surface Water Pollutants (12)
16. Selected Coastal Surface Water Pollutants in Shellfish (13)
17. Estuarine Eutrophication Conditions (14)
18. Contaminated Sediments (15)
19. Selected Point Source Loadings to Surface Water (16a)
20. Sources of Point Source Loadings Through Class V Wells to Ground Water (16b)
21. Nonpoint Source Sediment Loadings from Cropland (4)
22. Marine Debris (18)

Note: Each line above has a link to an Internet description of each indicator. For first indicator go to www.epa.gov/iwi/help/indic/fs1.html; replace "1" in URL with number given in parentheses above for other indicators.

Integrating Compatible Programs and Solutions

There is no "silver bullet" for protecting and restoring ecosystems and watersheds. A wide range of measures must be used to preserve existing values and improve degraded conditions. Watershed and ecosystem management measures include regulations, restoration projects, land acquisition, environmental monitoring, stewardship by land trusts and landowners, and education and research. Regulations on land use, polluting actions, and ecosystem-impacting practices take the form of permitting programs requiring compliance with rules or ordinances designed to protect lands, waters, and habitats. Although these regulations provide an important foundation for protective action, they are insufficient to achieve effective management. They may help to prevent further degradation, but improvement and restoration of watersheds and ecosystems often requires proactive measures to acquire, restore, steward, and monitor natural resources.

To accomplish this comprehensive array of measures, holistic ecosystem and watershed management must team with other programs with common and compatible objectives. Perhaps not surprisingly, a range of programs designed to provide economic and social benefits can also protect and enhance watersheds and ecosystems. These include programs to mitigate natural hazards, arrest soil erosion, preserve farmland, treat polluted runoff, protect drinking water sources, restore impaired/TMDL waters, manage forests, improve air quality, protect wetland benefits, manage fisheries, provide recreation and open space, and enhance the quality of life in our communities.

Watershed and ecosystem management add ecological dimensions to these human-related objectives, but most are very compatible. Successful programs take advantage of the synergies provided by coordination and collaboration of diverse initiatives. Such programs enjoy a broader base of support, greater acceptability, improved cost-effectiveness, and smoother implementation.

Achieving this collaboration is easier said than done. Public interests, groups, and agencies are often fragmented in their objectives and programs. Competition for scarce resources (time, money, institutional capacity) often pits one against the other. Successful programs have realized the advantages of building partnerships and pooling social, political, and financial capital into comprehensive efforts of common interest. Often this begins with appropriate institutional arrangements.

Institutional Arrangements for Ecosystem and Watershed Management

Ecosystem and watershed protection requires an integration of science, planning, policy, and politics. The nested or tiered approach (figure 10.1) applies not only to scientific understanding, but also to institutional and political organization. As we move from catchment to watershed to basin and from patch to matrix to ecosystem, the increasing geographic area captured crosses governmental jurisdictional boundaries. As we increase the number of jurisdictions, we complicate the institutional and political arrangements needed for effective management. Since watersheds and ecosystems rarely conform to jurisdictional boundaries, WSM usually requires interjurisdictional collaboration. However, parochial interests, competition, and past conflicts often inhibit meaningful cooperation among neighboring jurisdictions.

In addition, WSM also must involve private landowners and the public, as well as governmental agencies in a collaborative partnership. Although some regulatory land use controls are important, effective watershed protection depends on a range of voluntary measures, including land stewardship and watershed monitoring. Watershed associations and groups are critical players in WSM.

These institutional issues are well recognized by research on the practice of ecosystem and watershed management (Schueler, 2000; U.S. EPA, 1997). From 1999 to 2001, an interagency federal watershed protection team worked with local and state partners and watershed practitioners to assess the challenges to watershed health, recent successes of the watershed approach, and remaining obstacles. The process engaged more than 1,000 participants at 20 regional roundtable discussions, culminating in the National Watershed Forum in the summer of 2001 (Meridian Institute, 2001a, 2001b; U.S. EPA, 2001).

The roundtables and Forum concluded that the watershed approach offers the best hope for protecting and restoring the nation's waters. They gave much of the credit for successes to date to *local leadership and engagement*. "Citizens are leading the drive to reverse impacts to watershed health" (U.S. EPA, 2001).

The Forum also cited the importance of federal and state agencies for coordinating and supporting local watershed protection with financial and technical

TABLE 10.4 **Institutional Arrangements at Different Watershed Scales**

Scale	Participants	Roles and Actions	Examples
Region (subnational)	* Lead federal agency * Multiagency committee	* Federal commitment to watershed approach * Interagency agreements * Funding, technical support	* Federal unified policy * Regional teams
Basin (multistate)	* Lead federal agency * Multistate advisory group with federal and state reps, interest-group reps * Committees, task forces, stakeholders groups	* Multistate commitment * Basin plan * State/federal financial support	* River basin commissions * Great Lakes Joint Comm. * Chesapeake Bay program
Subbasin (state)	* Lead state agency * Statewide advisory committee with state and regional and interest group representatives * Committees, task forces, stakeholders groups	* State statutory/administrative directive for WSM * Statewide watershed protection plan * Requires regulatory "teeth" * Technical and financial assistance to watershed/subwatershed programs	* Oregon Plan for Salmon and Watersheds * Illinois River * Chesapeake Bay acts in Maryland and Virginia
Watershed (substate)	* Regional planning agency (e.g., COG, plan. district) * WS advisory committee of local governments, regional groups, other stakeholders	* Interjurisdictional plans and agreements * Guidance, technical and financial support	* Cuyahoga River, OH * San Miguel River. CO
Subwatershed (local)	* Watershed association (local government, landowners, interest groups) * Local watershed manager/coordinator	* Where the action is! * Land use controls * Stream/riparian restoration * Action limited without direction, financial, technical support from above	* Anacostia Watershed, DC * Matapole River, CA * East Fork of Little River, VA * Bronx River, NY
Catchment (site scale)	* Watershed association, Watershed coordinator * Landowners, developers, community groups	* Site development measures * Land stewardship * Stream/riparian restoration * Stream monitoring	* Haskell Slough, WA

support. Specifically, the Forum provided a range of recommendations, dealing largely with institutional issues of education, partnerships, planning, funding assistance, and implementation. Although scientific and technical factors are critically important in watershed and ecosystem management, these institutional issues continue to be the major challenges to effective protection and restoration.

Institutional Models for Watershed Management

Several organizational models for WSM and EM have emerged, but most involve a tiered approach and public-private-nonprofit partnerships. Although most management actions occur at the local level, larger-scale watershed and ecosystem institutional frameworks provide guidance and resources to smaller-scale planning and implementation efforts. Table 10.4 outlines participants and organizational units, roles and actions, and examples of WSM programs at various scales from subnational regions to site-level catchments.

Actions and measures are implemented at the subwatershed and catchment scale, but studies have shown that these programs often have limited effectiveness without technical and financial support from the regional subwatershed or state levels (Holst, 1999).

Research on local environmental planning has shown that key ingredients for successful community initiatives are a *committed elected official* who can advance the cause politically, a *skillful planner* who can generate and manage technical information, and an *active constituency* that contributes political support and local knowledge (Corbett and Hayden, 1981). This holds true for WSM as well. Support of elected officials is important to shepherd watershed protection regulations and funding. The "planner" is often played by the watershed manager. The constituency can be represented by the watershed association or stakeholders group, which not only provides political support but also monitors watershed conditions and implements restoration measures through voluntary action.

The Watershed Group/Association

A local watershed association often plays an important role for subwatershed and catchment planning and implementation. The association is usually composed principally of landowners in the subwatershed, but may also include government officials and interest groups. With landowner participation, the association can be instrumental in developing stewardship, monitoring, and other voluntary measures. In some cases, the group has legal authority, in some cases not. In either case, the association is well positioned to understand local problems and issues, to develop options to address them, and to implement these measures. At the subwatershed level, associations provide a mechanism for local governments and interest groups to gather watershed stakeholders to plan and implement protection and restoration. In the cases described in box 10.3 later in this chapter, the Bronx River Working Group and the Cuyahoga River Alliance are good examples of watershed associations.

Some associations have legal standing. For example, Virginia law allows the establishment of a watershed improvement district (WID) if voters and landowners approve such a district by large majorities. The WID is made up of landowners and has the authority to tax its members to fund watershed improvements. The Barcroft Reservoir WID in urban Fairfax County was established under this law in the 1970s. The district has developed a tax-supported fund to pay for monitoring and BMP retrofits. While the district has maintained the lake, its capacity to improve the watershed has been limited to lakeshore and tributary activities rather than upstream measures in the heavily urbanized watershed.

Most associations are voluntary groups. The East Fork (Little River) Watershed Association in Floyd County, Virginia, was established by local landowners with the help of the National Committee for the New River (NCNR) in the early 1990s. The agricultural watershed is made up of fiercely independent landowners—some long-term natives known for their taste for moonshine and some "urban refugees" who migrated from the northeast to enjoy a more communal life. While these groups are culturally very different, they both are distrustful of government, guard their property rights, and take pride in the fact that all water flows out of Floyd County. The perceived threat of government action on their impaired watershed drew these diverse landowners together in a common cause. NCNR helped educate this group about the watershed's problems and convinced them that they should take action themselves before state agencies came in and told them what to do. This argument struck a chord, and the group succeeded in developing a plan, acquiring grant funds, monitoring watershed quality, and implementing livestock fencing and other measures to reduce runoff pollution.

The Watershed Manager

The watershed manager is usually a paid staffer of local government or a large watershed association who plays a lead role in planning and coordinating watershed information, process, decisions, and implementation. The manager is usually the keeper of information on watershed data and analysis and on potential protection and restoration measures and costs. The manager will often coordinate the collaborative process, identifying stakeholders, setting up advisory committees, and organizing meetings.

Stakeholder Involvement and Advisory Committees

Stakeholder involvement is a critical part of watershed and ecosystem management. As discussed in chapter 4, stakeholders are those who effect change in the watershed and those who are affected by it. They include agencies, local governments, landowners and developers, and environmental, agricultural, and other interest groups. Stakeholder groups are used at all levels of watershed management, from basin to watershed to catchment scale.

Several approaches to stakeholder involvement were discussed in chapter 4. Stakeholder groups are organized as information task forces, working groups, or advisory committees. Representation on stakeholder groups varies with scale. At the basin level, committees are made up of representatives of federal and state agencies and national interests groups. At the watershed scale, stakeholder groups include state agency officials, local governments, and state or regional interest groups. At the subwatershed level, groups may be the same as watershed associations, including landowners and community groups.

Bauer (2001) and Keuhl (2001) each studied the collaborative process of stakeholder groups. Bauer showed that community-scale watershed groups are potentially more effective in learning and reaching consensus than basin-scale groups because they are closer to the problems and potential solutions. Keuhl (2001) investigated advisory committees in the Great Lakes Remedial Action Planning and found that the collaborative process led not only to consensus-building, but also to increased knowledge of water and watershed systems and improved understanding of problems and solutions.

Integrating Statewide and Local Watershed Programs

The plethora of case studies of the practice of WSM and EM has demonstrated the importance of local action (U.S. EPA, 2001; Williams, Wood, and Dombeck, 1997).

However, successful local programs rarely act alone. They often depend on administrative or statutory direction from above, guidance from basin and watershed plans produced at the state or regional level, technical assistance, and especially financial support from state and federal agencies. Likewise, statewide, basin, and watershed-level programs require not only local action but also consistent reporting and monitoring of local restoration and protection projects.

A good example of integrating statewide and local programs is Oregon's framework. The state-level *Oregon Plan for Salmon and Watersheds,* funding from the Oregon Watershed Enhancement Board, watershed level programs like the Willamette Restoration Initiative, and the 90 subwatershed councils around the state provide the institutional structure. The Watershed Restoration Reporting system provides consistent and timely feedback on local activities to the state so that progress can be effectively monitored. The Oregon framework is described in the next section.

Other states, like Wisconsin, Minnesota, North Carolina, and Maryland, among others, have integrated the WPA into their water quality programs. All of these states provide technical and funding support for local subwatershed planning and implementation. These programs often build on established state programs and agencies, such as soil and water conservation districts in rural areas. However, local watershed groups are critical, especially in urban and suburban areas.

Applications of Ecosystem and Watershed Management

Thousands of experiments in watershed and ecosystem management have been developed over the past decade (Bauer and Randolph, 2000; U.S. EPA, 1997, 2000b, 2002; Yaffee et al., 1996). Because they are experimental, there is a strong need to monitor and evaluate experiences to see what works and what doesn't. This section reviews some of these experiences. After a look at EM in the Forest Service, it reviews a few examples of community-based watershed management that show success depends on technical expertise, hard work, and elements of a social movement. The section concludes with a review of Oregon's Plan for Salmon and Watersheds, among the more comprehensive ecosystem/watershed management efforts.

Federal Agency Ecosystem Management

The first section of this chapter described the evolution within federal land agencies toward an EM approach. The Forest Service, the Park Service, the Bureau of Land Management, and the Fish and Wildlife Service have all modified their planning and management of public lands to incorporate emerging methods. This began with sustained yield and multiple use in the 1960s, NEPA requirements and environmental impact assessment in the 1970s, management planning in the 1980s, and more collaborative and ecosystem management in the 1990s (Phillips and Randolph, 1998; Randolph, 1987).

In the summer of 1992, Forest Service chief Dale Robertson announced the agency's intent to develop EM as "a strategic approach for sustaining desired conditions of ecosystem diversity, productivity, and resilience for the multiple uses and values of the national forests" (USDA, USFS, 1992; Salwasser, 1994). Although the Forest Service did not modify its planning and management regulations to reflect EM principles until 2000 (USDA, USFS, 2000), the agency began implementing EM principles in 1992.

Phillips and Randolph (1998) reviewed Forest Service plans produced in the mid-1990s in comparison to plans for the same units in the 1980s to assess the extent to which their plans and practices reflected EM principles. For this research, they developed 11 evaluation questions based on an extensive review of the growing ecosystem literature. They involved native species populations, ecological processes, ecosystem health and diversity, different spatial and temporal scales, ecosystem boundaries, collaborative decision making, scientific research, adaptive management, education, and evaluation.

Based on these questions, they conducted content analysis on mid-1980s and mid-1990s plans for George Washington, Francis Marion, and Texas National Forests. In all three cases, the mid-1990s plans addressed the EM criteria to a far greater extent than the mid-1980s plans.

For example, the 1993 George Washington National Forest Plan was developed after the 1986 plan was mired in conflict.

- The 1993 Plan was produced after a two-year collaborative planning process of diverse stakeholders (see chapter 4).
- It called for a 42 percent reduction in area suitable for timber sales, and clear-cutting was reduced by 62 percent compared with the 1986 Plan (close to the Forest Service's EM goal calling for a systemwide clear-cutting reduction of 70%).
- Conversion from native hardwood to non-native softwood species was no longer deemed appropriate.
- Riparian area practices called for "ecologically based width" buffers rather than no or standard width buffers in the 1986 Plan.
- Lands designated for old-growth conditions and unfragmented habitat increased by 19 percent and 13 percent, respectively, over the 1986 Plan.
- The 1993 Plan maintained 90 percent of the forest in "natural state" under visual quality objectives compared with just 38 percent in the 1986 Plan.

The study concluded that the mid-1990s plans demonstrated a marked change in the use of EM principles. In addition, the 1990s plans were all less controversial and enjoyed much smoother adoption than their 1980s counterparts. A related study also showed that by incorporating EM principles, these plans reflected the goals and objectives of NEPA to a greater extent than did the previous plans (Phillips and Randolph, 2000).

Watershed Success Stories

A number of collections of case studies are helpful guides to watershed management experience. Yaffee et al. (1996), Williams et al. (1997), Schueler and Holland (2000), and the U.S. EPA (1997, 2000b, 2001) chronicle community-based protection and restoration projects across the country. Box 10.3 gives four examples of the 30 watershed success stories presented in the EPA (2000b). The cases are from across the country and range from urban to rural applications. The common threads include local volunteerism and advocacy, planning and assessment, and government support.

Oregon Plan for Salmon and Watersheds

Perhaps one of the best examples of integrated WSM comes from Oregon. Faced with growing concerns over endangered salmon, the Pacific Northwest has tried to manage water and salmon while maintaining economic vitality. Twelve salmonoid species in Oregon have been listed under the federal ESA. In response, Oregon developed a comprehensive approach to restore the salmon species by restoring watersheds. The *Oregon Plan for Salmon and Watersheds* (OPSW) was developed in the mid-1990s and approved by the state legislature in 1997. In 1999, the governor expanded the scope of the plan to watershed health statewide.

The OPSW has been more than a technical exercise to improve watersheds and recover salmon habitat and species numbers; it has become a high-stakes social movement:

> There is a lot at stake. More than just the future of salmon. The nature of Oregon is at stake. Our environment—from the salmon in the streams to the employment opportunities our children will have—depends on the many decisions we make today....Our task is to conduct our human business in Oregon, in a manner that is compatible with sustaining productive soils, clean drinking water, recreation, cultural values, *and* native salmon populations. (OPSW, 2001)

The inclusive tone of the movement is set in the following quote from the 2001 status report on the Plan.

Who Is Responsible for Healthy Watersheds?

In a world where people often look for simple solutions to complex problems, some people suggest that saving salmon is the responsibility of loggers, or farmers, or fishers, or the tribes, or the people who operate the dams, or the people who build houses, or the people who protect seals, and so-on, and so-forth. That suggestion is *wrong*. Saving salmon—restoring healthy watersheds—will require willing participation of all of us, neighbors in the greater Oregon watershed. Saving salmon must not be viewed as someone else's responsibility—but as *my* responsibility. The reality is that many Oregonians *are* actively involved in the effort to sustain healthy watersheds, clean water, and native fish. (OPSW, 2001)

BOX 10.3—Four Watershed Management Success Stories (U.S. EPA, 2000b)

Bronx River, New York—*Community Cooperation in Urban Watershed Restoration*

The 56.4-square-mile Bronx River Watershed forms New York City's truly urban Bronx River that flows for 23 miles through the New York Botanical Garden, the Bronx Zoo, Soundview, Hunts Point, and other communities before emptying into the Long Island Sound. In the early 1800s, the Bronx River watershed had a magnificent oak forest and abundant wildlife, including beaver and trout. After nearly two centuries of degradation, the Bronx River Working Group was formed in 1997 to coordinate watershed restoration, education, and outreach efforts.

Supported by an EPA Wetlands Protection grant and other sources, the continuously expanding alliance of over 50 community groups, nonprofits, and businesses and government agencies is accomplishing significant watershed restoration and protection. It is acquiring land, restoring river channel hydraulics, stabilizing eroding riverbank with native vegetation, reclaiming wetlands and floodplains, improving habitat, and increasing public access to the river.

Many actions are underway, including a mile-long greenway project in the Soundview section of the watershed. A City of New York Department of Parks and Recreation initiative, the Adopt-The-River Program provides technical and financial assistance to community-based projects. In the fall of 1999 alone, 15 program community events focused on reopening riverside trails, removing debris from the river, restoring wildlife habitat, and developing waterfront access.

Conasauga River, Georgia and Tennessee — *Protecting Wildlife Habitat from Nonpoint Source Pollution*

The 91-mile Conasauga River is home to a remarkable diversity of species, including 25 that are considered rare. In 1999, the USDA Forest Service selected the watershed as one of 12 priority large watersheds, and the river has been identified as one of the most biologically important rivers in the southeast United States. The watershed is impacted by urban, forestry, and agricultural activities. Eighteen miles of the Conasauga River and 54 miles of tributaries are still in Georgia's List of Impaired Waters for fecal, metal, toxic chemical, sediment, and nutrient impacts. The Conasauga River watershed is classified as a Category 1 priority watershed in the state's Unified Watershed Assessment.

In 1994, the Limestone Valley Resource Conservation and Development Council undertook an ecosystem-based study and organized meetings of local stakeholders. Three years later, the council founded the Conasauga River Alliance, a partnership made up of local citizens, conservation groups, and federal, state, and local agencies. The alliance is addressing the degradation of habitat and water quality caused by erosion, sedimentation, excessive nutrients, and toxic chemicals in the watershed. The alliance has worked with landowners and agency representatives to support enrollment of nearly 200 acres of riparian area in the USDA Conservation Reserve Program. The alliance has also placed over 25 miles of riverbank and streambank under some form of conservation management and planted 11,000 trees.

Cuyahoga River, Ohio—*Restoring an American Heritage River*

The Cuyahoga River drains 813 square miles and travels 100 miles from Geauga County through the Cuyahoga Valley National Recreation Area located between the urban and industrial centers of Akron and Cleveland, before emptying into Lake Erie. The river first caught on fire in 1936. In 1969 a Cuyahoga River fire caught the attention of the nation, and the Cuyahoga became a "poster-child" for the environmental movement. After years of improvement, the Cuyahoga River was designated as 1 of 14 American Heritage Rivers in 1998, but pollution problems remain. The EPA classified portions of the watershed as 1 of 43 Great Lakes Areas of Concern, warranting development of a remedial action plan (RAP).

The Ohio Environmental Protection Agency formed the Cuyahoga River RAP Coordinating

Continued ➤

BOX 10.3—(continued)

Committee, consisting of 33 representatives from local, regional, state and federal agencies, private corporations, and citizen and environmental organizations. The mission of the RAP is to plan and promote the restoration and preservation of beneficial uses of the lower Cuyahoga River through remediation of existing conditions and prevention of further pollution and degradation.

Watershed restoration efforts like river and stream cleanups and biological stream monitoring by volunteers are supported by focused activities based in municipal and township units. The Big Creek Stream Stewardship Program involves locally based education and outreach activities, habitat improvement projects, data collection, and storm drain stenciling.

Noticeable environmental improvements have already been recorded in the Cuyahoga River. Studies in 1998 and 1999 documented usage of the river as a navigation channel for Lake Erie fish migration, including steelhead trout.

Haskell Slough, Washington —*Excavation Resurrects Aquatic Habitat*

Haskell Slough, a system of streams and ponds connected to the Skyhomish River, is an important fish overwintering and rearing area for Puget Sound chinook, coho, steelhead, and chum. In the 1930s, the system was diked upstream, and years of intermittent flooding and silt deposits isolated

the system from the Skyhomish River. Land development, roadway construction, and agricultural runoff filled in the channels between the system's ponds, and adult or juvenile salmon washed into the system could not escape.

In 1996, the Haskell Slough Salmon Restoration Project was initiated as a cooperative effort of private landowners and a coalition of nonprofit organizations, Native American tribes, and state and federal agencies. After two years of planning and design, the Salmon Habitat Restoration Project began in 1998. By 1999, a new channel was constructed, and 3.5 miles of river bed was restored by excavating 7,000 feet of stream channels connecting 11 existing large, groundwater-fed ponds. The excavation ensures year-round flow through the entire Haskell Slough. The project also installed rootwads, large woody debris, log weirs, and other structures to enhance the salmon-rearing habitat. Project participants monitor fish traps to track progress and the quantity of fish in the system. In 1999, after 50 years of limited or no production, about 10,000 coho salmon fry were counted swimming into the slough. Adult salmon have returned to the high water in the lower portion of the system. Within four years, several thousand adult coho will be produced by the system, as well as increased numbers of chinook, steelhead, and searun cutthroat.

The core values of the Plan, shown in the following list, illustrate the deep-seated ethical basis for the plan: Seek the truth; respect people and nature; share, act voluntarily, build partnerships, and strengthen community; let rivers be rivers and untame our watersheds. These values appear to have captivated agencies, communities, and citizens and have resulted in considerable action in watershed protection and restoration. This is reflected in the expanding range and number of participants, the increasing funding provided, and the growing number of restoration projects and actions taken since 1995.

Core Values of Oregon Plan for Salmon and Watersheds

Seek truth, learn, and adapt. Our knowledge of the world is imperfect. Understanding and behavior must evolve over time.

Be humble. Remember, Mother Nature does not answer to salmon or man. Both survive at her discretion.

Obey the law and live up to commitments. Honorable behavior earns trust. Get busy and earn it.

Respect people, respect nature. The two are inseparable.

Act voluntarily. Do one's best each day. Miracles don't spring from just trying to get by.

Exercise patience. Salmon have survived here for thousands of years. Our work won't be complete in a month, a year, or a decade. Our challenge is to build a world where both salmon and people can flourish on a greater time scale than most people comprehend.

Build partnerships, make friends, and strengthen community. No single person or organization has the power or understanding needed to keep the world safe for us all. We need each other.

Strive to let rivers be rivers, and untame, a little, our watersheds. People have changed the land and changed the waters of the West in ways that do not respect salmon or people. We must undo some of these changes to maintain a world in which we can thrive.

Share. Share information. Share the power to make decisions. Share the responsibility to act.

Consider our children's needs. They will inherit the world from us.

Never give up hope.

Principles of the Oregon Plan and Use of the Tiered Approach

The basic principles of the OPSW include the elements of watershed and ecosystem management:

- *Community-based Action:* Local watershed councils, soil and water conservation Districts (SWCD), landowners, and other grassroots players perform the key roles of preparing and implementing actions, as well as monitoring and improving them over time.
- *Governmental Coordination:* State and federal laws, policies, and funding programs provide the context, goals, and support for the program; agencies provide the oversight and technical assistance for community-based action.
- *Monitoring and Accountability:* Assessment of work and results is essential to ensure effective use of funds, monitor progress toward program goals, and support adaptive learning.
- *Adaptive Management:* Program participants must learn from the experience of local restoration efforts to enhance understanding of natural systems and improve restoration measures.

These basic principles illustrate the need for a tiered approach: while protection and restoration action is concentrated at the subwatershed and catchment (project) levels, that action must be informed and funded from the regional, basin, and watershed levels by state and federal laws, policies, agencies, and programs. And accountability, shared experience, and adaptive learning requires monitoring, reporting, and information flow from the project level to agencies at the watershed and basin levels. The Oregon case provides an excellent example of this tiered approach.

- *At the regional level:* The Oregon Plan is driven by federal law and mandates in the ESA for listed salmon and other species.
- *At the basin level:* The Northwest Power Planning Council (NPPC) supports work to restore watersheds and salmon populations throughout the Columbia River Basin. In addition, the National Marine Fisheries Service (NMFS) allocates funds to the Northwest states for ESA recovery in the Columbia River and coastal watersheds.
- *At the state level:* The Oregon Plan provides a statewide framework for implementing the federal requirements and enhances recovery of salmon habitat, water quality, and watershed integrity. Several state agencies, such as the departments of Fish and Wildlife, Agriculture, Forestry, Environmental Quality, and State Police (enforcement) play active roles in planning, data management, technical assistance, monitoring, and funding. The Oregon Watershed Restoration Board is the principal state funding agency for subwatershed and restoration project grants.
- *At the watershed level:* Watershed level plans guide subwatershed and project actions. In 1998, the citizen-based Willamette Restoration Initiative (WRI) was established and completed the Willamette Chapter of the Oregon Plan in 2001. The WRI strategy included 27 critical actions needed to protect and restore Oregon's largest and most critical watershed that is home to 70 percent of its population, 50 percent of its agriculture, and native runs of four species listed under the ESA.
- *At the subwatershed level:* The number of local watershed councils grew from a handful in 1993 to 90 in 2001. Working in partnerships with SWCD, these councils provide the critical institutional layer to coordinate catchment projects, apply for funding, and report to state agencies.
- *At the catchment level:* Here is where restoration projects occur. These are conducted by different parties, including state agencies, watershed councils, citizen groups, and landowners. Project reporting also originates here, so that lessons and learning can be shared with others in the watershed and basin.

Funding for Plan Implementation

Successful restoration depends on adequate funding from federal and state sources. Federal sources include the NPPC restoration funding ($100 million per year for the entire Columbia Basin), NMFS ($9–15 million a year to Oregon for salmon ESA Recovery), federal land agencies, and EPA funds for water quality improvement. State legislatively approved biennial funding for watershed restoration increased from $0.5 million in 1987–1989 to $5.5 million in 1996–1997 to $32 million in 1999–2001.

A critical step for state watershed restoration funding was the overwhelming voter passage of Ballot Measure 66, the so-called Salmon and Parks Measure, in

1998. The referendum dedicated 15 percent of Oregon lottery receipts to conservation programs, half to parks and half to salmon and watershed programs. These funds, as well as NMFS recovery funds, are administered by the Oregon Watershed Restoration Board (OWRB) for grants to local watershed restoration projects. In addition to state and federal sources, funding for watershed restoration comes from private industrial forest landowners, nonindustrial landowners, and citizen groups. Between 1995 and 2000 more than $100 million was spent on watershed restoration.

Summary

As we embark on the challenges of managing natural resources, lands, and waters in the new century, two related approaches have emerged as guiding paradigms: ecosystem management and watershed management. These approaches are still evolving, but already they show great promise from considerable experience at both the national and local level in the United States. International experience indicates that they have universal applications.

Ecosystem and watershed management share several common principles. They are fundamentally scientific, aiming to base decisions on the best available technical data and information. They aim also to add to the body of knowledge about natural systems and solutions through experimentation, monitoring and evaluation, and adaptive management. The approaches integrate different scales of space and time. Ecosystem projects may be small in scale but should be viewed as part of larger landscapes. Watersheds are "nested"; catchment projects should be guided by plans for the larger basins that contain them. Plans are guided by history, and have a long time horizon necessary to achieve a sustainable future. Ecosystem and watershed solutions should integrate a range of regulatory and nonregulatory methods into innovative packages that also address compatible objectives like natural hazard mitigation, recreation, water supply protection, and other economic benefits. The solutions aim to both protect and restore natural systems. As such, *management* is a more encompassing term than *protection*.

Finally, these approaches are collaborative, aiming to engage a wide range of participants and stakeholders not only in gathering information and viewpoints, but also in formulating decisions and implementing plans. The collaborative and adaptive nature of EM and WSM is perhaps their greatest quality, the characteristic that will sustain them well into the future. We have seen many examples of how WSM has become a social movement, engaging not only agencies, but also businesses, landowners, citizen groups, and schoolchildren in planning, monitoring, and implementing restoration and protection projects. This will give these approaches their staying power as they develop social, intellectual, and political capital. In addition, their adaptive nature fosters change, improvement, and evolution as participants learn better ways to provide for the needs of people within functioning natural ecosystems.

Environmental Land Use Principles and Planning Analysis

11 ■ Environmental Geospatial Data and Geographic Information Systems

Environmental planning and management is an information-intensive field. The chapters that follow apply a wide range of geologic, hydrologic, and ecological information to understand and communicate conditions and options to inform planning decisions.

Before exploring specific information and analytical methods, this chapter reviews the effective use and key sources of land-based or geospatial data. First, it reviews the role of information in environmental planning. The chapter then presents basic data sources, maps, aerial photos, and satellite imagery, as well as their availability in digital form. These digital data and local environmental data are increasingly available on the Internet. The chapter then describes geographic information systems (GIS). GIS have emerged as effective and powerful tools to store, analyze, and visually present environmental data. It is important to ground truth or test the accuracy of information from maps, photos, and other secondary sources, and the role of field data and monitoring is described. Finally, the chapter discusses the use of environmental and community data indicators to monitor change and make sense of the magnitude of information.

Role of Data and Information in Environmental Planning and Management

Environmental planning involves the integration of scientific, engineering, and economic information with normative perceptions and values. This integration is a challenge because of the wide range of both quantitative and qualitative information. The planning process determines the type and specificity of information needed. As shown in box 2.1, *Scoping* (Step 0) identifies data needs and develops

TABLE 11.1 **Tiered Approach to Information Gathering and Analysis**

	Level of Detail	*Information Sources*	*Products*
Rapid Assessment	General, coarse scale; little analysis	Readily available information Available maps; secondary sources, Internet sources	Hand-drawn working maps Internet maps Lists
Intermediate Assessment	More specific data; more analysis	Remote sensing images; detailed secondary data sources	Information matrices; more detailed map displays
Advanced Assessment	Detailed, refined, targeted info; detailed analysis	Primary data sources; local maps Local knowledge; field surveys	GIS product maps; integration of data and analysis

a work plan for collecting and analyzing data. *Analysis* (Step 2) focuses on information gathering and analysis, but this activity continues throughout the process.

A Tiered Process

Information gathering and assessment often follows a tiered process, first by looking at readily available and general information, followed by increasing levels of detail. Many processes start with a **rapid assessment** that takes a quick look at problems and available information and tries to move quickly to initial action (see, e.g., Sayre et al., 2000; TNC, 1999). Although moving to action quickly has many advantages, rapid assessment should also identify needs for more detailed analysis to follow. This is sometimes referred to as **gap analysis,** or the identification of data gaps in need of filling. **Intermediate and advanced assessment** involves increasing levels of detail, more analysis, and more sophisticated data products. This tiered approach is illustrated in table 11.1.

Collection of basic data is the first step. This may include map or remotely sensed information on topography, soils, geology, and land use/land cover. More specific information on wetlands, habitats, and culturally significant areas acquired from field monitoring or citizens' local knowledge can be part of this basic data collection. Performing derived studies aims to make sense of this data as the information is prioritized and interpreted. Specific data and mapped products depend on the management objectives. Assessing environmentally sensitive and critical areas requires information on land use, land ownership, development infrastructure, population growth, and other factors influencing land use change. Methods such as build-out and environmental impact assessment can clarify possible future effects. The resulting mapped information can be used as a basis for land use planning and management. It also serves as a baseline for further studies.

Considerations and Pitfalls in Use of Data and Information

The proper use, accuracy, and documentation of land-related information depends on the consideration of a number of data issues. These should be considered throughout the planning and analysis process, especially in the early stages. The issues include form, scale, accuracy, coverage, completeness, age, confidentiality, maintenance, paper trail to sources, communication, and appropriateness (Hirschman, Randolph, and Flynn, 1992).

1. *Form:* Are the data digital (e.g., latitudes and longitudes in a database), spatial (e.g., on a map), temporal (e.g., plotted on a graph with a time dimension), or a combination of these (figure 11.1)? Are data qualitative (e.g., groundwater moves rapidly) or quantitative (flow is 50 feet per day)?

2. *Scale:* How large or small is the mapped representation of a given land area? If two maps are the same size, the large-scale map will represent less land than the small-scale map. Accordingly, the large-scale map is more detailed. This is important when overlaying maps of different scale (see figure 11.4).

3. *Accuracy:* How well do the data or mapped locations of features reflect their actual existence or location on the land surface (or how much "slop" is there in the mapped representation)? For example, DRASTIC categories (see chapter 15) are accurate to 100 acres while soil map units in a soil survey (chapter 12) are commonly accurate to 2 acres. The various accuracies of different data sets become crucial when comparing or overlaying information. Note that there is a difference between accuracy and precision. While **accuracy** is the degree of agreement between sample or map data and reality, **precision** is how well you can reproduce the data values that you measure, monitor, or map.

4. *Coverage:* What states, counties, USGS quad sheets, and/or tax parcels are included in a data set? For example, detailed geology maps have been published for only one of the nine quadrangle maps covering Montgomery County, Virginia.

5. *Completeness:* What percentage or number of a given feature is actually presented in a data set? Not every incidence of an endangered species, sinkhole, cave, land use practice, or other feature in the real world is represented on a map or in a database. Likewise, factors such as water quality, slope, and soil permeability are based on a limited number of sample points.

6. *Age:* How old are the data? The age of data is more important for factors such as land use and tax parcel boundaries, which can change in short periods of time, than for factors like geology.

7. *Confidentiality:* Should there be restrictions on the dissemination, use, and communication of certain data? This is an issue with data on endangered species, caves, and archaeological sites where widespread dissemination of the data may lead to adverse impacts to the resource. For example, agencies provide only general information about the location of endangered species to prevent poaching or habitat damage (figure 11.2).

8. *Maintenance:* What must be done to keep the data up-to-date or otherwise useful? If data are to be used in the planning process, they should be maintained as new data become available and existing data become obsolete. This is a particularly important consideration for data that are inherently changeable, such as tax parcel boundaries, or delineations that depend on federal and state policies, such as jurisdictional wetland boundaries or facilities with discharge permits.

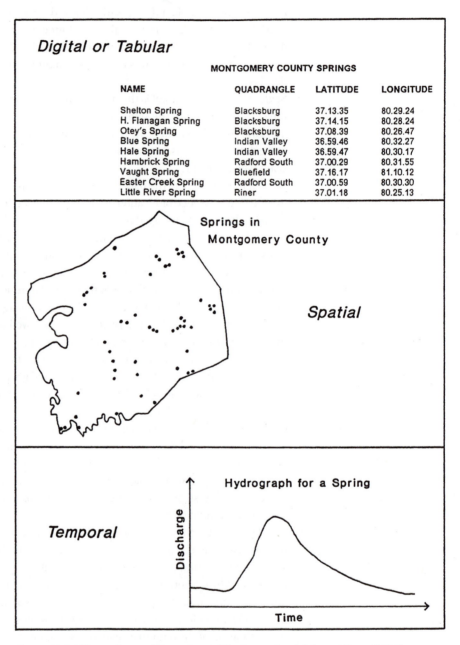

Figure 11.1 Different Forms of Data. *Source:* Hirschman, Randolph, and Flynn (1992).

9. *Paper Trail to Sources:* Creating a paper trail to the sources of a data product involves documenting the source agency, original scale, age, and information pertaining to accuracy for each data source used in a data analysis process. This documentation is critical if data products are to be used or procedures followed by other agencies, or if accuracy problems are to be analyzed. Data sources vary in quality according to the function, reliability, and reputation of source agencies, organizations, or personnel.

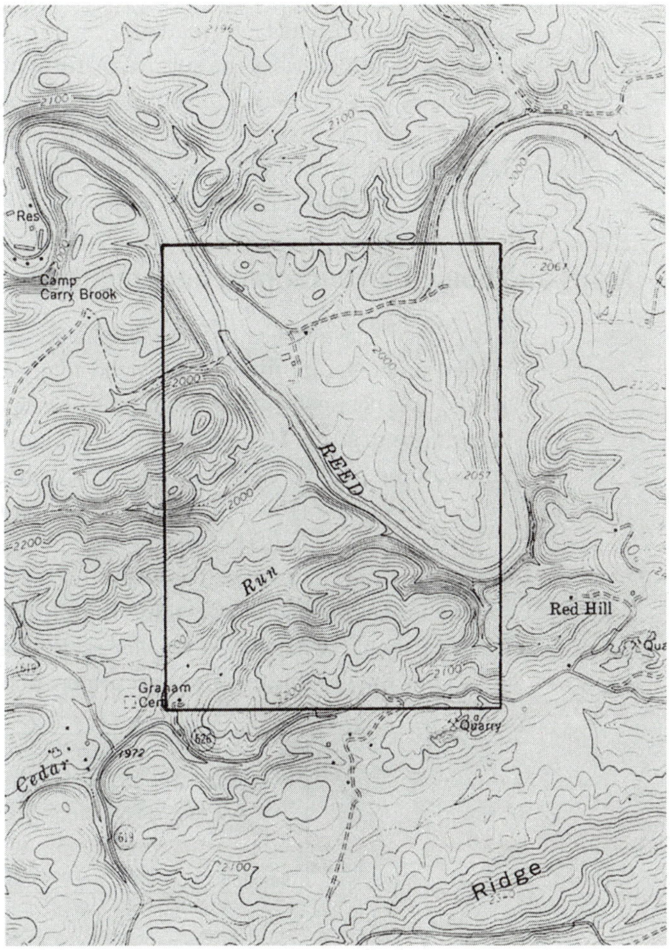

Figure 11.2 The Exact Location of an Endangered Species Is Confidential. Map shows a 1-minute longitude-latitude block to give general location only. *Source:* Hirschman, Randolph, and Flynn (1992).

10. *Communication with the Public and Decision Makers:* Is the data in a form that is understandable to laypeople, or does it require repackaging and interpretation for effective communication?

11. *Appropriateness:* How relevant are the data to a program's needs and applications? How can important qualitative data be used with quantitative data? What data and analytical methods will be most appropriate, accessible, and cost-effective for achieving program objectives?

Geospatial Information

There has been a revolution in the quality and availability of geospatial data, which, combined with GISs, have advanced the methods for land use and environmental planning. Before discussing these systems, it is important to understand some fundamentals of geospatial information.

Topography describes the surface features of the land including terrain, rivers and lakes, environmental resources, roads, and other man-made structures. Therefore, topographic investigation is an important first step in land analysis. Like most land information, topography is best represented in maps and remote sensing images like aerial photographs.

Maps and Some Cartographic Fundamentals

A map is a "masterpiece of false simplicity...(whose) secret meanings must be mulled upon, yet all the world is open to a glance" (Muehrcke and Muehrcke, 1998). Less poetically, maps are graphic descriptions of the surface features of the land drawn to scale. Map **scale** is the relationship of distance on the map to distance on the land. It can be represented as a graphical scale or as a fraction or ratio. For example, 1:24,000 means 1 inch on the map equals 24,000 inches or 2,000 feet on the land. The smaller the ratio or fraction value, the smaller is the scale. The ratio value is smaller when the second number (the land distance) of the ratio is larger. Therefore, counterintuitively, the smaller the scale, the larger the area shown. Remember: smaller scale = larger area; larger scale = smaller area. Only the graphical scale is accurate when the map is enlarged or reduced.

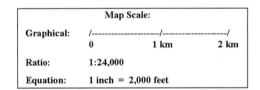

Figure 11.3 gives the map scales typically used in various planning studies, and figure 11.4 shows maps of four scales of the same area. The scales range from very large for project planning (e.g., 1:1,200 or 1 inch = 100 feet) to very small for state or regional planning (e.g., 1:1,000,000 or 1 inch = 16 miles). A map of larger scale shows a smaller area and usually more detail and accuracy.

Maps are two-dimensional, which creates a challenge to accurately represent scale for locations on the round earth. Geographic spherical **coordinate refer-**

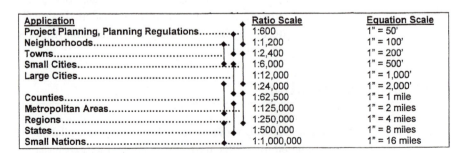

Application	Ratio Scale	Equation Scale
Project Planning, Planning Regulations	1:600	1" = 50'
Neighborhoods	1:1,200	1" = 100'
Towns	1:2,400	1" = 200'
Small Cities	1:6,000	1" = 500'
Large Cities	1:12,000	1" = 1,000'
	1:24,000	1" = 2,000'
Counties	1:62,500	1" = 1 mile
Metropolitan Areas	1:125,000	1" = 2 miles
Regions	1:250,000	1" = 4 miles
States	1:500,000	1" = 8 miles
Small Nations	1:1,000,000	1" = 16 miles

Figure 11.3 Scales of Maps Typically Used in Planning Studies

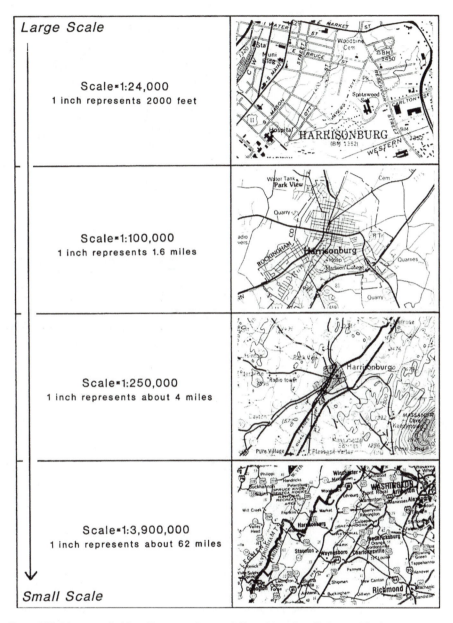

Figure 11.4 Large-scale Maps Represent Less and Show More Detail. *Source:* Hirschman, Randolph, and Flynn (1992).

encing uses longitude and latitude to accurately identify location. However, for flat maps representing scale in length, a grid coordinate system can identify location by x,y Cartesian planar coordinate system (see figure 11.5). The most used international plane grid system is the Universal Transverse Mercator (UTM) grid, which divides the earth into 60 longitudinal zones. A separate grid is made for each of the 60 zones. The method achieves an accuracy level of 1 part in 2,500 maximum error (Muehrcke and Muehrcke, 1998).

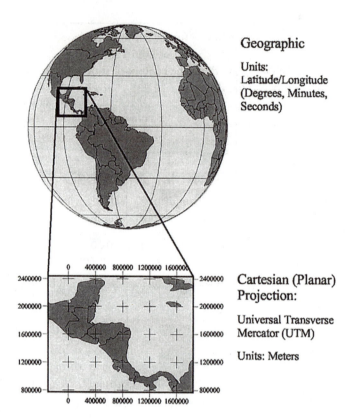

Figure 11.5 Coordinate Systems: Geographic versus Cartesian (Planar). *Source:* Sayre et al. (2000).

A **topographic** map is illustrated in figure 11.6. This standard USGS 1:24,000 quadrangle map shows a variety of land features, including water and forested land, and man-made features like roads, railroads, buildings, and communities. Topographic map symbols representing these features are described at: http://mac.usgs.gov/mac/isb/pubs/booklets/symbols/.

The topographic map also shows the area's vertical relief with **elevation contour lines.** These lines connect points on the land surface having the same elevation. The contour interval is the vertical distance between adjacent contour lines. The elevation above sea level is usually printed on every fifth contour line. The closer together the contour lines are, the steeper the terrain. The steepness or **slope** of the land is an important characteristic in determining its suitability for various uses and its susceptibility to erosion and landslides. A technique for measuring the slope of the terrain using elevation contour lines on a topographic map is described in chapter 12. These contour lines are also used to identify water drainage patterns; chapter 13 describes a method for using them to delineate drainage basin or watershed boundaries.

Planimetric maps do not show elevation contours and are usually used for **thematic** maps, which highlight specific information, such as geology or land use and land cover. **Land use/land cover maps** show vegetation type and how the land is used. Figure 11.7 gives examples of land use/land cover maps at 1:250,000 and

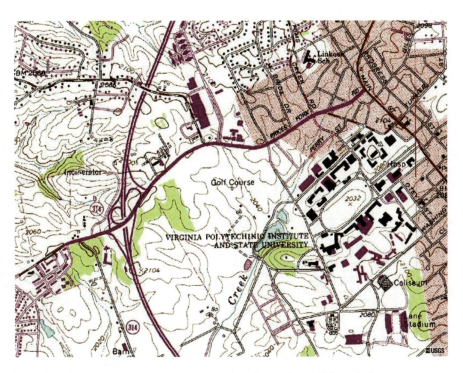

Figure 11.6 Portion of USGS 7.5-Minute Quadrangle Map for Blacksburg (VA)

1:24,000 scales. The numbers on the map refer to a standard classification system developed for these maps. The following list gives the categories for Levels 1 and 2 of the classification system. Level 1 has nine categories: urban or built-up land, agricultural, rangeland, forest, water areas, wetland, barren land, tundra, and perennial snow or ice. Each general class is subdivided into several detailed Level 2 classes.

USGS Level 1 and 2 Land Use and Land Cover Classification System

LEVEL 1	LEVEL 2
1 Urban/built-up land	11 Residential
	12 Commercial and services
	13 Industrial
	14 Transportation, utilities
	15 Industrial/comm. complexes
	16 Mixed urban or built-up land
	17 Other urban or built-up land
2 Agricultural land	21 Cropland and pasture
	22 Orchards, vineyards, nurseries, ornamental horticultural areas
	23 Confined feeding operations
	24 Other agricultural land
3 Rangeland	31 Herbaceous rangeland
	32 Shrub and brush rangeland

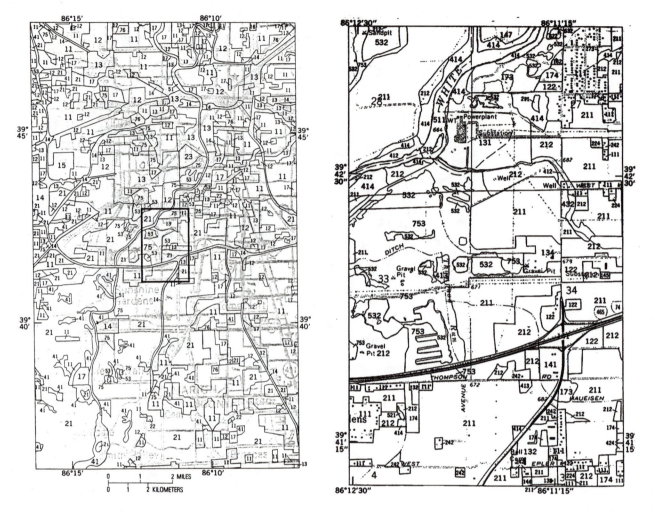

Figure 11.7 Land Use/Land Cover Maps: 1:250,000 (Level 2) and 1:24,000 (Level 3). *Source:* Anderson et al. (1976).

	33 Mixed rangeland
4 Forestland	41 Deciduous forestland
	42 Evergreen forestland
	43 Mixed forestland
5 Water	51 Streams and canals
	52 Lakes
	53 Reservoirs
	54 Bays and estuaries
6 Wetland	61 Forested wetland
	62 Nonforested wetland
7 Barren land	71 Dry salt flats
	72 Beaches
	73 Sandy areas other than beaches
	74 Bare exposed rock
	75 Strip mines, quarries, gravel pit

	76	Transitional areas
	77	Mixed barren land
8 Tundra	81	Shrub and brush tundra
	82	Herbaceous tundra
	83	Bare ground tundra
	84	Wet tundra
	85	Mixed tundra
9 Perennial snow/ice	91	Perennial snowfields
	92	Glacier

These land use/land cover maps are derived from aerial photos and satellite images. The 1992 series of land use/land cover data was based on Landsat data at the 1:100,000 and 1:250,000 scales. The series was updated in 2000 with Landsat 7 data (http://lcluc.gsfc.nasa.gov/ and http://edcwww.cr.usgs.gov/glis/hyper/guide/1_250_lulc).

Large-scale maps (e.g., 1:600 to 1:12,000) are usually produced by local agencies. The U.S. Geological Survey (USGS) National Mapping Program (NMP) is the best source of intermediate and smaller scale (1:24,000 and smaller) topographic maps in the United States. The agency produces maps at scales from 1:24,000 to 1:1,000,000. The most useful USGS maps for community planning are the so-called 7.5-minute series, which show areas 7.5 minutes latitude by 7.5 minutes longitude in size at a scale of 1:24,000 (1 inch = 2,000 feet). Figure 11.6 is from this series. In addition, the USGS produces a 15-minute series (1:62,500), as well as maps at scales of 1:125,000, 1:250,000, 1:500,000, and 1:1,000,000 (see figure 11.4 for examples). USGS also has completed land use–land cover maps for the entire United States at scales of 1:100,000 and 1:250,000.

Box 11.1 gives the graphical map products available from USGS. More information on map products is available from the NMP (http://mapping.usgs.gov/esic/index.html). The digital age is rapidly changing the production and access to maps. USGS has turned to map-on-demand (print-on-demand) in response to specific requests, replacing their traditional approach of printing and warehousing maps at the Rocky Mountain Mapping Center and hundreds of retail dealers. Finding and ordering maps online is provided by the USGS MapFinder website, which allows users to locate and order USGS by zip code or place name (see http://edcwww.cr.usgs.gov/Webglis/glisbin/finder_main.pl?dataset_name = MAPS_LARGE). Maps can be viewed online from USGS private partners (e.g., Microsoft's TerraServer, http://terraserver.homeadvisor.msn.com/default.asp).

Remote Sensing Information: Aerial Photos and Satellite Imagery

Remote sensing is simply the observation or measurement of data from a distance. Advances in remote sensing technologies in the last few decades have greatly improved our observation of the environment. Just as the first images of the earth from space raised global consciousness, digital photographic images and satellite data have raised our capabilities in monitoring, analyzing, and understanding the earth's processes and our impacts on them. Before looking at aerial photos and satellite data, we must address some fundamentals of remote sensing.

BOX 11.1 — Graphical Map Products Available from USGS

The production of digital cartographic data and graphic maps comprises the largest component of the Survey's NMP. Cartographic data are compiled from aerial photographs, other remotely sensed images, historical records, legal documents, and direct field observations and surveys and comply with standards of content, geometric accuracy, and presentation.

Printed Maps

Topographic Quadrangle Maps: The USGS's most familiar product is the 1:24,000-scale topographic quadrangle map. This is the scale of data produced and depicts greater detail for a smaller area than intermediate-scale (1:50,000 and 1:100,000) and small-scale (1:250,000, 1:2,000,000 or smaller) products, which show selectively less detail for larger areas.

Thematic Maps: Maps in which information on special subjects is geographically displayed on planimetric base maps or overlays registered to planimetric or topographic base maps. This category includes land use and land cover and associated maps, and National Atlas maps.

Other Format Maps: This category consists of maps in nonquadrangle format. These maps include a county map series, state base map series, U.S. base maps, a national park series, and outline maps of the world. Scales range from 1:960 to 1:80 million.

Other Map Products: Other map products, published to meet the special needs of federal agencies, include National Imagery and Mapping Agency (NIMA) 15-minute topographic maps, Antarctic map series, shaded relief topographic maps, satellite image maps, and U.S. border maps.

For more information see http://mapping .usgs.gov/www/products/1product.html and http://mapping.usgs.gov/www/products/ status.html.

Some Remote Sensing Fundamentals

Remote sensing technologies detect electromagnetic radiant energy reflected or emitted from objects and land surfaces. The characteristics of this radiation can be interpreted and analyzed to reveal practical information about those objects and surfaces. Figure 11.8 gives the electromagnetic spectrum, which shows a range of frequencies or wavelengths of the radiation from very short waves gamma rays and X-rays (<0.001 micrometers [microns]) to visible light (0.4–0.7 microns) to near infrared (0.7–0.9) to shortwave infrared (1.6–2.5) to thermal infrared (8–12) to microwaves and radio waves (>1000 microns).

All objects emit radiation. In addition, emitted radiation from the sun (and from active remote sensing devices, like radar) reflects off surfaces and objects. The reflected radiation is determined by the characteristics of the object, that is, its color, orientation, and thermal properties. Figure 11.9 gives the "spectral signatures" of different objects or surfaces in the visible and near-infrared wavelengths. In the visible range the reflected radiation is a function of the object's color. In the near-infrared range, it is a function of its temperature and thermal properties.

Passive remote sensing devices, like photographic and video cameras and thermal and multispectral scanners, simply detect the radiation reflected and emitted by surface objects. **Active** sensors, like radar and sonar, emit their own waves to illuminate features of interest, then measure the reflected wavelengths that return.

Photographic cameras use film emulsions that are sensitive to visible or infrared wavelengths and produce an image. Multispectral scanners, on the other

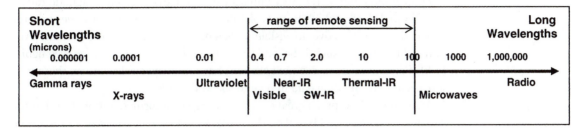

Figure 11.8 The Electromagnetic Spectrum and the Wavelength Range of Remote Sensing

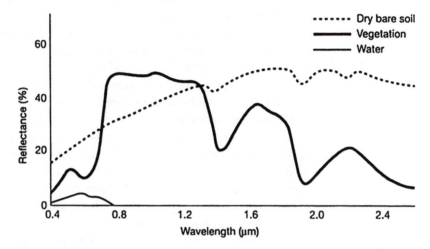

Figure 11.9 Spectral Reflectance of Vegetation, Water, and Bare Soil. *Source:* Thomas Lillesand and Ralph Kiefer, 2004, Remote Sensing and Image Interpretation, 4th edition. New York: John Wiley and Sons. Used with permission of Thomas Lillesand.

hand, actually measure radiation data separately in several spectral or wavelength bands. Having digital data in different wavelengths for the same object or surface permits more sophisticated computer analysis and interpretation.

Aerial Photos

Aerial photographs have long been a key source of topographic information. Aerial photos vary in **scale, view angle,** and **spectral characteristics,** all of which determine the type and usefulness of information they display. Most aerial photographs show a **vertical** view angle. **Oblique** photos are those taken at an angle less than perpendicular to the surface; they are often used by planners for visual assessments.

Scale depends on the elevation from which photos are taken and the lenses used. Only vertical photos are accurate in scale, and their accuracy depends on the elevation of the sensor. Vertical views taken from low to medium elevations are often distorted in scale toward the edges of the image. Objects at the edges are a greater distance from the sensor than are those at the center of the image and will appear relatively smaller than they are.

Photographic film can detect different wavelengths of electromagnetic radiation. Normal black-and-white and color film tries to replicate what we see and so is designed to be sensitive to visible wavelengths detected by the human eye. Infrared film senses slightly beyond the visible into the infrared range (see figure 11.8). Satellite sensors (see next section) have multispectral scanners that measure separately radiation data in several spectral bands.

Analysts can interpret a great deal of topographic information from the characteristics of photo images based on the image's texture, tone, the size and shape of objects, their site and association with other objects, and terrain. Terrain can be visualized from photographs by viewing them stereoscopically. Using a stereo-viewer, the observer focuses each eye on the same location in photo pairs, and a three-dimensional image emerges.

Spectral factors can also aid in interpretation. **Near-infrared** photos provide several distinct contrasts: wet areas (lakes, streams, wetlands) are very dark, dry meadows and woodlands are light, and conifers are darker than deciduous trees. In color infrared photos, healthy deciduous trees and lawns appear red, while conifers are a darker purple. **Thermal infrared** images can detect surface temperatures.

Microwave radar imagery differs from conventional photography in two ways. First, rather than a passive system sensing natural radiation, it uses an active sensing system, generating waves that bounce off objects on the land and are detected by the sensor. Second, it uses wavelengths well outside the visible spectrum, enabling sensing of surface features not detectable from natural radiation. Side-looking airborne radar (SLAR) produces images resembling air photos with a low-angle sun and shadow effects.

Aerial photos are used by planners for mapmaking, for identifying and interpreting terrain features (Way, 1978), for environmental inventories and monitoring, and as a source of data and digital images for GISs. For example, the USGS has used vertical aerial photographs to produce and update its topographic maps since 1928.

In the 1970s, USGS began producing **orthophotoquads** or nondistorted photomaps at the scale of the 7.5-minute quadrangle series. Using a photomechanical process, the Survey is able to eliminate the scale distortion of vertical photographs; then, information from the 7.5-minute map can be superimposed onto the so-called orthophotograph, producing the photomap. From 1980 to 1987, the USGS National High-Altitude Aerial Photography (NHAP) program produced the images for orthophotoquads. In 1987 the program was renamed and reconfigured as the National Aerial Photography Program (NAPP). The program produces standardized photos taken from a constant altitude of 20,000 feet taken at the center of each quarter section of each 7.5-minute quadrangle.

Each photo is 9″ × 9″ covering 5 square miles at a scale of 1:40,000. The photos are digitized and rectified to correct for distortion at the edges. For each location, new photos are produced every 5–7 years and serve as the main source for updates of USGS topographic maps. Since 1990 these photos have been taken in both black-and-white and color infrared. A color infrared digital orthophoto "quarter" quad (DOQQ) for Blacksburg, Virginia, is shown in figure 11.10. It shows one-quarter of the area of the Blacksburg quadrangle map.

Figure 11.10 Color Infrared Digital Orthophoto Quarter Quad Photo for Blacksburg (VA)

Satellite Images and Data

Satellite remote sensing has revolutionized environmental monitoring and data collection. It has two distinct advantages over traditional aerial photos: (1) using a multispectral scanner, it produces digital data in different wavelength bands for use in computer imaging and GIS; and (2) whereas aerial photos are a "snapshot in time," satellites provide recurring data of the same location at frequent intervals (e.g., 16 days for Landsat 7, one day for Terra's MODIS sensor), providing continual monitoring.

Satellite digital imagery measures the amount of radiation received from a specific location on the ground. The images are produced as picture elements or "pixels" of a given resolution grid-cell size. The finer the resolution, the more spatially detailed the resulting data. The Landsat 4 multispectral scanner (MSS) had a resolution of about 80 meters square or 1.5 acres. The Thematic Mapper (TM) sensor on Landsat 5 (launched in 1984) improved this resolution to about 30 meters or 0.2 acres. Landsat 7 (launched in April 1999) has the Enhanced Thematic Mapper Plus (ETM+) which has the same resolution of the TM but adds a panchromatic band with a 15-meter resolution. The French SPOT satellite data has a resolution of 10 meters or 1,000 square feet in certain bands. For SPOT satellite images, see http://www.spot.com.

The Terra satellite was launched in December 1999 and it contains five state-of-the-art sensor systems. The most practical data to-date have come from the ASTER (advanced spaceborne thermal emission and reflection radiometer) sensor, which senses 14 spectral bands (4 in the visible and near infrared [VNIR], [0.52–0.86 microns], 6 in the shortwave infrared [1.6–2.4 microns], and 5 in the thermal infrared [8.1–11.6 microns]) at varying resolutions. At 15 meters in the VNIR range, ASTER provides four times the resolution of Landsat 7. The MODIS sensor, also aboard the Terra, provides near daily repeat coverage of the entire globe. New commercial satellites, such as Space Imaging's IKONOS sensor launched in 2000, are producing even finer resolution in the 1-meter to 4-meter (10–160 sq. ft.) range for panchromatic images and 4-meter to 10-meter range for mulitspectral data. Further refinements are expected.

For examples of some amazing images from Landsat 7, ASTER, MODIS, and other Terra sensors, see Landsat 7 Image browser (http://edclxs2.cr.usgs.gov/L7ImgViewer.shtml), NASA's Visible Earth website (http://visibleearth.nasa.gov/) and USGS's EROS Data Center's Distributed Active Archive Center (DAAC) (http://edcaac.usgs.gov/dataproducts.html and http://edcaac.usgs.gov/samples). See also Space Imaging, Inc.'s website for images from the IKONOS sensor (www.spaceimaging.com). An example of use of satellite data in rapid ecological assessment is described in chapter 16 (see figure 16.7).

The satellite sensors record values in different spectral wavelength bands for each pixel. The data can be entered into computer programs, and the digital values for different bands can be retrieved individually or in combination for interpretation. Figure 11.11 shows how values from two bands can be interpreted to distinguish types of land cover. For example, areas with a Landsat band 7 value of 30–40 and band 5 value of 20–25 are dense forests. Pixels having specific digital values or combinations of values can be assigned certain colors by the programs

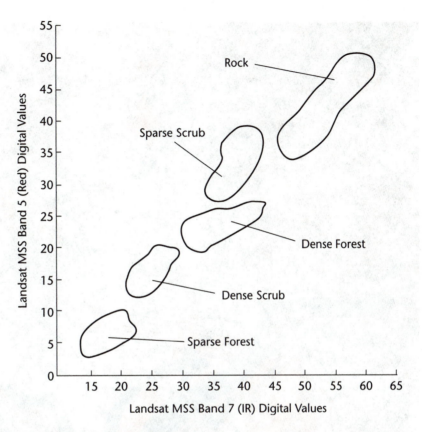

Figure 11.11 Data from Two Spectral Bands Combine to Indicate Land Cover. *Source:* James B. Campbell, 1983, Mapping the Land: Aerial Imagery for Land Use Information. Used with permission of the Association of American Geographers.

and can be displayed on a monitor and photographed or printed. Figure 11.12 gives an image from the ASTER sensor on Terra. The real usefulness of these data is that they are in digital form and can be used in combination with other spatial information in geographic information systems.

Aerial Photo and Satellite Image Availability

Box 11.2 gives remote sensing products available through USGS. The EROS Data Center (EDC) (http://edcwrw.cr.usgs.gov) is the main source for aerial photos and satellite images. EDC houses 8 million aerial photos dating back to the 1940s. NAPP has a user-friendly interface for searching, viewing, and ordering aerial photos called PhotoFinder, which, like MapFinder, allows users to search for and order aerial photos by zip code (http://edc.usgs.gov/Webglis/glisbin/finder_main.pl?dataset_name=NAPP). USGS's Earth Explorer (http://edcsns17.cr.usgs.gov/EarthExplorer/) data discovery and access tool (formerly the Global Land Information System [GLIS]) also provides online searching for specific products.

As they do for map products, USGS's private partners (Microsoft's TerraServer and MapMart) provide online services for searching, viewing, and ordering aerial

Figure 11.12 Washington, D.C., June 1, 2000, from the ASTER Sensor on Terra Satellite. This composite of three bands in visible and infrared range shows vegetation in red, water in dark greys and built-up areas in light blues. With 15-meter resolution, ASTER can see individual buildings. With revisit time of 4–16 days, ASTER can monitor changes on the earth's surface.

photos (see http://mapping.usgs.gov/partners/viewonline.html and http://mapping.usgs.gov/esic/esic.html). TerraServer provides viewing of orthophotoquads down to 1-meter resolution and downloading of .jpg image files. Try it: http://terraserver.homeadvisor.msn.com/default.asp.

Aerial photos of larger scale are available from other online vendors. For example, Vargis Eyemap (www.vargis.com) provides downloadable images down to 1-foot resolution. Many local governments and other agencies produce their own aerial photos at the coverage and scale they need. Often these are made available

BOX 11.2—Remote Sensing Products Available from USGS

Aerial Photographs

Aerial photographs archived and distributed by the USGS include the repository of multiagency National Aerial Photography Program (NAPP) photos at 1:40,000 scale in color, infrared, or black and white; National High Altitude Aerial Photography Program (NHAP) photos at 1:58,000 scale for color and infrared and 1:80,000 for black and white; and other aerial photos.

Orthophotoquads: Orthophotoquads are distortion-free aerial photographs that are formatted and printed as standard 7.5-minute, 1:24,000-scale quadrangles (15-minute in Alaska) or as quarter quadrangles at a scale of 1:12,000.

Satellite Images and Satellite-Derived Data

Satellite Photographs: From NASA.

Satellite Image Maps: Experimental multicolored or black-and-white image maps produced from digital data collected by Land Satellite (Landsat) and Systeme Probatoire d'Observation de la Terre (SPOT) sensors. Scales range from 1:24,000 (Point Loma, Calif.) to 1:7,500,000 (conterminous 48 states).

Photo Products Derived from Airborne and Satellite Sensor Data: These include color and black-and-white photographic products generated from advanced very high resolution radiometer (AVHRR), side-looking airborne radar (SLAR), land satellite (LANDSAT), and Systeme Probatoire d'Observation de la Terre (SPOT) imagery digital data.

to the public and private firms for a fee. The Landsat 7 Image Viewer gives users an opportunity to view online worldwide Landsat images. Three clicks of the mouse zeroes you in from a world map to the Landsat image of your region. Try it out: http://glovis.usgs.gov/.

NASA's EOS Data Gateway is a web-based query system that provides information on a variety of data sets, with documentation, image browsing, and ordering services (http://edcimswww.cr.usgs.gov/pub/imswelcome/).

Environmental Monitoring with Remote Sensing and Future Prospects

The increasing availability and quality of remote sensing data has resulted in greater application in environmental monitoring. Box 11.3 lists the variety of applications and data that can be derived from satellite and other sensors. In many places, such environmental data already exist at a larger scale and with more accuracy than remotely sensed data can provide. But keep in mind that much of the world's land is not even mapped at a practical scale, and satellite and other imagery provides the first look at this resource information. This is especially useful for rapid environmental assessment. Remote sensing also provides continual sensing at recurring intervals, which is essential to monitor environmental change. NAPP produces orthophotoquads and DOQQ at a 5- to 7-year interval. But satellite data from Landsat 7 has 16-day repeat coverage of the same location, and the MODIS sensor on the Terra satellite provides almost daily repeat cover-

---

BOX 11.3—Environmental Monitoring Applications of Remote Sensing

Natural Hazards

- Disaster assessment
- Hazard monitoring:
  Meteorological (storms, tornadoes, hurricane rainfall, flooding, snowfall, drought)
  Beach erosion
  Insect infestation (e.g., gypsy moth)
  Disease and forest fires

Water

- Hydrometeorology
- Watersheds
- Floodplain mapping
- Wetlands monitoring
- Impervious surface
- Ocean temperatures

Ecology, Conservation, Resource Management

- Vegetation and wetlands inventories
- Forestry (e.g., tree stand inventories, forest disease and pest infestation)

- Wildlife studies, habitat types, fragmentation
- Resource exploration and inventories

Soils

- Soil color, roughness, temperature, moisture

Landform, Land Use, Crop Production

- Landscape patches
- Land use/land cover
- Impervious surface
- Urban heat island (e.g., Stone and Rodgers, 2001)
- Urban sprawl (e.g., as measured by vegetation change or impervious surface)

(*Source:* Derived from Hart, 1999)

---

age, albeit at a smaller scale. For examples of satellite images depicting environmental change, see the Earthshots website (http://edcwww.cr.usgs.gov/earth shots/slow/tableofcontents).

Figure 11.13 shows how satellite data can be used to monitor impervious surface. Developed by Andrew Smith from the Mid-Atlantic Regional Earth Science Applications Center (RESAC) at the University of Maryland, the image of the Washington–Baltimore corridor shows highly concentrated impervious surfaces in red, moderate areas in blue, and low concentrations in green. It was developed with Landsat 7 data and data from the private 1-meter resolution IKONOS satellite sensor, operated by Space Imaging, Inc. From 450 miles up, the satellite collects space data images at the same resolution of DOQQ, but with far greater frequency than the 5- to 7-year return time of the DOQQ.

Considering the improvements in technology and data availability over the past 30 years, it is hard to imagine future possibilities. Further advances in spatial and spectral resolution are likely to create unforeseen applications. If we can "read a license plate from space," as some are predicting, we can count wildlife, monitor land use change, "witness" real-time environmental change, and greatly enhance environmental assessment and forecasting. Applications will depend on data availability and cost. Downloadable, perhaps "real-time," data from the Internet to GIS is likely, but costs may increase as remote sensing moves from subsidized government programs to private, for-profit enterprises.

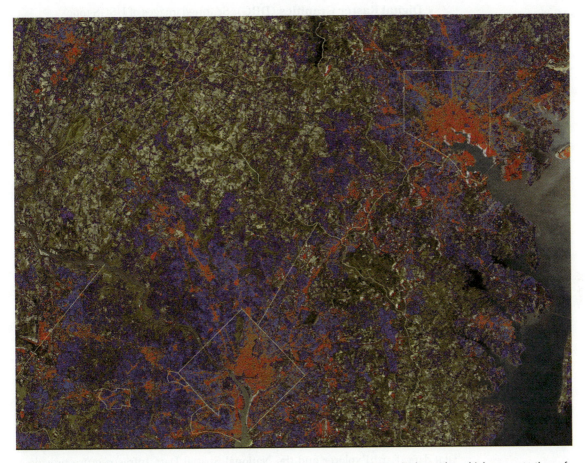

Figure 11.13 Extent of Impervious Surfaces in Washington, D.C., to Baltimore Region. Red areas have high concentrations of impervious surfaces, blue moderate concentrations and green low concentration. *Source:* Visible Earth (http://visibleearth. nasa.gov/cgi-bin/viewrecord?8152) Image produced by Andrew Smith, Mid-Atlantic RESAC, University of Maryland. Image courtesy Stu Snodgrass, NASA GSFC Scientific Visualization Studio, based on data from Landsat 7 and IKONOS.

Digital Map and Remote Sensing Data

The real revolution in spatial environmental data has come through the production and availability of geospatial digital data. Nearly all of the products discussed to this point are not only available in digital form but also downloadable from the Internet. The primary data include the following:

- **Digital Line Graphs (DLG):** Vector files containing line data, such as roads and streams, digitized from USGS topographic maps.
- **TIGER files:** Developed by the U.S. Census Bureau to support the 1990 Census, TIGER line files were among the first digital vector data available to the public for the entire United States. The database includes roads, railroads, rivers, lakes, political boundaries, census boundaries, and other data, including location in longitude and latitude.

- **Digital Raster Graphics (DRG):** Scanned images of USGS topographic maps. The image inside the map neatline is georeferenced to the earth's surface.
- **Digital Elevation Models (DEM):** Digital records of terrain elevations for ground positions at regularly spaced horizontal intervals. DEM's are developed from stereo models or digital contour line files derived from USGS topographic quadrangle maps.
- **Land Use and Land Cover (LULC):** LULC data are derived from thematic overlays registered to 1:250,000-scale base maps and a limited number of 1:100,000-scale base maps. Associated maps display information in five data categories: (1) political units, (2) hydrologic units, (3) census county subdivisions, (4) federal land ownership, and (5) state land ownership.
- **Digital Orthophoto Quarter Quads (DOQQ):** These are digital images of aerial photographs. The DOQQ combines the image characteristics of a photograph with the geometric qualities of a map. The standard DOQQ produced by the USGS is a black-and-white or color-infrared 1-meter ground resolution quarter quadrangle (3.75-minute) image.
- **Digital Satellite Data:** Products include advanced very high resolution radiometer (AVHRR) images, Landsat Thematic Mapper (TM) and Multispectral Scanner (MSS) digital data; and Terra ASTER and MODIS sensor data.

Several government Internet sites provide searching and ordering of these digital data. EarthExplorer and the National Spatial Data Infrastructure provide a clearinghouse search form to search data servers around the world. Satellite data is available from USGS's EROS Data Center's DAAC (http://edcaac.usgs.gov/dataproducts.html) and from the EOS Data Gateway (http://eorims.cr.usgs.gov/imswelcome), NASA's web-based query system. The Earth Explorer website gives data availability display for any location. Images and data can be ordered online. You can also preview some of the available images online, like DOQQs. Give it a look: http://edcsns17.cr.usgs.gov/EarthExplorer/.

High-resolution digital photos are available from private sources. VARGIS provides 1-foot resolution photos for use in GIS. It uses MrSID, a file compression and expansion software developed by LizardTech, Inc., to compress very large digital files at 20–1 without loss of image detail. Using MrSID, one CD can hold images for all of Washington, D.C., at 1-foot resolution. See www.vargis.com.

The digital form of data enhances accessibility and availability because it can be easily transferred via the Internet. However, the greatest benefit of digital geospatial data is that they are directly usable in GIS. GIS can manipulate and model the available data layers to generate product maps and visualizations for better understanding of environmental systems and change and better-informed planning (see GIS section later in this chapter).

Community Environmental Planning Data on the Internet

We live in the midst of an information revolution. Through the Internet, never before has so much data and information been so accessible to so many. Advances in software and hardware, the increasing electronic connectedness of the population, and government decisions to post all documents and data on the Internet have all contributed to this revolution. The hard part is making sense of it all, keeping pace with the rate of expansion, and ensuring the reliability of available information. An assumption here is that the most valid source of data is government sources; most private sources are reliable but should be subject to closer scrutiny.

Box 11.4 summarizes several sources of such data available for viewing and downloading from the Internet. One of the best sites is the USGS National Spatial Data Infrastructure Clearinghouse site. The USGS EarthExplorer site and the National Atlas Map Layers site are perhaps the best national sources of GIS data layers.

Internet Mapping and Data Monitoring

Software advances have brought interactive mapping to the Internet, allowing users to access environmental geospatial information they specify. Citizens now demand to do their own assessment of their local environment. Through new Internet software, citizens can access instantaneously local data in a form they request. In addition, interactive software allows agencies and groups to tap local knowledge and citizen monitoring via the Internet. ArcIMS (Internet mapping server) was developed by the Earth Science Research Institute (ESRI), Inc., to enable users to create a map service on the Internet. Several interactive mapping sites are available with a wealth of information. Although the results should always be reviewed for accuracy, they are useful for rapid assessment.

EPA's Enviromapper Storefront includes several community-level mapping links given in the following list. "Surf Your Watershed," for example, has links to environmental data in the watershed and offers the opportunity for the user to add information to the database. Other local mapping websites include the Wetlands Mapper Tool of the U.S. Fish and Wildlife Service and National Atlas Make-a-Map. Most use ArcIMS.

Internet Mapper Websites for Environmental Mapping

EPA EnviroMapper: http://www.epa.gov/enviro/enviromapper

Many states and local governments provide their own interactive mapping for use by their citizens; a good example is the Town of Blacksburg, Virginia: http://arcims2.webgis.net/blacksburg/default.asp?

EPA Window on My Environment: http://www.epa.gov/enviro/wme

EPA Surf Your Watershed: http://www.epa.gov/surf

EPA Brownfields: http://www.epa.gov/enviro/

EPA EnviroFacts: http://www.epa.gov/enviro/

EPA Superfund: http://www.epa.gov/enviro/

USFWS National Wetlands Mapper: http://wetlands.fws.gove/mapper_tool.htm

National Atlas Make-a-Map: http://www.nationalatlas.gov

BOX 11.4—Internet Sites for Viewing and Downloading Geospatial Data

Download Data Online

USGS National Spatial Data Infrastructure Clearinghouse: http://mapping.usgs.gov/nsdi/

USGS geographic data download: DEM, NED, DLG, LULC, NLCD, NHD: http://edcwww.cr.usgs.gov/doc/edchome/ndcdb/ndcdb.html

USGS EarthExplorer—view Landsat and DOQQ plus order Landsat, DOQQ, DEM, DRG, DLG, NAPP: http://edcsns17.cr.usgs.gov/EarthExplorer/

USGS EROS Data Center: http://edcwww.cr.usgs.gov/

USGS Geodata Explorer (Geologic Division)—access, view, and download geospatial databases: http://geode.usgs.gov/

USGS State Land Cover Data: http://edcw2ks15.cr.usgs.gov/lccp/nlcd_db.asp

National Atlas Map Layers: http://www.nationalatlas.gov

EPA Land Use and Land Cover data is repackaged for easy download: http://www.epa.gov/OWOW/watershed/andcover/onefile.html

SSURGO provides county-based soils map at 1:24,000: http://www.ftw.nrcs.usda.gov/ssur_data.html

ESRI site: Tigerline and Census data for download: http://www.esri.com/data/online/tiger/data.html.

GIS Data Depot—private site with many sources: http://www.gisdatadepot.com

Data Viewing and Ordering Online

Online maps and photos (USGS partners) (viewer): http://mapping.usgs.gov/partners/viewon line.html

Microsoft TerraServer (USGS partner) (view/download .jpg maps and photos): http://terraserver.homeadvisor.msn.com/default.asp

USGS Digital Backyard—describes topomaps, aerial photos, DRG, DOQQ: http://mapping.usgs.gov/digitalbackyard/

USGS PhotoFinder—locate, view, and order NAPP photos: http://edcwww.cr.usgs.gov/Webglis/glisbin/finder_main.pl?dataset_name=NAPP

USGS MapFinder—locate and order USGS maps: http://edcwww.cr.usgs.gov/Webglis/glisbin/finder_main.pl?dataset_name=MAPS_LARGE

USGS Land Use/Land Cover, Urban Dynamics Time Series: http://landcover.usgs.gov/urbanlandcover.html

Counties Soil Source (one example): http://www.vgin.state.va.us/localgovt/Wythe%20County.htm

USGS Landsat 7 Browse Image Viewer: http://glovis.usgs.gov/

National Atlas Make-a-Map: http://www.nationalatlas.gov

Geography network—collaborative system that connects data and services: http://www.geographynetwork.com

In addition to interactive mapping data, a wide range of other data forms are available on government Internet sites. For example, real-time water flow and 4-hour lag water quality data are available from USGS Water Watch (http://water.usgs.gov/waterwatch/) and EPA websites. Users identify monitoring locations on Internet maps. Other sites give biological data (http://www.nbii.gov/, http://www.gap.uidaho.edu/).

Considering recent expansion of data available on the Internet, it is difficult to anticipate what the future will hold. Clearly the trends toward improved public access, visualization of data, downloadable data, and timeliness of data are likely to continue. One potential change is the greater use of interactive information entry by monitoring groups, neighborhood organizations, and the public. Although data reliability issues must be addressed, capacity for such interactive information sharing has significant potential for tapping local knowledge, assisting government agencies in gathering and posting data, and improving community involvement.

Geographic Information Systems

The power of digital data has been realized with advances in GIS. The GIS has emerged as one of the most widely used and fundamental computer systems for any application requiring spatial information. It has revolutionized the field of cartographic analysis and mapmaking, rendering virtually obsolete the cartographic artisan with pen in hand. The advances have included:

- *Improvements in computer software:* Improved analytical capabilities, graphic display, user-friendliness, and affordability have expanded GIS users in 10 short years from sophisticated experts to every local government to home users.
- *Improvements in computer hardware:* From the 1970s to as recently as the early 1990s, GIS systems had to run on mainframe computers and produced blocky plotted maps that took considerable imagination to interpret. Improved software required improved hardware, including faster and larger-memory computers, higher-resolution monitors, and faster and higher-quality printers and plotters. As these hardware devices have become readily available, GIS moved from mainframe to desktop to laptop computers, and printed map products outpaced manual cartographic capabilities. At the same time, they became more affordable, attracting increasing numbers of users.
- *Improvements in spatial databases:* As software and hardware improved, the limiting factor in the use of computer GIS systems was digital data. Spatial data were available from maps and aerial photos, but they were not in digital form. Digitizing these data manually was tedious and costly. As already discussed, the scope, resolution, and availability of digital spatial data have exploded in the past 10 years. Like hardware and software, the increased availability and affordability of data have enabled a wide range of users. Finally, increased availability and affordability of global positioning systems (GPS) have enhanced the gathering and monitoring of digital field data for use in GIS.
- *Improvements in applications:* Success begets success. More and new uses of GIS have illustrated the possibilities and led to additional applications. These include new clients (e.g., the uses for commercial marketing are endless), new fields (e.g., bioinformatics), new dimensions (e.g., 3-D, fly-by, and fly-through projections), and new forms of product delivery (e.g., Internet mapping systems).

As a result of these advances, GIS has grown by 10 times from 1994 ($0.76 million) to a $7.7 billion industry in 2001. This figure includes $5.4 billion in GIS services, $1.1 billion in software sales, and $0.8 billion in related hardware sales. Earth Systems Research Institute (ESRI), Inc., makers of the Arc suite of products, including ArcInfo, ArcView GIS, ArcIMS, and others, now dominates worldwide GIS software market with a 35 percent share. Intergraph, Inc., is a distant second at 13 percent (Daratech, 2002).

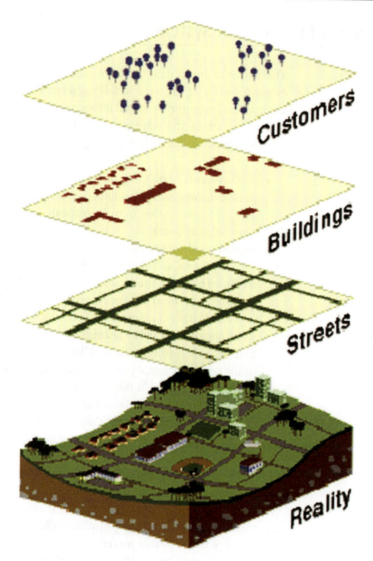

Figure 11.14 GIS Stores Data in Layers. *Source:* ESRI. Image reprinted courtesy of ESRI and used with permission. Copyright © ESRI. All rights reserved.

Some Fundamentals of GIS

A GIS is a set of interrelated computer technologies that achieve the entry, storage, processing, retrieval, and generation of spatial data (Carstensen, 1999). As discussed, advances in software, hardware, data, and training have brought GIS from the domain of the geographic specialist to that of any computer user. GIS is used to make and update maps, integrate maps and other information from a variety of sources, analyze spatial information, and inform decisions about land use, natural resources, demographics, commercial markets, and innumerable other applications with spatial dimensions.

GIS is often characterized as four components:

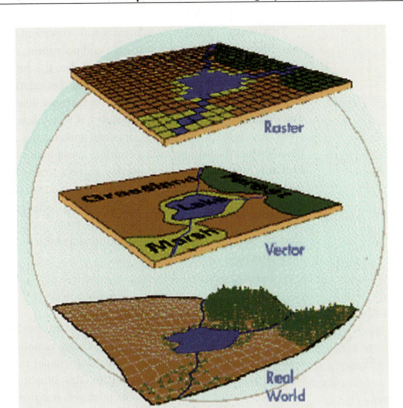

Figure 11.15 Raster and Vector Data Formats. *Source:* ESRI. Image reprinted courtesy of ESRI and used with permission. Copyright © ESRI. All rights reserved.

1. **Hardware** or the computer processing, memory, digitizing, and printing components
2. **Software** for data management, input, and manipulation and geographic query, analysis, and visualization
3. **Data** from a variety of sources, including digitized maps, satellite imagery and data, geographic data in tabular form, field data with GPS coordinates, digitized aerial photographs, and others
4. **People** to manage systems, design applications, and interpret results for a variety of purposes

Data Layers and Formats

As shown in figure 11.14, GIS stores spatial data in **layers** or themes. Each layer contains information "geocoded" in geographic coordinates indicating location. A variety of geographic coordinates can be used (e.g., longitude/latitude, address, census block, Cartesian grids from map projections). All layers must be represented by the same coordinate system so that they can be combined and manipulated to generate new spatial data products.

By linking information to geographic coordinates, a GIS user can access information for any location (what are the soils on my building site?) as well as locate specific information (where are the wetlands in my community?).

Three types of geographic information are represented in GIS: **points** (e.g., buildings); **lines** (e.g., roads and streams); and **polygons** (e.g., soils and wetlands). GIS works with two formats to store and manipulate this information (see figure 11.15). **Vector format** stores point, line, and polygon boundaries in x-y coordinates.

The vector format describes discrete features, like points and lines, very well, and produces very good maps. However, it is not as useful in describing continuously varying features like soils, or performing overlay analyses. **Raster format** is based on a grid model providing continuous data for each point or grid cell. Raster format is especially useful for overlay analysis since each data layer has the same grid system and layers can combine information for each grid cell. However, systems with large grid cells (limited resolution) will show discrete data in a crude "blocky" appearance. Finer resolution is more accurate but requires more data storage. Most GIS systems now accommodate both vector and raster formats, providing the benefits of both.

Operations and Analysis in GIS

At least seven potential tasks or processes are involved in GIS systems: data input, manipulation, management, query, analysis, visualization, and serving (ESRI, 2002). **Data input** used to require digitizing paper maps, but recent advances by data suppliers make most available data GIS-compatible and allow direct loading into a GIS. Improvements in global positioning systems (GPSs) and related software have enabled automated data input of field data into GIS (see chapter 13).

All geographic data are not in the same scale or format, so **data manipulation** is required to provide compatibility so that data can be overlain and integrated. Manipulation includes projection changes, data aggregation, filtering, scaling, and stretching. **Data management** includes storage, organization, and access in a database management system in which data are stored in a collection of tables. Common fields are used to link the different tables together (ESRI, 2002).

GIS operations use queries and spatial analysis. **Queries** simply ask questions that can be answered by using or combining information from different data layers. For example, "what is the dominant soil in a county's existing agricultural zones?" Answering this query requires use of the soils layer and the county zoning layer. A query used in the example in the next section is "what is the value of property impacted by a 50-foot buffer creek overlay district in Blacksburg in its Rural Residential zone?" This requires layers on streams, zoning, property parcel boundaries, and parcel value.

More sophisticated **spatial analysis** can assess patterns and trends, perform scenario development, incorporate statistical analysis, and develop spatial models. Two important examples of spatial analytical tools are proximity analysis and overlay analysis. **Proximity analysis** takes advantage of the horizontal spatial scale of GIS layers and measures data within a specified distance from a point, line, or polygon boundary. The example query in the previous paragraph requires proximity analysis to identify the stream buffer area. Proximity analysis can determine the population (potential customers) located within a mile of a store, the number of septic systems located within 200 yards of a lake, the boundary of a 100-yard buffer around wetlands, and so on.

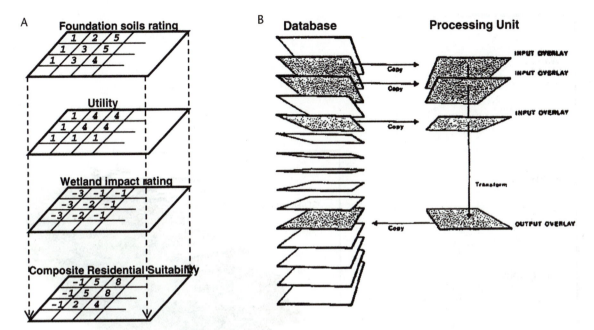

Figure 11.16 Overlay Analysis Is Used to Combine Date Layers to Produce Composite Maps That Are Then Added as New Layers in Database. *Source:* after Tomlin (1983).

Overlay analysis integrates different data layers to provide composite maps. Figure 11.16a shows how raster data layers on foundation soils, utility availability, and wetland impacts can be rated and combined to produce a new composite layer on residential suitability (for more on land suitability analysis, see chapter 18). Figure 11.16b illustrates how overlay operations are used to produce output overlays that become part of the stored database.

Additional GIS analytical capabilities include, among others, the following:

- spatial statistical analysis (e.g., what is the average property value in a land preservation zone?);
- network analysis and routing (e.g., what is the most efficient route from point A to point B?);
- computer-assisted design (CAD) (drawing capabilities and 3-D models);
- land information systems (combined mapping and database capabilities for parcels, including location, size, and land records);
- multimedia, hypertext, and hot links (use of sound, photos, video, links to text and other media); and
- simulation and spatial modeling (e.g., how would build out according to current zoning affect traffic congestion and runoff pollution loading in an undeveloped area?) (O'Looney, 2000).

An important GIS task is **visualization.** Mapmaking capabilities of GIS have enhanced the production of visual representations of land use, environmental

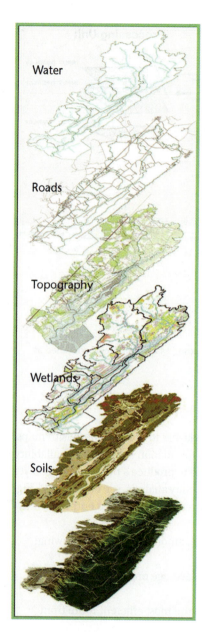

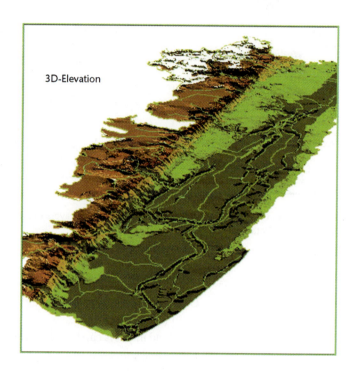

Figure 11.17 GIS Product Map Composite, 3-D Elevation View of Machopongo Watershed, Northampton County, Virginia. *Source:* Produced by Catherine Xu, Virginia Tech. Used by permission.

resources, land use change, and land use opportunities. Because of the visualization capabilities, GIS has become a useful tool in public communication. In fact, an entire subfield of GIS, PPGIS, is dedicated to the use of GIS in public participation. Visualization is enhanced by software that produces three-dimensional images using digital elevation data, as well as by the integration of digital aerial photographs, especially DOQQs. Figure 11.17 shows a 3-D projection composite map of the Machopongo watershed on the eastern shore of Virginia. It is an overlay composite of different layers: water, roads, topography, wetlands, and soils, as well as USGS digital elevation model (DEM) data.

Data and map serving has become an important GIS task both for accessing and delivering spatial data and for interactive mapping on the Internet. Earlier sections of this chapter discussed the many Internet sources of digital spatial data available for downloading. ESRI's ArcIMS (Internet Mapping Server) software has been used to serve interactive mapping capabilities for many environmental and land use applications. Users can choose locations and map layers they want in order to produce their own custom maps.

Performing GIS Operations

It is beyond the scope of this chapter to instruct the reader on how to use GIS software. Keep in mind, however, that GIS is just another software that has become easier and easier to use. Like spreadsheet and word-processing software, one can learn GIS by doing it.

There are a number of online tutorials and step-by-step applications that are very useful to get into the software and learn the tricks of the trade. Some of my students and I have developed some useful practice assignments and tutorials to help other students get started (see http://www.uap.vt.edu/classes/4374/Tutorial/tutsite/lesonweb/index.html for tutorial on ArcGIS 8.1 and http://www.uap.vt.edu/classes/uap4374/question.html for a practice question on ArcView 3.2). ESRI has a "virtual campus" with a large number of online tutorials on use of their full range of software as well as specific applications including agriculture, census, conservation, earth science, forestry, health, and hydrology, among others (http://campus.esri.com).

GIS Applications in Environmental Land Use Planning

The potential applications of GIS are endless, considering the systems can assist analysis and management of any spatial data. O'Looney (2000) and Greene (2000) identify a wide range of uses in public policy and government decision making, including economic development, housing, public works, transportation, law enforcement, human services, and public health, in addition to land use planning, environmental inventories and monitoring, emergency management, and citizen participation. A good source on different applications is the annual ESRI Map Book, which illustrates the state of the art of applications (http://www.esri.com/mapmuseum/index.html.)

This book shows a plethora of GIS products developed for environmental land use planning and management. In addition to this chapter, the following examples in other chapters illustrate the range of applications:

    Chapter 4: Collaborative design, Green maps
    Chapter 5: Greenway/green infrastructure planning
    Chapter 6: Smart development design, participatory design
    Chapter 7: Comprehensive planning and growth management

An Example in ArcView GIS 8.1: Land Values and Stream Buffers

It is useful here to at least introduce GIS software and its operations through the use of an example. Figure 11.18 gives the window for ArcMap, part of ESRI's ArcView GIS 8.1, a version of its basic GIS software introduced in 2000. The window shows a view of a map of Blacksburg, Virginia, already loaded into the software from five different shape (.shp) vector data files forming five different layers or themes. They include boundaries for census blocks, streams, town corporate limits, zoning districts, and land parcels. In addition, a table on the assessed value of each parcel was downloaded as a database file (.dbf). In figure 11.18, only the "streams" and "zoning" layers are turned on (the box next to the layer title is checked). Additional loaded layers can be viewed by simply checking the box. The vertical toolbar between the legend and the map view gives a number of commands to zoom in and out, scan, find, and identify map features. Colors, line widths, and other graphical variations of layer data can be easily modified to show desired effects.

This example uses these data layers to perform a query about the effect of a proposed creek buffer overlay zone on development and property values (for a description of toolbar commands and the completion of this query exercise, see http://www.uap.vt.edu/classes/4374/Tutorial/tutsite/lesonweb/index.html)

Visualization: Cameron/Holmes Run Watershed Characterization

GIS not only provides analytical capabilities but also helps bring data to life through visualization. A picture (or map) is worth a thousand words, and the capability of GIS to integrate colored maps, aerial and ground level photos, 3-D perspectives, and graphical data has made GIS extremely useful for environmental inventories, scenario development, and public participation. Three examples illustrate these capabilities. The first is a watershed characterization, the second is a landscape targeting study, and the third is a citizen-based watershed planning effort.

Figure 11.19 displays some product maps of a watershed characterization study conducted in northern Virginia (Bryant, Smith, Randolph, and Jeong, 2002). The Holmes Run study was done as part of a pilot project funded by USGS on urban

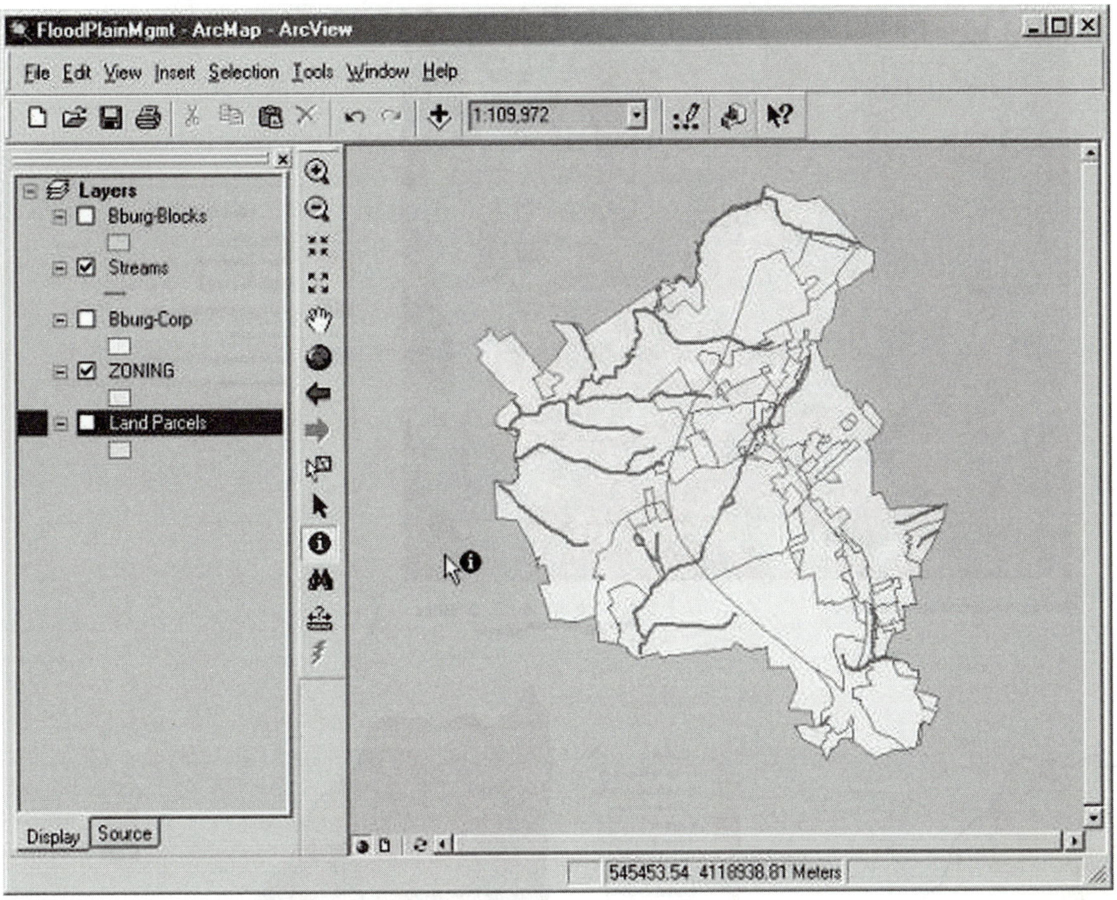

Figure 11.18 ArcGIS 8.1 ArcMap Window

biodiversity as part of its National Biological Information Infrastructure (NBII) program. Using a large number of data layers from federal and local agency sources, the study focused on land use that affected upland, riparian, and aquatic habitat in this heavily urbanized watershed.

Figure 11.19 shows some of the many GIS product maps, including land cover (A), land use (B), impervious surfaces (C), and protected lands (D and E). Protected lands include parklands, and stream corridors designated resource protection areas (RPAs) under Virginia's Chesapeake Bay Preservation Act. The study showed that even in a highly urbanized watershed such as this, remnant habitats exist, although they are limited. These remnants provide a foundation on which to extend and connect additional habitat elements.

Targeting Conservation Areas: The Nature Conservancy's Conservation by Design

The Nature Conservancy uses GIS to identify areas for potential acquisition and protection. After prioritizing areas based on broad ecoregional planning (see chap-

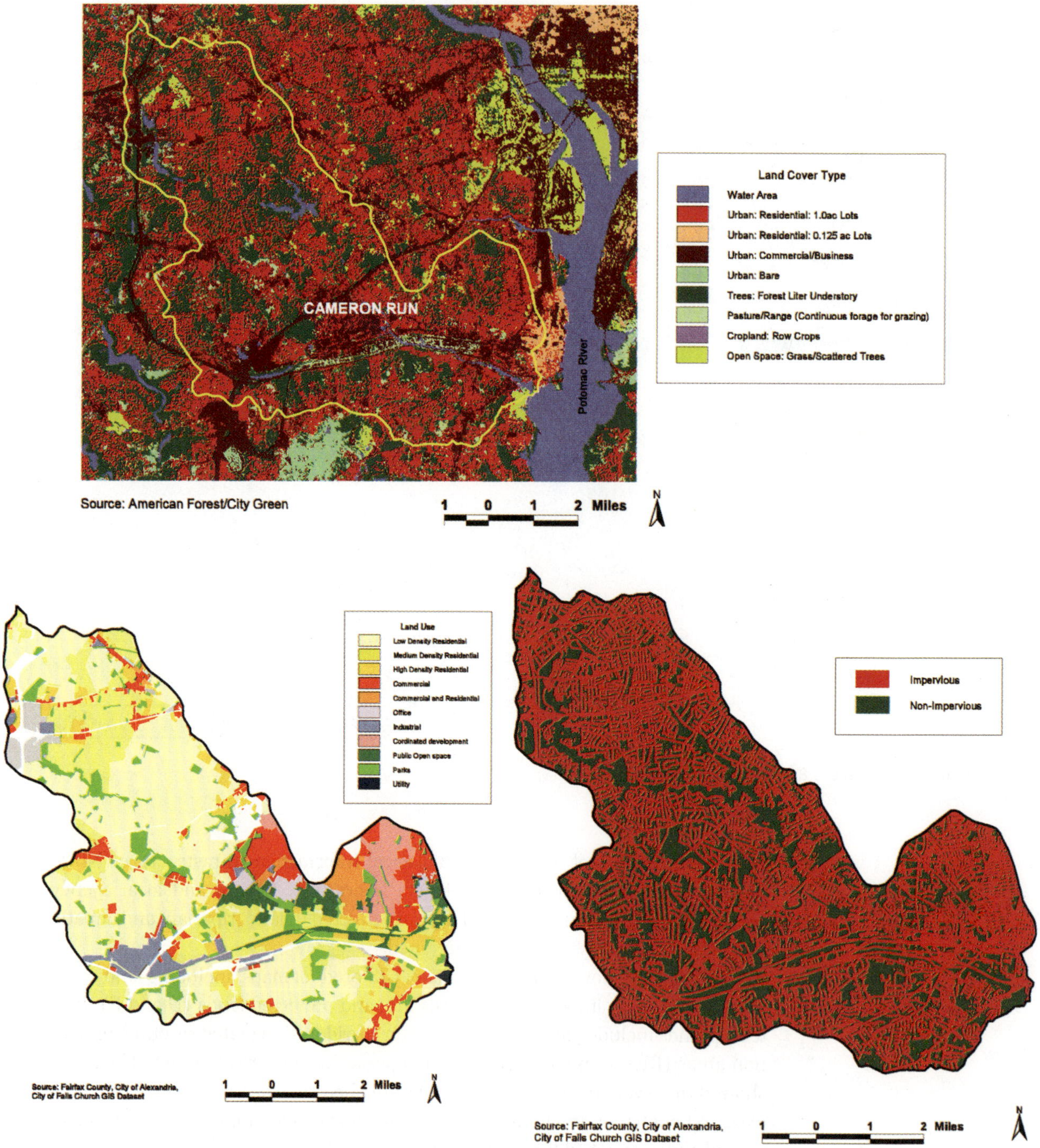
CAMERON RUN
Potomac River
Land Cover Type
Water Area
Urban: Residential: 1.0ac Lots
Urban: Residential: 0.125 ac Lots
Urban: Commercial/Business
Urban: Bare
Trees: Forest Liter Understory
Pasture/Range (Continuous forage for grazing)
Cropland: Row Crops
Open Space: Grass/Scattered Trees
Source: American Forest/City Green
1 0 1 2 Miles
N
Land Use
Low Density Residential
Medium Density Residential
High Density Residential
Commercial
Commercial and Residential
Office
Industrial
Cordinated development
Public Open space
Parks
Utility
Source: Fairfax County, City of Alexandria, City of Falls Church GIS Dataset
1 0 1 2 Miles
N
Impervious
Non-Impervious
Source: Fairfax County, City of Alexandria, City of Falls Church GIS Dataset
1 0 1 2 Miles
N

Figure 11.19 Product Maps of Cameron/Holmes Run Biodiversity Study. *Source:* Bryant et al. (2003).

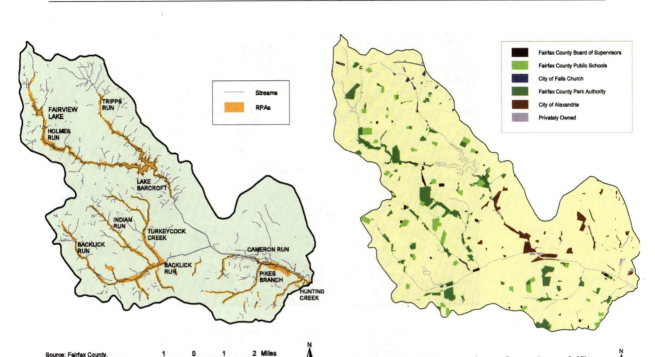

Streams
RPAs

Fairfax County Board of Supervisors
Fairfax County Public Schools
City of Falls Church
Fairfax County Park Authority
City of Alexandria
Privately Owned

Source: Fairfax County,
City of Alexandria GIS Dataset

1   0   1   2 Miles

Source: Fairfax County, City of Alexandria,
City of Falls Church GIS dataset

1   0   1   2 Miles

Figure 11.19 (continued)

ter 10), TNC aims to target specific parcels that it can patch together by acquisition or other means to protect functional ecosystems. Using GIS data layers on land use/land cover, parcels and ownership, and roads, TNC can identify blocks of unroaded natural areas that serve as functional landscapes. Figure 11.20 shows a GIS product inventory map produced that shows such roadless, forested blocks greater than 15,000 acres.

Public Participation GIS: Chattooga River Watershed Plan

In the early 1990s, grassroots environmental groups interested in the protection of the Chattooga River watershed, the headwaters of the Savannah River that encompasses portions of three states and three national forests, formed the Chattooga River Watershed Coalition, later renamed the Chattooga Conservancy. The coalition proposed to the Forest Service that the watershed's national forests should be managed as a coherent ecological unit rather than by political or forest boundaries. The Coalition teamed with Clemson University planners to use GIS to develop a plan focused on reestablishing large, continuous blocks of interior old growth forest and maintaining the diversity of forest types.

The project aimed to transfer data and expertise to the Coalition, have it develop in-house capabilities, and provide lessons transferable to other citizen and environmental groups. The Forest Service facilitated the process by providing their well-developed electronic database to the project.

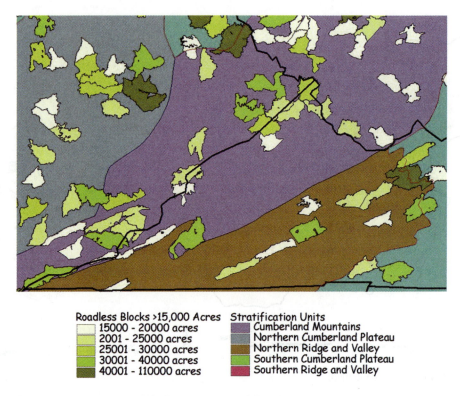

Roadless Blocks >15,000 Acres
- ☐ 15000 - 20000 acres
- ☐ 2001 - 25000 acres
- ☐ 25001 - 30000 acres
- ☐ 30001 - 40000 acres
- ☐ 40001 - 110000 acres

Stratification Units
- Cumberland Mountains
- Northern Cumberland Plateau
- Northern Ridge and Valley
- Southern Cumberland Plateau
- Southern Ridge and Valley

Figure 11.20 Large Forested Blocks Are Prime Candidates for Protection. *Source:* John Prince, The Nature Conservancy, 2000. Used with permission.

The process involved considerable data analysis and produced plan alternatives that were evaluated. A draft plan was completed in 1995, and a final plan was produced in large poster form in 1996 (see figure 11.21). Analyzed data and the final plan maps were transferred electronically to the national forests in the three states for their use as alternatives in development of their forest management plans (Chattooga Conservancy, 1996; Randolph and Zahm, 1998).

The GIS project was a critical part of the plan development and the attention it received both by the public and the Forest Service. Through data analysis and visualization, the GIS enabled this grassroots group to develop and present a professional plan that was considered a base element of the Forest Service planning effort.

The Power and Pitfalls of GIS

Geographic information systems have emerged as one of the most useful tools in environmental land planning, indeed in all applications that have a spatial dimension. As a result the technology has grown by a factor of ten from 1994 to a $7.7 billion industry in 2001. Advances in software, hardware, data availability, and user training have been accompanied by ever-increasing applications.

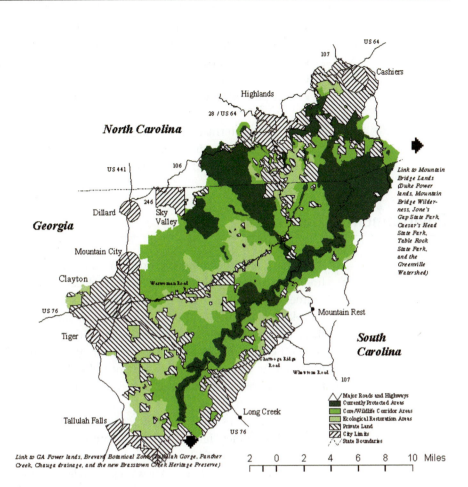

Figure 11.21 Chattooga Watershed Conservation Plan. *Source:* Chattooga Conservancy. http://www.chattoogariver.org/. Used with permission.

In environmental land planning, GIS facilitates land inventories, land analysis, visioning and scenario building, visualization and presentation, and participation. The ease of producing maps has enabled more analysis, alternatives, planning scenarios—more ideas and possibilities—than previously possible. As GIS has become more affordable and accessible, it has moved from the domain of the expert to that of any computer user. Community and environmental groups are now using GIS to produce their own plans that rival the sophistication of agencies and consultants but that incorporate their own values.

Although this penetration of the technology has largely been a good thing, it has also raised concerns, as people who have little or no cartographic knowledge are becoming mapmakers. Kent and Klosterman (2000) identified common mistakes made by GIS users that reduce the effectiveness of their products. Some of these were discussed at the beginning of the chapter. These pitfalls include:

- Failing to understand the purpose of the map
- Trying to improve accuracy by "zooming in"

- Neglecting map projections and coordinate systems
- Failing to evaluate and document map sources
- Not including necessary map elements, such as title, scale, or legend
- Presenting too much information
- Misrepresenting quantitative and qualitative data

Kent and Klosterman (2000) suggest that planners and other mapmakers test their products by showing them to others outside of their expertise to see if they communicate desired information effectively.

Environmental Field Data

As we have seen, environmental data and information are increasingly available from government and other sources. For local environmental planning, these sources are very useful, especially for "rapid assessment," but they do not replace local knowledge and field observation and monitoring of environmental conditions. It is often important to address some of the secondary data issues discussed earlier. Field studies can move the level of analysis beyond rapid assessment to intermediate and advanced assessment (table 11.1). They complement government monitoring and remote sensing data in three ways:

1. Field studies verify or "ground truth" secondary sources of information.
2. Field studies "fill in the blanks" of information not available from secondary sources.
3. Field studies tap "local knowledge" and field monitoring of groups, landowners, and residents who often know more about their local environment than government sources.

Many secondary sources of information are often not provided at sufficient accuracy or currency for specific applications. Field studies can check specific location, measurements, and changing conditions that may not be reflected in secondary data.

Secondary sources are often limited in scale or do not focus on the location or data needed for a specific planning application. Government stream water quality monitoring stations, for example, are located several miles apart on rivers and not available at all on many tributaries. They may not monitor the water contaminants that are needed for a planning study. Field monitoring can complement secondary sources by focusing on specific study locations and necessary data.

Increasingly, planners realize that secondary and professional sources of information often miss detailed information that is readily apparent to those living in an area. This "local knowledge" can contribute greatly to planning intelligence. Surveys, questionnaires, interviews, and workshops are all used to acquire local knowledge from residents and landowners (see chapter 4). These methods may be the only source of historical information about changing environmental conditions. In addition, agencies are constrained by budgets and personnel, and they often cannot monitor environmental conditions at the scale, accuracy, or frequency needed for informed decisions. Local voluntary monitoring programs can contribute greatly to agency databases and educate local groups about environmental conditions at the same time.

There are three basic approaches to field observation:

1. Monitoring: measuring and recording quantitative environmental data
2. Visual surveys: simple observation and recording of visual environmental conditions.
3. Mapping: spatially recording environmental conditions.

See chapter 13 for examples of field stream and riparian surveys and monitoring. Figure 13.22 describes a method for digital field monitoring using a handheld computer, GPS unit, digital camera, and GIS.

Community Indicators, Indexes, and Thresholds

Part of the difficulty in monitoring the environment is knowing what to monitor. Making sense of complex environmental systems and the growing reams of data and information is a challenge for both agencies and stakeholders. Increasingly, environmental indicators are used to simplify environmental assessment.

It is helpful to distinguish between an **indicator,** an **index,** and a **threshold:**

- An *indicator* is a single measure of a condition of an environmental element that represents the status or quality of that element. For example, fecal coliform content and dissolved oxygen in water and ozone concentration in the air are useful indicators of water and air quality.
- An *index* is a synthesis of several indicators that are combined into an overall measure of status or quality of an environmental element. It is usually derived by a sum-of-weighted-factors analysis. For example, the Air Quality Index (AQI) and the Index of Biological Integrity (IBI) are often used as measures of air quality and biodiversity.
- A *threshold* is the value of an indicator or index that represents a problem condition or a desirable outcome. A threshold is often defined by a goal that a community wants to achieve or by an established standard, such as an air or water quality standard. Thresholds should be attainable, meaningful, and integrated into the planning process.

Indicators and indexes aim to help identify problems, represent important factors and relationships, understand current conditions, establish community goals, and measure change, trends, and progress. Indicators must be measurable with available information, verifiable, reproducible, and meaningful and understandable to a range of users. An indicator or index can be used to monitor change and progress toward a desirable (or problem) threshold.

A variety of indicators and indexes are described in later chapters, and their use is an important component of watershed assessment (chapter 10) and environ-

TABLE 11.2 **Hypothetical List of Community Indicators, Relationships, Purposes, and Thresholds**

Indicator/Index (units)	Related to what outcome?	Community Purpose	Current Level	Goal or Threshold
Environmental				
Impervious surface (acres or % of total area)	Biodiversity in stream corridors(−) Stream impairment (+) Economic loss from flooding (+)	Improve stream health Reduce flooding	15% of total area	15% (maintain current levels)
Vehicle miles traveled (miles)	Air quality (−) Energy consumption (+) Congestion (+) Social stress (+)	Encourage efficient development patterns Reduce congestion Improve air quality	25,000 miles/day	Reduce by 5%
Days AQI in good range (# days/year)	Human health (+) Impact on tourism (+)	Improve air quality Improve human health	10 da/yr	5 da/yr
Stream miles "impaired" (not meeting WQ stds) (miles)	Aquatic habitat degradation (+) Aesthetic/recreation capacity (−)	Improve water quality Enhance recreation opportunities	25 miles	10 miles
Solid waste recycled (% of generated)	Material resource conservation (+) Landfill soil/GW pollution (−)	Minimize landfilling Reclaim materials	10%	25%
Land in open space (acres)	Aesthetic greenness (+) Urban wildlife habitat (+)	Preserve community character/recreation Enhance wildlife	10,000 acres	10,000 acres (maintain current levels)
Economic				
Unemployment (%)	Families on govt support (+) Personal Income (−) Poverty/homelessness (+)	Increase # jobs Ensure family income Reduce poverty	8%	4%
Income per capita ($/cap)	Economic vitality Tax revenues	Enhance family income Enhance local revenues	$25,000/ cap/yr	$30,000/cap/yr
Employed in locally owned businesses (%)	Local reinvestment	Enhance local economic self-reliance	40%	50%
Social				
Below poverty level (%)	Poverty, personal income	Reduce poverty	10%	8%
Homeless (# people)	Poverty, community character	Reduce homelessness	1,000	500
Access to adequate healthcare (% of pop)	Community health	Improve community health	75%	85%
Voting rate (% of eligible)	Community engagement	Improve democracy	50%	75%

mental impact assessment (chapter 18). A good case study of the use of indicators and thresholds is the Lake Tahoe region (chapters 8 and 18). The 22 indicators in EPA's Index of Watershed Indicators (IWI) were given in chapter 10.

Indicators have been used for national and global monitoring. Some, like gross domestic product (GDP), Consumer Price Index, unemployment rate, and poverty rate, have long been used to measure economic and social conditions. Recently, attention has been given to national ecological indicators (Dale and Beyeler, 2001; National Research Council, 1999).

The use of indicators in community planning has increased significantly. **Community indicators** include not only environmental factors but also economic and social conditions to reflect the objectives of sustainability. Several sources provide long lists of possible indicators (Livable Communities, http://www.lgc.org/center/about/center.html; Green Communities, http://www.epa.gov/region03/greenkit/index.html; Hart, 1999). However, the use of community indicators and thresholds should be viewed as a process that begins with engaging citizens, groups, firms, and other stakeholders in a dialogue about community issues, concerns, and goals. The choice of indicators and thresholds must be based on this process, and monitoring indicators should become a community activity.

Although the list of potential indicators is very long, the choice of indicators should be held to a manageable, measurable, and meaningful set selected by the community. It should be clear what each indicator is measuring or is linked to, and what community purposes it represents. Table 11.2 gives a hypothetical list of environmental, economic, and social indicators and illustrates the considerations needed in selecting them. Goals and thresholds for these indicators should be attainable.

Summary

This ambitious chapter has addressed the important topic of information and data in environmental planning. For informed and knowledgeable planning decisions, the proper collection, analysis, and presentation of appropriate information is a critical and fundamental task. A planner's role is to help decision makers, elected officials, the public, and other stakeholders make sense of the huge volume of potentially conflicting information.

For environmental issues relating to land use, spatial information is very important. Maps, aerial photos, and satellite images and data, increasingly available on the Internet, provide basic information. It is often important to complement this information with field data monitoring. The increasing availability of such information has helped planners assemble large amounts of data, but has made more difficult the planners' task to pare down available information into that which is meaningful and appropriate. Analytical and display tools, like GIS, have enhanced the quality of intermediate and advanced assessment and especially the visualization of information that helps communicate key issues, relationships, and options to stakeholders.

Although often viewed as a technical planning activity involving mapping and remotely sensed data, field data gathering and analysis is enhanced by community involvement. The use of environmental and community indicators helps planners make sense of available information, focusing assessment linking information and community-determined goals. Many of the fundamentals discussed in this chapter will come to life in subsequent chapters on more focused elements of environmental land use planning.

12 ▪ Soils, Topography, and Land Use

To understand the natural processes of the land, and to plan land use in accord with them, there is no more fundamental place to start than the soil. Soil is a living dynamic resource that supports plant life by providing a physical matrix, biological setting, and chemical environment for water, nutrient, air, and heat exchange (USDA, 1996). Soil controls decomposition of organic matter and biogeochemical cycles; affects surface and subsurface hydrology; determines inherent vegetation, habitat type, and agricultural potential; and supports human habitation and structures. As a result, many disciplines are interested in soils: the agronomist, the hydrologist, the wildlife biologist, the farmer, the builder, the engineer, and the land use planner, to name a few.

This chapter introduces soil quality and some land use properties of soils, discusses soil surveys and interpretation, and addresses major issues and assessment for agricultural lands and urban soils. It describes techniques for evaluation of soils used by planners, including soil quality indicators, soil suitability mapping, agricultural land assessment, and erosion prediction and sedimentation control. It also presents methods of slope analysis.

Land Use Properties of Soils and Soil Quality

Soils are made up of *inorganic minerals* (rock, clay, silt, and sand) that provide structure; *organic matter* (living and decomposing plant and animal material) that supplies nutrients and holds moisture; and *air, water, and dissolved nutrients*, essential for living organisms. Box 12.1 provides some soil fundamentals, including soil origin and processes (figure 12.1), and principal characteristics including texture, bulk density, biology, plasticity, permeability, among others. These characteristics affect the soil's quality and land use.

BOX 12.1 — Some Soil Fundamentals

The process of soil formation and depletion is a complex combination of physical, chemical, and biological processes (figure 12.1). Underlying rock provides the **parent material** and, through physical and chemical **weathering**, produces the soils' fine-grained minerals. Overlying vegetation and animals provide organic material or litter that, through various stages of biological **decomposition**, produces the soil's humus. Physical processes of **deposition** and **erosion** continually remove and replace surface materials. **Percolation** of water leaches materials from the surface to lower depths. It takes 100–400 years to form 1 centimeter of soil through these processes.

The vertical cross section of the soil, or **soil profile**, contains distinguishable **zones** or **horizons**. The O horizon is the organic litter above the A horizon or topsoil. A contains the most organic matter and has the greatest biological activity. Between A and B is the E or leached horizon which is the source of the downward removal of materials by leaching (the process of eluviation). B and C horizons are the subsoil. B has greatest accumulation of leached materials (the process of illuviation), and C contains weathered parent material.

Soil Taxonomy

The continental United States is dominated by 10 soil classes that are further distinguished by subclass. See the NRCS poster on the classification system and location of classes and subclasses at http://soils.usda.gov/research/results/posters/soil _tax.pdf.

Soil Characteristics

Texture is the relative proportion of different size particles. The following are particle definitions by diameter:

Cobbles	> 75 millimeters (mm)
Gravel	2.0–75 mm
Sand	0.05–2.0 mm
Silt	0.002–0.05 mm
Clay	< 0.002 mm

Of course, soils are generally mixtures of different-sized particles, so the Department of Agriculture has devised textural classes of soils depending on their composition of sand, silt and clay. These classes are described in figure 12.4. The texture of the soil has a great effect on its drainability, erodibility, bearing strength, and stability.

Bulk density is the unit volume weight of the soil. An ideal density is 1.33 megagrams per cubic meter (Mg/m^3). Values over 1.6 Mg/m^3 tend to inhibit plant root penetration. **Compacted soil** is compressed to a bulk density greater than 1.6.

Structure is determined by the shape of particle clusters, called *peds*. These can provide openings for percolation (downward movement of water) even in clay-rich soils.

Color can indicate the types of minerals present, the organic content, and seasonal water fluctuations. **Organic content** is the amount of humus, leaf mold, sawdust, and other organics in the soil, indicating better nutrient cycling. Reddish soils are highly weathered with a high content of oxidized iron; dark or black soils indicate high organic matter; gray soils have permanently high and stagnant water tables. Mottled soils showing spots of different colors indicate a fluctuating water table or poor drainability and thus can reflect seasonal wetness even when examined in dry periods.

Soil ecology broadly describes the biological activities of the soil. In most vegetated soils there is a complex soil ecosystem involving plants and organic residue, and several trophic levels of bacteria, algae, fungi, protozoa, nemotodes (worms), anthropods, and higher animals (gophers, mice, shrews, moles, woodchucks). Soils play a critical role in biogeochemical cycles.

Consistence is the degree and kind of adhesion and cohesion of the soil. Consistence is described under dry, moist, and wet conditions. Under dry and moist conditions, the hardness of the peds or the difficulty in crushing the ped by hand is noted. Under wet conditions, the stickiness and plasticity of the soil is noted. It affects the workability of the soil, its ability to support loads, and its tendency to shrink and swell.

Plasticity is determined by seeing how well the soil can be shaped into a "spaghetti wire" and then how well the wire can be manipulated. It is quantitatively defined in terms of the Atterberg limits, which are a soil's "plastic limit" (or the water content, in percent water, at which the soil begins to

Continued ➤

BOX 12.1 — (continued)

deform) and its "liquid limit" (or the water content at which the soil cannot retain its shape and begins to flow). The soil's plasticity index is the liquid limit minus the plastic limit. Shrink-swell soils generally have a high plasticity index.

Hydraulic conductivity or permeability is the ease with which gases and liquids pass through a given volume of soil. It can be measured by a percolation test in which a 2 ft. x 2 ft. x 2 ft. hole is filled with water and allowed to drain; the hole is filled with water again. The permeability is the distance the water drops in one hour; the percolation rate is the time it takes the water to drop one inch. Permeability is rated on a scale from rapid (greater than 6 in/hr) to slow (less than 0.2 in/hr). Coarse-grained soils (sands) have relatively large spaces between particles and thus have rapid permeability rates, whereas fine-grained soils (clays) have slow rates. The structure of fine-grained soils can affect permeability rate; the rate can be higher if there are avenues between peds for infiltration. **Soil porosity** is the percentage of the total soil volume not occupied by soil particles and indicates its water-holding capacity.

Hydric soils are those that are often saturated due to high water table and exhibit the coloration and mottling typical of poorly drained soils. They are a good indicator of the presence of wetland conditions.

Reaction indicates its pH or degree of acidity or alkalinity, affecting crop production and corrosion of materials. **Salinity** or the salt content of soil can inhibit vegetative growth.

Fertility of the soil is measured by a chemical analysis of plant nutrients and indicates the fertilizer needs of the soil to support crop growth. **Productivity** of the soil measures yield of a specific crop and depends on fertility, texture, structure, and other factors like slope.

The **stoniness** of the soil is the amount of course fragments from 10 to 24 inches in diameter in or on the soil. Stoniness is classified on a 0 to 5 scale: 0 indicates no or few stones, 4 indicates that stones make the use of machinery impractical.

The **rockiness** of the soil is the amount of the soil surface occupied by bedrock outcrops. A 0–5 scale similar to the stoniness scale is used to classify rockiness.

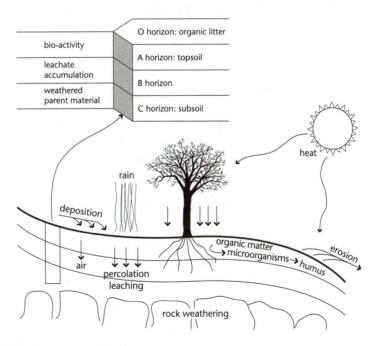

Figure 12.1 Soil Processes and Profiles

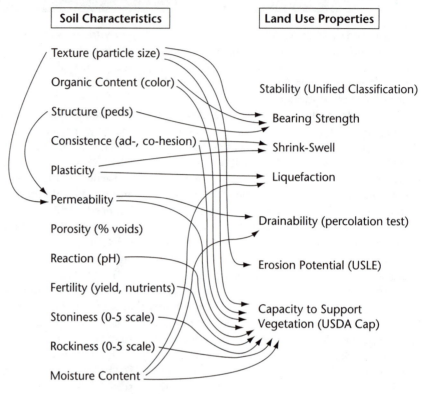

Figure 12.2 Land Use Properties of Soils

Land Use Properties of Soil

Soils exhibit properties that have a significant influence on land capabilities and should be an important consideration when planning land use. Figure 12.2 displays four important land use properties of soils and the types of soils and soil characteristics affecting their use in agricultural and urban settings. Certain soils may compress, shrink, swell, or shift, causing problems for structures. Others may drain surface water or septic effluent poorly or may be highly susceptible to erosion. Still others may have productive resource value—as prime agricultural soils or simply to support urban vegetation.

Soil Stability: Strength and Movement

The stability of the soil involves its susceptibility to compression or settling, shrinking and swelling, and spontaneous flow. Stability determines how well the soil can support structures and physical infrastructure. The potential for settling or compression of soil when subjected to a load depends on its **bearing strength,** which is related to the soil's bulk density or its dry weight per unit of bulk volume. In general, coarse soils such as gravelly soils have better bearing strength than loosely consolidated fill, water-saturated, clayey, or highly organic soils. Settlement is a particular problem on land "reclaimed" from lake or bay shores by filling in with dredge spoils, municipal wastes, or other materials. Especially when not properly compacted and when placed on soft bay muds, these materials will settle when supporting a load due to their own low strength and/or the low internal cohesion. Potential **settlement** of low-strength soils generally does not preclude construction but requires special engineering measures, such as compaction, surcharging, or the use of bearing or friction piles, to mitigate potential problems.

Shrink-swell potential depends on the soil's plasticity or water-bearing characteristics. Some clay soils (made up of such minerals as smectite or montmorillomite) will expand excessively when wetted and shrink when dried. These expansions and contractions can exert extreme pressures sufficient to crack foundations and roadways and dislodge structures. Other soils may also expand when frozen; these so-called **frost-heave** soils are generally fine soils that retain water. Spontaneous flow or **liquefaction** potential may be high where soil is made up of loosely packed, well-sorted fine-grained sands and silts and where high water tables are prevalent. When these soils are saturated, only a portion of the load of the overlying soil and structures is carried by the grain-to-grain contact of the soil particles. The remainder of the load is supported by the buoyant force of water between the particles. When shaken by an earthquake or other impulse, the contact between the grains may be lost, and the saturated soil will behave like a liquid. Any structure resting on the soil will also move.

The Unified Soil Classification system, described in table 12.1, rates soils in terms of their properties for structures and foundations based on bearing strength and potential expansion. The most important soil characteristic affecting these properties is texture, categorized by letters G (gravel), S (sand), and C (clay). Also important is the content of plastic clay and organic matter. The best engineering soils are uniformly large particle soils without plastic clay and organic material. Clayey and organic soils rate the worst.

Drainability

The Unified Soil Classification system also rates the drainability of the soil, which is important not only for buildings and roads, but also for other land uses such as crop production, septic and infiltration drainfields, and waste containment facilities. Drainability depends primarily on soil permeability (or the ease with which fluids pass through the soil [see box 12.1]), but also on soil depth and the depth of the water table or groundwater surface. Generally, coarse-grained soils that have relatively large spaces between particles have rapid permeability rates, whereas fine-grained soils have slow rates. Soil compaction reduces permeability and impedes drainability. Good drainage of soils is desirable for most land uses except waste or chemical containment facilities like sanitary landfills, lagoons, or underground storage tanks. In such cases, compacted clay or artificial liners are used to contain water drainage, which is often contaminated by waste leachate.

On-site wastewater or septic systems and drainfields are permitted and usually designed by public health engineers based on soil drainability. Septic drainfields can create water quality problems in two ways. First, soil drainability is often insufficient to drain effluents and surface seepage occurs. Second, when soil drainability is too high and/or drainfields are too close to receiving waters, insufficient fil-

TABLE 12.1   **Unified Soil Classification System**

Soil Group	USCS Symbol	Soil Description	Allowable Bearing (lb/ft²) with Medium Compaction	Drainage* Characteristics	Frost Heave Potential	Shrink-Swell Potential
Group I-Excellent	GW	Well-graded gravels, gravel sand mixtures, little or no fines	8,000	Good	Low	Low
	GP	Poorly graded gravels, gravel-sand mixtures, little or no fines	8,000	Good	Low	Low
	SW	Well-graded sands, gravelly sands, little or no fines	6,000	Good	Low	Low
	SP	Poorly graded sands, gravelly sands, little or no fines	5,000	Good	Low	Low
	GM	Silty gravels, gravel-sand-silt mixtures	4,000	Good	Medium	Low
	SM	Silty sands, sand-silt mixtures	4,000	Good	Medium	Low
Group II	GC	Clayey gravels, gravel-sand-clay mixtures	4,000	Medium	Medium	Low
Fair	SC	Clayey sands, sand-clay mixtures	4,000	Medium	Medium	Low
to Good	ML	Inorganic silts and very fine sands, rock flour, silty or clayey fine sands, or clayey silts with slight plasticity	2,000	Medium	High	Low
	CL	Inorganic clays of low to medium plasticity, gravelly clays, sandy clays, silty clays, lean clays	2,000	Medium	Medium	Medium
Group III	CH	Inorganic clays of high plasticity, fat clays	2,000	Poor	Medium	High
Poor	MH	Inorganic silts, micaceous or diatomaceous fine sandy or silty soils, elastic silts	2,000	Poor	High	High
Group IV	OL	Organic silts and organic silty clays of low plasticity	400	Poor	Medium	Medium
Unsatisfactory	OH	Organic clays of medium to high plasticity, organic silts	0	Unsatisfactory	Medium	High
	PT	Peat and other highly organic soils	0	Unsatisfactory	Medium	High

* Percolation rate for good drainage is >4 inches/hour, medium drainage is 2–4 inches/hour, poor is <2 inches/hour

G—gravelly soils >2 mm	W—uniform particle size, absence of clay
S—sandy soils	C—uniform particle size, binding clay fraction
M—fine inorganic sand and silt	P—non-uniform particle size, absence of clay
C—inorganic clay	L—low placticity (liquid limit <50)
O—organic silts and clays	H—high plasticity (liquid limit >50)
PT—peat, highly organic soils	

tration and biodegradation occur before effluent ends up in surface waters or groundwater. On-site wastewater systems and soils are discussed in a later section of this chapter.

Erodibility

Erodibility is another important land use property of soils. Soil loss through erosion on agricultural and silvicultural lands can reduce productivity; erosion from these lands and from construction sites often leads to sedimentation of water bodies. The process of water erosion, illustrated in figure 12.3, involves rainsplash, sheetwash, rill and gully, and channel erosion. **Rainsplash erosion** results from the direct impact of falling drops of rain on soil particles. The impact dislodges soil par-

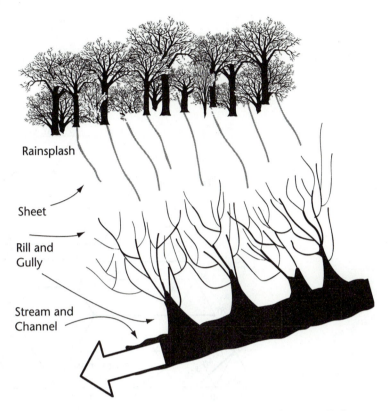

Rainsplash

Sheet

Rill and
Gully

Stream and
Channel

Figure 12.3 Four Types of Water Erosion. *Source:* G. Day and D. Smith, Virginia Tech.

ticles and splashes them into the air. The dislodged particles can then be easily transported by surface runoff. **Sheet erosion** removes a layer of exposed surface soil by the action of rainfall splash and runoff. The water moves in broad sheets over the land and is not confined to small depressions. **Rill and gully erosion** develops as flowing runoff concentrates in grooves, called rills, which cut several inches into the soil surface. Rills grow to deeper and wider gullies where concentrated flow of water moves over the soil. In **stream and channel erosion,** increased volume and velocity of runoff may cause erosion of the stream bottom, especially channel banks.

The loss of soil depends on soil type and, more importantly, on the surface slope (which affects the speed and erosive force of the runoff) and the vegetative cover (which intercepts raindrops, decreases runoff by increasing infiltration, and slows what runoff remains). Figure 12.4 gives the U.S. Department of Agriculture (USDA) Textural Triangle used to classify the soil texture by the composition of sand, silt, and clay. The most erodible soils are unvegetated sandy loams because of their high surface runoff potential due to their clay content and a low resistance to erosion due to their sand content. The soil erodibility factor and index, as well as the use of the Universal Soil Loss Equation (USLE) to estimate annual loss of soil from a parcel of land are discussed later in this chapter.

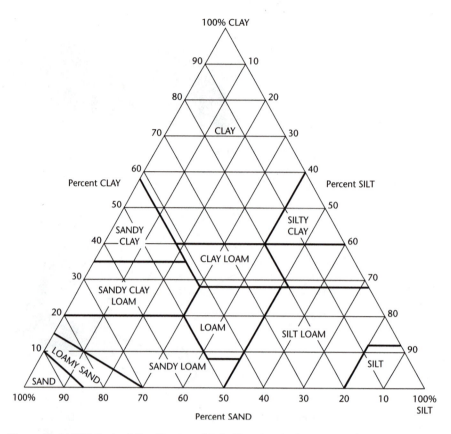

Figure 12.4 USDA Textural Classification of Soils. The triangle shows textural classes graphically depending on composition of sand, silt, and clay.

Capacity to Support Vegetation

Soil quality to support agriculture, silviculture, and urban vegetation is another land use property. The top horizons are critical for vegetation, as roots for even large trees extend only about 18 inches in depth. A number of factors affect the agricultural capability of soils, including fertility, reaction, texture, bulk density, drainability, stoniness, rockiness, and erodibility. Prime agricultural soils are fertile, well-drained soils on level or gently sloping lands and generally include floodplains, river valleys, and certain grassy plains. Flood deposit plains have the best potential with their alluvial (water-deposited) soils, flat topography, and limited utility for other uses. The USDA Agricultural Land Capability system considers these factors in rating cropland and is given in box 12.2. The issue of farmland conversion and the Land Evaluation and Site Assessment (LESA) system for evaluating farmland are discussed in the next section. Urban uses of soil, including landscaping, park and street boulevard management, and urban forestry, must also address soil quality. The removal, compaction, filling, and contamination of urban soils affect productive use. Agricultural lands and urban soils are discussed in later sections.

BOX 12.2 — USDA Agricultural Capability Classification

The USDA classifies lands based on their soils' capabilities to produce crops without deterioration. The system takes into account soil types, slope and drainage of the land, the erodibility and rockiness of the soil, and other factors. Land is classified into the eight categories given below. The higher the number, the more severe are the limitations to agriculture use. Often, specific limitations are identified by a letter following the Arabic or Roman numeral: "e" = erosion, "w" = wetness, "s" = internal soil problems, and "c" = climatic limitations. Classes 1 and 2 are "prime agricultural lands." The capability classification is an important input in the LESA system.

Class 1—few limitations for crop production
Class 2—moderate limitations that reduce crop choice
Class 3—severe limitations that reduce crop choice
Class 4—very severe limitations that reduce crop choice
Class 5—moderate limitations that make soils unsuitable for cultivation
Class 6—severe limitations that make soils unsuitable
Class 7—very severe limitations that make soils unsuitable
Class 8—limitations that preclude commercial crop production

Soil Quality and Soil Degradation

Soil quality is the fitness of a soil to function within its surroundings, support plant and animal productivity, maintain or enhance water and air quality, and support human health and habitation. The quality of a specific soil depends on the use to which it is put. Soil quality is evaluated by monitoring several indicators chosen to reflect the specific function and use of the soil. Indicators can show the health or degradation of the soil, point to improvement strategies, and provide the focus for monitoring change.

Soil degradation occurs in many ways. Most are caused or exacerbated by human activities. Erosion is probably the most important soil degradation process, removing potentially tons per acre per year from sites denuded of vegetation, either for crop production or land development. Grading for land development, mining, and other activities often removes valuable topsoil. Soil can be contaminated with pollutants, salts, or acidic or alkaline conditions that limit their useful functions. Soil can be compacted by human use, increasing bulk density and reducing drainability and capacity for root growth.

Just like community and environmental indicators discussed in chapter 11, soil quality indicators should be measurable, meaningful, and manageable and be determined by the user's objectives. Figure 12.5 gives a flowchart for selecting soil quality indicators based on a user's goals. Many of these indicators can be measured and monitored in the field. There are several field methods for measuring biological, chemical, and physical soil quality indicators. For example, an organic smell and visual inspection of the soil for fauna such as earthworms, fungi, and larva indicate a biologically healthy soil. Soil pH (acidity and alkalinity), salinity, and nitrate content are common chemical indicators. Infiltration rates, bulk density, and visual signs of erosion are physical characteristics.

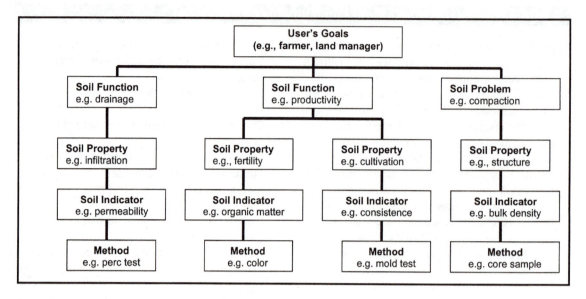

Figure 12.5 Chart for Selecting Soil Quality Indicators

Indicators should be used to identify soil degradation problems and to formulate plans for soil improvement. Monitoring indicators over time shows the effectiveness of improvement plans. For example, low organic matter reduces fertility and indicates poor structure. Soil amendments can increase organic matter, improving soil functions. Bulk density indicates soil compaction, which limits drainage, root growth, and gas exchange. Aeration methods can counter the impacts of compaction. Monitoring bulk density can show the effectiveness of aeration methods and frequency.

For more information on soil quality, see the USDA, NRCS Soil Quality Data Sheets (http://www.statlab.iastate.edu/survey/SQI/sqiinfo.html).

Soil Surveys and Interpretive Soils Mapping

Soil surveys provide the best available soils information for land planning. The USDA Natural Resources Conservation Service (NRCS, formerly the Soil Conservation Service [SCS]) has been producing soil surveys since the turn of the last century, and the process is continuous. Every year surveys are being revised to meet current needs, and new areas are being surveyed. Although soil surveys in the United States date back to 1896, the modern soil survey dates from about 1956 and reflects improved and standardized mapping and interpretation techniques. As of 2002, modern surveys are available for 1,557 counties (43%) of the United States, and another 842 (23%) are in process. About 365 counties (8%) have older out-of-date soil surveys (see updates at http://www.ftw.nrcs.usda.gov/jpg/ssa_small.jpg). Digital soil surveys that have digital maps and data were first produced in the 1990s and are available for 1,064 counties (as of August 2001).

Figure 12.6 Soil Survey Photomap and Base Map Showing Soil Map Units. *Source:* USDA, SCS (1985).

The modern surveys include three useful components:

1. **Text** describes the county, its general 5–10 types of soils (called *associations*), the 15–20 more specific types of soils (called *series*), and the 40–60 soil series-slope combinations (called *map units*).

2. **Maps** show the location of the soils by "map units or symbols," which denote soil series and complexes at different slopes. The maps are usually produced at a scale of 1:15,840 or 1:24,000. As shown in figure 12.6, aerial photographs are used as the base map, and the soils polygons and surface features, like roads and drainages, are included in the soils overlay. The polygon symbols on the soils overlay refer to the map units: The number denotes the soils series or complex, the letter denotes the slope.

3. **Tables** provide detailed information for each series and map unit. The tables include engineering, physical, and chemical properties and water characteristics, as well as interpretive information such as expected yields for various crops, woodland productivity and limitations, wildlife habitat potential, potential sources of construction mate-

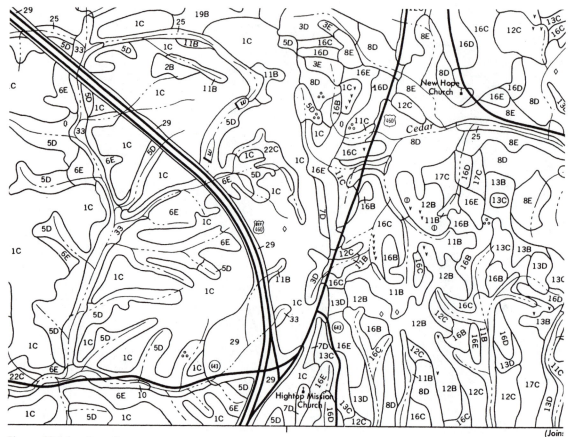

Figure 12.6 (continued)

rials, and limitations for building site development and for sanitary facilities (e.g., septic systems, landfills, etc.). Table 12.2 gives some examples of soil survey tables taken from the Montgomery County, Virginia, soil survey (USDA, SCS, 1985). In the actual survey the complete listing of the 55 map units are rated under each table heading.

Interpretive Soils Mapping Using the Soil Survey

Using the soil survey maps and tables, one can produce interpretive soils maps fairly easily. An interpretive map displays areas of similar soil properties in the same color or shading. For example, a septic suitability map would show in one color those areas with severe soil limitations for operation of septic drainfields, in another color those areas with moderate limitations, and in still another color those with slight limitations. These interpretive maps can be made for any of the specific factors given for each soil map unit in the tables or text of the soil survey, that is, those listed in tables 12.2. These maps can be very valuable for land use planning.

TABLE 12.2 Examples of Soil Survey Table Headings

TABLE 6 Yields per Acre of Crops and Pasture—

Soil Name and Map Symbol	Corn	Corn Silage	Oats	Wheat	Alfalfa Hay	Grass-Legume Hay	Pasture
	Bu	Ton	Bu	Bu	Ton	Ton	AUM*
15B: Glenelg	135	27	80	50	5.5	3.5	10.5

TABLE 7 Woodland Management and Productivity—

Soil Name and Map Symbol	Ordination Symbol	Management concerns				Potential productivity		
		Erosion Hazard	Equipment Limitation	Seedling Mortality	Wind-throw Hazard	Common Trees	Site Index	Trees to Plant
3E*: Lowell— (north aspect)	2c	Severe	Severe	Slight	Slight	Northern red oak — Yellow-poplar — Shortleaf pine — Virginia pine —	76 90 80 80	Yellow-poplar, eastern white pine, shortleaf pine

TABLE 8 Recreational Development—Limitations

Soil Name and Map Symbol	Camp Areas	Picnic Areas	Playgrounds	Paths and Trails	Golf Fairways
5D*, 6E*: Weikert —	Severe: slope, small stones, depth to rock	Severe: slope, small stones, depth to rock	Severe: slope, depth to rock, small stones	Severe: slope	Severe: slope thin later, small stones

TABLE 9 Wildlife Habitat—

Soil Name and Map Symbol	Potential for habitat elements							Potential as habitat for—		
	Grain and Seed Crops	Grasses and Legumes	Wild Herbaceous Plants	Hardwood Trees	Coniferous Plants	Wetland Plants	Shallow Water Areas	Openland Wildlife	Woodland Wildlife	Wetland Wildlife
8D*: Caneyville	Poor	Fair	Good	Good	Good	Very poor	Very poor	Fair	Good	Very poor

TABLE 10 Building Site Development—Limitations

Soil Name and Map Symbol	Shallow Excavations	Dwellings without Basements	Dwellings with Basements	Small Commercial Buildings	Local Roads and Streets	Lawns and Landscaping
8D*, 8E*: Caneyville—	Severe: depth to rock, slope	Severe: slope	Severe: dept to rock, slope	Severe: slope	Severe: low strength, slope	Severe: slope

TABLE 12.2 *(Continued)* **Examples of Soil Survey Table Headings**

TABLE 11 Sanitary Facilities—Limitations

Soil Name and Map Symbol	Septic Tank Absorption Fields	Sewage Lagoon Areas	Trench Sanitary Landfill	Area Sanitary Landfill	Daily Cover for Landfill
7D*: Berks—	Severe: depth to rock, slope	Severe: slope, depth to rock, seepage	Severe: slope, depth to rock, seepage	Severe: seepage, slope, depth to rock	Poor: small stones, slope, area reclaim

TABLE 13 Water Management—

Soil Name and Map Symbol	Limitations for—			Features Affecting—		
	Pond Reservoir Areas	Embankments, Dikes, and Levees	Aquifer-fed Excavated Ponds	Drainage	Terraces and Diversions	Grassed Waterways
8D*: Caneyville—	Moderate: depth to rock	Severe: thin layer, hard to pack	Severe: no water	Deep to water	Slope, depth to rock	Slope, depth to rock

TABLE 15 Physical and Chemical Properties of the Soils—

Soil Name and Map Symbol	Depth	Clay	Moist Bulk Density	Permeability	Available Water Capacity	Soil Reaction	Shrink-Swell Potential	Erosion Factors K	T	Organic Matter
8E*, 8E*: Caneyville—	In	Pct	G/cm3	In/hr	In/in	pH				Pct
	0–8	10–25	1.20–1.40	0.6–2.0	0.15–0.22	4.5–7.3	Low—	0.43	3	2.4
	8–32	36–60	1.34–1.60	0.2–0.6	0.12–0.18	4.5–7.3	Moderate—	0.28		

Source: USDA, SCS, Montgomery County (VA) Soil Survey, 1985

Using the soil survey tables, soils suitability maps can be developed for the following factors:

- crop productivity (e.g., corn yields per acre)
- woodland production (rated by a site index [height to which a tree species will likely grow in 50 years] and by management limitations)
- limitations for recreation development (slight, moderate, severe)
- wildlife habitat rating (good, fair, poor, very poor)
- limitations for dwellings with basements (slight, moderate, severe)
- limitations for dwellings without basements (slight, moderate, severe)
- limitations for local roads and streets (slight, moderate, severe)
- limitations for septic tank absorption fields (slight, moderate, severe)
- limitations for sanitary landfills (slight, moderate, severe)
- limitations for water management (slight, moderate, severe)
- source of construction materials
- engineering indices (e.g., texture, unified class, plasticity)
- physical/chemical properties (e.g., depth, shrink-swell, permeability, erosion index)

1. For the planning area to be assessed, prepare a soils base map from the soil survey map unit overlay maps or the photomaps. Make a copy of the soils base map for each soil suitability factor (e.g., septic drain fields, buildings with basements) to be assessed.

2. Make a list of the map units and soil series that occur in the planning area as the first two columns of a soil suitability matrix. Using the soil survey table for each factor or land use to be mapped, list the rating or limitation posed by the soil for that use and the reason. (See Step 2 table below.)

3. Group the map units having the same suitability rating or limitation. If one map unit is made up of two soil series having different ratings, you will not be able to tell from the map which series is present. For these units create a new rating (e.g., Moderate or Severe). (See Step 3 table below.)

4. Choose a color or shading scheme for the different ratings that makes sense. Usually, light shading is good for "slight" limitation or "good" rating, dark shading for "severe" limitation or "poor" rating. In color, the "red = stop", "yellow = caution", "green = go" approach works well.

5. On the soils base map, mark the individual map units with the shading or color corresponding to their rating.

6. Once all the series are marked, go back and color or shade in the map unit areas to produce the suitability map.

7. Prepare a map title and legend that keys the colors or shades to the ratings. Include the title and legend on the map. (See Step 5–7 maps next page.)

Step 2 Table

Map Unit	Soil Series	Factor: Dwellings with basements		Factor: Septic Tank Drainfield	
		Limitation	Reason	Limitation	Reason
1C	Berks	Moderate	slope/depth	Severe	depth
1C	Clymer	Moderate	depth/slope	Moderate	depth/slow perc/slope
7D	Berks	Severe		Severe	depth/slope
7D	Weikert	Severe	slope/depth	Severe	slope/depth
8D	Caneyville	Severe	depth/slope	Severe	depth/slow perc/slope
8D	Opequon	Severe	slope/depth/shr-swell	Severe	slope/depth/slow perc
11B	Duffield	Moderate	shrink-swell	Moderate	depth
11B	Ernest	Severe	wetness	Severe	slow perc/wetness
11C	Duffield	Moderate	slope/shrink-swell	Moderate	depth/slope
11C	Ernest	Severe	wetness	Severe	slow perc/wetness
12C	Frederick	Severe	shrink-swell	Moderate	slow perc/slope
12C	Vertrees	Moderate	slope/shrink-swell	Severe	slow perc
16B	Groseclose	Severe	shrink-swell	Severe	slow perc
16B	Poplimento	Severe	shrink-swell	Severe	slow perc
16C	Groseclose	Severe	shrink-swell	Severe	slow perc
16C	Poplimento	Severe	shrink-swell	Severe	slow perc
16D/16E	Groseclose	Severe	slope/shrink-swell	Severe	slow perc/slope
16D/16E	Poplimento	Severe	slope/shrink-swell	Severe	slow perc/slope

Continued ➤

BOX 12.3—(continued)

Step 3 Table: Soil Suitability for Dwellings with Basements

Slight	Moderate	Moderate or Severe	Severe
	1C	11B	7D
		11C	8D
		12C	16B
			16C
			16D/16E

Steps 5-7 Maps

Soil Limitations

	Moderate (Slope, depth to rock)		Moderate or Severe (Slope, depth to rock)		Severe (Shrink/swell, slope, depth to rock)

A Base Map

B Moderate: 1C

Continued ➤

As described in box 12.3, a base map is made from the survey maps showing the soil map units. Using the tables, map units are grouped by their rating or degree of limitation for the factor to be mapped, and each similarly rated group is assigned the same color. The box shows the steps in the process and the final interpretive soil suitability map for dwellings with basements.

BOX 12.3—(continued)

Composite Map

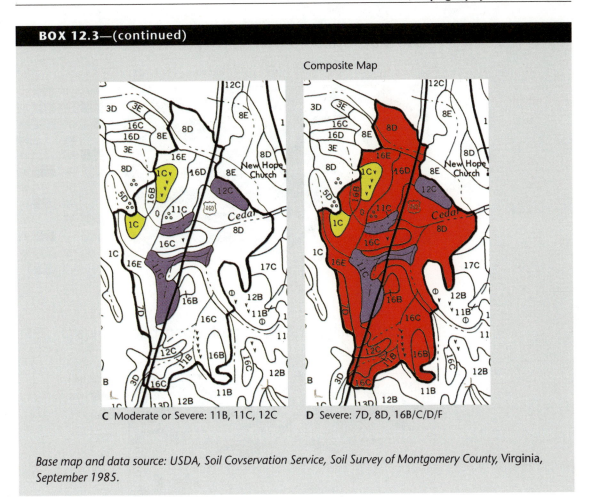

C Moderate or Severe: 11B, 11C, 12C   D Severe: 7D, 8D, 16B/C/D/F

Base map and data source: USDA, Soil Covservation Service, Soil Survey of Montgomery County, Virginia, September 1985.

Soil Surveys in the Digital Age

The interpretative mapping method discussed demonstrates the usefulness of soil survey information in land analysis. Because of the increased use of GIS for such purposes, NRCS has increased the availability of county soil survey maps in digital form. As of late 2001, NRCS has produced digital soil map data for 1,064 counties and has many in process through the Soil Survey Geographic Data Base (SSURGO). Figure 12.7 shows a soils map produced in a GIS system. Figure 12.7a shows map units in a bordered portion of the county. Using the same procedure as box 12.3 but with GIS, figure 12.7b shows a septic drainfield soil suitability map for same area.

The USDA NRCS, in partnership with Microsoft, Compaq, and ESRI, has developed a number of Internet tools to enhance access to soils information, especially in digital form. This so-called Lighthouse Project (http://www.lighthouse.nrcs.usda.gov/lighthouse/) includes three tools to deliver data and user software. The Geospatial Data Gateway (http://www.lighthouse.nrcs.usda.gov/gateway/) is being developed to provide a single access point to a variety of geospatial data. The Toolkit provides a collection of software tools (now for USDA employees only). The Soil

Soil Map Units

Soil Suitability for Septic tank absorption fields

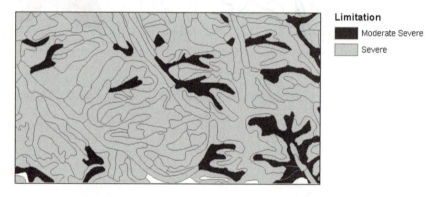

Figure 12.7 Soils Map Units and Interpretive Soil Suitability Maps in GIS

Data Viewer (http://lighthouse.nrcs.usda.gov/lighthouse/websdv/WebSDVHelp/ viewer.htm) provides online access to soils information. It is built as an ESRI ArcView extension to provide soils suitability maps in the same way as box 12.3 and figure 12.7. As of late 2001, this service is available only for those dozen or so counties for which detailed SSURGO data is available (http://ims2. ftw.nrcs.usda.gov/ statusmaps/ssurgo_nasis.jpg), but coverage will likely improve rapidly.

Limitations of Soil Surveys and New Advances

Although the soil survey is one of the best sources of natural resources information in the United States, there are certain limitations in using surveys, especially older surveys. A study by Gordon and Gordon (1981) indicates that earlier surveys have some internal inconsistencies. Surveys produced after the 1978 guidelines in the

National Soils Handbook are well-produced documents with national quality control. Still, even these modern documents are accurate only to about 2 acres. Therefore, when using soil surveys, Gordon and Gordon suggest four parallel approaches to provide some validation of information:

- Investigate local examples of existing development on soils in question to identify potential problems.
- Gather additional site-specific soils data.
- Seek additional advice from soils and engineering professionals.
- Obtain information on the costs of overcoming soil suitability limitations through design changes.

NRCS continues to improve the soil survey by improving field methods to increase accuracy and precision, providing more soil interpretation categories (e.g., limitations for stream buffers), increasing the availability of digital soils data and maps, and extending the application from agricultural to urban uses.

Useful Soil Survey Websites

Map of soil survey coverage in United States:
    http://www.statlab.iastate.edu/soils/soildiv/sslists/sslisthome.html
Soil survey manual: http://www.statlab.iastate.edu/soils/ssm/gen_cont.html
National Soil Survey Center: http://www.statlab.iastate.edu/soils/nssc/
NRCS home page: http://www.nrcs.usda.gov/
Lighthouse Project: http://www.lighthouse.nrcs.usda.gov/lighthouses
SSURGO county soil maps: http://www.ftw.nrcs.usda.gov/ssur_data.html

Slope Analysis

Soil survey map units indicate relative slope, but more accurate slope mapping is derived from topographic maps. The slope map shows the relative steepness of the land. This section describes procedures for measuring slope and producing a slope map from topographic maps or elevation data. It begins with the basic definitions of and equations for slope given in figure 12.8.

As shown in figure 12.8, terrain steepness or slope is characterized in four ways: as the **gradient,** as the **horizontal to vertical ratio,** as the **inclination or slope angle** in degrees, and most often as **percent slope.** Table 12.3 correlates the four measures of slope. Note that a 45° slope angle is a 100 percent slope. The following sections describe methods for determining slope for a specific site and for producing areawide slope maps from topographic maps.

Determining Slope of a Site from a Topographic Map

A simple technique for site analysis makes use of a ruler, map horizontal graphic scale, or a slope gauge that relates percent slope to the space between elevation

Percent (%) Slope $= \dfrac{100^*V_{12}}{H_{12}}$

where, H_{12} = horizontal distance, point 1 to point 2
$V_{12} = E_2 - E_1$ = vertical distance, pt.1 to pt. 2
E_i = elevation at point i

Slope angle $= °S = TAN^{-1} \dfrac{V_{12}}{H_{12}}$

Slope Gradient = "1 in H_{12}/V_{12}"; **HtoV ratio:** "H_{12}/V_{12}:1"

Example: H_{12} = 200 feet, E_2 = 540 ft, E_1 = 520 ft
$V_{12} = E_2 - E_1$ = 20 feet

% Slope $= \dfrac{100^*20}{200} = 10\%$

$°S = TAN^{-1} \dfrac{20}{200} = 5.7°$

Gradient = 1 in 10; **HtoV ratio** = 10:1

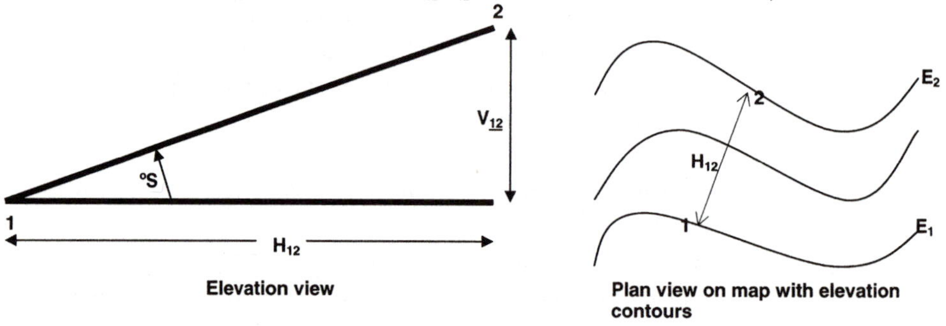

Elevation view

Plan view on map with elevation contours

Figure 12.8 Slope Terminology and Definitions

contour lines. The technique applies the basic equation for percent slope, given here and rewritten with map values and scales:

$$\% \text{ slope} = \frac{100 \times V}{H}$$

$$\% \text{ slope} = \frac{100 \times \text{contour scale (ft/interval)} \times \# \text{ intervals}}{\text{distance on horizontal graphical scale (when using graphical scale)}}$$

Figure 12.9 shows how a transparency of the horizontal graphical scale can be used to measure the average slope between two points. Simply count the contour intervals between the points and multiply the number counted by the contour scale to get the vertical elevation change between the points. Then place the horizontal scale over the map and read the horizontal distance between the points off the scale. The percent slope is 100 times the vertical elevation change divided by the horizontal distance.

TABLE 12.3 Correlating Different Slope Measures

Slope Angle, Degrees	Gradient	H/V Ratio	Percent Slope (%)
3	1 in 20	20:1	5
6	1 in 10	10:1	10
9	1 in 12.7	12.7:1	15
12	1 in 5	5:1	20
18	1 in 3.3	3.3:1	30
30	1 in 2	2:1	50
45	1 in 1	1:1	100

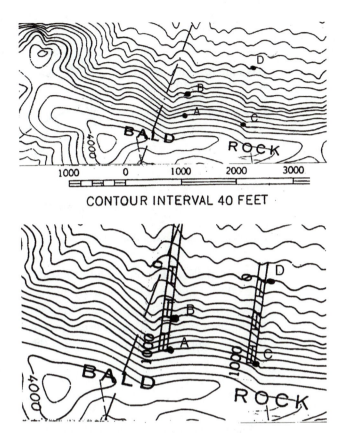

Figure 12.9 Using Horizontal Scale to Find "H" in Average Slope Measurements:
% slope AB = $\frac{100 \times 40 \times 5}{400}$ = 50%; % slope CD = $\frac{100 \times 40 \times 10}{100}$ = 40%

Alternatively, one can use a ruler or make a slope gauge to measure slope between points or between contour lines. The following variation of the percent slope equation is used:

% slope = $\dfrac{100 \times \text{contour scale (ft/interval)} \times \text{\# intervals}}{\substack{\text{gauge/ruler length} \times \text{horizontal scale (ft/in) (when using} \\ \text{a ruler or gauge)}}}$

A ruler can be placed on the map to measure the distance in inches between two points. This value is plugged into the denominator of the equation to calculate the percent slope.

To avoid having to make repeated calculations, gauges can be produced to read percent slope off the map. Using the equation, different gauges can be produced that measure the percent slope of different spacing between two adjoining contour lines.

Gauge width = $\dfrac{100 \times \text{contour scale (ft/interval)} \times \text{\# intervals}}{\text{% slope} \times \text{horizontal scale (ft/in)}}$

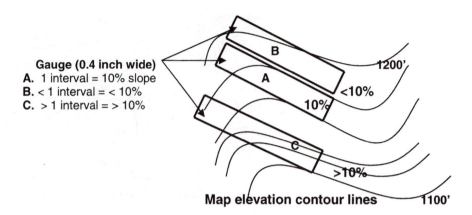

Figure 12.10 Using a Single-Interval Gauge to Read Percent Slope

For example, if the contour interval scale is 40 feet, and the horizontal scale is 1:12,000 or 1 inch = 1,000 feet, a 0.4-inch gauge width can be used to find areas of 10 percent slope on a map by measuring a single contour interval. As seen in figure 12.10, this gauge can be placed over the contour intervals to read where areas are 10 percent slope, greater than 10 percent slope, and less than 10 percent slope.

$$\text{Gauge width for 10\% slope} \quad = \quad \frac{100 \times 40 \text{ ft/interval} \times 1 \text{ interval}}{10 \times 1000 \text{ ft/in}} \quad = \quad 0.4 \text{ inch}$$

Such gauges can be made for different percent slopes. The second column of table 12.4 gives gauge widths for a single contour interval for different slopes. Since it is tedious to measure single intervals, gauges can be made for multiple intervals, as shown in the third and fourth columns of table 12.4. For example, if a 1-inch gauge is used on the sample map and 10 intervals are measured in the 1 inch gauge, it is a 40 percent slope; if 5 intervals are measured it is 20 percent; and if 1 interval is measured, it is less than 5 percent slope.

Producing an Areawide Slope Map

These same techniques can be used to produce slope maps. Slope maps distinguish areas of different steepness or classes of slope such as flat areas (e.g., 0–10%

TABLE 12.4 Relation of Gauge Width, Number of Contour Intervals and Percent Slope (e.g., 40 ft. contour, 1″ = 1000′)

Percent Slope (%)	Gauge Width, inches 1 interval	Gauge Width, inches 5 intervals	Gauge Width, inches 10 intervals
5	0.8	4.0	8.0
10	0.4	2.0	4.0
20	0.2	1.0	2.0
30	0.133	0.67	1.33
40	0.1	0.5	1.0

TABLE 12.5 **Gauges for Producing Slope Map (e.g., 40 ft. contour, 1 in. 1000 ft)**

Class	Focus on	Single-Interval Gauge, inches	1/2-inch Gauge # intervals	1-inch Gauge # intervals	2-inch Gauge # intervals
0–10%					
10–20%	10 to 11%	0.4	1 1/4+	2 1/2+	5+
20–40%	20 to 21%	0.2	2 1/2+	5+	10+
>40%	40 to 41%	0.1	5+	10+	20+

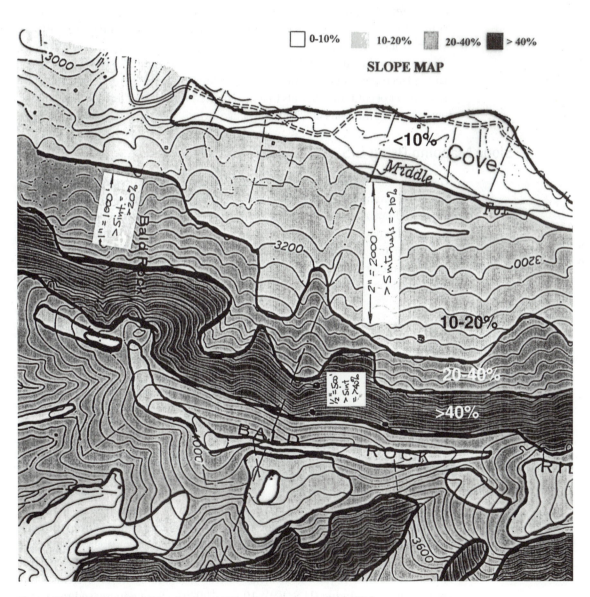

Figure 12.11 Working Slope Map Produced Using Slope Gauges in Table 12.5

slope) and steep areas (e.g., greater than 40% slope). One can use the same gauges produced in the last section. It is not necessary to measure slope at every point on the map, but rather only those points or lines where the slope changes from one class to another. For this purpose, a single-interval gauge for the slope between classes can be used to find where the slope changes from one class to another. Often, gauges that show a small number of intervals for these slope class changes are used. Table 12.5 shows a table of single and multiple interval gauges used for producing a slope map with 0–10 percent, 10–20 percent, 20–40 percent, and >40 percent steepness classes. For example, using the 1/2-inch gauge, where the number of intervals that fall within the gauge is just more than 5 intervals, the slope changes to more than 40 percent. That place should be marked as the boundary between the "20–40 percent" and ">40 percent" classes. The 0.1-inch single-interval gauge can also be used; finding the areas where just one interval fits within the gauge is exactly 40 percent slope; just more than one interval is >40 percent, just less than one interval is 20–40 percent. Figure 12.11 shows a working slope map produced using these gauges. The 1/2″, 1″, and 2″, shown as strips of paper placed perpendicular to the contour lines, indicate percent slope class by the number of contour intervals that are counted within their length. In each case more than five intervals fit within the gauge strips.

Slope Mapping Using GIS

The availability of digital elevation model (DEM) data and GIS have simplified the process of producing slope maps. The GIS can measure the relationship of elevation and horizontal scale (using the same relationship as the preceding equations) and produce a slope map. Figure 12.12 shows a slope map of Blacksburg, Virginia. Figure 12.12a displays the digital elevation model (DEM) data (see chapter 10) in meters above sea level, and figure 12.12b gives the derived slope map with four slope classes.

Soil Drainability: On-site Wastewater and Land Application of Wastes

Soil considerations are very important in land disposal and application of wastes. Soil drainability is one of the determining characteristics for on-site wastewater systems, waste lagoons, waste landfills, and land application of manure fertilizer. The latter application also depends on nutrient uptake by crops determined by a nutrient management plan.

Sanitary landfills for municipal wastes are designed to contain waste materials and leached liquids. Therefore, they are designed for zero drainage from the contained landfill. In the past, this was achieved by using low-permeability compacted clay as a landfill lining material, but continuing leaching problems led to federal landfill standards requiring artificial liners, leachate removal systems, and groundwater monitoring (U.S. EPA, 1993a, 1993b). Despite increased recycling,

Digital Elevation Model of Blacksburg

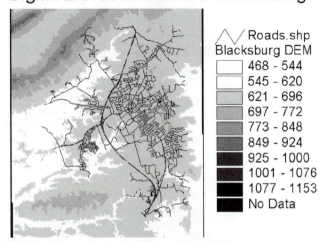

Roads.shp
Blacksburg DEM
- 468 - 544
- 545 - 620
- 621 - 696
- 697 - 772
- 773 - 848
- 849 - 924
- 925 - 1000
- 1001 - 1076
- 1077 - 1153
- No Data

Slope derived from Digital Elevation Model

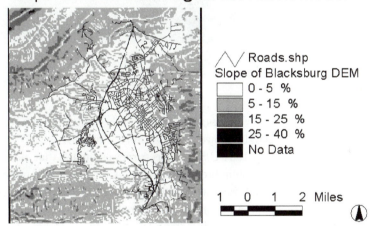

Roads.shp
Slope of Blacksburg DEM
- 0 - 5 %
- 5 - 15 %
- 15 - 25 %
- 25 - 40 %
- No Data

1 0 1 2 Miles

Figure 12.12 Elevation Map and Slope Map Using DEM Data and GIS

composting, and combustion, landfills were still used for 60 percent of municipal wastes in 2000 (U.S. EPA, 2002a).

On-site wastewater or septic systems are used by about 23 percent of the 115 million homes in the United States from a high of about 55 percent in Vermont to a low of 10 percent in California. More than half of these systems are more than 30 years old. Figure 12.13 shows a conventional on-site system. Main components are (1) a septic tank, which removes most settleable and floatable material and functions as a anaerobic bioreactor to partially digest retained organic matter and (2) a subsurface wastewater infiltration system (SWIS), which uses soils to absorb, filter, and biologically process the septic tank effluent that contains pathogenic organisms, nitrogen and phosphorus nutrients, and remaining organic matter. These systems can work effectively if they are placed in areas with appropriate soils and hydraulic capacities; are located appropriate distances from wells and

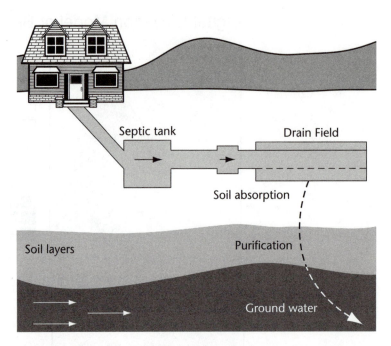

Figure 12.13 Conventional On-Site Wastewater System. *Source:* U.S. EPA (2002a).

water bodies; and are properly designed, installed, and maintained (U.S. EPA, 2002b). However, this is not always the case.

A 1997 U.S. Census survey estimated that more than 400,000 homes had septic system breakdowns during a three-month period in 1997. The EPA estimates failure rates at 10–20 percent, not including undetected systems that may be contaminating surface and groundwater. States with highest failure rates include Minnesota (50–70%), West Virginia (60%), Louisiana (50%), and Missouri (30–50%) (Angoli, 2001; U.S. EPA, 2002b).

Ineffective and failed septic systems result in contaminated ground and surface waters and public health problems. In 1996, the EPA estimated that 500 communities had public health problems caused by failed septic systems. Septic systems are cited as the third most common source of groundwater contamination. Systems contribute to surface water contamination as well, especially where they are located close to riparian, lake, and coastal waters. A study of Buttermilk Bay in Massachusetts found that 74 percent of the nitrogen entering the Bay came from septic systems (U.S. EPA, 2002b).

Because of the level of use and rates of failure, on-site wastewater septic systems are a major environmental problem in urbanizing areas as well as recreation areas. In some urbanizing areas, on-site systems were thought of as a temporary measure until centralized sewage systems were built. However, high costs of service extension and other factors have made these systems more permanent. As a result, public management of these systems has not been effective, and many communities have suffered the consequences.

An effective community management program for on-site systems includes clear program goals, public education, technical guidelines and standards, regular monitoring and maintenance, certification of providers, enforcement mechanisms, funding mechanisms, and program evaluation (U.S. EPA, 2002b).

Proper siting and design of new conventional systems requires an estimate of wastewater flow and a site and soils assessment. Soils must provide sufficient permeability and hydraulic capacity and depth to bedrock and water table. Other important characteristics include topography, surface drainage, vegetation, and proximity to surface waters, wells, wetlands, rock outcrops, and property lines. Soil investigations usually employ test pits or borings to determine soil depth, horizons, texture, structure, color, consistence, and redoximorphic features. Redoximorphic features are iron modules and mottles that form in seasonally saturated soils, which obviously are not good for absorption fields.

Finally, soil investigation measures infiltration, or the rate water is accepted by the soil, and hydraulic conductivity, or the rate water is transmitted through the soil. These are difficult to measure. The long-used percolation test measures the rate at which water drops in a two-foot square hole (see box 12.1). However, the test is flawed primarily because it is a snapshot in time, and it has been replaced by detailed descriptions of the soil profile that indicate longer-term conditions (U.S. EPA, 2002b).

Improved designs and new technologies have enhanced the effectiveness and longevity of on-site systems. These include redundant or reserve drainfields, sand/media filters, enhanced nutrient removal, sequenced batch reactors, disinfection, and others (see U.S. EPA, 2002b). Decentralized community-scaled systems offer an attractive alternative to both on-site systems and centralized sewers (English and Yaeger, 2002; U.S. EPA, 2000).

Agricultural Lands and Land Evaluation and Site Assessment

The conversion of prime agricultural lands to nonagricultural uses such as highways and suburban development has been an issue of concern for three decades. The USDA developed the land evaluation and site assessment (LESA) system to help planners determine the value of agricultural lands so that it could be considered in land planning decisions. Before discussing LESA, the following section introduces the agricultural land conversion process.

Agricultural Land Conversion

Although conversion of agricultural land may result in a higher economic return from the land, at least in the short term, it can also irreversibly remove from agriculture highly productive soils that have taken centuries to develop. In many areas, agricultural land use is an important contribution to the local economy and to the agrarian character that many communities would like to maintain.

Prime farmland is rural land with the best combination of physical and chemical characteristics for producing food, feed, forage, fiber, and oilseed crops and is available for these uses. It has USDA capability class 1 or 2 soils (box 12.2).

In the United States, prime farmland is 64 percent cropland, 15 percent forestland, 11 percent pastureland, and 6 percent rangeland. The rest is other rural land not in production. The biggest concentration of prime farmland is in the belt of four midwestern states (Ohio, Indiana, Illinois, and Iowa), in which more than half the nonfederal rural land is prime farmland (USDA, 2001b).

The National Resources Inventory (NRI) documents land use change in the United States every five years. The latest report covers the period 1992–1997 (USDA, 2001b). The estimated *331.8 million acres of prime farmland in 1997* was down 10 million acres from the 1982 total—including some 4.7 million prime farmland acres converted to urban and rural development. Forestland and cultivated cropland made up more than 60 percent of the 111.6 million acres converted to development between 1982 and 1997. Between 1992 and 1997, 645,000 acres per year of prime farmland was converted to development uses. In the latest 15 years, 30 percent of newly developed land was converted from prime farmland (USDA, 2001b).

In response to these trends, several states and localities in the United States have devised programs to preserve agricultural lands. These programs range from tax incentives and regulations to the purchase or transfer of development rights. Specific programs are discussed in chapters 5, 7, and 8. A first step for planners, however, is to assess farmlands to see what areas are most suitable for retention in agricultural use and which may be more suitable for development.

Land Evaluation and Site Assessment

In response to the Farmlands Protection Act of 1981, the SCS (now NRCS) developed the LESA system to help planners judge the relative agricultural suitability of lands near urban areas (USDA, SCS, 1983). County planners throughout the country have implemented the procedure. It involves two parts: first, the **Land Evaluation (LE)** rates the soils of the area, usually a county, for cropland; second, the **Site Assessment (SA)** identifies factors other than soils that are important to the quality of a site for agricultural use and rates specific sites based on those factors. Variations of the system can also be used to evaluate forestland and rangeland. Implementing the LESA system requires first establishing the rules of the system and, second, applying the system to individual sites.

Establishing the LESA System in a County

Although some states have developed statewide LESA programs, most applications are in individual counties. Since a number of subjective decisions are required to establish the system's rules, the procedure calls for a local LESA committee representing different agricultural, conservation, and development interests.

The first part of the system, the **Land Evaluation** (LE), involves an interpretation of information in the county soil survey. The LE rates 10 groupings of soil series based on their productivity or potential for growing an indicator crop selected by the LESA committee. The indicator crop is usually the most important crop in the county. Soil productivity indicates the expected yield for the indi-

TABLE 12.6 **LESA Worksheet #2 for Montgomery County (VA): Land Evaluation Groups and Relative LE Values**

LE Group	Land Capability Class	Important Farmland Class	Soil Potential Index	Soil Map Units	Acres in County	Percentage of County	Relative Value
1	2e/2w	Prime	100	28, 30B, 16B, 12B, 20B	10,105	3.9	100
2	2e/2w	Prime	84–96	13B, 15B, 19B, 33	7,695	3.0	90
3	2e/3e	Statewide	81–92	11B, 12C, 15C, 21C, 30C	11,881	4.6	87
4	3e/3w	Statewide	69–77	11C, 13C, 14, 17C, 31C	12,676	4.9	74
5	2e/3e/4w	Local	61–76	2B, 25, 2C	12,177	4.7	64
6	3e/3s	Local	48–57	1C, 26C, 10	11,102	4.3	55
7	3e	Statewide	45–53	22C, 16C	9,964	3.8	47
8	4e	Statewide	21–33	30D, 15D, 16D, 13D	12,668	4.9	22
9	4e	Local	13–17	9C, 3D, 26D	10,290	4.0	16
10	6e/6s/7s	—	—	3E, 4E, 5D, 6E, 7D, 8D, 8E, 9D, 29, 16E, 18B, 18C, 18D, 23C, 24D, 26E, 27E, 32B, 32C, 32D, 34E		61.8	0

cator crop under a high level of management; soil potential adjusts the productivity by considering the costs of measures to overcome capability limitations such as erosion or wetness and the continuing limitations after measures are taken. The soil groupings are also influenced by the USDA Land Capability classification (the 1–8 rating described in box 12.2) and an "important farmland" classification. This latter rating includes four categories (prime, statewide importance, local importance, and other) and can emphasize the importance of certain farmlands or uses regardless of their soil types, such as for specialty crops or animal production.

Given the indicator crop, NRCS offices will usually provide counties with the LE groupings. In a worksheet, NRCS groups all soil map units according to their Land Capability classification, important farmland designation, yield of the indicator crop in tons per acre (as given in the soil survey tables; see "table 6" in table 12.2), and productivity index. The index simply normalizes the yields to a 0–100 scale where 100 corresponds to the yield of the highest yield soils. Each of these ratings can affect the group into which the map unit is placed. Worksheet #2 (table 12.6) summarizes this information and computes a relative value for each group, from 0 to 100.

The LE thus provides a fairly objective means for assigning agricultural value on a 0–100 scale to the soils of the county. The 50 or so soil series and map units are aggregated to 10 groups of common agricultural *capability* for growing a specific indicator crop.

However, the *suitability* of land for agricultural use also depends on factors other than soils. The **Site Assessment** (SA) portion of LESA investigates these nonsoil factors that contribute to the suitability of specific parcels for retention in agricultural use. The procedure calls for a sum-of-weighted-factors approach. As

TABLE 12.7   Site Assessment Factors, Scoring, Weights (W) and Adjusted Weights (AW) for Montgomery County (VA)

		W	AW
1. Percent of Area in Agriculture Within Radius of the Property Boundary		7	1.8
10	95–100%		
8	75–95%		
6	50–75%		
4	24–50%		
2	10–25%		
0	0–10%		
2. Land Use Adjacent to Site		7	1.8
10	All sides of Site in Agriculture		
8	One Side of Site Adjacent to Non-agricultural Land		
5	Two Sides of Site Adjacent to Non-agricultural Land		
2	Three Sides of Site Adjacent to Non-agricultural Land		
0	Site Surrounded by Nonagricultural Land		
3. Zoning		8	2.1
10	Site and All Surrounding Sides Zoned for Agricultural Use		
8	Site and Three Sides Zoned for Agricultural Use		
5	Site and Two Sides Zoned for Agricultural Use		
2	Site and One Side Zoned for Agricultural Use		
0	Site Zoned for Nonagricultural Use and/or Site Zoned on all Sides for Non-agricultural Use		
4. Availability of Less Productive Land		8	2.1
10	More Than 2/3 of the Land Within a 2 Mile Travel Distance is Less Productive		
5	1/3 to 2/3 of the Land Within a 2 Mile Travel Distance is Less Productive		
0	Less than 1/3 of the Land Within a 2 Mile Travel Distance is Less Productive		
5. Compatibility With Comprehensive Plan		8	2.1
10	Agriculture Use Compatible With Plan		
0	Agriculture Use Incompatible With Plan		
6. Central Water Distribution System		6	1.6
10	No Public Water Within 1 Mile		
7	Public Water Within 2,000 Feet		
4	Public Water Within 500 Feet		
0	Public Water at or Adjacent to Site		
7. Central Sanitary Sewerage System		6	1.6
10	No Public Sewer Line Within 1 Mile		
7	Public Sewer Line Within 2,000 Feet		
4	Public Sewer Line Within 500 Feet		
0	Public Sewer Line at or Adjacent to Site		
8. Transportation		4	1.0
10	Site Access to Unimproved Road		
5	Site Access to Secondary Road		
0	Site Access to Primary Road		

TABLE 12.7 *(Continued)* **Site Assessment Factors, Scoring, Weights (W) and Adjusted Weights (AW) for Montgomery County (VA)**

		W	AW
9. Compatibility of Proposed Use With Surrounding Existing Land Use			
10	Incompatibility	8	2.1
0	Compatibility		
10. Site in Agricultural & Forestal District AFD			
10	In AFD	5	1.3
0	Not in AFD		
11. Soil Conservation District Plan Filed			
10	Active Plan	5	1.3
5	Inactive Plan		
0	No Plan		
12. Family Farm Value			
10	Three or More Generations	5	1.3
5	Two Generations		
0	One Generation		

discussed in chapter 2, the determination and evaluation of the factors using this approach is a value-laden process. It requires broad local participation to be fair in the eyes of local citizens and to be responsive to local, areawide, and national needs. Therefore, the procedure calls for the local LESA committee to determine and weigh the factors to be used in the site assessment, thus establishing the "rules" of the process.

An example of these rules, that is, the factors and weights, is shown in table 12.7. Given are 12 factors selected by the LESA committee in Montgomery County, Virginia. They range from "percentage of land in agriculture within 1/2 mile" of the site to "zoning" for the site to "central sewerage system availability"—each has some bearing on the suitability of the site for agriculture and alternative uses. Each factor has a maximum score of 10 and an assigned weight between 1 and 10 (in this case between 4 and 8). Multiplying the maximum score for each factor by its weight and summing the products yields a total maximum points (770). Because the procedure calls for a maximum SA score of 200, the weights are adjusted by multiplying by 0.26 (or 200/770). Multiplying the adjusted weights (e.g., 2.1 instead of 8) by the maximum scores for each factor and summing the products will yield the desired maximum total of 200. Individual sites can then be assessed by assigning the site values for these factors; a sum of the products of these factor values times their adjusted weights will give a total site assessment value between 0 and 200.

A total LESA score combines the LE and SA scores for a value between 0 and 300. Normally, the committee will determine a "cut-off" score, for example 200, which roughly separates higher and lower suitability agricultural sites.

Applying LESA to Specific Sites

Once the rules of the LESA procedure are established, it can be applied to specific parcels of land. Tables 12.8 and 12.9 and figure 12.14 illustrate the process. The land evaluation component assigns to each soil map unit on the site, the LE value (0–100) for the agricultural soil group that includes that series. Based on the acreage of each map unit, an average land evaluation value is computed for the site. The example in table 12.8 gives the LE value of 67. Recall that the best soils in *that* county for producing corn (the LESA committee's choice as the indicator crop) are rated 100.

The SA table shown in table 12.9 gives the 12 factors and their adjusted importance weights chosen by the committee in table 12.7. The product of the factor rat-

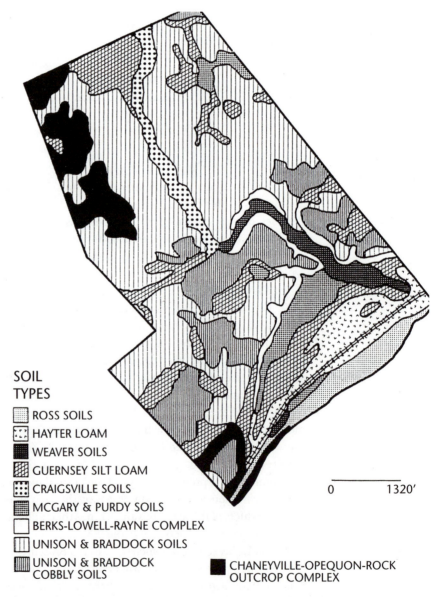

SOIL
TYPES

▦ ROSS SOILS

⦂ HAYTER LOAM

■ WEAVER SOILS

▨ GUERNSEY SILT LOAM

▦ CRAIGSVILLE SOILS

▤ MCGARY & PURDY SOILS

□ BERKS-LOWELL-RAYNE COMPLEX

▥ UNISON & BRADDOCK SOILS

▥ UNISON & BRADDOCK COBBLY SOILS

■ CHANEYVILLE-OPEQUON-ROCK OUTCROP COMPLEX

0   1320′

Figure 12.14 Soil Types, Whitehorne Site. *Source:* Montgomery County Planning Department (1984).

TABLE 12.8 **Land Evaluation for Whitethorne**

Map Unit	Soil Name	Slope	Acres	Agricultural Group
30B	Unison and Braddock Soils	2–7%	64.2	1
30C	Unison and Braddock Soils	7–15%	128.4	3
30D	Unison and Braddock Soils	15–25%	124.0	8
19B	Guernsey Silt Loam	2–7%	125.6	2
31C	Unison and Braddock Cobbly Soils	7–15%	101.8	4
28	Ross Soils	0–2%	27.8	1
33	Weaver Soils	0–2%	21.3	2
25	McGary and Purdy Soils	0–2%	13.3	5
10	Craigsville Soils	0–2%	21.6	6
20B	Hayter Loam	2–7%	47.1	1
3E	Berks-Lowell-Rayne Complex	25–65%	25.6	10
8E	Caneyville-Opaquon-Rock Outcrop Complex	25–65%	55.1	10

Map Unit	Agricultural Group	Relative Value	Acres	Acres % Relative Value
30B	1	100	64.2	6,420.0
30C	3	87	128.4	11,170.8
30D	8	22	124.0	2,728.0
19B	2	90	125.6	11,304.0
31C	4	74	101.8	7,533.2
28	1	100	27.8	2,780.0
33	2	90	21.3	1,917.0
25	5	64	33.3	2,132.2
10	6	55	21.6	1,188.0
20B	1	100	47.1	4,710.0
3E	10	0	25.6	0.0
8E	10	0	55.1	0.0
			775.8	51,883.2

Land Evaluation average relative site value = 51.883 + 775.8 = 67.0

ings (0–10) given to the site and the adjusted weights gives the "adjusted weights assigned points," which are summed to give the total SA score. This site has a value of 130.2. Recall that the maximum value is 200. The LE value of 67 and the SA value of 130.2 combine to give a LESA total of 197.2 on the 300-point scale (Montgomery County, 1984).

In some cases, counties will determine only LE scores for sites simply to provide an evaluation of agricultural capability. Indeed, the SA portion of the procedure has been looked upon by some counties as too subjective and potentially controversial.

Use and Critique of LESA

The implementation of LESA for agricultural lands by rural and urbanizing counties has increased steadily since it was established in the mid-1980s. Applications have included the following:

TABLE 12.9 **Site Assessment for Whitethorne**

Factor	Assigned Points	Adjusted Weight	Adjusted Weight Assigned Points
1. % of Area in Agriculture	6	1.8	10.8
2. Land Use Adjacent to Site	8	1.8	14.4
3. Zoning	0	2.1	0.0
4. Availability of Less Productive Land	10	2.1	21.0
5. Compatibility with Comprehensive Plan	10	2.1	21.0
6. Central Water	10	1.6	16.0
7. Central Sewer	10	1.6	16.0
8. Transportation	10	1.0	10.0
9. Compatibility with Existing Surrounding Land Use	10	2.1	21.0
10. AFU	0	1.1	0.0
11. Soil Conservation Plan	0	1.1	0.0
12. Family Farm Value	0	1.3	0.0
Site assessment value			**130.2**

Total LESA score = 67.0 + 130.2 = 197.2

- Evaluating rezoning and other development applications for sites currently zoned for agriculture
- Impact assessment
- Prioritizing or qualifying sites for inclusion in land protection programs such as agricultural districts, agricultural zones, development rights transfer or purchase areas, and so on
- Comprehensive land use plans: where community growth should be encouraged and discouraged

A survey by Coughlin et al. (1994) indicated the level of use and applications of LESA in its first decade. More than 212 state and local jurisdictions were using LESA by 1990. Most of the use was in the eastern and southern states. Popular applications include zoning, impact assessment, agricultural districting and development rights programs, and lending.

Since LESA has become the basic planning tool for evaluating agricultural lands throughout the country, some comments on its strengths and weaknesses are appropriate. In terms of strengths, LESA goes well beyond previous measures of agricultural land value (e.g., land capability classes) by incorporating nonsoil factors. LESA is designed to be flexible so that individual counties can tailor key factors in the process (i.e., indicator crop, SA factors and weights) to meet the county's needs and perceptions. Although the nature of the sum-of-weighted-factors process is value-laden (e.g., what is an appropriate indicator crop, what are the appropriate weights to assign to SA factors), the values are chosen by a committee of members representing diverse interests in the community.

With regard to weaknesses, LESA is fairly complex, requiring a good deal of time and effort on the part of the county and the committee to establish the rules of the process. However, once the rules are established, applying the procedure to individual sites is straightforward, requiring perhaps one-half of a person-day per site. Some have questioned the relative values assigned by the LESA procedure to soil (100) and nonsoil (200) factors; in many cases, they argue, soil factors should be given greater weight. Although LESA is designed to be flexible, flexibility may lead to misuse of the procedures. Preconceived notions, even existing programs for land protection, can bias the choice of factors to justify those notions or programs. Finally, whereas flexibility may serve individual counties, it does not serve regional or statewide interests since LESA values from one county cannot be compared with another. Some states have had to develop a statewide LESA system, separate from the county system, that allows comparative values for setting priorities for state farmland protection programs.

Urban Soils

Soils in urban areas do not receive the attention that agricultural soils do, but urban soils are important for urban forestry, landscaping, land development, and erosion and sediment control. As discussed earlier, soil strength and stability are important considerations for building and road construction. In addition, many of the same factors affecting agricultural land use are important for vegetation in urban areas, including urban woodlands, parklands, street boulevard trees, riparian buffers, and community gardens. This section describes common urban soil problems and remediation measures. Erosion and sediment control for urban land development and construction is discussed in the next section.

The following list shows common urban soil problems (USDA, Forest Service, Southern Region, 2001). A common concern is soil compaction that affects root growth and drainage on parklands, recreation fields, and landscaping, especially tree propagation in central urban areas dominated by impervious surfaces (Craul, 1999). Signs of soil compaction include very hard soil, standing water, excessive runoff, high bulk density, or poor plant growth. Compacted soil often behaves like impervious surfaces, inhibiting water infiltration and exacerbating runoff.

Urban Soil Problems

- *Soil compaction:* Increased bulk density caused by any weight on land surface, such as construction equipment, vehicles, and pedestrians. Compaction inhibits drainage, aeration, and root growth. Compacted soil often behaves like impervious surfaces, concrete or asphalt.
- *Impervious surfaces:* Surfaces like roads and parking lots interrupt exchange of gases, alter drainage, and increase soil temperature.
- *Soil erosion and stream sedimentation:* Land development and construction removes vegetative cover and disrupts natural hydrology, creating short- and long-term erosion and sedimentation problems.
- *Moving soils:* Moving soil through grading and clearing eliminates topsoil, increases erosion, and affects drainage and aeration.

- *Soil contamination:* Chemical spills, waste dumping, excessive fertilizer and pesticide use, and runoff pollution contaminate soils.
- *Fill dirt:* Use of fill dirt affects drainage, aeration, and compaction.

Compaction can be prevented by avoiding wet areas, limiting travel routes and parking, and applying mulch. For new planting sites, soil compaction problems can be resolved by tilling and mixing soil and mulching. For existing planted sites where tilling is not possible, core aeration, vertical mulching, and radial trenching can reduce soil compaction.

Urban soils are also subject to contamination by petroleum products from surface runoff and leaking underground storage tanks, heavy metals, and other chemicals, including excessive use of pesticides. One of the biggest challenges for brownfields redevelopment in urban areas is contaminated soils. Restoration of urban soils can improve conditions, reduce impacts, and enhance productivity. **Phytoremediation** uses green plants to remove contaminants from soils. It is especially effective in removing heavy metals (U.S. EPA, 1998). Aeration methods can help relieve compaction of heavily used areas like recreation fields and lawns. Soils for community gardens and landscaping can be improved by adding organic materials like compost to reduce density, diversify texture, and enhance fertility.

Soil Erosion and Assessment

Soil erosion is a worldwide problem caused by wind or water and is accelerated by the removal of vegetation. Erosion threatens agricultural production capacity and is the major source of damaging sediment in rivers, lakes, and estuaries. Figure 12.15 from the National Resources Inventory (USDA, 2000) shows wind and sheet and rill erosion estimates declined from 3.1 billion tons per year in 1982 to 1.9 billion tons in 1997. Most of this reduction came from a drop in erosion on highly erodible land (HEL), much of which was taken out of production by the federal Conservation Reserve Program (CRP). Under this program, farmers are paid a benefit not to farm highly erodible lands (see chapter 5).

Revised Universal Soil Loss Equation, Erodibility Index, and Highly Erodible Lands

The basis for most assessment of soil erosion is the Universal Soil Loss Equation (USLE), which was developed by W. H. Wischmeier and D. D. Smith (1960) from decades of data measured on experimental agricultural plots in several states. In the early 1990s, the USLE was revised (RUSLE), fine-tuning some of the parameter values and improving applications on nonagricultural lands.

The RUSLE calculates the expected annual potential soil loss per acre, based on rainfall pattern, soil composition, vegetative cover, slope, and conservation practices:

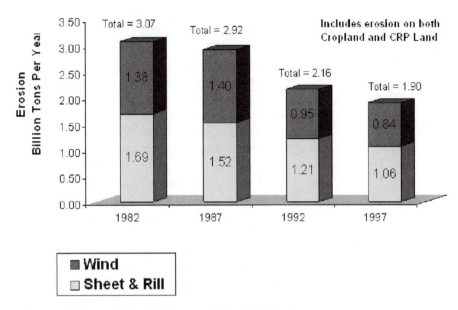

Figure 12.15 NRI Estimate of Erosion Soil Loss, 1982 to 1997. *Source:* USDA (2001a)

$$A = K \times R \times C \times LS \times P$$

where   A = average annual soil loss in tons per acre
        K = soil-erodibility factor
        R = rainfall erosion index
        C = crop management or plant cover factor
        LS = slope geometry, based on steepness and length
        P = conservation practice factors

The erodibility factor (K), rainfall index (R), and slope geometry (LS) (except for contouring) are based on the inherent site conditions. Plant cover (C) and conservation practices (P) are based on management of the site.

- Values for K can be estimated based on textural class and organic content from table 12.10, but values given for specific series in soil surveys are more accurate.
- Values for R can be obtained from figure 12.17.
- Given values for slope length and percent slope, LS values can be determined from figure 12.16.
- Values for plant cover (C) and conservation practices (P) depend on site conditions and land management. The C factor is the ratio of soil loss for given conditions to soil loss from a cultivated fallow field. For cropland, the determination of C is complicated by crop stage and crop manage-

ment practices (e.g. conservation tillage, winter seeding, etc.). Generalized C values are given table 12.11.

- Agricultural practices other than crop management can conserve soil and are reflected in the P value. If there are no conservation practices, P is 1.0. P values are given in table 12.12 for three conservation practices.

The Erodibility Index (EI), is defined by the inherent erosion properties of the site (K, R, and LS), and a tolerance (T) value of soil loss, usually 3–5 tons per acre. K and T values are given in soil surveys (see "table 15" in table 12.2).

$$\text{Erodibility Index (EI)} \quad = \quad \frac{K \times R \times LS}{T}$$

where   T = Erosion Tolerance (usually 3–5 tons per acre)

Highly erodible lands (HEL) are defined as lands with EI greater than 8. The CRP provides benefits to farmers to keep certain lands out of production. Since the early 1980s the program has focused on HEL, and thousands of these areas have been taken out of cultivation (CRP is also discussed in chapter 5). This is a main reason for the significant reduction in soil erosion from 1982 to 1997 estimated by the NRI (figure 12.15).

Example of RUSLE, EI, and HEL Calculations

Compare the expected erosion in tons per year from a 10-acre site with a 6 percent, 220-foot slope and 2 percent organic silt loam soil, in south-central Illinois, before and after the grass and weed cover is cultivated and laid fallow. Assume no conservation practices and T = 5. What is the erosion per year before and after cultivation? What is the land's EI? Is it HEL?

TABLE 12.10   **K, Soil-Erodibility Factor Values**

| Textural Class | Organic Matter (%) | | |
	0.5	2	4
Fine sand	0.16	0.14	0.10
Very fine sand	0.42	0.36	0.28
Loamy sand	0.12	0.10	0.08
Loamy very fine sand	0.44	0.38	0.30
Sandy loam	0.27	0.24	0.19
Very fine sandy loam	0.47	0.41	0.33
Silt loam	0.48	0.42	0.33
Clay loam	0.28	0.25	0.21
Silty clay loam	0.37	0.32	0.26
Silty clay	0.25	0.23	0.19

See soil survey for more accurate values

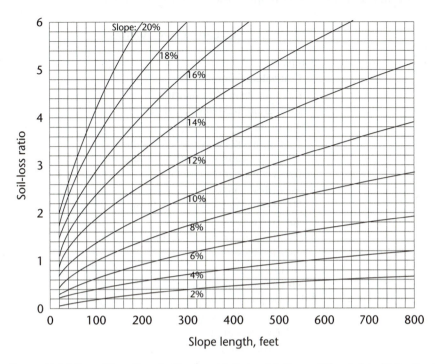

Figure 12.16 Slope Effect Chart for Topographic Factor, LS. *Source: Urban Soils* by Philip Craul, copyright © 1999, John Wiley and Sons. Reprinted with permission of John Wiley and Sons, Inc.

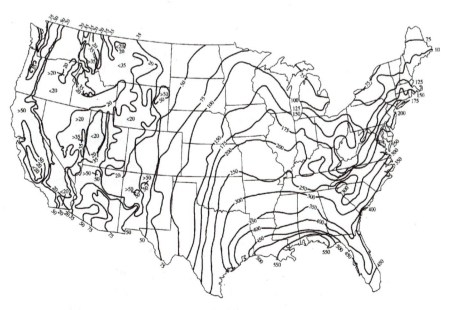

Figure 12.17 Rainfall Factor, R, for the Eastern United States. *Source: Urban Soils* by Philip Craul, copyright © 1999, John Wiley and Sons. Reprinted with permission of John Wiley and Sons, Inc.

TABLE 12.11   **C, Land Cover Values**

Cropland	
Cultivated, fallow field	1.0
Corn seedbed, after plowing	0.60
Corn grain, fall plow w/residue	0.33
Pasture, Range	
Established grass, legume meadow	0.004
Meadow, two months after seeding	0.05
Grass, weeds (80% cover)	0.013
Undisturbed Forest	
75–100% canopy, 90–100% litter	0.0001–0.001
45–70% canopy, 75–85% litter	0.002–0.004
20–40% canopy, 40–70% litter	0.005–0.009
Construction Sites	
No mulch	1.0
Straw/hay: tons/acres (t/a)	
1.0 t/a (<10% slope)	0.2
2.0 t/a (<16% slope)	0.06
(16–20% slope)	0.11
(>35% slope)	0.20
Crushed stone	
135t/a	0.05
240 t/a	0.02
Wood chips	
7 t/a	0.08
12 t/a	0.05
25 t/a	0.02

Solution:

k=0.42 (table 12.10); R=200 (figure 12.17); LS = 1.0 (figure 12.16);

C (before) =0.013 (table 12.11); C (after) = 1.0; P=1.0

$$A = K \times R \times LS \times C \times P = 0.42 \times 200 \times 1.0 \times 0.013 \times 1.0 = 1.092 \text{ T/ac} \times 10 \text{ ac} =$$
$$10.9 \text{ tons per year before cultivation}$$

$$A = K \times R \times LS \times C \times P = 0.42 \times 200 \times 1.0 \times 1.0 \times 1.0 = 84.0 \text{ T/ac} \times 10 \text{ ac} =$$
$$840 \text{ tons per year after cultivation}$$

$$EI = (K \times R \times LS)/T = 0.42 \times 200 \times 1.0/5.0 = 16.8$$

Yes, this is HEL.

Although the USLE was developed and is primarily used for erosion potential from cropland, it has been applied to other land uses that disturb soil cover such as rangeland, construction, and recreation. The RUSLE has improved its application to construction sites, mined lands, reclaimed lands, and other highly disturbed sites (Toy and Foster, 1998; USDA, NRCS, 2000).

TABLE 12.12 **P, Conservation Practice Values**

Percent Slope (%)	P_e Contouring (max. slope length in m)	P_a Strip Cropping	P Terracing and Contouring
Parallel to Field	0.8	—	—
1.1–2	0.6 (150)	0.30	—
2.1–7	0.5 (100)	0.25	0.10
7.1–12	0.6 (60)	0.30	0.12
12.1–18	0.8 (20)	0.40	0.16
18.1–24	0.9 (18)	0.45	—

Improvements and further applications continue. The USDA National Sedimentation Laboratory has developed analytical software for use of RUSLE (version 1.06b released January 2001) (http://www.sedlab.olemiss.edu/rusle). The RUSLE 2 is a more advanced Windows-based version released in summer 2001 (http://www.bioengr.ag.utk.edu/rusle2). Michigan State University provides a nice online interactive RUSLE for use with Michigan soils (http://www.iwr.msu.edu/~ouyangda/rusle). Finally, the Water Erosion Prediction Project (WEPP) is a simulation model that provides more detailed assessment than RUSLE at both field and watershed scales (http://topsoil.nserl.purdue.edu/nserlweb/weppmain/wepp.html).

Mitigating Soil Erosion from Agricultural Lands

Box 12.4 gives a number of control practices that can reduce soil erosion and sedimentation for different activities. Figure 12.18 illustrates some of these mea-

---

BOX 12.4 — Erosion and Sedimentation Practices for Various Land-Disturbing Activities

Crop Production

Conservation tillage, contour and/or strip cropping
Cover and green manure cropping
Mulching

Pasture and Grazing

Fencing for grazing management
Streambank protection (see chapter 14)
Filter strips, buffers (see chapters 14,16)

Forest Products Harvesting

Filter strips, buffers
Road and trail access system design
Revegetation

Mining

Bench drainage, toe berms
Filter strips
Revegetation
Check dams
Stream protection

Construction

Site design (see chapter 14)
Minimize extent of area exposed at one time
Mulching
Filter strips, buffers (see chapters 14, 16)
Sediment barriers
Revegetation

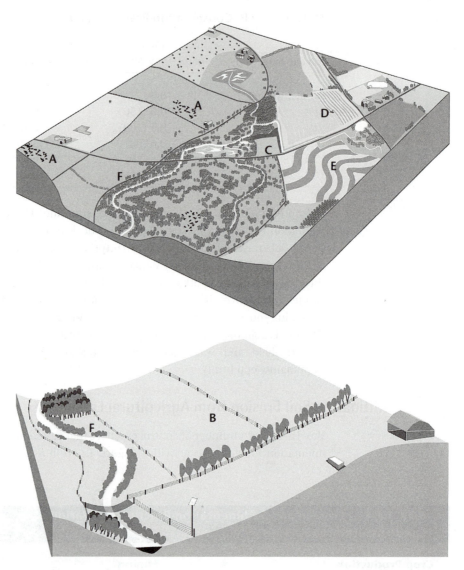

Figure 12.18 Agricultural Erosion Control.
- Tillage, seeding, fertility, pest management, and harvest operations should consider soil properties and topography in water and soil conservation and management.
- Grazing land management should protect environmental attributes, including native species protection, while achieving optimum, long-term resource use. Livestock exclusion and management with fencing reduces overgrazing and protects stream corridors, controlling both sheet and streambank and channel erosion (see **A** & **B** on figures).
- Where crops are raised and the land class allows, pastures should be managed with crop rotation sequences to provide vigorous forage cover while building soil and protecting water and wildlife qualities.
- Farm woodlots, wetlands, and field borders should be part of an overall farm plan that conserves, protects, and enhances native plants and animals, soil, water, and scenic qualities (**C**).
- Erosion control measures include: contour farming (**D**), conservation tillage, terracing (**E**), critical area planting, sediment basins, and filter strips (**F**).

Source: FISRWG (1998).

BOX 12.5—Erosion and Sediment Control Principles and Planning

Design Phase

1. Evaluate the site: topography, drainage, vegetation, soils, rainfall patterns.
2. Divide the site into the natural drainage areas.
3. Plan the development to fit the site.
4. Determine limits of clearing and grading. Divide the project into smaller phases, clearing small amounts of vegetation at a time.
5. Divert water from disturbed areas, minimize length and steepness of slopes, avoid soil compaction by restricting heavy equipment to limited areas.
6. Select temporary and permanent erosion and sediment control practices.

   a. Soil stabilization (soil cover: vegetative and nonvegetative covers)

   b. Sediment control (sediment filters, basins)
   c. Runoff control (diversion, check dams)

Construction Phase

7. Temporary structure practices

   a. Erosion control blankets
   b. Straw bale dike
   c. Silt fence
   d. Temporary swale
   e. Many others

Operation Phase

8. Maintain installed E&S practices (e.g., vegetative cover, diversion works, detention basins).

Sources: USDA, NRCS, 2000; Craul, 1999.

sures. The practices involve retaining or establishing a vegetative or other cover to the land, slowing runoff and filtering sediment, protecting streambanks, and carefully planning and designing the land disturbing activity. Erosion and sediment control from urban construction is discussed in the next section. Runoff control is discussed at length in chapter 14.

Urban Erosion and Sediment Control

Construction grading and filling removes vegetation and leads to erosion. In fact, studies of urban construction projects have shown they can produce a soil loss of 218 tons/acre compared with 5–20 tons/acre and less than 1 ton/acre for forestland (Craul, 1999). Such projects produce impervious surfaces on roads, parking lots, and the building footprint, taking soils out of use. However, exposure of unvegetated soil during construction, disruption of drainage patterns, and the impervious surfaces that increase runoff all contribute to removal of eroded soil from the site and off-site deposition of sediments in receiving waters. Sediment reduces water quality, increasing turbidity and nutrients, and lowering flow capacity. As a result, most states and localities implement erosion and sediment (E&S) control regulations for land construction and development.

The regulations often require temporary measures during construction as well as long-term design measures to control erosion and runoff. Before construction begins, the owner or contractor must prepare an erosion and sediment control plan incorporating E&S principles into the development design, construction, and operation (see box 12.5).

TABLE 12.13 **Effects of Management Practices on Controlling Erosion on a Road Bank using RUSLE**

Site Conditions		Soil Loss from Road Bank (t/a/y)	Sediment Yield at Base of Slope (t/a/y)
1st 6 mo	*2nd 6 mo*		
Bare	Bare	400	400
Bare	Bare, Silt Fence	400	250
Bare	Mulch, Seeded	140	140
Bare	Sod Diversion	40	5

Assumptions: roadside cut, 100 ft. long at 30% gradient; site disturbed March–June; soil loss and sediment yield during a single construction season; soil is silt loam; silt fence is placed at base of slope; diversion placed in middle of slope. (NRCS, 2000; Toy & Foster, 1998)

TABLE 12.14 **Effectiveness of Groundcovers in Reducing Runoff and Erosion for a Single Rain Event**

Material	Soil Loss (t/a)	Percentage of Rainfall Runoff	Percentage of Ground Cover Established
Bare soil w/partial cover	2.97	83	50
Woven mesh	0.18	68	61
Wood shavens in nonwoven polyester netting	0.36	74	69
Coconut fiber mat	0.48	76	58
Straw (2 t/a)	0.26	60	76
Grass sod	0.04	28	NA

Simulated rain event: 3.78 in/h; location: Univ. of MD research facilty; soil: loamy sand, sandy clay loam; % cover established one year after Kentucky 31 fescue grass seeded and covered by material (NRCS, 2000; Brady & Weil, 1999)

Good erosion and sediment control planning can avoid considerable problems and costs later in the process. Key considerations are topography, drainage ways, soils, and natural vegetation. A combination of slope gradient and length pose erosion hazards. Generally, slopes of 0–7 percent pose low erosion hazard (unless greater than 300 feet); 7–15 percent pose a moderate hazard (unless greater than 150 feet); and greater than 15 percent poses a high erosion hazard.

Erosion and sediment control practices include three types of measures:

- Soil stabilization: vegetation stabilization, top-soiling, erosion control matting, mulching, and tree protection.
- Runoff control: reduction, diversion, detention, infiltration (see chapter 14).

BOX 12.6—Example of Erosion and Sediment Control Project

1. Grassed diversion swale is constructed above the hillside cut for the building. It will drain in opposite directions.
2. The cut made for the building is stabilized with grasses and other slope erosion control measures.
3. Clearing of the forest and grass vegetation is done only where construction is necessary. Remaining vegetation is maintained.
4. Pond is constructed on the lower terrace nest to No Name Brook before land clearing begins for the cut slope, building pad, and parking lot. It is a permanent sediment and runoff control basin during and after construction.
5. Bridge is built over No Name Brook. Filter strips are placed around the abutment areas to prevent siltation of the fill. The abutments are stabilized after construction with grasses and erosion control blankets.
6. A grassed diversion swale is constructed above the proposed cut for the access road. It drains into No Name Brook well above the bridge abutment to minimize erosion at the abutment.
7. The access road entrance is stabilized so that sediment does not enter the lateral ditches for Sweet Road and Pine Creek.

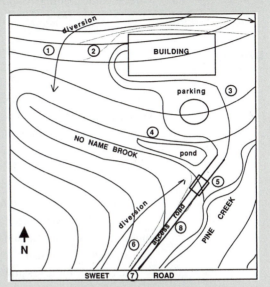

The development superimposed on the physical site. For numbered elements consult list to the left. The dark lines represent original contours; the lighter lines represent modified contour lines.

8. A filter fence is constructed along the access road and parallel to Pine Creek to prevent sediment from entering Pine Creek.

Source: Urban Soils by Philip Craul, copyright © 1999, John Wiley and Sons. Reprinted with permission of John Wiley and Sons, Inc.

■ Sediment control: vegetated buffers, sediment catchments, sediment traps. The amount of sediment removed depends on the speed of water, the time water is detained, and the size of the sediment particles.

The RUSLE and empirical studies provide useful data on different erosion and sediment control practices. Table 12.13 shows the effects of different practices on soil loss and sediment yield from a 100-foot, 30 percent slope road side cut in Nashville, Tennessee. Because of difference in R value, soil loss and sediment yields would be 35 percent and 80 percent less in Chicago and Denver, respectively.

Table 12.14 shows the effectiveness of different ground covers in reducing runoff and erosion. Straw cover applied at 2 tons per acre can reduce soil loss by 90 percent and runoff by 20 percent and increase ground cover after one year by 50 percent.

Box 12.6 illustrates an erosion and sediment control project. The construction of the building, access road, and parking lot has potential impact on sedimentation of

Pine Creek. Eight control measures are described in the list and shown on the figure. They include grading, runoff diversion, vegetation, filter fence, and detention pond.

Summary

Soils are a fundamental natural resource of the land that affects its capability to support vegetation and development. Land use is affected by soils' strength and stability, drainability, erodibility, and agricultural and resource potential. Soil quality is subject to degradation by human activities, including compaction, erosion, and contamination, and can be improved through remediation.

For agricultural and development uses, the soil survey is the best source of information. Soil survey information can be used to map soil suitability for a variety of uses and as a basis for assessing agricultural suitability using the LESA technique. Soil suitability also depends on slope, which can be assessed for both site and areawide needs using topographic maps.

Techniques for assessing soil erosion potential, such as the RUSLE, are useful to identify problems and controls. Urban soils are subject to erosion and sedimentation from land construction practices and are also plagued by contamination and compaction problems. Most states require erosion and sediment control plans for construct. Federal agricultural programs, like the CRP, have been effective in reducing the nation's soil erosion.

13 ▪ Land Use, Stream Flow, and Runoff Pollution

The next three chapters address hydrologic considerations in land use. This chapter discusses the effects of land use on stream flow, water quality, and stream integrity. Critical issues include storm flows and flooding that pose natural hazards to property and people, baseflows and low flows that affect aquatic ecology, and runoff pollution that affects both natural waters and sources of community water supplies. Chapter 14 discusses emerging approaches for stormwater management and stream restoration to address these impacts. Chapter 15 focuses on groundwater and land use. Chapters 9 and 10 also discuss related issues of watershed management and flood hazard mitigation.

The hydrologic cycle, described in figure 13.1, is intimately related to the land. Water evaporated from the land and the ocean ultimately precipitates as rain or snow. Precipitation that does not immediately evaporate and transpire through vegetation back to the atmosphere has one of two fates: (1) it infiltrates the soil and contributes to soil moisture, subsurface flow, and groundwater recharge; or (2) it runs off on the surface, contributing to surface streams, lakes, and rivers. Although runoff contributes the most to **stormwater flows,** much of the infiltrated subsurface flow later seeps to the surface and contributes the most to **baseflow** or stream flow between storms. Ground and surface waters may be important existing or future sources of **water supply** for people and communities. Land use in watersheds of surface supply and in the recharge areas of groundwater aquifers has a significant effect on the quality and viability of those water sources.

Urbanization, with its smooth **impervious** parking lots, streets and rooftops, tends to reduce infiltration and increase the rate of accumulation and the amount of stormwater runoff, which in turn exacerbates drainage and flooding problems and **channel erosion** downstream. This runoff carries with it **non-point source (NPS) water pollutants** that now exceed industrial and municipal "point" discharges in contributing to the pollution of lakes, rivers, and estuaries in the United States.

Figure 13.1 Hydrologic Cycle. The transfer of water from precipitation to surface water and groundwater, to storage and runoff, and eventually back to the atmosphere is an ongoing cycle. *Source:* FISRWG (1998).

The Water Balance

Precipitation patterns determine the distribution of water on and under the ground. The measurement of precipitation is straightforward, and gauging stations have been recording rainfall data throughout the United States for over 150 years. These historic data have been analyzed statistically to give average precipitation over a drainage basin or region and the frequency of storms of given intensities that are likely to occur in the future. Most of this analysis was done decades ago (U.S. Weather Bureau [USWB], 1961). This assumption that the future will resemble the past is a critical one in hydrology, and it assumes relatively constant climatic conditions. Climatic changes from global warming and other causes may affect this assumption and our use of long-term historic data.

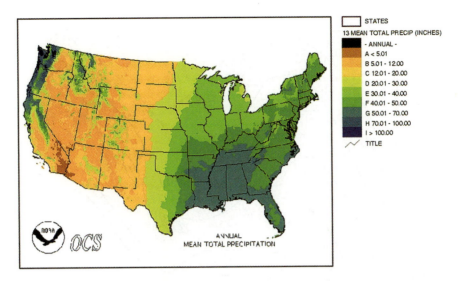

Figure 13.2 Annual Precipitation in United States

Figure 13.2 gives annual average precipitation for the United States. These data are available for most areas of the world. The semihumid eastern United States (30–60 inches per year) is distinguished from the semiarid west (0–30 inches per year). Not only do annual averages vary, but so do the seasonal variations and the **intensity** and **duration** of storms. It is this pattern of precipitation more than its average that determines runoff and flooding problems and stormwater management needs.

For this reason, historic precipitation data is analyzed in terms of the **frequency** of storms of different **durations** and **intensities,** and this information is available in a variety of forms. Maps such as figure 13.3 show intensity for storms of a specific duration and frequency; these maps are available for many durations and frequencies (see websites at USWB, 1961; National Weather Service [NWS], 2002). For a specific location, the intensity-duration-frequency data can be plotted in one curve as shown in figure 13.4. The figure shows the "return period" (frequency) for storms of different intensities (inches/hour) and durations. Figure 13.4 shows that although Seattle and Miami receive about the same annual precipitation on average (48 inches per year), the pattern of rainfall is far different in the two cities. For example, the recurrence of a one-hour, one-inch rainfall in Seattle is greater than 100 years, whereas the return period of such a storm in Miami is less than 2 years.

The frequency or return interval is a simple way of stating the probability of occurrence based on history. A 100-year storm does not mean that if we have such an event this year, we won't see another one for 100 years. It simply means that based on historic data the probability of the event occurring in any year is 1 in 100, or 1 percent. If we get such an event this year, we still have a 1 percent chance of a similar event next year, and we could get it next month.

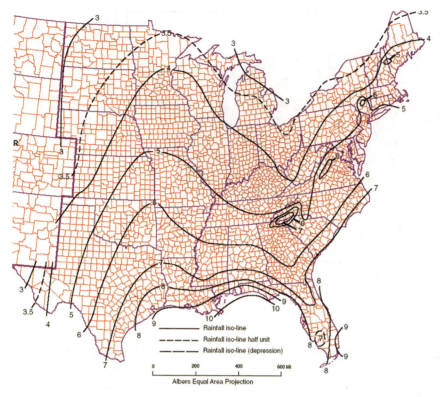

Figure 13.3 10-Year Frequency, 24-Hour Rainfall Inches Over Eastern and Midwestern United States. *Source:* USDA (1986).

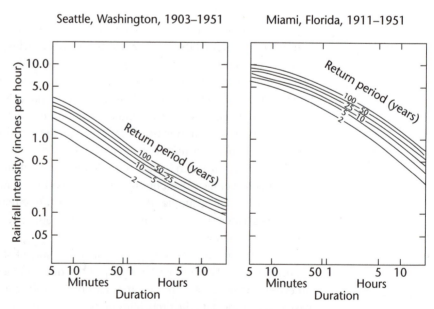

Figure 13.4 Intensity-Duration-Frequency Curves for Seattle and Miami. The differences between the two reflect differences in the climates of the two cities. *Source: Water in Environmental Planning* by Thomas Dunne and Luna Leopold, copyright © 1978. Reprinted with permission of W. H. Freeman and Company.

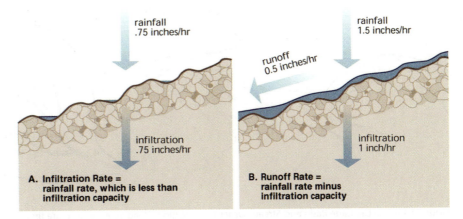

Figure 13.5 Precipitation Rate and Infiltration Rate Determine the Runoff Rate. Infiltration rate depends on soil texture, soil moisture, and vegetative cover. *Source:* FISRWG (1998).

Watersheds and Channel Processes

Precipitation that does not evaporate either infiltrates the ground or runs off on the surface as overland flow. Much of the infiltrated water ultimately seeps out of the ground, contributing to stream baseflow between storms. The texture of the soil determines its permeability and infiltration rate. But for all soils, as they become saturated from a given storm, a greater percentage of the precipitation will end up as surface runoff. Figure 13.5 shows this water balance between precipitation, infiltration, and runoff.

Overland Drainage: Runoff and Watersheds

Topography determines how surface water drains. It delineates **drainage basins,** also called **watersheds** or **catchments.** Rain falling within the **drainage boundary** or **divide** will drain through the basin exit channel. Other basin characteristics include:

- **basin or watershed area:** the area within the boundary;
- **basin length:** the distance from the first-order channel farthest upstream to the basin outlet; and
- **drainage density:** the length of all the channels divided by the basin area; generally, the greater the drainage density, the steeper the slopes in the basin and the higher the peak flows for a given rainfall.

Figure 13.6 shows a drainage basin and the convention for stream order classification. First-order channels are highest in the watershed and have no tributaries. First-order channels join to form second-order streams, second-order streams join to form third-order streams, and so on. Stream channels are also defined by how often water is present. **Perennial streams** (shown as a solid blue line on color topographic maps) normally run all year long. **Intermittent**

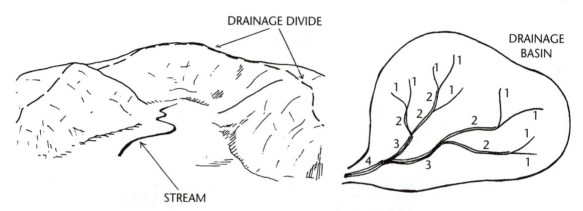

Figure 13.6 The Drainage Basin and Stream Order Classification. Headwater streams are first order, which combine to form second order streams, which combine to third order and so on.

streams (shown as dashed blue lines on topographic maps) run during the wet season. **Ephemeral streams** (not shown on topographic maps) run only during and immediately after storms.

Box 13.1 describes **watershed delineation,** a simple method for defining basins or watersheds using a topographic map. It is often important to identify "critical" watersheds or those deserving special attention. These may be a watershed of an existing or potential water supply reservoir, watersheds with potential drainage capacity problems, or those undergoing land development. It is the first step in watershed management (see chapter 10). The eight-step procedure begins by identifying the outlet point on a stream or river, which will define the watershed draining to that point. After identifying all of the "in" channels draining to the outlet, the procedure finds the "out" channels immediately outside the watershed, identifies high points between these "in" and "out" channels, and connects these high points by drawing connecting lines roughly perpendicular to the elevation contours.

Channel Processes and Geomorphology

Although topography affects drainage, drainage also affects topography through the processes of geomorphology, the formation of landforms by water erosion and deposition. The erosion and deposition processes of the river channel largely determine the landforms of the valley floor including the floodplain. Channels do not flow uniformly over time but are dynamic in nature. Channels have a natural tendency to meander or to develop a wavy pattern from a straight one. Figure 13.7 shows how the varying water velocities in the channel section produce this meandering effect. Faster water on the outside of the stream curves cause more erosion, while slower velocities in the inside cause deposition of sediment. Over time these processes cause the curves to enlarge. This process also contributes to the deep pool, shallow and stony riffle, and unobstructed run sequence in natural streams segments. It is this meandering process, not flooding, that actually causes the development of floodplains and the distinct landforms common to river valleys.

BOX 13.1—Delineating Watershed Boundaries

1. Identify the **outlet point** on a stream or river that defines the watershed draining to that point.
2. Find and trace drainage **channels within** the watershed. On color topo map, they are blue lines. "V" shape of elevation contours point upstream.
3. Find and "X" out neighboring **channels outside** the watershed. The watershed boundary will be between the channels in the basin (step 2) and these outside channels.
4. Consider yourself a drop of water and **check** the direction of drainage by inspecting the slope direction between the "in" and "out" channels.
5. Find and **mark the high points** (peaks and saddles) between the "in" and "out" channels. These will be on the watershed boundary.
6. **Connect these points** with light pencil, intersecting the contour lines at roughly a right angle.
7. Consider yourself a drop of water again and **check** where you would go if you fell inside or outside the line. Make corrections as necessary.
8. **Finalize** Map.

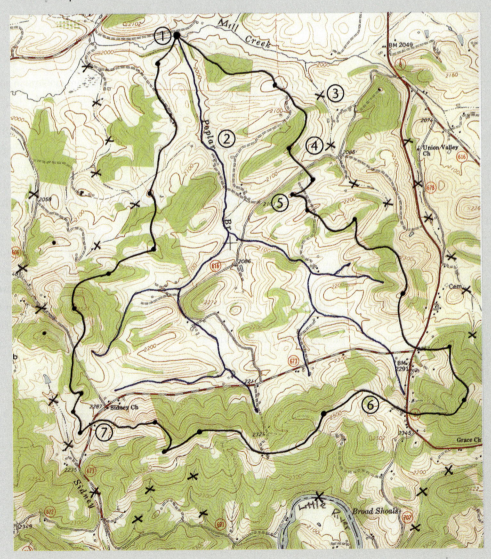

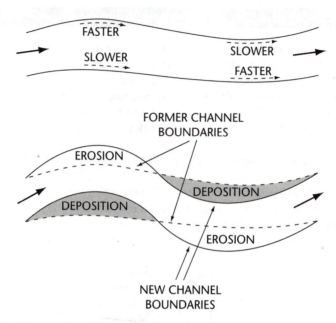

Figure 13.7 The Tendency of Streams to Meander at Shallow Slopes through Erosion and Deposition. This meandering process is what shapes floodplains.

Figure 13.8 delineates channel characteristics: bankfull depth and width and the hydrologic floodplain are channel dimensions with channel at maximum flow or its bankfull discharge. The bankfull discharge, also called the channel-forming or dominant flow, is defined as the flow that fills a stable alluvial channel to the elevation of the active or hydrologic floodplain. Greater flows will overtop the channel and spread out onto the topographic floodplain. Figure 13.9 gives the stream classification developed by Rosgen (1994). The system groups reaches of streams by slope, entrenchment in the valley, degree of meandering, bankfull width-depth ratio, and types of soils and geology (Riley, 1998). The figure shows channel types and corresponding slopes and flood-prone areas. A stream has a **longitudinal transition** along its length and a **lateral transition,** extending outward from the normal and bankfull channel to the floodplain to the extent of its riparian vegetation to its upland watershed boundary.

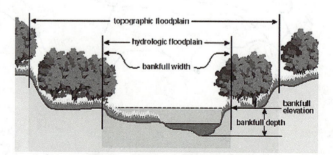

Figure 13.8 Bankfull Dimensions and Floodplain Definitions. *Source:* FISRWG (1998).

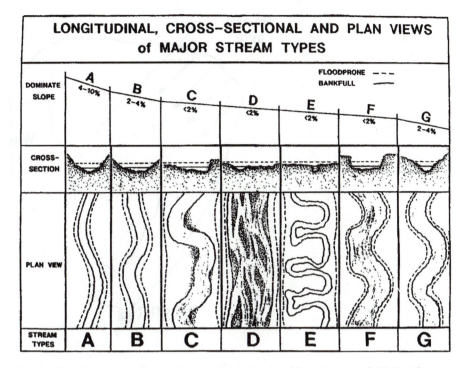

Figure 13.9 Stream Classification System. *Source:* Reprinted from *Catena*, vol. 22, David Rosgen, "A Classification of Natural Rivers," p.174, Copyright © 1994, with permission from Elsevier.

Streams and river channels change from headwaters to discharge to another receiving water body. Three zones vary in slope, stream discharge and mean flow velocity, channel width and depth, channel bed material grain size, and relative volume of stored alluvium or deposited materials from upstream. These include the following:

- Headwater zone with steeper slopes; higher velocity; larger bed material; and lower discharge, channel width and depth, and stored alluvium
- Transfer zone between headwaters and deposition zones
- Deposition zone with flat slope; lower velocity; smaller bed material; and higher discharge, channel width and depth, and stored alluvium

Effects of Land Use on Stream Flow and Predicting Peak Discharge

The **hydrograph** shows over time the response of channel flow at a specific point to a given storm over its watershed. A hypothetical hydrograph is shown in figure 13.10. The rainfall is generally given in a histogram showing the depth of rainfall

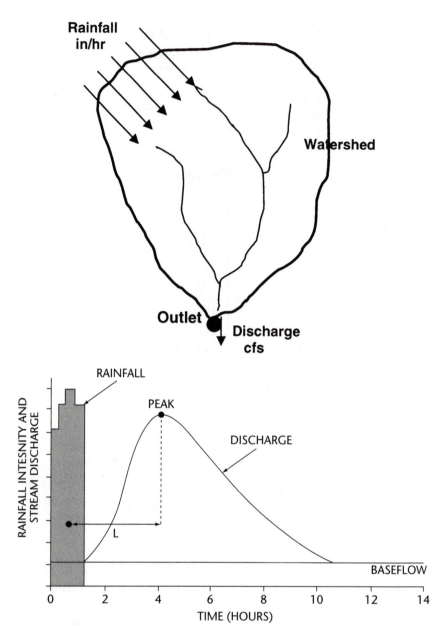

Figure 13.10 Hypothetical Hydrograph Showing the Response of Stream Flow. "L" is the lag time to peak discharge. Baseflow is stream flow without storm event.

for each hour of the storm. The curve that follows shows the channel discharge response as a flow rate that builds up to a peak, then drops back to the original baseflow. Important to note are the timing and magnitude of the peak. The peak will occur at some time after the center of mass of the storm, called the **lag time.** The **peak flow** is the maximum flow, at which time the water flow elevation is highest and flooding is the worst. The hydrograph relationship of rainfall to discharge depends on several characteristics of the watershed, principally soil cover,

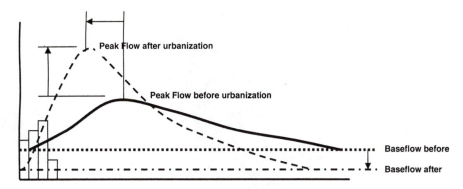

Figure 13.11 Effect of Urbanization's Impervious Surfaces on Peak Flows and Baseflows

slope, and channel length. Given the relationship, hydrologists can generate a peak discharge frequency based on rainfall frequency.

Land cover and drainage characteristics affect the accumulation of stormwater flow as well as the amount of baseflow between storms. The process of urbanization, that is, paving and covering the land with impervious surfaces and constructing drainage pipes and lined channels, acts to increase the peak discharge from a given storm event by (a) reducing the amount of water that infiltrates the ground, thus *increasing the volume* of surface runoff and, more important, and (b) *increasing the rate* at which the runoff accumulates, reducing the hydrograph lag time. Because of impervious surfaces, less water infiltrates the ground, and, thus, less is available for groundwater-contributed baseflow between storms, especially in dry weather periods. As a result, urban streams run faster and higher during storms, and often run dry between storms.

As shown in figures 13.11 and 13.12, the peak flows from a given storm event will be greater from a watershed after it has experienced land development than before. It also shows that the baseflow between storms will be much less. Baseflow and summer low flows are critical to support stream ecology and riparian vegetation. Finally, the stream geometry shows higher flood flows and a broader floodplain.

Land development and urbanization cause hydrologic changes, which have a number of damaging effects in the following list. This section focuses on the first. The latter three are discussed in following sections. Chapter 14 addresses measures and management practices to reduce these impacts.

1. The increased flows caused by land development can exacerbate **flooding downstream.**
2. Urban runoff carries **water contaminants** affecting the quality of receiving water; generally, as urban runoff increases, so does the pollution it carries.
3. Reduced infiltration reduces groundwater storage and reduced dry weather stream flows.
4. Urbanization directly and indirectly causes the **destruction of natural creeks and streams.**

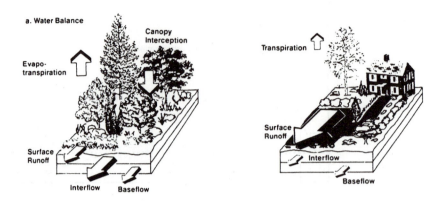

a. Water Balance

Evapo-transpiration

Canopy Interception

Transpiration

Surface Runoff

Interflow   Baseflow

Surface Runoff

Interflow

Baseflow

b. Streamflow

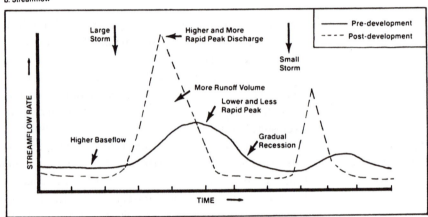

Large Storm

Higher and More Rapid Peak Discharge

Small Storm

Pre-development
Post-development

STREAMFLOW RATE

More Runoff Volume

Lower and Less Rapid Peak

Gradual Recession

Higher Baseflow

TIME

c. Response of Stream Geometry

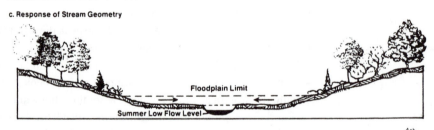

Floodplain Limit

Summer Low Flow Level

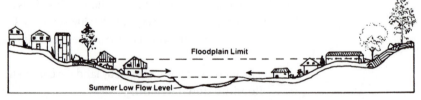

Floodplain Limit

Summer Low Flow Level

Figure 13.12 Changes in Watershed Hydrology as a Result of Urbanization. Note increase in peak flow, decrease in baseflow, and higher flood levels. *Source: Controlling Urban Runoff: A Practical Manual for Planning and Designing Urban BMPs*, by Tom Schueler, 1987. Reprinted with permission of Metropolitan Washington Council of Governments, 777 North Capital St., NE, Ste. 300, Washington, D.C. 20002-4239, 202-962-3256.

TABLE 13.1 **Hydrologic Cycle Changes of Impervious Surface Associated with Urbanization**

Land Use/Cover	Imperviousness (%)	Evapotranspiration (%)	Infiltration (%)	Runoff (%)
Natural Cover	0	40	50	10
Low Density Resid.	10–20	35	42	23
Urban Residential	35–50	35	35	30
Urban Center	75–100	30	15	55

(Source: EPA 1993)

Many analysts have argued that **impervious surface coverage** in a watershed is a good indicator of potential impact on stream health (see section on stream integrity). Table 13.1 shows the water cycle changes associated with impervious surfaces. Increasing density of urbanization increases imperviousness, which reduces infiltration and increases runoff.

Planning and designing stormwater drainage systems and managing land use effects on runoff require the ability to predict runoff flows from storm events. Planners and engineers also need to be able to assess the capacity of channels to carry stormwater flows and to design mitigation measures to reduce peak flows. In the past 30 years, a number of sophisticated computer simulation methods have been developed that model stormwater response to precipitation and estimate effects of land use and control measures on flows. A number of these runoff models are listed in table 13.2.

Some of the simpler techniques are presented here to illustrate how these models work and to understand the factors that influence land use impacts on water flows. They describe methods to estimate the peak discharge of a stream for a

TABLE 13.2 **Comparison of Stormwater Model Attributes and Functions**

| Attribute | Model | | | | |
	HSPF	SWMM	TR-55/TR-20	HEC-1	Rational Method
Sponsoring agency	USEPA	USEPA	NRCS (SCS)	CORPS (HEC)	
Simulation type	Continuous	Continuous	Single event	Single event	Single event
Water quality analysis	Yes	Yes	None	None	None
Rainfall/runoff analysis	Yes	Yes	Yes	Yes	Yes
Sewer system flow routing	None	Yes	Yes	Yes	None
Dynamic flow routing equations	None	Yes	Yes	None	None
Regulators, overflow structures	None	Yes	None	None	None
Storage analysis	Yes	Yes	Yes	Yes	None
Treatment analysis	Yes	Yes	None	None	None
Data and personnel requirements	High	High	Medium	Medium	Low
Overall model complexity	High	High	Low	High	Low

Source: PGC-DEM, 1999

storm of a given duration and intensity under current conditions and under conditions brought about by proposed development. Chapter 14 describes a method to size on-site detention to mitigate the expected impacts. Appendix 13.D describes methods for determining channel capacity and channel erosion problems, necessary techniques in natural drainage design, and stream corridor protection and restoration programs. Working through the techniques provides the reader the opportunity to understand quantitatively the factors that influence peak discharge, channel capacity, and stormwater detention.

The Rational Method

This technique, based on Mubraney's formula developed in 1851, has provided the design basis for almost all of the urban drainage systems built in the world up to about 1980. However, the method has been criticized for such applications as being unnecessarily conservative, leading to expensive and oversized systems. As a result, the 1970s saw considerable improvements in design methods. Still, the Rational Method provides a reasonable "first cut" approximation of peak discharge. The use of the Rational Method is limited to drainage areas of less than 200 acres. It involves the following simple equation for peak discharge:

$$Q = CiA \qquad \text{(Eq. 13–1)}$$

where, Q = peak discharge (cubic ft per second—cfs)
C = rational runoff coefficient, based on land cover
i = rainfall intensity (inches/hour)
A = drainage area (acres)

Values of the **runoff coefficient** (C) for various rural and developed land uses are given in table 13.3. If a drainage area of interest is made up of one or more types of soil cover, a weighted average can be computed by simply summing the products of the individual subarea's coefficient times its fraction of the total area. (See the following example.) The **rainfall intensity** (i) is determined from a rainfall intensity-frequency-duration curve such as figure 13.4 or figure 13.13. The intensity is read from the curve for a desired frequency and a duration equal to the **time of concentration** (T_c) for the drainage area (i.e., the time of flow from the most remote point in the basin to the design point, in minutes). The T_c depends on the length of travel, the drainage slope, the land cover, and channel type. It can be approximated by the nomograph given in figure 13.14.

Rational Method Example

Using the Rational Method, determine the peak discharge resulting from a 10-year frequency storm falling on an 80-acre drainage area in Richmond, Virginia, comprised of 30 percent rooftops, 10 percent streets and driveways, 20 percent lawns at 5 percent slope on sandy soil, and 40 percent woodland. The height of the most remote point above the outlet is 100 feet and the maximum length of travel is 3,000 feet; assume the combination of land covers produces the equivalent of a natural basin on bare earth.

TABLE 13.3 **Runoff Coefficients for Rational Method**

Land use	C
Business:	
Downtown areas	0.70–0.95
Neighborhood areas	0.50–0.70
Residential:	
Single-family areas	0.30–0.50
Multi-units, detached	0.40–0.60
Multi-units, attached	0.60–0.75
Suburban	0.25–0.40
Industrial:	
Light areas	0.50–0.80
Heavy areas	0.60–0.90
Parks, cemeteries	0.10–0.25
Playgrounds	0.20–0.35
Railroad yard areas	0.20–0.40
Unimproved areas	0.10–0.30
Streets:	
Asphaltic	0.70–0.95
Concrete	0.80–0.95
Brick	0.70–0.85
Drives and walks	0.75–0.85
Roofs	0.75–0.95
Lawns:	
Sandy soil, flat, 2%	0.05–0.10
Sandy soil, average, 2–7%	0.10–0.15
Sandy soil, steep, 7%	0.15–0.20
Heavy soil, flat, 2%	0.13–0.17
Heavy soil, average, 2–7%	0.18–0.22
Heavy soil, steep, 7%	0.25–0.35
Agricultural land:	
Bare packed soil	
Smooth	0.30–0.60
Rough	0.20–0.50
Cultivated rows	
Heavy soil no crop	0.30–0.60
Heavy soil with crop	0.20–0.50
Sandy soil no crop	0.20–0.40
Sandy soil with crop	0.10–0.25
Pasture	
Heavy soil	0.15–0.45
Sandy soil	0.05–0.25
Woodlands	0.05–0.25

Note: The designer must use judgment to select the appropriate C value within the range. Generally, larger areas with permeable soils, flat slopes and dense vegetation should have lowest (C) values. Smaller areas with dense soils, moderate to steep slopes, and sparse vegetation should be assigned highest (C) values.

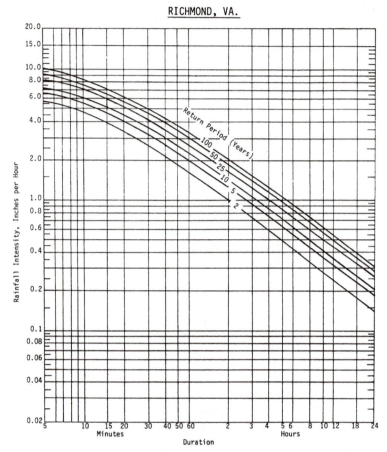

Figure 13.13 Rainfall Intensity-Duration-Frequency Curve for Richmond, Virginia. *Source:* VDCR (1992).

$C = (.9)(.30) + (.9)(.10) + (.15)(.20) + (.10)(.40) = .43$
  (rooftops) (streets)   (lawns)   (woodland)   (from table 13.3)
        $T_c = 14$ minutes (from figure 13.14, ht = 100, length = 3,000)
        $i = 5.4$ inches (from figure 13.13, dur. = 14 min, freq. = 10 yr)
        $A = 80$ acres
        $Q = CiA = (.43)(5.4)(80) = 185.76$ cubic feet per sec.

TR 55 Peak Discharge Graphical Method

This technique is described in the Soil Conservation Service (now NRCS) Technical Release No. 55 (TR 55), *Urban Hydrology for Small Watersheds* (USDA, 1986). It is considered more accurate than the Rational Method for larger urban drainage areas (up to about 2,000 acres) because it takes into account more factors and involves less judgment on the part of the user (particularly in the choice of the time of concentration). The peak discharge method can also be used to produce hydrographs for larger areas (up to 20 sq. miles) using a tabular hydrograph

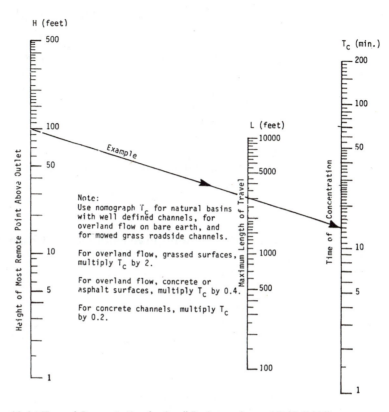

Figure 13.14 Time of Concentration for Small Drainage. *Source:* VDCR (1992).

method also described in TR 55. For further information on this hydrograph method, see SCS (USDA, 1986) http://www.wcc.nrcs.usda.gov/hydro/hydro-tools-models-tr55.html. Though it is less sophisticated than many computer models, TR 55 is heavily used in state and local stormwater and erosion and sediment control programs (see section on stormwater management practices in chapter 14) and land analysis software like CITYgreen (see chapter 16).

The TR 55 graphical peak discharge method described here determines the peak flows resulting from a "design" 24-hour storm over a specific drainage area. By modifying the land use and cover conditions in the drainage area, it can be used to predict the peak discharge effects of different land use scenarios. The process is illustrated in table 13.4. The method employs a number of data tables, charts, and four worksheets. For blank worksheets see http://www.wcc.nrcs.usda.gov/water/quality/common/tr55/tr55.pdf. We will only be working with Worksheets 2, 3, and 4 in this chapter and Worksheet 6 in the next. The worksheet, figure, and example numbering from TR 55 have been retained to ease cross-referencing the source.

STEP 1 Worksheet 2 computes the watershed Curve Number (*CN*) and Runoff (*Q*).

(Data needed: Design 24-hour storm (inches), watershed acres, acres in various land uses/covers, HSG)

TABLE 13.4 **TR-55 Process for Graphical Discharge Method**

Data to calculate Tc?	If no, TR 55 not applicable
Hydrograph or subareas required?	If no, proceed below. If yes, consult TR-55 document, chapter 5
Step 1: Compute Watershed Curve Number and Runoff:	Worksheet 2
Step 2: Compute Watershed Time of Concentration (Tc):	Worksheet 3
Step 3: Compute Peak Discharge:	Worksheet 4
Step 4: Compute Storage to Reduce Peak Discharge:	Worksheet 6

TABLE 13.5a **Runoff Curve Numbers for Urban Areas (TR55 table 2–2)**

		Curve Numbers For			
Cover Description	*Avg % impervious[1]*	*Hydrologic Soil Group (HSG)*			
Cover Type and Hydrologic Condition		*A*	*B*	*C*	*D*
Open space (lawns, parks, golf courses, cemeteries, etc.)[2]:					
Poor condition (grass cover <50%)		68	79	86	89
Fair condition (grass cover 50% to 75%)		49	69	79	84
Good condition (grass cover >75%)		39	61	74	80
Impervious areas:					
Paved parking lots, roofs, etc.		98	98	98	98
Streets and roads: Paved; curbs and storm sewers		98	98	98	98
Gravel (including right-of-way)		76	85	89	91
Urban districts:					
Commercial and business	85	89	92	94	95
Industrial	72	81	88	91	93
Residential districts:					
1/8 acre or less (town houses)	65	77	85	90	92
1/4 acre	38	61	75	83	87
1/3 acre	30	57	72	81	86
1/2 acre	25	54	70	80	85
1 acre	20	51	68	79	84
2 acres	12	46	65	77	82

[1]The average percent impervious shown was used to develop the composite CN's. Other assumptions are as follows: impervious areas are directly connected to the drainage system and have a CN of 98, and pervious areas are considered equivalent to open space in good hydrologic condition. CN's for other combinations of conditions may be computed using figure 13.20.

[2]CN's shown are equivalent to those of pasture. Composite CN's may be computed for other combinations of open space cover type.

TABLE 13.5b **Runoff Curve Numbers for Cultivated and other Agricultural Lands (TR55 table 2–2)**

Cover Description		*Hydrologic*	*Curve Numbers For Hydrologic Soil Group*			
Cover Type	*Treatment*	*Condition*	*A*	*B*	*C*	*D*
Fallow	Bare soil	—	77	86	91	94
	Crop residue cover (CR)[1]	Poor	76	85	90	93
		Good	74	83	88	90
Row crops	Straight row (SR)[1]	Poor	72	81	88	91
		Good	67	78	85	89
	SR + CR[1]	Poor	71	80	87	90
		Good	64	75	82	85
Pasture, grassland, or range[2]		Poor	68	79	86	89
		Fair	49	69	79	84
		Good	39	61	74	80
Meadow—mowed for hay		—	30	58	71	78
Brush—brush-weed-grass[2]		Poor	48	67	77	83
		Fair	35	56	70	77
		Good	30	48	65	73
Woods—grass combination (orchard or tree farm).[3]		Poor	57	73	82	86
		Fair	43	65	76	82
		Good	32	58	72	79

[1]Poor: Factors impair infiltration and tend to increase runoff.
Good: Factors encourage average and better than average infiltration and tend to decrease runoff.
[2]Poor: <50% ground cover or heavily grazed with no mulch.
Fair: 50 to 75% ground cover and not heavily grazed.
Good: >75% ground cover and lightly or only occasionally grazed.
[3]Poor: Forest litter, small trees, and brush are destroyed by heavy grazing or regular burning.
Fair: Woods are grazed but not burned, and some forest litter covers the soil.
Good: Woods are protected from grazing, and litter and brush adequately cover the soil.

The curve number (*CN*) is a measure of the land cover influence on infiltration and runoff, similar to the C factor in the Rational Method. It ranges in value from about 30 to 98. It depends on the vegetative or impervious cover, land use practice, and hydrologic soil group (HSG). Based on their texture and infiltration rates, soils are classified in HSG A (sands and sandy loams), B (silt loam and loam), C (sandy clay loam), and D (clay, clay loam, sandy clay, silty clay). Other factors, like soil compaction or high water table, can supercede the effect of texture. Soil surveys list HSG for different soils and map units.

Table 13.5 gives *CN* values for various agricultural and urban land covers and uses. Values range from 30 (for meadow and woods in HSG A) to 98 (for impervious surfaces). The first step in Worksheet 2 is to compute a weighted average *CN* value for the drainage area or watershed. The various land covers of the area and their acreages are entered on the worksheet; *CN* values for these covers are looked up on table 13.5 and entered. The *CN* values are multiplied by the acreage, and the sum of these products is divided by the total acreage to yield the average CN value.

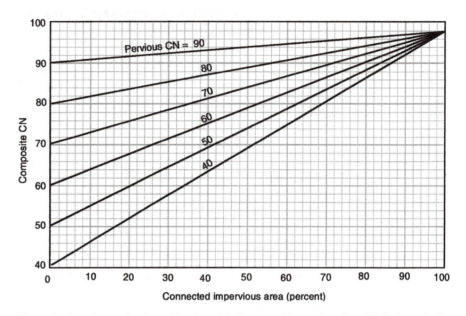

Figure 13.15a Composite Curve Number with Connected Impervious Area (TR55 figure 2–3). *Source:* USDA (1986).

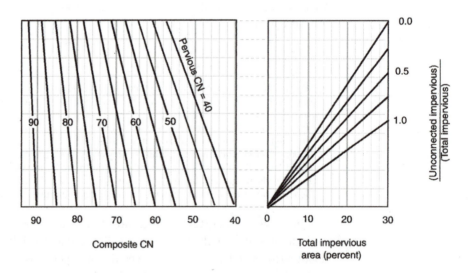

Figure 13.15b Composite Curve Number with Unconnected Impervious Areas (TR55 figure 2–4). *Source:* USDA (1986).

$$CN \text{ average} = \frac{\sum CN_i \times A_i}{\sum A_i} \qquad (Eq. \ 13\text{–}2)$$

where CN_i is the CN for each land cover, i

A_i is the area for each land cover, i

Table 13.5 values assume that urban uses have the percent impervious cover in the table and that the surfaces are hydraulically connected to drainage works. To determine CN when all or part of the impervious area is not directly connected to

TABLE 13.6 **Converting from Rainfall Depth to Runoff Depth for Different Curve Numbers (CN) (TR55 table 2–1)**

Runoff Depth for Curve Number of—

CN→	40	45	50	55	60	65	70	75	80	85	90	95	98
Rainfall					------	*inches*	------						
1.0	0.00	0.00	0.00	0.00	0.00	0.00	0.00	0.03	0.08	0.17	0.32	0.56	0.79
1.2	.00	.00	.00	.00	.00	.00	.03	.07	.15	.27	.46	.74	.99
1.4	.00	.00	.00	.00	.00	.02	.06	.13	.24	.39	.61	.92	1.18
1.6	.00	.00	.00	.00	.01	.05	.11	.20	.34	.52	.76	1.11	1.38
1.8	.00	.00	.00	.00	.03	.09	.17	.29	.44	.65	.93	1.29	1.58
2.0	.00	.00	.00	.02	.06	.14	.24	.38	.56	.80	1.09	1.48	1.77
2.5	.00	.00	.02	.08	.17	.30	.46	.65	.89	1.18	1.53	1.96	2.27
3.0	.00	.02	.09	.19	.33	.51	.71	.96	1.25	1.59	1.98	2.45	2.77
3.5	.02	.08	.20	.35	.53	.75	1.01	1.30	1.64	2.02	2.45	2.94	3.27
4.0	.06	.18	.33	.53	.76	1.03	1.33	1.67	2.04	2.46	2.92	3.43	3.77
4.5	.14	.30	.50	.74	1.02	1.33	1.67	2.05	2.46	2.91	3.40	3.92	4.26
5.0	.24	.44	.69	.98	1.30	1.65	2.04	2.45	2.89	3.37	3.88	4.42	4.76
6.0	.50	.80	1.14	1.52	1.92	2.35	2.81	3.28	3.78	4.30	4.85	5.41	5.76
13.0	.84	1.24	1.68	2.12	2.60	3.10	3.62	4.15	4.69	5.25	5.82	6.41	6.76
8.0	1.25	1.74	2.25	2.78	3.33	3.89	4.46	5.04	5.63	6.21	6.81	7.40	7.76
9.0	1.71	2.29	2.88	3.49	4.10	4.72	5.33	5.95	6.57	7.18	7.79	8.40	8.76
10.0	2.23	2.89	3.56	4.23	4.90	5.56	6.22	6.88	7.52	8.16	8.78	9.40	9.76
11.0	2.78	3.52	4.26	5.00	5.72	6.43	7.13	7.81	8.48	9.13	9.77	10.39	10.76
12.0	3.38	4.19	5.00	5.79	6.56	7.32	8.05	8.76	9.45	10.11	10.76	11.39	11.76
13.0	4.00	4.89	5.76	6.61	7.42	8.21	8.98	9.71	10.42	11.10	11.76	12.39	12.76
14.0	4.65	5.62	6.55	7.44	8.30	9.12	9.91	10.67	11.39	12.08	12.75	13.39	13.76
15.0	5.33	6.36	7.35	8.29	9.19	10.04	10.85	11.63	12.37	13.07	13.74	14.39	14.76

the drainage system, (1) use figure 13.15a (TR 55 figure 2–3) if total impervious area is less than 30 percent or (2) use figure 13.15b (TR 55 figure 2–4) if the impervious area is equal to or greater than 30 percent, because the absorptive capacity of the remaining pervious areas will not significantly affect runoff. See Appendix 13.A for examples using these figures.

Once the average CN value is calculated, the runoff (Q) can be determined for the design storm (P) from table 13.6, and the value is entered in the last entry on the worksheet. The design storm depends on the recurrence frequency of the 24-hour storm. Figure 13.2 gives data for a 10-year event for the eastern and midwestern United States. The TR 55 document gives data for 2-, 10-, 25-, and 100-year 24-hour storms (USDA, 1986; see the web address given previously).

TR 55 Step 1 Example: The watershed covers 250 acres in Dyer County, northwestern Tennessee. Seventy percent (175 acres) is a Loring soil, which is in HSG C. Thirty percent (75 acres) is a Memphis soil, which is in group B. The event is a 25-year frequency, 24-hour storm with total rainfall of 6 inches. Cover type and conditions in the watershed are different for each example. The example illustrates how to

Worksheet 2: Runoff curve number and runoff

Project Heavenly Acres	By WJR	Date 10/1/85
Location Dyer County, Tennessee	Checked NM	Date 10/3/85

Check one: ☐ Present ☒ Developed   175 Acres residential

1. Runoff curve number

Soil name and hydrologic group (appendix A)	Cover description (cover type, treatment, and hydrologic condition; percent impervious; unconnected/connected impervious area ratio)	CN [1] Table 2-2	Figure 2-3	Figure 2-4	Area ☒ acres ☐ mi² ☐ %	Product of CN x area
Memphis, B	25% impervious 1/2 acre lots, good condition	70			75	5250
Loring, C	25% impervious 1/2 acre lots, good condition	80			100	8000
Loring, C	Open space, good condition	74			75	5550

[1] Use only one CN source per line

Totals ➡ 250 | 18,800

$$\text{CN (weighted)} = \frac{\text{total product}}{\text{total area}} = \frac{18{,}800}{250} = 75.2 \quad ; \quad \textbf{Use CN} \blacktriangleright \boxed{75}$$

2. Runoff

		Storm #1	Storm #2	Storm #3
Frequency .... yr		25		
Rainfall, P (24-hour) .... in		6.0		
Runoff, Q .... in (Use P and CN with table 2-1, figure 2-1, or equations 2-3 and 2-4)		3.28		

use TR 55 Worksheet 2 to compute CN and Q. Two other examples with different land use situations that illustrate use of figure 13.15 are given in appendix 13.A.

Example 2–2: Seventy percent (175 acres) of the watershed, consisting of all the Memphis soil and 100 acres of the Loring soil, is 1/2-acre residential lots with lawns in good hydrologic condition. The rest of the watershed is scattered open space in good hydrologic condition. Using table 13.5 CN values, the worksheet calculates a composite CN of 75. Given the 24-hour design storm of 6 inches, the runoff Q from table 13.6 is 3.28 inches.

STEP 2 Worksheet 3 computes the time of concentration (T_c).

(Data needed: hydraulic parameters, channel length, slope, shape, and surface roughness for the top of watershed to outlet.) (See figure 13.16.)

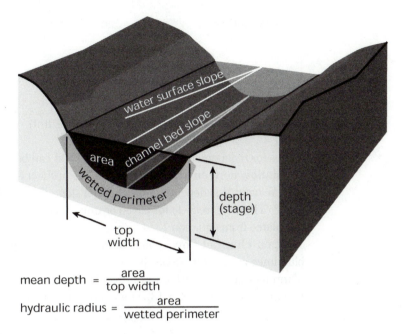

mean depth $= \dfrac{\text{area}}{\text{top width}}$

hydraulic radius $= \dfrac{\text{area}}{\text{wetted perimeter}}$

Figure 13.16 Hydraulic Parameters. *Source:* FISRWG (1998).

The time of concentration (T_c) is time for the runoff to travel from the hydraulically most distant point of the watershed to the point of interest or outlet. It is the sum of the travel times (T_t) for consecutive channel segments.

$$T_c = T_{t1} + T_{t2} + T_{t3} + \dots T_{tm} \qquad \textit{(Eq. 13–3)}$$

where T_c = time of concentration (hr)
         T_t = travel time (hr)
         m = number of flow segments

$$T_t = \frac{L}{3600V} \qquad \textit{(Eq. 13–4)}$$

where T_t = travel time (hr)
         L = flow length (ft)
         V = average velocity (ft/s)
         3600 = conversion factor from seconds to hours

The tricky part of Worksheet 3 is determining the flow velocity, V. There are three ways to calculate it depending on the type of water flow.

Sheet flow is flow over plane surfaces and usually occurs in the headwater of streams. It depends on the frictional resistance to flow, measured by Manning's roughness coefficient, n. For sheet flow of less than 300 feet, the following equation applies:

$$T_t = \frac{0.007\,(nL)0.8}{(P_2)^{0.5}\,s^{0.4}} \qquad\qquad (Eq.\ 13\text{–}5)$$

where n = Manning's roughness coefficient
   L = flow length (ft)
   P_2 = 2-year, 24-hour rainfall (in)
   s = slope of hydraulic grade (land slope, ft/ft)

Values for n depend on surface conditions and can be estimated from table 13.7.

Shallow concentrated flow is the fate of sheet flow after a maximum of 300 feet. Velocity, V, is dependent on channel slope and can be estimated with figure 13.17 (TR 55 figure 3–1) for paved or unpaved channels. Travel time can then be calculated from equation 13–4.

Open channel flow applies to intermittent and perennial channels (where blue lines appear on USGS quadrangle sheets). Flow velocity is determined by Manning's equation, which requires information on channel shape, slope, and roughness. (See appendix 13.D for open channel roughness [n].)

$$V = \frac{1.49r^{2/3}s^{1/2}}{n} \qquad\text{(Manning's equation)}\qquad (Eq.\ 13\text{–}6)$$

where V = average velocity (ft/s)
   r = channel full hydraulic radius (ft)
   $r = a/p_w$, where a = cross-sectional flow area (ft²)
     p_w = wetted perimeter (ft) (see figure 13.16)
   s = slope of hydraulic grade line (channel slope, ft/ft)
   n = Manning's roughness coefficient for open channel flow

TABLE 13.7   Roughness Coefficients (Manning's n) for Sheet Flow (TR55 table 3–1)

Surface Description	n^1
Smooth surfaces (concrete, asphalt, gravel, or bare soil)	0.011
Fallow (no residue)	0.05
Cultivated soils:	
Residue cover ≤20%	0.06
Residue cover >20%	0.17
Grass:	
Short grass prairie	0.15
Dense grasses[2]	0.24
Bermudagrass	0.41
Range (natural)	0.13
Woods:[3]	
Light underbrush	0.40
Dense underbrush	0.80

[1]The n values are a composite of information compiled by Engman (1986).

[2]Includes species such as weeping lovegrass, bluegrass, buffalo grass, blue grama grass, and native grass mixtures.

[3]When selecting n, consider cover to a height of about 0.1 ft. This is the only part of the plant cover that will obstruct sheet flow.

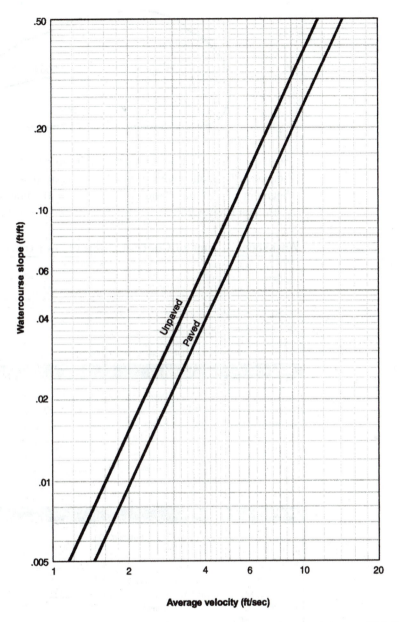

Figure 13.17 Velocity for Shallow Concentrated Flow. (TR55 figure3–1) *Source:* USDA (1986).

The T_t is calculated for each flow segment using Worksheet 3. The T_c is the sum of the T_ts.

Example 3-1: The sketch below shows a watershed in Dyer County, northwestern Tennessee. The problem is to compute T_c at the outlet of the watershed (point D). The 2-year 24-hour rainfall depth is 3.6 inches. All three types of flow occur from the hydraulically most distant point (A) to the point of interest (D). To compute T_c, first determine T_t for each segment from the following information (see Worksheet 3):

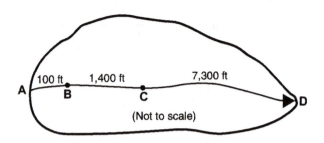

Segment AB: Sheet flow; dense grass; slope (s) = 0.01 ft/ft; and length (L) = 100 ft.
Segment BC: Shallow concentrated flow; unpaved; s = 0.01 ft/ft; and L = 1,400 ft.
Segment CD: Channel flow; Manning's n = .05; flow area (a) = 27 ft2; wetted perimeter (pw) = 28.2 ft; s = 0.005 ft/ft; and L = 7,300 ft.

Worksheet 3: Time of Concentration (T_c) or travel time (T_t)

Project *Heavenly Acres*	By *DW*	Date *10/6/85*
Location *Dyer County, Tennessee*	Checked *NM*	Date *10/8/85*

Check one: ☐ Present ☒ Developed

Check one: ☒ T_c ☐ T_t through subarea

Notes: Space for as many as two segments per flow type can be used for each worksheet.
Include a map, schematic, or description of flow segments.

Sheet flow (Applicable to T_c only)

	Segment ID	AB	
1.	Surface description (table 3-1)	Dense Grass	
2.	Manning's roughness coefficient, n (table 3-1)	0.24	
3.	Flow length, L (total L ≤ 300 ft) .... ft	100	
4.	Two-year 24-hour rainfall, P_2 .... in	3.6	
5.	Land slope, s .... ft/ft	0.01	
6.	$T_t = \dfrac{0.007\ (nL)^{0.8}}{P_2^{\,0.5}\ s^{0.4}}$　　Compute T_t .... hr	0.30 +	= 0.30

Shallow concentrated flow

	Segment ID	BC	
7.	Surface description (paved or unpaved)	Unpaved	
8.	Flow length, L ....ft	1400	
9.	Watercourse slope, s .... ft/ft	0.01	
10.	Average velocity, V (figure 3-1) .... ft/s	1.6	
11.	$T_t = \dfrac{L}{3600\ V}$　　Compute T_t .... hr	0.24 +	= 0.24

Channel flow

	Segment ID	CD	
12.	Cross sectional flow area, a .... ft²	27	
13.	Wetted perimeter, p_w .... ft	28.2	
14.	Hydraulic radius, $r = \dfrac{a}{p_w}$ Compute r .... ft	0.957	
15	Channel slope, s .... ft/ft	0.005	
16.	Manning's roughness coefficient, n	0.05	
17.	$V = \dfrac{1.49\ r^{2/3}\ s^{1/2}}{n}$ Compute V ....ft/s	2.05	
18.	Flow length, L .... ft	7300	
19.	$T_t = \dfrac{L}{3600\ V}$ Compute T_t .... hr	0.99 +	= 0.99
20.	Watershed or subarea T_c or T_t (add T_t in steps 6, 11, and 19) .... Hr		1.53

TABLE 13.8 I$_a$ Values for Runoff Curve Numbers (TR55 table 4–1)

Curve Number	I$_a$ (in)	Curve Number	I$_a$ (in)
40	3.000	70	0.857
41	2.878	71	0.817
42	2.762	72	0.778
43	2.651	73	0.740
44	2.515	74	0.703
45	2.444	75	0.667
46	2.348	76	0.632
47	2.255	77	0.597
48	2.167	78	0.564
49	2.082	79	0.532
50	2.000	80	0.500
51	1.922	81	0.469
52	1.816	82	0.439
53	1.77	83	0.410
54	1.704	84	0.381
55	1.636	85	0.353
56	1.571	86	0.326
57	1.509	87	0.299
58	1.448	88	0.273
59	1.360	89	0.247
60	1.333	90	0.222
61	1.279	91	0.198
62	1.226	92	0.174
63	1.175	93	0.151
64	1.125	94	0.128
65	1.077	95	0.105
66	1.000	96	0.083
67	0.985	97	0.062
68	0.941	98	0.041
69	0.899		

STEP 3 **Worksheet 4 computes the peak discharge.**

(Needed: drainage area, design storm (P), CN, and Q [from Worksheet 2], T_c [from Worksheet 3])

The peak discharge, q_p, for the design 24-hour storm over the watershed is calculated by the following equation:

$$q_p = q_u A_m Q F_p \qquad\qquad (Eq.\ 13–7)$$

where q_p = peak discharge (cfs)
          q_u = unit peak discharge (csm/in: cfs per mi^2 per inch of runoff)
          A_m = drainage area (mi^2)
          Q = runoff (in)
          F_p = pond and swamp adjustment factor

The drainage area, A_m, is known and the runoff, Q, was calculated in Worksheet 2. The pond and swamp adjustment factor, F_p, takes account of the potential

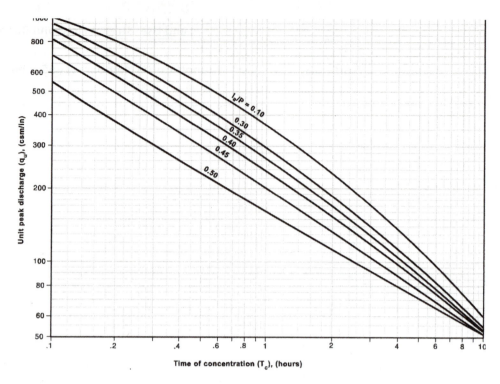

Figure 13.18 Unit Peak Discharge for Type II Rainfall Distribution. (TR55 exhibit 4–II) *Source:* USDA (1986).

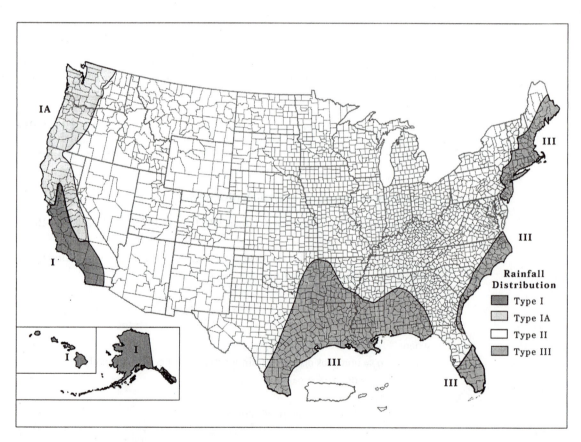

Figure 13.19 Rainfall Distribution Types. *Source:* USDA (1986).

Worksheet 4: Graphical Peak Discharge method

Project Heavenly Acres	By RHM	Date 10/15/85
Location Dyer County, Tennessee	Checked NM	Date 10/17/85

Check one: ☐ Present ☒ Developed

1. Data

Drainage area .... A_m = _____0.39_____ mi² (acres/640) _____

Runoff curve number .... CN = _____75_____ (From worksheet 2), _____Figure 2-6_____

Time of concentration .... T_c = _____1.53_____ hr (From worksheet 3), _____Figure 3-2_____

Rainfall distribution .... = _____II_____ (I, IA, II III) _____

Pond and swamp areas sprea
throughout watershed .... = _____– –_____ percent of A_m (_____– –_____ acres or mi² covered)

	Storm #1	Storm #2	Storm #3
2. Frequency .... yr	25		
3. Rainfall, P (24-hour) .... in	6.0		
4. Initial abstraction, I_a .... in (Use CN with table 4-1)	0.667		
5. Compute I_a/P	0.11		
6. Unit peak discharge, qu .... csm/in (Use T_c and I_a/P with exhibit 4– II)	270		
7. Runoff, Q .... in (From worksheet 2). Figure 2-6	3.28		
8. Pond and swamp adjustment factor, F_p .... (Use percent pond and swamp area with table 4-2. Factor is 1.0 for zero percent pond ans swamp area.)	1.0		
9. Peak discharge, q_p .... cfs	345		

(Where $q_p = q_u A_m Q F_p$)

reduction in time of concentration, and therefore peak discharge, caused by ponding or wetlands in the watershed. Table 13.9 gives values for F_p for pond and swamp areas up to 5 percent of the watershed area. The unit peak discharge, q_u, is the peak discharge per square mile per inch of runoff. It is estimated using figure 13.18, based on the rainfall distribution type, time of concentration (T_c), and a ratio, I_a/P, called the initial abstraction over P. Values of I_a depend on CN values and are given in table 13.8. Rainfall distribution type is given in figure 13.19. Worksheet 4 is used to calculate q_p.

Example 4–1: Compute the 25-year peak discharge for the 250-acre watershed described in examples 2–2 and 3–1: CN = 75, Q = 3.28 in., T_c = 1.53h. Worksheet 4 is used to compute q_p as 345 cfs.

TABLE 13.9 **Adjustment Factor (_Fp_) for Pond and Swamp Areas that are Spread Throughout the Watershed (TR55 table 4–2)**

Percentage of Pond and Swamp Areas	Fp
0	1.00
0.2	0.97
1.0	0.87
3.0	0.75
5.0	0.72

Effects of Land Use on Water Quality

In addition to affecting runoff quantity, land use also impacts water quality as surface runoff from cultivated, disturbed, and developed land carries water contaminants to receiving waters. Before focusing on land use and nonpoint source pollution, the following section provides some water quality fundamentals.

Water Quality Fundamentals

In the United States, we have made considerable progress in the past 30 years cleaning up our waterways and improving the safety of water for humans and aquatic life, primarily through improved engineering treatment at municipal sewage treatment plants and industrial facilities. We have doubled the number of waterways safe for fishing and swimming, doubled the number of Americans served by adequate sewage treatment, and reduced soil erosion from cropland by one-third. However, much remains to be done (U.S. EPA, 2000a, 2000b, 2002).

- In 1998, about 70 percent of Americans lived within 10 miles of polluted waters, and 300,000 miles of rivers and 5 million acres of lakes did not meet water quality standards.
- One-third of the 1,062 beaches reporting to the EPA had at least one health advisory or closing.
- More than 2,500 fish consumption advisories or bans were issued where fish were too contaminated to eat.
- The EPA estimates at least a half-million cases of illness annually can be attributed to microbial contamination of drinking water. In 1999, community water systems serving 1 of every 10 people reported a health standard violation.

- Of our waters that were monitored in 2000, 39 percent of river miles, 45 percent of lake area, and 54 percent of estuary area were too polluted for safe fishing or swimming.

The primary focus has shifted from municipal and industrial dischargers to runoff pollution from nonpoint sources (NPS). Indeed, national water quality assessments indicate that 60 to 70 percent of the nation's waters not meeting water quality standards are impaired by NPS pollution.

Before addressing NPS pollution, this section introduces some water quality fundamentals, including water pollutants and standards. The following sections review stream quality assessment and sources and impacts of NPS. Measures and programs to control stormwater quality problems are discussed in the next chapter.

Water Pollutants

Water quality is a complex subject, and it is useful to provide an overview of some basic scientific concepts. Table 13.10 describes the major classes of water contaminants, including sources, effects, measurement, and controls. Major pollutants carried by surface runoff include the following:

- **Oxygen-demanding** or **organic wastes** deplete water's **dissolved oxygen (DO)** that is needed to support aquatic life through biological decomposition. Water bodies gain oxygen from atmospheric aeration and photosynthesizing plants. But they also consume oxygen through respiration by aquatic life, decomposition, and various chemical reactions. Wastewater from runoff or treatment plants contains organic materials that are decomposed by microorganisms, using oxygen in the process. The strength of the wastes is measured by the oxygen required to decompose them, so-called biochemical oxygen demand (BOD). Biological treatment uses the natural decomposition process to stabilize organic waste.
- **Plant** or **inorganic nutrients,** such as phosphorus and nitrogen, contribute to excessive growth of algae and other undesirable aquatic vegetation in water bodies. Phosphorus is the limiting nutrient in most fresh waters, so even a modest increase in phosphorus can set off a chain of undesirable events in a stream, including accelerated plant growth, algae blooms, low dissolved oxygen, and the death of certain aquatic animals. Nitrogen is also an essential nutrient and is present in organic form as well as inorganic ammonia (NH_3), nitrates (NO_3), and nitrites (NO_2). Total Kjeldahl nitrogen (TKN) is the sum of ammonia and organic nitrogen. Together with phosphorus, nitrates and ammonia in excess amounts can accelerate aquatic plant growth and change the types of plants and animals that live in the stream. This, in turn, affects dissolved oxygen, temperature, and other indicators. Nutrients can be removed by advanced physical and chemical treatment, but biological treatment using vegetation uptake is also effective.

TABLE 13.10   **Water Pollutants, Sources, and Effects**

Water Pollutant	Sources	Effects	Measurement	Controls
Organic oxygen demanding wastes	Sewage, industry, runoff	Depletes DO; alters life forms; fish kills	BOD_5	Biological treatment
Plant nutrients	Sewage, agricultural and urban runoff, industry	Algae growth, waterweeds	Nitrogen, phosphorus	Advanced treatment, biological treatment
Thermal effluent	Power plants, industry, impervious surfaces	Accelerates decomp., biological activity; reduces DO solubility	Temperature	Cooling towers, ponds
Sediment, suspended particles	Runoff	Reduces clarity; smothers bottom life	Turbidity	Settling
Minerals, salts	Agricultural runoff	Taste; inhibits freshwater plants	Total dissolved solids (TDS)	Desalination; chemical treatment
Synthetic, volatile organic chemicals: e.g., oil, pesticides	Industry, spills, agri. runoff, air pollution	May be toxic to aquatic life, humans; subject to biomagnification	Chemical analysis	Activated carbon filtration
Inorganic chemicals (e.g. acids, heavy metals)	Industry, mining runoff, air pollution	May be toxic to aquatic life, humans; may be subject to biomagnification	Chemical analysis	Chemical treatment
Radioactive substances	Nuclear fuel cycle, medical wastes, industry	Toxic to aquatic life, humans	Chemical analysis, beta count	Isolation, chemical treatment
Pathogenic organisms	Sewage	Disease transmission	Fecal coliform count	Disinfection

▪ **Suspended solids** cause sedimentation in receiving waters. They
include particles that will not pass through a 2-micron filter, including silt
and clay, plankton, algae, fine organic debris, and other particulate matter. They can serve as carriers of toxics like pesticides, which readily cling
to suspended particles. Solids are removed by settling in detention facilities.

▪ **Dissolved solids** consist of calcium, chlorides, nitrate, phosphates, iron,
sulfur, and other ions particles that will pass through a filter with pores of
around 2 microns (0.0002 cm). Dissolved solids affect the water balance
in the cells of aquatic organisms. Removal requires advanced physical
treatment like reverse osmosis or desalination.

▪ **Acidity and alkalinity** are measured by pH on a scale from 1.0 (very
acidic) to 14.0 (very alkaline), with 7.0 being neutral. pH affects many
chemical and biological processes in the water. For example, different
organisms flourish within different ranges of pH. Most aquatic animals
prefer a range of 6.5–8.0. pH outside this range reduces the diversity in
the stream. Low pH can also allow toxic compounds to become available
for uptake by aquatic plants and animals. Alkalinity is a measure of the
capacity of water to neutralize acids.

- **Synthetic volatile organic chemicals (VOC)** are used in petroleum products and pesticides, which are toxic to humans and aquatic life. Biological treatment can reduce concentrations, but carbon filtration is most effective.
- **Inorganic chemicals,** such as toxic heavy metals, include mercury, lead, zinc, copper, and cadmium. They can biomagnify in concentration in higher levels of the food chain and are a prevalent cause of fish advisories.
- **Disease-causing microorganisms** include pathogenic bacteria, viruses, and protozoans that also live in human and animal digestive systems. Members of two bacteria groups, coliforms and fecal streptococci, are used as indicators of possible sewage contamination because they are commonly found in human and animal feces. Disinfection reduces microbial contamination. In addition, natural waters can provide breeding areas for carriers of disease, such as mosquitoes, which carry malaria and the West Nile virus.

Water Bodies and Beneficial Uses

The effects of these pollutants depend on the quality and beneficial uses of the natural waters that receive them. The major types of water bodies include freshwater streams and rivers, freshwater lakes and wetlands, mixed fresh- and saltwater estuaries, coastal and marine waters, and groundwater. **Streams'** self-flushing and aerating action gives them some assimilative capacity for conventional pollutants such as organics, nutrients, suspended particles, and waste heat. However, the natural quality of streams varies widely from pristine headwaters to more nutrient-enriched downstream waters. Streams and rivers are used for a wide range of **beneficial uses,** including water supply, recreation, fish propagation, agricultural and industrial use, and waste assimilation.

Lakes have much lower assimilative capacity because of poor flushing. As a result, pollutants tend to accumulate in lakes; sediments fill up lake bottoms, nutrients contribute to growth of algae and other undesirable vegetation, and organics consume dissolved oxygen. This is a natural process called **eutrophication,** or aging of lakes, and it will ultimately reduce the lake's beneficial uses for water supply, fish propagation, recreation, and aesthetics. Under natural conditions this process may take centuries. However, runoff pollution containing nutrients and sediments can accelerate this natural process. This human-induced "cultural" eutrophication can occur in decades. Natural lakes and human-made reservoirs are both subject to the same process of aging. Lakes have a much longer residence time (so pollutants will accumulate more) but have a smaller watershed (which may be easier to manage). Reservoirs have a shorter residence time and more through-flow and flushing, but their much larger watersheds can contribute more pollutants and be more difficult to control.

Estuaries are subject to some of the same processes as lakes and rivers, since some have flows and flushing (including intertidal mixing) like rivers, and others are more stagnant bays that behave like lakes. As important breeding and development habitats for fish and shellfish, estuaries have special needs because pollution can easily disrupt fish growth or contaminate populations with resulting economic impacts. **Coastal** and especially **marine waters** have the largest assimilative capacity for water pollutants, but pollution can impact coastal waters for recreation and fishing.

Groundwater is the fourth type of water body. As we shall see in chapter 15, groundwater encounters complex flow, filtering, and chemical processes. Because groundwater from private wells is often used for domestic water supply without treatment, groundwater quality concerns relate more to human health than to ecological health.

Water Quality Criteria and Standards

The 1972 federal Clean Water Act (CWA), as amended in 1977 and 1987, provides the framework for the nation's management of water quality. The Act sets forth a national goal of achieving a level of quality in all waters to support recreation and fish consumption, so-called *fishable and swimmable* quality. To define this threshold, the Act, and its administering agency the U.S. EPA, called on the states to establish water quality standards for their water bodies, monitor compliance, and manage pollutant discharges to meet these standards. The CWA's management programs for nonpoint sources are discussed in the next chapter.

The process of establishing water quality standards begins by the states' designating the beneficial uses of individual water bodies. The Act's goals call for minimum standards for recreation and propagation of aquatic life, but certain water bodies or reaches of streams may have beneficial uses (e.g., sources of community water supply or trout waters) that require higher standards. The states then determine criteria, such as chemical-specific thresholds or descriptive conditions, that aim to protect these beneficial uses. In addition, the Act provides an antidegradation policy to prevent waters that meet the standards from deteriorating from current conditions (U.S. EPA, 2000a). Natural surface waters are classified based on their natural quality and their beneficial uses, and water quality standards are assigned to different classifications.

Table 13.11 gives the classification system used in Washington State as an illustration. Five different classes of waters are assigned to each water body in the state. The table lists the basic criteria for different classes of fresh water. The same classes are assigned to marine waters as well, but with different standards. Management of both point and nonpoint sources of water pollution aims to achieve and maintain these water quality standards (Washington State Code, 1997). For water quality standards (WQS) for each state see http://www.epa.gov/ost/wqs/.

Impaired Waters in the United States

Section 305(b) of the CWA calls on the states to assess every two years the health of their waters and progress toward meeting the standards and goals of the Act. In addition, section 303(d) requires the states to identify and prioritize all of their "impaired" waters, or those that do not meet their water quality standards. States group their assessed waters into the following categories:

TABLE 13.11   **Classification of Waters and Fresh Water Quality Standards in Washington State[7]**

Class	Fecal Col[1]	DO[2]	Temp[3]	pH[4]	Turbidity[5]	Toxics[6]
AA (outstanding)	50	9.5	16	6.5–8.5	5	Max. 31
A (excellent)	100	8.0	18	6.5–8.5	5	Max. 31
B (good)	200	6.5	21	6.5–8.5	10	Max. 31
C (fair)	200	4.0	22	6.5–8.5	10	Max. 31
Lake[8]	50	Nat'l	Nat'l	Nat'l	5	Max. 31

[1]Fecal coliform count: maximum colonies per 100 milliliters (ml)
[2]Dissolved oxygen: minimum milligrams/liter
[3]Temperature: maximum °C
[4]pH: within range
[5]Turbidity: maximum nephelometric turbidity units (NTU)
[6]Toxics: maximum levels of 31 listed toxic, radioactive, deleterious materials
[7]WQS also provided for marine waters; all fresh and marine waters are assigned a classification
[8]Lake class: DO, Temp, pH shall not exceed natural conditions
(Source: WAC, 1997)

1. Attaining WQS

   a. Good/Fully Supporting: meets WQS

   b. Good/Threatened: meets WQS but may degrade in near future

2. Impaired, Not Attaining WQS

   a. Fair/Partially Supporting: meets WQS most of the time but occasionally exceeds them

   b. Poor/Not Supporting: does not meet WQS

3. WQS not attainable

   a. Use-attainability analysis shows that one or more designated uses is not attainable because of specific conditions.

Table 13.12 summarizes the *2000 National Water Quality Inventory* results (U.S. EPA, 2002). It shows five types of surface water bodies, their total length or area, the percentage that was assessed, and the assessment ratings. This assessment is becoming more comprehensive each time it is done. In 2000, 180,000 more stream miles were assessed than in 1996. Percent impairment increased from 1998 to 2000 for all categories except the Great Lakes.

Table 13.13 shows the uses impaired and stressors (pollutants) and sources of impairment for rivers and streams, lakes, and estuaries. Common uses impaired for all three water bodies are aquatic life, fish consumption, and swimming. Thirty-eight percent of assessed rivers are impaired for fish consumption, 34 percent for aquatic life, 28 percent for primary contact like swimming, and 14 percent for drinking water supply. Several pollutants are problematic, led by pathogens, sil-

TABLE 13.12   **Quality of Nation's Waters, 2000**

Water Body	Total Length or Area	Assessed (%)	Assessment			
			Good (%)	Good, But Threatened (%)	Impaired 2000 (%)	Impaired 1998 (%)
Rivers, streams	3.69 million miles	19	53	8	39	35
Lakes, ponds, reservoirs	40.6 million acres	43	47	8	45	45
Estuaries	31,072 sq. mi.	36	45	<4	51	44
Ocean shoreline waters	66,600 miles	5	79	7	14	12
Great Lakes shoreline waters	5,500 miles	92	0	22	78	96

Source: U.S. EPA, 2000a, 2002

TABLE 13.13   **Causes and Sources of Impaired Waters in United States, 2000 (With Percent of Assessed Waters Impaired for Uses and by the Stressors and Sources)**

	Rivers and Streams	Lakes, Ponds, and Reservoirs	Estuaries
Uses Impaired	Fish consumption (38%) Aquatic life (34%) Swimming (28%) Drinking water (14%)	Fish consumption (35%) Aquatic life (29%) Swimming (23%) Drinking water (17%)	Aquatic life (52%) Fish consumption (48%) Shellfishing (25%) Swimming (15%)
Stressors	Pathogens (Bacteria) (35%) Siltation (Sedimentation) (31%) Habitat alterations (22%) Oxygen demanding (21%) Nutrients (20%)	Nutrients (50%) Metals (Primarily mercury) (42%) Siltation (Sedimentation) (21%) Total dissolved solids (19%) Oxygen demanding (15%)	Metals (Primarily mercury) (52%) Pesticides (38%) Oxygen demanding (34%) Pathogens (30%) Toxic organic (23%)
Sources	Agriculture (48%) Hydrologic modifications (20%) Habitat modifications (14%) Urban runoff (13%)	Agriculture (41%) Hydrologic modifications (18%) Urban runoff/storm sewers (18%) Other nonpoint sources (14%)	Municipal point sources (37%) Urban runoff/storm sewers (32%) Industrial discharges (26%) Atmospheric deposition (24%)

Source: EPA, 2002

tation, organics, nutrients, and metals. Main sources of impairment are agricultural and urban runoff and stream modification.

For lakes, 35 percent are impaired for fish consumption, 29 percent for aquatic life, 23 percent for primary contact, and 17 percent for drinking water supply. Main pollutants causing impairment are nutrients (50%), metals (42%), siltation, organics, and dissolved solids (each 15–20%). Main sources are agricultural runoff (41%), hydromodification (18%) and urban runoff (18%). Hydromodification is conversion of natural channels or shoreline construction. Pathogens, organics, pesticides, metals, and nutrients from municipal point sources, urban runoff, and atmospheric deposition are the major causes of impairment in estuaries. Fish consumption (48%), aquatic life (52%), and shellfishing (25%) are the main estuary uses not supported (U.S. EPA, 2000a).

The Great Lakes are the most assessed and impaired of the nation's waters. Major uses impaired are fish consumption (78%) and aquatic life (12%). Toxic organic and other organic chemicals, pesticides, and nutrients from atmospheric deposition and discontinued sources are the main sources of impairment. The discontinued industrial discharges and contaminated sediments are the legacy of past pollution (U.S. EPA, 2000a).

Figure 13.20 shows the percentage of impaired waters within watersheds for 1998. All of these data on the nation's water quality demonstrate that despite significant improvements in the past 30 years since the passage of the Clean Water Act, we are far from achieving the goals of the Act. They also show that the main sources of remaining pollution are not the traditional industrial and sewage pipe discharges, but more diffuse land runoff and atmospheric deposition.

Indicators of Water Quality

Water quality criteria and standards provide the basis for most indicators of water quality. Thousands of monitoring stations throughout the country operated by state and federal agencies measure many of the traditional physical and chemical constituents: dissolved oxygen, biochemical oxygen demand, forms of nitrogen and phosphorus, pesticides, heavy metals, and others. These data are stored in two national water databases, STORET (1999 and after) and the Legacy Data System (before 1999), and are accessible on the Internet (see http://www.epa.gov/storet/about.html). Some of these data are available in real time.

Water monitoring has historically focused on chemical and physical constituents. In the past decade, a broader range of indicators have been used to monitor water quality to represent expanding interests in aquatic ecology and watershed health. For example, the EPA has developed a database from various sources to indicate overall watershed integrity. Box 10.2 lists the 22 indicators of watershed integrity (IWI) (www.epa.gov/iwi/help/indic/fs1.html).

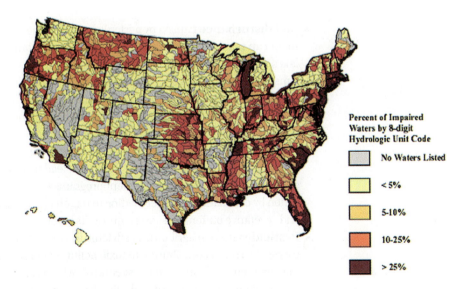

Percent of Impaired Waters by 8-digit Hydrologic Unit Code

No Waters Listed
< 5%
5-10%
10-25%
> 25%

Figure 13.20 Percentage of Impaired Waters by Eight-Digit Hydrologic Unit Code. *Source:* U.S. EPA (2000b).

Biological monitoring samples fish and macroinvertebrate species that indicate overall health of water systems rather than a snapshot look at water quality constituents. Different approaches to water body assessment include watershed surveys and habitat assessment for measuring physical conditions, macroinvertebrate sampling to measure biological condition, and measuring water quality constituents to reveal chemical conditions. See later section and appendices 13.B–C.

Because national data monitoring cannot address all local water quality problems, agencies have encouraged volunteer groups to provide information they monitor. As discussed later in this chapter, volunteer water quality monitoring, through groups like the Izaak Walton League's Save Our Streams (SOS) program, has improved in sophistication and reliability. By the early 1990s, 38 states had volunteer programs with over 24,000 participants monitoring 1,000 streams; 2,800 lakes, ponds, and wetlands; and four major estuaries. These programs have gained the respect of state and federal environmental agencies, which have adopted volunteer-gathered data in their water quality databases.

Land Use Practices and Nonpoint Sources (NPS) Pollution

As already mentioned more than half of the pollutants entering the nation's waters comes from runoff. The most pervasive problem is agricultural sources (affecting more than 60% of all river basins), followed by urban sources (runoff, hydro-modification, discharges) (affecting 50%), mining runoff (10%), and silvicultural runoff (10%).

Figure 13.21 gives an overview of land use practices that cause runoff pollution (first column), the results and consequences to receiving waters (second and third columns), and potential controls (fourth column). The table is divided into the major land uses and practices causing NPS pollution: agriculture crop production, agriculture animal production, forestry, mining, and urban development. Some examples include the following:

- **Soil disturbance** caused by agricultural cultivation and land development can result in erosion that will cause sedimentation of streams, lakes, or estuaries, which can smother bottom feeding or benthic organisms. Conservation tillage (which leaves some crop residue to reduce erosion), contour cropping, or filter strips aim to control agricultural erosion at the source, while level spreaders, filters strips, ponds, and wetlands can remove suspended solids before they enter waterways.
- **Excessive use of fertilizer** in agriculture or urban uses can result in runoff laden with plant nutrients, which can lead to algal growth in lakes and estuaries. Nutrient management programs aim to control excess application by calculating fertilizer loading to match plant uptake. Filter strips and vegetative buffers can absorb nutrients before they enter waterways.
- **Pesticides** used in agriculture, silviculture, and urban land uses, can be carried by runoff contributing to toxic pollution of receiving waters. Input management and integrated pest control (which relies on nonchemical means of pest management and selective chemical use) can reduce pesticide pollution.

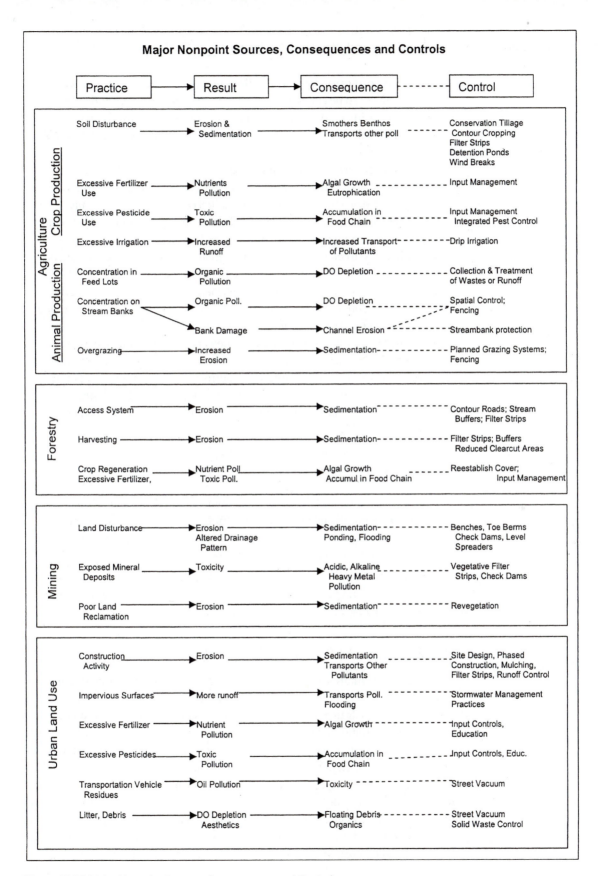

Figure 13.21 Major Nonpoint Sources, Consequences, and Controls

- **Animal concentration in feedlots** produces large amounts of organic wastes that can be carried by runoff in high concentrations and overload receiving waters, depleting the water's dissolved oxygen and causing fish kills. For such concentrated facilities, collection and treatment of runoff is generally required.
- **Animals grazing in open pasture** can overgraze available grass, exposing soil and creating erosion problems. In addition, animals tend to concentrate on stream banks, the so-called *cows-in-creeks syndrome,* which causes organic pollution and destruction of channel banks. Spatial control through fencing is necessary to reduce impact.
- **Mining disturbs the land,** not only creating conditions for erosion, but also often altering drainage patterns. Benches cut into slopes, check dams, and level spreaders can help alleviate runoff and pollution problems during operations. Extensive reclamation and revegetation of mined lands is necessary to solve long-term erosion and NPS problems.
- In forestry operations, **cutting of access roads and harvesting methods** increase erosion, particularly in proximity to stream channels and with greater land disturbance. Controls include building roads and trails along contours and providing vegetated or artificial filter strips to intercept runoff, and maintaining natural buffers along water bodies.
- **Urban runoff** carries
  - sediment from construction activities;
  - nutrients and pesticides from excessive uses on lawns, gardens, and golf courses;
  - organic material and floating debris from roadside litter; and
  - petrochemicals and toxic substances from transportation residues and air pollution fallout. More than one-half of the substances on EPA's list of 129 priority toxic chemicals have been found in urban runoff.
- **Hydraulic modification** of channels, shorelines, and riparian areas for drainage or land development is another source of pollution into waterways and cause of channel and habitat destruction.

Urban Runoff and the First Flush Effect

Urban runoff pollutants are carried in highest concentration during the first part of a storm event, the so-called **first flush** effect. Monitoring and modeling research in the early to mid-1970s established a simple standard that was adopted by many communities trying to control stormwater pollution: Size your stormwater control measure to capture the runoff from the first portion of a storm, and you'll treat 90 percent of the annual pollutant load. As a result, urban stormwater pollution control strategies normally focus on a storm's initial runoff or use a lower frequency or smaller design storm. For example, an area's 1-year 24-hour storm may be 2 inches and its 10-year 24-hour storm is 5 inches. Although we may wish to control stormwater from the larger storm to mitigate flooding, controlling runoff from the smaller storm may be sufficient to manage water quality.

For many years it was believed that this 90 percent objective could be achieved by capturing and treating the first half-inch of runoff in any storm. This "half-inch" rule was adopted in many ordinances, but field studies showed that though it was effective in areas of 30 percent and less impervious cover, the half-inch runoff carried less than 90 percent at greater imperviousness. One study showed that at 50 percent impervious cover, the first half-inch carried 75 percent of TSS, and at 70 percent it carried only 53 percent (Chang, Parrish, and Souer, 1990).

As a result, rather than assuming the first "half-inch" rule, stormwater controls now calculate the **"water quality volume"** (WQ_v) or the volume of storage needed to capture and treat 90 percent of the average annual stormwater pollutant load, based on impervious surface. These calculations are discussed in the next chapter.

Estimating Runoff Pollution: The Simple Method

The Simple Method was developed by Schueler (1987) to estimate pollutant loads from an urban site or catchment. The method has been shown to give reasonable results compared with more complex models (Ohrel, 1996).

The **pollutant load equation** for chemical contaminants is the following:

$$L = 0.226 \times R \times C \times A$$

where L = Annual load (lbs)
R = Annual runoff (inches)
C = Pollutant concentration (mg/l)
A = Area (acres)
0.226 = Unit conversion factor

The modified equation for bacteria is:

$$L = 103 \times R \times C \times A$$

where L = Annual load (Billion Colonies)
R = Annual runoff (inches)
C = Bacteria concentration (1,000/ ml)
A = Area (acres)
103 = Unit conversion factor

The **annual runoff (R)** is the product of annual rainfall, and a runoff coefficient (R_v).

$$R = P \times P_j \times R_v$$

where R = Annual runoff (inches)
P = Annual rainfall (inches)
P_j = Fraction of annual rainfall events that produce runoff (usually 0.9)
R_v = Runoff coefficient

TABLE 13.14 **Pollutant Concentrations from Source Areas**

Constituent	TSS	TP	TN	F Coli	Cu	Pb	Zn
Land Use/Units	mg/l	mg/l	mg/l	1000 col/ml	µg/l	µg/l	µg/l
Urban average	55	0.26	2.0	1.5	51	129	11.1
Residential roof	19	0.11	1.5	0.26	20	21	312
Res./com. parking	27	0.15	1.9	1.8	51	28	139
Residential street	172	0.55	1.4	37	25	51	173
Lawns	602	2.1	9.1	24	17	17	50
Gas station	31	—	—	—	88	80	290
Heavy industry	124	—	—	—	148	290	1600

Sources: New York, 2002; Schueler, 1999; Smullen and Cave, 1998; Clayton and Schueler, 1996; Steuer, et al., 1997

The **runoff coefficient (R_v)** is calculated based on impervious cover in the sub-watershed.

$R_v = 0.05 + 0.9 I_a$
  where I_a = Impervious fraction

The stormwater **pollutant concentration (C)** is usually estimated from national data. Table 13.14 gives average data from a number of monitoring studies of urban stormwater for concentrations of pollutants from various urban land uses. The Simple Method assumes these values. If a catchment or site has a mix of land covers, an average value weighted by the percentage of the land cover should be calculated.

Example:

Using the Simple Method, calculate the stormwater pollutant load of suspended solids (TSS) of a 2-inch, 24-hour storm from a 2-acre urban site that is 30 percent impervious and has typical urban runoff pollutant concentrations.

$C = 55$ mg/l
$R_v = 0.05 + 0.9(I_a) = 0.05 + 0.9(0.30) = 0.32$
$R = P \times P_j \times R_v = 2 \times 0.9 \times 0.32 = 0.52$ in
$L = 0.226 \times R \times C \times A = 0.226 \times 0.52 \times 55 \times 2 = 12.9$ lbs TSS

Effects of Land Use on Stream Integrity

The effects of land use on peak flows and runoff pollution damage the physical and biological integrity of natural channels. In addition, reduced infiltration reduces groundwater storage and reduced dry weather stream flows. Urbanization directly and indirectly causes the **destruction of natural creeks and streams.**

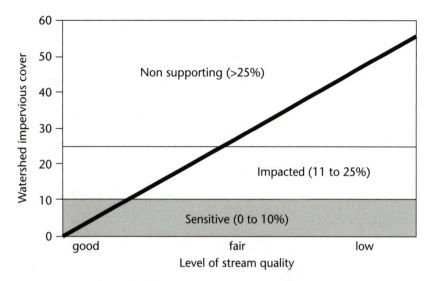

Figure 13.22 Relationship of Watershed Impervious Surface Coverage to Stream Health. *Source:* Tom Schueler, 2000, "Basic Concepts in Watershed Planning." Reprinted courtesy of Center for Watershed Protection.

- **Lower base- and dry-weather flows** adversely affect stream ecology and riparian vegetation.
- **Traditional stormwater engineering practices** often convert natural channels to underground pipes and culverts or concrete lined chutes in an effort to increase drainage capacity; however, this destroys the aesthetic and environmental amenities these creeks provide.
- Further, the higher, more frequent and faster-moving flows caused by land development exacerbate **stream erosion,** undermining waterside trees and residential property.
- Erosion damage and more frequent downstream flooding create additional **pressure for conversion** of creeks to lined channels.

Stream Integrity and Impervious Surfaces

Many analysts have argued that **impervious surface coverage** in a watershed is a good indicator of potential impact on stream health. As discussed earlier, urbanization increases impervious cover, reducing infiltration and increasing runoff during storms and reducing stream baseflows between storms (table 13.1). Figure 13.22 gives Schueler's simple relationship between imperviousness and stream health. According to the model, more than 10 percent impervious surface in a watershed can impact stream health, while more than 25 percent can degrade stream health to nonsupporting beneficial uses (Schueler, 2000).

Others have argued that imperviousness alone may be too simplistic to capture the effects of urban development on stream quality. First, the effects of impervious surfaces will depend on if they are *hydraulically connected* to the stormwater drainage system. Second, there are land use practices that can lessen the effects of development on runoff, NPS pollution, and other stream impacts. Although many aim to reduce imperviousness, others increase infiltration and slow the accumulation of runoff through various detention devices. These practices reduce the **effective impervious area** (EIA) or the directly connected impervious area to the storm drain system in a catchment or watershed. These measures are described in the next chapter. The following section discusses methods used to assess the integrity and capacity of natural channels as well as stream water quality.

Stream Assessment

Stream assessment is important for monitoring stream integrity, identifying restoration problems and opportunities, as well as evaluating stream or watershed projects. A monitoring program should follow a clear strategy with defined objectives, an assessment design including sampling and data interpretation, and a reporting program. The evaluation objectives will determine the assessment tools and indicators, as shown in table 13.15.

There are four approaches to stream monitoring:

- Watershed survey to identify watershed boundaries, upland land use, pollution sources, and stream corridor physical dimensions and conditions.
- Habitat assessment to determine riparian conditions including vegetation, erosion, and other impairment.

TABLE 13.15 Stream Assessment Objectives and Evaluation Tools and Indicators

General Objectives	Evaluation Tools and Indicators
Assess watershed trends	Land use/land cover
	Land management
	Topography and soil types
Evaluate hydrologic changes	Channel dimensions
	Water depth and velocity
	Rates of bank and bed erosion
	Flood stage surveys
Improve riparian habitat	Percent vegetative cover
	Buffer width and condition
	Wildlife use, species diversity
Improve aquatic habitat	Pool/riffle composition, water depth
	Percent cover and shading
	Bed material composition
	Biological assessments
Improve water quality	Dissolved oxygen
	Priority pollutants
	Turbidity, suspended solids, floating matter
	Biological assessments

Adapted from: U.S. EPA, Watershed Academy, 2000

- Macroinvertebrate sampling to indicate aquatic habitat and water quality integrity and impairment.
- Water quality sampling to measure water quality and identify water pollution.

The tiered framework for doing stream assessments includes four progressively more complex activities:

- Stream or watershed walk to gather visual and dimensional data
- Streamside biosurvey to collect and evaluate macroinvertebrates at the side of the stream
- Channel capacity and erosion assessment
- Intensive biosurvey to collect biotic species and water samples and analyze them in the laboratory

Visual surveys and streamside biosurveys are described here based on two publications, EPA's *Volunteer Stream Monitoring: A Methods Manual* (1997) and NRCS's *Stream Visual Assessment Protocol* (1998). The procedures in these publications draw heavily from other protocols (e.g., Izaak Walton League of America, 1994; California Department of Fish and Game, 1996). Most of these approaches modify professional assessment protocols for volunteer implementation. Thus, they are made to be straightforward, simple, and quite appropriate for our discussion.

Watershed Survey

The watershed survey begins by delineating the watershed of the stream reach being assessed. This procedure using a topographic map was described in box 13.1. Quite often the causes of stream impairment are upland uses and nonpoint pollution sources. Walking the land of the watershed and sketching onto the watershed map land uses, impervious cover, potential runoff pollution sources, drainage characteristics, vegetative cover, and other characteristics can reveal watershed improvements needed for stream restoration. Existing maps, aerial photos, and other available information can be very useful in watershed assessments.

Stream Walk and Visual Assessment

A systematic stream walk using an accepted protocol provides a useful assessment of the conditions of the riparian habitat and stream banks. Channel dimensions can also be measured for use in channel capacity calculations (see next section). The NRCS visual assessment protocol gives a good illustration of procedures and results (USDA, NRCS, 1998), but other methods are also available. Some of the useful measures gathered in the stream walk include stream channel and bank characteristics relating to width and depth, pools and riffles, substrate (channel bottom), shading, and cover. Also included are water characteristics like appearance, odor, and temperature. Some of these dimensions are used to assess channel capacity, velocity, and erosion. Box 13.2 describes things to look for in a stream walk.

The NRCS protocol assesses up to 15 indicators that are combined into an index score of overall stream condition. The indicators include the following:

- Channel condition
- Hydrologic alteration
- Riparian zone
- Bank stability
- Water appearance
- Nutrient enrichment
- Instream fish cover
- Barriers to fish movement
- Pools
- Insect/invertebrate habitat
- Canopy cover: coldwater or warmwater fishery (if applicable)
- Manure presence (if applicable)
- Salinity (if applicable)
- Riffle embeddedness (if applicable)
- Macroinvertebrates observed (if applicable)

Appendix 13.B gives the assessment form and the scoring procedure for each indicator. Assessment scores are logged on the form, and an average score (the sum of the scores divided by the number of indicators used) is calculated.

A visual biological survey notes the presence of fish, fish barriers, aquatic vegetation, and algae. Fish can indicate stream quality sufficient for other organisms. Aquatic plants provide food and cover for aquatic organisms. Algae are simple, unrooted plants that mainly live in water and provide food for the food chain. Excessive algal growth may indicate excessive nutrients (organic matter or a pollutant such as fertilizer) in the stream.

Streamside Biosurvey

The streamside biosurvey assesses stream macroinvertebrates or nonfish species. The presence, absence, and abundance of both sensitive and tolerant species serve as a useful indicator of stream health and water quality. Biosurvey methods have been used by water quality agencies and volunteer monitoring programs for two decades. The Izaak Walton League of America institutionalized the method in its Save Our Streams (SOS) program and variations have been used throughout the United States. Several thousand monitoring groups now assess streams, and the results have proven to be so reliable that state and federal agencies now accept them in their water quality databases.

A biosurvey protocol is discussed in appendix 13.C. It is drawn from the EPA's *Volunteer Stream Monitoring: A Methods Manual* (1997). The method gathers, sorts, and counts macroinvertebrates present in a sampling reach and computes a stream health indicator based on the abundance and distribution of species.

BOX 13.2—Useful Measures Gathered in a Stream Walk

- *Stream bank and channel characteristics*
- *Location of pools, riffles, and runs; depth of runs and pools*
- *Width of the stream channel, hydrologic and topographic floodplains; depth of thalweg and bankfull channel (see figure 13.8)*

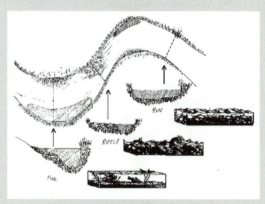

- *Stream bottom (substrate)* is the material on the stream bottom. Identify what substrate types are present:

    Silt/clay/mud—This fine-particle substrate has a sticky, cohesive feeling. Sediments behave like ooze.

    Sand (up to 0.1 inch)—Tiny, gritty particles of rock smaller than gravel, coarser than silt.

    Gravel (0.1–2 inches)—From quarter-inch pebbles (fine pea gravel) to 2-inch rocks (coarse gravel).

    Cobbles (2–10 inches)—Between 2 and 10 inches (tennis ball to basketball size).

    Boulders (greater than 10 inches)—Most of the rocks range from basketball to car size.

    Bedrock—Solid rock; rocks bigger than a car

    Embeddedness—The extent to which gravel, cobbles, and boulders are sunken into the stream bottom

- *Stream velocity:* Mark off a 20-foot section of stream run and measure the time it takes a stick, leaf, or other floating object to float the 20 feet. Repeat 5 times and pick the average time. Velocity = 20 ft/average time.
- *Shape of the stream bank, the extent of artificial modifications and erosion.*

Vertical or undercut bank—A bank that rises vertically or overhangs the stream. Although this type of bank can provide good cover for macroinvertebrates and fish and be resistant to erosion, if seriously undercut, it might be vulnerable to collapse.

Steeply sloping—A bank that slopes at more than a 30-degree angle. This type of bank is very vulnerable to erosion.

Gradual sloping—A bank that has a slope of 30 degrees or less. Although this type of stream bank is highly resistant to erosion, it does not provide much streamside cover.

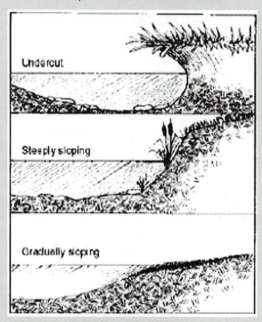

- *Presence of logs or woody debris* that slows or diverts water can provide important fish habitat.
- *Streamside cover* information helps determine the quality and extent of the stream's riparian zone.
- *Stream shading* is the extent to which the stream itself is overhung and shaded by the cover.

Water Characteristics

- *Water appearance* can be a physical indicator of water pollution.

    Clear—colorless, transparent

Continued ➤

BOX 13.2—(continued)

Milky—cloudy-white or gray, not transparent; might be natural or due to pollution

Foamy—might be natural or due to pollution, generally detergents or nutrients

Turbid—cloudy brown due to suspended silt or organic material

Dark brown—might indicate that acids are being released into the stream due to decaying plants

Oily sheen—multicolored reflection might indicate oil floating in the stream, although some sheens are natural

Orange—might indicate acid drainage

Green—might indicate excess nutrients being released into the stream

▪ *Water odor* can be a physical indicator of water pollution

No smell or a natural odor

Sewage—might indicate the release of human waste material

Chlorine—might indicate overchlorinated sewage treatment/water treatment plant

Fishy—might indicate the presence of excessive algal growth or dead fish

Rotten eggs—might indicate sewage pollution (the presence of methane from anaerobic conditions)

▪ Water temperature

Digital Field Monitoring

Field monitoring by volunteer groups relies on paper forms for recording information, but these forms are not optimal for efficient data collection, entry, and display. Recently, these accepted protocols have been adapted to allow the digital entry and storage of data using handheld computers or personal digital assistants (PDAs), global positioning systems (GPSs), digital water quality sensors, and digital cameras (for visual assessments) (see figure 13.23). The use of these tools and emerging software (e.g., CyberTracker™, Excel, ArcView/ArcGIS, and ArcIMS) allows an efficient means of collecting, recording, storing, analyzing, and mapping stream, watershed, habitat, and wildlife data, then presenting the results in an interactive format on the Internet.

CyberTracker™ is a data collection tool developed in South Africa to tap the unique knowledge and expertise of illiterate South African bushmen to monitor the movements and behavior of wildlife. Programmed into a PDA with a GPS unit, bushmen simply point at an icon on the screen when they see a species, tracks, or other indicator (figure 13.23b), and the data and GPS location are automatically stored. Anderson (2001) adapted the fully programmable, freeware software for stream survey data collection. Data monitored in the field are entered onto the PDA touchpad. The GPS automatically enters into the PDA the spatial location of the data and any digital photos taken. Back in the office, the data are downloaded into a spreadsheet, checked, and then transferred to a GIS, complete with location coordinates. Figure 13.23d shows the GIS project file with digital topographic map on which red pluses indicate the data collection locations. By clicking the mouse on a location, the data and photo pop up. Anderson (2001) tested the tools and protocol using both experienced stream surveyors and schoolchildren with great success.

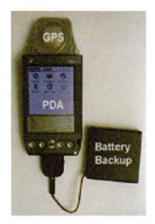

a

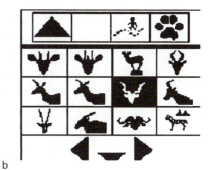

b

c

d

Figure 13.23 Tools for Digital Monitoring: PDA, GPS (A), CyberTracker (B), Digital Camera (C). GIS ArcView project resulting from Stream Survey (D). Click on map location (red pluses) and stream data and photo pop up. (Anderson, 2001)

Assessing Channel Capacity and Excessive Channel Erosion

Urban streams face a survival challenge as a result of upstream impervious surface. More frequent and higher storm flows reach and exceed the bankfull capacity of channels more often, resulting in excessive flooding and channel erosion. The typical remedy is to "improve" the drainage characteristics of the channel by straightening, widening, and lining. Unfortunately, this destroys the natural ecological, aesthetic, and other environmental benefits of natural creeks. Efforts to preserve and restore natural streams must consider the flow capacity and erosive forces of the channels. Stream preservation efforts must assess hydraulic characteristics of the channel, including its flow capacity and erosion problems.

Assessment methods for channel capacity use open channel flow calculations based on two equations (see figures 13.8 and 13.16):

Manning's Equation:
$$V = \frac{1.49\, R^{2/3}\, S^{1/2}}{n} \qquad (Eq.\ 13\text{--}6)$$

where V = the average velocity in the channel (ft/sec)

            n = Manning's roughness coefficient, based on the lining of the channel

            R = the hydraulic radius (feet)

            S = the slope of the channel (elevation drop (ft)/linear foot)

The Continuity Equation:
$$Q = AV$$

Where Q = flow in the channel (cfs)

            A = cross-sectional area of the channel (sq. ft)

            V = average velocity in the channel (ft/sec)

This method is used to determine **bankfull velocity** and **bankfull capacity** (see figure 13.8). A channel is considered to be "adequate" if: (1) its capacity is greater than the streamflow of a design frequency storm, and (2) the channel is resistant to the erosion from the bankfull flow velocities. If the assessment of a natural channel fails the first test (i.e., insufficient capacity), measures must be considered to reduce runoff flows in the watershed; or the channel may have to be modified to increase its capacity. If the channel fails the velocity test, the segments of the stream susceptible to erosion can be treated with vegetation and/or rocks to reduce the erosion potential (see chapter 14).

The procedure for assessing natural streams and designing human-made or restored channels is essentially the same. For channel design, you assess an assumed channel size using the procedure; if it is too big or small, you adjust the size and test it again. The procedure has three main steps:

1. Determine the "required" flow capacity (i.e., the peak discharge from the design storm) and the "permissible" velocity of the channel (i.e., the maximum velocity without erosion for the channel lining or banks).

2. Calculate the channel velocity using the Manning Equation and the channel capacity using the Continuity Equation.
3. Compare the results from (1) to those from (2): If the channel velocity is greater than the "permissible velocity," excessive erosion is likely; if the channel capacity is less than the "required" capacity, excessive flooding is likely. Remedial action or a modified design is required.

To solve the Manning and Continuity equations, you need stream data from a stream walk survey as well as some design tables. The procedure and design tables are given in appendix 13.D.

Summary

Water has a major effect on the landform, shaping the land through erosion and deposition. Likewise, land use has a significant influence on water balance, affecting infiltration and runoff, peak and baseflows. Although any land disturbance will change the water balance, land development and urbanization and their associated impervious surfaces inhibit infiltration and speed runoff. These effects combine to cause higher peak discharges and greater stormwater and flooding problems during major storm events and reduced baseflows and low flows between storms and during drought. While much attention has been given to land development impacts on peak flows because of potential economic damages, impacts on low flows have a significant effect on stream ecology. It is not uncommon for urban streams to dry up during drought because reduced infiltration limits subsurface baseflow for the streams. In addition, increased storm flows carry with them a range of water pollutants.

Several methods now exist to assess the effect of changing land use on water flows, including peak storm flows, runoff pollution, and stream integrity. This chapter and appendices describe a number of these techniques, including the Rational Method, TR 55, the Simple Method, stream surveys, and testing channel capacity. Managing stormwater and natural channels involves applying these and other analytical methods to inform land development and design as well as preservation and restoration decisions. The next chapter presents approaches to stormwater management and stream restoration, including a range of stormwater management practices.

Appendix 13.A

TR 55 Step 1 Examples

See Step 1 example 2–2 in chapter 13 text.

Example 2–3

This example is the same as example 2–2 in chapter 13, except that the 1/2-acre lots have a total impervious area of 35 percent. For these lots, the pervious area is lawns in good hydrologic condition. Since the impervious area percentage differs from the percentage assumed in table 13.5 (2–2 in TR 55), use figure 13.15a (2–3 in TR 55) to compute *CN*.

Worksheet 2: Runoff curve number and runoff

Project	Heavenly Acres	By	WJR	Date	10/1/85
Location	Dyer County, Tennessee	Checked	NM	Date	10/3/85

Check one: ☐ Present ☒ Developed

1. Runoff curve number

Soil name and hydrologic group (appendix A)	Cover description (cover type, treatment, and hydrologic condition; percent impervious; unconnected/connected impervious area ratio)	Table 2-2	Figure 2-3	Figure 2-4	Area ☒ acres ☐ mi² ☐ %	Product of CN x area
Memphis, B	35% impervious 1/2 acre lots, good condition		74		75	5550
Loring, C	35% impervious 1/2 acre lots, good condition		82		100	8200
Loring, C	Open space, good condition	74			75	5550

1/ Use only one CN source per line

Totals ➡ 250 | 19,300

$$CN \text{ (weighted)} = \frac{\text{total product}}{\text{total area}} = \frac{19,300}{250} = 77.2 \quad ; \quad \text{Use CN} \rightarrow \boxed{77}$$

2. Runoff

		Storm #1	Storm #2	Storm #3
Frequency	yr	25		
Rainfall, P (24-hour)	in	6.0		
Runoff, Q	in	3.48		

(Use P and CN with table 2-1, figure 2-1, or equations 2-3 and 2-4)

Example 2–4

This example is also based on example 2–2, except that 50 percent of the impervious area associated with the 1/2-acre lots on the Loring soil is "unconnected," that is, it is not directly connected to the drainage system. For these lots, the pervious area *CN* (lawn, good condition) is 74 percent and the impervious area is 25 percent. Use figure 13.5b (2–4 in TR 55) to compute the *CN* for these lots. *CN*s for the 1/2-acre lots on Memphis soil and the open space on Loring soil are the same as those in example 2–2.

Worksheet 2: Runoff curve number and runoff

Project: Heavenly Acres	By: WJR	Date: 10/1/85
Location: Dyer County, Tennessee	Checked: NM	Date: 10/3/85

Check one: ☐ Present ☒ Developed

1. Runoff curve number

Soil name and hydrologic group (appendix A)	Cover description (cover type, treatment, and hydrologic condition; percent impervious; unconnected/connected impervious area ratio)	CN [1] Table 2-2	CN [1] Figure 2-3	CN [1] Figure 2-4	Area ☒ acres ☐ mi² ☐ %	Product of CN x area
Memphis, B	25% connected impervious 1/2 acre lots, good condition	70			75	5250
Loring, C	25% impervious with 50% unconnected 1/2 acre lots, good condition			78	100	7800
Loring, C	Open space, good condition	74			75	5550

[1] Use only one CN source per line

Totals ▶ 250 | 18,600

$$CN \text{ (weighted)} = \frac{\text{total product}}{\text{total area}} = \frac{18,600}{250} = 74.4 \quad ; \quad \textbf{Use CN ▶} \quad \boxed{74}$$

2. Runoff

		Storm #1	Storm #2	Storm #3
Frequency	yr	25		
Rainfall, P (24-hour)	in	6.0		
Runoff, Q	in	3.19		
(Use P and CN with table 2-1, figure 2-1, or equations 2-3 and 2-4)				

Appendix 13.B

USDA Stream Visual Assessment

The NRCS protocol assesses up to 15 indicators that are combined into an index score of overall stream condition. The indicators include the following:

- Channel condition
- Hydrologic alteration
- Riparian zone
- Bank stability
- Water appearance
- Nutrient enrichment
- Instream fish cover
- Barriers to fish movement
- Pools
- Insect/invertebrate habitat
- Canopy cover: coldwater or warmwater fishery (if applicable)
- Manure presence (if applicable)
- Salinity (if applicable)
- Riffle embeddedness (if applicable)
- Macroinvertebrates observed (if applicable)

The assessment form is given here (see figure 13.B.1 and table 13.B.1). The stream reach and environs are sketched and described on the form. Assessment scores are determined for each factor based on the 1–10 scoring system on the following pages. The scores are logged on the form and an average score (the sum of the scores divided by the number of indicators used) is calculated. A score of >9.0 is excellent; a score of <6.0 is poor.

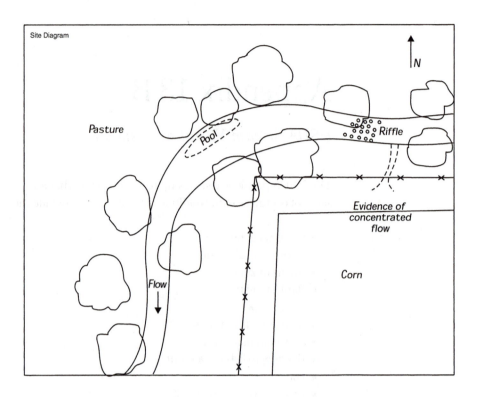

Assessment Scores

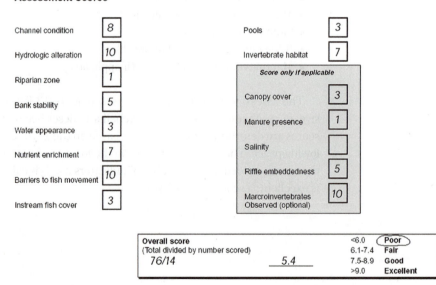

Channel condition	8
Hydrologic alteration	10
Riparian zone	1
Bank stability	5
Water appearance	3
Nutrient enrichment	7
Barriers to fish movement	10
Instream fish cover	3

Pools	3
Invertebrate habitat	7

Score only if applicable

Canopy cover	3
Manure presence	1
Salinity	
Riffle embeddedness	5
Marcroinvertebrates Observed (optional)	10

Overall score (Total divided by number scored)		<6.0	Poor
		6.1-7.4	Fair
76/14	5.4	7.5-8.9	Good
		>9.0	Excellent

Figure 13.B.1 USDA Stream Visual Assessment

TABLE 13.B.1   **Factors and Scoring Descriptions for Visual Stream Assessment (USDA, NRCS, 1999)**

Channel Condition

Natural channel; no structures, dikes. No evidence of downcutting or excessive lateral cutting.	Evidence of past channel alteration, but with significant recovery of channel and banks. Any dikes or levies are set back to provide access to an adequate floodplain.	Altered channel; <50% of the reach with riprap and/or channelization. Excess aggradation; braided channel. Dikes or levees restrict floodplain width.	Channel is actively downcutting or widening. >50% of the reach with riprap or channelization. Dikes or levees prevent access to the floodplain.
10	7	3	1

Hydrologic Alteration

Flooding every 1.5 to 2 years. No dams, no water withdrawals, no dikes or other structures limiting the stream's access to the floodplain. Channel is not incised.	Flooding occurs only once every 3 to 5 years; limited channel incision. or Withdrawals, although present, do not affect available habitat for biota.	Flooding occurs only once every 6 to 10 years; channel deeply incised. or Withdrawals significantly affect available low flow habitat for biota.	No flooding; channel deeply incised or structures prevent access to flood plain or dam operations prevent flood flows. or Withdrawals have caused severe loss of low flow habitat. or Flooding occurs on a 1-year rain event or less.
10	7	3	1

Riparian Zone

Natural vegetation extends at least two active channel widths on each side.	Natural vegetation extends one active channel width on each side. or If less than one width, covers entire flood plain.	Natural vegetation extends half of the active channel width on each side.	Natural vegetation extends a third of the active channel width on each side. or Filtering function moderately compromised.	Natural vegetation less than a third of the active channel width on each side. or Lack of regeneration. or Filtering function severely compromised.
10	8	5	3	1

Bank Stability

Banks are stable; banks are low (at elevation of active floodplain); 33% or more of eroding surface area of banks in outside bends is protected by roots that extend to the baseflow elevation.	Moderately stable; banks are low (at elevation of active floodplain); less than 33% of eroding surface area of banks in outside bends is protected by roots that extend to the baseflow elevation.	Moderately unstable; banks may be low, but typically are high (flooding occurs 1 year out of 5 or less frequently); outside bends are actively eroding (overhanging vegetation at top of bank, some mature trees falling into steam annually, some slope failures apparent).	Unstable; banks may be low, but typically are high; some straight reaches and inside edges of bends are actively eroding as well as outside bends (overhanging vegetation at top of bare bank, numerous mature trees falling into stream annually, numerous slope failures apparent).
10	7	3	1

TABLE 13.B.1 (*Continued*)   **Factors and Scoring Descriptions for Visual Stream Assessment**
(**USDA, NRCS, 1999**)

Water Appearance

Very clear, or clear but tea-colored; objects visible at depth 3 to 6 ft (less if slightly colored); no oil sheen on surface; no noticeable film on submerged objects or rocks.	Occasionally cloudy, especially after storm event, but clears rapidly; objects visible at depth 1.5 to 3 ft; may have slightly green color; no oil sheen on water surface.	Considerable cloudiness most of the time; objects visible to depth 0.5 to 1.5 ft; slow sections may appear pea green; bottom rocks or submerged objects covered with heavy green or olive-green film. or Moderate odor of ammonia or rotten eggs.	Very turbid or muddy appearance most of the time; objects visible to depth <0.5 ft; slow-moving water may be bright green; other obvious water pollutants; floating algal mats, surface scum, sheen or Heavy coat of foam on surface. or Strong odor of chemicals, oil, sewage, other pollutants.
10	7	3	1

Nutrient Enrichment

Clear water along entire reach; diverse aquatic plant community includes low quantities of many species of macrophytes; little algal growth present.	Fairly clear or slightly greenish water along entire reach; moderate algal growth on stream substrates.	Greenish water along entire reach; overabundance of lush green macrophytes; abundant algal growth, especially during warmer months.	Pea-green, gray, or brown water along entire reach; dense stands of macrophytes clog stream; severe algal blooms create thick algal mats in stream.
10	7	3	1

Instream Fish Cover

>7 cover types available	6 to 7 cover types available	4 to 5 cover types available	2 to 3 cover types available	None to 1 cover type available
10	8	5	3	1

Cover types: Logs/large woody debris, deep pools, overhanging vegetation, boulders/cobble, riffles, undercut banks, thick root mats, dense macrophyte beds, isolated/backwater pools, other: _____.

Barriers to Fish Movement

No barriers	Seasonal water withdrawals inhibit movement within the reach.	Drop structures, culverts, dams, or diversions (<1 foot drop) within the reach.	Drop structures, culverts, dams, or diversions (>1 foot drop) within 3 miles of the reach.	Drop structures, culverts, dams, or diversions (>1 foot drop) within the reach.
8	5		3	1

Pools

Deep and shallow pools abundant; greater than 30% of the pool bottom is obscure due to depth, or the pools are at least 5 feet deep.	Pools present, but not abundant; from 10 to 30% of the pool bottom is obscure due to depth, or the pools are at least 3 feet deep.	Pools present, but shallow; from 5 to 10% of the pool bottom is obscure due to depth, or the pools are less than 3 feet deep.	Pools absent, or the entire bottom is discernible.
10	7	3	1

TABLE 13.B.1 (*Continued*) **Factors and Scoring Descriptions for Visual Stream Assessment (USDA, NRCS, 1999)**

Insect/Invertebrate Habitat

At least 5 types of habitat available. Habitat is at a stage to allow full insect colonization (woody debris and logs not freshly fallen).	Three to 4 types of habitat. Some potential habitat exists, such as overhanging trees, which will provide habitat, but have not yet entered the stream.	One to 2 types of habitat. The substrate is often disturbed, covered, or removed by high stream velocities and scour or by sediment deposition.	None to 1 type of habitat.
10	7	3	1

Cover types: Fine woody debris, submerged logs, leaf packs, undercut banks, cobble, boulders, coarse gravel, other: _____

Macroinvertebrates Observed

Community dominated by Group I or intolerant species with good species diversity. Examples include caddisflies, mayflies, stoneflies, hellgrammites.	Community dominated by Group II or facultative species, such as damselflies, dragonflies, aquatic sowbugs, blackflies, crayfish.	Community dominated by Group III or tolerant species, such as midges, craneflies, horseflies, leeches, aquatic earthworms, tubificid worms.	Very reduced number of species or near absence of all macroinvertebrates.
15	6	2	−3

Coldwater Fishery Canopy Cover (if applicable)

>75% of water surface shaded and upstream 2 to 3 miles generally well shaded.	>50% shaded in reach. or >75% in reach, but upstream 2 to 3 miles poorly shaded.	20 to 50% shaded.	<20% of water surface in reach shaded.
10	7	3	1

Warmwater Fishery Canopy Cover (if applicable)

25 to 90% of water surface shaded; mixture of conditions.	>90% shaded; full canopy; same shading condition throughout the reach.	(intentionally blank)	<25% water surface shaded in reach.
10	7		1

Appendix 13.C

Streamside Biosurvey

The streamside biosurvey assesses stream macroinvertabrates or nonfish species. The presence, absence, and abundance of both sensitive and tolerant species serve as a useful indicator of stream health and water quality. Biosurvey methods have been used by water quality agencies and volunteer monitoring programs for two decades. The Izaak Walton League of America institutionalized the method in its Save Our Streams (SOS) program and variations have been used throughout the United States. Several thousand monitoring groups now assess streams, and the results have proven to be so reliable that state and federal agencies now accept them in their water quality databases. The protocol discussed below is drawn from EPA's *Volunteer Stream Monitoring: A Methods Manual* (1997). The method gathers, sorts, and counts macroinvertebrates present in a sampling reach and computes a stream health indicator based on the abundance and distribution of species.

To do a Streamside Biosurvey, you need the necessary tools and equipment. This includes a "kick net" with a #30 or #35 mesh for sampling substrates, a "D-frame net" for gathering samples under logs, a bucket, and waders or creek shoes. Recording forms are useful for entering data and calculating index scores. In planning a survey, you must determine the stream habitats present (e.g., substrates, snags and logs, vegetated beds and banks), select sampling sites (figure 13.C1), and determine the number of jabs or samples to take from each site (with a goal of 20 total). Using the kick-net and D-frame net methods shown in figure 13.C2, you collect macroinvertebrate organisms. The collected organisms are sorted, identified, counted, and released.

You group the macroinvertebrates into three categories based on pollution tolerance and sensitivity. The three categories are given in box 13.C. Group I (sensitive organisms) includes pollution-sensitive organisms, like mayflies and stone-

Figure 13.C.1 Stream Riffles Shown at the Top and Bottom of This Photo Are Good Sample Points for Benthic Macroinvertebrates. *Source:* U.S. EPA, 1999.

Figure 13.C.2 Kicknet (left) and Dipnet or D-Frame Net (right) Techniques for Gathering Benthic Organisms. *Source:* U.S. EPA, 1999.

BOX 13.C—Stream Macroinvertebrates Used in Biosurveys

Group I Taxa

Pollution-sensitive organisms found in good-quality water.

1. **Stonefly: Order Plecoptera.** 1/2" to 1 1/2", 6 legs with hooked tips, antennae, 2 hairline tails. Smooth (no gills) on lower half of body.

2. **Caddisfly: Order Trichoptera.** Up to 1", 6 hooked legs on upper third of body, 2 hooks at back end. May be in a stick, rock, or leaf case with its head sticking out. May have fluffy gill tufts on underside.

3. **Water Penny: Order Coleoptera.** 1/4", flat saucer-shaped body, 6 tiny legs and fluffy gills on the other side. Immature beetle.

4. **Riffle Beetle: Order Coleoptera.** 1/4", oval body with tiny hairs, 6 legs, antennae. Walks slowly underwater. Does not swim on surface.

5. **Mayfly: Order Ephemeroptera.** 1/4" to 1", brown, moving, platelike or feathery gills on the sides of lower body, 6 large

hooked legs, antennae, 2 or 3 long hairlike tails. Tails may be webbed together.

6. **Gilled Snail: Class Gastropoda.** Shell opening covered by thin plate called operculum. As opening faces you, shell usually opens on right.

7. **Dobsonfly (Hellgrammite): Family Corydalidae.** 3/4" to 4", dark-colored, 6 legs, large pinching jaws, 8 pairs feelers on lower half of body with paired cottonlike gill tufts along underside, short antennae, 2 tails, and 2 pairs of hooks at back end.

Group II Taxa

Somewhat pollution-tolerant organisms can be in good-/fair-quality water.

8. **Crayfish: Order Decapoda.** Up to 6", 2 large claws, 8 legs, resembles small lobster.

9. **Sowbug: Order Isopoda.** 1/4" to 3/4", gray oblong body wider than it is high, more than 6 legs, long antennae.

10. **Scud: Order Amphipoda.** 1/4", white to gray, body higher than it is wide, swims

Continued ➤

BOX 13.C—(continued)

sideways, more than 6 legs, resembles small shrimp.

11 **Alderfly Larva: Family Sialedae.** 1" long. Looks like small Hellgramite but long, branched tail at back end (no hooks).

12 **Fishfly Larva: Family Cordalidae.** Up to 1 1/2" long. Looks like small hellgramite but often a lighter reddish-tan color, or with yellowish streaks. No gill tufts underneath.

13 **Damselfly: Suborder Zygoptera.** 1/2" to 1", large eyes, 6 thin hooked legs, 3 broad oar-shaped tails, positioned like a tripod. Smooth (no gills) on sides of lower half of body. (See arrow.)

14 **Watersnipe Fly Larva: Family Athericidae (Atherix).** 1/4" to 1", pale green, tapered body, caterpillarlike legs, conical head, feathery "horns" at back.

15 **Crane Fly: Suborder Nematocera.** 1/3" to 2", milky, green, or light brown, plump caterpillar-like body, 4 fingerlike lobes at back end.

16 **Beetle Larva: Order Coleoptera.** 1/4" to 1", light-colored, 6 legs on upper half of body, feelers, antennae.

17 **Dragonfly: Suborder Anisoptera.** 1/2" to 2", large eyes, 6 hooked legs. Wide oval to round abdomen.

18 **Clam: Class Bivalvia.**

Group III Taxa

Pollution-tolerant organisms can be in any quality of water.

19 **Aquatic Worm: Class Oligochaeta.** 1/4" to 2", can be very tiny, thin wormlike body.

20 **Midge Fly Larva: Suborder Nematocera.** Up to 1/4", dark head, wormlike segmented body, 2 tiny legs on each side.

21 **Blackfly Larva: Family Simulidae.** Up to 1/4", one end of body wider. Black head, suction pad on other end.

22 **Leech: Order Hirudinea.** 1/4" to 2", brown, slimy body, ends with suction pads.

23 **Pouch Snail and Pond Snails: Class Gastropoda.** No operculum. Breathe air. When opening is facing you, shell usually open to left.

24 **Other Snails: Class Gastropoda.** No operculum. Breathe air. Snail shell coils in one plane.

Source: Izaak Walton League (1994), USDA, NRCS (1998).

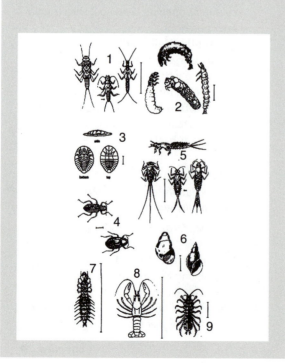

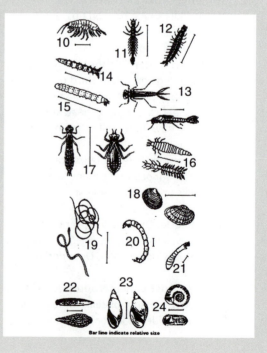

Bar line indicate relative size

flies, typically found in good-quality water. Group II (somewhat sensitive organisms) includes somewhat pollution-tolerant organisms, such as crayfish, sowbugs, and clams, found in fair-quality water. Group III (tolerant organisms) includes pollution-tolerant organisms, like worms and leeches, found in poor-quality water.

You count the specimens found in each sensitivity category and determine whether they are rare (**R: 1–9 organisms** found in a sample), common (**C: 10–99 organisms**), or dominant (**D: 100 or more organisms**). You then add the numbers of Rs, Cs, and Ds in each category and multiply each by the appropriate weighting factor (table 13.C1a). You add the scores to a total score and compare it to the water quality rating scale (table 13.C1b).

TABLE 13.C.1a **Weighting Factors Used in Calculating Stream Water Quality Ratings**

| | Weighting Factor | | |
Abundance	Group I Sensitive	Group II Somewhat Sensitive	Group III Tolerant
Rare (R)	5.0	3.2	1.2
Common (C)	5.6	3.4	1.1
Dominant (D)	5.3	3.0	1.0

TABLE 13.C.1b **Tentative Rating Scale for Streams in Maryland**

Score	Rating
>40	Good
20–40	Fair
<20	Poor

TABLE 13.C.1c Macroinvertebrate Count

Identify the macroinvertebrates in your sample and assign them letter codes based on their abundance:
R (rare) = 1–9 organisms; C (common) = 10–99 organisms; and D (dominant) = 100 plus organisms.

Group I Sensitive	Group II Somewhat-Sensitive	Group III Tolerant
C (50) Water penny larvae	R (4) Beetle larvae	R (5) Aquatic worm
R (2) Hellgrammites	_____ Clams	_____ Blackfly larva
_____ Mayfly nymphs	_____ Crane fly larvae	_____ Leeches
_____ Gilled snails	R (6) Crayfish	_____ Midge larvae
_____ Riffle beetle adult	_____ Damselfly nymphs	C (50) Snails
C (25) Stonefly nymphs	D (100) Scuds	
_____ Non net-spinning caddisfly larvae	D (150) Sowbugs	
	R (8) Fishfly larvae	
	_____ Alderfly larvae	
	C (27) Net-spinning caddisfly larvae	

TABLE 13.C.1d Sample Calculations of Index Values for Volunteer Creek

Group I Sensitive	Group II Somewhat Sensitive	Group III Tolerant
1 (No. of R's) × 5.0 = 5.0	3 (No. of R's) × 3.2 = 9.6	1 (No. of R's) × 1.2 = 1.2
2 (No. of C's) × 5.6 = 11.2	1 (No. of C's) × 3.4 = 3.4	1 (No of C's) × 1.1 = 1.1
	2 (No. of D's) × 3.0 = 6.0	
Index Value for Group I = 16.2	Index Value for Group II = 19.20	Index Value for Group III = 2.3

Total Index = 16.2 + 19.2 + 2.3 = 37.7 (Fair)

Tables 13.C1c and 13.C1d illustrate the scoring system for a hypothetical site. Three species were found in Group I; two were common, and one was rare. Six species were found in Group II; three were rare, one common, and two dominant. Two species were in Group III, one rare and one common. The number of Rs, Cs, and Ds in each group are multiplied by the weights and summed to a total index of 37.7 or a fair rating.

Appendix 13.D

Procedure for Testing Channel Capacity

Obtain information from the stream walk survey that is necessary for computing channel capacity:

- Draw a typical profile of the channel bottom.
- Select central points along the channel at which measurements are made; sufficient points should be selected so that data will adequately describe the stream.
- Measure the shape and dimensions of the stream cross section at the control points and others as necessary to determine an average cross section.
- Describe the channel between control points including the material of the channel bed and banks, vegetation, meander, and obstructions to flow.

The information is used in the three-step procedure:

Step 1

- Determine the "required" peak flow (Q_r) the channel must carry from peak discharge calculations for a design storm (e.g., 2-year or 10-year storm).
- Determine the "permissible" velocity (V_p) for erodible channels. For man-made grass-lined channels V_p values are given in table 13.D.2; for natural channels, V_p should be determined for the most erodible section of the stream, that is, areas of exposed soil. Values for various earthen channels are given in table 13.D.1. These values may be increased by 50 percent where dense vegetation exists naturally or is applied; or the erosion potential can be nearly eliminated by applying riprap (rocks) to highly erodible sections.

Step 2

- Determine the channel velocity (V) using Manning's equation.

$$V = \frac{1.49 R^{2/3} S^{1/2}}{n} \qquad \textit{(Eq. 13–6)}$$

TABLE 13.D.1 **Permissible Velocities for Unlined Earthen Channels**

Soil Types	Permissible Velocity
Fine Sand (noncolloidal)	2.5 ft/sec
Sandy Loam (noncolloidal)	2.5 ft/sec
Silt Loam (noncolloidal)	2.5 ft/sec
Ordinary Firm Loam	3.5 ft/sec
Fine Gravel	5.0 ft/sec
Stiff Clay (very colloidal)	5.0 ft/sec
Graded, Loam to Cobbles (noncolloidal)	5.0 ft/sec
Graded, Silt to Cobbles (colloidal)	5.5 ft/sec
Alluvial Silts (noncolloidal)	3.5 ft/sec
Alluvial Silts (colloidal)	5.0 ft/sec
Coarse Gravel (noncolloidal)	6.0 ft/sec
Cobbles and Shingles	5.5 ft/sec
Shales and Hard Pans	6.0 ft/sec

TABLE 13.D.2 **Permissible Velocities for Grass-lined Channels**

Channel Slope	Lining	Permissible Velocity
0–5%	Bermudagrass	6 ft/sec
	Reed canarygrass	5 ft/sec
	Tall fescue	
	Kentucky bluegrass	
	Grass-legume mixture	4 ft/sec
	Red fescue	2.5 ft/sec
	Redtop	
	Sericea lespedeza	
	Annual lespedeza	
	Small grains	
	(temporary)	
5–10%	Bermudagrass	5 ft/sec
	Reed canarygrass	4 ft/sec
	Tall fescue	
	Kentucky bluegrass	
	Grass-legume mixture	3 ft/sec
Greater than 10%	Bermudagrass	4 ft/sec
	Reed canarygrass	3 ft/sec
	Tall fescue	
	Kentucky bluegrass	

This is the most complicated part of the procedure. First, the channel geometry must be approximated for natural channels. Given in figure 13.D1, the channel geometry will determine the cross-sectional area (A) and the hydraulic radius (R). The slope (S) of the channel comes from the channel profile.

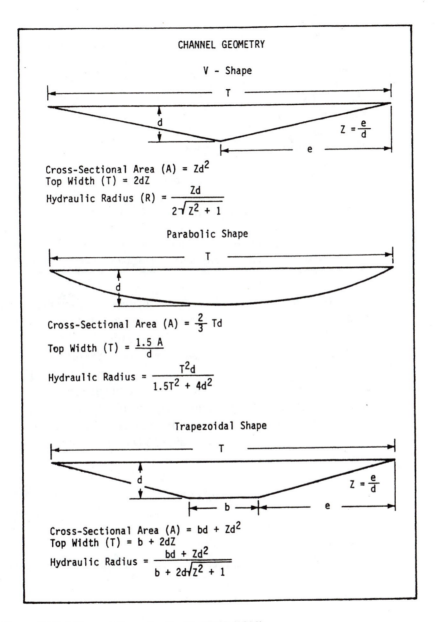

Figure 13.D.1 Channel Geometry. *Source:* VDCR (1992).

TABLE 13.D.3   Roughness Coefficients for Man-made (n) and Selected Natural Channels (n_b)

Boundary	Manning Roughness, n Coefficient
Smooth concrete	0.012
Ordinary concrete lining	0.013
Vitrified clay	0.015
Shot concrete, untroweled, and earth channels in best condition	0.017
Straight unlined earth canals in good condition	0.020
Rivers and earth canals in fair condition—some growth	0.025
Winding natural streams and canals in poor condition— considerable moss growth	0.035
Mountain streams with rocky beds and rivers with variable sections and some vegetation along banks	0.040–0.050

All that remains to solve Manning's equation is the roughness coefficient (n), which depends on the channel lining. For riprap linings, $n = 0.0395\,D$, where $D =$ the median stone size in feet in the riprap mixture.

For natural channels, several factors affect n. The procedure involves assuming a "basic n" for the channel bottom material (n_b) given in table 13.D3, then modifying the "basic n." Modifying factors include the irregularity of the channel surfaces (n_1); the variations in channel shape or size (n_2); obstructions in the channel (n_3); vegetation in the channel (n_4); and channel meandering (m). Values for these modifiers are also given in table 13.D4. The total roughness coefficient is given by:

$$n = (n_b + n_1 + n_2 + n_3 + n_4) \times (m)$$

Given the input values (R, S, and n) the channel velocity (V) can be determined by Manning's equation.

- Determine the channel capacity using the Continuity Equation:

$$Q = AV$$

Step 3

- Compare the channel capacity to the required capacity:

    if $Q < Q_r$, the channel capacity is inadequate

- Compare the channel velocity to the permissible velocity:

TABLE 13.D.4 **Roughness Coefficient _n_ Value Adjustments for Natural Channels**

	Channel Conditions	n Value Adjustment	Example
n^1 : Degree of irregularity	Smooth	0.000	Compares to the smoothest channel attainable in a given bed material.
	Minor	0.001–0.005	Compares to carefully dredged channels in good condition but having slightly eroded or scoured side slopes.
	Moderate	0.006–0.010	Compares to dredged channels having moderate to considerable bed roughness and moderately sloughed or eroded side slopes.
	Severe	0.011–0.020	Badly sloughed or scalloped banks of natural streams; badly eroded or sloughed sides of canals or drainage channels; unshaped, jagged, and irregular surfaces of channels in rock.
n^2 : Variation in channel cross section	Gradual	0.000	Size and shape of channel cross sections change gradually.
	Alternating occasionally	0.001–0.005	Large and small cross sections alternate occasionally, or the main flow occasionally shifts from side to side owing to changes in cross-sectional shape.
	Alternating frequently	0.010–0.015	Large and small cross sections alternate frequently, or the main flow frequently shifts from side to side owing to changes in cross-sectional shape.
n^3 : Effect of obstruction	Negligible	0.000–0.004	A few scattered obstructions, which include debris deposits, stumps, exposed roots, logs, piers, or isolated boulders, that occupy less than 5 percent of the cross-sectional area.
	Minor	0.005–0.015	Obstructions occupy less than 15 percent of the cross-sectional area and the spacing between obstructions is such that the sphere of influence around one obstruction does not extend to the sphere of influence around another obstruction. Smaller adjustments are used for curved smooth-surfaced objects than are used for sharp-edged angular objects.
	Appreciable	0.020–0.030	Obstructions occupy from 15 to 20 percent of the cross-sectional area or the space between obstructions is small enough to cause the effects of several obstructions to be additive, thereby blocking an equivalent part of a cross section.
	Severe	0.040–0.050	Obstructions occupy more than 50 percent of the cross-sectional area or the space between obstructions is small enough to cause turbulence across most of the cross section.
n^4 : Amount of vegetation	Small	0.002–0.010	Dense growths of flexible turf grass, such as Bermuda, or weeds growing where the average depth of flow is at least two times the height of the vegetation; supple tree seedlings such as willow, cottonwood, arrowweed, or saltcedar growing where the average depth of flow is at least three times the height of the vegetation.
	Medium	0.010–0.025	Turf grass growing where the average depth of flow is from one to two times the height of the vegetation; moderately dense stemmy grass, weeds, or tree seedlings growing where the average depth of the flow is from two to three times the height of the vegetation; brushy, moderately dense vegetation, similar to 1- to 2-year-old willow trees in the dormant season, growing along the banks and no significant vegetation along the channel bottoms where the hydraulic radius exceeds 2 feet.

TABLE 13.D.4 *(Continued)* **Roughness Coefficient *n* Value Adjustments for Natural Channels**

	Channel Conditions	n Value Adjustment	Example
	Large	0.025–0.050	Turf grass growing where the average depth of flow is about equal to the height of vegetation; 8- to 10-year-old willow or cottonwood trees intergrown with some weeds and brush (none of the vegetation in foliage) where the hydraulic radius exceeds 2 feet; bushy willows about 1 year old intergrown with some weeds along side slopes (all vegetation in full foliage) and no significant vegetation along channel bottoms where the hydraulic radius is greater than 2 feet.
	Very Large	0.050–0.100	Turf grass growing where the average depth of flow is less than half the height of the vegetation; bushy willow trees about 1 year old intergrown with weeds along side slopes (all vegetation in full foliage) or dense cattails growing along channel bottom; trees intergrown with weeds and brush (all vegetation in full foliage).
m : Degree of meandering	Minor	1.00	Ratio of the channel length to valley length is 1.0 to 1.2.
	Appreciable	1.15	Ratio of the channel length to valley length is 1.2 to 1.5.
	Severe	1.30	Ratio of the channel length to valley length is greater than 1.5.

(adjustment values apply to flow confined in the channel and do not apply where down-valley flow crosses meanders) (m)

BOX 13.D—Example of Procedure for Testing Channel Capacity

Given the following characteristics of a stream, test its capacity to carry a two-year peak flow of 400 cfs without overtopping or without excessive channel bank erosion.

- Cross section → trapezoidal: T = 25'; d = 4'; b = 9'; e = 8'.
- Stream profile slope → 0.015 feet per foot.
- Channel is earthen in fair condition.
- Channel banks are 1/3 shales, 1/3 fine gravel, and 1/3 firm loam.
- Channel size changes occur gradually, its surface has moderate irregularity, there are minor obstructions, and for each 20 feet of straight channel length there are 25 feet of meander length.
- Vegetative growth has a moderate influence on channel roughness.

if $V > V_p$, sections of the channel will be subject to excessive erosion

STEP 1 "Required" peak flow: $Q_r = 400$ cfs

"**Permissible**" velocity: $V_p = 3.5$ ft/sec (from table 13.D1 for the most erodible section, firm loam)

STEP 2 Determine channel velocity *V*:

a. *channel cross section:* $A = bd + zd^2$, $z = e/d = 8/4 = 2$

$A = (9)(4) + (2)(4)^2$

$= 36 + 32 = \textbf{68 ft}^2 = A$

b. **hydraulic radius:** $R = \dfrac{bd + 2d^2}{b + 2d(z^2+1)^{1/2}} = \dfrac{(9)(4) + 2(4)^2}{9 + (2)(4)(2^2+1)^{1/2}} = 2.53$

c. **roughness:**

$n = (n_b + n_1 + n_2 + n_3 + n_4) \times (m)$

n_b: earthen, fair condition	◊ 0.025	(from table 13.D3)
n_1: moderate irregularity	◊ 0.010	
n_2: gradual size changes	◊ 0.000	
n_3: minor obstructions	◊ 0.012	
n_4: vegetation	◊ 0.015	

m: *meander* $= 25/20 = 1.25$ ◊ 1.15

$n = (0.025 + 0.010 + 0.000 + 0.012 + 0.015)\,(1.15)$

$= (0.062)\,(1.15) = 0.070 = n$

Manning Equation: $V = \dfrac{1.49\,R^{2/3}\,S^{1/2}}{n} = \dfrac{1.49(2.53)^{2/3}(0.015)^{1/2}}{0.07} = \textbf{4.5 ft/sec} = V$

Channel Capacity $= Q = AV = (68)\,(4.5) = 306\ \text{cfs} = Q$

STEP 3

$Q\,(306) < Q_R\,(400)$ ◊ capacity inadequate

$V\,(4.5) > V_R\,(3.5)$ ◊ excessive erosion of firm loam banks

14 ▪ Stormwater Management and Stream Restoration

This chapter first discusses emerging approaches for comprehensive stormwater management, including means of integrating water quantity and quality and point and nonpoint source pollution. It then describes measures for the control and treatment of stormwater that also enhance infiltration and baseflows and reduce channel eroding flows. As we better control storm flows and improve baseflows, our natural channels can better handle the effects of development and impervious surfaces. The final section describes means of natural stream restoration.

Comprehensive Stormwater Management

Managing stormwater and the effects of land use has changed significantly in recent decades as we have broadened our objectives and improved mitigation measures. The following list ("Increasing Complexity and Effectiveness of Stormwater Management") describes the changing nature of stormwater management in the United States. Historically, managing stormwater meant building drainage works to get the water out more quickly so it would not accumulate and flood the land. These works include pipes, culverts, and widened and straightened channels with concrete or rock "armor," which destroyed natural channels. However, speeding up the drainage of water out of one area often meant that storm flows increased downstream, increased stormwater flows carried more pollution to waterways, and natural channels were being destroyed to accommodate higher flows.

Since the 1970s engineers and planners began to understand better the effects of impervious surfaces on storm flows, the pollution carried by stormwater, the public's desire to maintain natural drainage systems, the limitations of traditional engineering works, and the range of new measures available. As a result, stormwater management has become more complex and more comprehensive in addressing both storm flows and baseflows, water quality, flood damage mitigation, natural drainage, and stream restoration.

Control measures have evolved from centralized structures to distributed and on-site practices and from structural methods to natural and biological measures. Management used to focus on tax-supported public works but now emphasizes on-site development ordinances and stormwater impact fees. Stormwater management used to be the domain of the engineer; now the range of stakeholders also includes landowners, land use planners and designers, and citizen volunteers.

Increasing Complexity and Effectiveness of Stormwater Management

Before 1970

- **Objectives:** Provide adequate stormwater drainage from developed land; try to control flood flows.
- **Means:** Structural methods: Increase drainage capacity by guttering streets, using pipes and culverts underground, and enlarging and lining natural channels; "armor" natural channels with concrete and rocks to prevent channel erosion and loss of property; use stormwater detention as necessary.
- **Design methods:** Size capacities based on the Rational Method and other rudimentary techniques.
- **Financing and implementation:** Public works funded by tax dollars.

1970s to 1980s

- **Objectives:** Provide adequate drainage, manage new floodplain development, mitigate storm flows closer to the source, apply erosion and sediment controls and best management practices (BMPs) for runoff pollution.
- **Means:** Structural methods: Mitigate storm flows by on- and off-site detention; increase drainage capacity as necessary.
- **Design methods:** Analyze effects of land use change on stormwater quantity and quality and size capacities using sophisticated computer modeling techniques.
- **Financing and implementation:** Stormwater ordinances require developers bear costs in projects, stormwater fees, and tax dollars.

1990s to 2000s

- **Objectives:** Provide adequate drainage by on-site mitigation of stormwater flows; enhance infiltration to support baseflows and low flows; treat runoff; maintain nonerosive channel velocities; protect and restore natural drainage channels, provide passage of flood flows through floodplain management and building relocation.
- **Means:** More effective on-site and other decentralized runoff control and treatment; encouraging or mandating "low-impact" development designs and integrated stormwater control practices; infiltration; bioengineering to restore natural channels.

- **Design methods:** Use of both computer models and simpler sizing and design methods to estimate land use impacts and apply appropriate on-site measures.
- **Financing and implementation:** More effective prescriptive or performance-based stormwater ordinances; impact fees; citizen volunteers (stream monitoring and restoration).

Stormwater Management Programs and Ordinances

Stormwater management ordinances are designed to mitigate or offset stormwater impacts of development through regulations on land development and construction practices. They should address three concerns: flooding, stormwater quality, and channel erosion. The first stormwater ordinances focused on construction practices to control runoff, soil erosion, and sedimentation. As stormwater issues became more complex, ordinances were developed to require developers to achieve postconstruction criteria for runoff quantity, quality, channel capacity and erosive velocities, groundwater recharge, and natural channel improvement. Table 14.1 compares the on- and off-site effects of conventional stormwater management techniques to more innovative "low-impact development" (LID) practices. Specific practices are described in a later section.

Zero Impact and Low-Impact Development Programs

Most adopted stormwater ordinances require postconstruction runoff from all developed sites not to exceed predevelopment runoff for a design storm. The design storm varies among ordinances, but is generally a 1-, 10-, or 100-year 24-hour storm. Detention and infiltration measures can be used to mitigate expected flows to predevelopment levels and must be demonstrated by calculation, using methods like TR 55 or accepted computer models. Some ordinances require annual groundwater recharge rates be maintained after development by promoting infiltration using structural and nonstructural methods. Some of the more innovative stormwater ordinances and programs have been developed by the Center for Watershed Protection (CWP) (http://www.cwp.org). Many are posted at the Stormwater Manager's Resource Center that is run by CWP with a grant from the EPA. The virtual center is perhaps the single best source of stormwater management information (http://www.stormwatercenter.net/).

There are some excellent recent examples of stormwater management programs and ordinances. New York's (State of New York, 2001) statewide stormwater regulations and design manual and Virginia's (1999, 2001) stormwater handbook and model ordinance illustrate comprehensive approaches. Maryland's Prince George's County's (1999, 2002) **low-impact development** (LID) program is a good example of local government implementation.

LID measures can be implemented by regulation through a performance or prescriptive requirement in the stormwater ordinance, by incentive, or by education. Incentives can offer density bonuses, streamlined approval, or other financial benefits, if developers incorporate LID measures. Educational programs assist

TABLE 14.1 **Stormwater Management Effects of Conventional and "Low-Impact" Approaches**

Hydrologic Parameter	*Conventional*	*Low-Impact Development*
On-site		
Impervious cover	Encouraged to achieve effective drainage	Minimized to reduce impacts
Vegetation/natural cover	Reduced to improve efficient site drainage	Maximized to maintain predevelopment hydrology
Time of concentration	Shortened, reduced as a by-product of drainage efficiency	Maximized and increased to approximately predevelopment conditions
Runoff volume	Large increases in runoff volume not controlled	Controlled to predevelopment conditions
Peak discharge	Controlled to predevelopment design storm (2 year)	Controlled to predevelopment conditions for all storms
Runoff frequency	Greatly increased, especially for small, frequent storms	Controlled to predevelopment conditions for all storms
Runoff duration	Increased for all storms because volume is not controlled	Controlled to predevelopment conditions
Rainfall abstractions (Interception, infiltration, depression storage)	Large reduction in all elements	Maintained to predevelopment conditions
Groundwater recharge	Reduction in recharge	Maintained to predevelopment conditions
Off-site		
Water quality	Reduction in pollutant loadings but limited control for storm events that are less than design discharge	Improved pollutant loading reductions; full control for storm events that are less than design discharge
Receiving streams	Severe impacts documented—channel erosion and degradation; sediment deposition; reduced baseflow habitat suitability decreased, or eliminated	Stream ecology maintained to predevelopment
Downstream flooding	Peak discharge control reduces flooding immediately below control structure but can increase flooding downstream	Controlled to predevelopment conditions

Source: PGC-DEM, 1999

implementation by informing contractors and designers as well as their customers (potential home buyers) of LID benefits.

The LID approach used in Prince George's County, Maryland, employs the following five components (Prince George's County, 1999):

- LID *site planning* defines the development envelope, minimizes impervious areas and connectedness, and increases drainage pathways.
- LID *hydrologic analysis* delineates watershed and microwatershed boundaries, using modeling techniques like TR 55 to establish predevelopment baseline conditions and to evaluate site planning benefits and integrated management practices.
- LID *integrated management practices (IMPs)* are measures to control runoff. This step assesses hydrologic control needs and site constraints and screens, evaluates, and selects appropriate IMPs.
- LID *erosion and sediment control (E&SC)* to indicate how LID can provide E&SC compliance.
- LID *public outreach and education* to inform developers and consumers.

New York's program requires on-site measures to mitigate effects of development on water quality, natural channels, overbank flooding, and extreme flooding. Sizing criteria require on-site measures to be sized in order to

- hold and treat the **water quality volume** (WQ_v) or the runoff from about a one-inch rainfall. The exact WQ_v depends on the area of the catchment and the percent impervious cover;
- detain the **channel protection volume** (Cp_v) or the runoff from the postdevelopment 1-year 24-hour storm;
- control the **overbank flood** (Q_o) or the peak discharge from the 10-year storm to 10-year predevelopment rates; and
- control the **extreme flood** (Q_f) or the peak discharge from the 100-year storm to 100-year predevelopment rates.

A later section describes the measures and explains how they can achieve these criteria.

Stormwater Utilities and Development Impact Fees

Beyond stormwater regulations, communities can use incentives to stimulate use of effective measures. Several cities have established stormwater utilities to provide incentives as well as generate revenues for public stormwater management and stream preservation and restoration. Bellevue, Washington, developed one of the first stormwater utilities. Storm and surface water drainage service charges are based on the area of property and the percentage of impervious surface (roofs, plazas, parking lots, etc.) (http://www.ci.bellevue.wa.us/page.asp?view = 2156).

Often used in conjunction with stormwater regulations for new development, a stormwater utility can address both new and existing developments. Property owners are assessed a stormwater conveyance and treatment fee based on the unmitigated or hydraulically connected impervious surface of their site. Not only do the utilities generate revenues for improvements, but also the fee acts as an incentive for property owners to retrofit mitigation measures or reduce impervious surface.

Development impact fees are used to compensate local government for the cost of public services or other impacts resulting from new development. These can include stormwater impact fees, and some localities use this approach in lieu of establishing a formal stormwater utility.

Integrated Management of Nonpoint and Point Source Water Pollution

Under the Clean Water Act (CWA) of 1972, early attention by the EPA and the states focused on industrial and municipal sewage discharges. The EPA established national effluent standards for these discharges based on the best practicable technologies. These standards served as the basis for effluent permits issued by the states for those discharging into waters meeting the water quality standards. For waters not meeting the standards, so-called nonattainment or impaired waters, the states were to base permits on more stringent effluent limitations.

Managing Nonpoint Source Pollution

Despite considerable progress in cleaning up the nation's waterways, by 2000, 40 percent of the nation's waters still did not achieve the fishable and swimmable standards of the CWA. Runoff pollution is now the cause of most of our impaired waters. An estimated 60–70 percent of our remaining water pollution comes from these nonpoint sources (NPS). However, runoff pollution is far more difficult to manage than the point source pollution coming from discrete and accountable pipe discharges. NPS pollution requires more than just treatment technologies; it requires improvements in land use practices.

The CWA tried to address NPS pollution, first with section 208 wastewater treatment plans (which had to incorporate NPS after a mid-1970s court case), then with section 319 under the 1987 amendments. One of the few regulatory components of the 1987 amendments classifies large city stormwater discharges as sources requiring a National Pollution Discharge Elimination System (NPDES) discharge permit, basically treating them as point sources. Section 319 is essentially nonregulatory and aims to provide clearer direction and more funding to NPS programs by means of federal pass-through grants issued by the states to local NPS initiatives. It called on the states (with EPA approval) to (1) develop NPS assessment reports, (2) adopt NPS management programs, and (3) implement the management programs over a multiyear time frame. From FY1990 through FY1999, $877 million in grants were issued by the EPA for section 319 assistance. Funds available increased to $200 million in FY1999 (U.S. EPA, 2000a).

In 1990, Congress enacted the Coastal Zone Act Reauthorization Amendments (CZARA). Section 6217 created a new coastal NPS pollution control program to be incorporated into both state section 319 CWA programs (administered by the

EPA) and state Coastal Zone Management Act (CZMA) programs. It *requires* that states with federally approved coastal zone management programs (now 30 states) develop and implement coastal NPS pollution control programs. The programs must implement management measures published as EPA guidance (U.S. EPA, 1993) and additional measures as necessary to attain and maintain state water quality standards. These state programs must contain enforceable policies and mechanisms to ensure implementation (U.S. EPA, 2000a).

Other agencies and programs are also involved in runoff pollution problems. For agricultural runoff, the Natural Resources Conservation Service (NRCS) and related agencies in the Department of Agriculture, as well as state soil and water conservation agencies, provide funding and technical assistance to farmers to implement mostly voluntary runoff pollution controls.

Total Maximum Daily Load (TMDL)

The last several years have seen the resurrection of a mechanism for comprehensive management of pollutant discharges for nonattainment or impaired waters: the total maximum daily load, or TMDL, approach. The CWA set forth a national goal of achieving a level of quality in all waters to support recreation and fish consumption, so-called fishable and swimmable quality. It required states to establish water quality standards (WQS) for their water bodies, monitor compliance, and manage pollutant discharges to meet these standards. To assist in state permitting of point sources, the EPA established basic effluent limitation standards for each type of discharger (i.e., industry type, sewage treatment) based on the best practicable control technology.

For many impaired waters, these "technology standards" were not enough, and to meet WQS, states were to require more stringent permitted effluent limitations. The CWA stipulated that to determine the appropriate limitations, states were to calculate the TMDL of each violated pollutant that could be discharged into a water body and still attain the standard. That TMDL would then be allocated to various sources, including industrial and municipal dischargers, human-made nonpoint sources, and natural NPS. The allocated load to point dischargers would serve as the basis for their effluent permits. The allocated load to human-made NPS would serve as a basis for NPS treatment. For nonattainment waters, the TMDL is the basis for setting permits:

Total discharge allocations to regulated sources = TMDL – Natural NPS

In other words, the permitted allocations plus natural and unregulated sources must not exceed the TMDL.

Little attention was given to this approach until the early 1990s when many water quality advocacy groups, impatient over progress to achieve WQS, began suing their states and the EPA to implement the approach. TMDL lawsuits have been filed in 39 states. Advocates thought this approach was a means to improve NPS control, reduce water pollution, attain the WQS, and finally achieve the goals of the CWA. However, the approach is complex and difficult to implement.

The TMDL approach requires the following:

1. Determining the TMDL to achieve WQS—this often requires sophisticated monitoring data and modeling of discharges, receiving waters, and, for NPS, watersheds.
2. Allocating TMDL to sources—this requires factoring in equity and economic considerations.
3. Basing permits of regulated sources on TMDL allocations.
4. Managing unregulated sources to achieve TMDL allocations.

In July 2000, the EPA issued draft regulations for the states to implement the TMDL approach over 10 years. However, Congress's General Accounting Office (GAO) issued two critical reports, suggesting the lack of sufficient data for TMDLs and questioning the EPA's economic analysis. A National Academy of Sciences (NAS) 2001 report countered the GAO report by arguing that data and scientific methods are sufficient to implement the approach. It suggested that the program focus on attainment of WQS rather than administrative outcomes, encompass a range of water conditions including biological criteria and habitat restoration, combine monitoring and modeling, and employ "adaptive implementation" to reduce uncertainty and to assess progress. The report affirmed the need to move away from an effluent-based approach to an ambient water quality approach that is fundamental to TMDLs. In response, the EPA decided in late 2001 to delay implementation for one year to reconsider the NAS findings (NAS, 2001; Rogers and Hazlett, 2001; U.S. EPA, 2001).

In March 2003, the EPA withdrew the July 2000 TMDL rule, which was to go into effect April 30, 2003. The agency stated "significant changes would need to be made to the July 2000 rule before it could represent a workable framework for an efficient and effective TMDL program. Furthermore, EPA needs additional time beyond April 30, 2003, to decide whether and how to revise the currently-effective regulations implementing the TMDL program in a way that will best achieve the goals of the CWA. The withdrawal of the July 2000 rule will not impede ongoing implementation of the existing TMDL program" (U.S. EPA, 2003).

Stream Restoration

Urban streams have been assaulted for decades. Greater watershed impervious surfaces decrease baseflows and increase peak flows, flooding, runoff pollution, and channel erosion. As a result, many natural stream channels have been deepened or widened to increase their drainage capacity and "armored" with buried pipes, rocks, or concrete to reduce erosion. These degraded channels often become ugly backdrops to the urban scene, rather than the natural streams that once provided environmental, ecological, and aesthetic benefits to their communities. Degraded natural streams seemed to be an inevitable cost of urbanization.

However, new comprehensive efforts to manage stormwater have shown that measures can stabilize and reduce peak flows, runoff pollution, and channel erosion, arresting what appeared to be an irreversible trend in urban stream degradation. As a result, effective stormwater management has enhanced the viability and integrity of natural channels and reduced pressure for destructive stream modification. In many areas, these efforts have been complemented by stream restoration projects that aim to bring back to life degraded urban streams. Often conducted by volunteer groups, these projects have stabilized stream banks with "bioengineering" measures, replanted riparian vegetation, and restored stream gravels and fish habitat. In some urban areas, buried streams have been uncovered and restored to natural conditions and have become valuable components of urban greenways. These measures and projects are discussed further in the last section of this chapter.

Stormwater Management Measures

Stormwater management measures aim to reduce peak flows, control runoff pollution, and increase infiltration. These effects protect and enhance natural streams and riparian property by reducing flooding and channel erosion, increasing baseflows, and improving natural water quality. This section describes the wide array of measures, synthesizing numerous approaches labeled by others as runoff controls, best management practices (BMPs), stormwater treatment, and low-impact development integrated management practices (IMPs).

These measures can be grouped into three categories. First, **land use planning, design, and management** refer to several approaches to prevent excessive runoff and pollution in urban and agricultural land uses. They strive to conserve vegetation, minimize impervious cover, and prevent pollution. Examples in this category include grazing management, forest harvest and revegetation planning, cluster development, phased grading and development, and avoidance of erodible areas. Second, **pollutant source reduction** aims to reduce the application of or clean up potential contaminants before rainfall events convert them to runoff pollutants. Examples here include nutrient management plans, integrated pest management, urban street vacuuming, and litter control. Third, **stormwater control and treatment** includes practices to control runoff and remove pollutants, often before they leave the site and at least before they enter receiving waters. Examples are bioretention, ponds, wetlands, filtration, infiltration, and conveyance measures. Although prevention and source reduction are higher priority practices, they are often limited in their ability to achieve stormwater management objectives. Therefore, most attention is given to runoff control and treatment practices.

Land Use Design and Management

Better land use design and management can reduce the generation of runoff and pollution by preserving natural conditions, limiting the aerial extent of impervious surfaces, and preventing pollution. For example, plans for grazing management, forest harvest, and land development can address runoff problems by avoiding streams, wetlands, and other sensitive areas; retaining and maintaining buffers, filter strips, and other vegetation; and phasing activities over time and space. Fencing can partition pasture and grazing land to avoid overgrazing and allow

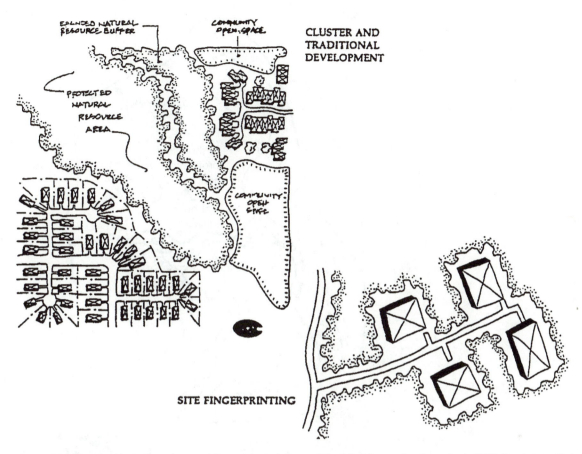

Figure 14.1 Site Planning, Clustering, and Fingerprinting. *Source: Watershed Restoration SourceBook*, 1992. Reprinted with permission of Metropolitan Washington Council of Governments, 777 North Capital St., NE, Ste. 300, Washington, D.C. 20002-4239, 202-962-3256.

grazed sections to recover, reducing runoff, erosion, and sedimentation. Fencing can also keep stock out of streams, arresting the "cows in creeks syndrome," one of the major sources of stream degradation in pasture farmland. In forestry plans, harvest sequence, access roads, proximity to streams and drainage, harvest methods, use of buffers, and timing of revegetation all affect runoff and pollution.

In land development, conservation design can reduce runoff and pollutants by retaining open spaces and natural vegetation areas, minimizing and "disconnecting" impervious surfaces, and preserving natural drainage. Disconnecting impervious areas from one another reduces the **effective impervious area** (EIA) or the impervious area that is directly connected to the storm drain system in a catchment or watershed.

Called "conservation and minimization" IMPs in low-impact development, these design measures include clustering development, site "fingerprinting" or clearing only the area needed and retaining site vegetation, using narrower streets and permeable pavements like grid pavers or porous asphalt, and retaining vegetation and buffers, among others. Figure 14.1 shows clustering and fingerprinting. Incorporating these measures into site design can be more effective than costly retrofits.

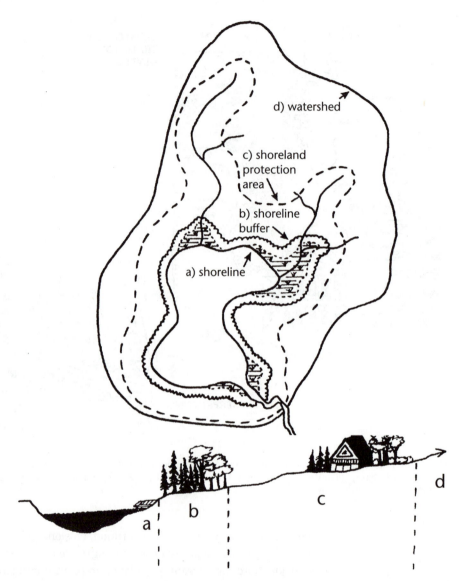

Figure 14.2 Four Zones of Lake Protection. *Source:* Karen Cappiella and Tom Schueler, 2001, "Crafting a Lake Protection Ordinance." Reprinted courtesy of the Center for Watershed Protection.

Lakeshore Protection

Land planning and design are the primary methods of runoff and pollution control for lake protection. There are four major zones to be considered in lake protection: the actual **shoreline,** a forested **shoreline buffer** extending landward, a **shoreland protection area** extending further, and a **watershed** zone used to control pollutant loadings to the lake. Figure 14.2 shows the boundaries of these zones on a hypothetical lake area.

TABLE 14.2 **Development Criteria for the Four Zones of a Lake Protection Ordinance**

Criteria	Shoreline	Shoreline Buffer	Shoreland Protection Area	Watershed
Defined as:	High water mark (HWM)	50 to 150 ft from HWM, 300 ft for source water	250 to 1000 feet from HWM	Divide of contributing watershed
Vegetation target for the zone	Maintain natural shoreline, no disturbance w/out permit	Forest or native veg., Max. view corridor 30′	Max. clearing limits on lots: 25 to 50%	Forested buffers to tributary streams
Allowable uses	Bioengineered 1 pier/ dock per frontage, 1 stairway	Walkways, boathouse within view corridor	Residential homes, septic systems	Most are allowed
Restricted uses	Boathouses and other accessory structures, riprap, bulkheads	No permanent structures, no impervious surface or land-disturbing activity	Commercial or industrial zones or uses with hazmat spill risk	Uses with hazmat spill risk
Septic systems	N/A	Not allowed	Setback 100–200 feet from HWM	Design/inspection criteria to reduce failure
Stormwater	No pipe outfalls to lake	No stormwater practices allowed	Achieved by environmentally sensitive design	Stormwater treatment practices to remove target phosphorous
Lot requirements	N/A	N/A	Minimum lot size, minimum frontage, maximum impervious cover, limit rooftop runoff	Open-space subdivisions and better site design to reduce impervious cover
Zoning	Establish requirements and density in a lake protection overlay district of a comprehensive plan			
Enforcement	Local or state permit	Local development review process		
Education	Lake association and/or resource agency			Watershed association

Source: Cappiella and Schueller (2001)

Cappiella and Schueler (2001) list the following primary considerations in lake protection. They demonstrate that lake areas, especially shorelines, are unique in terms of their ecology, intensity of use, property values, and management.

1. Shorelines are prime real estate that attract dense development oriented toward the lake.
2. Lake water quality requires reducing inputs of phosphorous, usually the limiting nutrient
3. Preserving the natural shoreline is critical for protection of aesthetic, ecological, and property values.
4. Shoreline vegetation is very important for fish and wildlife.
5. Intense pressures exist for shoreline modification and clearing to enhance views and install structures.
6. Water-based recreation is a primary use and management concern.
7. Septic systems are prominent and often cause serious water quality problems.

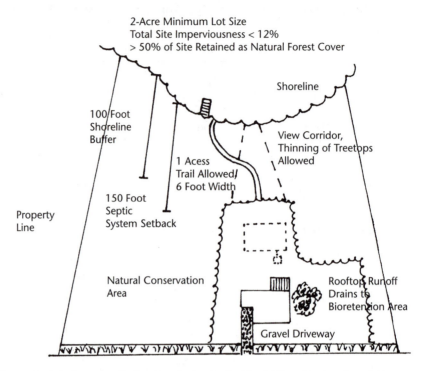

Figure 14.3 Environmentally Sensitive Design for Residential Shoreline Lot. *Source:* Karen Cappiella and Tom Schueler, 2001, "Crafting a Lake Protection Ordinance." Reprinted courtesy of the Center for Watershed Protection.

8. Lake associations can be effective for lake protection enforcement and education.
9. Lake ordinances must be customized for unique lake conditions and water quality goals.

Table 14.2 gives some model development criteria for use in a lake protection ordinance. The criteria vary with the four zones and include vegetation, allowable and restricted uses, septic systems and stormwater, lot requirements, zoning, enforcement, and education. Figure 14.3 incorporates several of these criteria in an environmentally sensitive design for a residential shoreline lot.

Pollutant Source Reduction

Removing pollutants at the source before runoff occurs prevents NPS pollution. Urban sources can be controlled by street vacuuming and litter control. Source controls also include education programs for homeowners, household hazardous waste collection, companion animal waste control ordinances, and community roadside and streamside cleanup programs.

In agricultural areas, source reduction is used to control excess application of fertilizers and pesticides that often end up as nutrient and toxic runoff pollution. Fertilizer application should be limited to the rate at which plants or crops can utilize them. **Nutrient management** plans specify fertilizer applications based on calculations of plant uptake. When fertilizer application is balanced by plant

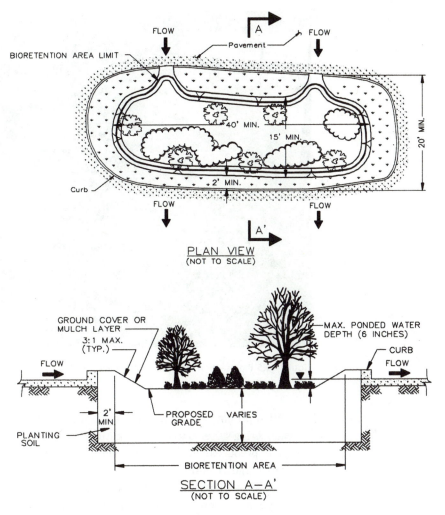

Figure 14.4 Bioretention Plan and Section View. *Source:* Commonwealth of Virginia (1999).

uptake, little residual remains to be carried away by runoff (see USDA, 1999). **Integrated pest management (IPM)** programs aim to reduce applications of potentially polluting pesticides by employing a variety of pest control measures, including biological controls (i.e., natural enemies and reproductive disruption), cultural methods (i.e., temporal and spatial adjustments to planting and harvesting cycles), and reduced amounts of pesticides that are selective to the species (USDA, 1999).

Stormwater Management Practices

Land planning and pollution source prevention are important first steps in controlling runoff and NPS pollution, but they are usually insufficient to achieve stormwater management objectives, especially in urban and urbanizing areas. Stormwater management practices (SMPs) aim to reduce runoff, increase infiltration, and provide settling, filtering, and biological treatment of the remaining runoff. Some of these measures are most effective on-site, providing detention and

Figure 14.5 Bioretention in Residential Application. *Source:* Commonwealth of Virginia (1999).

infiltration primarily through the site's landscape. Others are carefully designed bioengineering systems that mimic nature. The goal of all of these measures is to maintain predevelopment runoff volume, quality, and time of concentration (Prince George's County, 1999).

There are six categories of SMPs. Each is described and illustrated next, followed by a discussion of effectiveness and sizing criteria.

- **Bioretention:** a vegetated sink that detains and filters runoff, providing some infiltration
- **Stormwater ponds:** wet or dry ponds detain and store runoff for slow release
- **Constructed wetlands:** detains and biologically treats runoff
- **Filtration:** engineered sand filtration systems
- **Infiltration:** excavated trenches or drains that provide infiltration of runoff to subsurface flow
- **Conveyance and open channels:** moves runoff slowly from site or to pervious areas

Bioretention

In bioretention, landscaping features are usually located in parking lot islands or residential land depressions, which contain mulch, soil, and vegetation designed to provide natural pollutant removal mechanisms. After filtering through the

Figure 14.6 Bioretention "Green Alley" and Parking Lot. *Source:* Commonwealth of Virginia (1999).

mulch and soil bed, runoff is usually collected in a perforated underdrain and returned to the storm drain system. (See figures 14.4, 14.5, and 14.6.)

Bioretention channels: similar to a wet swale, it provides conveyance, filtration, and infiltration.

Bioretention benches: deposited soil bed, mulch, and vegetation as a bench on slopes to slow, store, and filter runoff.

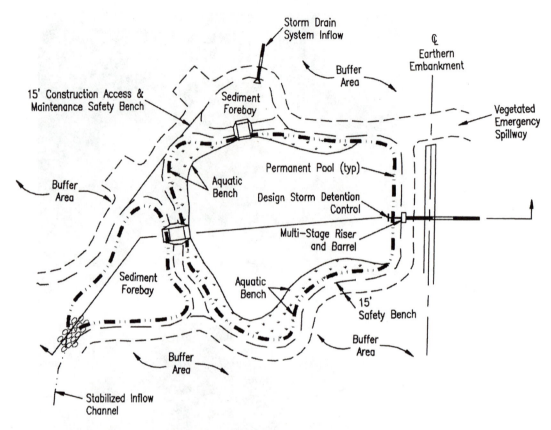

Figure 14.7 Wet Stormwater Retention Pond with Earthen Embankment. Schematic shows different pool heights for different storage levels. *Source:* State of New York (2001).

Stormwater Ponds

This category includes a combination of permanent pool, extended detention, or shallow marsh equivalent to WQ_V; ponds treat runoff by settling and algal uptake of nutrients. (See figures 14.7 and 14.8.)

Wet pond: provides all WQ_V in a permanent pool, cost-effective, widely used, limited in highly urbanized areas and arid climates; documented improvements in property value.

Wet extended detention pond: split between permanent pool and storage provided above the pool from which storm volume is released over 12 to 24 hours. Half the treatment volume in permanent pool. Consumes less space than wet pond.

Multiple pond system: water quality storage in two or more cells.

"Pocket" pond: drains smaller area than traditional pond. Permanent pool is maintained by intercepting groundwater.

Dry pond: detention pond without permanent pool drains completely; slows runoff but provides minimal treatment.

Other storage: parking lot storage, rooftop storage, cisterns, downspout barrels all provide storage but no treatment.

Figure 14.8 Dry Stormwater Detention Pond between Storms and During Storm. *Source:* Commonwealth of Virginia (1999).

Stormwater Wetlands

Stormwater wetlands are constructed wetlands similar to ponds that also incorporate wetland plants. Pollutants are removed by settling and biological uptake. Designed specifically for detaining and treating stormwater, these wetlands have less biodiversity than natural wetlands, but they are the most effective stormwater practices in terms of removal of pollutants and aesthetic value. (See figures 14.9 and 14.10.)

Figure 14.9 New Stormwater Wetland with First Signs of Wetland Vegetation. *Source:* Commonwealth of Virginia (1999).

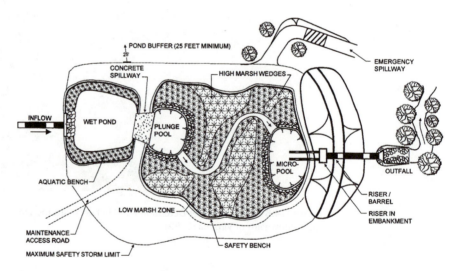

Figure 14.10 Stormwater Wetland Schematic. *Source:* State of New York (2001).

Shallow marsh: most of the storage and treatment volume is in shallow high and low marsh depths, although there is usually a forebay and micropool outlet. Because of limited depth, shallow marshes have a high surface-to-volume ratio and require more land area to achieve sufficient volume. Wildlife habitat potential.

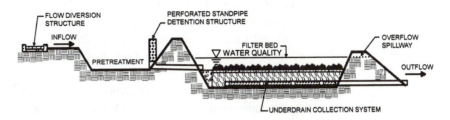

Figure 14.11 Sand Filter Schematic. *Source:* State of New York (2001).

Figure 14.12 Sand Filter Installation at the Perimeter of Parking Lot. Note pretreatment trough and curb-cuts for drainage from lot. *Source:* Commonwealth of Virginia (1999).

Extended detention (ED) wetland: like a shallow marsh, the ED wetland provides additional volume above the marsh, thus providing a lower surface-to-volume ratio. Plants must be selected that can tolerate longer periods of wet and dry conditions than shallow marsh vegetation.

Wetland-pond system: combines a wet pond with a shallow marsh, providing more storage volume.

"Pocket" wetland: like a pocket pond, the bottom intercepts groundwater to maintain a permanent pool. With a small storage volume, the pocket marsh is effective only for small drainage areas.

Filtering Measures

These measures provide maximum treatment using filtering media to remove pollutants. (See figures 14.11 and 14.12.)

Surface sand filter: this most widely used filtering system has above-ground sediment basin and filter chamber. It is usually employed offline to capture the water quality volume, although designed for only small water quality events. Treated runoff is collected for exfiltration or discharge.

Underground sand filter: all sediment chamber and filter components are underground. They are expensive, but consume little space, so are well suited for highly urbanized areas.

Perimeter underground filter: underground sediment chamber and filter designed on the perimeter of parking lot. Runoff flows from the parking lot into the chamber though perimeter grating drains (see figure 14.12).

Organic filter: a surface filter system with organic matter (e.g., peat, compost, charcoal) used instead of or mixed with sand to enhance filtering of nutrients or trace metals.

Filter strip: a grass or vegetated slope onto which a level spreader evenly distributes runoff to be filtered and treated by vegetation.

Infiltration Measures

Infiltration measures are designed to allow runoff to infiltrate to groundwater. They can reduce runoff and enhance baseflows, as well as provide treatment. However, to protect groundwater adequate treatment is essential for infiltration, and pretreatment is often required. (See figures 14.13 and 14.14.)

Infiltration trench: a rock-filled trench with no outlet designed to receive runoff that has passed through some pretreatment such as a swale or detention pond. Collected runoff is stored in the voids between stones and infiltrates through the bottom into the soil. Requires sufficient soil permeability and limited pollutant source.

Infiltration basin: a shallow impoundment with only a high elevation outlet, designed to infiltrate stormwater into the soil. Pretreatment is usually necessary. Although basins have a high pollutant removal capacity, they are highly dependent on soil permeability, and failure rates are relatively high.

Porous pavements: permeable pavement surface with underlying gravel or stone reservoir that temporarily stores runoff before being infiltrated into the ground. Permeable surfaces may be porous asphalt or pervious concrete, both of which appear like conventional paving but are manufactured without "fine" materials to incorporate voids for infiltration. The surfaces may also be so-called grass pavers made of precast, interlocking concrete blocks with open areas designed to allow grass to grow. Although they can be an effective infiltration and treatment practice, porous pavers require a high level of maintenance.

Dry wells: includes Dutch drains and deep sump wells that provide infiltration and groundwater recharge. Not effective for treatment and without pretreatment may be a potential source of groundwater contamination.

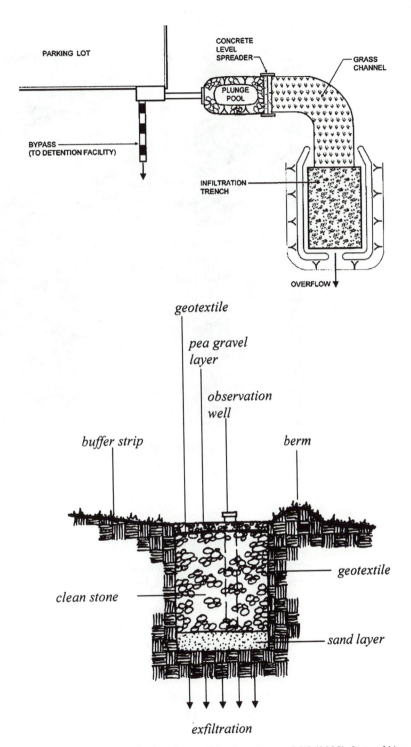

Figure 14.13 Infiltration Trench Plan View and Section. *Sources:* PGC (2002), State of New York (2001).

Figure 14.14 Newly Installed Parking Lot Infiltration Trench. *Source:* Commonwealth of Virginia (1999).

Conveyance and Open Channels

Swales, spreaders, and flow diverters move runoff slowly from site or to pervious areas. (See figures 14.15, 14.16, and 14.17.)

Dry swales: similar to bioretention. Existing soil is replaced by a fabricated soil/sand bed meeting permeability requirements. Runoff is filtered through the bed and discharged to the stormwater system through an underdrain (see figure 14.16).

Wet swales: behaves like a linear wetland cell, incorporating a shallow permanent pool and wetland vegetation. Ideal for highway runoff, wet swales are used less in residential/commercial areas because shallow standing water is often regarded as a nuisance. Check dams can enhance storage to achieve water quality volume (see figure 14.15).

Level spreaders: direct runoff to pervious areas for level discharge (see figure 14.17).

Diversion berms: divert runoff from impervious to pervious areas, disconnecting impervious areas.

Figure 14.15 Open Channel Swale and Check Dams. *Source:* Commonwealth of Virginia (1999).

Effectiveness of Urban Stormwater Management Practices

The effectiveness of urban SMPs depends on the functional goals of the application. As discussed earlier, stormwater management objectives include improving **stormwater quality,** controlling **stream channel erosion,** reducing **flooding,** and enhancing **groundwater recharge.** Practices can control flooding and channel erosion by slowing runoff and reducing peak storm flows. Practices that

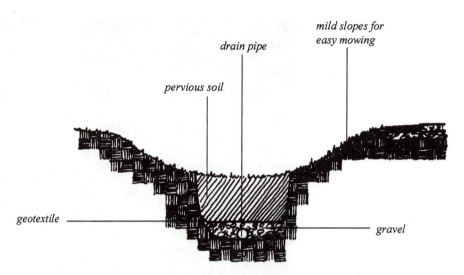

Figure 14.16 Section of Dry Swale. *Source:* PGC (2002).

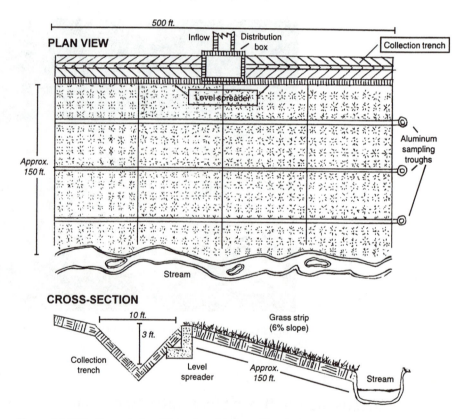

Figure 14.17 Yu Concrete Level Spreader with Grass Filter Strip. *Source:* CWP (1994).

increase infiltration will enhance groundwater recharge. Improving water quality through stormwater treatment is more difficult.

Table 14.3 compares stormwater control and treatment measures, based on data provided by several sources given in the table. Each measure is rated for its capability to remove pollutants, recharge groundwater through infiltration, reduce erosive velocities of runoff to protect natural channels, and reduce peak discharge to provide flood protection. In addition, the table gives pollutant removal values, drainage area limitations, and a rating of cost, maintenance, and acceptability.

As the table shows, bioretention practices provide good pollutant removal and infiltration for small drainage areas at reasonable cost and public acceptability. As a result, they are a primary measure for on-site low-impact development. Ponds and wetlands provide good detention volume and therefore reduce flooding and channel erosion. Wet ponds and wetlands also have good pollutant removal, but dry ponds do not. Because ponds and wetlands are effective for drainage areas greater than 25 acres, they are primary measures for large properties or concentrated flow. The TR 55 method for sizing detention volume to reduce peak discharge to predevelopment conditions is discussed in a later section.

Filtering and infiltration measures provide very good treatment, and infiltration also improves recharge, but these measures are more expensive and higher maintenance than other practices. Both wet and dry swales have good treatment capabilities.

If stormwater treatment is an important management objective, the Center for Watershed Protection (CWP) provides useful guidance for selection of measures. Effective measures can capture and treat the full water quality volume (WQ_v) and are capable of removal of 80 percent of total suspended solids (TSS) and 40 percent of total phosphorus. They should also have a pretreatment mechanism and an acceptable lifetime in the field (State of New York, 2001).

The WQ_v is the volume of storage needed to capture and treat 90 percent of the average annual stormwater pollutant load. For many years it was believed that this 90 percent objective could be achieved by capturing and treating the first half-inch of runoff in any storm as a result of the "first-flush" effect. This "half-inch" rule was adopted in many ordinances, but field studies showed that while it was effective in areas of 30 percent and less impervious cover, the half-inch runoff carried less than 90 percent at greater imperviousness. One study showed that at 50 percent impervious cover, the first half-inch carried 75 percent of TSS, and at 70 percent it carried only 53 percent (Chang, Parrish, and Souer, 1990). More recent design applications, like New York's (State of New York, 2001) *Stormwater Design Manual* prepared by CWP, do not use the "half-inch" rule, but base WQ_v on impervious surface (see later).

Stormwater ponds, wetlands, infiltration, bioretention, filtration, and swales can meet these treatment criteria if they are designed to store and treat the full WQ_v (table 14.4). As a result, these are the only measures recommended by the CWP. The Center does not recommend filter strips, dry wells, ditches, and grass channels that do not store the full volume. It also discourages use of oil/grit chambers and dry detention because of limited treatment capabilities, and porous pavements because of high maintenance and high failure rates (Center for Watershed Protection, 2000).

TABLE 14.3   **Comparison of Urban Stormwater Control and Treatment Practices**

SWC&T Practice	Capabilities				% Pollutant Reduction				Cost/ Acceptance		
	Pollutant Removal	Recharge	Chan Prot.	Flood Prot.	TSS	TP	TN	DA	Cost	Maint.	Accept.
Bioretention	G	G	L	L	NA	65	49	<2	2½	2	2
Ponds											
Dry	L	L	G	G	7	19	5	—	—	—	—
Wet	G	L	G	G	79	49	32	>25	2	1½	1½
Wet ED	G	L	G	G	80	55	35	>25	2	2	2
Multiple	G	L	G	G	91	76	NA	>25	3	2	1½
Pocket pond	G	L	G	G	87	78	28	<5	1½	4	3
Wetlands											
Shallow	G	L	G	G	83	43	26	>25	3	3½	2
ED wetland	G	L	G	G	69	39	55	>25	3	3	2½
Pond/wetland	G	L	G	G	71	56	19	>25	3	2	1½
Pocket marsh	G	L	L	M	57	57	44	<5	2	4	3
Filtering											
Surface sand	G	G	M	L	87	59	32	<10	4	3½	2½
UG sand	G	L	L	L	80	50	35	<2	4.5	4	1
Perimeter sand	G	L	L	L	79	41	47	<2	4	3½	1
Organic	G	L	L	L	88	61	41	<10	4	3½	2½
Infiltration											
Trench	G	G	M	M	100	42	42	<5	3½	5	2
Basin	G	G	M	M	90	65	50	<10	3	5	4
Porous pavement	G	G	M	M	95	65	83	<5	3	5	1
Open channels											
Dry swale	G	G	L	L	93	83	92	<5	2½	2	1½
Wet swale	G	L	L	L	74	28	40	<5	2	2	1½
Grass channel	L	L	L	L	81	34	31	—	—	—	—

Sources: CWP, WPTN #64; New York, 2001; Schueler, 2000; Winer, 2000; PGC-ERM, 2002.

Pollutant Removal . . . Pollutant removal capability
Recharge . . . Groundwater recharge capability
Chan Protection . . . Channel protection capability
Flood Protection . . . Overbank flood protection
TSS . . . Total suspended solids removal
TP . . . Total phosphorous
TN . . . Total nitrogen
DA . . . Max. drainage area, acres
Cost . . . Initial cost, 1 = low, 5 = high
Maint . . . Maintenance, 1 = low, 5 = high
Accept . . . Community acceptance, 1 = high, 5 = low
Ratings, depending on design:
  G = Good
  M = Marginal
  L = Little or none

TABLE 14.4 **Pollutant Removal Capabilities (%) of Stormwater Treatment Practices**

Practice	n	TSS	TP	TN	Carbon	Bacteria	HC	Metals
Stormwater ponds[a]	44	80	51	33	43	70	81	50–74
Stormwater wetlands	39	76	49	30	18	78	85	40–69
Infiltration	6	95	70	51	54	ND	ND	98–99
Filters[b]	19	86	59	38	54	37	84	49–88
Swales[c]	9	81	34	84	69	(−25)	62	42–71
Ditches	11	31	(−16)	(−9)	18	5	ND	0–38

Sources: Schueller (2000), Brown and Schueller (1997), Winer (2000).

Values are median percentage removal before and after treatment practice.
n = number of performance studies
TSS = total suspended solids
TP = total phosphorus
TN = total nitrogen
Carbon = organic carbon (BOD, COD or TOC)
Bacteria = mean removal rates of fecal coliform bacteria
HC = total petroleum hydrocarbons
Metals = range for cadmium, copper, lead and zinc
ND = not determined
[a]Includes wet ponds and excludes conventional dry detention ponds.
[b]Includes a variety of sand filters and bioretention and excludes vertical sand filters and vegetated filter strips.
[c]Includes biofilters, wet swales and dry swales.

Selection and Sizing Considerations for Urban Stormwater Management Practices

Selection and sizing of SMPs depend on various factors, including management objectives and applications. The CWP has developed a number of useful guidelines for use in manuals and regulations in New York and Virginia (State of New York, 2001; Commonwealth of Virginia, 1999). Table 14.5 gives a selection matrix for choosing the appropriate SMP for different land uses. "Hotspots" are areas of potentially high pollution, like industrial areas, and "ultraurban" refers to areas where space is limited and original soils have been disturbed. The "N" and "?" ratings are based on ability to achieve needed water quality volume, land area needed, and cost/maintenance compared with other options.

Low-impact development (LID) emphasizes on-site bioretention, grass swales, and infiltration. On-site LID measures are normally more cost-effective and lower in maintenance than applications after flow is concentrated. However, LID does not preclude the need for concentrated flow measures, and all sites may not be suitable for LID, depending on soil permeability, depth to water, and slope. LID maintenance includes such measures as mowing grass swales, remulching and revegetating bioretention areas, and vacuuming permeable pavements. Because most LID measures are located on private property, maintenance requires a commitment by property owners or action by homeowners' associations (Prince George's County, 1999, 2002; U.S. EPA, 2000).

TABLE 14.5   **Stormwater Management Practice Selection Matrix for Various Land Uses**

SMP Group	SMP Design	Rural	Residential	Roads and Highways	Commercial High Density	Hotspots	Ultra Urban
Bioretention	Bioretention	?	?	Y	Y	A2	Y
Pond	Micropool ED	Y	Y	Y	?	A1	N
	Wet pond	Y	Y	Y	?	A1	N
	Wet ED pond	Y	Y	Y	?	A1	N
	Multiple pond	Y	Y	?	?	A1	N
	Pocket pond	Y	?	Y	?	N	N
Wetland	Shallow wetland	Y	Y	?	?	A1	N
	ED wetland	Y	Y	?	?	A1	N
	Pond/wetland	Y	Y	N	?	A1	N
	Pocket wetland	Y	?	Y	?	N	N
Infiltration	Infiltration trench	?	?	Y	Y	N	?
	Shallow I-basin	?	?	?	?	N	?
	Dry well[1]	?	Y	N	?	N	?
Filters	Surface sand filter	N	?	Y	Y	A2	Y
	Underground SF	N	N	?	Y	Y	Y
	Perimeter SF	N	N	?	Y	Y	Y
	Organic SF	N	?	Y	Y	A2	Y
Open channels	Dry swale	Y	?	Y	?	A2	?
	Wet swale	Y	N	Y	N	N	N

Source: CWP, New York, 2001.
Y = Yes. Good option in most cases.
? = Depends. Suitable under certain conditions, or may be used to treat a portion of the site.
N = No. Seldom or never suitable.
A1 = Acceptable option, but may require a pond liner to reduce risk of groundwater contamination.
A2 = Acceptable option, if not designed as an exfilter.
[1]The dry well can only be used to treat rooftop runoff.

Stormwater treatment needs and objectives also affect the type and size of SMPs. These measures use settling of solids, filtering, and biological processes to treat stormwater. Table 14.6 shows that these treatment measures have varying capabilities for critical pollutants like phosphorus. The table provides a guide for selecting measures of different sizes for higher pollutant removal needs associated with higher impervious surfaces.

Table 14.7 describes the sizing criteria for stormwater management practices developed by CWP for New York State. Individual or a combination of measures are sized to meet design volumes for water quality treatment (WQ_v), channel erosion protection (Cp_v), peak discharge reduction to reduce overbank flooding (Q_o) and extreme flooding (Q_f). The formulas for WQ_v are given in the table. Cp_v is the runoff volume from the 1-year 24-hour storm as determined by TR 55. The volumes for peak discharge mitigation for the 10- and 100-year storm are determined by TR 55 detention calculations given in the next section.

TABLE 14.6   **Processes of Stormwater Treatment and Guide for Phosphorus Removal**

Stormwater Treatment Practice	Settling	Filtering	Biological Processes	Phosphorus Removal (%)	Percent Impervious (%)
Vegetated filter strip		X		10	16–21
Grassed swale (w/check dams)	X	X		15	16–21
Constructed wetlands	X	X	X	30	22–37
Extended detention ($2 \times WQ_v$)	X			35	22–37
Retention basin ($3 \times WQ_v$)				40	22–37
Bioretention basin/filter		X	X	50	38–66
Retention basin ($4 \times WQ_v$)	X		X	50	38–66
Infiltration ($1 \times WQ_v$)		X		50	38–66
Retention ($4 \times WQ_v$ + aquatic bench)	X		X	65	66–100
Sand filter		X		65	66–100
Infiltration ($2 \times WQ_v$)		X		65	66–100

Source: CWP, New York, 2001.

TABLE 14.7   **Stormwater Management Practice Sizing Criteria for New York State (2001)**

WQ_v Water Quality Volume	**90% Rule:** $WQ_v = [(P)(R_v)(A)]/12$ in acre-feet. $R_v = 0.05 + 0.009(I)$ I = Impervious Cover (Percent) Minimum $R_v = 0.2$ P = 90% Rainfall event number (about 1 inch, may vary with location) A = site area in acres
Cp_v Channel Protection Volume	**Default Criterion:** Cp_v = 24-hour extended detention of postdeveloped 1-year, 24-hour storm event **Option for Sites Larger Than 50 Acres:** Distributed runoff control—geomorphic assessment to determine the bankfull channel characteristics and thresholds for channel stability and bedload movement.
Q_o Overbank Flood	Control the peak discharge from the 10-year storm to 10-year predevelopment rates.
Q_f Extreme Storm	Control the peak discharge from the 100-year storm to 100-year predevelopment rates Safely pass the 100-year storm event

Example: Size SMP for a 5-acre development site converted from meadow to a 30 percent average impervious surface development. Assume P = 1 inch. Selection: retention basin (wet pond).

WQ_v: $R_v = 0.05 + 0.009(30) = 0.32$
      $WQ_v = (1)(0.32)(5)/12 = 0.133$ acre-feet

Cp_v: Find runoff volume and velocity for 1-year, 24-hour storm for postdevelopment site and compare to bankfull capacity and permissible velocity using methods in chapter 13.

Q_o, Q_f: Find storage volume needed to reduce postdevelopment peak to predevelopment peak for both 10-year and 100-year storms using TR 55 storage volume method (see next section).

     Size wet pond to assure WQ_v storage plus extended volume to meet Cp_v and storage needed for Q_o and Q_f.

Sizing Detention Ponds Using TR 55

A number of techniques are available to size detention ponds to reduce peak water flows. Flood or flow routing techniques determine the effect of stream or pond storage on stream flow. They are based primarily on the **Continuity Equation:**

$$q = AV$$

where q = channel flow (cfs)
         A = channel cross sectional area (ft²)
         V = average channel velocity (ft/sec)

and its derivative, the **Storage Equation:**

$$q_i - q_o = dV_s/dt$$
$$q_i dt - q_o dt = dV_s$$
$$V_s = \int q_i dt - \int q_o dt$$

where t = time (s)
         q_i = inflow into the stream reach or storage device (cfs)
         q_o = outflow from the stream reach or storage device (cfs)
         V_s = the volume storage in the stream reach or storage device (ft³)

     The integrals indicate the areas under the inflow and outflow hydrographs during the early stages of a storm's drainage. A storage volume equal to the difference between the two areas will essentially convert the inflow hydrograph coming into the detention pond to the outflow hydrograph going out. Figure 14.18 shows this graphically. Shown is the change in the hydrograph after suburban development in the watershed: a shorter lag time and a higher peak. The difference between the hydrographs before the outflow peak (areas A + B) is the detention storage volume required to reduce the high peak hydrograph (i.e., inflow) to the low peak hydrograph (i.e., outflow), thus offsetting the runoff effects of the development. A

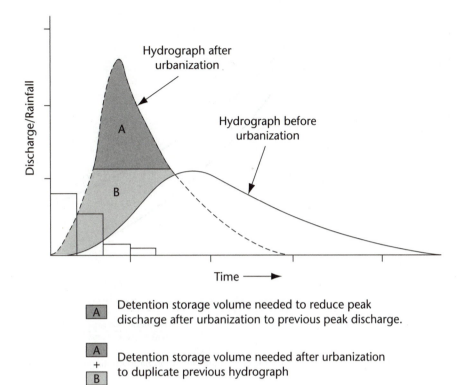

Detention storage volume needed to reduce peak discharge after urbanization to previous peak discharge.

Detention storage volume needed after urbanization to duplicate previous hydrograph

Figure 14.18 Mitigating the Effect of Urbanization on Peak Discharge with Stormwater Detention after Concentration.

detention volume equal to area A would be sufficient to reduce the peak flows to the original peak.

A simple method to estimate detention volume is given in TR 55 (USDA, 1986). It utilizes results from the peak discharge method described in chapter 13 and uses an additional Worksheet 6. The method and an example are given below.

Worksheet 6 Sizes Detention Volume to Reduce Peak Discharge (USDA, 1986)

(Needed: drainage area (A_m), peak inflow ($q_i = q_p$, worksheet 4), peak outflow (q_o), watershed runoff from design storm (Q, worksheet 1), rainfall distribution type.)

The method computes the ratio peak inflow/peak outflow or q_i/q_o. The ratio of volume of storage to volume of runoff, V_s/V_r, is determined from figure 14.19. V_s is computed by multiplying this ratio by V_r.

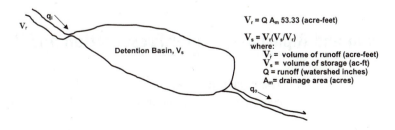

$V_r = Q\ A_m\ 53.33$ (acre-feet)

$V_s = V_r(V_s/V_r)$
where:
    V_r = volume of runoff (acre-feet)
    V_s = volume of storage (ac-ft)
    Q = runoff (watershed inches)
    A_m = drainage area (acres)

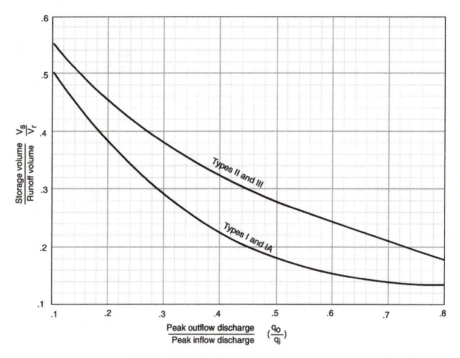

Figure 14.19 Approximate Detention Basin Routing (TR55 Figure 6–1). *Source:* USDA (1986).

Example 6–1: Estimating V_s, Single-Stage Structure (USDA, 1986)

A development is being planned in a 75-acre (0.1170 mi^2) watershed that outlets into an existing concrete lined channel designed for present conditions. If the channel capacity is exceeded, damages will be substantial. The watershed is in the type II storm distribution region. The present channel capacity, 180 cfs, was established by computing discharge for the 25-year frequency storm by the graphical peak discharge method (worksheet 4 in chapter 13). The developed-condition peak discharge (q_i) is computed by the same method is 360 cfs, and runoff (Q) is 3.4 inches. Since outflow must be held to 180 cfs, a detention basin having that maximum outflow discharge (q_o) will be built at the watershed outlet.

How much storage (V_s) will be required to meet the maximum outflow discharge (q_o) of 180 cfs, and what will be the approximate dimensions of a rectangular weir outflow structure?

Figure 14.19 and Worksheet 6a are used to estimate required storage ($V_s = 5.9$ acre-ft). The worksheet can also be used to estimate the maximum elevation or stage of storage with an outlet crest of 100 feet. For more information on storage stage and outlet types, see the TR 55 documentation (USDA, 1986).

Stream and Riparian Corridor Preservation and Restoration

The **riparian zone,** shown in figure 14.20, refers literally to banks beside water bodies, but also commonly refers to lands proximate to lakes, streams, and estuar-

Worksheet 6a

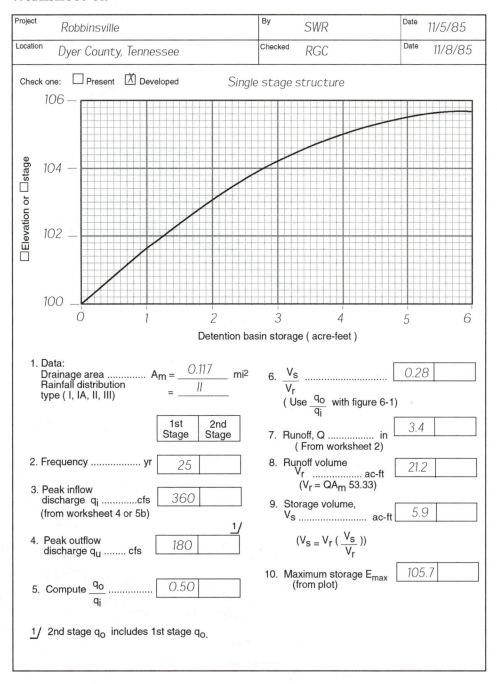

Project	Robbinsville	By	SWR	Date	11/5/85
Location	Dyer County, Tennessee	Checked	RGC	Date	11/8/85

Check one: ☐ Present ☒ Developed   *Single stage structure*

1. Data:
   Drainage area .... A_m = __0.117__ mi²
   Rainfall distribution
   type (I, IA, II, III) = __II__

	1st Stage	2nd Stage
2. Frequency .... yr	25	
3. Peak inflow discharge q_i ....cfs (from worksheet 4 or 5b)	360	
4. Peak outflow discharge q_u .... cfs	180	1/
5. Compute $\dfrac{q_o}{q_i}$	0.50	

6. $\dfrac{V_s}{V_r}$ .... | 0.28 |
   (Use $\dfrac{q_o}{q_i}$ with figure 6-1)

7. Runoff, Q .... in | 3.4 |
   (From worksheet 2)

8. Runoff volume V_r .... ac-ft | 21.2 |
   ($V_r = QA_m$ 53.33)

9. Storage volume, V_s .... ac-ft | 5.9 |

   $(V_s = V_r \left(\dfrac{V_s}{V_r} \right))$

10. Maximum storage E_{max} | 105.7 |
    (from plot)

1/ 2nd stage q_o includes 1st stage q_o.

ies. The riparian zone divides the aquatic zone and the upland zone, but it is physically and ecologically related to both. As shown in figure 14.20b, the riparian zone filters upland runoff, stabilizes stream banks, provides critical edge and corridor wildlife habitat, shades water, and provides cover and food supply for aquatic species. The riparian zone is characterized by vegetation requiring large amounts of water, creating unique habitat conditions for wildlife. Riparian zones are distin-

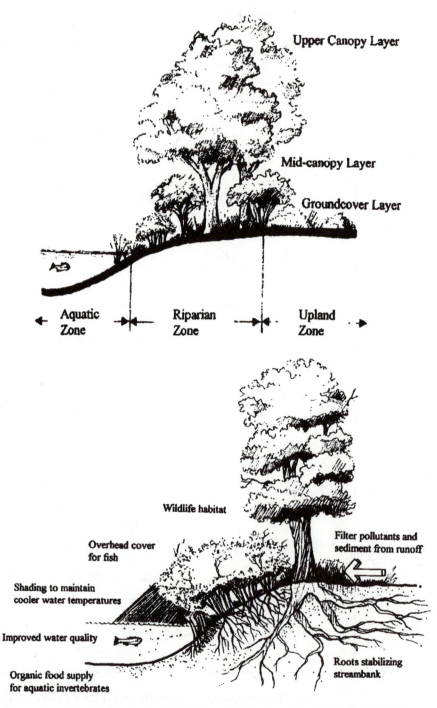

Figure 14.20 Riparian Zone and Its Functional Elements. *Source:* USDA, NRCS (undated).

Figure 14.21 Destruction of Stream Riparian Corridors in Agricultural and Urban Landscapes. Typical straightening and "armoring" of channels in urban areas using concrete mattresses and sacks are shown in *b* and *c* (B: Boneyard Creek, Urbana-Champaign, IL) and riprap (C-Galindo Creek, Concord, CA). *Sources:* FISRWG (1998) (*a*), Riley (1998) (*b, c*)

guished by the type of water source and may extend well beyond the water line. **Lentic habitats** are proximate to standing waters, such as lakes and ponds. **Lotic habitats** are associated with running waters, such as rivers and streams.

Principles and Process of Stream Corridor Protection and Restoration

Our national land use history has not been kind to stream corridors. Agricultural land use has maximized agricultural productivity at the expense of riparian vegetative diversity, habitat value, and water quality (figure 14.21a). In urban areas, natural drainage patterns are often seen as "getting in the way." Instead of embracing these riparian features and designing with them, planners and developers often destroy them, cover them up, armor and culvert them in a sea of impervious surface (figure 14.21b and 14.21c), only to see the ghosts of streams past rise again in recurring flood flows and runoff pollution.

Recurring flooding and pollution problems are not the most serious impacts of such practices. Lost are potential environmental services, ecological benefits, aesthetic beauty, and economic property values provided by the riparian and stream corridor. As a result, a national movement has surfaced to resurrect and restore impacted stream corridors to their natural functions and renew these riparian benefits. With the aid of federal and state agencies to farmers, stream corridor restoration is being applied to rural agricultural areas. Community groups and local governments have taken the lead in restoration efforts in urban and urbanizing areas.

Restoration is the process of returning a damaged ecosystem to its condition prior to disturbance (National Research Council, 1992) (see chapter 10). Stream corridor restoration is not easy. It requires careful planning and a broad understanding of hydrologic, physical, chemical, and biological processes. Stream restorers have to play engineer, biologist, ecologist, landscape architect, and planner. As a result, stream restoration is best conducted by an interdisciplinary team. Indeed, a major federal initiative to develop practical guidance for stream corridor restoration required a multiagency working group with representatives from the NRCS, Forest Service, National Oceanic and Atmospheric Administration, Corps of Engineers, Housing and Urban Development, Fish and Wildlife Service, Park Service, U.S. Geological Survey, Environmental Protection Agency, Federal Emergency Management Agency, and others (FISRWG, 1998).

This section outlines some basic principles of stream corridor restoration, including restoration's goals and techniques and a design and planning process. It then describes measures and practices to restore and maintain natural channels. Stream data gathering and analysis are important in this process. Chapter 13 and appendices described two of several procedures used for stream assessment. The first was visual and biological stream surveys. They require field stream walks, visual inspection, and documentation of the stream condition, and sampling stream biota, usually macroinvertebrates, to indicate stream health. The second method was calculating channel flow capacity and channel bank erosion problems and potential (see chapter 13, appendices 13.B, 13.C, and 13.D).

The Federal Interagency Stream Restoration Working Group (1998) outlines a process for developing a stream restoration plan. It follows our basic process given in box 2.1. Step 2 calls for assessing existing stream condition along a **condition continuum** from pristine to heavily degraded. This not only helps to understand the current situation but also to envision possible futures: Where along this continuum will the stream be if we do nothing? Where do we want it to be and what do we need to achieve that? Table 14.8 gives urban stream restoration goals and techniques used to achive them.

The restoration process should:

- work within a watershed/landscape context;
- involve an interdisciplinary team;
- develop clear, achievable, and measurable goals;
- use reference sites within the watershed;
- aim to preserve and protect resources (don't wait until restoration is needed);

TABLE 14.8 **Urban Stream Restoration Goals and Techniques**

Urban Stream Restoration Goals	*Techniques/Methods*
Control urban hydrologic regime.	Upstream structural retrofits. Parallel pipe systems.
Remove urban pollutants.	Source control pollution prevention efforts. Upstream structural retrofits. Increased/enhanced stream buffers. Elimination of illicit connections. Erosion and sediment controls.
Restore instream habitat structure.	Create pools/riffles. Confine and deepen low flow channels. Provide structural complexity. Provide in-stream fish cover.
Stabilize channel morphology.	Enhance channel geometry (length to width ratio, meander patterns, etc.). Stabilize severe bank erosion. Stabilize channel and bed to accommodate bankfull discharge. Provide enhanced tree canopy over headwater streams.
Replace/augment riparian cover.	Stabilize stream banks. Provide in-stream overhead cover. Revegetate stream banks and buffers. Erosion and sediment controls.
Protect critical stream substrates.	Riffle creation. Mechanical stream substrate cleanout ("mudsucker"). Enhance steam buffers. Remove fish migration barriers.
Recolonize stream community.	Selectively reintroduce predisturbance native fish community.

- restore ecological integrity, natural structure, natural function;
- design for self-sustainability, using "passive" restoration, natural fixes, and bioengineering; and
- monitor and adapt where changes are necessary and anticipate future changes.

Stream restoration should take a watershed approach and look beyond the stream and corridor to the upland sources of runoff. Therefore, it involves the following:

- **In-stream techniques:** (channel reconfiguration and realignment to restore geometry, meander, sinuosity, substrate composition, structural complexity, reaeration, stream bank stability)
- **Riparian techniques:** (reestablishment of vegetative canopy, increasing corridor width, restrictive fencing)

> ▪ **Upland or watershed techniques:** (control of NPS pollution, impervious surface, SMPs)

There is an important design element to stream urban restoration, and as in most planning, it is important to engage stakeholders in the process. Visualizing the possibilities is an important step for generating support and funding for projects. Photo simulation can give people an idea of the opportunities. Figure 14.22 gives a photo pair produced by Steve Price for The Friends of Baxter Creek in Richmond, California.

Designing Restored Stream Channels, Meanders, and Floodplains

The heart of the stream restoration process is the design and selection of alternatives. Restoration measures address four main components of the steam corridor: the **stream channel,** the **in-stream habitat,** the **streambank,** and **riparian habitat and buffers.** The extent of the measures depends on the condition of the stream and the restoration objectives. Projects can range from minor stream bank treatment to major re-creation of a natural stream channel from a straightened, armored, or buried drainage channel. Major restoration requires engineering design of channel meander and floodplain dimensions. The following list outlines a process for designing re-created channels taken from Riley (1998) and FISRWG (1998).

Designing Restored Stream Channels, Meanders, and Floodplains

1. **Preliminary Bankfull Dimensions:** Determine restoration bankfull width and depth based on existing, historic, or desirable conditions (see figure 14.23).
   a. Measure width, depth, slope, cross-sectional area of existing channels, terraces, and floodplains.
   b. If stream is being re-created in urban area, measure reference streams in different drainage areas that appear to be in "urban equilibrium," that is, stable under existing development conditions.
   c. Consult historic photographs; interview residents with local knowledge.
   d. Conduct calculations of channel capacity and velocities for design storms and discharges for existing and proposed channel dimensions (see chapter 13).
2. **Meander Design:** If stream meander is part of restoration: (see figure 14.23)
   a. Estimate the channel meander based on prior conditions, other streams in the region, or calculation:
   Meander wavelength $(L) = 11$ x bankfull width;
   Meander amplitude $(M_A) = 2.7$ x bankfull width;
   Radius of curvature (r_c) is $0.2\ L$ and averages 2.3 x bankfull width.
3. **Floodplain Design:** Draw restoration meander and channel dimensions and design floodplain based on dimensions in 1.a. More floodplain is better than less.

Figure 14.22 Photo Simulation of Potential Restoration of Baxter Creek, Richmond, California. *Source:* Steve Price, Urban Advantage. Used with permission.

    a. Transfer dimensions to site map and adjust meander shape and flood-plain area to fit existing land use, streets, and utilities. Consider opportunities for relocation of structures.

    b. Stream bank slopes should be 1:1 to 1:3; natural banks average 1:2, but 1:3 is better for people access.

    c. Floodplain elevation should be greater than the top of the bankfull channel.

4. **Check Design Against Site Dimensions and Discharge Flows:**

    a. Measure elevation and slope between upstream and downstream boundaries of restoration site.

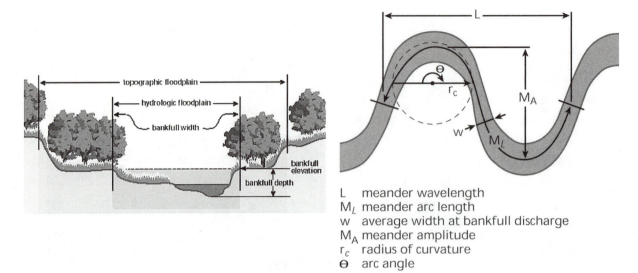

L   meander wavelength
M_L meander arc length
w   average width at bankfull discharge
M_A meander amplitude
r_c radius of curvature
Θ   arc angle

Figure 14.23 Stream Bankfull and Meander Dimensions. *Source:* FISRWG (1998).

   b. Compare slope, meander, bankfull, and floodplain dimensions to refer-
      ence streams. If channel is too short or slope is too great, energy of the
      stream may have to be dissipated by in-stream measures, such as a
      step-pool or weir.
   c. Draw flood elevations for 25-, 60-, and 100-year floods. See if bankfull
      and floodplain cross sections can accommodate them.
   d. Calculate the velocities for different storm discharges. If above 6
      ft/sec, larger floodplain or channel bank bioengineering are needed
      (see next section).

Bioengineering Measures to Restore Stream Corridors and Control Bank Erosion

Growing experience in stream restoration has resulted in developing several measures to improve the stability, water quality, and ecological integrity of stream corridors. Some excellent source materials for information on these measures are
available, including the NRCS conservation practices website (USDA, undated),
NRCS bioengineering reports (e.g., USDA, 2002), FISRWG (1998), and the Center for Watershed Protection (http://www.cwp.org). The most effective measures
involve good planning and "bioengineering" methods that include restoration construction practices using mostly vegetative materials.

Most stream corridor restoration projects deal with streams that, while
degraded, do not need to be redesigned or re-created. Restoration measures for in-
stream habitat, stream banks, and riparian vegetation and habitat do not require

the engineering analysis of channel and meander design. The following list outlines procedures for designing these measures. Specific measures are described next. The design and selection of measures are based on restoration goals and objectives and assessment of existing conditions (table 14.8). This assessment employs visual and biological stream assessment methods discussed in chapter 13.

Designing In-Stream Habitat, Streambank, and Riparian Habitat Restoration Measures

1. In-stream Habitat Restoration:
   a. Assess bed material size distribution, pools, riffles, confinement of low-flow channel
   b. Promote greater structural complexity across the streambed using check dams, wing deflectors, boulder clusters; deepen low-flow channel confinement areas.
   c. Establish appropriate riffle spacing (pool-riffle spacing = 3–10 × channel widths (6 is average; 4 on steeper, 8–9 on gradual slopes).
   d. Protect critical stream substrates: gravels, boulders, overhead cover; fish spawning areas; promote recolonization of the stream community.
2. Streambank Protection Restoration:
   a. Calculate allowable (permissible) velocity at bankfull flows (see appendix 13.D).
   b. Stabilize channel morphology with appropriate methods: vegetative methods (plantings, revetment); indirect methods (dikes, flow deflectors, weirs); or (last resort) armor methods (riprap, grid pavers, concrete).
3. Riparian Vegetation and Habitat Restoration:
   a. Reforestation of native cover; changes in mowing to allow succession of vegetation.
   b. Removal of exotics and invasive species.
   c. Promote overhead cover for fish habitat.
   d. Vegetative buffers:
      i. 3-zone buffer system: streamside, middle zone (100-year floodplain plus undevelopable steep slopes 4 ft per percent slope, adjacent wetlands or critical habitats), outer zone (25 ft beyond middle zone) (see figure 14.28, box 14.1).
      ii. pre-development vegetative target.
      iii. minimum 100-ft buffer width, but buffer contraction and expansion depending on conditions.
      iv. maintain unbroken corridor with design of buffer crossings.
      v. use upland BMPs as well as buffers: buffers can treat stormwater from only 10 percent of watershed.

The following figures in box 14.1 illustrate measures for riparian buffers, streambank erosion control, and in-stream habitat enhancement. Box 14.1 lists several measures under these three categories.

BOX 14.1 — Stream Corridor Restoration Measures

In-stream Habitat Restoration Measures

Boulder clusters: provide overhead cover and create deep areas used by juvenile fish

Boulder or log weirs, channel constrictors: constrict flow increasing water force, deepen channel, provide cover

Cobble or gravel liners: add riffle and spawning materials to streambed materials

Fish passages: provide access to desirable and migrating fish

Log, brush, or rock shelters: trap detritus for organisms that feed fish and provide shade and cooling

Migration barrier: controls nuisance species

Tree cover: trees felled and anchored along stream bank to provide overhead cover and substrate for organisms

Stream Bank Protection and Restoration

Bag, log, rootwad, tree and boulder revetment: facing of stone or other materials to prevent erosion of banks

Bank shaping and vegetating: reduces bank slope, preparatory for other bank stabilization

Brush mattress: layer of live branch cuttings that sprout and restores riparian vegetation, habitat (figure 14.24)

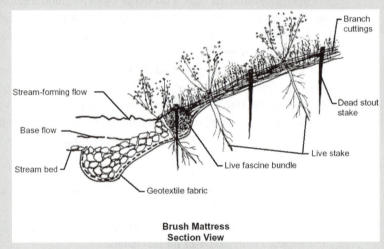

**Brush Mattress
Section View**

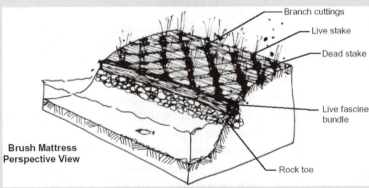

**Brush Mattress
Perspective View**

Figure 14.24 Brush Mattress. *Source:* CSD-MSU (undated).

Continued ➤

BOX 14.1 — (continued)

Coconut fiber roll: cylindrical, flexible rolls of coconut husk fibers that mold to and protect slopes

Double and single wing deflectors: rocks wings create midchannel pools

Erosion blanket, hydroseeding: spray seeding can be enhanced by degradable blanket

Groynes: structures jutting into channel that divert high velocity currents away from outer banks

Live cribwall: interlocking timbers filled with alternating layers of soil and live branches to protect steep banks

Live stakes: dormant woody cuttings inserted into toe or stream bank (figure 14.25)

Live fascine: bundles of dormant, live cuttings bound together in cylindrical form and attached to bank (figure 14.25)

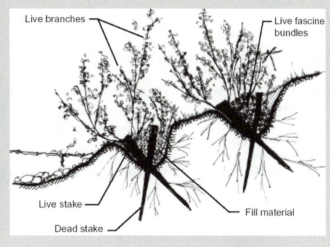

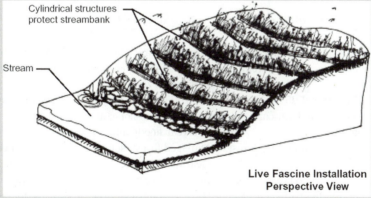

Figure 14.25 Live Fascine: Rooting Stakes. *Source:* CSD-MSU (undated).

Continued ➤

BOX 14.1 — (continued)

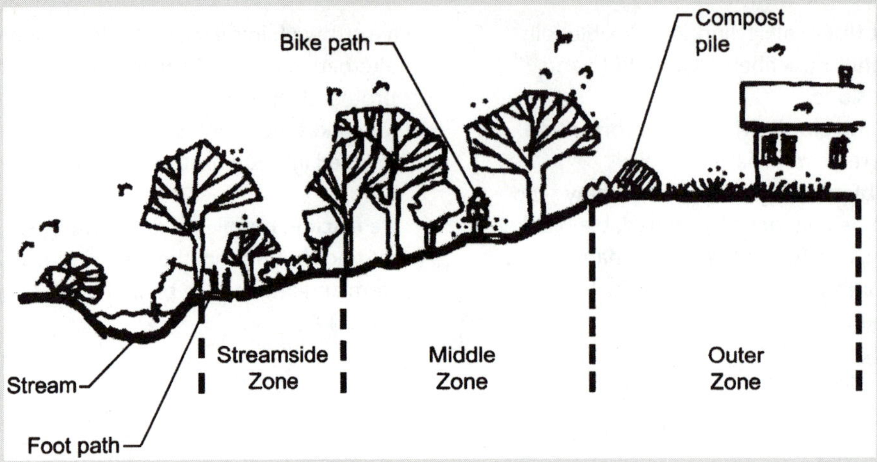

Figure 14.26 Riparian Buffer Zone. *Source:* CSD-MSU (undated).

Vegetated rock gabions: basket of heavily galvanized wire mesh filled with rock and laced together on bank

Streambank "armor": riprap, grid pavers, concrete placed or molded on shaped streambanks with high velocities

Riparian Habitat Restoration

Forested and vegetated buffers (figure 14.26)
Buffer zonation (table 14.9)

Source: Center for Sustainable Design (undated).

TABLE 14.9 **Riparian Buffer Zones and their Characteristics**

Characteristics	*Streamside Zone*	*Middle Zone*	*Outer Zone*
Function	Protect the physical integrity of the stream ecosystem.	Provide distance between upland development and streamside zone.	Prevent encroachment and filter backyard runoff.
Width	Minimum of 25 ft plus wetlands and critical habitat.	50–100 ft depending on stream order, slope, and 100-year floodplain.	25-ft minimum setback to structures.
Vegetative Target	Undisturbed mature forest; reforest if grass.	Managed forest, some clearing allowable.*	Forest encouraged, but usually turfgrass.
Allowable Uses	Very restricted (e.g., flood control, footpaths, etc.).	Restricted (e.g., some recreational uses, some stormwater BMPs, bike paths).	Inrestricted (e.g., residential uses, including lawn, garden, compost, yard wastes, most stormwater BMPs).

*100-year floodplain plus undevelopable steep slopes 4 ft per percent slope, adjacent wetlands or critical habitats

Summary

Stormwater management was once the sole domain of the engineer who could calculate flows and design structures to enhance drainage. The engineer is still involved, but because of expanding objectives for water quality, infiltration and low flow protection, natural drainage and stream restoration, and mitigation of impervious surfaces, stormwater management now has a large number of stakeholders and problem solvers. Stakeholders include landowners, local watershed groups, and volunteer stream monitors, among others, and the professionals involved include environmental planners and landscape architects, as well as engineers.

Creative solutions to stormwater management, like wetlands and bioretention, imitate nature and its processes for biological water treatment, retention, and infiltration. These innovative measures are finding their way to state and local stormwater programs and ordinances with the hope that new development will not have the impacts of the past and that we may reduce future damage on our remaining natural streams in urbanizing areas. A greater challenge is correcting the 'sins' of the past by retrofitting stormwater management practices, disconnecting impervious surfaces, and restoring and in some cases uncovering natural drainage channels, and bringing back to life the urban streams that add so much to the aesthetic, recreation, and ecological worth of our communities.

15 ▪ Land Use and Groundwater

Just as the use of the land impacts surface water flows and quality, it also affects groundwater. Water infiltrating the land surface becomes part of the subsurface groundwater flow. Impervious surfaces inhibit infiltration and recharge of groundwater, and pollution sources on the land contribute to groundwater contamination. Before exploring these impacts and discussing approaches to land and groundwater management, it is important to understand some concepts and terminology related to hydrogeology and groundwater use.

Groundwater Hydrology Fundamentals

Figure 15.1 gives an overview of groundwater relationships and introduces groundwater terms. Subsurface water must occupy the voids or interstices within soil and rocks that are not occupied by solid material. The degree of voids existing in soil or rock material is measured by its **porosity,** or the ratio of the volume of voids to the total volume of soil or rock. If the interstices are connected so that a fluid can move from one to another, the material is said to be permeable. Recall from chapter 12 that **permeability** is the capacity to transmit fluids under pressure. (The coefficient of permeability is measured in volume of water transmitted through an area under a standard pressure and temperature.) Generally, subsurface materials having high porosity and permeability make good water-bearing formations.

Aquifers and Recharge

Formations that contain enough water and have sufficient permeability to be used as water supply sources are called **aquifers.** An **aquiclude** (such as clay) is usually porous and may contain groundwater but transmits it slowly and is not a good water supply source. An **aquifuge** (such as rock) neither stores nor transmits water. Aquicludes and aquifuges can serve as confining layers **(aquitards)** above or below aquifers. The occurrence of aquifers, their recharge, and the movement of groundwater are determined by geologic factors including surface and subsur-

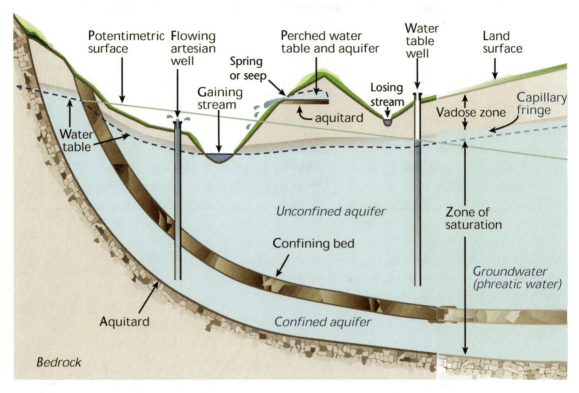

Figure 15.1 Groundwater System, Illustrating Major Terms. *Sources:* USGS (1972), FISRWG (1998).

face materials, stratigraphy, and structure. Porosity and permeability of materials determine their water-bearing potential. The potential of unconsolidated materials depends on texture and degree of sorting. Some rock materials such as sandstones and limestones may have sufficient voids and permeability to provide good aquifer potential. Other rock materials (igneous and metamorphic rock, shale) have poor potential unless a high degree of weathering and fracturing has produced voids. Table 15.1 gives porosities and permeabilities for selected materials and types of openings in water-bearing rocks.

Unconfined or **free aquifers** have direct vertical contact with the atmosphere through the open pores in the soil, and recharge comes from infiltration above. The top of an unconfined aquifer is the groundwater table (see figure 15.1). Below the water table is the saturated zone, above it is the unsaturated or aeration zone, also called the **vadose zone.** The **water table** level fluctuates with periods of rainy and dry weather. Unconfined **perched aquifers** produce **seeps** or **springs** where underlying layers force water to spill out of the ground. Figure 15.2 shows aquifer recharge areas for a typical unconfined aquifer in a river valley made up of unconsolidated alluvial and colluvial deposits having good porosity and permeability. The primary recharge area is directly above the aquifer. Secondary recharge comes from runoff from mountain flanks, which flows into the primary area. Tertiary recharge comes from runoff higher up the watershed, which contributes to stream flow in the river.

TABLE 15.1   **Porosities and Coefficients of Permeability for Common Materials**

		Porosity (%)	Permeability (gal/ft²/da)
	Clay	45	0.01
Good	Sand	35	1,000
Water-	Gravel	25	100,000
Bearing	Gravel and Sand	20	10,000
Materials	Sandstone	15	100
	Shale	5	1.0
	Granite	1	0.01

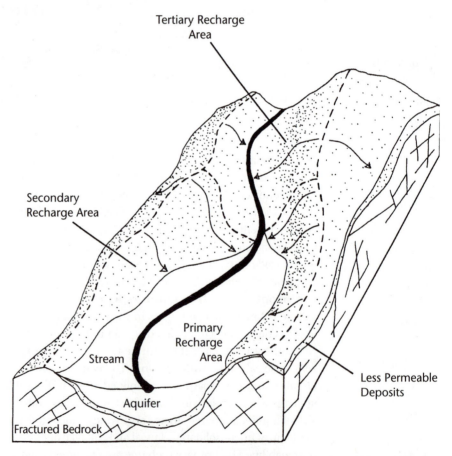

Figure 15.2 Aquifer Recharge Areas. *Source:* Jon Witten and Scott Horsley. 1995. *A Guide to Wellhead Protection.* Planning Advisory Service Report 457/458. Used with permission of the American Planning Association.

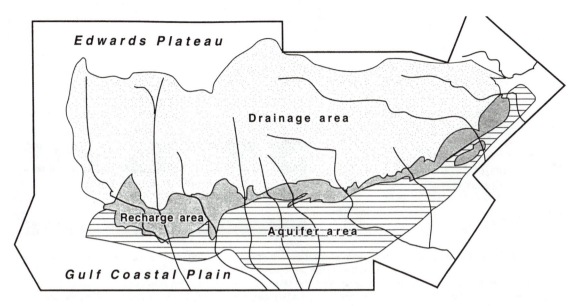

Figure 15.3 Edwards Aquifer. *Source:* Jon Witten and Scott Horsley. 1995. *A Guide to Wellhead Protection.* Planning Advisory Service Report 457/458. Used with permission of the American Planning Association.

If the aquifer is overlain by a geologic layer through which water cannot move, it is said to be **confined.** Stratigraphy and structure influence the recharge of confined aquifers. **Stratigraphy** is the study of layered rock material in the Earth's crust. Layers of different types of geologic material may fold and bend, occasionally cropping out to the surface, occasionally dropping to significant depths. As shown in figure 15.1, a confined aquifer is a layer of good water-bearing material bounded by confining layers or materials of low permeability. Thus, a confined aquifer is recharged where its permeable stratum intercepts the ground or by connection to another aquifer or surface water sources. Connection to such sources can result from subsurface **structure** or faults and fractures, which provide avenues for water movement. **Semiconfined aquifers** are those that are recharged at their interception with the ground surface and by fractures through their confining layer that may extend to the ground surface. Figure 15.3 shows the semiconfined Edwards Aquifer in Texas. Runoff and streamflow from the drainage area flows into the recharge area; faults and fractures in the recharge area provide the principal avenues for aquifer recharge from the streamflow.

Potentimetric (Piezometric) Surface and the Cone of Depression

When a well is drilled or pipe sunk into an aquifer, the water in it will rise to a certain level. The height of that water above some arbitrary datum, usually sea level, is called the **head** or **potentimetric** or **piezometric surface.** For an unconfined aquifer, this level will be the water table. As shown in figure 15.1, for confined aquifers this level is determined by the height of water in the confined column below its recharge area. It may be above the water table (an artesian well) or below the water table (a subartesian well). If the pressure is great enough for the

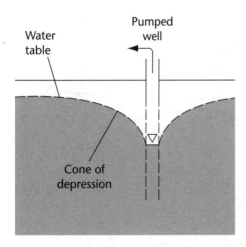
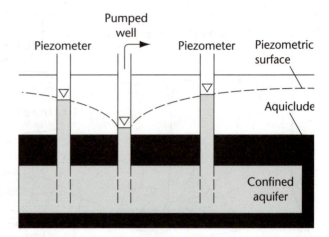

Figure 15.4 Cones of Depression. Pumping from a well lowers the piezometric surface. In unconfined aquifers (left), this lowers the water table. In confined aquifers, it lowers the piezometric surface which can be measured with piezometers. For large aquifers, the cone can extend for several miles and take years to recover, even after adequate recharge. *Source: Water in Environmental Planning* by Thomas Dunne and Luna Leopold, copyright © 1978. Reprinted with permission of W. H. Freeman and Company.

water to actually rise above the ground surface and flow freely, it is called a flowing artesian well.

Pumped wells can dramatically affect the piezometric potential and cause adverse effects. As shown in figure 15.4, pumping causes a **cone of depression** that lowers the potentimetric surface not only at the well but also in the surrounding area. With several wells tapping the same aquifer, competition can result, as one deep well can lower the surface below neighboring shallower wells. The piezometric depressions in Tidewater Virginia, where large industrial wells are used by pulp and paper mills in Franklin and West Point, have caused a drop in the piezometric surface of 100–160 feet that extend as far as 50 miles from the wellhead.

Figure 15.5 shows that along a stream, a cone of depression can lead to surface-to-groundwater flow. In times of drought the stream can be completely drained in this way. Along the coast, heavy pumping of groundwater can lead to **saltwater intrusion.** Lighter fresh groundwater occurs as a wedge above heavier saline groundwater. The height of the wedge above sea level is 1/40 of its depth below. Pumping fresh water raises saltwater 40 times faster than it depresses the cone of freshwater. If the cone is depressed to sea level, saltwater intrudes into the well, reducing water quality, even though there is adjacent fresh water.

Groundwater Flow and Relationship with Surface Water

Groundwater flow is determined by piezometric pressure and aquifer materials. Shallow groundwater generally conforms to surface topography. This is not always true for confined aquifers. In the recharge-discharge process of a typical groundwater system, subsurface movement may be relatively rapid in shallow systems, whereas the groundwater in deep confined aquifers may take decades to move from recharge to discharge.

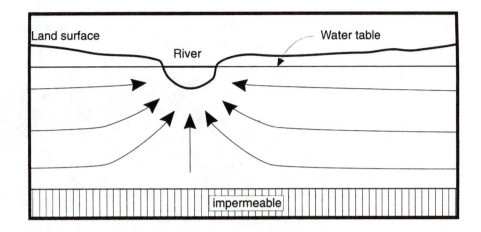

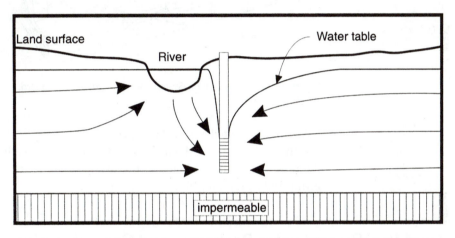

Figure 15.5 Cone of depression can turn a gaining stream into a losing stream. *Source:* Jon Witten and Scott Horsley. 1995. *A Guide to Wellhead Protection.* Planning Advisory Service Report 457/458. Used with permission of the American Planning Association.

Discharge from shallow groundwater flow is an important component of stream-flow between storms. The "effluent" or "gaining" stream shown in figures 15.1 and 15.5 (top) gains surface flow from subsurface flow when the water table is above the surface water. An "influent" or "losing" stream loses surface flow to groundwater when the water table is below the surface water. Figure 15.5 (bottom) shows that a well's cone of depression can turn a gaining stream into a losing stream.

Figure 15.6 shows the karst hydrologic system and the interaction of surface and groundwater movement. Not only does karst provide direct avenues for unfiltered flow from surface to groundwater, but landowners often try to fill sinkholes associated with karst with wastes that contribute toxic materials to the groundwater (see also karst section of chapter 9).

A graduate student's study near Blacksburg, Virginia, demonstrated the rapid movement of groundwater flow (and the contaminants it may carry) in karst systems. He injected a dye tracer into two sinkholes in the Lusters Gate area. He intended to monitor possible release of the dye into surface seeps near the Roa-

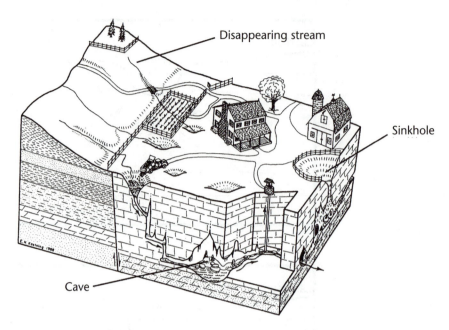

Figure 15.6 Karst Hydrologic System. *Source:* Virginia Cave Board.

noke River three miles away by inspecting the seeps at daily intervals for several months. To his surprise the dyes were present on his first inspection of the seeps the next day, within 24 hours of the dye injection (Hirschman, Randolph, and Flynn, 1992; Hayman, 1972).

Land Use, Groundwater Recharge, and Contamination

Land use impacts groundwater in much the same way as it affects surface waters. All groundwater originates on the land. Impervious surfaces inhibit infiltration, subsurface water flow, and groundwater recharge. Most groundwater contaminants originate from land activities and seep into groundwater by subsurface flow. Managing groundwater quantity and quality requires understanding the groundwater system, maintaining recharge, and controlling sources of contamination. This requires managing land use development and land use practices.

Impervious Surface and Groundwater Recharge

We have seen in chapters 13 and 14 that impervious surfaces have a critical impact on surface water flows and quality. Since they inhibit infiltration, they reduce shallow groundwater flow that contributes to stream flow between storms. They also reduce deeper groundwater flow that contributes to aquifer recharge. Communities dependent on groundwater for water supply have a special challenge to understand their groundwater system and to manage development to protect recharge areas. The first step is to delineate recharge areas. Figure 15.3 shows the important Edwards Aquifer in Texas, the location of its recharge area, as well as the drainage area that contributes to that recharge. The next step is to control land use development and practices that can potentially impact aquifer recharge.

Groundwater Contamination

Although land use can affect groundwater recharge, especially through construction of impervious surfaces, its more significant impact is groundwater contamination. Concerns over groundwater contamination stem from three factors:

- Groundwater is out of sight and therefore generally out of mind. It is difficult to monitor, and problems are usually not discovered until damage has occurred.
- Groundwater contamination is far more difficult to treat and remediate than surface water pollution.
- Groundwater use in private wells is usually used for domestic and drinking water needs without treatment.

Because groundwater is used for drinking water, contaminants of concern are those related to human health effects. These are distinguished between those causing acute health effects and those resulting in chronic effects. **Acute effects** are immediate effects, appearing within hours or days. They can result from exposure to pathogens (disease-causing organisms) or nitrates in drinking water. Pathogens are waterborne bacteria, viruses, protozoa, and parasites that cause gastrointestinal illness and, in extreme cases, death. Protozoa *Giardia lamblia* and *Cryptosporidium* have caused several disease outbreaks in the United States during the past 15 years. Nitrates in drinking water can cause acute health effects in infants, causing methemoglobinemia, or "blue baby syndrome."

Chronic health effects result from exposure to a drinking water contaminant over many years. Effects include birth defects, cancer, and other long-term health effects. Contaminants causing chronic health effects include lead and other metals and volatile organic chemicals, like pesticides, solvents, and other petrochemicals.

Groundwater contamination comes from several sources introduced on the land surface (e.g., liquid or solid wastes, road salt, animal feedlots, fertilizer and pesticides, airborne particulates), above the water table (e.g., leaching landfills, septic systems, leaking underground storage tanks, leaking pipelines, stormwater dry wells), or below the water table (e.g., abandoned wells, exploratory wells, waste injection wells, mines, saltwater intrusion). Land use involves the first two categories. The primary sources of groundwater contamination from surface land use are listed below:

- **Septic systems** can be a problem when located too close to wells in soils having very high permeability or structural avenues for rapid wastewater movement.
- **Leaking underground storage tanks** containing petroleum products have caused considerable contamination and abandonment of wells.

- Contamination from **landfills** and **lagoons** has led to stricter standards and controls, including dual liners and groundwater monitoring.
- **Surface runoff** from agricultural, urban, mining, and industrial lands have all contributed to contamination. Nitrogen fertilizers and pesticides on agricultural lands have created human health-related problems.

The movement of contaminants depends on the groundwater flow regime discussed previously. It also depends on the characteristics of the pollutant, including its density and its chemical and physical properties that may affect its reaction and filtration when in contact with subsurface materials. Pollutants having the same density as water will follow the groundwater flow path. Those denser will sink and not migrate laterally as quickly. Those less dense may actually float on top of the water table.

Assessing Groundwater Resources

Managing groundwater and preventing groundwater contamination at the local level involves four components:

1. Understanding the groundwater system
   a. Hydrogeologic investigations
   b. DRASTIC studies
   c. Wellhead protection area (WHPA) delineation
2. Inventorying and assessing threats and potential sources of contamination
3. Monitoring groundwater
4. Developing a groundwater management program
   a. Remediation
   b. Prevention

      Regulatory measures
      Nonregulatory measures

Improved groundwater assessment methods have helped communities better understand their groundwater systems. Hydrogeologic investigations, DRASTIC studies, and WHPA delineation techniques can provide communities a scientific basis for programs to protect them. The next section describes hydrogeologic and DRASTIC mapping studies, and wellhead protection and other groundwater management programs are discussed in the one that follows.

Understanding the Groundwater System: Hydrogeologic Investigations

Community groundwater investigations can assess groundwater potential and problems. They describe the physical setting of the community (i.e., physiography, hydrology, and soils), the hydrogeology (geologic formations and aquifer systems), groundwater quality, groundwater problems, and groundwater development potential. The location of recharge areas is important to apply land use strategies for groundwater protection.

Figures 15.7 and 15.8 illustrate some results of the Roanoke County Groundwater Study (Breeder and Dawson, 1976). The study describes the hydrogeology of the county, giving the geologic formations and their water-bearing characteristics; both aerial and sectional views are given to show the stratigraphy and structure as well as the surface materials.

Figure 15.7 identifies the main aquifer recharge areas. In this case, they are associated with the fault lines and river valleys. The figure also identifies where urbanization has interfered with recharge through the construction of impervious surfaces and where artificial recharge is provided. Figure 15.8 denotes specific groundwater problem areas. It shows land subsidence areas and where poorly sited developments (landfills and industrial operations) have caused groundwater contamination; included is the Dixie Caverns Landfill. The name advertises the waste landfill's inappropriate location in a karst and cave area. Not surprisingly, this site became a national Superfund site.

The study concluded that the aquifers could safely yield 50 to 60 million gallons per day (mgd) in addition to current withdrawals of 10 mgd; but to protect this resource, the study recommended that groundwater recharge zones be maintained as open space areas (VSWCB, 1976). Despite this potential, Roanoke County determined in the late 1980s that groundwater contamination in this urbanizing area posed too great a risk and decided to develop surface water for long-term water supply.

The Edwards Aquifer, shown in figure 15.3, was the first in the nation to be designated a "sole source aquifer" under the provisions of the Safe Drinking Water Act (SDWA) of 1974. Studies showed that major recharge areas are where the limestone reservoir crops out of the impervious tight clay and where large crevices and cracks occur in the streambeds along the Balcones Fault zone. The direct recharge by surface flow through this fault zone and various solution openings makes the aquifer susceptible to runoff pollutants. As early as the 1970s, land use control programs were developed to protect the aquifer from runoff pollution, including a special permit required for development in the area draining to the aquifer. Permits are based on a point system that assesses the risk of a proposed development to contaminate the groundwater. Managing the Edwards Aquifer is discussed further in the section "Groundwater Source Protection."

DRASTIC: Mapping Groundwater Contamination Susceptibility

In the late 1980s, the U.S. EPA, in conjunction with the American Water Well Association, developed a method to help counties assess and map susceptibility to groundwater contamination based on hydrogeologic factors (Aller, Bennett, Lehr, Petty, and Hackett, 1987). The DRASTIC method is a sum-of-weighted-factors technique that considers the following seven factors:

D: Depth to Water (feet): greater D—> less susceptibility
R: Net **R**echarge (inches): greater R—> greater susceptibility

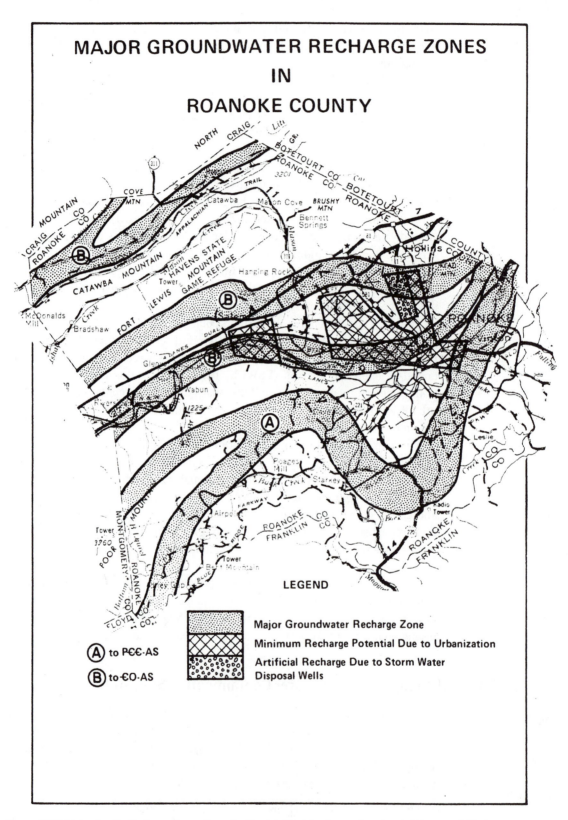

Figure 15.7 Major Aquifer Recharge Areas, Roanoke County, Virginia. *Source:* Breeder and Dawson (1976).

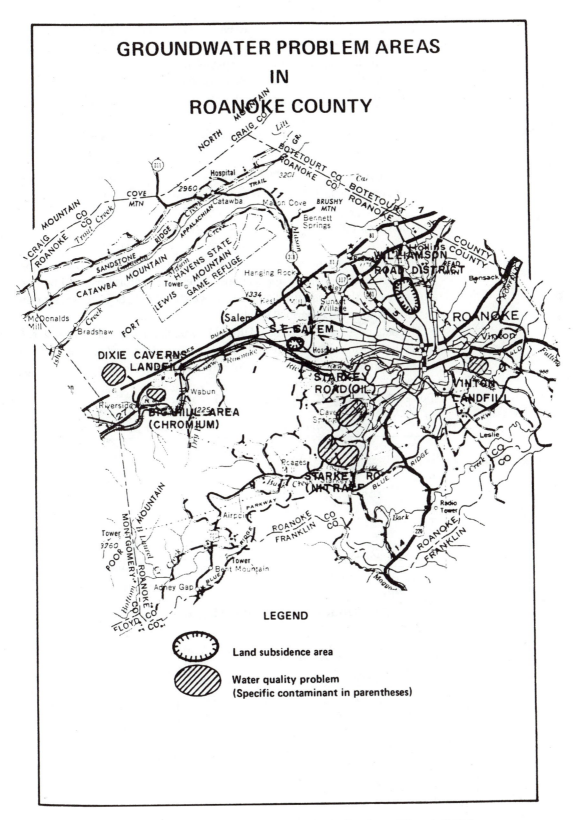

Figure 15.8 Groundwater Problems in Roanoke County, Virginia. *Source:* Breeder and Dawson (1976).

A: Aquifer Media (material): more porous/permeable—> greater susceptibility

S: Soil Media (material): more porous/permeable—> greater susceptibility

T: Topography (slope): greater T—> less susceptibility

I: Impact of the Vadose Zone (material): more porous/permeable—> greater susceptibility

C: Conductivity (gallons per day per ft^2): greater C—> greater susceptibility

The calculation of a DRASTIC score for a specific area involves adding together the products of the factor ratings (r) and the factor weights (w):

$$\text{DRASTIC score} = D_r D_w + R_r R_w + A_r A_w + S_r S_w + T_r T_w + I_r I_w + C_r C_w$$

The factor weights between 1 and 5 are given in table 15.2. The basic DRASTIC weights are used in normal applications. Where agricultural use and pesticides are a concern, the agricultural or pesticide weights should be used. Factor ratings on a 1 to 10 scale are described in table 15.3a-g.

The data necessary to perform DRASTIC calculations are fairly complex. Soil surveys, geologic maps, county government information, and local industry and university studies are especially useful sources of data. However, for many areas

TABLE 15.2 DRASTIC Weights (1 to 5 scale)

Factor	Basic Weight	Agricultural Weight
D	5	5
R	4	4
A	3	3
S	2	5
T	1	3
I	5	4
C	3	2

TABLE 15.3a Ranges and Ratings for Depth to Water

D	Depth To Water (Feet)	
Range		Rating
0–5		10
5–15		9
15–30		7
30–50		5
50–75		3
75–100		2
100 +		1
Weight: 5		Pesticide Weight: 5

TABLE 15.3b **Ranges and Ratings for Net Recharge**

R Range	Net Recharge (Inches) Rating
0–2	1
2–4	3
4–7	6
7–10	8
10+	9
Weight: 4	Pesticide Weight: 4

TABLE 15.3c **Ranges and Ratings for Aquifer Media**

A Range	Aquifer Media Rating	Typical Rating
Massive Shale	1–3	2
Metamorphic/Igneous	2–5	3
Weathered Metamorphic/Igneous	3–5	4
Glacial Till	4–6	5
Bedded Sandstone, Limestone and Shale Sequences	5–9	6
Massive Sandstone	4–9	6
Massive Limestone	4–9	6
Sand and Gravel	4–9	8
Basalt	2–10	9
Karst Limestone	9–10	10
Weight: 3		Pesticide Weight: 3

TABLE 15.3d **Ranges and Ratings for Soil Media**

S Range	Soil Media Rating
Thin or Absent	10
Gravel	10
Sand	9
Peat	8
Shrinking and/or Aggregated Clay	7
Sandy Loam	6
Loam	5
Silty Loam	4
Clay Loam	3
Muck	2
Nonshrinking and Nonaggregated Clay	1
Weight: 2	Pesticide Weight: 5

TABLE 15.3e **Ranges and Ratings for Topography**

T   *Topography (Percent Slope)*

Range	Rating
0–2	10
2–6	9
6–12	5
12–18	3
18+	1
Weight: 1	Pesticide Weight: 3

TABLE 15.3f **Ranges and Ratings for Impact of the Vadose Zone Media**

I   *Impact of the Vadose Zone Media*

Range	Rating	Typical Rating
Confining Layer	1	1
Silt/Clay	2–6	3
Shale	2–5	3
Limestone	2–7	6
Sandstone	4–8	6
Bedded Limestone, Sandstone, Shale	4–8	6
Sand and Gravel with significant Silt and Clay	4–8	6
Metamorphic/Igneous	2–8	4
Sand and Gravel	6–9	8
Basalt	2–10	9
Karst Limestone	8–10	10
Weight: 5		Pesticide Weight: 4

TABLE 15.3g **Ranges and Ratings for Hydraulic Conductivity**

C   *Hydraulic Conductivity (GPD/FT²)*

Range	Rating
1–100	1
100–300	2
300–700	4
700–1000	6
1000–2000	8
2000+	10
Weight: 3	Pesticide Weight: 2

data on all of the DRASTIC factors are not available. To help implement DRASTIC where detailed data may not be available, the method provides information on **hydrogeologic settings** for different groundwater regions of the country. Figure 15.9 shows the 11 groundwater regions. For each region, different hydrogeologic settings are identified, and for each setting, DRASTIC factor values are estimated and DRASTIC scores are calculated. Table 15.4 lists all the hydrogeologic settings and their DRASTIC scores.

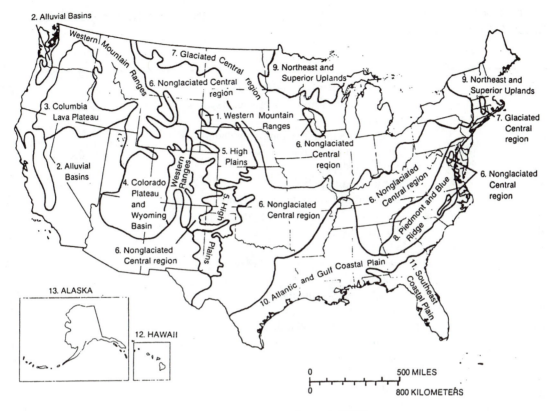

Figure 15.9 Groundwater Regions of the United States. *Source:* Aller et al. (1987).

TABLE 15.4 Hydrogeologic Settings and Associated DRASTIC Indexes Sorted by Ground-Water Regions

Settings	Descriptions	Rating
1Aa East	Mountain Slopes	65
1Ab West	Mountain Slopes	70
1Ba East	Alluvial Mountain Valleys	128
1Bb West	Alluvial Mountain Valleys	146
1Ca East	Mountain Flanks	83
1CB West	Mountain Flanks	106
1D	Glacial Mountain Valleys	180
1Ea East	Wide Alluvial Valleys (External Drainage)	158
1Eb West	Wide Alluvial Valleys (External Drainage)	180
1F	Coastal Beaches	196
1G	Swamp/Marsh	139
1H	Mud Flows	130
2A	Mountain Slopes	74
2B	Alluvial Mountain Valleys	132
2C	Alluvial Fans	122
2D	Alluvial Basins (Internal Drainage)	122
2E	Playa Lakes	110
2F	Swamp/Marsh	127
2G	Coastal Lowlands	202

TABLE 15.4 (*Continued*)   **Hydrogeologic Settings and Associated DRASTIC Indexes Sorted by Ground-Water Regions**

Settings	Descriptions	Rating
2Ha	River Alluvium with Overbank Deposits	163
2Hb	River Alluvium without Overbank Deposits	191
2I	Mud Flows	149
2J	Alternating Sandstone and Shale Sequences	112
2K	Continental Deposits	96
3A	Mountain Slopes	86
3B	Alluvial Mountain Valleys	168
3C	Hydraulically Connected Lava Flows	146
3D	Lava Flows Not Connected Hydraulically	105
3E	Alluvial Fans	105
3F	Swamp/Marsh	139
3G	River Alluvium	147
4A	Resistant Ridges	86
4B	Consolidated Sedimentary Rock	87
4C	River Alluvium	152
4D	Alluvium and Dune Sand	102
4E	Swamp/Marsh	176
5A	Ogalala	109
5B	Alluvium	107
5C	Sand Dunes	150
5D	Playa Lakes	110
5E	Braided River Deposits	185
5F	Swamp/Marsh	196
5Ga	River Alluvium with Overbank Deposits	129
5Gb	River Alluvium without Overbank Deposits	143
5H	Alternating Sandstone, Limestone and Shale Sequences	80
6A	Mountain Flanks	103
6B	Alluvial Mountain Valleys	152
6C	Mountain Flanks	105
6Da	Alternating Sandstone, Limestone and Shale-Thin Soil	139
6Db	Alternating Sandstone, Limestone and Shale-Deep Regolith	125
6E	Solution Limestone	195
6Fa	River Alluvium with Overbank Deposits	126
6Fb	River Alluvium without Overbank Deposits	187
6G	Braided River Deposits	190
6H	Triassic Basins	106
6I	Swamp/Marsh	144
6J	Metamorphic/Igneous Domes and Fault Blocks	71
6K	Unconsolidated and Semiconsolidated Aquifiers	101
7Aa	Glacial Till Over Bedded Sedimentary Rock	103
7Ab	Glacial Till Over Outwash	137
7Ac	Glacial Till Over Solution Limestone	139
7Ad	Glacial Till Over Sandstone	109
7Ae	Glacial Till Over Shale	88
7Ba	Outwash	176
7Bb	Outwash Over Bedded Sedimentary Rock	158

TABLE 15.4 (*Continued*) **Hydrogeologic Settings and Associated DRASTIC Indexes Sorted by Ground-Water Regions**

Settings	Descriptions	Rating
7Bc	Outwash Over Solution Limestone	186
7C	Moraine	135
7D	Buried Valley	158
7Ea	River Alluvium with Overbank Deposits	134
7Eb	River Alluvium without Overbank Deposits	191
7F	Glacial Lake Deposits	135
7G	Thin Till Over Bedded Sedimentary Rock	121
7H	Beaches, Beach Ridges and Sand Dunes	202
7I	Swamp/Marsh	150
8A	Mountain Slopes	75
8B	Alluvial Mountain Valleys	162
8C	Mountain Flanks	106
8D	Regolith	100
8E	River Alluvium	176
8F	Mountain Crests	70
8G	Swamp/Marsh	120
9A	Mountain Slopes	75
9B	Alluvial Mountain Valley	180
9C	Mountain Flanks	106
9Da	Glacial Till Over Crystalline Bedrock	113
9Db	Glacial Till Over Outwash	139
9E	Outwash	190
9F	Moraine	166
9Ga	River Alluvium with Overbank Deposits	146
9Gb	River Alluvium without Overbank Deposits	191
9H	Swamp/Marsh	120
9I	Bedrock Uplands	118
9J	Glacial Lake/Glacial Marine Deposits	120
9K	Beaches, Beach Ridges and Sand Dunes	181
10Aa	Regional Aquifers	82
10Ab	Unconsolidated and Semiconsolidated Shallow Surficial Aquifer	184
10Ba	River Alluvium with Overbank Deposits	142
10Bb	River Alluvium without Overbank Deposits	187
10C	Swamp	202
11A	Solution Limestone and Shallow Surficial Aquifers	218
11B	Coastal Deposits	191
11C	Swamp	224
11D	Beaches and Bars	190
12A	Mountain Slopes	154
12B	Alluvial Mountain Valleys	184
12C	Volcanic Uplands	165
12D	Coastal Beaches	201
13A	Alluvium	140
13B	Glacial and Glaciolacustrine Deposits of the Interior Valleys	141
13C	Coastal Lowland Deposits	140
13D	Bedrock of the Uplands and Mountains	92

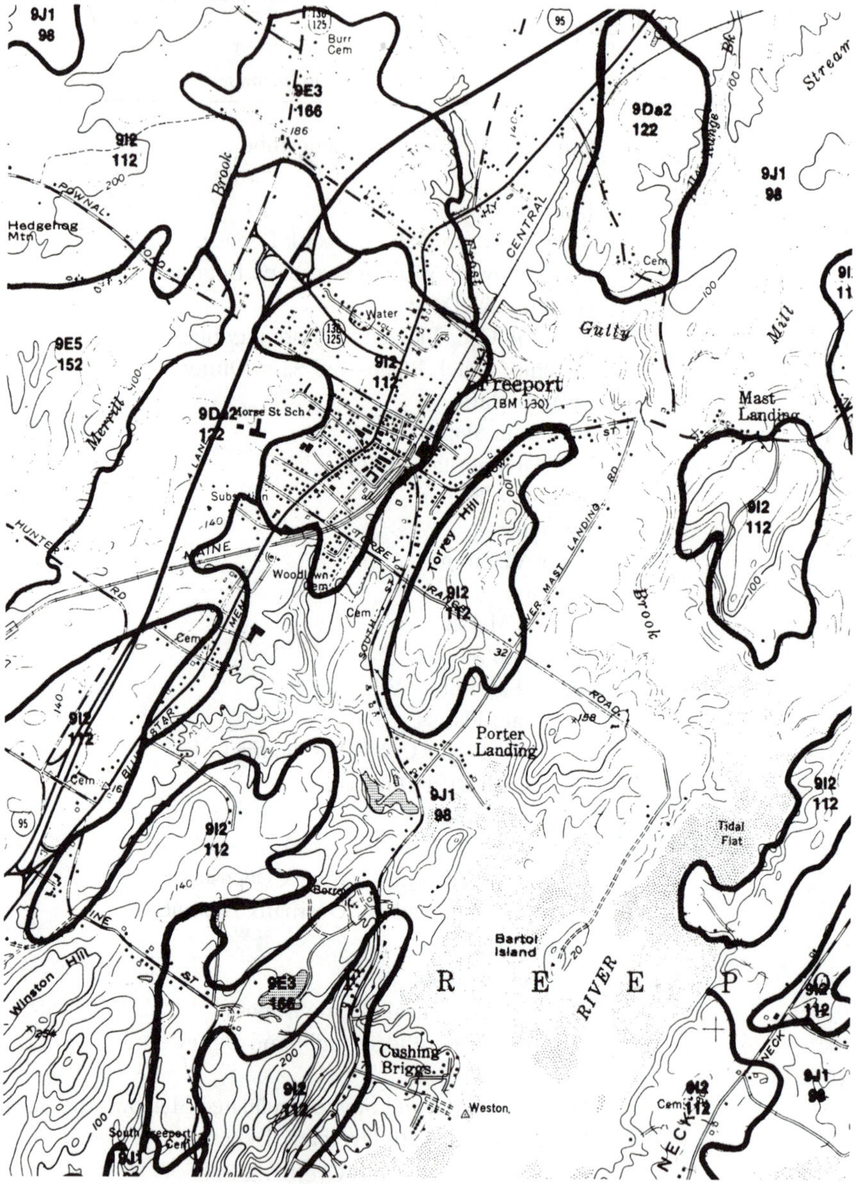

Figure 15.10 Working DRASTIC Map. *Source:* Aller et al. (1987).

The procedure for conducting a DRASTIC study culminating in a county DRASTIC map involves the following steps:

1. Gather available data on DRASTIC factors from soil surveys, geologic maps and studies, and other sources.
2. For each factor, prepare a map overlay displaying the values for the factor.
3. If data are not available for certain areas or factors, identify the hydrogeologic settings for the areas and consult the provided factor data for these settings. Fill in gaps in factor overlays as necessary (see figure 15.10).

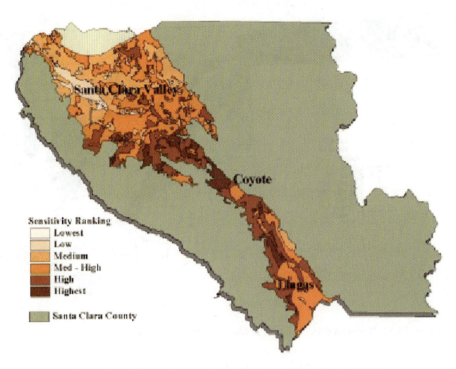

Figure 15.11 DRASTIC Map for Santa Clara Valley, California. *Source:* Santa Clara Valley Water District (2001).

4. Overlay individual factor maps and delineate boundaries of combined factors.
5. Combine overlays of all factors and delineate boundaries of all combinations of factors.
6. Calculate total DRASTIC scores for each delineated area.
7. Group areas into 20-point categories (i.e., 0–19, 20–39, 40–59, etc.), and color map by category.
8. Provide legend for the map and provide interpretation in accompanying text.

Figures 15.11 and 12 give examples of final DRASTIC maps. Visually they show by color areas of relative potential for groundwater contamination. Efforts continue to improve the DRASTIC method (USGS, 1999; Fritch, McKnight, Yelderman, and Arnold, 2000). When producing DRASTIC maps and interpreting their results, it is important to consider the major assumptions used in the development of the procedure:

1. The contaminant is introduced at the ground level.
2. The contaminant is flushed into the groundwater by precipitation.
3. The contaminant has the mobility of water.
4. The area evaluated using DRASTIC is 100 acres or larger.

This final assumption is perhaps the most important. Because of the lack of precision in the method, it cannot be used for small areas. No area on the DRASTIC map

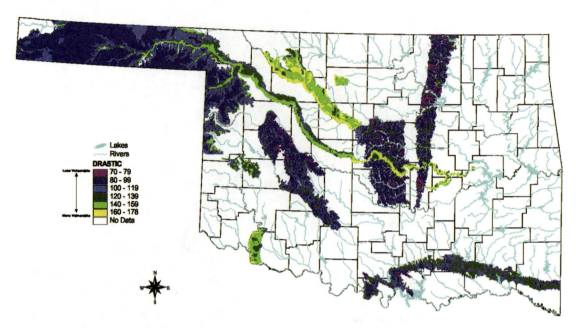

Figure 15.12 Oklahoma DRASTIC Study of Major Aquifers in the State. *Source:* Osborn, Eckenstein, and Koon (1998).

can be less than 100 acres. As discussed in the following section, DRASTIC maps can be used to target high potential areas for action or special standards. Still, the 100-acre limitation inhibits the use of the DRASTIC map as the sole basis for overlay zoning.

Groundwater Source Protection

The SDWA was passed in 1974 and amended in 1986 and 1996. It provided detailed community drinking water standards and water supply monitoring and reporting requirements. The recent amendments recognized the limitations of relying on water treatment to ensure safe drinking water supplies and stressed protection of water sources. Source waters of public drinking water are classified as groundwater, surface water, and groundwater under the influence of surface water. This latter category is groundwater subject to surface pollution like protozoa and turbidity.

Under the SDWA, states are required to conduct **source water assessment** for each public water system (PWS). There are 161,000 public water systems (PWSs). These include 53,400 community water systems (CWSs) that serve 270 million people in the United States, 18,700 nontransient, noncommunity water systems (NTNCWSs) such as schools and factories that serve the same people more than 6 months but not year-round, and 89,000 transient noncommunity water systems (TNCWSs) like restaurants on wells. All federal regulations apply to CWSs, most requirements apply to NTNCWSs, and only regulations for contaminants that pose immediate health risks (like microbial contamination) apply to TNCWSs, unless they rely on surface sources. In that case they must have filtration and disinfection. Of the CWSs, 84 percent serve 3,300 or fewer people, and 7 percent serve more than 10,000 and 81 percent of the population (Tiemann, 2003).

The source water assessment includes:

- delineation of the source water protection area (the watershed or groundwater recharge area that may contribute pollution);
- contamination source inventory, which identifies potential sources of pollution;
- susceptibility determination, which indicates potential for contamination; and
- dissemination of source water assessment results to the public.

Source water assessments aim to protect public health, prepare water systems for possible problems, and identify cost-effective ways for communities to achieve safe water standards. For surface water sources, source water protection focuses on the watershed of the source; for groundwater sources, it focuses on wellhead protection (U.S. EPA, 2000).

Sole Source Aquifers

The SDWA also established the **Sole Source Aquifer (SSA) Program** to protect important groundwater sources. A sole source or principal source aquifer is one that supplies at least 50 percent of the drinking water consumed in the area overlying the aquifer. The Edwards Aquifer in Texas, was the first SSA designated in the country. By 2000, there were 70 designated SSAs in the United States.

Development projects having the potential to contaminate designated SSAs are subject to EPA review by a groundwater specialist. For example, these projects might include highways, wastewater or stormwater treatment facilities, agricultural projects, and others. This review can result in requirements for design improvements, groundwater monitoring, and other measures.

As the major water supply for central Texas including the cities of San Antonio and Austin, the Edwards Aquifer has become one of the most managed groundwater systems in the country. The coordinated effort is administered by the Texas Natural Resources Conservation Commission (see http://gis.tnrcc.state.tx.us/website/iredwards1/viewer.htm and http://www.tnrcc.state.tx.us/admin/topdoc/rg/011.pdf), the regional Edwards Aquifer Authority (see http://www.edwardsaquifer.org/), as well as the cities and counties relying on the water source. Austin's drinking water protection zone is an important part of its land use controls (see figure 7.6).

Wellhead Protection Planning

Section 1428 of the 1986 SDWA Amendments established the **Wellhead Protection Program (WHP).** It aims to help communities protect vulnerable groundwater supplies by controlling land use development and practices around public drinking water wells. All but one of the states have EPA-approved WHPs. To establish a WHP, communities must delineate the source water protection area, identify sources of contamination, and develop regulatory and nonregulatory measures to manage contamination.

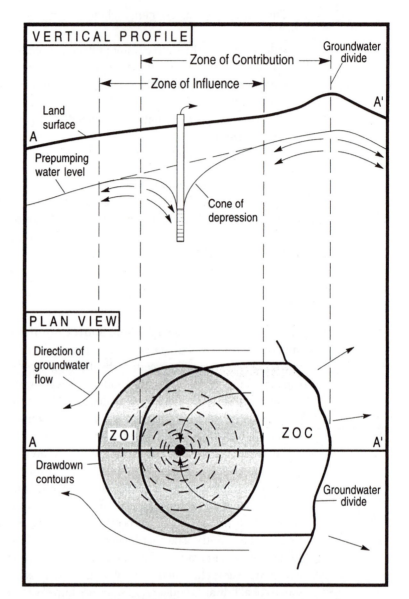

Figure 15.13 Zone of Influence (ZOI) and Zone of Contribution (ZOC). *Source:* Jon Witten and Scott Horsley. 1995. *A Guide to Wellhead Protection.* Planning Advisory Service Report 457/458. Used with permission of the American Planning Association.

Delineation of Wellhead Protection Areas

The first step in wellhead protection is delineating the protection area. Although DRASTIC provides a countywide view of its hydrogeology, wellhead protection focuses on individual wells and the land area that must be controlled to protect the water supply. The wellhead protection area (WHPA) does not necessarily include the entire aquifer and its recharge area. As shown in figure 15.14, the WHPA tends to be a smaller part of the total aquifer. A technical challenge is determining the boundaries of that area. First some definitions are illustrated in figure 15.13:

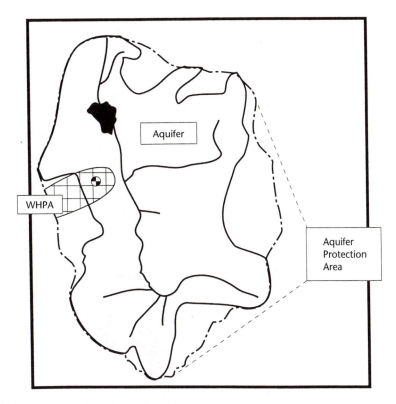

Figure 15.14 Aquifer Recharge versus Wellhead Protection Areas. *Source:* Jon Witten and Scott Horsley. 1995. *A Guide to Wellhead Protection.* Planning Advisory Service Report 457/458. Used with permission of the American Planning Association.

- **Zone of Influence:** the surface projection of the boundaries of the cone of depression around the well.
- **Zone of Contribution:** the surface projection of the boundaries of the portion of the aquifer recharge area that contributes water to the well. This normally extends to a localized groundwater divide on the upflow side and to a portion of the cone of depression on the downflow side.

Delineation of the WHPA can be done in different ways depending on available data and analysis. Figures 15.14 and 15.15 show two examples of WHPAs. The example in figure 15.14 uses three WHPA zones. The first uses a fixed radius around the well, the second zone is the primary recharge area, and the third is the secondary recharge. Figure 15.15 shows a private well protection zone based on a fixed radius of 100 feet around the well plus a 200-foot buffer up the groundwater flow gradient.

Figures 15.16 and 15.17 show the integration of hydrogeologic studies and WHPA delineation by the Hamilton to New Baltimore (OH) Groundwater Consortium (HNBGC). The multijurisdictional consortium used aquifer, DRASTIC, and subsurface time of travel studies to identify critical recharge zones for their groundwater sources (HNBGC, 2003).

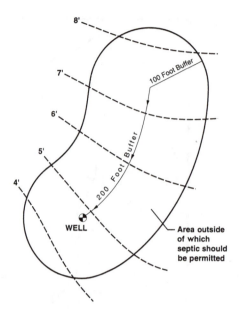

Figure 15.15 Private Well Protection Zone. *Source:* Jon Witten and Scott Horsley. 1995. *A Guide to Wellhead Protection.* Planning Advisory Service Report 457/458. Used with permission of the American Planning Association.

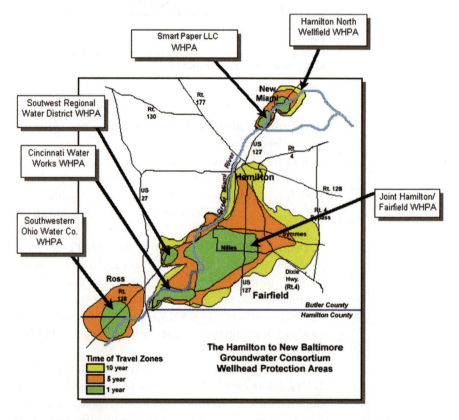

Figure 15.16 The Hamilton to New Baltimore Groundwater Consortium Wellhead Protection Areas. *Source:* HNBGC (2003).

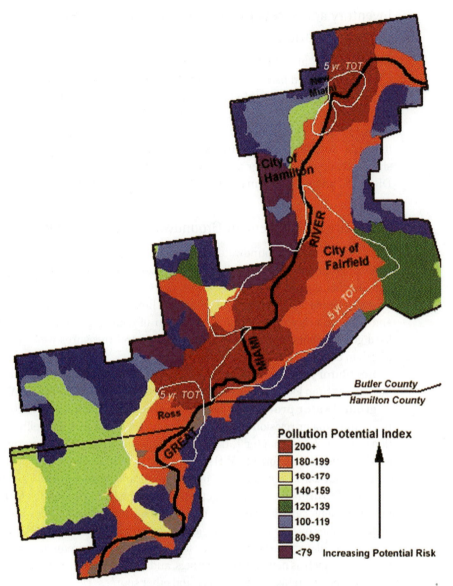

Pollution Potential Index

- 200+
- 180-199
- 160-179
- 140-159
- 120-139
- 100-119
- 80-99
- <79   Increasing Potential Risk

The Hamilton to New Baltimore
Groundwater Consortium
Drastic Ratings Map

Figure 15.17 Hamilton to New Baltimore (OH) DRASTIC Map. *Source:* HNBGC (2003).

Inventory and Assess Threats and Potential Sources of Contamination

Both DRASTIC and WHPA delineation are based on hydrogeology, but they do not consider what land uses and sources may contribute to contamination. An inventory of potential sources of contamination is necessary to identify existing and future problems. An inventory includes locations of waste landfills and lagoons, areas of septic system use, gas stations and other underground storage tanks, industrial facilities with hazardous materials, and agricultural areas with extensive pesticide and fertilizer use. These threats can be mapped and overlaid onto DRASTIC and/or WHPA maps (Crowley and Tulloch, 2002).

Formulate and Implement Groundwater Protection Measures

EPA's programs for groundwater are not regulatory. There are no enforceable national groundwater standards. Federal groundwater programs generally coordinate, facilitate, educate, and assist with protection of groundwater. Management largely depends on state and local initiatives. Box 15.1 gives examples of regulatory and nonregulatory measures for protection of source groundwater available to local governments. Most of these land use control measures were discussed at length in chapters 5 and 7.

Regulatory measures include land use zoning to prevent potentially polluting sources from locating in susceptibility or wellhead protection areas. **Wellhead or groundwater protection overlay zoning** is an effective approach that does not require major revision of existing ordinances. Illustrated for wellhead protection in figure 7.4 in chapter 7, the overlay is placed on top of existing zoning. The overlay zone will conform to WHPA boundaries. Within the zone, special conditions or standards are required of proposed land uses. Figure 7.5 illustrates Austin's (TX) drinking water protection zone for the Edwards Aquifer. Cluster zoning regulations can also be tailored to wellhead protection by allowing development densities on-site while setting aside sensitive areas, including WHPAs.

Other regulatory measures include local permitting requirements for groundwater sources, such as new wells and springs, and for potential contamination sources, such as septic systems, waste lagoons, and other sources. Depending on groundwater protection needs, specific conditions, standards, or restrictions may apply.

Nonregulatory measures include public education, household hazardous waste collection, continuous groundwater monitoring, and land acquisition of protection areas, among others. A good example of land acquisition is the Edwards Aquifer in Texas (see figure 15.4). Government Canyon is the recharge zone for the Edwards Aquifer. A proposal to build 766 homes and an 18-hole golf course in the Canyon sparked formation of a public-private coalition in San Antonio that purchased the land for $2 million. The City of Austin voted to authorize $20 million in bonds to purchase critical watershed land for open space (U.S. EPA, 2001).

Mapping of susceptibility, protection areas, and threats does not indicate if there is a groundwater problem. **Groundwater monitoring** is necessary to see if there is contamination and where it occurs. Comprehensive groundwater moni-

BOX 15.1—Regulatory and Nonregulatory Measures for Wellhead Protection Areas

Regulatory Tools

Land Use Controls: Zoning ordinances, subdivision controls, cluster and planned unit development

Prohibitions or conditional permitting of potentially contaminating uses: Gas stations, landfills, industries handling hazardous chemicals

Health regulations: Septic system controls

Nonregulatory Measures

Public education

Land purchase, conservation easements

Groundwater monitoring

toring is not available in most areas, so existing well data often must be used to get a snapshot of groundwater conditions.

The Virginia Cooperative Extension Service at Virginia Tech implemented an effective household well and spring monitoring program in several Virginia counties with the dual objectives of providing assistance to households with wells and gathering onetime samples of groundwater quality. The program advertises a public well water quality workshop to which well and spring users are invited to bring water samples from their sources. At the workshop, presenters talk generally about good well and springbox maintenance and water handling. At a second workshop, results of lab testing of the samples and source-specific recommendations are provided to the households. Testing includes bacteria, inorganic chemicals such as iron and sulfur, hardness, nitrates, and in some cases pesticides. The data are also used to provide a baseline of groundwater quality. Knowing the location of the samples, the data can be mapped to show hot spots of well-water pollution.

Given the information from susceptibility and protection area mapping, inventory of potential threats, and groundwater monitoring, a locality is prepared to develop a groundwater management program. If monitoring discovers severe problems, some groundwater **remediation** may be necessary.

Summary

Groundwater is an important source of drinking water. Although most of population in the United States uses surface water supplies, about 80 percent of public water systems and nearly all individual systems depend on groundwater sources. Most individual groundwater sources are used without treatment.

Groundwater is closely related to the land since nearly all of it comes from infiltration recharge from the land surface. Impervious cover on the land surface inhibits infiltration and recharge. Unconfined shallow aquifers are closely connected to surface waters. Groundwater contributes baseflows to gaining streams and is recharged by losing streams. In fractured or karst geology, there are direct conduits between surface waters and groundwaters. Because of its close connection to the land surface, groundwater is susceptible to contamination from surface sources, including underground storage tanks of petroleum and other chemical products, landfills and other waste areas, polluted stormwater, septic systems and wastewater lagoons, among others.

As a result, management of groundwater requires planning and management of the land. It is important to understand groundwater flow and recharge as well as susceptibility to contamination. In recharge areas, impervious surfaces should be minimized, and potential sources of contamination should be restricted. DRASTIC and other hydrogeological studies can help understand surface-groundwater relationships and guide land use decisions.

Special care should be taken to manage land use in the vicinity of wellheads of public water supplies. Overlay zoning and other land regulations are appropriate to restrict land uses to protect public health.

16 ▪ Landscape Ecology, Urban Forestry, and Wetlands

Urbanization and other intensive use of land and related water resources result in significant impacts on natural ecosystems, the habitats and wildlife they support, and the environmental functions they provide to human society. At the same time, people have increasingly recognized the values associated with natural features and the ecological integrity of the landscape. These values have been translated into increased property values and greater public acceptance of land use management and development decisions that reflect sensitivity to greenspace, ecosystems, and habitats.

This chapter deals with planning considerations and methods involved in gathering, analyzing, and displaying ecological information for purposes of guiding land use and resource development and conservation. It employs the simple four-step planning process given in box 2.2: inventories (what do we have?); needs assessment (what are our problems, objectives, and priorities?); management strategies, plans, and programs (what should we do?); and implementation and monitoring (let's do it!).

The discussion in this chapter focuses primarily on applying this process to vegetation and urban forestry and wetlands, riparian, and coastal ecosystems. Chapter 17 expands this discussion to wildlife habitats and planning for biodiversity.

Fundamentals of Landscape Ecology

Although the methods and techniques discussed herein do not necessitate a detailed background in ecological science, it is important to understand a set of fundamental principles, which serve as the basis for managing and protecting natural ecosystems. **Ecology** is the study of the interrelationships of living organisms with one another and with the physical environment. It can focus on an individual, a species population, an ecological community, or ecosystems of various scales from regional to local. **Biodiversity** is simply defined as the variety of life and all processes that keep life functioning (Keystone Center, 1991). It is studied at genetic, species, and ecosystem levels. Global efforts to manage biodiversity aim to arrest species extinction and preserve intact natural ecosystems. Box 16.1 provides an

BOX 16.1—Some Basic Ecological Concepts

Energy and Material Flow in Ecosystems

Simple food chains or webs are often used to characterize the flow of energy and minerals in ecosystems (figure 16.1). Through photosynthesis, plants are able to convert radiant solar energy into chemical energy. They store this energy in their biomass for their own use and for the use of all other forms of life. Plants are therefore called **producers** or **autotrophs** ("self-feeding") as distinguished from the **consumers** or **heterotrophs** ("other feeding"). The levels of the food chain are called **trophic levels,** where I is the primary or plant level, II is the plant eater or herbivore level, III is the eater of the plant eater or first carnivore level, and so on.

About 80–90 percent of energy consumed by the various life-forms is required for maintenance and **respiration,** energy that is ultimately lost as heat. As a result, the carnivorous occupants of higher trophic levels require tremendous quantities of plant biomass to support their food chain. Thus, they usually require very large habitats. This concept of food chain respiration and biomass requirements is also the basis of **biomagnification** of contaminants. Animals must absorb large amounts of food compared to their body weight since so much of the energy must be expended for respiration. If that food source contains contaminants that do not pass through but tend to be stored in fats and tissues, those contaminants will concentrate quite readily. And as one moves up the food chain, one is exposed to food with higher concentrations. This is why Great Lakes fish contain high concentrations of toxins and are subject to human consumption advisories.

Whereas energy flows through ecosystems, minerals cycle around them, changing from organic form in living matter to inorganic form in the nutrient pool and back again. **Decomposers** (fungi, bacteria, and other microorganisms) play the crucial role of converting excrement and other dead organic material into the inorganic nutrients that plants can absorb and reconvert to organic plant material. The important elements of life—carbon, hydrogen, oxygen, nitrogen, phosphorus, potassium, sulfur—all are involved in individual cycles called **biogeochemical** cycles; the name indicates the various forms the elements can take.

Succession and Productivity

Like their respective members, ecosystems develop from a young to a mature state through the process of **ecological succession.** For example, a shallow lake over time may convert to a swamp, then a meadow, and finally a forest. The mature state is called the **climax community.** The type of vegetation that characterizes it depends largely on the physical parameters of the area, principally its **temperature, sunlight, moisture,** and **soil conditions.** Thus, succession results from the

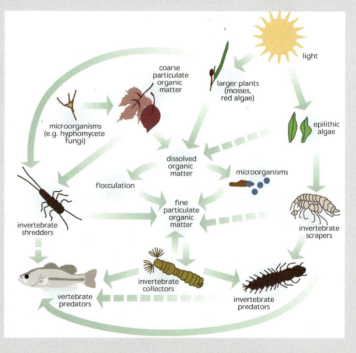

Figure 16.1 Aquatic Food Web. *Source:* FISRWG (1998).

Continued ➤

BOX 16.1—(continued)

modification of the physical environment by the community, but the physical environment determines the pattern, rate of change, and limits of succession (Odum, 1971). Figure 16.2 shows the climax vegetative communities, so-called biotic regions or **biomes,** associated with the various environmental conditions of North America.

In the process of maturing, an ecosystem, like an individual organism, enjoys an early period of high growth. This physical growth slows, ultimately ceasing by maturity. Growth is measured by **net community production** or the conversion of sunlight to a net increase in total biomass. Figure 16.3 shows that **gross primary production** (or the total photosynthesized primary energy) and **net primary production** (or the gross production minus plant respiration) begin low, grow, then level out at a maximum when the climax community is achieved. On the other hand, net community production rises initially to a peak, then falls off to zero at climax. The large net primary production is absorbed by heterotrophic respiration, particularly that of the decomposers. The following table below shows that net primary productivity varies considerably for different ecosystems, topped by salt marshes, freshwater wetlands, and tropical rain forests.

Net Productivity of Selected Ecosystems[*]

Salt marsh	2300	Cultivated land	750
Freshwater wetland	2000	Grassland	700
Tropical rainforest	2000	Boreal forest	500
Warm temperate mixed forest	1000	Desert	150
Cold deciduous forest	1000		

grams/m²/year

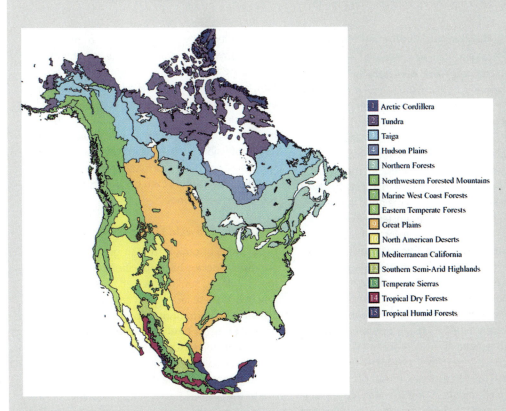

Figure 16.2 Major Biotic Regions of North America. *Source:* Commission for Environmental Cooperation (1997).

1 Arctic Cordillera
2 Tundra
3 Taiga
4 Hudson Plains
5 Northern Forests
6 Northwestern Forested Mountains
7 Marine West Coast Forests
8 Eastern Temperate Forests
9 Great Plains
10 North American Deserts
11 Mediterranean California
12 Southern Semi-Arid Highlands
13 Temperate Sierras
14 Tropical Dry Forests
15 Tropical Humid Forests

Continued ➤

BOX 16.1—(continued)

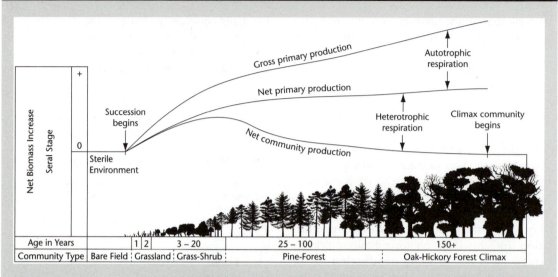

Figure 16.3 Ecological Succession and Productivity. In the early stages of succession, the ecosystem acts like a nutrient sponge, assimilating available nutrients into biomass. The magnitude of the sponge decreases as the climax community is approached. At climax, the same mass of nutrients leaves the ecosystem, primarily by decomposition, as enters it. Net community production drops to zero.

Diversity, Habitat and Ecological Niches

As an ecosystem develops toward maturity it tends to acquire greater **diversity** or a greater variety of organisms. Diversity can be measured in a number of ways, the simplest being **species richness** or the number of species per 1,000 individuals in an ecosystem. Other measures aim to incorporate species "evenness" or the apportionment of individuals to species. In most cases, diversity is directly correlated with the **stability** of an ecosystem, or its ability to maintain in the presence of some upsetting circumstance like drought or disease. High rates of species extinction have made protection of **biodiversity** an important objective in land and ecosystem management. It is the basis for the Endangered Species Act and other programs aiming to protect diversity at various scales: from the regional landscape to ecological communities to species populations and habitats to genetic diversity (Wilson, 1988, 2002).

An ecosystem provides a **habitat** or **habitat niche** for its member species, thus supplying them with their life needs of food, water, cover, and space. An ecosystem may provide only a limited number of habitat niches. Modifying an ecosystem may alter its ability to supply the needs of its members. Conversely, individual species themselves contribute to the complete fabric of the ecosystem. Each plays a functional role or occupies a special **ecological niche** in the ecosystem. Odum (1971) draws the analogy that a species' habitat niche is its "address," while its ecological niche is its "profession," ecologically speaking. If that species is removed from the ecosystem, either another species must then occupy its niche or the ecosystem will change.

Organism Growth: Liebig's Law

Populations of organisms can grow if conditions are right. Species have specific requirements for food nutrients, sunlight, water, and other factors. Any one of these factors can constrain or limit the growth of an organism or population. This is the basis of **Liebig's Law of the Minimum.** It states that under steady-state conditions, an organism's or population's growth is limited by the essential nutrient or factor present in the least amount relative to the species' needs. If that nutrient or factor is increased, the population will grow; if it is decreased, the population will decline.

Continued ➤

BOX 16.1—(continued)

The Concept of Carrying Capacity

Although Liebig's Law deals with the influence of specific factors on the population growth of individual species in an area, the concept of carrying capacity deals with the ability of the area to support them. The **carrying capacity** of an area is the number or biomass of organisms that can be sustained without adversely affecting that area. The term comes from the study of population dynamics and involves the concepts of **biotic potential** (or maximum reproduction rate) and **environmental resistance** (or the sum of environmental limiting factors that prevent the biotic potential from being realized) (Odum, 1971).

The most common growth pattern on populations in nature follows a sigmoid or S-shaped curve. In this case the environmental resistance to growth does not occur suddenly but increases gradually in response to greater population density. It can take the form of increased competition for food and space (and light for vegetation), increased transmission of disease, and increased predation. The rate of population growth starts slowly in the establishment phase, rises exponentially, then slows as it encounters increasing environmental resistance, and finally levels off at a sustainable population, which defines the area's carrying capacity. In reality, populations may oscillate around the carrying capacity, rising above it in favorable times only to fall below when conditions are unfavorable. In some cases, exceeding the carrying capacity may result in its reduction. For example, overgrazing can result in excessive erosion that may reduce grassland productivity and ultimately the grasslands carrying capacity. A further discussion of the application of the carrying capacity concept to managing human settlements is given in chapter 18.

overview of several concepts, including energy and mineral flow in ecosystems, ecological succession, biodiversity, limiting factors, and carrying capacity.

Ecology addresses a wide range of spatial scales, from a small local area like a stream section or reach to a catchment to a larger watershed to a still larger landscape scale to a regional scale. This "nesting" of scales is an important approach to bound a study area but recognize the area's relationship to smaller and larger ecosystems (see figure 10.1). A landscape is defined as an area having a repeated pattern of components including both natural and human-altered areas (FISRWG, 1998). Landscapes can range in size from a few to several thousand square miles. Landscape ecologists organize spatial structure with four basic components: matrix, patch, corridor, and mosaic (figure 16.4). These structural elements can be applied at multiple scales.

- **Matrix** is the land cover that is dominant and interconnected over majority of land surface (e.g., forest, agriculture, urban).
- **Patch** is a nonlinear polygon area less abundant than and different from matrix.
- **Corridor** is a linear or elongated patch that links other patches in the matrix.
- **Mosaic** is a collection of patches, none of which are dominant enough to be interconnected throughout landscape.

At the landscape scale, patches and corridors can be described as discrete ecosystems. Corridors play an important role as primary pathways for movement of

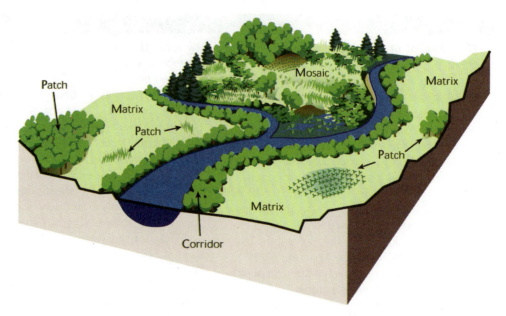

Figure 16.4 Spatial Structure in Landscape Ecology. *Source:* FISRWG (1998).

energy, materials, and organisms. They connect patches and are conduits between ecosystems and external environments.

Vegetation

Have you thanked a green plant today? Ecologically, plants are the producers of useful energy and materials for all of life. Environmentally, vegetation provides a variety of functions in erosion control, runoff control, slope and dune stabilization, atmospheric purification, and cover for wildlife. And in human settlements vegetation contributes to the quality of life in its value for forest products, recreation, aesthetics, windbreaks, and sun shading and temperature control. This section highlights the benefits of vegetation and methods of inventorying and assessing urban vegetation.

Box 16.2 lists the urban benefits of vegetation. Many of the environmental control benefits, such as erosion, runoff, and NPS pollution control and slope stability were discussed in earlier chapters. In addition, vegetation can help control noise and microclimatic conditions. The U.S. EPA has suggested the use of vegetation to counter the "urban heat island" effect by increasing cities' albedo (reflected solar radiation) and evapotranspiration cooling. The ecological benefits in wetland and coastal environments are discussed later in this chapter.

Classifying, Inventorying, and Mapping Vegetation

Vegetation information is usually displayed on maps showing vegetative types, existing woodlands and tree types, open lands, active farmland, wetlands, and other areas. An example is given in figure 16.5, a map of vegetative types in San

BOX 16.2 Benefits of Vegetation in Urban Areas

Environmental Control

- Erosion control
- Slope stability
- Runoff control
- NPS pollution control
- Dune stabilization
- Noise attenuation
- Glare and reflection reduction

Microclimate Control

- Temperature reduction (counters urban "heat island" effect)

- Wind control
- Shading

Architectural and Aesthetic Benefits

- Articulation of space
- Natural aesthetics

Ecological Benefits

- Wildlife habitat

Mateo County, California. These vegetation inventory maps can provide a base map for urban forestry programs and special studies of visual quality or special ecological zones such as wetlands, riparian lands along streams and lakes, dune systems along coasts, and habitats of specially classified or desirable wildlife species. They can provide guidance for land use policies and programs to protect vegetative and ecological features.

Vegetation inventory maps can be produced using available map and aerial photograph information. As discussed in chapter 11, the USGS 7.5-minute quadrangle series distinguishes forested from nonforested areas. More useful are land use and land cover maps, available for much of the United States at scales of 1:100,000 and 1:250,000. Illustrated in figure 11.7, the land cover information distinguishes types of forests, agricultural lands, rangeland, wetlands, and barren land, as well as developed land. (See "USGS Level 1 and 2 Land Use and Land Cover Classification System" in chapter 11.)

Aerial photographs are a useful source of vegetation information. Vegetative cover types can be distinguished from photographs by investigating differences in tone, texture, and pattern, as shown in the following list. The later section on urban forestry describes other methods for inventorying and assessing urban vegetation.

Interpreting Aerial Photos for Vegetation Inventories

1. Woodlands and forests are easily distinguished from nonforested lands:

   - Deciduous stands show branched texture in winter photos; show red in summer infrared color; and appear lighter than coniferous stands in infrared black and white.
   - Coniferous stands show fuller and darker than deciduous stands in winter photos and infrared black-and-white summer photos; appear dark purple in infrared color photos.

2. Orchards show a repetitive pattern.

3. Nonforested lands can be further interpreted:

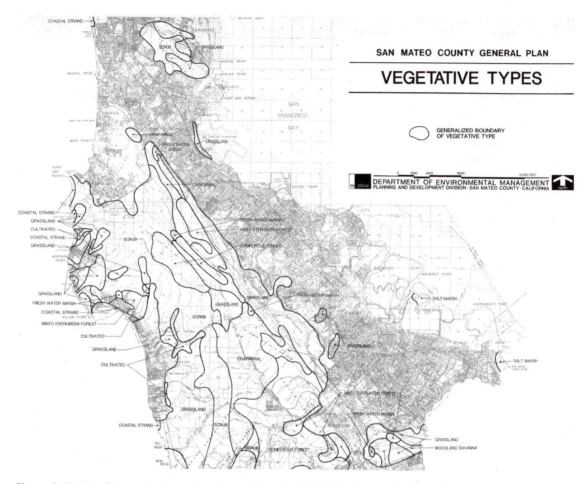

Figure 16.5 Map of Vegetative Types, San Mateo County (CA) General Plan. *Source:* San Mateo County (1984).

- Cropland can be distinguished by the presence of plowed furrows or the straight line pattern of the previous season's crop rows.
- Pasture land has a uniform texture on the photographs.
- Nonpasture open land will generally appear less uniform as the processes of succession may have begun with shrubs, bushes, and small trees contributing to the mixed texture.

When conducting vegetation studies, it is useful to categorize the existing vegetation. There are a variety of classification schemes; one useful for land cover inventories is described in figure 16.6 from Marsh (1978). It has four levels including vegetation structure, plant types, size and density, and site. **Vegetation structure** is indicated by the life-form of the vegetation, such as forest, brush, or wetland. The dominant individual **plant types** are indicated in the second level by common name (e.g., oak, cattail, etc.). The third level, **size and density,** involves the range of stem diameters and the number of stems per acre, or simply percent cover for grasses and shrubs. And the fourth level gives the **site features** or habitat type, such as greenbelt, farmland, tidal marsh, and so on.

Level I (vegetative structure)		Level II (dominant plant types)	Level III (size and density)	Level IV (site and habitat or associated use)	Level V (special plant species)
Forest (trees with average height greater than 15 ft with at least 60% canopy cover)		E.g., oak, hickory, willow, cottonwood, elm, basswood, maple, beach, ash	Tree size (diameter at breast height) Density (number of average stems per acre)	E.g., upland (i.e., well-drained terrain), floodplain, slope face, woodlot, greenbelt, parkland, residential land	Rare and endangered species; often ground plants associated with certain forest types
Woodland (trees with average height greater than 15 ft with 20–60% canopy cover)		E.g., pine, spruce, balsam fir, hemlock, douglas fir, cedar	Size range (difference between largest and smallest stems)	E.g., upland (i.e., well-drained terrain), floodplain, slope face, woodlot, greenbelt, parkland, residential land	Rare and endangered species; often ground plants associated with certain forest types
Orchard or plantation (same as woodland or forest but with regular spacing)		E.g., apple, peach, cherry, spruce, pine	Tree size; density	E.g., active farmland, abandoned farmland	Species with potential in landscaping for proposed development
Brush (trees and shrubs generally less than 15 ft high with high density of stems, but variable canopy cover)		E.g., sumac, willow, lilac, hawthorn, tag alder, pin cherry, scrub oak, juniper	Density	E.g., vacant farmland, landfill, disturbed terrain (e.g., former construction site)	Species of significance to landscaping for proposed development
Fencerows (trees and shrubs of mixed forms along borders such as road, fields, yards, playgrounds)		Any trees or shrubs	Tree size; density	E.g., active farmland, road right-of-way, yards, playgrounds	Species of value as animal habitat and utility in screening
Wetland (generally low, dense plant covers in wet areas)		E.g., cattail, tag alder, cedar, cranberry, reeds	Percent cover	E.g., floodplain, bog, tidal marsh, reservoir backwater, river delta	Species and plant communities of special importance ecologically and hydrologically; rare and endangered species
Grassland (herbs, with grasses dominant)		E.g., big blue stem bunch grass, dune grass	Percent cover	E.g., prairie, tundra, pasture, vacant farmland	Species and communities of special ecological significance; rare and endangered species.
Field (tilled or recently tilled farmland)		E.g., corn, soybeans, wheat; also weeds	Field size	E.g., sloping or flat, ditched and drained, muckland, irrigated	Special and unique crops; exceptional levels of productivity in standard crops

Figure 16.6 Four-Level Vegetation Classification System. Source: William Marsh, *Environmental Analysis: For Land Use and Site Planning*, 1978, McGraw-Hill. Reprinted with permission of McGraw-Hill Companies.

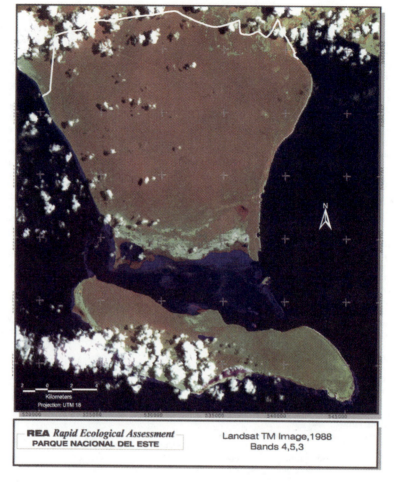

Figure 16.7 Example Maps from Rapid Ecological Assessment in the Dominican Republic. *Source:* Sayre et al. (2000).

Rapid Ecological Assessment

Rapid ecological assessment (REA) is a flexible, accelerated, and targeted biodiversity survey of vegetation types and species in a terrestrial area. It uses remotely sensed data and images, reconnaissance overflights, field monitoring, and spatial information visualization for conservation planning. Most applications by TNC and partner organizations in the last decade have been in critical ecosystems in mostly Latin American developing countries where limited ecological data exists for conservation planning. REA emphasizes speed (less than a year from start to finish), upfront planning, landscape-level (coarse filter by remote sensing) and species-level (fine filter by field monitoring) assessments, GIS mapping techniques, scientific documentation, and capacity building and partnerships (Sayre et al., 2000).

REA has three objectives:

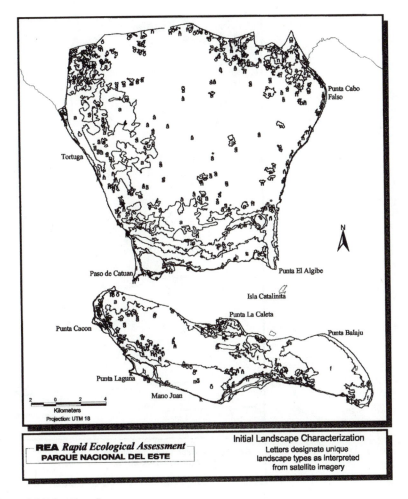

Figure 16.7 *(continued)*

1. Characterize vegetation types from remote sensing imagery interpretation and assess biodiversity of these habitats by field study.
2. Assign biodiversity significance priorities to habitat units for informed conservation management.
3. Recommend candidate areas for permanent conservation.

To achieve these objectives, REA includes the following steps:

1. Acquisition and interpretation of satellite and aerial photograph images of the study area, including current color-infrared, Landsat TM, high-resolution satellite data, and targeted reconnaissance overflights, as available.
2. Planning and training workshops for involved personnel.
3. Field monitoring of samples of vegetative types from image interpretation for verification of vegetation type and collection of species data. Paper or electronic (e.g., handheld computers, GPS, and Cyber-

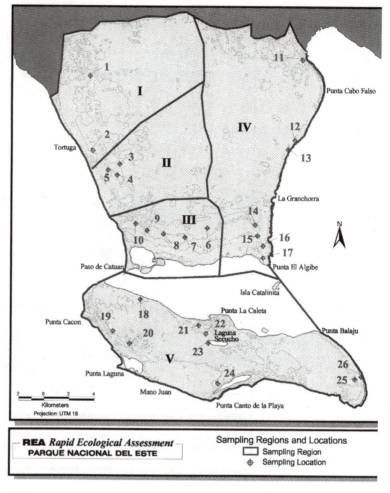

Figure 16.7 *(continued)*

tracker software [see chapter 13]) logging forms are used for field monitoring.

4. Synthesis and visualization of information in map form using GIS.
5. Assignment of biodiversity significance levels (i.e., highest, high, moderate, minor) based on biodiversity, condition and extent of habitat, connectivity potential, landscape congruity, and threats.
6. Recommendations for management strategies and candidate sites for permanent conservation.

Figure 16.7 illustrates four products of 1994 REA for the Parque Nacional del Este (National Park of the East) in the Dominican Republic (TNC, 1997). Figure 16.7a gives a color-infrared satellite image of the park. The color-infrared bands (Landsat TM bands 4, 5, and 3) are useful for terrestrial vegetation mapping. Figure 16.7b shows the initial landscape characterization from image interpretation. Spectrally unique areas are identified as polygons and

Figure 16.7 *(continued)*

labeled, even if the specific vegetation class is unknown. More detailed aerial photographs or reconnaissance overflights may be necessary to identify specific classes. Figure 16.7c stratifies the site into sampling regions delineated for ecological or logistic reasons. Field monitoring sampling locations are chosen to represent unique communities of the initial landscape characterization. Figure 16.7d gives proposed zonation for conservation-oriented management of the park (Sayre et al., 2000).

Vegetative Buffers

Vegetative buffers use permanent vegetation strategically located to enhance ecological functions and landscape conditions, including:

- stable and productive soils;
- cleaner water;

Figure 16.8 Riparian Forest Buffers. *Source:* USDA, NRCS (1998).

- enhanced aquatic and terrestrial wildlife habitat and populations;
- protected crops, livestock, and structures;
- enhanced aesthetics and recreation opportunities; and
- sustainable landscapes.

After a 1993 National Research Council report recommended the increased use of buffers, the Natural Resources Conservation Service (NRCS) established the National Conservation Buffer Initiative (NCBI) in 1996. The Initiative now involves more than 100 conservation agencies, agribusinesses, and agricultural and environmental organizations, all partnering to promote use of conservation buffers (USDA, 1999).

NRCS identifies several different vegetative buffers, six of which are described in box 16.3: riparian buffers, filter strips, contoured grass strips, grassed waterways, windbreaks, and field cross-wind traps. Other buffers include living snow fences (similar to windbreaks) and alley cropping.

Riparian buffers are perhaps the most important. These areas of trees and shrubs next to streams, lakes, and wetlands protect water bodies by intercepting surface runoff and the sediment and pollutants it carries. In addition, buffers provide food and cover for wildlife, shade to lower shoreline water temperatures, slow flood flows, stabilize stream banks and shorelines, and provide litter and woody debris for aquatic organisms. The wildlife corridor benefits of buffers are discussed further in chapter 17.

Forest buffers provide the widest range of benefits (figure 16.8). As figure 16.9 shows, riparian vegetative buffers include three zones. Zone 1 is closest to the stream or water body and includes water-loving vegetation like willows or cottonwoods. This

BOX 16.3—Six Variations of Vegetative Buffers

Riparian Buffers

A riparian buffer is an area of trees and shrubs located adjacent to streams, lakes, ponds, and wetlands. It intercepts contaminants from surface runoff and shallow subsurface water flow. The buffer also can be designed to enhance wildlife habitat, impact water temperature, and aid in stream bank stability.

Filter Strips

A filter strip is an area of grass or other permanent vegetation used to reduce sediment, organics, nutrients, pesticides, and other contaminants from runoff and to maintain or improve water quality. It slows the velocity of water, filters suspended soil particles, and increases infiltration of runoff and soluble pollutants and adsorption of pollutants on soil and plant surfaces. Filter strips also can be designed to enhance wildlife habitat.

Cross-Wind Trap Strips

Cross-wind trap strips are areas of herbaceous vegetation that are resistant to wind erosion and grown as nearly as possible perpendicular to the prevailing wind direction. These strips catch windborne sediment and other pollutants, such as nutrients and pesticides, from the eroded material before it reaches water bodies or other sensitive areas. They are filter strips for windborne material.

Grassed Waterways

A grassed waterway/vegetated filter system is a natural or constructed vegetated channel that is shaped and graded to carry surface water at a nonerosive velocity to a stable outlet that spreads the flow of water before it enters a vegetated filter.

Windbreak/Shelterbelt

A windbreak or shelterbelt is a single or multiple row of trees or shrubs that protects the soil from wind erosion, protects sensitive plants, manages snow, improves irrigation efficiency, protects livestock and structures, and creates or enhances wildlife habitat.

Contour Buffer Strips (Contour Grass Strips)

Contour Buffer strips are of perennial vegetation alternated with wider cultivated strips that are farmed on the contour. Contour buffer strips slow runoff and trap sediment. They help reduce sediment, nutrients, pesticides, and other contaminants in runoff as they pass through the buffer strip. Vegetative strips can also be designed to provide food and cover for wildlife.

Source: USDA (1999).

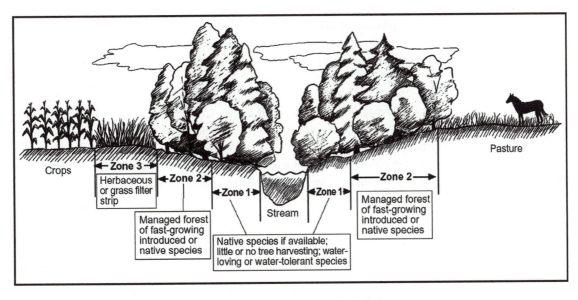

Figure 16.9 Three Zones of Riparian Forest Buffers. *Source:* USDA, NRCS (1998).

critical zone provides habitat, litter, shading, and shoreline stabilization. Zone 2 is adjacent to and upslope from zone 1. Vegetation in zone 2 intercepts and filters runoff sediment and pollution. Zone 2 can be managed to provide timber, wood fiber, and horticultural products. Zone 3 is established if periodic and excessive water flows, erosion, and sediment from upslope fields or tracts are anticipated. Zone 3 is generally composed of herbaceous plants or grass and a diversion or terrace, if needed, and it is a "first defense" to ensure proper functioning of zones 1 and 2 (USDA, 1998).

NRCS recommends minimum forest buffer widths to maximize benefits. Buffer zone 1 and 2 width should be 30 percent of the active floodplain width. Minimum buffer width for floodplains greater than 333 feet is 100 feet; for those less than 333 feet, 45 feet; for those on one side only, 60 feet; and for no floodplain, 35 feet.

Forest Health

Managing the health of forest ecosystems has become an important objective of the U.S. Forest Service, not only for national forests but also for private and urban forests. The Forest Service identifies several health concerns (USDA, 2003):

- **Wildfire threat:** Fuel buildup and overcrowding from fire suppression and other management practices has increased the threat of catastrophic fire on 39 million acres of the national forests. Ex-urban residential development at the **wildland/urban interface** has increased the threat to human safety and property.
- **Invasion of exotic pests:** Gypsy moth, Asian long-horned beetles, hemlock wooly adelgid, and other introduced pests have caused extensive damage to forests, woodlands, and urban trees.
- **Air pollution:** Acid rain and ozone pollution can transport long distances and impact forest ecosystems, especially in the eastern United States. Ozone and nitrogen oxide impacts are also prevalent in the southwestern United States.
- **Degraded riparian areas:** High-quality forest riparian areas are critical for runoff and sediment control and wildlife habitat. This has been a serious problem in the southwestern United States where 65 percent of animals depend on riparian habitats during all or part of their life cycles.

Large areas of U.S. forestland are at risk from disease or insect mortality. Almost 10 percent of the nation's 737 million acres of forests are at risk. About 47 percent of the at-risk acres are on National Forests, 53 percent are on other lands. Four groups account for about 70 percent of the acres at risk: gypsy moth in the east, root diseases in the interior west, southern pine beetle in the south, and bark beetles in the west.

Urban Forestry

The urban forest includes all woody vegetation within the environs of human populated places. Forested land in urban and metropolitan areas constitutes a surprising 25 percent of the U.S. forest canopy (McPherson, 2003). Although such forests do not provide significant timber production, they enhance the quality of human settlements through climate control, air quality enhancement, watershed protection and runoff control, noise reduction, habitat for urban wildlife, recreation opportunities, and aesthetics—"they clean the air we breathe and the water we drink, protect us from the summer heat and winter winds, and nourish our emotional and spiritual lives" (Laundauer, 2001). Thus, management of the urban forest is an important local environmental issue.

Benefits of the Urban Forest

- Increase property values
- Decrease energy costs
- Improve air quality
- Reduce storm water runoff
- Decrease soil erosion
- Improve water quality
- Create wildlife habitat
- Increase community pride
- Increase recreational opportunities
- Improve health and well-being
- Reduce noise levels
- Create buffer zones

However, few cities adequately manage their trees and forests. The U.S. Forest Service recently reported that 13 southeastern states are expected to lose 30 million acres of prime forestland to urban development over the next four decades. The advocacy group American Forests (AF) has demonstrated significant reductions in urban and metropolitan tree canopy, what they call "the national urban tree deficit" (AF, 2001a). Figure 16.10 shows the reduction of tree cover (shown in lighter shade) in the Atlanta metro region from 1974 to 1996.

In metro Atlanta, heavy tree cover (where canopy covers more than half of the land surface) declined from about half of the metro area in 1974 to about one-quarter in 1996. Areas with less than 20 percent cover increased from 44 to 71 percent. Average tree cover dropped from 45 to 29 percent (AF, 2001b).

About 30 percent of urban trees are publicly owned, principally located in parks, street and other rights-of-way, and grounds of public buildings (Grey and Deneke, 1992). Management of urban forests involves three areas: management of municipally owned trees; regulation of tree removal and planting during construction and development on private property; and campaigns for community-wide tree planting.

There are significant benefits of forest and tree protection, retention, and planting, but a healthy urban forest requires a monetary investment. Costs involved in urban forestry including planting, maintenance and removal, infrastructure repair, litigation and liability, storm cleanup, and administration. McPherson, Nowak, and Rowntree's (1994) research in Chicago showed that a tree needs to live 9–18 years before the benefits outweigh the costs to the community. To achieve this longevity, efforts should be taken to "protect the investment" by ensuring proper sites and trees, proper planting techniques, long-term maintenance, and monitoring and protecting tree health.

Urban and Regional Forest Canopy Analysis

American Forest recently developed a GIS application software called CITYgreen for urban forestry planning and education. CITYgeen version 5.0 is designed to work with ESRI's ArcView 3.2. It uses aerial photos, field surveys, and other data to create an inventory and benefit analysis of vegetation at the neighborhood scale. Remote sensing images are interpreted for tree canopy, structures, and impervious surfaces. Field data includes tree species, health, height, truck diameter, soil, and slope (AF, 2002a).

CITYgreen uses this data to compute economic benefits of tree cover resulting from stormwater runoff reduction, air pollution mitigation, and energy savings. Stormwater runoff benefits are based on TR 55 (USDA, 1986; see chapter 13). Air quality benefits are derived from the urban forest effects (UFORE) model, which calculates the carbon sequestered and the amount of ozone, carbon monoxide, sulfur dioxide, and nitrogen dioxide deposited or absorbed by the tree canopy. Energy benefits are based on the home heating and cooling energy reductions from shading and wind attenuation.

Since 1995 AF has applied CITYgreen to ecosystem analyses in several cities and metropolitan areas, including Atlanta, Chattanooga, Houston, Roanoke (VA), Washington (DC), Puget Sound, Willamette Valley (Portland, OR), Colorado Front Range, and Chesapeake Bay region, among others. These assessments have followed a similar methodology. It involves the following steps:

1. Larger metropolitan or regional scale analysis uses Landsat MSS and TM images (and more recently high-resolution satellite data) to quantify tree canopy change from the 1970s to the 1990s (see figures 16.10 and 16.11).
2. Local area or neighborhood scale analysis uses ground surveys and aerial photos of sample sites representing different land uses to assess trees, grass, and impervious surfaces. Most recent studies have shown that high-resolution satellite images can provide similar data detail for an entire area without sampling (AF, 2001b).
3. Using CITYgreen software, ecosystem benefits (stormwater, air quality, and energy) are calculated for sample sites, then extrapolated to the entire region based on total area for each land use and tree canopy category (see table 16.1).

Table 16.1 shows the results from the Willamette/Lower Columbia area, which extends from Vancouver, Washington, to Eugene, Oregon, and the Chattanooga (TN) studies. As figure 16.11 shows, the trends for the Willamette area are different from the other areas. Whereas the others show a decrease of heavy canopy (>50% tree cover) from the 1970s to the 1990s, the Willamette area shows a decline to 1986, then an increase to 2000. American Forest believes this trend reversal was the result of Oregon's use of urban growth boundaries to contain sprawling development that impacts forest canopy.

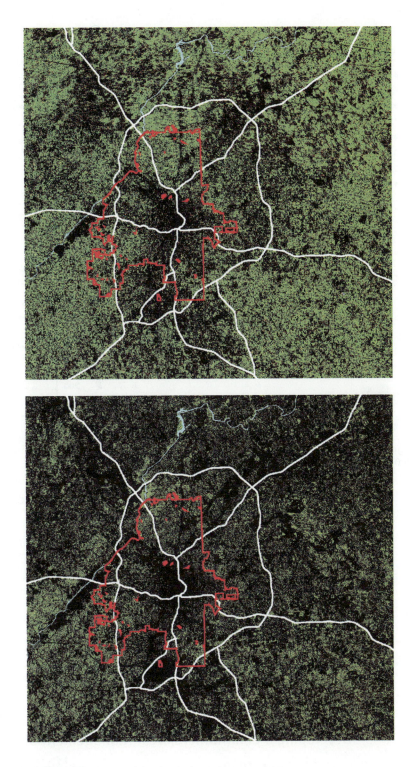

Figure 16.10 Reduction of Tree Cover in Metro Atlanta from 1974 to 1996. *Source:* American Forests, *Urban Ecosystem Analysis, Atlanta Metro Area,* 2001b. Reprinted with permission of American Forests.

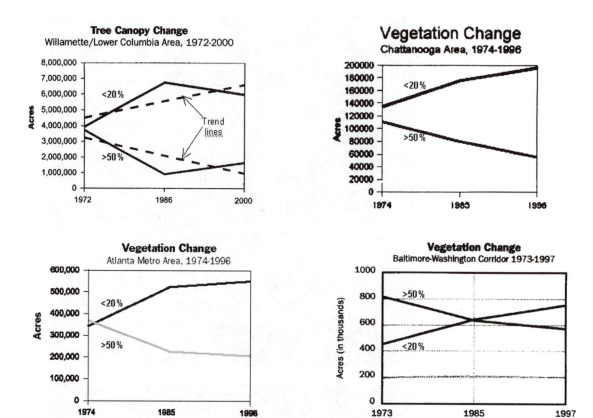

Figure 16.11 Trend Lines for Tree Canopy Area in Four American Forests Study Areas. *Source:* American Forests (1999, 2001b, 2001c, 2002b). Reprinted with permission of American Forests.

TABLE 16.1   **Results from American Forests Ecosystem Analyses for Willamette Valley and Chattanooga**

| | Willamette/Lower Columbia | | | Chattanooga | | |
	1972	2000	Loss/Gain	1974	1996	Loss/Gain
Area >50% tree cover	47%	21%	−56%	50%	21%	−50%
Area <20% tree cover	50%	75%	+51%	51%	75%	+46%
Stormwater value*	$22.6B	$20.6B	−$2.4B	$1.04B	$0.76B	−$0.28B
Air quality value**	$741M	$419M	−$322M	$19M	$13M	−$6M
Stored Carbon**	131Mt	73Mt	−58Mt	3.6Mt	2.4Mt	−1.2Mt

* one-time benefit; ** annual benefit

Developing a Community Forest Management Strategy

Figure 16.12 describes a simple planning process for urban forestry following the basic approach outlined in box 2.2 and the planning process in box 2.1. The inventory stage assesses not only the resource but also public and stakeholder concerns and attitudes. Agents of change include factors instrumental in affecting future

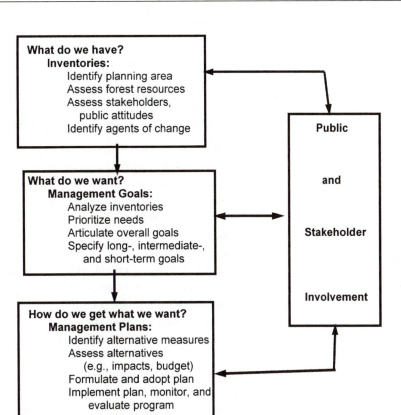

Figure 16.12 Urban Forestry Planning Process

conditions, such as tree diseases and damage, agency personnel, and available budget. Management goals, objectives, and priorities follow inventories and set the stage for specific action. Management plans follow the normal planning process in identifying alternatives and their impacts and formulating, adopting and implementing the plan and its measures and programs.

What do we have? A first step is to assess the forest and tree resources. This may involve an inventory of tree numbers classified by species, condition, age, and location; canopy cover by location; and problem areas (see later subsection "Inventorying and Evaluating the Urban Forest"). In addition, a review may be made of the current management framework and practices, including ordinances, guidelines, and municipal tree maintenance. Identifying public stakeholders can help develop support and build a constituency for urban forestry.

What do we want? Identifying needs and goals is based on the assessment of resources and existing management and on stakeholder involvement. The resource itself has biological needs, such as increasing species and age diversity or increasing the rate of tree planting. Management needs may include adequate tree protection and landscaping ordinances or financial and personnel resources. Community needs stem directly from stakeholder and public involvement and represent public perceptions and needs for education, technical assistance, and forest conservation.

Needs assessment helps identify goals or the specific ends that a management strategy aims to achieve. Goals should be quantifiable in some way, so that progress toward the goals can be monitored. The International Society of Arboriculture's (ISA, 2001) *Guidelines for Developing and Evaluating Tree Ordinances* suggests nine possible urban forestry and tree program goals, as listed in the following:

Typical Urban Forestry Program Goals

1. Establish and maintain maximum tree cover.
2. Maintain trees in a healthy condition through good cultural practices.
3. Establish and maintain an optimal level of age and species diversity.
4. Promote conservation of tree resources.
5. Select, situate, and maintain street trees appropriately to maximize benefits and minimize hazard, nuisance, hardscape damage, and maintenance costs.
6. Centralize tree management under a person with the necessary expertise.
7. Promote efficient and cost-effective management of the urban forest.
8. Foster community support for the local urban forestry program and encourage good tree management on privately owned properties.
9. Facilitate the resolution of tree-related conflicts between citizens.

How do we get what we want? The heart of the process is the formulation and implementation of the urban forestry plan and management strategy. The strategy will include an appropriate set of management tools, such as mitigation and other guidelines, ordinances and other regulations, assistance and incentive programs, planting programs, and public education. Once the urban forestry program is adopted, individual components must be implemented. This may require passing ordinances, budgeting funding, hiring an arborist, establishing a tree commission, appointing a citizen advisory board, and developing a tree master plan, among other steps.

After implementation, it is important to monitor and evaluate progress toward meeting program goals. This requires process or program evaluation (i.e., have administrative objectives been met?) and, more important, outcome evaluation of progress toward physical urban forest goals (i.e., increase in forest cover, increase in forest diversity). Some methods for forest inventory and evaluation are discussed in the next section.

Inventorying and Evaluating the Urban Forest

Much like vegetation inventories discussed previously, urban forest inventories are normally prepared from remote sensing and field observation. The emphasis is on forests, individual trees, and the functions they provide. These techniques are useful not only for initial inventories, but also for postimplementation program evaluation to see if program goals are being met. A number of methods are used for inventory and evaluation studies (ISA, 2001):

- **Sampling from populations.** Short of counting and documenting every tree, inventories often use sampling methods to assess cover, count,

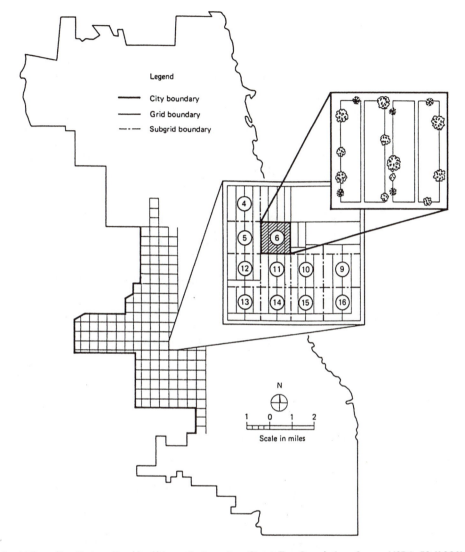

Figure 16.13 Subgrid Sampling System Used in Chicago to Inventory Street Tree Population. *Source:* USDA, FS (1990).

and condition. Figure 16.13 illustrates a grid-cell-sampling scheme developed by Geiger and others for Chicago in the 1970s that allows detailed inventory with reduced cost and labor.

- **Photogrammetry and remote sensing techniques.** Stock aerial photographs or other aerial imagery can be used to assess tree canopy cover quickly and cost-effectively. For regional studies, satellite data can be used to assess forest cover (figure 16.10). Two methods of analyzing aerial photos are described after this list.

- **Ground survey.** For many applications, the ground survey is still the simplest and most accurate means for collecting detailed data on the urban forest. "Windshield" and walking surveys can be used.

- **Photo points.** Photographs taken from the ground or the air can provide graphic and obvious evidence of changes in tree condition and cover. It is

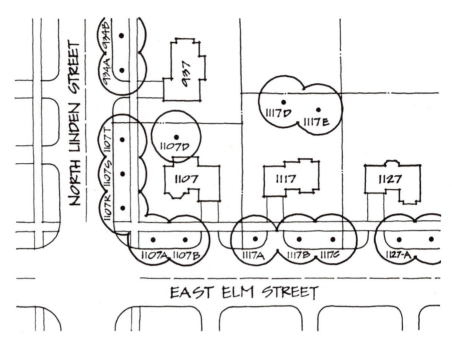

Figure 16.14 Lotline/Letter Method for Locating Trees for Database. *Source:* USDA, FS (1990).

important that photo points be consistent and repeatable to show change over time.

▪ **Public polling.** People are an integral part of the urban forest, and involving them incorporates not only their attitudes but also their local knowledge.

▪ **Record keeping and analysis.** Well-maintained records and databases can be analyzed to provide a wealth of information on forest condition and ordinance performance. The use of GIS and other computer techniques enhances the gathering, storage, analysis, and visualization of information. Figure 16.14 illustrates a lotline address/lettering method of identifying neighborhood trees for a tree database that may include data on species, size, and condition.

Figure 16.15 illustrates two techniques for analyzing aerial photos to estimate forest canopy cover. Figure 16.15a shows a digital dot grid overlay. Triangles were used because they are easier to see; the triangle vortex serves as the dot. The number of dots touching the dark canopy were counted and compared to the total number of dots. Figure 16.15b illustrates how ImageTool software converts the photo into a digital black-and-white image, showing canopy as black and other areas as white. The software counts the pixels in black and compares the count to the total pixels to estimate canopy cover. This method produces a result of 20.8 percent canopy, whereas the dot grid method gave 21.4 percent. The dot grid method took four hours less time (ISA, 2001).

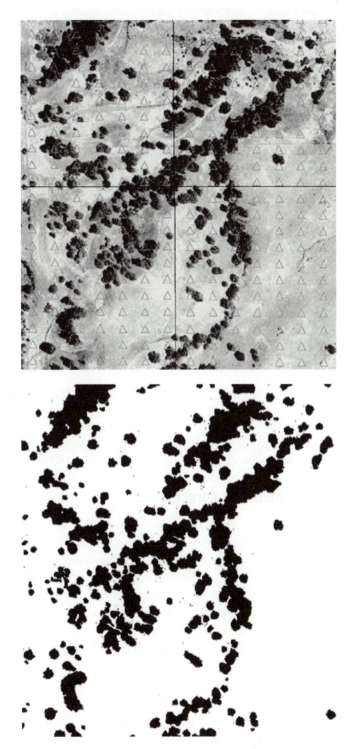

Figure 16.15 Dot Grid Overlay and ImageTool Methods for Estimated Forest Canopy. *Source:* USDA, FS, Southern Region (2001).

BOX 16.4—Manageability of Urban Forest Lands

Directly Manageable Urban Forests	Indirectly Manageable Urban Forests
City parks	Utility easements
Public squares	Other ownerships
Grounds of city buildings	Federal and state lands
Monuments and cemeteries	Private lands
Boulevard medians	Existing tree preservation
Streetsides	Site planning and design
Parking lots	Tree planting
Riparian areas	

A standard method for assessing street tree canopy is the **canopy cover at the edge of pavement (CCEP).** It measures the amount of shading that streets receive from street trees and can be used with aerial photos or ground survey. On aerial photos, a ruler or point dots are laid along the visible edge of the pavement. The analyst counts the number of points that fall on the tree crowns and the total number of points, then calculates the %CCEP:

$$\% \text{ CCEP} = 100 \times (\text{points with canopy cover/total number of points})$$

A ground survey can reveal the same data at evenly spaced points, say every three steps. An advantage of measuring CCEP by ground survey is that additional survey information like tree measurements and conditions can be assessed (ISA, 2001).

Managing the Urban Forest

Managing the urban forest depends on the specific program goals and on the "manageability" of forest lands, which is fundamentally based on ownership. Box 16.4 gives examples of directly manageable forests, which are primarily those owned by the local government and indirectly manageable forests, most of which are privately owned.

Most urban forestry programs address one or more of the following priorities:

- Managing trees on publicly owned lands:

    Public buildings and grounds

    Boulevards and streetsides

    Public parks and riparian areas

- Education and technical assistance for trees management on privately owned lands
- Ordinances for landscaping and planting in new developments
- Ordinances for protection of existing trees in new developments
- Tree planting plans, incentives, and programs

Tree Protection and Preservation

Much of the reduction in urban and metropolitan forest canopy has resulted from construction and land development activities. Construction activities typically cause more damage below ground than above ground, since most tree roots are within the top 18 inches of soil and extend well beyond the spread of the tree canopy. Land clearing, grading, trenching, and paving; vehicle and pedestrian movement; and toxic leaks and spills have serious impacts on established trees.

Protecting trees requires action before, during, and after construction. First, the early site design process should include a site and tree evaluation to identify trees to save, remove, and transplant. The evaluation should assess tree species, age, size, health, value, and critical root zone.

Second, site development plans should incorporate existing natural vegetation, especially areas of environmental and economic value. Preserving groups of trees or "tree save islands" is recommended because stands of trees can better tolerate disturbance and offer aesthetic and environmental benefits. The plans should assess impacts of construction activities and identify measures to mitigate them. For example, impervious surface locations should avoid critical root zones. Third, construction practices should be sensitive to tree protection needs. The following list shows a number of tree protection techniques (USDA, Forest Service, Southern Region, 2001).

Tree Protection Techniques

- Organize site activities to avoid impacts on trees.
- Minimize land disturbance.
- Trench before clearing and grading along limits of disturbance.
- Account for underground utilities.
- Adapt to pavement.
- Install protective tree fencing around the critical root zone.
- Mulch in the critical root zone.
- Ensure quality of fill material.
- Prune branches for vehicle clearance.
- Maintain trees before, during, and after during construction: fertilize, prune, water, aerate.
- Restore site.

Tree Planting Programs

Global deforestation and impacts on global warming and climate change have spurred efforts for tree planting worldwide. For example, the Global ReLeaf program is an international effort by the forest advocacy group AF. For every dollar donation to the Global ReLeaf Fund, AF plants one tree in 1 of their 500 projects in every U.S. state and 21 countries. Many projects are in urban areas to shade, cool, and beautify communities, and others are part of ecosystem restoration projects in less-developed areas. As of August 2001, Global ReLeaf had planted more than 19 million trees.

In late 2001, AF released its "National Urban Tree Deficit" study that estimated that there was a deficit of more than 634 million trees in U.S. urban areas. Based on its analysis of high-resolution satellite image data in 10 regional studies (described in the preceding section, "Urban and Regional Forest Canopy Analysis"), the organization estimated forest canopy for urban areas in the 48 contiguous states. These studies of urban landscape change over the past 20 years (e.g., figures 16.10 and 16.11) also served as the basis for the following recommended levels of tree cover for eastern U.S. metropolitan areas (lower levels were recommended for the plains and dryland western states):

- 40 percent overall average
- 60 percent for suburban areas
- 25 percent for urban residential areas
- 15 percent for commercial areas

The study compared the results of current satellite data analysis to the recommended levels to estimate the national urban tree deficit of 634 million trees (AF, 2001a).

Urban tree planting programs are proactive activities to enhance urban environments and arrest the decline of tree cover. Although such programs are not complex, a number of factors should be considered depending on program objectives, site conditions, planting type, species, and stock. For example, a public street tree planting plan in Minneapolis emphasizes species diversity because of Dutch elm disease mortality in the city.

Designing Urban Forestry Ordinances

The heart of most urban forestry programs affecting private property is the urban forestry or landscaping ordinance. There are three categories of such ordinances: **street tree ordinances** primarily cover the planting, maintenance, and removal of trees within public rights-of-way and parking lots; **tree protection ordinances** aim to protect native mature trees or trees with historical significance; and **view or solar access ordinances** help resolve conflicts between property owners when trees block views or sunlight.

Ordinances vary widely in form, content, and complexity, but an effective tree ordinance should meet the following criteria (ISA, 2001):

1. *Goals* should be clearly stated and ordinance provisions should address the stated goals.
2. *Responsibility and authority* should be designated to a tree commission to set policy and to a city arborist and other staff to conduct operations and enforcement.
3. *Basic performance standards* should indicate which practices, conditions, and performance are acceptable and which are not. Standards should be specific and quantifiable. Typical standards included in tree ordinances are given in table 16.2.
4. *Flexibility* must be maintained in meeting provisions and in enforcement.
5. *Enforcement* methods should be clear.

TABLE 16.2 **Typical Standards Included in Tree Ordinances**

Standard	Description
Tree planting	How to prepare the planting area, planting techniques, and postplanting procedures.
Tree care	Activities that will improve tree health and protect trees from construction damage, such as pruning, fertilization, mulching, and watering. Techniques to prevent soil compaction and reduced aeration are also covered.
Tree species	What species should and should not be planted in a given situation.
Tree selection	How to select healthy tree stock.
Transplanting	Procedures on how to transplant trees.
Tunneling for utilities	Requirements for utility installation and maintenance near trees, and suggest alternatives to trenching through roots such as tunneling.
Aeration system	How to determine if an aeration system is needed and how to install a system.
Design	Requirement that a tree protection plan be submitted with the land-development permit. These standards are often linked to the land-development process.
Minimum tree coverage or replacement	Requirement measured as canopy cover, number of trees per acre, or minimum basal area (square foot of tree area measured cross section at diameter at breast height) of trees per acre.
Encroachment	Techniques to be used during clearing, trenching, and grading to prevent damage to the protected root zone.
Landscape strip and buffer	Requirements for landscape strips and buffers, such as widths of strips, curb stops, parking lot landscape islands, species selection, and percent coverage in trees.
Special	Special standards can apply to unique characteristics of a site, such as a vegetative buffer along a stream tributary within the property boundaries.

Source: USDA, FS, 2001.

6. The ordinance should be part of a *comprehensive urban forest management strategy*. The lack of integration between urban forest management and tree ordinances is common.

7. The ordinance should be developed with *community support*.

A model ordinance prepared for Atlanta, Georgia, area communities illustrates the main components of an urban forestry program. They include

- the establishment of an urban forestry or tree commission;
- the appointment of a municipal arborist; and
- the development of regulations and guidelines for managing publicly and privately owned trees.

Figure 16.16 Typical Tidal Salt Marsh. *Source:* Good et al. (1998).

The guidelines include the establishment of a **Tree Protection Zone** within the community, which comprises publicly owned land as well as private property planned for development or within 50 feet of a street right-of-way. Within the zone, a permit is required for removing or damaging more than 50 percent of the trees, ditching within 10 feet of any tree, or placing impervious surface that impedes passage of water, air, or fertilizer to tree roots. For other tree protection and urban forestry ordinances see the ISA website (http://www.ISA-arbor.com) and U.S. Forest Service website (http://www.urbanforestrysouth.usda.gov).

Wetlands Mitigation and Management

Wetlands are defined as areas where saturation with water is the dominant factor determining the nature of soil development and the types of plant and animal communities living in the soil and on its surface (Cowardin, Carter, and LaRoe, 1979). The Clean Water Act defines wetlands as "those areas that are inundated or saturated by surface or ground water at a frequency and duration sufficient to support, and that under normal circumstances do support, a prevalence of vegetation typically adapted for life in saturated soil conditions. Wetlands generally include swamps, marshes, bogs and similar areas" (40 CFR 230.3[f]).

As part of the National Wetlands Inventory program, the U.S. Fish and Wildlife Service (FWS) developed a wetlands and deepwater classification system, which is described in figure 16.17. In December 1996 this "Cowardin system" was designated the national standard for wetland mapping. The main subsystems (marine, estuarine, riverine, lacustrine [lake], and palustrine) are further distinguished by

Marine: Open ocean overlying the continental shelf and associated high-energy coast line. Examples of wetland types within this system are subtidal and intertidal aquatic beds, reefs, and rocky shores.

Estuarine: Deepwater tidal habitats and adjacent tidal wetlands that are usually semi-enclosed by land but have open, partially obstructed, or sporadic access to the ocean and in which ocean water is at least occasionally diluted by freshwater runoff from the land. Examples of estuarine classes include subtidal and intertidal emergent wetlands, forested wetlands, and rock bottom.

Riverine: Wetland and deepwater habitats contained within a channel with two exceptions: 1) wetlands dominated by trees, shrubs, persistent emergent plants, emergent mosses or lichens, and 2) habitat with water containing ocean-derived salts in excess of 5 ppt (parts per thousand). Rivers and streams fall within this system and subsystems include tidal, perennial, or intermittent watercourses.

Lacustrine: Wetlands and deepwater habitats with all of the following characteristics: 1) situated in a topographic depression or a dammed river channel; 2) less than 30 percent area coverage by trees, shrubs, persistent emergent vegetation, emergent mosses, or lichens; and 3) total area exceeds 8 hectares (20 acres). Lakes typify lacustrine wetland systems.

Palustrine: All nontidal wetlands dominated by trees, shrubs, persistent emergent vegetation, emergent mosses or lichens, and all such wetlands that occur in tidal areas where salinity due to ocean-derived salts is below 5 ppt. This system also includes wetlands lacking such vegetation if they are less than 8 hectares, lack wave-action or bedrock shoreline features, and, at the deepest spot are no deeper than 2 meters at low water. Examples include ponds, bogs, and prairie potholes.

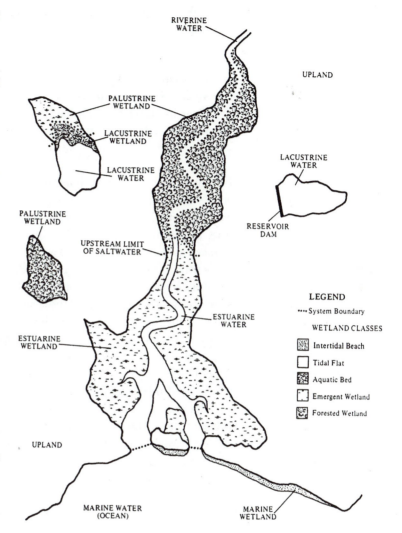

Figure 16.17 Wetland Systems Definitions. *Source:* Cowardin, 1979.

class, usually defined as bottom type for deep water and as vegetative type for wetlands. Palustrine or inland, freshwater wetlands account for about 95 percent of the wetlands in the coterminous United States; the remainder are estuarine wetlands, mostly of the emergent class.

The National Research Council (1995) lists several major vernacular classes of U.S. wetlands and some plants associated with each:

- **Freshwater marsh:** fresh water-saturated area having aquatic vegetation and grasses, sedges, and herbs.
- **Tidal salt and brackish marsh:** saltwater saturated area subject to tidal influence and having aquatic vegetation and salt tolerant grasses and rushes (see figure 6.16).
- **Prairie potholes:** shallow depression occurring in outwash or till plain resulting from glacial retreat, having grasses, sedges, and herbs.

- **Fens:** peat-accumulating wetland receiving water from surface runoff or seepage, having sedges, grasses, shrubs, and trees.
- **Bogs:** nutrient poor, acidic wetland dominated by waterlogged spongy mat of sphagnum moss that forms acidic peat, fed primarily by rainwater and no inflow or outflow; also has shrubs and trees.
- **Swamp bottomland:** area intermittently or permanently covered with water, having shrubs or trees, usually cypress, gum, and red maple.
- **Mangrove forest:** water-saturated or submerged area with water-tolerant black, red, and white mangrove trees.

Wetland types are diverse, but they all possess hydrologic, soil, and biotic characteristics that distinguish them from upland or other aquatic ecosystems. **Hydrological characteristics,** that is, the duration, flow, amount, and frequency of water on a site, are the *primary factors* that determine soil and vegetation elements. Wetland hydrology occurs when a site is wet enough to produce soils that can support hydrophytic or "water-loving" vegetation. Wetland soils are called **hydric soils** and are saturated with water for all or part of the year. Saturated soils become anaerobic as water drives the oxygen out of the spaces between soil particles. This changes the soil's structure and chemistry (Somers, Bridle, Herman, and Nelson, 2000).

As a result of waterlogged and anaerobic conditions, wetlands are hostile to most terrestrial plants. As a result, they are dominated by **hydrophytic plants** that are adapted to these conditions. Wetland plant species include emergent plants (cattails, sedges, and rushes), submerged plants (pondweeds, eelgrass), floating plants (e.g., duckweed), trees (cypress, red maple, and swamp oak), shrubs (willows and bayberry), moss, and other types of vegetation (Somers et al., 2000).

Because wetlands exist at the land-water interface, they are used by animals from both wet and dry environments. Many invertebrate, fish, reptile, and amphibian species depend on wetland water cycles to survive or complete their life cycles. Nearly all amphibians, approximately 75 percent of all commercial marine fish species, and at least 50 percent of migratory birds use wetlands regularly (NRC, 1995).

Benefits of Wetlands

Historically, wetlands have been viewed as wasted land, which could be put into productive use only through draining and earth filling. As a result, well over half of the original 215 million acres of wetlands in the lower 48 states has been converted to other uses. However, the values and benefits of wetlands have been better recognized in the past 25 years and in response, efforts to control wetland conversion have grown considerably.

Box 16.5 lists some of the benefits of wetlands. Not only do wetlands provide important ecological benefits for wildlife and natural systems, but they also support human activities through flooding and erosion control, water quality treatment, groundwater recharge, and recreation. Most wetlands in the United States are located in the southeast coastal plain, Lower Mississippi Valley, the prairie potholes region, Great Lakes States, and in upper New England. Such lands have been called "the cradle of life" for waterfowl, fisheries, endangered species, countless small birds, mammals, and a wide variety of plant life.

BOX 16.5—Benefits of Wetlands

Flood Damage Reduction

Wetlands often function like natural tubs or sponges, storing water and slowly releasing it. Trees and other wetland vegetation help slow floodwaters. This combined action, storage and slowing, can lower flood heights. A Corps of Engineers' study of the Charles River Basin in Massachusetts concluded that the loss of 8,100 acres of forested wetlands would result in millions of dollars of annual flood damages downstream (U.S. Army Corps of Engineers, 1976).

Shoreline Erosion Control

Wetlands dissipate wave energy and erosive potential, thus buffering shorelines and upland areas from erosion.

Water Quality Improvement

Wetlands intercept surface runoff and remove nutrients, organic wastes, and sediment before it reaches open water, helping to improve water quality, including groundwater and sources of water supply.

Groundwater Recharge

Since fresh water wetlands occur at the outcrop of the water table, they are an important interface between surface and groundwater and contribute to the recharge of aquifers.

Healthy Fisheries

About 75 percent of commercial fish and shellfish depend on estuaries and their wetlands. Most fresh-water fish are dependent on marshes and riparian wetlands where they spawn during spring floods.

Ecological Benefits to Wildlife and Biological Diversity

Wetlands are among the most biologically productive natural ecosystems in the world. They can be compared to tropical rain forests and coral reefs in the diversity of species they support. An estimated 46 percent of the listed threatened and endangered species rely directly or indirectly on wetlands for their survival. Wetlands provide critical habitats for 50–80 percent of the continental waterfowl, 80 percent of North America's breeding birds, 190 species of amphibians, as well as many mammals, including muskrat, beaver, mink, raccoon, marsh and swamp rabbits, and other small mammals.

Recreation, Aesthetics, Education, and Research

Wetlands provide opportunities for popular activities such as hiking, fishing, and boating. For example, an estimated 50 million people spend approximately $10 billion each year observing and photographing wetlands-dependent birds.

Source: NRC (1995).

Wetland Conversion and Alteration

An estimated 52 percent of the original 221 million acres of wetlands in the United States have been converted to other uses, about 80 percent for agricultural use. The United States is continuing to lose wetlands but the loss has slowed considerably in the last three decades. As shown in box 16.6, annual wetland loss of 458,000 acres in the 1950s to the early 1970s slowed to less than 300,000 acres by 1980s. Latest estimates for 1986–1997 are about 100,000 acres per year, with a net loss of 58,500 acres as a result of wetland creation and restoration (U.S. Department of the Interior, 2000). In most cases, new wetland acres are of less quality than lost acres. Historically, agricultural activities have caused by far the greatest impact on wetlands, but land development contributed half of the wetland loss from 1992 to 1997 according to the latest *National Resources Inventory* (USDA, 2001).

BOX—16.6 Improved Wetlands Loss Trends and Contributing Factors in Lower 48 States

Wetlands Losses, 1950s–1990s

1950s–1970s	458,000 acres per year
1970s–1980s	290,000 acres per year
1986–1997	58,500 acres per year (net loss)

Factors contributing to the marked decline in the loss rate during the last decade include

■ implementation of the *section 404 wetlands permitting* program of the Clean Water Act (CWA);

■ *state and local* wetland regulatory programs;

■ increased *public awareness* and support for conservation;

■ expansion of federal, state, local, and private-sector *restoration programs* that have contributed *78,000 acres a year* to the national wetlands base;

■ enactment of *Swampbuster measures* in the farm bills since 1985; and

■ a decline in the profitability of converting wetlands due to the *tax reform of 1986*.

Agricultural and land development activities damage wetlands in a number of ways. Most damage is caused by physical alterations, like draining, filling, and dredging, but chemical and biological changes also reduce wetland benefits. Box 16.7 describes several methods of wetland alteration.

Wetland Protection, Mitigation, Restoration, and Creation

With growing awareness of the benefits of wetlands, wetlands advocates and environmental agencies have worked to develop policies and strategies to arrest the alteration, conversion, and destruction of wetlands. The progress made is reflected in the declining rate of wetland loss (box 16.6). Since 1990 the federal government has had a policy of "no net loss" of wetlands. The Clinton administration wanted to achieve a net gain of 100,000 wetland acres per year by 2005. The estimated current net loss of 58,000 acres per year suggests we have not achieved "no net loss" much less "net gain." Even if we did, it does not imply that wetlands would not be damaged. "No net loss" means that for every wetland lost, another will be restored or created. Indeed, federal and state permitting programs aiming to protect wetlands (discussed later) allow damage to wetlands as long as mitigation is provided.

Figure 16.18 gives a wetlands protection hierarchy. Given the benefits of wetlands as well as the hassle to the landowner posed by permit requirements, costly mitigation, and negative public opinion, the best action is to avoid wetlands impacts altogether. Next, landowners should minimize impacts, and third, mitigate or compensate for unavoidable impact. Figure 16.19 illustrates wetland avoidance and mitigation in a development project (Salveson, 1994).

Under the federal CWA section 404 regulatory program, applicants are permitted to mitigate wetlands impacts only after they have taken every effort to avoid and minimize the impact. Mitigation can be through restoration of previously damaged wetlands, enhancement of existing wetlands, or creation of new wetlands. Lewis (1990) provides the following definitions for these terms:

BOX 16.7—Methods of Altering Wetlands

Physical Alterations

Filling—adding any material to change the bottom level of a wetland or to replace the wetland with dry land.

Draining—removing water from a wetland by ditching, tiling, or pumping.

Excavating or **dredging water away**—preventing the flow of water into a wetland by removing water upstream or lowering groundwater tables.

Flooding—raising water levels either behind dams, by pumping, or otherwise channeling water into a wetland, often done to create livestock watering ponds, irrigation ponds, detention ponds, or water hazards on golf courses.

Fragmenting—bisecting wetlands with roads that create barriers to normal flow of water and normal activity of wildlife, also creating a source of mortality for wetland animals migrating from one portion of the wetland to another.

Shading—placing pile-supported platforms or bridges over wetlands, causing vegetation to die.

Conducting activities in adjacent areas—disrupting the interconnectedness between wetlands and adjacent land areas, or incidentally impacting wetlands through activities at adjoining sites.

Chemical Alterations

Changing levels of nutrients—increasing or decreasing levels of nutrients within the local water and/or soil system, forcing changes in the wetland plant community

Introducing toxins—adding toxic compounds to a wetland either intentionally (e.g., herbicides and/or pesticides) or unintentionally (e.g., stormwater runoff from nearby roads containing oils, asbestos, heavy metals, and others), which adversely affect wetland communities.

Biological Alterations

Grazing—consumption and compaction of vegetation by large numbers of domestic livestock.

Disrupting natural populations—altering the number or abundance of existing species, introducing exotic or domestic species, or otherwise disturbing resident organisms.

Source: Somers et al. (2000).

---

1. Avoid Impact

2. Minimize Impact

3. Mitigate or Compensate Unavoidable Impact:

    a. Restore Damaged Wetlands

    b. Enhance Existing Wetlands

    c. Create New Wetlands

Increasing Difficulty and Cost ↓

Figure 16.18 Wetlands Protection and Mitigation Hierarchy

Restoration: Returning a degraded or former wetland to as close to the preexisting condition as possible.

Enhancement: Increasing one or more of the functions performed by an existing wetland beyond what currently or previously existed in the wetland. There may be an accompanying decrease in other functions.

Creation: Converting a nonwetland (either dry land or deep water) to a wetland.

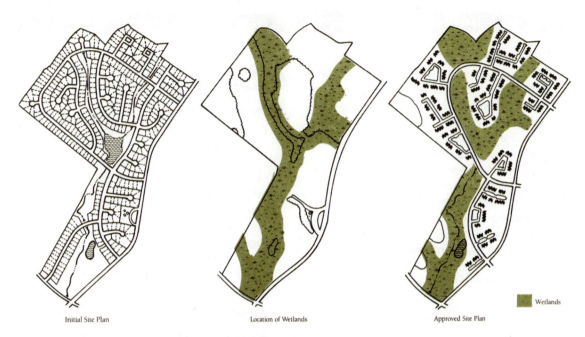

Figure 16.19 Initial and Approved Plans for the Village of Thomas Run, Maryland. *Source: Wetlands: Mitigating and Regulating Development Impacts* by David Salveson, 1994. Reprinted with permission of the Urban Land Institute.

The first method for renewing functions in mitigation is the **passive approach,** or removing the factors causing wetland degradation or loss and letting nature do the work of restoration. However, an **active approach** may be necessary if passive methods are not enough to restore the natural system. Active methods involve direct control of wetland processes when a wetland is severely degraded or in the case of wetland creation and most enhancements.

Wetland creation is the most difficult mitigation measure. Chapter 14 discussed the benefits of created wetlands for runoff and NPS pollution control, but it is very difficult to replicate the full range of benefits provided by natural wetlands. Before wetland vegetation will thrive, hydrologic conditions and hydric soils must be established. Wetland enhancement and restoration is easier because wetland hydrologic or soil conditions may be present.

Conducting a Wetland Restoration Project

Of course, some wetlands are easier to restore than others, and a first step is to assess restoration potential. Restoration potential depends on the degree of disturbance of both the site and its surrounding landscape, but the site's condition is more important (NRC, 1992).

The Interagency Workgroup on Wetland Restoration has produced a nice public guide to wetland restoration (IWWR, 2002). The guide tries to demystify wetland restoration. Although wetlands are complex, much can be done to improve degradation through simple assessment and measures based on local knowledge and experience. A first step is gathering information on the wetland site or sites. Topographic and floodplain maps, soil surveys, aerial photos, and national wetland inventory

TABLE 16.3 **Where to Find Information on Your Watershed/Landscape and Site**

Information	Where to Find Information Resources
Aerial photography	Local geological survey (USGS) office, NASA (satellite photos such as those from the Thematic Mapper); Farm Services Agency (FSA); local aerial photography companies; state natural resource agencies.
Flood elevations and floodplains	County, city, or town zoning and planning offices; Federal Emergency Management Agency (FEMA); flood hazard maps; district offices of the Army Corps of Engineers; state natural resource agencies.
National Wetlands Inventory (NWI) maps	For map status and free desktop printing of areas and acreage status (42% of US available) use the Wetland Interactive Mapper at http://wetlands.fws.gov. To purchase paper maps (90% of US available) call the USGS Earth Science Information Center at 1-888-ASK-USGS or contact a state distribution center from the list at http://wetlands.fws.gov/state_distribution_centers.htm.
Soil surveys	Local office of NRCS; find the field office directory at: http://www.ncg.nrcs.usda.gov/perdir.html.
Topographic maps	Local USGS office or USGS's "Map Finder" at: http://edcwww.cr.usgs.gov/Webglis/glisbin/finder_main.pl?dataset_name=MAPS_LARGE or call 1-800-ASK-USGS; local map or sporting goods stores.

information are the primary general sources of information (table 16.3), but the guide emphasizes acquiring local knowledge to assist in the restoration process.

Federal Wetlands Regulation

The principal federal program to protect wetlands is section 404 of the CWA, which regulates the discharge of dredged and fill material into waters of the United States, including wetlands. The basic premise of the program is that no discharge of dredged or fill material can be permitted if the nation's waters would be significantly degraded or a practicable alternative exists that is less damaging. In other words, when you apply for a permit, you must show that you have (1) taken steps to avoid wetland impacts where practicable; (2) minimized potential impacts to wetlands; and (3) provided compensation for any remaining, unavoidable impacts through activities to restore, enhance, or create wetlands.

The EPA and the Army Corps of Engineers (Corps) jointly administer the program. In addition, the FWS, the National Marine Fisheries Service, and state resource agencies play advisory roles. The Corps administers the day-to-day program, including individual permit decisions; develops policy and guidance; and enforces section 404 provisions. The EPA develops and interprets environmental criteria used in evaluating permit applications; has authority to veto the Corps's permit decisions (section 404[c]); identifies activities that are exempt; and reviews/comments on individual permit applications. Section 404(f) exempts some activities from regulation, including many ongoing farming, ranching, and silviculture practices.

A permit review process controls regulated activities, including discharges, filling, land clearing, ditching, and channeling. An individual permit is usually required for potentially significant impacts. However, for most discharges that will have only minimal adverse effects, the Corps often grants up-front general nationwide permits. These may be issued on a nationwide, regional, or state basis for particular categories of activities (e.g., minor road crossings, utility line backfill, and bedding) as a means to expedite the permitting process.

The application of 404 has been controversial. This is not surprising as it is one of the few federal programs regulating land use. Major issues include definitions of what constitutes a wetland and regulated land use activity under the program, what can be included in "nationwide" permits, regulation of isolated wetlands, and compensation for landowners whose property values are diminished by the regulation. Even though the CWA has not been reauthorized or amended since 1987, continual policy directives and court cases since have tried to clarify the wetlands program.

For example, several cases have argued the extent of the government's regulation of "isolated" wetlands or those not physically adjacent to navigable surface waters. In January 2001, the U.S. Supreme Court ruled 5–4 that the Corps's denial of a permit for wetland damage solely on the basis of impact on migratory birds exceeded its authority. Although the EPA and the Corps issued an interpretation of the decision allowing some continuation of federal regulation of isolated wetlands, the future of a strong federal role in this area is uncertain. The responsibility for isolated wetlands may fall to state and local wetland protection programs (Zinn and Copeland, 2003).

There has also been debate about whether to treat all wetlands equally or to classify them based on size, functions, or values. Several legislative proposals have called for a three-tier system, from highly valuable wetlands that would have the greatest protection to the least valuable wetlands on which alterations would be allowed. In practice, the Corps and EPA do not use a tiered system, but they provide flexibility in permit implementation based on the wetland, the size of the project, and the degree of impact (Zinn and Copeland, 2003).

In addition to the CWA, the federal farm bills have had a major effect on wetlands conversion. In recognition that agriculture has had a dramatic impact on wetlands, the farm bills established the Swampbuster, Wetlands Reserve, and Conservation Reserve programs to use incentives and disincentives to protect and restore wetlands. The Wetlands Reserve Program gives landowners payments for placing permanent easements on farmed wetlands. By 1997, agriculture wetland conversion dropped from over 50 percent of all conversion to 25–30 percent (USDA, 2001; USDI, 2000).

Wetland Mitigation Banking

Mitigation banking refers to the restoration, creation, enhancement, and, in some cases, preservation of wetlands or other aquatic habitats for the purpose of providing compensatory mitigation *in advance* of wetland damage permitted under the section 404 regulatory program (Zinn, 1997).

It creates a market-based program for wetland mitigation, including "sellers" and "buyers." Sellers are any group that restores wetlands and "banks" the mitigation credits with the Corps of Engineers. Buyers are landowners needing mitigation to get a wetland permit for their land use activity. By creating a "market" for wetland restoration, this program has prompted many civic-minded groups into entrepreneurial wetland restoration, knowing they will be compensated for their efforts. It has also eased the delays and regulatory burden on land developers who can achieve required wetland mitigation simply by buying credits of wetlands already restored.

This program also solves another problem of mitigation: knowing whether promised mitigation will actually work. Without banking, permits were issued based on mitigation plans by landowners, but there is often some question whether the plans will be fully implemented or if the restoration will work. Under mitigation banking, the project has already been completed, so there is more certainty that the restoration is successful.

The wetland mitigation banking process involves the following five steps:

1. A group or firm identifies degraded wetlands, documents their conditions, and proposes restoration to the Corps of Engineers under the mitigation banking program.
2. The group or firm restores the wetland, using labor and capital.
3. After restoration, the group or firm and the Corps document the restoration and assign wetland mitigation credits to the project.
4. When a landowner in the watershed applies for a wetlands permit for a wetland-disturbing activity, the Corps will seek evidence that the applicant has attempted to avoid and minimize impacts. If wetland impacts are deemed unavoidable, the applicant seeks to mitigate the impacts by purchasing wetland mitigation credits.
5. The Corps of Engineers decides what appropriate level of mitigation credits the applicant requires, and it requires a fee from the applicant for the credits. The fee is used to compensate the group or firm who conducted the restoration.

State and Local Wetland Protection Programs

Although the federal section 404 program gets the most attention, some of the earliest and most effective wetland programs are in the states. The federal wetland program is limited, and state and local programs are needed to "fill in the blanks" to provide protection for wetlands not addressed by federal jurisdiction, such as isolated wetlands. Table 16.4 summarizes six state wetland programs. Some of these states, such as Massachusetts, California, and Florida, initiated programs well before the federal permitting program began in 1975. Some (New Jersey, Michigan, California, and Massachusetts) regulate more activities than the federal program. New Jersey, California, and Massachusetts require buffer zones around wetlands. Several apply mitigation ratios; more mitigation acreage than impacted acreage may be required. Four of the states allow mitigation banking. Only one of the states (Michigan) has assumed implementation of the federal program.

TABLE 16.4   **Wetlands Protection Programs in Six States**

State	Legislative Authority and Regulatory Agency	Activities Regulated	Buffer Zones	Typical Mitigation Ratios	Mitigation Banking Allowed?	Assumption of Federal 404 Program?
Florida	Warren S. Henderson Wetlands Protection Act (1984); Department of Environmental Regulation	Dredge and fill	None	2.5:1–4:1[1]	Yes	No
New Jersey	Freshwater Wetlands Protection Act (1987) and the Wetlands Act (1970); Department of Environmental Protection	Removal, fill, dredge, alteration	25–150 feet (for freshwater wetlands)	1:1–7:1[2]	Yes	Working on it
Michigan	Goemaere-Anderson Wetlands Protection Act (1979); Department of Natural Resources	Removal, fill, dredge, drain	None	1:1	No	Yes
California	McAteer-Petris Act (1969) and the California Coastal Act (1976); California Coastal Commission and the San Francisco Bay Conservation and Development Commission	BCDC—chiefly beach access and removal and fill; CCC—very broad range of activities	100 feet required by CCC, none by BCDC	1:1	Yes	No
Oregon	Removal-Fill Law (1985); Division of State Lands	Removal and fill	None	1:1–6:1[3]	Yes	Decided against
Massachusetts	The Wetlands Protection Act (1972); Department of Environmental Protection	Removal, fill, dredge, alteration	Up to 100 feet	1:1	No	No

Source: *Wetlands: Mitigating and Regulating Development Impacts* by David Salveson, 1994. Reprinted with permission of the Urban Land Institute.
1. 2.5:1 for created wetlands, higher (4:1 and up) for enhanced wetlands.
2. 1:1 minimum, 7:1 for enhancement.
3. 1:1 for nontidal wetlands, up to 6:1 for tidal.

Local wetland protection programs can also complement federal and state programs. Most localities with urban forestry, urban wildlife, or riparian protection programs include wetlands. The following list outlines a simple process for developing a local wetlands protection program. The first step is the identification and evaluation of the wetlands in the area. Wetlands can be identified from a number of sources given in table 16.3. A local wetlands map derived from these sources should be field-checked to clarify any boundary differences.

Developing a Local Wetlands Protection Program

1. *Define goals and objectives.* Why should we protect wetlands?

   ▪ e.g., stormwater storage, wildlife habitat, economic value, recreational value

2. *Inventory and prioritize the resource.* What do we have and what is important?

- Review existing maps, aerial photos, FWS national wetland inventory maps, soil surveys (hydric soils), field investigation
- Prioritize wetlands based on size, public perceptions, functional uses, etc.

3. *Identify methods of protection.* What should we do?

- Acquisition: e.g., purchase, conservation easements, land trusts
- Regulations: legal restrictions or permitting, overlay zones

4. *Provide sufficient program funding.* What will it cost and where do we get funds?

- User fees, local bonds, state and federal conservation funds

5. *Provide appropriate public involvement.* Who are the stakeholders and what do they want?

- The public can provide political support for program and help in data collection and implementation.

6. *Implement program and monitor results.*

Coastal Ecology and Management

Coastal marshes, backbays, and estuaries are the transitional zone between marine and upland ecosystems, and they provide unique conditions for the propagation of fish, shellfish, and wildlife (see figure 16.20). The diversity of the estuarine environment includes the **marsh and baygrass community** of aquatic, riparian, and land species; the microorganism **plankton community** of both plants (phytoplankton) and animals (zooplankton); the **nekton community** of free-swimming larger species; and the **benthic community** of bottom dwellers. Estuaries play an important role in the life cycle of many species, including shrimp and anadramous fish.

Protection of coastal ecology depends on both habitat and water quality protection. Habitat protection requires managing shoreline and marshland uses, including the establishment of buffer zones between water and development and other intensive human use. Water quality protection requires management of development, land uses, and wastewater discharges not only in the coastal zone but also in the larger watershed draining into the estuary.

Efforts to protect the Chesapeake Bay, for example, illustrate the complexities and the challenge. Initial strategies focused on wastewater discharges into the Bay and its finger estuaries. Attention then turned to land use on its shores, then to uses surrounding the Bay. The comprehensive Chesapeake Bay program now focuses on "tributary strategies" including land uses in all of the basins draining into the Bay.

Coastal Zone Management

Because of the ecological value of the coastal zone, its management has become a national priority. Although the federal government has refrained from regulating private land use, it has recognized the need for coastal zone planning and has provided funds for such activities by state and local governments. The **Coastal Zone Management Act (CZMA) of 1972** aimed to stimulate land use planning and controls in coastal areas due to the environmental values, natural hazards, and

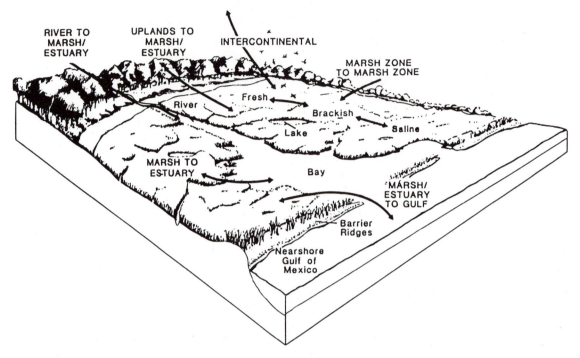

Figure 16.20 Deltaic marshes are closely linked to sea and upland ecosystems. *Source:* Clark et al. (1980).

development pressures coincident in these areas. The objectives of the Act are to centralize control of development decisions in coastal areas from fragmented local governments to the regional or state level. The program is administered by the Office of Ocean and Coastal Resources Management (OCRM) of the National Oceanic and Atmospheric Administration (NOAA).

The Act aimed not to specify how coastal zone lands should be used, but rather to establish state-developed plans, procedures, and institutions through which land use decisions could be made. The program provides two incentives for states to participate voluntarily and develop and implement coastal zone management (CZM) programs. First, under section 306, the Act provides grants to the states for program development and operation. Second, the Act provides that once a state program is approved, federal activities must be consistent with the program. In addition, the Act offers grants to states with approved plans to acquire land to preserve natural areas under the National Estuarine Sanctuary Program and for coastal rehabilitation projects. To qualify for the grants, the state program plans must include a number of required items, such as a definition of permissible uses, means by which land and water uses are to be controlled, and an organizational structure for implementation.

In general, CZM planning involves the following process:

1. Delineation of the coastal zone, participating agencies, jurisdictions, and stakeholders.
2. Inventory and analysis of coastal environmental, economic, and social resources.

3. Establishment of management objectives, such as: maintain a high quality environment, protect species diversity, conserve critical habitats and ecological processes, control pollution, identify lands for development, protect against natural hazards, restore damaged ecosystems, encourage participation.

4. Development of integrated strategies by appropriate agencies and stakeholders to achieve objectives, including regulatory programs and nonregulatory programs, such as land trusts, conservation easements, education.

5. Implementation of strategies and monitoring of progress and effectiveness.

Model Programs for Coastal Zone Management

In the late 1990s, NOAA's Office of Ocean and Coastal Resources Management (OCRM) commissioned evaluation studies of the effectiveness of the CZM program. Three separate studies were conducted, each focusing on a specific CZMA objective: protecting of beaches, dunes, bluffs, and rocky shores (Bernd-Cohen and Gordon, 1998); protecting estuaries and coastal wetlands (Good, Weber, Charland, Olson, and Chapin, 1998); and redeveloping urban ports and waterfronts (Goodwin, Hastings, and Ferguson, 1997). The studies' results measured progress not only in program implementation, but also of the practice of CZM in the United States. Based on the data available, they demonstrated improvement in CZM.

The beach and dune protection study found that coastal states are utilizing a variety of tools to achieve resource protection. These include regulatory setbacks and controls over shoreline development in combination with planning, stewardship of state lands, coastal land acquisition, and research and public education about shoreline processes and human interaction.

Regulatory controls are the most important tools, since the majority of the oceanfront shoreline is in private ownership and subject to development pressures. Protection is achieved through setbacks; regulation of shoreline development and shoreline stabilizations; restrictions on pedestrian and vehicular access; habitat protection; and permit compliance/permit tracking systems. Setbacks are particularly effective—acting as natural buffer areas and reducing hazard risks (see figure 9.18). Planning tools offer long-range vision and site-specific goals for the protection and development of selected coastal areas. Stewardship of coastal lands, through state land management and acquisition, is also an important component of all state coastal programs (Bernd-Cohen and Gordon, 1998).

Competing policies and demands for the use of the shoreline continue to pose a dilemma for coastal management. States and localities struggle with decisions regarding competing demands for recreation and tourist development, protection of threatened sensitive areas, the rights of private property owners, and public health and safety (Bernd-Cohen and Gordon, 1998).

Based on the results of the evaluation, Bernd-Cohen and Gordon (1998) summarized the elements of an effective CZM program for the protection of beaches, dunes, bluffs, and rocky shores. It includes elements of the following:

1. Regulation: coastal setbacks, construction controls, shoreline stabilization, access restrictions, and habitat protection.
2. Planning: adopted plans and enforceable policies for resources protection, beach nourishment, inlet management, dunes restoration, and so on.
3. Management and acquisition: inventory of public coastal land holdings, public land management and stewardship, coastal land acquisition.

The evaluation study of CZM protection of estuaries and wetlands yielded similar results. Good et al. (1998) concluded that most states consider estuary and coastal wetland protection highly important. For those states having sufficient data, the overall performance and effectiveness of their coastal management programs gets moderate to high ratings for protecting estuaries and coastal wetlands. However, they found that management of nontidal, freshwater wetlands is more limited, and nonregulatory wetland restoration is underutilized.

The study recommended that OCRM and the states (a) improve nontidal, freshwater wetland management in the coastal zone, (b) establish a national performance evaluation system so that states' activities can be more easily monitored, and (c) establish a coastal wetland restoration policy. "OCRM should establish explicit national CZM policy goals for wetland restoration, including (1) no net loss of wetland area and function in the short term, implemented through regulatory programs; and (2) a net gain of wetland area and function over the long term, implemented through non-regulatory restoration programs" (Good et al., 1998).

Based on their study, Good et al. (1998) developed a list of elements of a model state CZM program for protecting estuaries and wetlands. These elements include the following:

1. Information and research: wetland inventory and function assessment, monitoring of wetland change, GIS mapping.
2. Regulations: permit programs for wetlands, no-net-loss policy, mitigation at > 1:1 ratio, evaluation of regulatory outcomes.
3. Planning: local land use plans based on state standards for estuary and wetland protection, special area management planning (SAMP), reliable outcome data.
4. Acquisition: conservation easements for land and wetland protection.
5. Nonregulatory tools: public and landowner education, wetland restoration to achieve a net gain of wetland area and function.
6. Coordination: memoranda of agreement, joint permitting, coordination with 404 permitting.

State CZM Programs: The California Coastal Commission

The evaluation studies of the CZM program reviewed state planning and implementation, and provided some examples. Maryland and California were cited for effective programs for protection of wetland and estuarine resources, Washington and Wisconsin were among the exemplary programs for waterfront redevelopment, and California, Oregon, North Carolina, and Maryland are noted for protection of dunes and bluffs (Bernd-Cohen and Gordon, 1998; Good, et al., 1998; Goodwin et al., 1997). The California program illustrates the breadth of state programs.

The California coastal program was established by public referendum in 1972. The California Coastal Commission (CCC) was modeled after the effective San Francisco Bay Conservation and Development Commission that was established by the state legislature in 1965 (see chapter 8). The CCC oversees the state coastal program, which combines mandatory local planning and permitting and state coastal resource and land acquisition.

The program requires local coastal programs (LCPs) with CCC certification and oversight. Each LCP must identify specific coastal resources, hazard areas, coastal access, use priorities, and significant cumulative development impacts on coastal resources and access; and adopt a land use plan, zoning ordinances, and zoning district maps to reflect the level and pattern of development consistent with the Coastal Act. CCC certification of an LCP results in delegation of coastal development permit authority.

Local Planning and Permitting

There are 126 LCP segments statewide, of which 88 have CCC-certified programs and local permit delegation responsibilities. Certified LCPs vary regarding development of oceanfront property. Some impose rigorous guidelines for any new development and encourage purchase of remaining undeveloped properties; 24 coastal jurisdictions recognize coastal geologic hazards through designation of special zones, geologic hazard ordinances, or comparable techniques. Regarding bluff-top development, some local jurisdictions use predetermined, fixed setbacks that vary from 10 to 320 feet. Others employ a cliff retreat rate, most commonly over a 50-year period. Most communities compromise safe setback considerations in "infilling" areas. The lack of state guidelines for safe beach-level development has led to some continued development and reconstruction in hazardous locations (Good et al., 1998).

Coastal Land Acquisition

Nearly half (47%) of California's 1,100-mile-long coastline is in public ownership and active public management. The state's Department of Parks and Recreation (DPR) manages over 375 miles or 34 percent of the ocean shoreline in the state parks system. There are 87 bluff-front state parks and 32 rocky shore state parks. The DPR acquisition program for beaches and dunes, through special site-specific legislation and some bond funds, has acquired 26,838 acres of state beaches, 6,000 acres of unclassified beach areas, 27.3 miles of land in five state parks and one state reserve, and 2.8 miles of dunes (Good et al., 1998).

Coastal Zone Restoration

The Coastal Conservancy awards grants to local governments and nonprofit organizations for coastal restoration, coastal resources enhancement projects, resource protection zones, and buffer areas surrounding public beaches, parks, natural areas, and fish and wildlife preserves in the coastal zone. Between 1978 and 1995, 600 projects were initiated and 400 projects were completed involving access, wetlands protection, trail, recreational pier restoration, and farmlands protection.

Between 1978 and 1992, $175 million general obligation bonds acquired 29,000 acres (Good et al., 1998).

Estuarine and Wetland Protection

The San Francisco Bay Conservation and Development Commission (BCDC) preceded and served as a model for the CCC. Wetland loss due to filling has dramatically reversed, from 2,300 acres/year from 1940 to 1965 (before BCDC), to 20 acres/year from 1965 to 1986 (post-BCDC and early CZM), to 4 acres/year from 1987 to 1991 (recent CZM). Mitigation has more than compensated for these losses, with more than 30 acres/year net gain since 1987. The entire Bay is in a high protection zone, and four special area management plans provide for more detailed protection and restoration (Bernd-Cohen and Gordon, 1998). See figure 8.2.

Summary

Vegetation, the ecological producers, provides the foundation of food webs and ecosystems. Take care of the vegetation and you will do much to care for the ecosystem. Landscape ecology teaches us that terrestrial ecological functions depend on the interrelationships of the dominant land use/cover matrix with vegetative patches and corridors. People are an integral part of ecosystems and not surprisingly, vegetation provides to us significant economic, environmental, aesthetic and spiritual benefits. To preserve those benefits it is necessary to manage vegetative cover and the tree canopy.

Urban forestry has emerged as the basic discipline for managing the tree canopy in urban and metropolitan areas. Fundamental objectives include maintaining and protecting existing trees and increasing tree planting to expand the urban forest canopy. Studies by AF show that forest canopy has declined significantly in urban and metropolitan areas across the United States. Heavy canopy (>50% cover) in urban areas has decreased typically from 40–50 percent to 20 percent of total land area from the 1970s to the 1990s. AF recommends an average metropolitan canopy cover of 40 percent to maximize stormwater management, air quality, and energy benefits. It estimates a national urban tree deficit of 634 million trees, the number needed to be planted to achieve this 40 percent canopy level.

Some of the most important ecological areas are wetlands and the coastal zone at the land-water interface. Recognition of the economic, environmental, and social benefits of wetlands has helped establish a variety of programs to protect them. These programs have reduced the rate of conversion of wetlands to other uses, but we still have not achieved a no-net-loss status that is our national policy.

Coastal zones are critical environmental areas because they combine environmental sensitivity and development pressures. During the past three decades, federally supported state CZM programs have increased land use planning and management in these areas with mixed success. Some states, like California and Maryland, have developed effective programs that may inform other state and local governments.

17 ▪ Land Use, Wildlife Habitats, and Biodiversity

Approaches to wildlife management have evolved during the past 40 years. For decades, management focused on **"indicator" species,** usually sport and commercial species. It was assumed that if the numbers of these indicator species were well managed, remaining species would be in good shape. In the early 1970s, attention turned to threatened and endangered species as special indicator species. It became apparent that to manage stressed wildlife effectively required managing their **habitats.** This habitat-approach evolved into the perception that ALL wildlife are important as part of a larger functioning whole—the ecosystem. In the 1990s, **ecosystem management** has emerged as the organizing concept for managing wildlife, habitats, and biodiversity.

Biodiversity is defined simply as the variety of life and all processes that keep life functioning (Keystone Center, 1991). It is studied at genetic, species, and ecosystem levels. Global efforts to manage biodiversity aim to arrest species extinction and preserve intact natural ecosystems. Local efforts have traditionally focused on wildlands, but the last decade has seen new approaches to biodiversity of working landscapes and urban biodiversity.

This chapter applies some of the ecological concepts discussed earlier to managing wildlife and biodiversity. The primary focus is managing wildlife, habitats, and biodiversity in human-modified agricultural and urbanizing landscapes. Special attention is given to habitat conservation planning under the Endangered Species Act.

Some Fundamentals of Wildlife Habitats and Biodiversity

A **habitat** is the arrangement of **food, water, space,** and **cover** (for protection, hiding, and reproduction) that is required by a species individual or population. The arrangement determines a limited number of **habitat niches** that animals fill in the ecosystem. Plant communities provide habitat food, water, and cover;

Habitat Variable	Successional Stage (see figure)					
	1-GF	2-SS	3-PS	4-Y	5-M	6-OG
Plant diversity	●●	●●●●●	●●●	●	●●	●●●
Vegetation height		●	●●	●●●	●●●●	●●●●●
Canopy volume		●	●●	●●●	●●●●●	●●●●
Canopy closure	●	●●	●●●●	●●●●	●●●●	●●●
Structural diversity	●	●●●●	●	●	●●	●●●●●
Forage potential	●●●●●	●●●	●	●	●●	●●●
Browse potential	●	●●●●●	●	●	●●	●●●
Animal diversity	●●●	●●●●	●	●●	●●●●●	●●●●

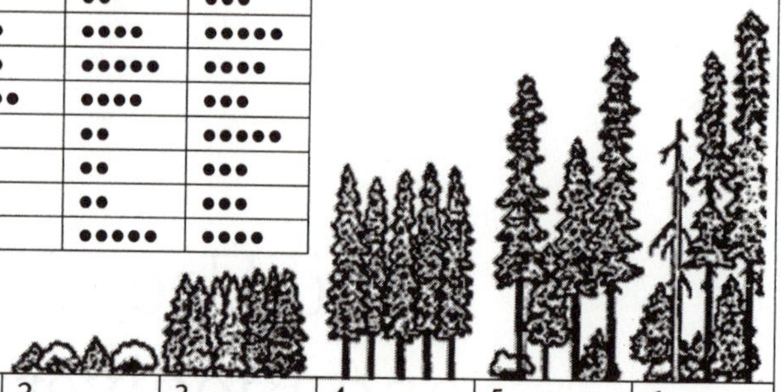

1 Grass-forb	2 Shrub-seedling	3 Pole-sapling	4 Young	5 Mature	6 Old growth

Six successional stages

Figure 17.1 Forest Successional Stages and Their Relationship to Habitat Variables. *Source:* USDA, Forest Service.

therefore, the **plant community type** is used to define the **type of habitat.** Habitat types are defined by plant associations (e.g., woodland, wetland, meadow, pond) and dominant plant species (e.g., pine, oak-hickory).

Although a plant community type is a unique combination of plants that occur in an area, the community is usually defined by the dominant single species of the climax community, even though several community types may exist at that time. The plant community during succession from bare ground to the climax vegetation passes through various **successional stages,** each of which may have different community types and thus different habitats. Figure 17.1 shows forest successional stages and their effect on habitat attributes.

Edges are produced where different plant communities or successional stages come together. **Ecotones** are formed where these different communities and stages overlap or intersperse. Edges and ecotones exhibit attributes of different communities and thus can provide greater plant diversity, more habitat niches, and greater habitat richness (or a greater number of wildlife species residing in an area). Figure 17.2 (1) shows that wildlife adapted to plant community A are likely to spill over to ecotone C, where A's influence extends into community B; likewise wildlife of community B will likely spill over into ecotone D (2). In addition, there may be species particularly adapted to the combined ecotone E (3).

Although edges can enhance diversity, wildlife need **core or interior habitat** for sufficient protected space and cover. Reduction and fragmentation of core habitat has the greatest impact on urban wildlife. Core habitat, edge buffers, and corridors connecting cores are essential habitat elements in agricultural and urbanizing areas (see figure 17.4). Water is a key for habitat vitality and richness not only as a primary need of wildlife, but also for the unique vegetative types, increased edges, and special habitats that occur near water bodies. This **riparian habitat** zone also provides distinct microclimates and migratory corridors for wildlife.

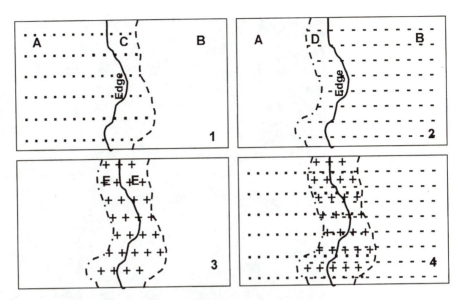

Figure 17.2 Edges, Ecotones, and Species Richness

The shelter and reproductive requirements of wildlife are enhanced by the presence of potential **nesting and den areas.** In terrestrial habitats, dead standing trees (snags), dead and downed logs in various stages of decay, cliffs, caves or talus, and broken up rocks at the base of steep slopes provide these habitat elements. In aquatic habitats, pools, underwater live and dead vegetation, and spawning gravels are important elements.

Habitat Cores, Corridors, Connectivity, and Fragmentation

Wildlife studies in agricultural and urbanizing landscapes show that perhaps the major landscape change impacting the viability of wildlife is **habitat fragmentation.** This is the incremental conversion of natural areas to other uses, reducing and isolating core habitats. Landscape ecology principles have proven very useful in understanding and responding to these impacts. Recall from chapter 16 that landscape ecology views the landscape as a **matrix** (dominant land use), **patches** (isolated vegetative types or habitats), **corridors** (natural or induced linear areas that link patches), and **mosaic** or **structure** (the overall collection of patches and corridors in the landscape). Figure 17.3 shows agricultural and urban matrixes.

Patches need to be large enough to provide interior or core habitat. For many species, interior habitat begins to develop about 150 feet from the patch edge. Habitat fragmentation reduces the capacity of a landscape to support healthy wildlife populations by diminishing original habitat, reducing patch size, increasing edge, increasing isolation of patches, and modifying natural changes or disturbances (e.g., fire suppression). Individual effects such as these may be small, but they are cumulative over time and can easily add up to major impacts (USDA, NRCS, 1999).

Figure 17.3 Landscape Elements in Agricultural Matrix Landscape Scale and Urban Matrix Stream Corridor Scale. *Source:* FISRWG (1998).

Connectivity becomes a critical issue when movements across landscapes become constricted by fragmentation. In unaltered landscape, natural species movements and ecological pathways provide connectivity. When wildland is fragmented by land conversion to development or agriculture, habitats lose their capacity to provide ecological pathways (Scott and Allen, undated). Beier and Loe (1992) list the functions of corridors: "Corridors provide avenues along which (1) wide ranging animals can travel, migrate, and meet mates...(2) plants can propagate...(3) genetic interchange can occur...(4) populations can respond to environmental change...[and] (5) locally extirpated populations can be replaced from other areas."

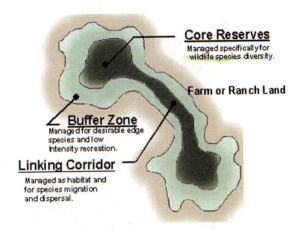

Figure 17.4 Habitat Core, Buffers, and Corridors. *Source:* USDA, NRCS (1999).

In response to problems of habitat fragmentation, landscape ecologists and wildlife managers have recognized the need to preserve and connect core habitats. Figure 17.4 defines some of the basic elements of wildlife habitat management in agricultural and urbanizing landscapes. The core reserve is the key element, providing essential space and cover for wildlife. But the effectiveness of core reserves is greatly reduced if they are encroached on or isolated by agriculture or development. Patches need to be large enough to provide interior or core habitat. Interior habitat begins to develop about 150 feet from the patch edge, although some species require a much larger buffer. Buffers gradually change habitat conditions from the core reserve to surrounding land use. Corridors provide secure habitat conditions for wildlife migration from one core reserve to another. Figure 17.5 illustrates landscapes with high and low degrees of connectivity.

Scott and Allen (undated) argue that effective corridors must provide "functional connectivity." This includes not only opportunities for movement, but also the contribution to (1) population parameters (e.g., growth rate, demographics, genetic structure) and (2) ecological processes (e.g., flows of water and nutrients, trophic/species interactions, recovery from disturbance). Corridor needs are species dependent. Remnant or remaining natural corridors are more effective at providing these functions than introduced corridors. Figure 17.6 illustrates that simply "squaring up" fields can enlarge both patches and corridors while increasing farming efficiency.

A number of landscape planning principles for managing habitat are illustrated in figure 17.7. These apply to both urbanizing and agricultural landscapes. Patches need to be as large as possible, connected, unified, redundant, and near to one another. Corridors should be continuous, wide as possible, redundant, and reflective of natural and historic conditions. Landscape structure needs to be horizontally and vertically diverse and incorporate native vegetation and the matrix other than patches and corridors also needs to be managed with wildlife in mind (USDA, NRCS, 1999).

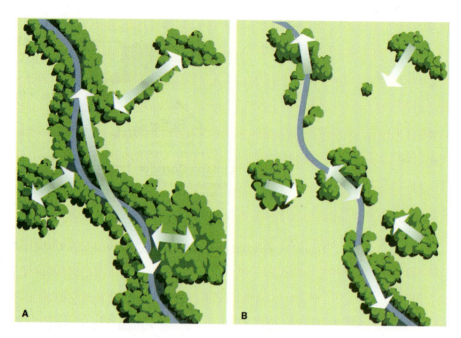

Figure 17.5 Landscapes with High and Low Levels of Connectivity. Connected landscape provides enhanced ecological functions over fragmented landscapes. *Source:* FISRWG (1998).

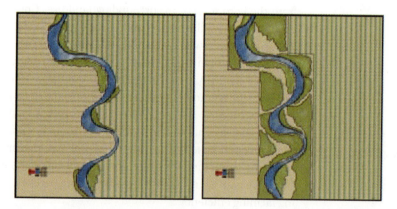

Figure 17.6 Squaring Up Farm Fields Can Enlarge Patches and Corridors While Increasing Farm Efficiency. *Source:* USDA, NRCS (1999).

PATCHES

A Large reserves/patches are better than small reserves/patches.

B Connected reserves/patches are better than separated reserves/patches.

C Several reserves/patches (redundancy) are better than one reserve/patch.

D Nearness is better than separation.

CORRIDORS

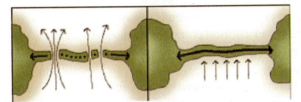

E Continuous corridors are better than fragmented corridors.

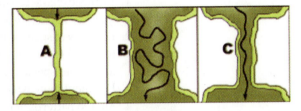

F Wider corridors are better than narrow corridors.

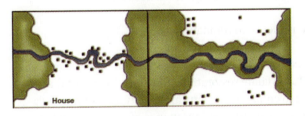

G Natural connectivity should be maintained or restored.

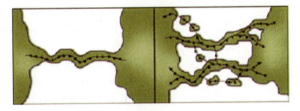

H Two or more corridor connections between patches (redundancy) are better than one.

STRUCTURE

I Structurally diverse corridors and patches are better than simple structure.

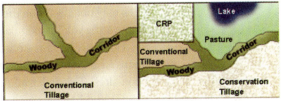

J Native plants are better than introduced plants.

Figure 17.7 Wildlife Planning Principles for Patches, Corridors, Matrix, and Structure. *Source:* USDA, NRCS (1999).

Functional Connectivity and Habitat Restoration

Although these simple concepts are very useful in assessing habitat change and planning for protection and restoration, providing effective habitats in a complex ecosystem is not quite so simple. Planners and wildlife specialists may be quick to include patches and corridors, but they rarely assess whether these linkages are optimal or even sufficient for all species, much less for the ecosystem processes needed to sustain them. All corridors are not the same. Some species need more corridor than others. Rather than define wildlife movement by corridors, it may be more prudent to define it by: (1) the forces and motivation creating species' need to move, (2) the possible avenues of movement, and (3) the target or destination of movement. There are cases where the combination of motivation and target overwhelms the obstacles of pathway, just as there may be cases where a lack of motivation keeps wildlife out of suitable corridors (Scott and Allen, undated).

Scott and Allen (undated) describe several factors that can impede movement and functional connectivity even when corridors exist:

1. Intrinsic characteristics of the corridor (e.g., corridor habitat is inadequate or too heterogeneous to provide unbroken pathways)
2. Diversity of species using corridors (most corridors are justified by large mammal movement, even though fragmentation is more devastating for smaller species and plants)
3. Fragmentation, which alters patterns of ecosystem dynamics
4. Altered patterns of movement (corridors replace unbroken regions, and thus may alter movement and adversely impact viability)
5. Inadequate corridor width (width is important but does not determine functions)
6. Reliance on introduced rather than remnant corridors

These factors should be considered in habitat restoration undertaken in response to habitat damage. Most wildlife restoration efforts are "passive," that is, habitat is re-created or restored to enhance the natural capacity of wildlife populations to grow and colonize unoccupied areas. Restoration is often done as mitigation for destroyed habitat in an exchange of acres gained for acres lost. "Active" wildlife restoration involves active manipulation of wildlife movement and demography. Passive approaches are less costly, but they rely on the premise that wildlife will migrate to new habitat conditions ("build it and they will come"). However, this may not always be the case, and habitat restoration is an uncertain means for recovering wildlife populations (Scott, Wehtje, and Wehtje, 2001).

Passive wildlife restoration assumes that animals (and therefore other populations) will flow down a gradient of density from surrounding habitats onto restoration sites. This is based on island biogeography theory (MacArthur and Wilson, 1967) and habitat patches (Diamond, 1975; Forman and Godron, 1986), which consider patches like islands in a hostile sea of human-dominated landscapes (Scott et al., 2001). Distance, connectivity, and island or patch size will determine migration. Impediments to movement occur at the landscape scale (the mosaic of patches of varying size, age class, and plant species) and the species scale (motivation, movement needs).

Habitat restoration must be planned to maximize the potential for colonization in challenged landscapes. The probability of restoration site colonization depends on proximity of the site to the target species' geographic distribution, the size of the site relative to species' needs, the level of patch isolation, and the social or behavioral characteristics of the species. Although evaluating colonization potential of a target species is difficult, evaluating ecosystem restoration is far more complex. It requires a regional perspective and coordination of restoration projects (Scott et al., 2001).

Another critical issue in habitat restoration is **invasive** or **exotic species.** These species, especially plants, destroy more habitat each year in the United States than urban growth. The U.S. Fish and Wildlife Service estimates that 4,600 acres of habitat are lost *each day* to invasive species. Removing and managing these invaders is a major component of restoration work (Interagency Workgroup on Wetland Restoration [IWWR], 2002).

Habitat Inventories and Evaluation

An important part of planning for wildlife and biodiversity is the inventory and evaluation of habitats. These range from simple to very complex studies, depending on needs and resources. Habitat assessment and evaluation are useful for management planning, impact assessment, and mitigation. They can compare the habitat value at different locations at the same point in time (e.g., today) or at the same location at different times (e.g., five years ago and today). Generally, evaluation procedures are based on two principles: (1) the habitat has a **carrying capacity** to support wildlife populations, and (2) the **suitability** of a habitat for a species can be based on its vegetative, physical, and chemical conditions. Assessment techniques include simple wildlife inventories, GAP analysis, the qualitative species-habitat matrix, indicator species studies, and diversity and habitat indices. More detailed ecological studies are necessary for habitat conservation plans, discussed in the next section.

Habitat inventories can be very useful at a variety of planning scales. They can be used to "red flag" areas of concern to be considered in land use and development. The inventories simply identify species and groups of organisms and special natural areas and display the information on a series of maps in which symbols and numbers identify species, habitats, and habitat use. (See box 17.1.)

GAP analysis is a "coarse-filter" assessment of the conservation status and potential for species in a region or watershed. It is based on vegetation communities, but also considers land ownership and management practice. The analysis produces a species richness map, which highlights areas with high biodiversity potential, and a GAP map, which compares this potential with existing conservation management practice, showing a "gap" in the protection of wildlife (USDA, NRCS, 1999). Box 17.2 gives a procedure for GAP analysis (see also figure 10.3).

Habitat evaluation procedures generally use an indicator species or a habitat or diversity index.

BOX 17.1—Data Needs for Wildlife and Habitat Inventories

Wildlife Species Data Needs

- Wildlife present in the planning area
- Nongame species
- Game species
- Threatened and endangered species (federal and state listed species)
- GAP data (where available)
- Vulnerable populations of a species
- Historical species (once present but no longer reside in the watershed)
- Population characteristics for species of concern
- Culturally important species (especially those tied to Native Americans or valuable to limited income groups for subsistence)

Wildlife Habitat Data Needs

- GAP data (where available)
- Existing vegetation
- Historical vegetation
- Wildlife species/plant communities relationships
- Land cover types
- Land ownership
- Habitat features
- Patches with high biodiversity
- Patches with vulnerable populations
- Migration and dispersal corridors
- Special areas (e.g., calving sites)
- Potential habitats
- Species ranges for species of concern
- Water availability and historical hydrology

Source: USDA, NRCS (1999).

BOX 17.2—Procedure for GAP Analysis Process

Species Richness Map

1. Determine those species that occur in the region that are of concern or interest.
2. Collect and compile habitat relationship and occurrence data for those species.
3. Create a map of where the habitats occur in the region based on existing vegetation.
4. Overlay the wildlife habitat data with the habitat map to determine areas of rich species diversity.

GAP Map (see figure 10.3)

1. Prepare a general land ownership map that classifies lands into public and private ownership.
2. Assign a management status of 1 to areas that are managed for wildlife, such as wildlife refuges, Nature Conservancy lands, and so on.
3. Assign a management status of 2 to areas that are managed for natural conditions such as U.S. Fish and Wildlife Service (FWS) refuges managed for recreational uses and Bureau of Land Management (BLM) areas of critical environmental concern.
4. Assign a management status of 3 to areas that are prevented from being permanently developed, including most BLM and USFS lands.
5. Assign a management status of 4 to private and public lands not managed for natural conditions.
6. Overlay this map with the habitat relationship data to determine habitats that are offered the least protection in the region, with status 1 lands providing the highest protection.

Source: USDA, NRCS (1999).

Indicator Species

An indicator species is an organism whose presence or absence, population density or dispersion, or reproductive success can indicate habitat conditions that are too difficult to measure for other species (Federal Interagency Stream Restoration Working Group [FISRWG], 1998). Indicator species are used to indicate effects of contamination, population trends, and habitat quality. The assumption is that if the habitat is suitable for the indicator species, it is suitable for others. However, each species is different in its habitat needs and habitat niche, so the effectiveness of indicator species to fully represent a wide range of species and habitats is limited.

If an indicator species is used, care should be taken so that:

- It is sensitive to and responds directly to changes in environmental attributes of concern, such as water quality or habitat fragmentation. For example, high-profile game species (e.g., bear or elk) are usually not good indicators of habitat quality since their populations are affected by hunting mortality that can mask environmental effects.
- It has a larger home range and population density than other species to ease measurement. For example, rare and endangered species have special importance, but they are not good indicators because they are difficult and expensive to measure.

Habitat Limiting Factors and Management Prescriptions

The Natural Resources Conservation Service (NRCS), in conjunction with its Wildlife Habitat Management Institute and the Wildlife Habitat Council, has prepared a number of fish and wildlife habitat leaflets to assist in evaluation and management of habitats for specific species. They outline a procedure for assessing habitat elements compared to a formulated list of habitat requirements for the species.

Diversity Indices

Biological diversity measures species abundance and variety in an area. It is measured at different levels of complexity depending on the objectives of the study: genetic, population/species, community/ecosystem, and landscape (Noss and Cooperrider, 1994), the latter three being most appropriate for environmental planning. In addition to overall diversity, studies often focus on subsets of habitats, such as native species, rare species, habitat guilds (species having common habitats, like cave dwellers), or taxonomic groups (e.g., amphibians, breeding birds) (FISRWG, 1998).

Diversity is usually measured at a defined scale: a single community (so-called **alpha diversity**), across community boundaries **(beta diversity),** or in large areas with many communities **(gamma diversity).** While planning for alpha diversity may increase localized diversity, Noss and Harris (1986) suggest that this may create a less diverse regional or gamma diversity. They recommend that diversity studies and wildlife habitat plans have a landscape context even when focusing on a specific community.

Richness indices are the most widely used diversity measures. They measure the number of species or the number of species divided by the overall population. **Abundance measures** account for the evenness of distribution of species. Other measures are based on **proportional abundance** and combine richness and evenness. Applying diversity indices to species subsets can enhance their effectiveness. For example, Pielou (1975) suggests three indices for terrestrial ecosystems: plant diversity, habitat diversity, and local rarity.

Habitat Suitability Index (HSI)

The HSI is a species-specific measure of suitability based on a habitat's vegetative, physical, and chemical characteristics. The index ranges from 0 (unsuitable) to 1 (optimum habitat). HSI models have been developed for different species by the U.S. FWS. A basic unit used is the habitat unit (HU), which aims to integrate habitat quantity and quality. It is defined as follows:

$$HU = AREA \times HSI$$

where   HU is the number of habitat units (in units of area)
               AREA is the areal extent of the habitat
               HSI is the Habitat Suitability Index

Habitat evaluation can assess change in HUs over time or as a result of some negative action, such as a land development proposal, or a positive action, like a habitat restoration project (FISRWG, 1998).

Conservation Corridor Planning in Rural Areas

In rural areas, there is a relative abundance of core wildlife habitats, but agricultural, transportation, and resource development activities cause their fragmentation and isolation. As a result, efforts to enhance rural habitats have focused on protecting, maintaining, and establishing conservation corridors that connect patches and core habitats (USDA, NRCS, 1999).

Principles of Conservation Corridor Planning

Corridors provide substantial benefits for wildlife by increasing habitat area and connectivity. Corridors that connect with each other and adjacent patches facilitate immigration and colonization of wildlife. They provide access to wildlife needs including food, water, and cover. Connected landscapes provide improved ecological functions and thereby increase the diversity of niches and species richness. In addition to wildlife benefits, corridors have recreation, education, and aesthetic value, as well as erosion and stormwater control, energy conservation, and enhanced property values (USDA, NRCS, 1999).

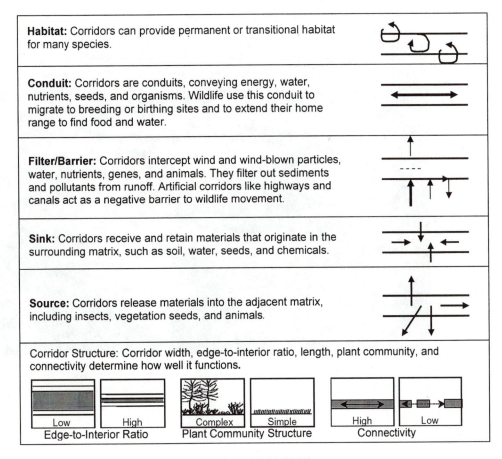

Habitat: Corridors can provide permanent or transitional habitat for many species.

Conduit: Corridors are conduits, conveying energy, water, nutrients, seeds, and organisms. Wildlife use this conduit to migrate to breeding or birthing sites and to extend their home range to find food and water.

Filter/Barrier: Corridors intercept wind and wind-blown particles, water, nutrients, genes, and animals. They filter out sediments and pollutants from runoff. Artificial corridors like highways and canals act as a negative barrier to wildlife movement.

Sink: Corridors receive and retain materials that originate in the surrounding matrix, such as soil, water, seeds, and chemicals.

Source: Corridors release materials into the adjacent matrix, including insects, vegetation seeds, and animals.

Corridor Structure: Corridor width, edge-to-interior ratio, length, plant community, and connectivity determine how well it functions.

Low High
Edge-to-Interior Ratio

Complex Simple
Plant Community Structure

High Low
Connectivity

Figure 17.8 Corridor Functions and Structure. *Source:* USDA, NRCS (1999).

Corridors provide a number of ecological functions, illustrated in figure 17.8: habitat, conduit, filter/barrier, sink, and source. In addition, the structure of the corridor, including its width, connectivity, and plant community architecture, determines its ecological and aesthetic value.

Process and Tools for Conservation Corridor Planning

In rural landscapes, a tiered approach to conservation corridor planning provides consideration of gamma level diversity through areawide or watershed scale planning and alpha level diversity planning at the property, parcel, or farm conservation plan scale. Figure 17.9 illustrates an areawide network of conservation corridors. Box 17.3 gives a planning process for areawide conservation planning, and

Figure 17.9 Areawide Network of Interconnected Riparian and Upland Corridors. *Source:* USDA, NRCS (1999).

box 17.4 gives the site-scale conservation planning process. Both of these are variations of our basic environmental planning process given in box 2.1.

Urban Biodiversity and Wildlife Management

Through the late 1970s and 1980s, increasing interest in urban wildlife issues developed. On the one hand, people began to appreciate nature, and the presence of wildlife was a kind reminder of their connection to the environment. On the other hand, it became increasingly apparent that certain species adapted quite well to the urban environment, and there was a need to not only attract but also manage wildlife populations (Adams and Dove, 1989; Leedy, Maestro, and Franklin, 1978).

More recently this interest in urban wildlife has broadened to encompass **urban biodiversity.** This apparent oxymoron has come into vogue for two reasons: (1) Studies have shown urban areas often contain more biological diversity than their surrounding farmland, and (2) remaining natural areas in cities provide not only habitat for many species but also treasures to a human populous that increasingly values natural surroundings. Although the context for urban biodiversity is far different from wildland and rural biodiversity, many of the same principles and approaches apply.

BOX 17.3—Areawide /Watershed Scale Conservation Corridor Planning Process

Preplanning: Assess preconditions; identify stakeholders; generate local support; organize interdisciplinary, interagency, public/private planning team; establish trust among stakeholders

Step 1: Delineate study area, identify resource problems, and determine data needs.

Step 2: Develop a vision statement, and determine goals and objectives.

Step 3: Inventory resources at appropriate scale.

Step 4: Analyze resource data.

Step 5: Formulate landscape scale alternatives and evaluate them based on goals and objectives and compatibility with watershed resources and local values.

Step 6: Select a plan.

Step 7: Implement the plan.

Step 8: Evaluate plan effectiveness.

Source: USDA, NRCS (1999).

However, successful protection and restoration of urban biodiversity and the benefits it provides both people and wildlife depend on the integration of biodiversity objectives with other compatible programs for environmental management, recreation, and natural hazard mitigation. The following discussion reviews urban wildlife planning and focuses on the challenges of urban biodiversity.

Urban Wildlife Planning

The main challenge of urban wildlife planning is providing habitat needs, especially of wildlife not well adapted to urban environments. The basic needs of wildlife discussed earlier include **food, water, cover,** and **space** for breeding and group territories, all of which are constrained in urban areas. Although natural areas and habitats exist in urban areas, including parks and open space, fringe area woodlands and fields, and wetlands, lakes and streams, they are highly fragmented by urban roads and land development.

BOX 17.4—Site-Scale Conservation Corridor Planning Process

Preplanning: Assess preconditions and planning resource materials.

Phase 1: Collection and Analysis at Conservation Plan Scale

    Step 1: Identify problems and opportunities.

    Step 2: Determine objectives.

    Step 3: Inventory resources.

    Step 4: Analyze resources.

Phase 2: Decision Support at the Conservation Plan Scale

    Step 5: Formulate alternatives: Integrate map layers on existing habitat

resources, habitat functions, and potential habitat and new plantings into a synthesis map layer.

    Step 6: Evaluate alternatives.

    Step 7: Make decisions.

    Step 8: Implement plan.

    Step 9: Evaluate plan.

Source: USDA, NRCS (1999).

Urban wildlife habitat planning and management aims to provide core habitat as patches in the urban matrix, buffers between core habitat and urban uses, and connecting corridors. Edge habitats benefit only certain species (e.g., opossums, raccoons, skunks, cowbirds, red-tailed hawks, white-tailed deer, and northern cardinals) often at the expense of interior habitat species. Most wildlife species inhabiting edges are considered habitat generalists. Interior core habitat is generally unaffected by its edge and is necessary for certain interior species like bobcats, wood thrushes, bobolinks, and ovenbirds (Barnes, 1999).

Scale is an important factor in providing core habitat. Landscapes of less than 250 acres support only a limited set of species and may not be large enough to include a diversity of habitat patches. Smaller animals may thrive, but medium-sized animals are compromised, and large animals are usually rare or transient. A landscape of interconnected patches of 250 to 12,000 acres begins to be large enough to support populations of medium-size animals such as coyotes, bobcats, and hawks. At this size, the region may encompass the variety of habitats these animals need to live and reproduce. Landscapes greater than 12,000 acres begin to protect ecosystem integrity and function. These large areas may be included in a large regional park or wildlife preserve that is part of a metropolitan wildlife plan.

As discussed earlier, connecting corridors are critical for wildlife in fragmented landscapes like urban areas. Wildlife planners have learned to focus on corridors, but these efforts have a number of common failings, as shown in the following list.

Common Failings in Designing Corridors to Provide Connectivity

- A homogenous corridor is assumed to provide connectivity for a heterogeneous array of species and ecosystem functions.
- A proposed corridor transects a highly heterogeneous landscape in a manner that may restrict use, often because pathways are blocked by unsuitable habitats.
- The level of habitat degradation affects the capacity of a proposed corridor to support species movement.
- The width or length of proposed corridors fail to provide unimpeded pathways for movement.
- The degree of permeability across the landscape matrix approaches the permeability of a wildlife corridor.
- Limited funds and time demand that each land acquisition has the maximum functional significance to populations and ecosystems, and proposed corridors are judged in isolation (*Source:* USDA, NRCS, 1999).

An urban wildlife conservation program begins by *minimizing negative habitat impacts* from development and continues by *providing permanent protection* of important habitat core patches, buffer areas, and corridors. Several methods of development practice designed to reduce or mitigate environmental and natural hazard impacts discussed in previous chapters (e.g., stormwater, soil erosion, landslides, flooding, nonpoint source pollution, tree canopy, etc.) are very compatible with habitat mitigation. For example, cluster development aims to group development on portions of the site most favorable to building while leaving the remainder preserved as open space. This can both preserve habitat and reduce other environmental impacts. The following list gives some guidelines for urban development sensitive to wildlife.

Guidelines to Reduce Impacts of Urban Development on Wildlife

- Before development, maximize open space and protect the most valuable wildlife habitat by placing buildings on less important portions of the site.
- Design stormwater controls like bioretention and constructed wetlands to benefit wildlife.
- Retain and plant native plants that have value for wildlife as well as aesthetic appeal.
- Provide habitat-enhancing elements like bird-feeding stations and nest boxes for cavity-nesting birds.
- Educate residents about wildlife conservation and provide opportunities for wildlife observation, such as a nature trail through open space (*Source:*Barnes, 1999).

However, reducing impacts is not sufficient because project-by-project development can incrementally consume and isolate core habitats. Fragmentation can only be arrested by more proactive wildlife planning on a landscape scale, requiring permanent habitat and corridor protection through land acquisition, conservation easements, habitat restoration, and other means.

Urban Biodiversity

Efforts to manage urban biodiversity aim to minimize and mitigate those impacts, protect and connect remaining habitats, and restore damaged natural areas. Many communities across the United States have been engaged in urban biodiversity conservation, whether they call it that or not. Programs for watershed protection and restoration, urban forestry, green infrastructure, parks and recreation, conservation design, and stormwater management have their own objectives, but if done appropriately, they can also advance the core objectives of urban biodiversity.

A good example of an urban biodiversity program is the **Chicago Wilderness,** a partnership of 68 community and environmental organizations, private firms, and local, state, and federal agencies dedicated to enhancing the Chicago region's biodiversity. Its foundation is 200,000 acres of protected conservation land, some of the largest and best surviving woodlands, wetlands, and prairies in the Midwest (see figure 17.10). In addition to these lands and a larger matrix of public and private lands that support nature, the Wilderness purposely includes as prominent members the people of the region who protect and live compatibly with it. These lands are documented in the Chicago Wilderness *Atlas of Biodiversity,* and the program's Biodiversity Recovery Plan is "both a plan and a process" that sets out eight biodiversity and public involvement goals and strategies to achieve them. The program's intent is that the plan be a living document to evolve during the

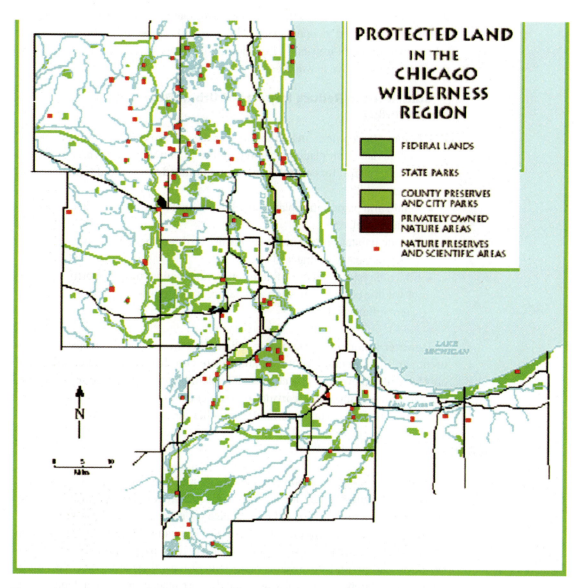

Figure 17.10 Protected Land in the Chicago Wilderness Region. *Source:* Chicago Wilderness, *An Atlas of Biodiversity.* Used with permission.

long-term effort of biodiversity recovery (Chicago Wilderness, 1999). The goals include the following:

- Preserve more land with existing or potential benefits for biodiversity.
- Manage more land to protect and restore biodiversity.
- Protect high-quality streams and lakes through watershed planning and mitigation of harmful activities to conserve aquatic biodiversity.
- Continue and expand research and monitoring.
- Apply both public and private resources more extensively and effectively to inform the region's citizens of their natural heritage and what must be done to protect it.

- Adopt local and regional development policies that reflect the need to restore and maintain biodiversity.

Randolph and Bryant (2002) explored issues of urban biodiversity in a study of the highly urbanized Holmes Run/Cameron Run watershed in Fairfax County, Falls Church, and Alexandria (VA) (see figures 17.11 and 11.19). The watershed is about 40 percent impervious surface and no portion of the landscape has escaped significant alteration. The areas that appear "natural" are highly fragmented in most cases, affected by various pollutants and stormwater flows, and filled with exotic species. The study identified some important issues of urban biodiversity:

1. *Protecting what's left:* Offsetting some of these assaults on biotic integrity is the fact that a significant portion of the riparian corridor in the watershed is in public ownership or protection, due in part to its designation as a Resource Protection Area (RPA) by the Chesapeake Bay Preservation Act. The Holmes Run/Cameron Run case study suggests that, although such highly urbanized settings lack the biodiversity of urban fringe and wildland settings, the ecological and sociological functions of remnant natural areas are still important, perhaps more important because there is so little left.

2. *Managing exotic and native species:* In such a landscape, invasive and exotic species are rampant. Bradshaw (1999) notes that, although the original ecosystems of city centers have largely been destroyed, cities still harbor a great diversity of life due to nature's ability to exploit every possible opportunity. These ecological niches are often subject to physical conditions that are more harsh than those found outside the city. The result is that generalist species are favored, and invasive exotic species often have a competitive advantage. Wildland biodiversity protection aims to prevent and eradicate non-native invasive species. In urban areas where non-native species are pervasive, a different approach is warranted. Efforts to protect and restore native species are important in urban areas, but elimination of exotic species is a financial and practical impossibility in most cases.

3. *Balancing urban core versus suburbs, the value of near nature, and Smart Growth management:* Smart Growth management strategies aim to contain urban development in areas of existing and planned infrastructure, to infill, redevelop, and revitalize existing communities, and to prevent sprawl that impacts outlying greenfields, habitats, and working landscapes. What does this emphasis imply for urban biodiversity? Does Smart Growth sacrifice urban core open space and biodiversity for the sake of enhanced ex-urban biodiversity? On a regional level, Smart Growth's urban containment may protect and enhance suburban or exurban biodiversity, but its infill development may put additional pressure on remaining urban patches and corridors, reducing habitat potential in the urban core. Although biodiversity is limited in the core, such areas still need to provide parks and protect floodplains and riparian corridors that have habitat value. Urban redevelopment,

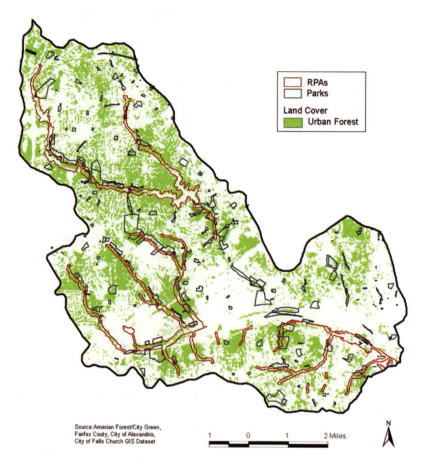

Figure 17.11 Key Elements of Urban Biodiversity in the Highly Urbanized Holmes Run Watershed. *Source:* Bryant et al. (2003).

also a part of Smart Growth, can offer opportunities to incorporate conservation designs to enhance biodiversity.

4. *Engaging stakeholders:* Enhancing urban biodiversity requires engagement of researchers, property owners, citizen groups, educational organizations, and local agencies. As a result, it needs to engage a constituency to help set priorities, gather data through volunteer monitoring, educate the community, and ultimately act on the information through land conservation and stewardship. Enhancing urban biodiversity requires a commitment, and it is this constituency who can communicate the community value of biodiversity treasures in the political process. The Chicago Wilderness program is an excellent example.

5. *Integrating objectives, tools, and programs:* Few communities will dedicate large financial resources to biodiversity protection. However, significant resources are available for a variety of local, federal, and state programs, the objectives of which are very compatible with urban biodiversity protection. These include water quality protection, stormwater management, floodplain management, stream restoration, parks and recreation, urban forestry, and greenway creation, among others. The regulatory and

nonregulatory tools used by these programs are also appropriate for urban biodiversity protection. They include overlay zoning, stormwater ordinances, land acquisition, conservation easements, education programs, and others. By partnering with these programs, urban biodiversity can be advanced with little or no additional financial investment.

Endangered Species and Habitat Conservation Planning

The federal Endangered Species Act (ESA) of 1973 established legal requirements for the protection of threatened species and set in motion a complex program for identifying, listing, and preserving endangered species and their habitats. The U.S. FWS and National Marine Fisheries Service (NMFS) (for marine species) manage the variety of ESA programs. Most states also administer state laws protecting such species. In the 1980s, The Nature Conservancy (TNC) established the National Diversity Information Program, which had operations in each state. The program aimed to identify locations of the habitats of unique species so that their disturbance could be avoided. The classification of special species contains several categories that are given in box 17.5. Included are the federal and state classifications, which have legal requirements, and state and global ranks, which do not.

Most states took over operation of the National Diversity program in the late 1980s. State Natural Heritage agencies maintain lists and locations of special species habitats by jurisdiction. In Virginia and other states, lists are available on the Internet (see table 17.1 and the following website: http://www.state.va.us/~dcr/dnh/coindex.htm). Mapped locations for individual species are not provided as public record, mainly to protect the habitat. Generalized statewide distribution maps of rare plants, animals, and communities are available.

Table 17.1 gives a partial list of the 74 specially classified species and communities in Montgomery County, Virginia. This long list, typical for most localities, underscores the need to be sensitive to the legal and conservation needs of threatened species in the process of land use and development.

Conservation Tools of ESA and Habitat Conservation Planning

Box 17.6 shows the status of nearly 45,000 ranked species and the variety of program tools that have developed under ESA. Under the 1973 ESA (Section 9), any "take" of a classified species or its habitat on public or private land is illegal. Recovery plans and their implementation agreements are developed by FWS and NMFS for listed endangered species. As the number of species on the federal lists grew, many became concerned that this provision would preclude any development in certain urban areas or resource development in natural areas, especially since it was estimated that 90 percent of endangered species habitats are at least partially on private land (General Accounting Office, 1994). In addition, the law focused on listed species and had few proactive elements to manage species and habitats to prevent their being listed.

BOX 17.5—Federal and State Classification of Specially Classified Species

Federal Status

The standard abbreviations for federal endangerment developed by the U.S. FWS, Division of Endangered Species and Habitat Conservation.

LE—Listed Endangered
LT—Listed Threatened
PE—Proposed Endangered
PT—Proposed Threatened
C—Candidate (formerly C1—Candidate category 1)
SOC—Species of Concern (formerly C2—Candidate category 2)

State Status–Virginia Example

The Virginia Division of Natural Heritage uses similar abbreviations for state endangerment.
LE—Listed Endangered
PE—Proposed Endangered
SC—Special Concern
LT—Listed Threatened
PT—Proposed Threatened
C—Candidate State Rank

State and Global Ranks

The following **ranks** are used by state agencies to set protection priorities for natural heritage resources. These ranks should not be interpreted as legal designations.

S1—Extremely rare; usually 5 or fewer populations or occurrences in the state; or may be a few remaining individuals; often especially vulnerable to extirpation.
S2—Very rare; usually between 5 and 20 populations or occurrences; or with many individuals in fewer occurrences; often susceptible to becoming extirpated.
S3—Rare to uncommon; usually between 20 and 100 populations or occurrences; may have fewer occurrences, but with a large

number of individuals; may be susceptible to large-scale disturbances.
S4—Common; usually >100 populations or occurrences, may be fewer with many large populations; may be restricted to only a portion of the state; usually not susceptible to immediate threats.
S5—Very common; demonstrably secure under present conditions.
SA—Accidental in the state.
SB—Breeding status of an organism within the state.
SH—Historically known from the state, but not verified for an extended period, usually >15 years; this rank is used primarily when inventory has been attempted recently.
SN—Nonbreeding status within the state. Usually applied to winter resident species.
SU—Status uncertain, often because of low search effort or cryptic nature of the element.
SX—Apparently extirpated from the state.
SZ—Long-distance migrant whose occurrences during migration are too irregular, transitory, and/or dispersed to be reliably identified, mapped, and protected.

Global ranks are similar, but refer to a species' rarity throughout its total range. Global ranks are denoted with a "G" followed by a character. Note that GA and GN are not used and GX means apparently extinct. A "Q" in a rank indicates that a taxonomic question concerning that species exists. Ranks for subspecies are denoted with a "T." The global and state ranks combined (e.g., G2/S1) give an instant grasp of a species' known rarity.

In response to these concerns and to make the ESA more flexible, new approaches for wildlife planning were developed in the 1980s and 1990s. They include habitat conservation planning, safe harbor agreements, candidate conservation agreements, and state conservation agreements. What has emerged is a complex conservation program that engages private landowners in the conservation process, provides incentives and assurances that actions taken will not lead to

TABLE 17.1 **Natural Heritage Resources of Montgomery County, Virginia (Some of 74 listed species and communities)**

Scientific Name	Common Name	Global Rank	State Rank	Federal Status	State Status	Seen in County Since 1980?
** Amphibians						
Cryptobranchus Alleganiensis	Hellbender	G4	S2S3	SOC	SC	N
** Communities						
Appalachian Cave Drip Pool/ Epikarstic Comm.		G2	S2			N
** Fish						
Noturus Gilberti	Orangefin Madtom	G2	S1S2	SOC	LT	Y
** Geologic Features						
Significant Cave						Y
** Invertebrates						
Allocapnia Simmonsi	Simmons' Slndr Wintr Stnfly	G2G4	S1			Y
** Mammals						
Myotis Sodalis	Indiana Bat	G2	S1	LE	LE	N
** Vascular Plants						
Buckleya Distichophylla	Piratebush	G2	S2	SOC	LE	Y

further requirements, and focuses on species and habitat conservation before they are listed (see box 17.6 for descriptions of these programs).

Habitat conservation planning aims to produce plans for the conservation of classified species habitats while accommodating some development in the vicinity of the habitats. Many wildlife advocates criticize this development as a serious diminution of endangered species protection, but others argue that habitat conservation planning is a proactive approach to species protection and that some accommodation of development is necessary to prevent repeal of the ESA at a time of increasing political interest for private property rights.

In the early 1980s, an experimental plan was developed for San Bruno Mountain, an economically valuable undeveloped area just south of San Francisco. The mountain was home to several classified species, including unique butterflies. The experimental plan aimed to provide preservation of the species through conservation of their habitat and to identify areas that could be developed with minimal impact on the habitat. Based on the San Bruno experience, the ESA was amended in 1982, and a new provision, section 10(a)(1)(B), was added to achieve more flexibility.

The section provides that the FWS can allow land or resource development in the vicinity of an endangered or classified species habitat by issuing an "incidental take permit" if the landowner or developer has prepared a satisfactory habitat conservation plan (HCP). The basic objective of the HCP is to demonstrate how the endangered species habitat will be conserved while allowing for land development in habitat area. According to the regulations,

BOX 17.6—Endangered Species Act Conservation Tool Continuum (44,359 total species ranked as of 2001)

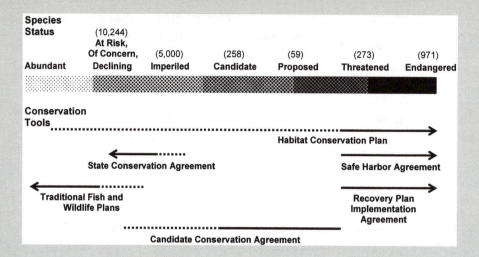

Habitat Conservation Plan (HCP) (1984): plan for species conservation allowing for "incidental take" of habitat to accommodate species needs while allowing some development to continue.

Recovery Plan (1973): plan for species population and habitat improvement to lead to delisting of endangered species.

Safe Harbor Agreement (1999): voluntary arrangement between FWS/NMFS and non-federal landowner intending to benefit endangered species while giving landowners assurances from additional restrictions. Agreements must assure "net conservation benefit" to the species and establish baseline conditions that may include population or habitat characteristics.

"No Surprises" Assurances (1994): under an HCP, landowners are assured that if "unforeseen" circumstances arise, the federal government will not require additional land, water, or other resources beyond the level agreed to in the HCP as long as the permittee is implementing the terms of the HCP in good faith.

Candidate Conservation Agreement (CCA) (1999): agreements between the FWS/NMFS and landowners or other participants to provide actions to stabilize or restore candidate species so that listing the species is no longer necessary. CCA "with assurances" provides landowners with assurances that their efforts to stabilize or restore candidate species will not result in future regulatory obligations in excess of those in the CCA.

State Conservation Agreement (emerging): a proactive, voluntary approach led by state wildlife or natural heritage agencies to develop partnerships among government agencies, nongovernment organizations and land trusts, and landowners, to develop agreements to protect precandidate species and ecological communities before they become imperiled.

Source: IAFWA (2001).

an "incidental take permit" can be issued if the HCP identifies

- impacts on endangered species,
- measures to minimize and mitigate impacts,
- alternatives are considered and action is justified,

and if the plan shows that

- taking, if any, is incidental,
- taking will not appreciably reduce likelihood of survival,
- applicant will minimize/mitigate to the maximum extent possible, and
- adequate funding is assured for plan implementation.

HCPs are not required to contribute to recovery of the listed species, but rather to ensure that its prospects for recovery are not reduced. Typical measures used to minimize and mitigate impacts of development are land acquisition (sometimes at another site), conservation easements, translocation of species, habitat restoration, removal of exotic species, and funding to support research on the species (James, 1999).

The following list outlines the habitat conservation planning process given in FWS's *HCP Handbook* (1996). Key elements include engaging all stakeholders early in the process, gathering and analyzing biological data, projecting "take" levels, developing mitigation measures, and developing funding and monitoring schemes.

The Habitat Conservation Planning Process as Outlined by the FWS

I. Preplanning Process
   A. Determine the applicant
   B. Gather steering committee members—representative of all stakeholders involved
   C. Designate a neutral facilitator
   D. Consult with the FWS
II. Plan Development
   A. Define the land area to be included in the HCP
   B. Gather biological data
      1. *Determine the species to be included in the HCP*
      2. *Gather and review existing data*
      3. *Develop new data through new biological studies as needed*
   C. Identify activities to be included in the HCP land area
   D. Determine the anticipated lake levels resulting from proposed activities
   E. Develop mitigation measures (the following in descending priority as given by FWS)
      1. *Avoid the impact*
      2. *Minimize the impact*
      3. *Rectify the impact*
      4. *Reduce or eliminate the impact over time*
      5. *Compensate for impact*

F. Develop monitoring measures for determining success and/or problems with the HCP

G. Plan for unforeseen circumstances and plan amendments

H. Develop a funding scheme to pay for HCP and any mitigation measures

I. Describe alternatives considered and reasons why alternative not chosen

III. Submit Plan for Permitting to FWS

IV. If Permitted, Implement the Plan

A. Implement mitigation measures

B. Monitor

C. Amend plan as necessary (USFWS/NMFS, 1996)

First-Generation HCPs

Table 17.2 gives the results of one "first-generation" HCP, the well-studied 1992 Balcones Canyon Conservation Plan (BCCP) for an area near Austin, Texas. The area is home to several classified species, including the black-capped vireo, the golden-cheeked warbler, and different karst species in the Edwards Aquifer region. The city, county, FWS, other public agencies, TNC, developers, and landowners were participants in the process. The planning process resulted in a preserve implementation plan including a federal wildlife refuge, acquisition of preserve lands, lands protected through a resolution trust corporation, and other public lands. Table 17.2 gives the area protected and unprotected by the plan. Just over half of the occupied warbler habitat is protected, about one-third of the potential vireo habitat and one-fifth of the potential karst habitat is protected. Figure 7.5 shows the BCCP protected lands.

The BCCP also illustrated the costs associated with first-generation HCP preparation and implementation. Just preparing the plan cost $760,000 ($200,000 for biological study, $400,000 for plan preparation, and $160,000 for the environmental impact statement). The many stakeholders contributed funds for the planning studies. Land acquisition costs associated with the plan were estimated at $56 million, not including management and administrative costs. Core funding came from a $22 million public bond referendum that was passed by city and county voters. Additional funding came from a $1,500 per acre mitigation fee

TABLE 17.2 **Remaining Habitat to be Protected in the BCCP Preserve System**

Type of Habitat	Total Protected	Percentage Protected (%)	Total Unprotected	Percentage Unprotected (%)
Potential karst invertebrate[1]	9,298 acres	20.5	36,070 acres	79.5
Occupied black-capped vireo[2]	1,164	56.3	904	43.7
Potential black-capped vireo[3]	10,503	38.9	16,475	61.1
Golden-cheeked warbler[4]	13,969	36.9	23,870	63.1

Source: Smith, 1995.

BOX 17.7—Issues from First-Generation HCPs

1. Extent to which habitat is protected: *How much protection is enough?*
2. Biological adequacy of conservation measures and long-term viability of habitat, given limited knowledge: *Do we really know what will happen?*
3. Ability to promote constructive political compromise: *With a wide range of stakeholders, how can we make effective and acceptable decisions?*
4. Ability to implement compromise: *Can an agreement hold together over time?*
5. Costs of HCP efforts: *What are equitable, efficient, and acceptable means of generating the large revenues required?*
6. Time for plan preparation and approval: Delays affect both development costs and opportunities and habitat impacts. *How long is this going to take?*
7. Uncertainties to landowners that new habitats or constraints are discovered after HCP investments: *What surprises await?*

BOX 17.8—HCP Checklist Based on First-Generation Plans

1. Incorporate thorough biological and scientific information base.
2. Represent stakeholders.
3. Integrate HCP into local regional plans.
4. Develop long-term equitable funding.
5. Protect simultaneously habitat for multiple species.
6. Dovetail HC with other community goals: open space, recreation, water quality.

on development in the area, and a building fee surcharge on development activities throughout the city and county. Revenues were pooled into a Habitat Mitigation Trust Fund (Beatley, 1994).

Box 17.7 lists several key issues concerning the adequacy and implementation of HCPs identified by several studies of first-generation HCP experience (Beatley, 1994; Smith, 1995). Beatley (1994) also provides a useful checklist for future HCPs that may improve their effectiveness and ease of preparation and implementation (box 17.8).

Points 3, 4, and 5 advance the notion that HCPs should not be stand-alone plans, but should be integrated into regional and other local plans and should focus on multiple species when possible.

"No-Surprises" Policy and Second-Generation HCPs

By 1992, 10 years after the 1982 ESA amendments, only 14 HCPs had been prepared. Among the reasons for this low level of activity are the issues listed in box 17.7, especially the last one. Land and resource developers believed that once they began the HCP process, they acknowledged the presence of endangered habitats and became committed to preservation at all costs. Future "surprise" information could constrain any development and require unanticipated costs for species protection. So most declined to enter into the HCP process.

Recognizing these constraints, Bruce Babbitt, the Interior Secretary, promulgated a new HCP policy in 1994, intended to remove the cloud of uncertainty from potential HCP activity. The "No-Surprises" policy stated that if, in the course of development, a landowner invests money and land to protect species covered in an approved HCP, the government will not later require that the landowner pay more or provide additional land even if the needs of species change over time (Fisher, 1996).

Some ESA advocates criticized the policy, saying that nature is full of surprises and that land and resource developers should be required to respond to them for the sake of endangered species. Others acknowledged that the policy was necessary to move the HCP process forward. It was better to engage the land and resource development community in proactive habitat protection planning than to have them sit on their hands and incrementally consume and impact habitats.

If the objective was to increase HCP activity, it worked. Between 1994 and June 2003, FWS and NMFS approved 408 HCPs, 215 amendments, and 661 permits (USDI, FWS, 2003). They included collaborative HCPs like Balcones Canyon, involving land developers; federal, state, and local governments; environmental groups; and land trusts. They also included HCPs by natural resources firms for company-owned lands. Some case studies of newer plans showed improved quality and content of HCPs (Slingerland, 1999).

However, there continued to be a cry for greater scientific integrity of the plans and an ecological, multispecies approach rather than a single-species approach (Noss, O'Connell, and Murphy, 1997). In response, the National Center for Ecological Analysis and Synthesis and the American Institute of Biological Sciences sponsored the most comprehensive study of HCPs completed to date. The study, involving eight universities and 106 graduate students, reviewed 208 of the 225 HCPs approved by 1997, 43 of which were examined in greater detail (Kareiva et al., 1999). The study found the following:

1. Eighty-two percent of the HCPs focused on a single species.
2. Many had insufficient data to support recommendations.
3. Only half estimated species "take" quantitatively.
4. Most provided no data that proposed mitigation measures would succeed.
5. Only 7 of 43 plans studied in detail had a clear monitoring plan.

The study recommended that the following steps be taken:

1. More explicit scientific standards should be developed.
2. When information is lacking, greater mitigation should be applied to provide a margin for error.
3. Adaptive management should be employed, that is, management and monitoring should provide new information.
4. The scientific community should be engaged in reviewing plans.

BOX 17.9—Critique of Habitat Conservation Planning That Led to California's Natural Community Conservation Planning (NCCP) Act

Criticisms of the Project-by-Project Approach

- Interfering with development projects impedes economic growth, conflicts with private property rights, and creates backlash against the endangered species laws.
- Project-by-project approach leads to patchy, ad hoc mitigation measures and does not prevent the fragmentation of habitat and ecosystems.
- Separate review of each development project creates costly delays, red tape, and uncertainty.
- Emphasis on individual projects is reactive and limits the ability to plan for species recovery or prevent species from declining.
- Enforcement of the "project-by-project" approach is contentious, often ending in costly court battles.

Criticisms of the "Single-Species" Approach

- Ecosystems require large areas of unfragmented landscapes encompassing large-scale natural processes and multiple habitat types (not just the immediate areas where the listed species live).
- Functioning ecosystems depend on the interactions of a wide variety of plant and animal species, not just those that happen to be listed.
- The single-species approach is an "emergency room" model that did not enforce protections until a given species' habitat and populations are so badly eroded that recovery is difficult or impossible.
- Single-species conservation efforts can be undermined by new listings or new information (as occurred with the Stevens' kangaroo rat in Riverside County).

Source: Pollak (2001b).

Natural Community Conservation Planning in California: Regional Conservation for Multiple Species

In 1991, California established its own program for endangered species protection. At the time, both conservation advocates and development interests were critical of habitat conservation planning under the federal ESA because it focused on one species and one project at a time (box 17.9). To property owners and developers, this was burdensome, costly, and unpredictable. To conservationists, this did not address overall needs of species and populations at risk, did not prevent fragmentation of habitats and ecosystems, and did not provide habitat enhancement often needed for ecosystem conservation.

The NCCP Act of 1991 aimed to be broader, more flexible, and more predictable than rules under the federal HCPs. The goal was to overcome the species-by-species and project-by-project approach by focusing on regional ecosystems and multiple species (both listed and nonlisted). It shared the HCP goal to provide effective conservation of the state's wildlife heritage while continuing to allow appropriate development and growth.

Although the legislative history was quite critical of the federal approach, the federal FWS and the Department of Interior encouraged establishment of the Cal-

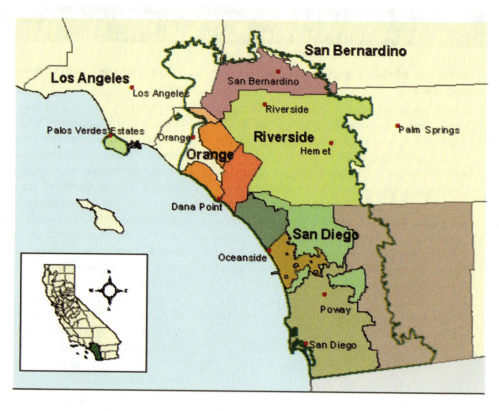

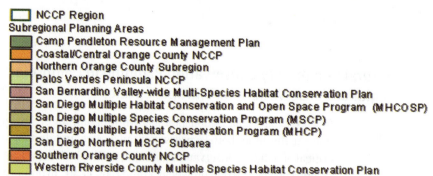

Figure 17.12 Map of Southern California Multispecies NCCP Areas. *Source:* State of California DFG (2003a).

ifornia program, believing it to be a useful proving ground for new approaches to habitat conservation that could be incorporated into the HCP process.

The act established a pilot program in Southern California, where controversy raged over the HCP prepared for the kangaroo rat in Riverside County. The main habitat of concern was the coastal sage scrub, which is home to several endangered species and was being rapidly converted to development. At the time of the NCCP Act, it was estimated that about 343,000–444,000 acres of coastal sage scrub remained in California, only 14–18 percent of its historic extent. The coastal sage scrub is the habitat of a small bird, the California gnatcatcher, which was being considered for state and federal listing of endangered species. It was feared

TABLE 17.3   **Comparative Data for Two Completed NCCPs**

	Orange County Central-Coastal NCCP	San Diego MSCP
Date Approved	April-97	August-98
Planning Area	209,000 acres	582,243 acres
Acres of Habitat in Planning Area	104,000 acres	315,940 acres
Acres of Habitat to be Conserved	37,378 acres	171,920 acres
Percent of Habitat to be Conserved	36%	54%
Percent of Conserved Habitat Already Publicly Owned or Dedicated at Time of Plan Adoption*	88%	48%
Percentage of Coastal Sage Scrub to be Protected	55%	62%
Total Additional Land Needing Protection at Time of Plan Adoption	750 acres	90,170 acres
Plan's Projection of Land Acquisition Costs	$8–9 million	$262–360 million
Local Government Share	750 acres	13,500 acres
State and Federal Share	n/a	13,500 acres
Developer Mitigation/Exaction Share**	Up to $7.5 million**	63,170 acres
Number of Species Covered	39	85

*In Orange County, includes lands designated for future dedication under existing development agreements.

**The Orange County plan imposes coastal sage scrub mitigation fees on nonparticipating landowners that can be used to fund land acquisition or habitat management. This could generate revenues of up to $7.5 million.

this species could provoke a "birds vs. economy" conflict like the northern spotted owl in the Pacific Northwest. Its fate was also seen as an indicator of conflicts to come as Southern California's many diverse habitats became imperiled (see box 17.10) (Pollak, 2001a). This regional landscape seemed ideal for testing a regional multispecies approach.

The pilot program has been ambitious and complex, with a goal of reconciling the needs of ecosystems with development pressure in a highly urbanized 6,000-square-mile area containing a human population of 17.5 million. The pilot called for several subplanning areas shown in figure 17.12. Two of these plans were completed by 2001: the Orange County Central-Coast NCCP (1996) and the San Diego Multispecies Conservation Plan (MSCP) (1997). Planning efforts continue (see http://www.dfg.ca.gov/nccp/cssreg.htm).

Table 17.3 gives some relevant data for the two completed plans. The San Diego MSCP is more comprehensive in terms of planning area, habitat area, areas needing protection, species covered, and total cost (see figure 17.13). Land acquisition costs for implementation of the San Diego MSCP are estimated to be about $1/3 billion. Orange County and San Diego County plans are truly multispecies and regional in coverage. The Orange County NCCP has 200,000 acres and 39 species, of which 15 are listed. The San Diego County MSCP has 800,000 acres and 85 species, of which 31 are listed.

The cost of plan implementation is considerable, but California voters have supported the NCCP process. In 2000, they passed Proposition 12, the Safe Neighborhood Parks, Clean Water, Clean Air, and Coastal Protection Bond Act,

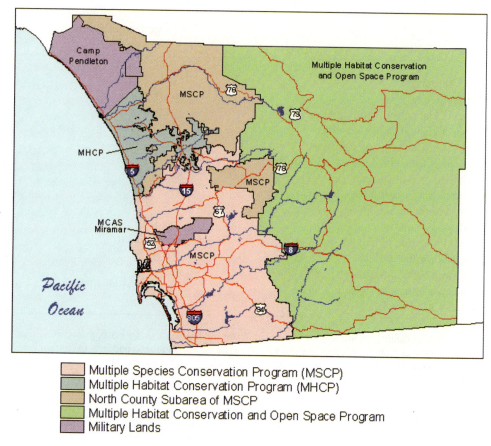

Figure 17.13 San Diego MSCP Conservation Targets. *Source:* State of California DFG (2003b).

which included $100 million that may be appropriated by the Legislature to the Wildlife Conservation Board for the acquisition of land for NCCP plans (the full $100 million was subsequently appropriated in the 2000–01 budget). In addition, the Act provided $50 million for the Department of Parks and Recreation to acquire lands "that are a high priority for both the state parks system and for habitat purposes, with priority given to projects that protect habitat for rare, threatened, or endangered species pursuant to a natural community conservation plan." (Pollak, 2001a)

Daniel Pollak of the California Research Bureau prepared an evaluation of the NCCP process through 2001 at the request of Senator Byron Sher. Based on a historical review of the legislative history, development of the program and the two completed plans, the two-part study outlined achievements of the process to date, conclusions and lessons from the completed plans, and recommendations for future NCCPs (Pollak, 2001a, 2001b).

Pollak (2001b) identified four important achievements of the process in moving beyond the limitations of single-species, project-by-project conservation:

BOX 17.10—The California Gnatcatcher: Much Ado About a Little Bird

The California gnatcatcher has served as the "poster child" of the state's great experiment in ecosystem conservation. Although the 1991 NCCP Act aimed to broaden the single-species, project-by-project approach of federal habitat conservation planning to a multispecies and regional ecosystem approach, the gnatcatcher served as a reminder that a single threatened species and its protecting rules remain the regulatory backbone of conservation efforts. The NCCP program floundered in its first few years as a result of political conflict between the many stakeholders in conservation and development.

The controversy came to a head when the state Fish and Game Commission declined to list the California gnatcatcher on its threatened and endangered list in 1993. Many thought this would diminish the clout of any NCCP in the coastal sage scrub pilot program. However, in March 1993, Interior Secretary Bruce Babbitt announced that the gnatcatcher would be listed as threatened under the federal ESA. Under section 4(d) of the ESA, the U.S. FWS has great latitude to develop special regulations for species listed as "threatened," and Babbitt stated that rules issued under section 4(d) would mesh the listing with the NCCP process. The take of gnatcatchers would be allowed as long as the take resulted from activities conducted in accordance with NCCP plans. During the interim period of plan development, the take would be allowed as long as it was in accordance with conservation guidelines developed by the NCCP Scientific Review Panel. In its August 1993 guidelines, the NCCP Panel recommended that loss of coastal sage scrub in the planning region be limited to 5 percent of the existing habitat during the planning process. This was formally adopted as federal policy when the final 4(d) rule for the gnatcatcher was published in December 1993 (see the following table).

The 4(d) rule did much to diffuse tension about the NCCP program, and the rule turned out to be one of the definitive events in the evolution of the NCCP pilot program. Interior Secretary Babbitt viewed the compromise as having national importance: "We have to be able to point to one community and prove they were able to, from start to finish, protect both a species and the local economy.... This may become an example of what must be done across the country if we are to avoid the environmental and economic train wrecks we've seen in the last decade" (Pollak, 2001a, p. 25).

The gnatcatcher 4(d) rule also put the federal government squarely in the center of the NCCP process. The U.S. FWS would hold the regulatory "hammer" and would become more intimately involved in plan development and approval. The new federal role also carried the promise of more federal funding, further bolstering optimism about the program.

Source: Pollak (2001a).

Interim Loss of Coastal Sage Scrub Under the Federal Gnatcatcher 4(d) Rule

County	Coastal Sage Scrub (CSS)	Maximum Allowable CSS Loss (5%)	CSS Loss to Date	Allowable Future CSS Loss
Los Angeles	1,252	63	57	6
Orange	30,125	1,506	1,064	442
San Diego	120,327	6,016	1,472	4,544
Riverside	162,031	8,102	593	7,509
TOTAL	313,735	15,687	3,186	12,501

- *Forward-looking planning.* The NCCP process has encouraged planners to develop plans that look ahead for many years, addressing regional habitat conservation needs in relation to future growth and development, rather than simply reacting to a series of species versus development crises.
- *Large, interconnected reserve areas.* The NCCP process has resulted in large habitat reserves with large blocks of habitat that strive to preserve or restore connectivity across a fragmented landscape. The reserves are based on comprehensive planning on a long-term, regional ecosystem scale, taking into account dozens of species, both listed and unlisted, and a variety of habitats.
- *Framework for collaboration.* The NCCP approach has created a framework for collaboration and brought to bear the energies and resources of many participants who would not normally work together. Development interests have modified project plans, contributed funding, or agreed on mitigation of development impacts.
- *Regulatory streamlining and improved certainty.* Local governments and landowners have received incidental take authorizations for a wide variety of species, including species not yet listed as endangered. Under the NCCP approach, the permit holders and beneficiaries will have a more streamlined approval process, and assurances barring or limiting additional regulatory requirements.

Pollak (2001b) also noted issues that continue to plague the effectiveness in the NCCP process.

Recurring Issues in the NCCP Program

- *The timing conundrum:* To protect imperiled resources that could be lost without timely action, NCCP plans require a great deal of scientific data and knowledge that takes time and effort to gather.
- *Never enough knowledge:* There will always be insufficient baseline data and understanding about many key ecosystem variables, such as the size, demography, distribution, and genetic variability of populations, and of causal processes governing population sizes and ecosystem functioning.
- *Decisions without standards:* NCCPs will be forced to make decisions about plan design and incidental take with incomplete scientific information, standards, or criteria.
- *Intersection of habitats and development pressures:* Every place where an NCCP approach is applied will be where there are serious human threats to the ecosystems.
- *Stakeholders grow impatient or dissatisfied:* Developers and localities want reliable regulatory assurances, and conservation advocates will want strong, clearly defined habitat protection.
- Complex plans require long-term compliance and monitoring.
- *Extensive long-term funding* is required for implementation, land acquisition, and adaptive management.

- *Adaptive management and monitoring* are critical to offset limitations in existing knowledge. Few managers know how to monitor necessary resources, let alone adaptively manage them.

Finally, Pollak (2001b) provides recommendations for future NCCP activities, which are relevant to all wildlife planning and management:

- *Invest up front in strong resource assessments.*
- *Establish clear standards for species coverage.* What standards should be met to consider that a species is adequately conserved?
- *Consider linking assurances to risks and conservation measures.* For example, perhaps a species at high risk, or a species about which little is known, should not be the subject of a 75-year "No Surprises" guarantee without strong, guaranteed conservation measures. Regulatory assurances should be stronger when the permit holders are able to "front-load" their plans' funding and conservation measures.
- *Improve oversight and accountability.* NCCP plans need reliable, coordinated oversight and enforcement to ensure that the many parties to these complex agreements fulfill their commitments.
- *Strengthen confidence in the assurances.* The NCCP program must maintain the confidence of regulated parties that they will benefit from regulatory streamlining and certainty.
- *Address interim development impacts.* Given how long the NCCP process takes, what should be done to ensure that interim development projects do not compromise the resources needed for successful NCCP plans?
- *Realistically assess the capabilities of adaptive management.* To what extent can adaptive management rectify gaps in our current knowledge or overcome mistakes in our initial plan design?
- *Implement monitoring and adaptive management.* How should monitoring and adaptive management be funded and coordinated? How can we more effectively ensure that it will be carried out in an effective and expeditious manner?

Summary

Land use planning for wildlife conservation and biodiversity has taken on new meaning in recent years, with increased attention in both urban and agricultural landscapes. Landscape ecology has contributed greatly to understanding the basic building blocks and management tools for habitat protection. Habitat core patches and functional corridors can help arrest the habitat fragmentation in converted landscapes, and retain or restore wildlife habitats.

Implementation of the federal Endangered Species Act through habitat conservation planning has led to collaborative efforts to analyze and protect threatened habitats. The Natural Community Conservation Planning program in California is developing multispecies and regional ecosystem approaches. Still, much improvement is needed in conservation planning to meet complex and competing objectives of financial and implementation feasibility, scientific reliability, and stakeholder acceptability.

As interest in protecting natural areas in urban settings continues to increase, conflicts between habitat conservation and development pressures and property values will escalate. Lessons from habitat planning for listed species, especially as they are applied to multiple species in a regional context, will inform other communities wishing to enhance their urban biodiversity.

18 ▪ Integration Methods for Environmental Land Analysis

The preceding chapters addressed principles of soils, geology, hydrology, and ecology and how they affect and are affected by human use of the land. For example, certain soils are well suited for human-built structures, whereas others lack the necessary strength, are susceptible to movement, or have superior alternative value for agriculture. Some land areas are susceptible to geologic hazards due to slope, instability, subsidence, or seismic activity; others are prone to flooding or provide important aquifer recharge or watershed value. And certain land areas have important ecological features, including productive wildlife habitats or valued aesthetic qualities. One primary objective of environmental land use planning and management is to consider these natural factors in planning, designing, and regulating land development to avoid construction and damage costs and to protect productive and valued natural systems. This chapter reviews some useful methods to integrate these considerations for use in decision making.

The **environmental land inventory** involves gathering and usually mapping a number of natural and often socioeconomic factors that have a bearing on land use. The inventory information can be displayed on hand-drawn maps or be entered into a computer data set of a GIS. The inventory itself can help guide development, or the information can be further analyzed. **Rapid assessment** is a term given to initial data gathering, usually at a general or coarse scale, from readily available information and secondary sources. Like environmental inventories, there is little analysis but some interpretation, and products take the form of hand-drawn or rudimentary maps and preliminary reports.

Land suitability analysis combines inventory information to produce composite maps that display the relative suitability for a specific use (in siting studies) or a number of uses (in comprehensive planning). Both hand-drawn maps (using transparent overlays) and GIS maps can be used for land suitability analysis. These techniques are closely related; in fact, one builds on the other. Inventories can stand alone or serve as the database for GIS and land suitability studies.

Human carrying capacity studies aim to determine the level or impact of human population that an area can support based on natural (e.g., land area, soils, etc.) and/or socioeconomic factors (e.g., water or sewer capacity). Variations of the carrying capacity model are used in "ecological footprint" studies and Limits of Acceptable Change studies for wilderness area management. **Environmental impact assessment** is a well-used technique for forecasting impacts associated with project development; it has many practical applications in the assessment of land use and development. Finally, **build-out analysis** is a form of impact assessment that is useful to portray visually the implications of full implementation of community land use plans and zoning ordinances. Figure 18.1 shows the potential relationships among these land analysis methods.

The Environmental Inventory

The environmental land inventory has become a routine task in land use planning. There are four objectives of the inventory:

   a. to provide a useful display of land information in maps;
   b. to "red flag" areas of concern for planners, citizens, landowners, and developers;
   c. to provide base data for siting and environmental impact studies; and
   d. to provide input for GISs and land suitability analysis.

Typically, an inventory simply maps spatial information with little or no evaluation of the information. The components of the inventory will vary with the area being studied, its conditions, and planning objectives. Generally, maps are included on soils and geologic conditions or limitations, slope and elevation, watersheds and flooding potential, vegetation and habitats, and other natural factors. In addition, the inventory often includes information on the built environment such as land use, transportation systems, land ownership, storm and sanitary sewerage, and so on, and cultural information like historic and archaeological sites.

The data displayed in an environmental inventory comes primarily from available sources, sometimes with interpretation and analysis. The previous chapters outlined a number of procedures for interpreting specific sources to produce inventory maps. Those sources include topographic maps, aerial photographs, soil surveys, geologic maps, floodplain maps, vegetation and habitat maps, and other locally produced maps and studies. Sometimes field studies may be necessary to validate the map information. Computer-based inventories can utilize Landsat digital imagery and other remote sensing as source information.

The inventory information can be displayed on hand produced maps or, if it is in digital form, used in a GIS from which maps can be produced. A GIS can facilitate updating, analyzing, and aggregating the inventory information.

The usefulness of the inventory depends not only on the completeness and accuracy of the information but on the quality of the graphic presentation. Useful maps should do more than simply display data; information should jump out at the

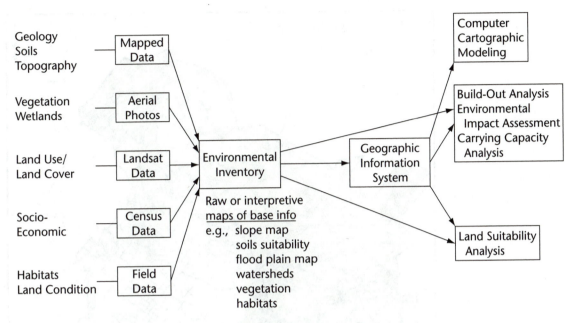

Figure 18.1 Potential Relationship of Environmental Land Analysis Methods

TABLE 18.1 Factors Inventoried in "Growth Management for Blacksburg's Environmental Sensitive Areas"

	Sources of Information
I. ENVIRONMENTAL INVENTORY	
Base Map	Uses 7 1/2′ Quad Map
Elevation	derived from USGS Quad
Slope	derived from USGS Quad
Geologic Hazards	USGS 7 1/2′ Geologic Map
Watersheds, Floodplains, and Stormwater	FEMA Floodplain Maps, Blacksburg P.W. Dept.
Drainage Capacity	SCS Soil Survey
Erosion Potential	SCS Soil Survey
Suitability of Soils for Septic Tanks	SCS Soil Survey
Suitability of Soils for Agriculture	1″–200′ Aerial Photos; Natural
Vegetation and Habitats of Specially Classified Species	Diversity Prog.
Historic Sites	Town Historic Inventory
Visual Resources: Corridors, Viewsheds	Field Study
II. LAND USE AND GROWTH POTENTIAL	
Generalized Land Use	Town data
Zoning	Zoning ordinance
Blacksburg Land Use Plan	Comprehensive Plan
Major Land Owners; Properties with Use-Value Assessment,	
Agricultural Districts	County, Town data
Sewer Availability	Public Works Dept.
Land Development Potential	Interpreted

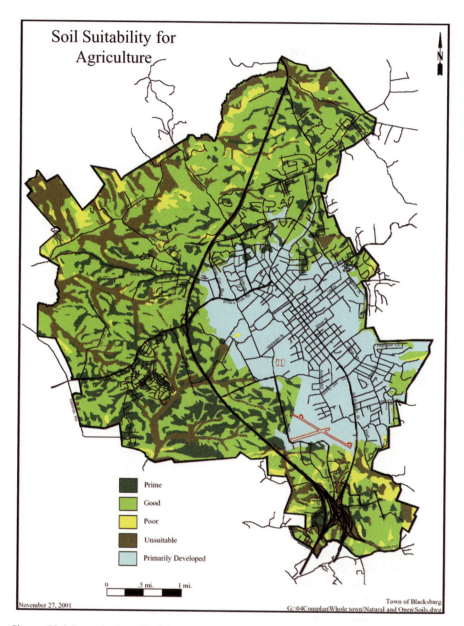

Figure 18.2 Examples from Blacksburg's Environmental Inventory. *Sources:* Anderson et al. (1981), Town of Blacksburg (2001).

map user. Line weights, textures, colors, symbols, and text should be carefully chosen to provide emphasis, order, and readability. Major factors should be shown in the strongest colors or tones. For example, a critique of the map in figure 18.2a is that the color for prime land is too close to the color for unsuitable, and therefore it is hard to distinquish them. Maps should not try to present too much information.

The following describes a few environmental inventory studies to illustrate the types of information gathered, the variety of data displays, and the use of the

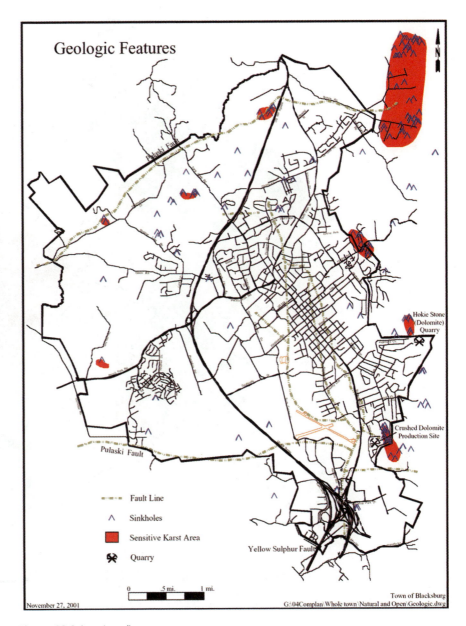

Figure 18.2 (continued)

inventory. An example of how an environmental inventory can be used in the development of a community comprehensive plan is given in chapter 7.

Blacksburg, Virginia. In 1981, the Town of Blacksburg, a rural college town of 30,000, conducted an environmental inventory in hopes of integrating information on **"environmentally sensitive" areas** into its growth management program. These were defined as (a) areas having environmental value (e.g., important habitats, prime agricultural soils, scenic areas) and (b) areas posing a natural

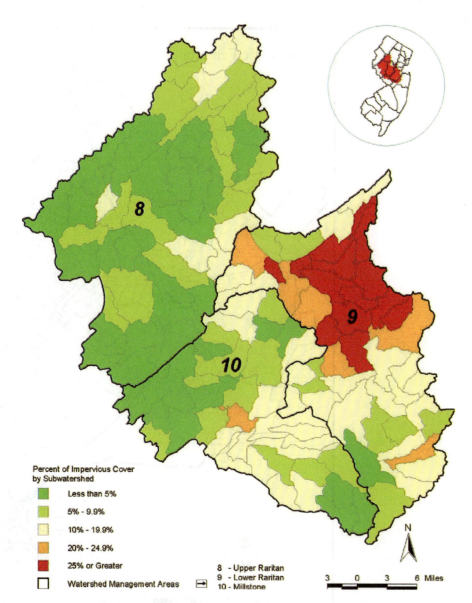

Percent of Impervious Cover by Subwatershed

- Less than 5%
- 5% - 9.9%
- 10% - 19.9%
- 20% - 24.9%
- 25% or Greater
- Watershed Management Areas

8 - Upper Raritan
9 - Lower Raritan
10 - Millstone

3 0 3 6 Miles

Figure 18.3 Two Environmental Inventory Products for the Raritan Watershed. *Source:* RBWMP (2002).

hazard to development (e.g., floodplains, steep slopes). In addition, the inventory included certain socioeconomic factors that reflected or created development pressures so that **"environmentally critical" areas**—those environmentally sensitive areas subject to development pressure—could be identified. In addition, the inventory was used to determine how well the town could accommodate future growth while protecting environmentally sensitive areas (Anderson, Conn, Loeks, and Randolph, 1981). Table 18.1 lists the maps produced as part of the inventory and the sources of information. Figure 18.2a and 18.2b illustrates two recent updates of the original maps, one showing soil suitability for agriculture, the other geologic features, fault lines, and karst areas.

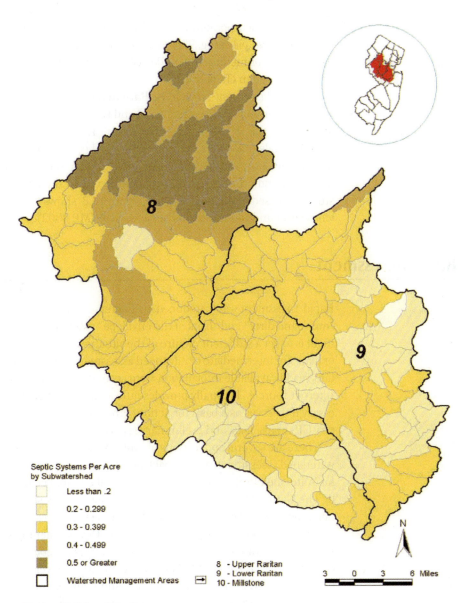

Septic Systems Per Acre
by Subwatershed

- Less than .2
- 0.2 - 0.299
- 0.3 - 0.399
- 0.4 - 0.499
- 0.5 or Greater
- Watershed Management Areas

8 - Upper Raritan
9 - Lower Raritan
10 - Millstone

3   0   3   6 Miles

Figure 18.3 (continued)

One of the Blacksburg maps was an inventory composite, which combined information from several maps. The map indicates areas of steep slopes and floodplains, areas with severe limitations to septic systems, and areas sewered or within easy sewer access. The acreage of currently sewered areas not subject to slope or flooding hazards was computed from the map and was found to well exceed the acreage required to accommodate even high projections of population growth. The report recommended a number of options the town could use to manage growth to protect environmentally sensitive areas, including encouraging infill development in existing sewered areas. In particular the consultants suggested that developers conduct a predesign environmental assessment to alert themselves and town planners to potential problems.

The town incorporated much of the study's information into its subsequent comprehensive planning. The inventory has had lasting value as it was used for baseline environmental data in Blacksburg's award-winning 1996 Comprehensive Plan, discussed in chapter 7.

Raritan Basin, New Jersey. The Raritan Basin Watershed Management Project (RBWMP) produced seven technical and two background reports to characterize and assess the 1,100-square-mile basin. Factors included in the inventory included soils, elevation, waters, water quality, riparian areas, wetlands, floodplains, land use, impervious cover, groundwater recharge areas, septic system inventory, and others. The information served as the basis for a land suitability study discussed in the next section. Figure 18.3 shows inventory maps for impervious cover and septic systems per acre (RBWMP, 2002).

Rapid Assessment

Rapid assessment was introduced in chapters 11 and 16. Sometimes referred to as "quick and dirty" and "back of the envelope" assessment, the goal of rapid assessment is to get a sufficient picture of the situation so that some action can be taken or plans for intermediate or advanced assessment can be made. Rapid assessment taps readily available information from secondary sources, like maps, photos, and Internet sources. It usually provides little analysis, although interpretation is necessary if it serves as a basis for action. Products include hand-drawn or rudimentary GIS maps, lists, and preliminary reports.

There are several applications of rapid assessment. Chapter 10 discussed rapid watershed assessment, an approach developed for watershed groups by the Center for Watershed Protection. Chapter 16 described rapid ecological assessment used by The Nature Conservancy (TNC) to develop a quick sense of ecological protection problems and opportunities in developing regions (Sayre et al., 2000).

TNC's Center for Compatible Economic Development (CCED) developed the Pathways program to build community initiatives for compatible economic development (CCED, 1998). TNC defines "compatible development" as the "production of goods and services, the creation and maintenance of businesses, and the pursuit of land uses that conserve the environment, enhance the local economy and achieve community goals." The Pathways process shows that rapid assessment plays a very important role.

The rapid assessment is done in three parts: environment, community, and economy. Box 18.1 gives the steps involved in the environmental assessment. It begins with a base map and a brief natural history of the area studies. Environmental inventories are conducted of natural resources, ecosystem communities, and plant and animal species. Priority lists are made for resources, communities, and species based on suggested criteria. Finally, perceived threats to the environment are interpreted from the assessment.

The procedures for the community and economic rapid assessments are similar, although the information gathered is different. Based on the assessment, local

---

BOX 18.1—Steps Involved in The Nature Conservancy's Rapid Environmental Assessment

Rapid Environmental Assessment

1. Secure a base map.
2. Prepare a brief natural history.
3. Identify renewable natural resources:

   Surface water, groundwater, air, forests, grasslands, farmland, fisheries, wildlife

4. Identify natural communities and ecosystems.

   Forest, grassland, desert, mountain, subterranean, beach and dune, marsh and estuary, wetland, aquatic

5. Identify species of animals and plants.

   Animals: mammals, migratory birds, resident birds, fish, reptiles, amphibians, arthropods (insects, spiders, crustaceans), other invertebrates (mollusks, sponges, worms)
   Plants: trees, shrubs, wildflowers, grasses and sedges, ferns, mosses, and liverworts

6. List the highest priority elements of the environment.
7. Identify threats to the environment.

Checklist for Ranking Environmental Elements:

Renewable natural resources: scope of distribution, abundance of resource; value to ecological health and well-being; importance or potential importance to the economy; ecological functions (e.g., salt marsh serves as nursery for fish; wetlands help control flooding); other importance (e.g., aesthetic or cultural)

Natural communities: high-quality example of the natural community; rarity of natural community type; potential contribution to larger-scale environmental integrity; scope or abundance of distribution; other importance (e.g., aesthetic or cultural)

Animal and plant species: rarity of the species; quality of the local occurrence; importance for recreational uses; importance or potential importance for the economy; other importance (e.g., aesthetical or cultural)

Source: TNC (1999).

---

community groups are prepared to articulate community threats, opportunities, and visions; to set priorities; and to formulate action plans.

Land Capability and Suitability Analysis

Although environmental land inventories and rapid assessments can aid land planning without extensive analysis, the ability to combine information on different variables enhances their usefulness. For example, maps displaying locations of different natural hazards such as flooding, shrink/swell soils, steep slopes, and karst areas can be combined to show a composite of all natural hazards. Areas can be rated as poor, fair, or good for development based on the combination of hazards present. This composite or combination approach is the basis of land suitability studies.

A basic assumption of such studies is that land has an intrinsic suitability for particular land uses that can be determined by combining information on individual factors. The objective of land suitability analysis is to determine the appropriate locations for certain uses based on those intrinsic characteristics (McHarg, 1969). The appropriate location is determined by identifying the land's natural features that indicate the *vulnerability* of certain areas to impact or damage as a result of development (e.g., habitats, resources, aesthetic values, erosion, slope stability), and those features that indicate the *attractiveness* of certain areas for development (e.g., absence of natural hazards, good soils for foundations, permeable soils for septic systems, road access, etc.). The analysis may involve information on natural features and information on the built environment such as proximity to highways and railroads, areas served by sewers and water, and existing land use.

Strictly speaking, a distinction can be made between land **capability** and land **suitability.** Capability refers to the physical capacity of the land to support development whereas suitability refers to the physical capacity plus the social acceptability and economic feasibility of development. It is often difficult to distinguish between capacity and acceptability, however, so related studies, whether they go beyond natural factors or not, are often called **suitability studies.**

Land suitability studies involve different approaches, but some general characteristics apply to all. All involve the display of land information in individual maps and combine the information by overlaying the maps either by hand or in a GIS to form a composite. That composite map can present several possible results depending on the objectives of the study. Usually, it will identify the areas most attractive for a particular use.

Land suitability procedures can be applied to **siting studies** and **comprehensive planning.** The objective of siting studies is to identify the best location for a *specific use,* such as a park, a landfill, a shopping center, a powerline, or a power plant. By combining in some fashion the maps containing information deemed important to that use, a composite can be produced to show the most suitable alternative locations. The composite for a park might combine maps on vegetation, unique habitats, slope, existing roads, and so on; for a landfill, it might combine maps on soils, slope, floodplains, existing land use, and other factors.

Alternatively, the goal may be to develop a **comprehensive plan** identifying the most suitable locations for a variety of land uses, such as housing, commercial and industrial development, and open space. A composite map is made for each use, again combining the factors perceived as important to each, perhaps based on public or agency criteria. These resulting composite maps can likewise be overlaid to identify areas suitable for more than one use, thus identifying potential land use conflicts. The final land use plan may be based on the composite as modified by certain social, economic, or environmental issues that were not part of the mapping procedure.

Methods of Combination

The basic procedure used in most land suitability studies is the same—determine objectives and data needs, develop inventory and data maps, and combine them to form a composite. However, several variations are worthy of description and comparison. The following discussion below, drawn heavily from Hopkins (1977), outlines these variations and some concerns and gives examples of their use.

Gestalt Method

The Gestalt method of land suitability determination is different from the other methods in that it does not rely on the combination of specific factors to form a composite. Instead, using aerial photographs or site surveys, it divides the area under study into homogeneous units and implicitly specifies the units' relative suitability for a particular use. The method assumes that the nature of the land can be described by its "Gestalt" or total appearance. The technique of terrain analysis developed by Douglas Way (1978) is essentially a Gestalt method. Using aerial photographs, Way's procedure identifies the landform of the area under study and, using drainage characteristics, texture, tone, and other parameters interpreted from the photographs, divides the area into homogeneous units. Using rules of thumb, the procedure implicitly assigns the suitability of these units for development.

The disadvantage of this method is that it is implicit, relying entirely on the perceptions, judgment, and experience of the analyst. The results may be difficult to explain, validate, or justify. But the technique is simple, essentially letting the picture of the land determine its use; fundamental constraints for development can be identified.

Ordinal Combination Method

The ordinal combination method involves simple nonweighted overlays. Maps of specific factors such as slope, soils, and vegetation, are divided into classes of similar conditions or value (e.g., >15% slope). For a specific land use, a factor class may pose certain problems or opportunities for development. The classes are rated against one another in terms of their suitability for the specific use being investigated, and this suitability is indicated by a shade of gray or color. The darker the shade, the less suitable is the factor class for that use. After this is done for all the factors, transparent overlays of each factor map are produced. A composite made by overlaying these transparencies will show areas suitable for development in light shades and areas less suitable in dark shades.

Ian McHarg popularized this technique in several notable land suitability studies in the 1960s, including the Richmond Parkway Study and the Twin Cities Metropolitan Area Study. In the Twin Cities Study, for example, McHarg and his associates used factors of geology, slope, and soils to determine the suitability for residential development. Factor values (e.g., classes of slope) were ranked according to their suitability for residential construction; those most suitable were specified for higher-density development, those less suitable for lower density. A composite of the three factors identified areas suitable for various residential densities.

Until GIS came into use for many of the combination procedures, this hand-drawn overlay technique was the most used land suitability method. It has two inherent problems, however. First, it adds together factors influencing land suitability, assuming they are of equal importance, when in fact one may be more important to a particular use than another. Second, the ordinal method assumes

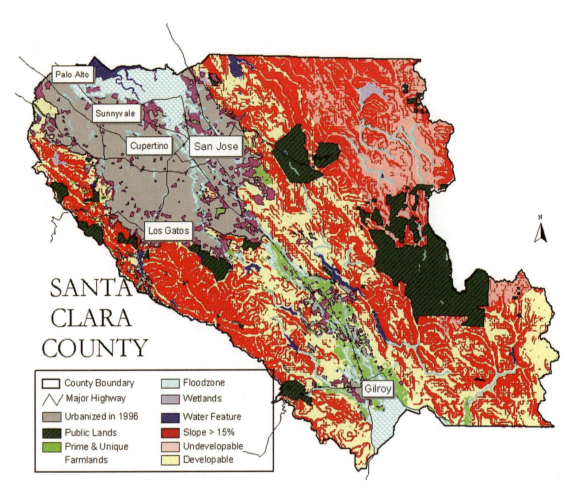

Figure 18.4 Development Suitability Map for Santa Clara County. *Source:* CHCD (2000).

that individual factors are completely independent. However, some factors may act synergistically, combining to form limitations or values greater than the simple sum of their individual effects. For example, the occurrence of certain slope, soils, and underlying geologic materials together can result in severe slope stability problems. But simply adding the individual effects of these values might not show such a severe limitation.

Linear Combination Method

The linear combination method for land suitability analysis attempts to solve one of the problems of the ordinal combination method by weighting factors by their relative importance. The method uses numbers to denote the relative suitability of factor classes and also to denote the relative importance of factors to the land use under question. By multiplying factor value numbers by the factor weights, commensurate scores can be assigned to each factor value. By "overlaying" factor maps a composite number can be determined for each distinct area by simply

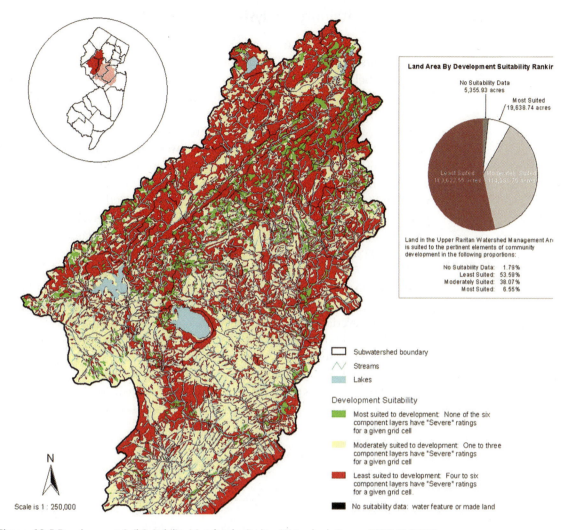

Figure 18.5 Development Soil Suitability Map for the Raritan Watershed. *Source:* RBWMP (2002).

adding the weighted factor scores. While numerical overlays can be done by hand, they work especially well in GIS land suitability analysis. Hand-produced overlays can incorporate only a limited number of factors, but computer GIS-based quantitative linear combination can accommodate a large number of factors. Ease of use permits iterative combinations using different weights to show the sensitivity of the analysis to the weights assigned (see figure 11.15).

Intermediate Factor Combination Method

The linear combination method, though very useful, does not solve the factor interdependence problem. The intermediate factor combination method aims to do this by initially combining interactive factors (e.g., slope, soils, and geology) into intermediate interpretive maps (e.g., slope stability). These interpretive maps are then used in the same way factor maps are used in the linear combination method.

Examples of Land Suitability Analysis

Figures 18.4 and 18.5 illustrate two product maps from recent land suitability projects. The first is an example from California's comprehensive housing suitability analysis conducted to identify development projections and constraints through 2020 (California Department of Housing and Community Development, 2000). In addition to assessing housing needs, the study mapped physical and environmental constraints, including flood-prone areas, steep slopes, water features, wetlands, and prime farmlands. Developable lands were those undeveloped lands that were free of those constraints. This analysis was done for each county, and figure 18.4 gives the suitability map for Santa Clara County. This map is a constraint map in which limiting factors for development are shown directly on the map rather than being combined to show a development rating. This is often preferred in suitability studies so that the reviewer can see where specific constraints are located. See CHCD (2000) for several other examples.

Figure 18.5 gives a composite map showing development suitability based on soils factors in the Raritan Basin Watershed. Six soils factors, including ratings for foundations, roads, septic system drainfields, and lawns and landscapes, were mapped and overlayed to produce the development suitability map. The ordinal combination did not weight the factors. Development suitability was rated based on the number of soils factors that had a severe rating. According to this analysis, only 7 percent of the watershed is "most suited" to development (no severe rating for any of the six factors), 38 percent is "moderately suited" (severe rating for one to three of the factors), and 54 percent is "least suited" (severe rating for four to six of the factors) (RBWMP, 2002).

Human Carrying Capacity Studies

Assessment of an area's carrying capacity is a land analysis approach related to land suitability. Carrying capacity was first applied to wildlife and range management; *capacity* was defined as the maximum population of a particular species that a habitat can accommodate (Dasmann, 1964). As introduced in chapter 16, *carrying capacity* involves the level of population or development that can be sustained in an area without adversely affecting that area beyond an acceptable level. It is characterized by the asymptote of the S-shaped growth curve shown in figure 18.6a.

The shape of the growth curve is based on environmental resistances the population confronts during its growth. For natural populations, the resistances relate to losses due to factors like predation, disease, and competition for food. For human populations, they relate to costs of development, costs to offset the adverse effects of development, costs of adding infrastructure (e.g., water supply), public opposition, and controls on development. Theoretically, the resistances are initially small, and there is increasing growth early; but as population grows, environmental resistances increase and greater resources are required to overcome them. Growth slows as resources required for the next increment of growth increase, until growth stops when the costs of obtaining the next increment is greater than the benefits of growth it allows. In natural systems, uncertainty and innovation resulting from adaptation and succession act to modify carrying capacity (figure 18.6b). In human systems, technological innovation can change the capacity for growth (figure 18.6d).

In natural systems, the resources expended to overcome resistances for the sake of growth are generated internally, and thus growth rates are usually self-regulated. However, in human systems, the costs can also come from external sources (e.g., subsidies for water and sewage systems), and these do not act to regulate growth. In addition, the human system does not depend on the natural system for survival. As a result, human population often grows beyond the carrying capacity without incurring the costs of growth and causes deterioration of the environment. Thus, human carrying capacity must be socially determined, and growth must be socially controlled if deterioration beyond an acceptable level is to be avoided (see figure 18.6c).

A variety of limiting factors can be investigated in carrying capacity studies depending on local conditions. Factors that can determine an area's carrying capacity or ability to support growth include total land area, soil limitations for septic systems, sewer capacity, stormwater drainage capacity, water supply capacity, air quality and meteorological conditions, water quality, visual quality, even school or hospital capacity.

The application of the carrying capacity concept in managing human systems hinges on two determinations: first, the level of adverse effect that is "unacceptable," and second, the threshold of population or development at which that level is reached. The approach is complicated by two considerations. The first is that determining what is "unacceptable," that is, what a community is willing to put up with in terms of the effects of population growth, is largely based on the values of the community. Thus determining the human carrying capacity, although it is based on certain scientific information, is ultimately a judgmental act, requiring community involvement through the planning and political process.[1] The Sanibel Island case (see sidebar) shows that even when a community tries to base a population threshold on environmental and infrastructure factors, it is determined more by political negotiation than by technical information.

---

1. The case of Los Angeles offers a nice example of the concepts of human carrying capacity. A number of natural factors in the LA area affect its capacity to support human population. In the early part of this century, water supply was a limiting factor to growth, which determined a level of carrying capacity. Through intervention, however, increasing amounts of water were imported into the basin, elevating that limit and increasing growth capacity. Developable land is constrained by natural hazards associated with slope stability, beach storm potential, seismic hazards, and forest fire potential, yet many residents chose to develop and live in such areas, finding the hazards "acceptable" compared with the benefits of living there. By imposing a strict grading ordinance in unstable slope areas, the city was able to reduce the damage hazard and thus increase the carrying capacity. Finally, air quality is perhaps LA's most significant environmental constraint. The air emissions resulting from the area's population, development, and lifestyle exceeded the capacity of the air basin to absorb them. Yet local governments in the LA basin have chosen not to limit growth to the air basin's carrying capacity but have "accepted" the level of air degradation associated with higher levels of development. They await technological improvements (e.g., electric or fuel cell cars) to allow the carrying capacity to "catch up" to the basin's population.

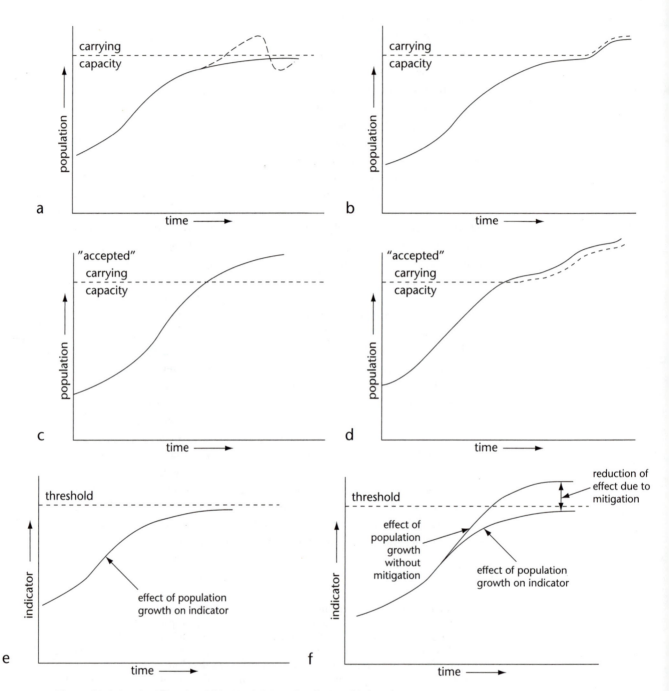

Figure 18.6 Carrying Capacity and Its Use in Managing Human Settlements

SIDEBAR 18.1   *Controlling Population Based on Carrying Capacity: Sanibel Island, Florida* In November 1974, the citizens of Sanibel Island incorporated the island as a city and initiated an effort to manage growth and development to avert storm damages and to protect the island's natural values. The new city hired Wallace, McHarg, Roberts, and Todd, and a citizens' organization hired the Conservation Foundation; the two groups coordinated work on an inventory of the island's natural systems. With the inventory in hand the city developed a plan based on the island's carrying capacity.

The carrying capacity was based on two limiting factors: the assimilative capacity of the island's wetlands to absorb pollutants and the capacity of the causeway linking the island to the mainland for evacuation of residents in the event of a hurricane. Based on projected impacts of different levels of development (from 6,000 to 24,000 units, compared with 4,000 existing units at the time), the Planning Commission recommended 6,000 units as the island's carrying capacity. Through the political process of public hearings, another 1,800 units were provided, for a capacity of 7,800 units or 3,800 above existing levels. The plan distributed these units to the various ecological zones of the island based on their tolerance for development. Specific performance standards were also adopted to minimize the impacts of these developments (Clark, 1976).

A second complicating consideration is that human intervention can increase the population limit for a given level of acceptable quality. Increasing the population carrying capacity can occur in two ways. First, the capacity of some important or limiting factor can actually be expanded, for example, by importing water or annexing land. Second, the effect each additional person has on the factors of interest can be reduced (a) by changing behavior to a more conserving lifestyle (e.g., use of bicycles rather than automobiles creates less air pollution), or (b) by technological improvements (e.g., water conservation devices, land use designs that reduce runoff).

From Population Levels to the Attribute-Indicator-Threshold Approach

This latter issue raises questions about defining human carrying capacity in terms of a population limit. What is important is not necessarily the overall population, but the *effect* that population has on the environment or on one or more factors of interest. Figures 18.6e and 18.6f show the carrying capacity curve not in terms of population but in terms of a specific environmental attribute of interest (e.g., air quality, water supply, visual quality) measured by a specific indicator (e.g., pollutant concentration, gallons per day capacity, visibility in miles). The carrying capacity is given by the acceptable threshold for that factor measured by that indicator. As figure 18.6f shows, innovation resulting from behavioral changes (affecting what each person does) and technological mitigation (affecting the impact of what each person does) can reduce the effect of a given growth of population on that indicator.

Whereas some applications of human carrying capacity have been based on an acceptable population threshold (like the Sanibel Island example), more recent attempts have recognized that the overall objective is to control not population numbers per se, but rather the effect of that population on specific environmental factors or resources of interest. This offers a good illustration of the well-known environmental impact equation popularized by Barry Commoner:

$$I = PAT \rightarrow Impact = Population \times Affluence \times Technology$$

This means that the impact on the environment is not just a matter of population levels. It also depends on the level of affluence of that population (as measured by the impact per person associated with lifestyle and consumption) and on the mitigation of impact that technology provides. For example, the impact on water supply depends not only on the number of people (population) but also on the average use per person (water-consuming lifestyle) and on technology used to mitigate the impact (water conservation devices like low-flow showerheads and toilets).

Using impact thresholds instead of population has become the basis for carrying capacity studies. This **threshold approach** is the basis for the Limits of Acceptable Change method for wilderness area management and for environmental management in the Lake Tahoe Basin, both discussed later.

The approach first identifies a number of important environmental components, resources, or variables. The variables may involve the **natural environment** (air quality, water quality, fish and wildlife habitat, noise, etc.), **human-built infrastructure** (water supply, sewage capacity, road capacity, etc.), or **community perceptions** (visual quality, congestion, etc.). For each component, one or more **indicators** are identified that measure the quality of the component. For example, for the variable water quality, the indicator may be the concentration of a specific pollutant, water clarity measured by Secchi disk test, dissolved oxygen content, or all three.

Specific **thresholds** for these variables are determined from scientific study (e.g., for healthful air quality) and/or community involvement (e.g., for visual quality). Specific programs and/or regulations are then developed to ensure achievement or compliance with the thresholds.

This **variable-indicator-threshold approach** has certain advantages over applying a population threshold. It better matches the objectives of the human carrying capacity concept to control the effect of population rather than the population per se. It provides for human and technological innovation to reduce the impacts per person. And it is far more systematic and far less arbitrary, which supports its use and protects it from legal challenge.

Environmental Thresholds in the Lake Tahoe Basin

The Lake Tahoe area of California and Nevada (figure 8.7) exhibits exceptional environmental amenities, and, perhaps for that reason, it has experienced extreme development pressures. A long history of attempts to manage growth and the environment culminated in the 1986 Tahoe Regional Plan (Tahoe Regional Planning Agency [TRPA], 1986). A brief history of the planning effort and the plan itself are described in chapter 8. The carrying capacity concept and the use of environmental thresholds played an important part in the environmental management of the basin.

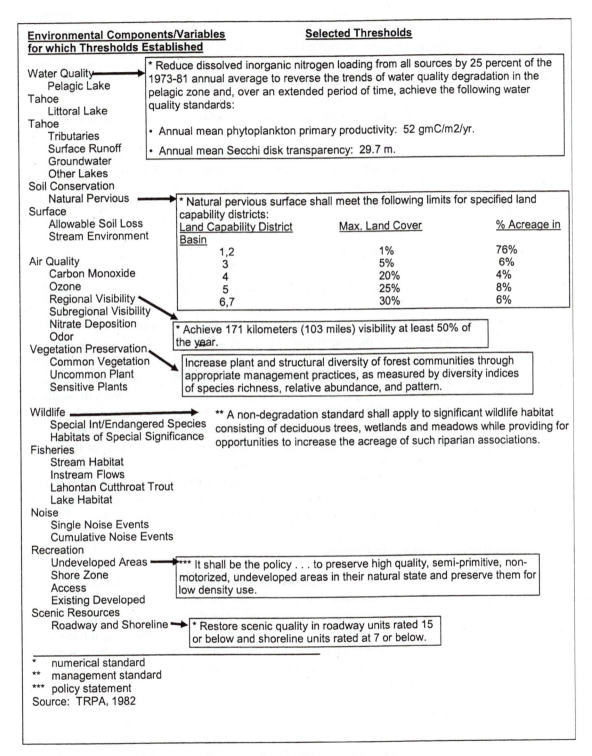

Environmental Components/Variables for which Thresholds Established | **Selected Thresholds**

Water Quality
  Pelagic Lake Tahoe
  Littoral Lake Tahoe
  Tributaries
  Surface Runoff
  Groundwater
  Other Lakes

> * Reduce dissolved inorganic nitrogen loading from all sources by 25 percent of the 1973-81 annual average to reverse the trends of water quality degradation in the pelagic zone and, over an extended period of time, achieve the following water quality standards:
>
> • Annual mean phytoplankton primary productivity: 52 gmC/m2/yr.
>
> • Annual mean Secchi disk transparency: 29.7 m.

Soil Conservation
  Natural Pervious Surface
  Allowable Soil Loss
  Stream Environment

> * Natural pervious surface shall meet the following limits for specified land capability districts:
>
> | Land Capability District Basin | Max. Land Cover | % Acreage in |
> |---|---|---|
> | 1,2 | 1% | 76% |
> | 3 | 5% | 6% |
> | 4 | 20% | 4% |
> | 5 | 25% | 8% |
> | 6,7 | 30% | 6% |

Air Quality
  Carbon Monoxide
  Ozone
  Regional Visibility
  Subregional Visibility
  Nitrate Deposition
  Odor

> * Achieve 171 kilometers (103 miles) visibility at least 50% of the year.

Vegetation Preservation
  Common Vegetation
  Uncommon Plant
  Sensitive Plants

> Increase plant and structural diversity of forest communities through appropriate management practices, as measured by diversity indices of species richness, relative abundance, and pattern.

Wildlife
  Special Int/Endangered Species
  Habitats of Special Significance

> ** A non-degradation standard shall apply to significant wildlife habitat consisting of deciduous trees, wetlands and meadows while providing for opportunities to increase the acreage of such riparian associations.

Fisheries
  Stream Habitat
  Instream Flows
  Lahontan Cutthroat Trout
  Lake Habitat
Noise
  Single Noise Events
  Cumulative Noise Events
Recreation
  Undeveloped Areas
  Shore Zone
  Access
  Existing Developed

> *** It shall be the policy . . . to preserve high quality, semi-primitive, non-motorized, undeveloped areas in their natural state and preserve them for low density use.

Scenic Resources
  Roadway and Shoreline

> * Restore scenic quality in roadway units rated 15 or below and shoreline units rated at 7 or below.

*   numerical standard
**   management standard
***   policy statement
Source: TRPA, 1982

Figure 18.7 Environmental Thresholds for the Lake Tahoe Basin. *Source:* TRPA (1982).

The TRPA defined environmental threshold carrying capacity as "an environmental standard necessary to maintain a significant scenic, recreational, educational, scientific, or natural value of the region or to maintain public health and safety within the region" (TRPA, 1982). The process used to develop the thresholds employed considerable public participation. It involved the following six steps:

1. Identify the environmental components or variables for which thresholds would be established.
2. Identify variables affecting the components.
3. Determine which measures would be appropriate as threshold indicators.
4. Determine the acceptable threshold level for each appropriate indicator.
5. Evaluate mechanisms to achieve each threshold to see if it is meaningful and possible.
6. Adopt the thresholds.

The environmental variables for which indicators and thresholds were established are given in figure 18.7, along with selected thresholds. Thresholds took three different forms: a **numerical standard** or quantifiable level that can be monitored; a **management standard** or nonquantifiable level of quality for which certain actions are prescribed; and a **policy statement** or decision to carry out a chosen course of action. Threshold statements could thus be made about variables that do not lend themselves to quantitative measurement. In addition, by including policy statements and management standards, the thresholds, once adopted, offered considerable guidance to the development of the regional plan (see chapter 8). A major challenge of the plan was that many of the adopted numerical threshold standards were already exceeded. The plan had to provide actions to improve quality while still accommodating some additional development. Monitoring the thresholds in 2001 showed that some are being met and some are not, some are improving and some are not (see table 8.2).

Limits of Acceptable Change

For decades the federal resource agencies have struggled with the challenges of providing for mandated multiple uses of the public lands while managing these lands' natural conditions. For example, recreational overuse of the national parks, national forests, and other lands often damages the resource and diminishes the natural experience of users, especially in wilderness areas. The Park Service has tried to use the carrying capacity concept to determine appropriate levels of recreation use to achieve their mandate of serving the greatest number of people while still protecting the natural ecosystems. The 1978 National Parks and Recreation Act required the Park Service to determine each park's "visitor capacity," the amount of use that allows for quality experiences while not resulting in unacceptable impacts to the park's significant resources (National Park Service, 2001).

After many attempts to quantify visitor carrying capacity and manage visitor population, the agencies have turned to the threshold approach. Stankey et al. (1985) developed the Limits of Acceptable Change (LAC) process for wilderness area planning in the national forests. A variation of this method, the Visitor Experience and Resource Protection (VERP) framework was developed for the national parks (National Park Service, 1997). Both rely on determining acceptable thresholds or desirable future conditions and formulating planning and management actions to achieve these thresholds or conditions.

For wilderness areas, the LAC process aims not to prevent any human-induced change to the wilderness, but rather to decide how much change will be allowed to occur and where and what actions are needed to control that change. LAC requires deciding what kinds of natural resource conditions and social experience conditions are acceptable, then prescribing actions to protect or achieve those conditions. The LAC process consists of nine steps in four major components given in the following list. Implementing the process requires considerable resource inventory as well as public (user) participation to determine desirable conditions and thresholds. By emphasizing conditions, impacts, and thresholds rather than numbers of users, LAC and VERP apply the carrying capacity concept in an objective and systematic way that can achieve desirable resource and social results through management actions.

Limits of Acceptable Change Process for Wilderness Area Management

I. Identify Issues, Concerns, Opportunities
  1. Identify area issues and concerns.
  2. Define and describe recreational opportunity classes (based on recreational opportunity spectrum from pristine to primitive to semiprimitive nonmotorized to roaded natural), including resource, social, and management descriptions for each.
II. Determine Present Condition of Wilderness Area
  3. Select indicators of resource conditions (e.g., trail erosion, campsite scars) and social conditions (e.g., solitude, noise).
  4. Inventory existing resource and social conditions.
  5. Specify measurable thresholds or standards for the resource and social indicators selected for each recreational opportunity class.
III. Determine Action Plan
  6. Compile information from components I and II and identify alternative opportunity class allocations.
  7. Identify what management actions would be needed to meet thresholds for each alternative allocation from 6.
  8. Evaluate and select a preferred alternative. This will be the action plan.
IV. Implement and Monitor the Action Plan
  9. Implement actions for the preferred alternative and monitor conditions. (*Source:* Stankey et al., 1985)

The Ecological Footprint

The concept of the **ecological footprint** is like the inverse of carrying capacity. Whereas carrying capacity tries to measure the capability of an area to support and sustain a population within acceptable limits, the ecological footprint tries to measure the corresponding area of productive land and aquatic ecosystems required to produce the resources used, and to assimilate the wastes produced, by a defined population wherever on Earth that land area might be located (Rees, 1996; Wackernagel and Rees, 1995). It accounts for the fact that unlike most natural habitats, human settlements are not contained ecosystems. Our communities import energy, food, water, and material resources from around the world, and export wastes far beyond their borders. For example, Rees (1996) calculated the ecological footprint of an average citizen in his hometown of Vancouver, British Columbia. Based on the average Canadian food diet, wood and paper consumption, fossil energy consumption, and corresponding carbon emissions, each Vancouverite requires 4.2 hectares of land to support these needs. With a population of 472,000, Vancouver has an ecological footprint of 2 million hectares, 174 times its city area of 11,400 hectares. Based on these per capita needs of 4.2 hectares, the population carrying capacity of Vancouver's area would be just 2,500 people.

The ecological footprint concept is useful for recognizing the impact of our patterns of consumption in a world of limited resources. Rees (1996) advances the measure as an indicator of community sustainability, but poor community-specific data often limit its effectiveness.

Environmental Impact Assessment in Land Use and Development

Environmental impact assessment (EIA) is one of the most mandated and useful tools in environmental planning. Created initially by the National Environmental Policy Act of 1969, the method has been adopted by half of the states in the United States and by foreign governments around the world. Its major applications are in large planning and resource development projects conducted, funded, or approved by a government agency. Still, the method has useful applications in land use and development and is used by several localities and states to assess the environmental impacts of development projects.

The objective of EIA is simply to identify and predict the impacts of prospective actions or projects so that that information can be used in the development design and ultimately the approval of the project. Usually, mitigation measures are identified to offset or reduce the impacts, and these are incorporated into the final design. In its evolution over 25 years, two uses of EIA have emerged. First, EIA is a "planning tool," a rational means of gathering and analyzing information intended to influence management and development decisions. Second, EIA is a "political tool," a means of influencing the attitudes of top officials, a mechanism that has increased the status and strategies of project opponents. After all, the EIA intends to "hang out dirty laundry," to clearly identify the impacts, including negative aspects of a proposal. Ortolano and Shepherd (1995) note: "the ultimate purpose of the EIA is not just to assess impacts; it is to improve the quality of decisions." This is done through both planning and political negotiation.

Ortolano and Shepherd (1995) go on to describe potential effects of EIA on project development. As shown in box 18.2, they include effects on projects and on

Box 18.2—Possible Effects of Environmental Impact Assessment

Possible Effects of EIA on Projects

- Withdrawal of unsound project
- Legitimization of sound project
- Selection of improved project location
- Reformulation of plans
- Redefinition of goals
- Mitigation of project impacts
  Dropping damaging elements of proposed project
  Minimizing adverse effects by scaling down or redesigning project
  Repairing or restoring environment adversely affected
  Creating or acquiring environments similar to those adversely affected

EIA as an Impetus for Administrative Change

- Often increases access of citizens, NGOs, and other agencies to information on project
- Enhances interagency coordination
- Affects power relations between ministries, increases power of environmental agencies

Source: Ortolano and Shepherd (1995).

administrative actions. One desirable project effect is that information on environmental impacts be considered from the very beginning in planning and design.

"With–Without" Analysis: Impact Variables, Indicators, and Thresholds

In conducting an EIA, it is important to assess the environment systematically. Generally, the assessment focuses on indicators of change. The following list defines impact variables or important components of the environment, indicators of change, and thresholds or standards for those indicators. This framework is the same one used in the threshold (or impact) approach to carrying capacity discussed earlier.

Environmental Impact Variables, Indicators, and Thresholds

- *Impact Variables:* Components of the environment that are important (e.g., water quality)
- *Impact Indicators:* Measures that indicate change in an impact variable (e.g., dissolved oxygen)
- *Impact Thresholds or Standards:* Values of impact indicators above or below which there is a problem; used to evaluate the impact (e.g., 5 ppm minimum of dissolved oxygen)

EIA aims to predict future change in impact indicators that are likely to result from the proposed action. "With–Without" (W–W/O) analysis is used to do this (see figure 18.8). The future change of a selected indicator is predicted with the proposed action and plotted on the graph. It is important to know the change that actually results from the action, so it is necessary to also plot the change in the

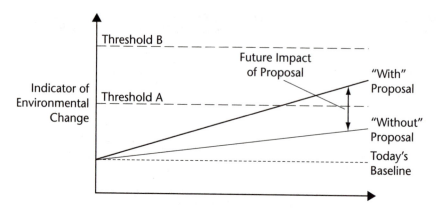

Figure 18.8 Environmental Impact Assessment "With–Without" Analysis

indicator that would result if the action were not undertaken. The "without" line plots this change. The "impact" of the proposed action is the difference between the "with" and "without" lines, not the difference between the "with" line and today's value or baseline.

The figure also illustrates the use of thresholds or standards in the evaluation of impacts. If the accepted threshold or standard for the indicator is Threshold B, neither the "with" or "without" would approach it, and the impact may be deemed of minor importance. However, if the standard is Threshold A, the "without" case would not exceed the threshold, while the "with" case would. Therefore, the impact of the proposal is far more significant.

The EIA Process

The following list gives an outline of a generalized EIA process. It begins with an early scoping exercise intended to gather key parties and stakeholders to design the process and identify key issues, impact variables, and impact indicators. The process is designed to be flexible so that it can be adapted to the individual case at hand. Scoping, data studies, and impact identification come early in the process. Prediction of impacts is really the heart of the process and generally the most important. Many of the techniques discussed in previous chapters can be used for data studies, impact identification, and impact prediction. For example, peak discharge analysis, channel erosion and capacity analysis, soils suitability mapping, DRASTIC, wellhead protection, vegetation, wetland and habitat inventories, and other methods are especially useful. In addition to prediction, however, evaluation and presentation of impacts are also critical because interpretation, discussion, and negotiation about impacts will determine how decisions are affected by the EIA.

Generalized Environmental Impact Assessment Process

1. *Scoping:* Design the process; draft work program; identify issues, impact variables, parties to be involved and methods to be used.
2. *Baseline Data Studies:* Collect initial information on baseline conditions and important impact variables, which may include socioeconomic as well as environmental parameters.

3. *Identification of Impacts:* Concurrent with baseline studies, identify and screen impacts of alternative actions: variables, indicators, and thresholds.
4. *Prediction of Impacts:* Estimate the magnitude of change in important impact variables and indicators that would result from each alternative using W–W/O analysis. Employ project outputs, simple algorithms, simulation models as needed.
5. *Evaluation of Impacts and Impact Mitigation:* Compare indicator impacts to thresholds; determine relative importance of impacts to help guide decisions; evaluate plans for mitigation of impacts.
6. *Presentation of Impacts:* Present impacts of alternatives in concise and understandable format.

Use of EIA in Land Development

As mentioned, in the United States, EIA is required of major federal government actions affecting the environment. It is also required of government agency actions in about half the states. Five of those states require EIA for all "public" actions, so EIA extends to the actions of local governments. In Washington State, those local actions specifically include permitting decisions of private land development. In other states, some localities have incorporated EIA into their development review process. Washington's State Environmental Policy Act (SEPA) process illustrates how EIA can be used effectively in assessing and mitigating environmental impacts of development (State of Washington, 1998).

The SEPA process begins with a threshold determination. If the proposed project is not exempt (e.g., building a single house is exempt), the threshold determination depends on whether the expected impact is significant or not. This is a critical decision, because if the proposal's impact is declared significant, the applicant must prepare a costly and time-consuming environmental impact statement (EIS). The applicant must prepare an assessment form to provide information for this determination. The checklist asks for responses on the project's description and its impact on a list of environmental variables or elements. The lead agency evaluates the checklist responses and often asks for more information or negotiates with the applicant before making the threshold determination.

If the agency declares that the proposal will likely pose a significant environmental impact, the applicant must prepare an EIS. A draft is prepared for 30-day public review, followed by a final EIS that responds to comments received. Based on the EIS, the lead agency must decide whether the proposal, including impact mitigation, should be permitted under SEPA. Even if the proposal meets existing zoning and other local ordinances, it can still be ruled in violation of SEPA because of excess environmental impact. Therefore, project approval becomes a "discretionary" decision based on environmental impacts rather than simply a "ministerial" decision based on meeting local codes. Local officials have two points of leverage on local development proposals. First, early in the process in the threshold determination, they can offer a nonsignificant impact determination in exchange for project design changes or mitigation measures that lessen the environmental impact. Second, and more obvious, they can grant a permit only if certain measures or changes are included in the proposal.

Common Problems in EIA Implementation

The following list shows a number of perennial problems that limit the effectiveness of EIA to achieve its objectives. These are taken from a wide range of experience, primarily in U.S. federal implementation as well as that in other countries (Ortolano and Shepherd, 1995). The major concerns are that EIA comes too late in the planning process, EIA information is not integrated into decisions, and cumulative impacts that extend beyond an individual project are not assessed. Efforts should be made to generate information early so that it can be integrated into planning decisions and to consider impacts beyond the project's primary effects (Randolph and Ortolano, 1976). Despite these limitations, EIA has emerged as one of the most useful tools for environmental planning and project assessment. Phillips and Randolph (2000) found that effective EIA and NEPA compliance and ecosystem management can go hand in hand for federal agencies.

Perennial Problems in EIA Implementation (Ortolano and Shepherd, 1995)

- EIA requirements are often avoided.
- EIA is often not carefully integrated into planning.
- EIA doesn't ensure environmentally sound projects.
- EIA is done primarily for projects, not programs or policies.
- Cumulative impacts are not assessed frequently.
- Public participation in EIA is often inadequate.
- Proposed mitigations may not be implemented.
- Postproject monitoring is rarely conducted.
- Assessments of risk and social impacts are often omitted from EIAs.

Build–Out Analysis

Build-out analysis was developed at the Center for Rural Massachusetts as a method to assess the impacts of community plans and zoning ordinances. As shown in figure 18.9, communities will build out over time. Build-out analysis applies existing rights provided by the zoning ordinance, builds it out, shows it visually in maps, then assesses the environmental and social impacts.

Build-out analysis is essentially EIA, not of a project, but of a large-scale community vision. Conceptually the analysis is quite simple. It follows the steps given in the following list. After preparing a base map of environmental features and existing development, the analysis takes the zoning ordinance and shows on the map the virtual implementation of the densities and uses allowed. The use of GIS can greatly facilitate this step. The resulting build-out map can show dramatically, both visually and through impact assessment, what the existing ordinance will

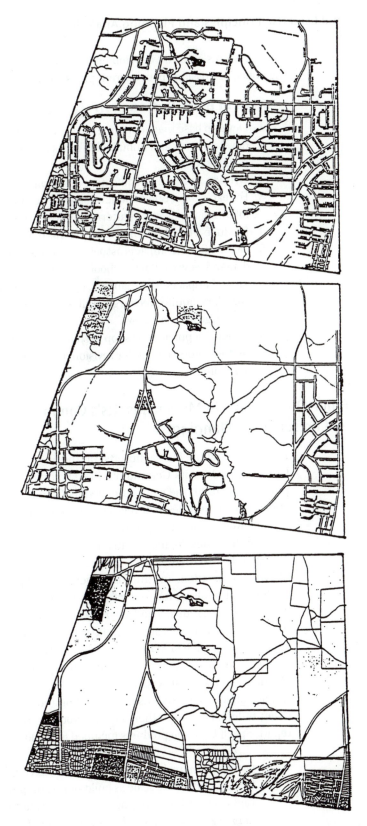

Figure 18.9 Incremental Build-out of Longmeadow, Massachusetts: 1942 (bottom), 1957 (middle), 1987 (top). *Source:* Jeffrey Lacy, *Manual of Build-Out Analysis,* 1990. Courtesy, Center for Rural Massachusetts, University of Massachusetts-Amherst.

mean in terms of future development. The analysis can be very useful in prompting public discussion about current plans and ordinances.

Steps in Build-Out Analysis

1. Develop base map including environmental inventory; identify existing developments and unbuildable areas (extremely steep slopes, floodplains, etc.
2. Overlap zoning map indicating development types and densities.
3. For each zone, build out development according to the allowed density following the existing patterns of development for those densities.
4. Produce a build-out map showing this development.
5. Determine the impacts associated with the build-out, including water demand, sewage flows, school population, road traffic, and environmental impacts (e.g., habitats, open space, agricultural lands, stream corridors, aquifer recharge, well heads, impervious surface and peak discharge and baseflow).
6. Conduct a public workshop to solicit comment on the build-out analysis and potential need for revision of the comprehensive plan and zoning ordinance.

Build-Out Analysis in Massachusetts's Community Development and Preservation Planning

In December 2002, Massachusetts was the first state to be awarded an EPA Smart Growth Award for its Community Preservation Initiative and build-out analysis program. In 1999, the state launched its Community Preservation Initiative "to empower communities to develop a vision and plan for their future." The Initiative was followed a year later with Executive Order 418 that provided state assistance for community development plans. The Community Preservation Act was enacted in September 2000. It allowed localities to establish a local fund for open space, historic preservation, and affordable housing and provided state matching funds.

Build-out analysis was one of the analytical centerpieces of the community preservation programs. The Department of Environmental Affairs, working with the 13 regional planning agencies and private planning firms, provided a full build-out analysis for each of Massachusetts's 351 cities and towns, GIS data layers and orthophotomaps for each community's own study, and tools for alternative futures planning and fiscal impact assessment.

Each build-out analysis used local zoning and land use maps, zoning and subdivision ordinances, and other data to produce three GIS maps and an impact report. Specifically, the products included the following:

1. *Orthophotomap:* base map image and GIS DOQQ data "clipped" for each locality at the same scale as build-out maps, providing a zoomable aerial view to check other map accuracy and locate community features.
2. *Map 1: Zoning and Absolute Development Constraints:* includes lands already developed, permanently protected (e.g., conservation

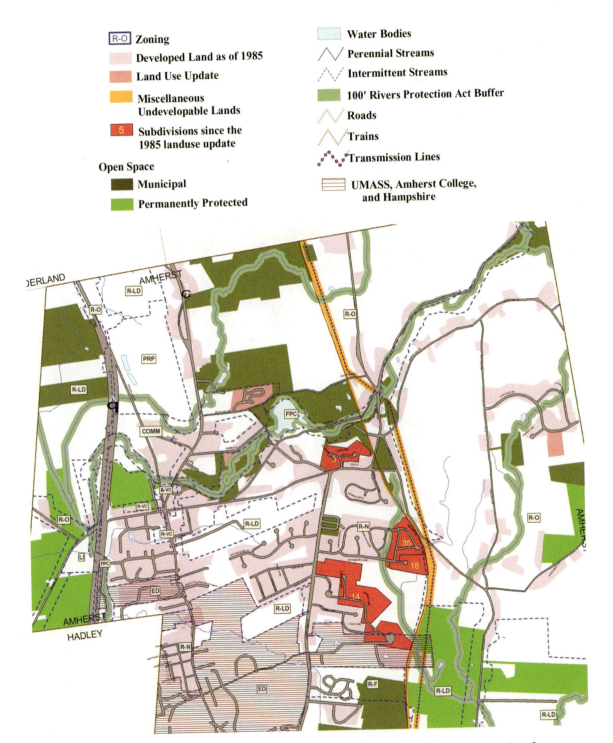

Figure 18.10 Build-out Map 1 for portion of Amherst (MA): Zoning and Absolute Development Constraints. *Source:* Commonwealth of Massachusetts (2003).

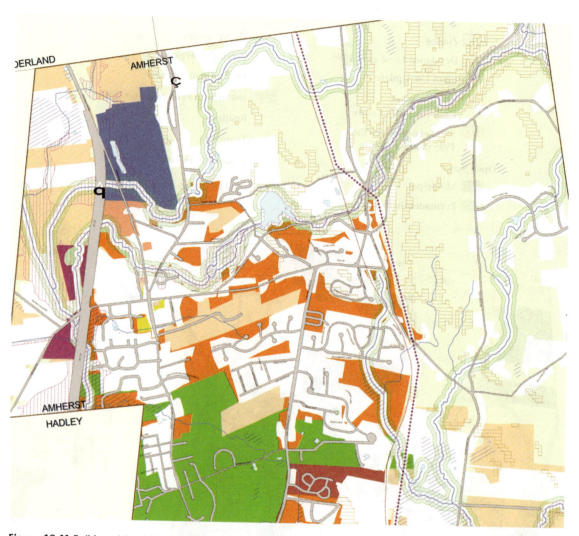

Figure 18.11 Build-out Map 2: Developable Lands and Partial Constraints. *Source:* Commonwealth of Massachusetts (2003).

easements), and other absolute constraints to development (e.g., 100-foot buffers under the Massachusetts Rivers Protection Act [MRPA]). Land available for development appears in white (see figure 18.10 for a portion of Amherst).

3. *Map 2: Developable Lands and Partial Constraints:* includes lands available for future development (white areas in Map 1). In color, the map distinguishes each zoning district. Partial constraints are those included in the zoning district ordinances (e.g., minimum lot sizes) and other partial constraints (e.g., second 100-foot buffer under MRPA) (see figure 18.11).

4. *Build-out Tables:* data provided in Map 2 for each zoning district including acres available for development and calculations on buildable area, commercial space, dwelling units, water demand, solid waste, new roads, number of students (see figure 18.11).

		Land Area (Acres)	Lots	Comm./Ind. Floor Area (Square Feet)	Res. Water Use (GPD)	Comm/Ind Water Use (GPD)	Municipal Solid Waste (Tons)	New Students	New Roads (Miles)
District B-G Developable Area:									
Total Area:									
including wetlands		2.9	9	87,164				3	
not including wetlands		2.9	9	87,164	1,769	6,537	12	3	0.02
District B-L Developable Area:									
Total Area:									
including wetlands		20.3	14	495,190				5	
not including wetlands		18.7	11	455,575	2,162	34,168	15	4	0.03
Wetlands Area:		1.6	0	0				0	
District B-VC Developable Area:									
Total Area:									
including wetlands		13.7	11	304,354				4	
not including wetlands		13.6	11	301,310	2,162	22,598	15	4	0.03
100 Year Flood Plain:		1.2	2	23,993				1	
Rivers Protection Area 100'-200':		1.8	3	0				1	
Wetland Area:		0.1	0	0				0	

Zoning Districts

R-LD	Low Density Residence
R-O	Outlying Residence
R-N	Neighborhood Residence
R-G	General Residence
R-F	Fraternity Residence
R-VC	Village Center Residence
B-VC	Village Center Business
B-L	Limited Business
B-G	General Business
COMM	Commercial
OP	Office Park
PRP	Professional Research Park
LI	Light Industrial
ED	Educational
FPC	Flood Prone Conservancy

Figure 18.11 (continued)

5. *Map 3: Composite Development Map*: simplifies the information on the first two maps by showing in purple all areas available for development, in yellow all areas unavailable for development, and in a shaded pattern all of the partial constraints that limit growth (see figure 18.12).
6. *Summary Build-out Statistics*: aggregates the build-out tables to reveal total impacts of build-out (see table 18.2).

For Amherst, build-out according to existing plans and zoning would add about 12,500 residents in 4,652 units, 2,779 new students, 1.3 million gpd of water use, 93 miles of new roads, and 6,500 tons of solid waste.

The program is described in detail in *The Buildout Book* (Commonwealth of Massachusetts, 2002). The build-out methodology is described at http://www/ state/ma/us/mgis/buildout.htm and the build-out maps and analyses and GIS data layers for each city and town are available at http://commpres.env.state.ma. us/content/buildout.asp.

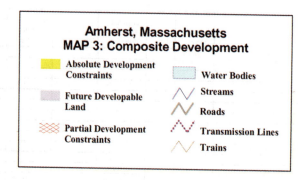

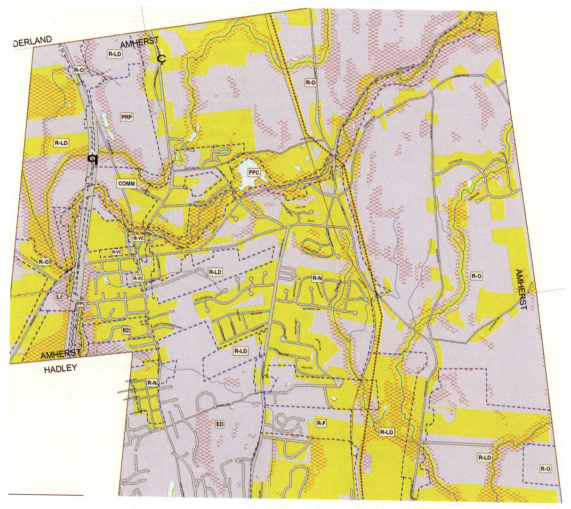

Figure 18.12 Build-out Map 3: Composite Development. *Source:* Commonwealth of Massachusetts (2003).

TABLE 18.2 **Summary Build-out Statistics for Amherst, Massachusetts (Additional Development and Impacts)**

Developable land area (sq ft)	331,648,523
Total residential lots	4,632
Comm./industrial buildable floor area (sq ft)	4,846,298
Comm./industrial water use (Gal/day)	363,472
Dwelling units	4,632
Future residents	12,599
Residential water use (Gal/day)	944,950
Municipal solid waste (tons)	6,463
Nonrecycled solid waste (tons)	4,596
Students	2,779
New roads (miles)	93

Summary

Previous chapters presented a wide range of techniques used to gather and analyze environmental information for use in planning and management. Rarely are these methods used alone. More often, planners, publics, and decision makers need to make sense of the results of these analyses and to integrate them into comprehensive or holistic assessments.

The methods presented in this chapter aim to provide this integration. The environmental inventory simply assembles spatial data in an understandable form, without analysis, so the user can make his or her own conclusions. Rapid assessment aims to gather and interpret information quickly as a basis for immediate action or to identify needs for intermediate or advanced assessment. Land suitability analysis takes baseline information further, combining sometimes diverse spatial data to assess the land's intrinsic capability for different uses. It can be used to screen sites for a particular use, gauge vulnerability of sensitive areas for certain uses, evaluate development pressure, and develop comprehensive land use plans.

Carrying capacity is an ecological concept originally used for wildlife and range management. It has had considerable appeal for managing human settlements but proved ineffective when used to estimate appropriate population levels. When applied to the impacts of population growth, however, the concept became more useful. Instead of an optimal level of population, this approach sets acceptable levels of thresholds of impact measured by indicators of change or condition in selected environmental and socioeconomic attributes. The "impact threshold" approach to carrying capacity has been used effectively in managing development in the Lake Tahoe Basin and in managing visitor use in wilderness areas.

Environmental impact assessment is one of the most used environmental analysis methods in the world. Despite its limitations, EIA has been a consistent source of environmental information for federal decision making. Its use in community land use and development is limited, but states like Washington and California, which use EIA routinely in local land use and development planning and decisions, have proven its potential value. EIA needs to occur early in the development process to be effective.

Build-out analysis is simply EIA for land use plans and zoning ordinances. It assumes a site or community will realize the full density of development permitted by ordinance and builds it out. When shown in map form along with impact analyses, the visual image of a community's future by right as well as assessment of its environmental and community impacts, can spur planners, citizens, and elected officials to question existing plans and seek more environmentally compatible alternatives. Massachusetts has employed build-out analysis through GIS as a key element of its community preservation planning program.

References

Chapter 1

Beatley, T. 1994. *Ethical Land Use: Principles of Policy and Planning*. Baltimore: Johns Hopkins Press.

Bernard, T., and J. Young. 1997. *The Ecology of Hope: Communities Collaborate for Sustainability*. Gabriola Island, British Columbia, Canada: New Society Publishers.

Bruntland Commission. 1987. *Our Common Future*. Final Report of the World Commission on Environment and Development. Oxford: Oxford University Press.

Caldwell, L. 1970. *The Environment: A Challenge for Modern Society*. Garden City, NY: American Museum of Natural History.

Campbell, S. 1996. "Green Cities, Growing Cities, Just Cities? Urban Planning and the Contradictions of Sustainable Development." *Journal of the American Planning Association* 62(3): 296–312.

Carson, R. 1962. *Silent Spring*. Boston: Houghton Mifflin.

Colby, M. 1991. "Environmental Management in Development: the Evolution of Paradigms." *Ecological Economics* 3(3): 193–213.

Goldsmith, E. 1993. *The Way: An Ecological World View*. Boston: Shambhala.

Hardin, G. 1968. "The Tragedy of the Commons." *Science* 162:1243–48.

Hawken, P., A. Lovins, and L. H. Lovins. 1999. *Natural Capitalism: Creating the Next Industrial Revolution*. Boston: Little, Brown.

Leopold, A. 1949. *The Sand County Almanac*. New York: Oxford University Press

Meadows, D. 1994. "Seeing the Population Issues Whole," In *Beyond the Numbers*, edited by L. Mazur, pp. 23–33. Washington, DC: Island Press.

Nash, R. 1989. *The Rights of Nature: A History of Environmental Ethics*. Madison: University of Wisconsin Press.

Nash, R. 1990. *American Environmentalism: Readings in Conservation History*. New York: McGraw-Hill.

Prugh, T., R. Costanza, and H. Daly. 2000. *The Local Politics of Global Sustainability*. Washington, DC: Island Press.

Stone, C. 1974. *Should Trees Have Standing? Toward Legal Rights for Natural Objects*. Los Altos, CA: W. Kaufmann.

Chapter 2

Arendt, R. 1999. *Growing Greener, Putting Conservation into Local Plans and Ordinances*. Washington, DC: Island Press.

Arnstein, S. 1969. "The Ladder of Citizen Participation." *Journal of American Institute of Planners* 35:216–24.

Barber, B. 1984. *Strong Democracy: Participatory Politics for a New Age*. Berkeley: Univeristy of California Press.

Braisoulis, H. 1989. "Theoretical Orientations in Environmental Planning: An Inquiry into Alternative Styles." *Environmental Management* 13(4): 381–93.

Calthorpe, P., and W. Fulton. 2001. *The Regional City*. Covelo, CA: Island Press.

Conn, W. D. 1986. "Review of Techniques for Weighing or Valuing the Benefits Associated with Environmental Quality Improvements." Report prepared for the International Joint Commision. Windsor, Ontario: Great Lakes Science Advisory Board. 31pp.

Corbett, J., and M. Corbett. 2000. *Designing Sustainable Communities, Learning from Village Homes*. Washington, DC: Island Press.

Corbett, J., and T. Hayden. 1981. "Local Action for a Solar Future." *Solar Law Reporter* 2(5): 957.

Duany, A., E. Plater-Zyberk, and J. Speck. 2000. *Suburban Nation: The Rise of Sprawl and the Decline of the American Dream*. New York: North Point Press.

Findley, R., and D. Farber. 2000. *Environmental Law in a Nutshell* (5th ed.). St. Paul: West Group.

Forester, J. 1989. *Planning in the Face of Power*. Berkeley: University of California Press.

Forester, J. 1999. *The Deliberative Practitioner: Encouraging Public Participatory Planning Processes*. Cambridge, MA: MIT Press.

Friedmann, J. 1987. *Planning in the Public Domain: From Knowledge to Action*. Princeton, NJ: Princeton University Press.

Hart, J. 1996. *Storm over Mono: The Mono Lake Battle and the California Water Future*. Berkeley: University of California Press.

Holling, C. S. 1978. *Adaptive Environmental Assessment and Management*. New York: John Wiley.

King, C., K. Feltey, and B. O'Neill. 1998. "The Question of Participation: Toward Authentic Participation in Public Administration." *Public Administration Review* 58(4): 317–26.

Lindblom, C. 1959. "The Science of Muddling Through." *Public Administration Review* 19:79–88.

Loomis, J. 1993. *Integrated Public Land Management*. New York: Columbia University Press.

McAllister, D. 1980. *Evaluation in Environmental Planning: Assessing Environmental, Social, Economic, and Political Trade-offs*. Cambridge, MA: MIT Press.

Myers, D., and Kitsuse, A. 2000. "Constructing the Future in Planning: A Survey of Theories and Tools." *Journal of Planning Education and Research* 19(3): 221–32.

Neuman, M. 1998. "Planning, Governing, and the Image of the City." *Journal of Planning Education and Research* 18(1): 61–71.

Sayre, R., E. Roca, G. Sedaghatkish, B. Youg, S. Keel, R. Roca, and S. Sheppard. 2000. *Nature in Focus: Rapid Ecological Assessment*. The Nature Conservancy. Washington, DC: Island Press.

Stone, C. 1974. *Should Trees Have Standing? Toward Legal Rights for Natural Objects*. Los Altos, CA: W. Kaufmann.

Susskind, L., and C. Ozawa. 1984. "Mediated Negotiation in the Public Sector: The Planners as Mediator." *Journal of Planning Education and Research* 3(3): 5–15.

Westman, W. 1985. *Ecology, Impact Assessment, and Environmental Planning*. New York: John Wiley.

Chapter 3

Anderson, L. 1995. *Guidelines for Preparing Urban Plans*. Chicago: Planners Press.

Arendt, R. 1996. *Conservation Design for Subdivisions*. Washington, DC: Island Press.

Arendt, R. 1999. *Growing Greener, Putting Conservation into Local Plans and Ordinances*. Washington, DC: Island Press.

Audirac, I., ed. 1997. *Rural Sustainable Development in America*. New York: John Wiley.

Barnett, J., and G. Hack. 2000. "Urban Design." In *The Practice of Local Government Planning* (3rd ed.), edited by C. J. Hoch, L. C. Dalton, and F. S. So, pp. 307–40. Washington: International City/County Management Association (ICMA).

Benfield, F. K., M. D. Raimi, D. T. Chen. 1999. *Once There Were Greenfields: How Urban Sprawl Is Undermining America's Environment, Economy, and Social Fabric*. Washington: National Resources Defense Council.

Calthorpe, P., and W. Fulton. 2001. *The Regional City*. Washington, DC: Island Press.

Dalton, L. C., C. J. Hoch, and F. S. So. 2000. "Introduction: Planning for People and Places." In *The Practice of Local Government Planning* (3rd ed.), edited by C. J. Hoch, L. C. Dalton, and F. So, pp. 3–17. Washington: ICMA.

Duany, A., E. Plater-Zyberk, J. Speck. 2000. *Suburban Nation: The Rise of Sprawl and the Decline of the American Dream*. New York: North Point Press.

Federal Emergency Management Agency. 2003. *Disaster Factsheets and Backgrounders*. Retrieved June 13, 2003, from http://www.fema.gov/library/factshts.shtm.

Garrett, J. 1999. "Looking At Limits for Urban Sprawl Controlling Suburban Development Becomes Next Century's Challenge for Nation's Cities." *Detroit Free Press* (March 11). Retrieved June 30, 2003, from http://www.freep.com/news/metro/GREENqsprawl11.htm.

Golley, F. B., and J. Bellot. 1999. *Rural Planning from an Environmental Systems Perspective*. New York: Springer.

Hoch, C. J., L. C. Dalton, and F. S. So. 2000. *The Practice of Local Government Planning* (3rd ed.). Washington: ICMA.

Kaiser, E., D. Godshalk, and F. S. Chapin. 1995. *Urban Land Use Planning* (4th ed.). Urbana: University of Illinois Press.

Kostoff, S. 1991. *The City Shaped, Urban Patterns and Meanings through History*. Boston: Little, Brown.

Lang, R. E., and P. A. Simmons. 2001. "'Boomburgs': The Emergence of Large, Fast-Growing Suburban Cities in the United States." *Fannie Mae Foundation Census Note 06* (June). Washington, DC: Fannie Mae Foundation.

Lynch, K. 1981. *Good City Form*. Cambridge, MA: MIT Press.

National Wildlife Federation. 2001. *Paving Paradise: Sprawl's Impact on Wildlife and Wild Places in California*. Retrieved June 13, 2003, from http://www.nwf.org/smartgrowth/pavingparadise.html.

Neuman, M. 1998. "Planning, Governing, and the Image of the City." *Journal of Planning Education and Research* 18(1): 61–71.

Sargent, F. O., P. Lusk, J. A. Rivera, and M. Varela. 1991. *Rural Environmental Planning for Sustainable Communities*. Washington, DC: Island Press.

The Nature Conservancy. 1999. *Pathways: Building a Local Initiative for Compatible Economic Development*. Center for Compatible Economic Development. Arlington, VA: The Nature Conservancy.

Probst, K. and D. Konisky. 2001. *Superfund's Future: What Will It Cost?* Washington, DC: Resources for the Future.

U.S. Council on Environmental Quality. 1974. *The Costs of Sprawl*. Washington: U.S. GPO.

U.S. Department of Agriculture (USDA), NRCS. 2001. *National Resources Inventory*. Washington: U.S. GPO. Retrieved June 13, 2003, from www.nrcs.usda.gov/technical/NRI.

U.S. Department of Interior, Fish and Wildlife Service. 2000. *Status and Trends of Wetlands in the Coterminous United States, 1986 to 1997*. Washington, DC: Author. Retrieved June 13, 2003, from http://wetlands.fws.gov/bha/SandT/SandT Report.html.

U.S. EPA. 1996. *The Watershed Protection Approach*. EPA 840-S-96-001. Washington, DC: U.S. EPA Office of Water. Retrieved June 13, 2003, from http://www.epa.gov/owow/watershed/framework.html.

U.S. EPA. 1997. *Community Based Environmental Protection*. EPA 230-B-96-003. Washington, DC: U.S. EPA Office of Policy, Planning and Evaluation. Retrieved June 13, 2003, from http://www.epa.gov/ecocommunity/pdf/coverrev.pdf.

U.S. EPA. 2000. *EPA's BEACH Watch Program: 2000 Update*. EPA-823-F-00-012. Washington, DC: U.S. EPA Office of Water. Retrieved June 13, 2003, from http://www.epa.gov/OST/beaches/.

U.S. EPA. 2001. *Update: National Listing of Fish and Wildlife Advisories*. EPA-823-F-01-010. Washington, DC: U.S. EPA Office of Water. Retrieved June 13, 2003, from http://www.epa.gov/waterscience/fish/links.htm.

Yaro, R., R. Arendt, H. Dodson, and E. Brabec. 1988. *Dealing with Change in the Connecticut River Valley*. Center for Rural Massachusetts, Environmental Law Foundation, Lincoln Institute for Land Policy (LILP). Cambridge, MA: LILP.

Chapter 4

Barber, B. 1984. *Strong Democracy: Participatory Politics for a New Age*. Berkeley: University of California Press.

Bauer, M., and J. Randolph. 2000. "Characteristics of Collaborative Environmental Planning and Decision-Making Processes." *Environmental Practice* 2(2): 156–65.

California Local Government Commission (CLGC). 2003. *Participation Tools for Better Participation and Land Use Planning*. Retrieved June 13, 2003, from http://www.lgc.org/freepub/land_use/participation_tools/visual_surveys.html.

Calthorpe Associates, Fregonese Calthorpe Associates, Envision Utah. 2000. *Envision Utah: Producing a Vision for the Future of the Greater Wasatch Area*. Berkeley, CA: Author.

Calthorpe Associates. Undated. *I-35W Build-out Study*. Twin Cities Region, Minnesota. Summary. Berkeley, CA: Author. Retrieved June 28, 2003, from http://www.calthorpe.com.

Daniels, S., and G. Walker. 1996. "Collaborative Learning: Improving Public Deliberation in Ecosystem-Based Management." *Environmental Impact Review* 16:71–102.

Dryzek, J. 1990. *Discursive Democracy: Politics, Policy, and Political Science*. New York: Cambridge University Press.

Forester, J. 1999. *The Deliberative Practitioner: Encouraging Public Participatory Planning Processes*. Cambridge, MA: MIT Press.

Gray, B. 1989. *Collaborating: Finding Common Ground for Multi-party Problems.* San Francisco: Jossey-Bass.

Fisher, R., W. Ury, and B. Patton, eds. 1991. *Getting to Yes: Negotiating Agreement Without Giving In* (2nd ed.). New York: Penguin.

Healey, P. 1997. *Collaborative Planning.* Hampshire, England: Macmillan.

Innes, J. 1996. "Planning Through Consensus Building: A New Perspective on the Comprehensive Planning Ideal." *Journal of the American Planning Association* 62:460–72.

Innes, J., J. Gruber, M. Neuman, and R. Thompson. 1994. *Coordinating Growth and Environmental Management Through Consensus Building.* Berkeley: California Policy Seminar.

John, D. 1994. *Civic Environmentalism.* Washington: Congressional Quarterly Press.

Keuhl, D. 2001. *From Collaboration to Knowledge: Planning for Remedial Action in the Great Lakes.* Ph.D. diss., Environmental Design and Planning, Virginia Tech, Blacksburg, Virginia.

London, S. 1995. "Collaboration in Action: A Survey of Community Collaboratives." A paper prepared for Pew Partnership for Civic Change. Retrieved from http://www.scottlondon.com/reports/ppcc-survey.html.

Margerum, R. 2002. "Collaborative Planning: Building Consensus and Building a Distinct Model for Practice." *Journal of Planning Education and Research* 21:237–53.

Margerum, R. 1999. "Getting Past Yes: From Capital Creation to Action." *Journal of the American Planning Association* 65(2): 181–92.

Maser, C. 1997. *Resolving Environmental Conflict.* Delray Beach, FL: St.Lucie Press.

Phillips, C., and J. Randolph. 1998. "Does the Forest Service Do Ecosystem Management?" *Journal of Forestry* 96(5): 40–45.

Phillips, C., and J. Randolph. 2000. "Ecosystem Management and Implementation of NEPA." *Environmental Management* 26(1): 1–12.

Porter, D., and D. Salvesen. 1995. *Collaborative Planning for Wetlands and Wildlife.* Washington, DC: Island Press.

Putnam, R. D. 1996. "The Strange Disappearance of Civic America." *The American Prospect* 7(24). Retrieved June 13, 2003, from http://www.prospect.org/print/V7/24/putnam-r.html.

Putnam, R. D. 2000. *Bowling Alone: The Collapse and Revival of American Community.* New York: Simon & Schuster.

Randolph, J., and M. Bauer. 1999. "Improving Environmental Decision-making Through Collaborative Methods." *Policy Studies Review* 16(3/4): 168–91.

Randolph, J., and R. Rich. 1998. "Collaborative Environmental Management: An Emerging Approach and Experience in Virginia." *Virginia Issues and Answers* 5(1): 11–19.

Randolph, J., and D. Zahm. 1998. "Information Technologies and Participation: Enhancing Communication and Interaction." In *Planning in Virginia, 1998,* edited by J. Randolph. Richmond: Virginia Chapter of the American Planning Association,

Regional Environmental Center for Central and Eastern Europe. 1996. *Awakening Participation: Building Capacity for Public Participation in Environmental Decision-making. Szentendre, Hungary.* Retrieved June 13, 2003, from http://www.rec.org/REC/Publications/PPTraining/cover.html.

Ury, W. 1993. Getting *Past No: Negotiating Your Way from Confrontation to Cooperation* (Revised ed.). New York: Bantam Doubleday.

USDA. Forest Service. 1996. *Collaborative Planning and Stewardship*. Retrieved June 30, 2003, from http://www.fs.fed.us/forum/nepa/colweb.htm.

U.S. EPA. 1997. *Volunteer Stream Monitoring: A Methods Manual*. EPA-841-B-97-003. Washington, DC: U.S. EPA Office of Water. Retrieved June 13, 2003, from http://www.epa.gov/OWOW/monitoring/vol.html#methods.

Weber, E. P. (1998). *Pluralism by the Rules: Conflict and Cooperation in Environmental Regulation*. Washington, DC: Georgetown University Press.

Wondolleck, J., and S. Yaffee. 2000. *Making Collaboration Work: Lessons from Innovation in Natural Resource Management*. Washington, DC: Island Press.

Zahm, D., and J. Randolph. 1999. "Participation and Partnerships in Planning." Online tutorial prepared for the American Planning Association (APA) and American Institute for Certified Planners (AICP). Available at http://www.uap.vt.edu/cdrom/default.htm.

Chapter 5

American Farmland Trust. 2001. *Fact Sheet: Agricultural Conservation Easements*. Farmland Information Center. Retrieved June 13, 2003, from http://www.farmland info.org/fic/tas/index.htm#fs.

American Farmland Trust. 2002. *Fact Sheet: Farmland Protection Toolbox*. Farmland Information Center. Retrieved June 13, 2003, from http://www.farmlandinfo.org/fic/tas/index.htm#fs.

Arendt, R. 1999. *Growing Greener, Pitting Conservation into Local Plans and Ordinances*. Washington, DC: Island Press.

Becker, G., and J. Womach. 2002. "The 2002 Farm Bill: Overview and Status." Washington, DC: Library of Congress. Congressional Research Service. Retrieved from http://www.cnie.org/NLE/CRSreports/Agriculture/ag-112.pdf.

Benedict, M., and E. McMahon. 2002. *Green Infrasructure: Smart Conservation for the 21st Century*. The Conservation Fund. Washington, DC: Sprawl Watch Clearinghouse. Retrieved June 13, 2003, from http://www.sprawlwatch.org/greenin frastructure.pdf.

Chicago Region Biodiversity Council. (undated). *Chicago Wilderness: An Atlas of Biodiversity*. Retrieved June 13, 2003, from http://www.epa.gov/glnpo/chiwild/.

City of Boulder. 2001. *Greenways Master Plan*. Boulder, CO: Author. Retrieved June 13, 2003, from http://www.ci.boulder.co.us/publicworks/depts/utilities/projects/greenways/index.htm.

Daniels, T. 2001. "State and Local Efforts in Conserving Privately-Owned Working Landscapes." Background paper for National Governors Association, Private Lands, Public Benefits: A Policy Summit on Working Lands Conservation.

Greenways, Inc. "Our Projects." Retrieved June 13, 2003, from http://www.green ways.com/pages/projects.html.

Hollis, L., and W. Fulton. 2002. "Open Space Protection: Conservation Meets Growth Management." Washington, DC: Brookings Institution Center on Urban and Metropolitan Policy.

Land Trust Alliance. 2003. About LTA; Local Land Trust Success Stories. Retrieved June 30, 2003, from http://www.lta.org/.

Metzger, P. 1983. "Mill Hollow: One Land Trust Transaction by the National Lands Trust." *Letter. A Monthly Report on Environmental Issues*. Washington, DC: The Conservation Foundation.

Salkin, P., J. Cintron, and J. Fleming. 2001. "Conservation of Private Lands: Opportunities and Challenges for the States." Background paper for National Governors Association, Private Lands, Public Benefits: A Policy Summit on Working Lands Conservation.

Smith, D., and P. Hellmund, eds. 1993. *Ecology of Greenways: Design and Function of Linear Conservation Areas.* Minneapolis: University of Minnesota Press.

State of Maryland. 2001. *GreenPrint Project Assessment: Factors Considered to Establish Ecological Value.* Retrieved from June 13, 2003, http://www.dnr.state.md.us/greenways/greenprint/.

Stokes, S., A. E. Watson, and S. Mastran. 1997. *Saving America's Countryside: A Guide to Rural Conservation* (2nd ed.) Baltimore: Johns Hopkins University Press.

The Conservation Fund. (undated). *Land and Water Conservation Fund: An Assessment of Its Past, Present, and Future.* Arlington, VA: Author.

The Nature Conservancy. 2001. *Conservation by Design: A Framework for Mission Success.* Arlington, VA: Author. Retrieved June 13, 2003, from http://nature.org/aboutus/howwework/files/cbd_en.pdf.

Trust for Public Land. 2002. *Local Greenprinting for Growth, Volume I.* Retrieved June 13, 2003, from http://www.tpl.org/tier3_cd.cfm?content_item_id=10648&folder_id=175.

UNC-CH, Graduate Student Workshop. 2001. *Kinston/Lenoir County Green Infrastructure Plan for the Neuse River Floodplain.* Department of City and Regional Planning, Chapel Hill.

UNC-CH, Graduate Student Workshop. 2002. *Linking Natural and Historic Assets: Green Infrastructure as Economic Development in Lenoir County, North Carolina.* Department of City and Regional Planning, Chapel Hill.

USDA. NRCS. 2001. *National Resources Inventory.* Washington: U.S. Government Printing Office. Retrieved June 28, 2003, from www.nrcs.usda.gov/technical/NRI.

Wright, J. 1993. "Conservation Easements: An Analysis of Donated Development Rights." *Journal of the American Planning Association* 59(4): 487–93.

Zinn, J. 2002a. "Land and Water Conservation Fund: Current Status and Issues." *Congressional Research Service.* Retrieved June 13, 2003, from http://www.cnie.org/nle/crsreports/public/pub-1.pdf.

Zinn, J. 2002b. "Protecting Natural Resources and Managing Growth: Issues in the 107th Congress." *Congressional Research Service.* Retrieved June 13, 2003, from http://www.cnie.org/nle/crsreports/natural/nrgen-16.pdf.

Zinn, J. 2002c. "Soil and Water Conservation Issues." *Congressional Research Service.* Retrieved June 13, 2003, from http://www.cnie.org/nle/crsreports/agriculture/ag-18.pdf.

Chapter 6

Arendt, R. 1994. *Rural by Design,* Chicago: American Planning Association Press.

Arendt, R. 1996. *Conservation Design for Subdivisions.* Washington, DC: Island Press.

Arendt, R. 1999. *Growing Greener, Pitting Conservation into Local Plans and Ordinances.* Washington, DC: Island Press.

Audirac I. 1999. "Stated Preference for Pedestrian Proximity to Community Facilities: An Assessment of New Urbanism 'Sense of Community'." *Journal of Planning Education and Research* 19(1): 53–66 and *JPER* Errata, 19(2):164.

Beamguard, J. 1999. "Packing Pavement." *The Tampa Tribune* (July 18). Retrieved June 28, 2003, from http://www.silcom.com/~rdb/share/bguard.html.

Beatley, T. 2000. *Green Urbanism*. Washington, DC: Island Press.

Benfield, F. K., M. D. Raimi, and D. Chen. 1999. *Once There Were Greenfields*. Washington, DC: Natural Resources Defense Council.

Birch, E. 2002. "Having a Longer View on Downtown Living." *Journal of American Planning Association* 68(1): 5–21.

California Local Government Commission (CLGC). 2003. *Participation Tools for Better Participation and Land Use Planning*. Retrieved June 13, 2003, from http://www.lgc.org/freepub/land_use/participation_tools/visual_surveys.html.

Calthorpe, P. 1993. *The Next Metropolis: Ecology and the American Dream*, Princeton, NJ: Princeton Architectural Press.

Calthorpe, P., and W. Fulton. 2001. *The Regional City*. Washington, DC: Island Press.

Calthorpe Associates. (undated). *I-35W Build-out Study*. Twin Cities Region, Minnesota. Summary. Berkeley, CA: Author. Retrieved June 28, 2003, from http://www.calthorpe.com.

Calthorpe Associates. 2000. *St. Croix Valley Redevelopment Study*. Prepared for the Metropolitan Council (MN). Berkeley, CA: Author. Retrieved June 13, 2003, from http://www.metrocouncil.org/planning/stcroixvalley/stcroixdev.htm.

Calthorpe Associates, Fregonese Calthorpe Associates, Envision Utah. 2000. *Envision Utah: Producing a Vision for the Future of the Greater Wasatch Area*. Berkeley, CA: Author.

Center for Excellence in Sustainable Development (CESD). 2002. "Green Development Success Stories." Retrieved June 13, 2003, from www.sustainable.doe.gov/greendev/stories.shtml.

City of Austin. 2001. *Green by Design: 7 Steps to Green Building*. Retrieved June 13, 2003, from http://www.ci.austin.tx.us/greenbuilder/

Congress for the New Urbanism. 2002a. *The Coming Demand*. Retrieved June 13, 2003, from http://www.cnu.org/cnu_reports/Coming_Demand.pdf.

Congress for the New Urbanism. 2002b. About CNU. Retrieved June 13, 2003, from http://www.cnu.org/.

Corbett, J., and M. Corbett. 2000. *Designing Sustainable Communities: Learning from Village Homes*. Washington, DC: Island Press.

Corbett, M. 1981. *A Better Place to Live*. Emmaus, PA: Rodale Press.

Duany, A., E. Plater-Zyberk, J. Speck. 2000. *Suburban Nation: The Rise of Sprawl and the Decline of the American Dream*. New York: North Point Press.

Kuntsler, J. 1993. *The Geography of Nowhere: the Rise and Decline of America's Manmade Landscape*. New York: Simon & Schuster.

Kuntsler, J. 2001. *The City in Mind: Meditations on the Urban Condition*. New York: Free Press.

Lund, H. 2002. "Pedestrian Environments and Sense of Community." *Journal of Planning Education and Research* 21: 301–12.

McHarg, I. 1969. *Design with Nature*. Garden City, NY: American Museum of Natural History.

Myers, D., and E. Gearin. 2001. "Current Preferences and Future Demand for Denser Residential Environments." *Housing Policy Debate* 12 (4): 633–59.

National Association of Home Builders. 1987. *Land Development*. Washington: Author.

Rocky Mountain Institute. 1998. *Green Development*. New York: John Wiley.

Simmons, P., and R. Lang, 2001. *The Urban Turnaround: A Decade-by-Decade Report Card on Postwar Population Change in Older Industrial Cities.* Fannie Mae Foundation Census Note 01. Washington, DC: Fannie Mae Foundation.

Sohmer, R., and R. Lang. 2001. *Downtown Rebound.* Fannie Mae Foundation Census Note 03. Washington, DC: Fannie Mae Foundation.

Talen, E. 1999. "Sense of Community and Neighborhood Form: An Assessment of the Social Doctrine of New Urbanism." *Urban Studies* 36(8): 1361–79.

Talen, E. 2001. "Traditional Urbanism Meets Residential Affluence: An Analysis of the Variability of Suburban Preference." *Journal of American Planning Association* 67 (2): 199–216.

Talen, E., and A. Duany. 2002. "Transect Planning." *Journal of American Planning Association* 68(3): 245–66.

U.S. EPA. 2000. *Brownfields Economic Redevelopment Initiative.* EPA 500-F-00-241. Washington, DC: U.S. EPA Solid Waste and Emergency Response (5105). Retrieved June 13, 2003, from http://www.epa.gov/brownfields/pdf/econinit.pdf.

U.S. EPA. 2001a. *Road Map to Understanding Innovative Technology Options for Brownfields Investigation and Cleanup* (3rd ed.) EPA 500-F-01-001. Washington, DC: U.S. EPA Office of Solid Waste and Emergency Response. Retrieved June 13, 2003, from http://clu-in.org/roadmap.

U.S. EPA. 2001b. *Transforming Brownfields Industrial Eyesores into Recreational and Open Space Attractions.* EPA 500-F-01-345. Washington, DC: U.S. EPA Solid Waste and Emergency Response.

U.S. EPA. 2002. Restoring Brownfields for Residential Reuse Puts EPA Right at Home. EPA 500-F-02-035. Washington, DC: U.S. EPA Solid Waster and Emergency Response.

U.S. EPA. 2003. *Brownfields Success Stories.* Retrieved June 13, 2003, from http://www/epa/gov/brownfields/success.htm.

Van der Ryn, S., and P. Calthorpe. 1984. *Sustainable Communities.* San Francisco: Sierra Club Books.

Yaro, R., R. Arendt, H. Dodson, and E. Brabec. 1988. *Dealing with Change in the Connecticut River Valley.* Center for Rural Massachusetts, Environmental Law Foundation, Lincoln Institute for Land Policy (LILP). Cambridge, MA: LILP.

Chapter 7

Arendt, R. 1994. *Rural by Design.* Chicago: American Planning Association Press.

Arendt, R. 1999. *Growing Greener, Putting Conservation into Local Plans and Ordinances,* Washington, DC: Island Press.

Arigoni, D. 2001. *Smart Growth and Affordable Housing.* Washington, DC: Smart Growth Network.

Benfield, F. K., J. Terris, and N. Vorsanger. 2001. *Solving Sprawl: Models of Smart Growth in Communities Across America.* Washington, DC: NRDC.

Boulder Valley Comprehensive Plan. 1996. Year 2000 update. Retrieved June 13, 2003, from http://www.ci.boulder.co.us/planning/BVCP2000/bpbvcp2000.htm.

City of Austin. Undated (a). Smart Growth Initiative. Retrieved June 13, 2003, from http://www.ci.austin.tx.us/smartgrowth/.

City of Austin. Undated (b). Smart Growth Matrix. Retrieved June 13, 2003, from http://www.ci.austin.tx.us/smartgrowth/matrix.htm.

City of Boulder. 2001. *Greenways Master Plan*. Boulder, CO: Author. Retrieved June 13, 2003, at http://www.ci.boulder.co.us/publicworks/depts/utilities/projects/greenways/index.htm.

Coughlin, R. 1991. Formulating and Evaluating Agricultural Zoning Programs. *Journal of the American Planning Association* 57(2):183–92.

Fairfax County (VA). 1991. *General Policy Plan*. Fairfax, VA: Author.

Fannie Mae Foundation. 2000. *Fair Growth*. Prepared for Association of Collegiate Schools of Planning Conference, November. Washington, DC: Author.

Fleissig, W., and V. Jacobsen. 2002. *Smart Growth Scorecard for Development Projects*. Congress for the New Urbanism. Washington, DC: U.S. EPA.

Hollis, L., and W. Fulton. 2002. *Open Space Protection: Conservation Meets Growth Management*. Washington, DC: Brookings Institution Center on Urban and Metropolitan Policy.

King County. Comprehensive Plan. 2000. Retrieved June 13, 2003, from http://www.metrokc.gov/exec/orpp/compplan/.

Lucero, L., and J. Soule. 2002. "A Win for Lake Tahoe: The Supreme Court Validates Moritoriums in a Path-breaking Decision." *Planning* 68(6): 4–7.

Montgomery County, Maryland. 2002. Special Protection Area Program, Annual Report 2001. Rockville, MD: Departments of Environmental Protection and Permitting Services. Retrieved June 13, 2003, from http://www.montgomerycountymd.gov/mc/services/dep/SPA/home.htm#Documents.

Montgomery County, Maryland. 2003. Agricultural Preservation Initiatives. Retrieved June 13, 2003, from http://www.montgomerycountymd.gov/siteHead.asp?page=/content/ded/AgServices/aginitiatives.html.

Morris, D. 1982. *Self-Reliant Cities: Energy and the Transformation of Urban America*. San Francisco: Sierra Club Books.

Natural Resources Defense Council (NRDC). 1977. *Land Use Controls in the United States*. New York: Dial Press/John Wade.

Nelson, A. C., and J. Duncan. 1995. *Growth Management: Principles and Practices*. Chicago: American Planning Association.

Northwest Environment Watch. 2002. *Sprawl and Smart Growth in Greater Seattle-Tacoma*. Seattle: Author. Retrieved June 13, 2003, from http://www.northwestwatch.org/press/seattle_sprawl.pdf.

1000 Friends of Minnesota. 2003. TDR Conceptual Overview. Retrieved June 23, 2003, from http://www.1000fom.org/Tool%20Box/TDR-concept.pdf.

Pruetz, R. 2003. *Beyond Takings and Givings: Saving Natural Areas, Farmland and Historic Landmarks with Transfer of Development Rights and Density Transfer Charges*. Burbank, CA: Arje Press.

Randolph, J. 1981. The Local Energy Future: A Compendium of Community Programs. *Solar Law Reporter* 3(2): 253–82.

Richardson, J. 2002. *Dillon's Rule and Growth Management in 50 States*. Washington, DC: Brookings Institution.

Town of Blacksburg, VA. 1997. Zoning Ordinance. Retrieved June 13, 2003, from http://www.blacksburg.gov/ordinances.php.

Town of Blacksburg. 2001. Comprehensive Plan. Retreived June 28, 2003, from http://www.blacksburg.gov/comp_plan/.

Witten, J. and S. Horsley. 1995. *A Guide to Wellhead Protection*. Planning Advisory Service. U.S. EPA. PAS Report 457/458. Chicago: American Planning Association.

Chapter 8

Adirondack Park Agency, State of New York. 2001. Adirondack Park State Land Master Plan Approved November 1987. Updated 2001. Retrieved June 13, 2003, from http://www.northnet.org/adirondackparkagency/.

American Planning Association. 1999. *Planning Communities for the 21st Century.* Chicago: Author.

American Planning Association. 2002. *Planning for Smart Growth. State of the States.* Chicago: Author.

Bosselman, F., and D. Callies. 1974. *The Quiet Revolution Is Land Use Control.* Prepared for the U.S. Council on Environmental Quality. Washington, DC: U.S. GPD.

Calthorpe Associates. 2000. *St. Croix Valley Redevelopment Study.* Prepared for the Metropolitan Council (MN). Berkeley, CA: Author. Retrieved June 13 2003, from http://www.metrocouncil.org/planning/stcroixvalley/stcroixdev.htm.

Calthorpe, P., and W. Fulton. 2001. *The Regional City.* Covelo, CA: Island Press.

ECONorthwest. 2000. *Willamette Valley Alternative. Futures Project.* Eugene, OR: Author.

Frece, J. 1997. "Lessons from Next Door: "'Smart Growth' in Maryland." *Planning in Virginia 1997.* Midlothian, VA: Virginia Chapter of the American Planning Association.

Frece, J. 2000. "Smart Growth in Maryland." Presentation at Blacksburg, Virginia, October.

Leonard, H. J. 1982. *Managing Oregon's Growth: The Politics of Development Planning.* Washington, DC: Conservation Foundation.

Metropolitan Council (Twin Cities, MN). 2002. Blueprint 2030. St. Paul, MN: Author. Retrieved June 13, 2003, from http://www.metrocouncil.org/planning/blueprint2030/overview.htm.

National Governors Association. 2001. Growth and Quality of Life Tool Kit. Retrieved June 13, 2003, from http://www.nga.org/center/growth.

Natural Resources Defense Council (NRDC). 1977. *Land Use Controls in the United States.* New York: Dial Press/John Wade.

New Jersey Pinelands Commission. Undated. A Summary of the New Jersey Pinelands Comprehensive Management Plan. Retrieved June 13, 2003, from http://www.state.nj.us/pinelands/.

New Jersey Pinelands Commission. 2002. *The Third Progress Report on Implementation.* Retrieved June 13, 2003, from http://www.state.nj.us/pinelands/planrev.pdf.

Northwest Environment Watch. 2002. *Sprawl and Smart Growth in Metropolitan Portland.* Seattle: Author. Retrieved June 13, 2003, from http://www.northwestwatch.org/press/portland_sprawl.html

1000 Friends of Oregon. 2003. Measure 7/Takings Information. Retrieved June 13, 2003, from http://www.friends.org/issues/m7.html.

Oregon Department of Land Conservation and Development. 1997. Oregon Statewide Planning Program. Salem, OR: Author. Retrieved June 28, 2003, from http://www.lcd.state.or.us/fastpdfs/brochure.pdf.

Phillips, C., and J. Randolph. 1998. "Has Ecosystem Management Really Changed Practices on the National Forests?" *Journal of Forestry* 96(5): 40–45.

Randolph, J. 1987. "Comparison of Approaches to Public Lands Planning: Forest Service, Park Service, Bureau of Land Management, Fish and Wildlife Service." *Trends* 24(2): 36–45.

San Francisco Bay Conservation and Development Commission. 1998. *San Francisco Bay Plan*. Retrieved June 13, 2003, from http://www.bcdc.ca.gov/.

State of Washington. 1998. *SEPA Handbook*. Olympia: Department of Ecology.

Tahoe Regional Planning Agency. 1986. *Regional Plan for the Lake Tahoe Basin*. Stateline, NV: Author. Retrieved June 2003, from http://www.trpa.org/Goals/preface.html.

Tahoe Regional Planning Agency. 2002. *2001 Threshold Evaluation Report*. Stateline, NV: Author. Retrieved June 2003, from http://www.trpa.org/News/2001_Thresholds.html.

U.S. Council on Environmental Quality. 1974. *The Costs of Sprawl*. Washington: U.S. GPO.

Chapter 9

American Society of Civil Engineers. 1998. *Minimum Design Loads for Buildings and other Sturctures*. ACSE Standard ASCE 7-98. Author: Reston, VA.

Association of Bay Area Governments. 1995. On Shaky Ground. Earthquake ground shaking maps. Retrieved June 27, 2003, from http://www.abag.ca.gov/bay area/eqmaps/pickcity.html.

Belo, B. 2003. *Natural Hazard Mitigation Planning for Karst Terrains in Virginia*. Master's thesis, Master of Urban and Regional Planning, Virginia Tech, Blacksburg, Virginia.

California Department of Conservation. 2003. Seismic Hazard Mapping Program. Retrieved June 22, 2003, from http://gmw.consrv.ca.gov/shmp/index.htm.

Clark, J., J. Banta, and J. Zinn. 1980. *Coastal Environmental Management: Guidelines for Conservation of Resources and Protection against Storm Hazards*. The Conservation Foundation. Prepared for six federal agencies. Washington, DC: U.S. Government Printing Office.

Douglas, B., M. Crowell, and S. Leatherman. 1998. "Considerations for Shoreline Position Prediction." *Journal of Coastal Research* 14(3): 1025–33.

FEMA. 1979. Flood Insurance Study including FHBM and FIRM (1980) for Blacksburg, VA. Retrieved June 28, 2003, from FEMA Map Store online at http://store.msc.fema.gov/webapp/wcs/stores/servlet/StoreCatalogDisplay?storeId10001&catalogId=10001&langId=-1&userType=G.

FEMA. 1998. *Property Acquisition Handbook for Local Communities: State Summary*. Washington, DC: Author.

FEMA. 2000a. Hazards website for fact sheets and other information on natural hazards available at http://www.fema.gov/hazards/.

FEMA. 2000b. *Project Impact: Building Disaster Resistant Communities*. Retrieved June 27, 2003, from http://www.fema.gov/impact/impact00.htm.

FEMA. 2000c. *Coastal Construction Manual* (3rd ed.) Washington, DC: Mitigation Directorate. Project Impact.

FEMA. 2002a. "Hazard Mitigation Planning and Hazard Mitigation Grant Program." *Federal Register* 67(38). February 26.

FEMA. 2002b. "Hazard Mitigation Planning and Hazard Mitigation Grant Program." *Federal Register* 67(190). October 1.

FEMA and ESRI. Project Impact: Helping to Build Disaster Resistant Communities. Online hazard maps accessed at http://www.esri.com/hazards.

FireWise Communities. 2001. *FireWise Communities.* Quincy, MA: National Wildland/Urban Interface Fir Program. Retrieved June 29, 3002, from http://www.firewise.org/communities.

General Accounting Office. 2002. *Proposed Changes to FEMA's Multi-hazard Mitigation Program Presents Problems.* RPT Number GAO-02-1035. Washington, DC: Author.

Godshalk, D., T. Beatley, P. Berke, D. Brower, and E. Kaiser. 1999. *Natural Hazard Mitigation: Recasting Disaster Policy and Planning.* Washington, DC: Island Press.

Griggs, G. and J. Gilchrist. 1983. *Geologic Hazards, Resources, and Environmental Planning.* Belmont, CA: Wadsworth.

Hudson, M. and K. Murray. 2003. Geologic Map of the Ponca Quadrangle, Newton, Boone, and Carroll Counties, Arkansas. Washington, DC: USDI, U.S. Geological Survey. Full map retrieved June 28, 2003, from http://pubs.usgs.gov/mf/2003/mf-2412/mf-2412.pdf.

Institute for Business and Home Safety (IBHS). 2001. *Community Land Use Evaluation for Natural Hazards.* Tampa, FL: Author. Retrieved from http://www.ibhs.org/research_library/downloads/95.pdf.

Jaffe, M., J. Butler, and C. Thurow. 1981. *Reducing Earthquake Risks: A Planners Guide.* PAS Report 364. Chicago: American Planning Association.

Kemmerly, P. 1993. "Sinkhole Hazards and Risk Assessment in a Planning Context." *Journal of the American Planning Association* 58(2): 222–33.

Nelson, A. C., and S. French. 2002. "Plan Quality and Mitigating Damage from Natural Disasters." *Journal of the American Planning Association* 8(2): 194–207.

Nilsen, T., R. Wright, T. Vlasic, and W. Spangle. Relative Slope Stability and Land-Use Planning in the San Francisco Bay Region, California. USGS Professional Paper 944. Menlo Park, CA: USGS.

Oregon Department of Land Conservation and Development. 2000. *Planning for Natural Hazards.* Salem, OR: Author.

Roth, R., J. Randolph, and C. Zipper. 1991. "Coal Mining Subsidence Regulation in Six Appalachian States." *Virginia Environmental Law Journal* 10(2): 311–43.

U.S. Army Corps of Engineers. 1984. *Roanoke River Upper Basin.* Final Interim Feasibility Report and Environmental Impact Statement for Flood Damage Reduction. Wilmington, NC: Wilmington District.

U.S. Geological Survey. 1982. *Goals and Tasks of the Landslide Part of a Ground-Failure Hazards Reduction Program.* USGS Circular 880. Reston, VA: Author.

U.S. Geological Survey. 1995. Saving Lives through Better Design Standards. Fact sheet 176-95. Menlo Park, CA: Author. Retrieved June 27, 2003, from http://quake.wr.usgs.gov/prepare/factsheets/BetterDesign/.

U.S. Geological Survey. 2000a. Land Subsidence in the U.S Fact Sheet-165–00. Washington, DC: Author. Retrieved June 23, 2003, from http://water.usgs.gov/wid/index-hazards.html.

U.S. Geological Survey. 2000b. Glacier Peak—History and Hazards of a Cascade Volcano. Fact sheet 058-00. Retrieved June 30, 2003, from http://wrgis.wr.usgs.gov/fact-sheet/fs058-00/fs058-00.pdf.

U.S. Geological Survey. 2001. Earthquake Shaking—Finding the Hotspots. Fact sheet 001–01. Washington, DC: Author.

U.S. Geological Survey. 2003a. National Seismic Hazards Mapping Project. Retrieved June 28, 2003, from http://geohazards.cr.usgs.gov/eq/.

U.S. Geological Survey. 2003b. Volcano Hazards Assessments—Reports and Maps. Retrieved June 22, 2003, from http://vulcan.wr.usgs.gov/Publications/hazards_reports.html.

Veni, G. 2002. "Revising the Karst Map of the United States." *Journal of Cave and Karst Studies* 64(1): 45–50.

Zipper, C., W. Balfour, R. Roth, and J. Randolph. 1997. "Domestic Water Supply Impacts by Underground Coal Mining Operations in Virginia, USA." *Environmental Geology* 29(1/2): 84–93.

Chapter 10

Bauer, M. 2001. *Collaborative Environmental Decisionmaking: A Power Sharing Process that Achieves Results through Dialogue.* Ph.D. diss., Environmental Design and Planning, Virginia Tech, Blacksburg, Virginia.

Bauer, M., and J. Randolph. 2000. "Characteristics of Collaborative Environmental Planning and Decision-Making Processes." *Environmental Practice* 2(2): 156–65.

Bower, D. E., C. Lowery, M. A. Lowery, and N. M. Hurley. 1999. "Development of a 14-Digit Hydrologic Unit Code Numbering System for South Carolina." U.S. Geological Survey WRIR-99-4015. Retrieved June 23, 2003, at http://sc.water.usgs.gov/publications/wrir99-4015.html.

Clewell, A., J. Rieger, and J. Munro. 2000. *Guidelines for Developing and Managing Ecological Restoration Projects.* Retrieved June 23, 2003, from http://www.ser.org/reading.php?pg = guidelines4er.

Commonwealth of Virginia. 1999. *Virginia Stormwater Management Handbook.* Richmond: Department of Conservation and Recreation.

Corbett, J., and T. Hayden. 1981. "Local Action for a Solar Future." *Solar Law Reporter* 2(5): 957.

Federal Interagency Stream Restoration Working Group (FISRWG). 1998. *Stream Corridor Restoration: Principles, Processes, and Practices.* Washington, DC: Government Printing Office.

Fitzsimmons, A. 1999. *Defending Illusions: Federal Protection of Ecosystems.* Lanham, MD: Rowman & Littlefield.

Flick, W., and W. King. 1995. "Ecosystem Management as American Law." *Renewable Resources Journal* 13(3).

Goldstein, B. "The Struggle Over Ecosystem Management at Yellowstone." *BioScience* 42(3): 183–87.

Grumbine, R. 1994. "What Is Ecosystem Management?" *Conservation Biology* 8(1): 27–38.

Holst, D. 1999. *Statewide Watershed Protection and Local Implementation: A Comparison of Washington, Minnesota, and Oregon.* Master's thesis, Master of Urban and Regional Planning, Virginia Tech, Blacksburg, Virginia. Retrieved June 22, 2003, from http://scholar.lib.vt.edu/theses/available/etd-042199-181520/unrestricted/MajorPaper.pdf.

Keuhl, D. 2001. *From Collaboration to Knowledge: Planning for Remedial Action in the Great Lakes.* Ph.D. diss., Environmental Design and Planning, Virginia Tech, Blacksburg, Virginia.

Meridian Institute. 2001a. *Discussion Group Proceedings of The National Watershed Forum.* Arlington, Virginia.

Meridian Institute. 2001b. *Final Report of The National Watershed Forum, June 27–July 1, 2001*. Arlington, Virginia.

National Research Council. 1992. *Restoration of Aquatic Ecosystems: Science, Technology, and Public Policy*. Washington, DC: National Academy Press.

Oregon Plan for Salmon and Watersheds. 2001. Retrieved June 22, 2003, from http://www.oregon-plan.org/.

Phillips, C., and J. Randolph. 1998. "Has Ecosystem Management Really Changed Practices on the National Forests?" *Journal of Forestry* 96(5): 40–45.

Phillips, C., and J. Randolph. 2000. "The Relationship of Ecosystem Management to NEPA and its Goals." *Environmental Management,* 26(1):1–12.

Randolph, J. 1987. "Comparison of Approaches to Public Lands Planning: Forest Service, Park Service, Bureau of Land Management, Fish and Wildlife Service." *Trends* 24(2): 36–45.

Salwasser, H. 1994. "Ecosystem Management: Can It Sustain Diversity and Productivity?" *Journal of Forestry* 92(8): 6–10.

Schueler, T. 1987. *Controlling Urban Runoff: A Practical Manual for Planning and Designing Urban BMPs*. Washington, DC: Metropolitan Washington Council of Governments.

Schueler, T. 1997. "The Economics of Watershed Protection." *Watershed Protection Techniques* 2(4): 469–81.

Schueler, T. 2000. "Basic Concepts of Watershed Planning," In *The Practice of Watershed Protection,* edited by T. Schueler and H. Holland, pp. 145–61. Ellicott City, MD: Center for Watershed Protection.

Schueler, T. and H. Holland, eds. 2000. *The Practice of Watershed Protection*. Ellicott City, MD: Center for Watershed Protection.

Smith, T. 1995. *Habitat Conservation Planning Under the Endangered Species Act: Is It Ecosystem Management?* Masters thesis, Urban and Regional Planning. Blacksburg, VA: Virginia Tech.

Society for Ecological Restoration (SER). 2002. *The SER Primer on Ecological Restoration*. Retrieved June 23, 2003, from http://www.ser.org/Primer.pdf, http://ecologicalrestoration.info/, and http://www.ser.org/reading.php?pg = rejournal.

State of New York. 2001. *New York State Stormwater Management Design Manual*. Prepared by Center for Watershed Protection. Albany: NY Department of Environmental Conservation.

The Nature Conservancy. 2001. *Conservation by Design: A Framework for Mission Success*. Arlington, VA: Author. Retrieved June 22, 2003, from http://nature.org/aboutus/howwework/files/cbd_en.pdf.

USDA. Forest Service. 1992. *Ecosystem Management of the National Forests and Grasslands*. Memorandum 1330-1. Washington, DC: Author.

USDA. Forest Service. 2000. "National Forest System Land Resource Management Planning: Final Rule." *Federal Register* 65(218): 67514–81

U.S. EPA. 1995. *Watershed Protection: A Project Focus*. (WH-553) EPA 841-R-96–003. Office of Water. Washington, DC: Author.

U.S. EPA. 1996. *The Watershed Protection Approach*. Office of Water. Washington, DC: Author.

U.S. EPA. 1997. *Top 10 Watershed Lessons Learned*. OWOW (4501F) EPA 840-F-97–001. Office of Water. Washington, DC: Author.

U.S. EPA. 2000a. *Watershed Analysis and Management (WAM): A Guide for Tribes*. Washington, DC: Author.

U.S. EPA. 2000b. *Watershed Success Stories: Applying the Principles and Spirit of the Clean Water Action Plan.* Washington, DC: Author.

U.S. EPA. 2001. *Protecting and Restoring America's Watersheds: Status, Trends, and Initiatives in Watershed Management.* (4204) EPA-840-R-00–001. Office of Water. Washington, DC: Author.

U.S. EPA. 2002. Watershed Initiative: Encouraging Successful Watershed Partnerships to Protect and Restore Water Resources. Retrieved June 27, 2003, from http://www.epa.gov/owow/watershed/initiative.

Williams, J., C. Wood, and M. Dombeck, eds. 1997. *Watershed Restoration: Principles and Practices.* Bethesda, MD: American Fisheries Society.

Yaffee, S., A. Phillips, I. Frentz, P. Hardy, S. Maleki, and B. Thorpe. 1996. *Ecosystem Management in the United States: An Assessment of Current Experience.* Washington: Island Press.

Chapter 11

Anderson, J., E. Hardy, J. Roach, and R. Witmer. 1976. *A Land Use and Land Cover Classification System for Use with Remote Sensor Data.* Geological Survey Professional Paper 964. Washington, DC: U.S. GPO.

Bryant, M., B. Smith, J. Randolph, M. Jeong, and M. Lipscomb. 2003. Urban Biodiversity in the Holmes Run/Cameron Run Watershed. Urban Biodiversity Information Node (UrBIN) Pilot. National Biological Information Infrastructure (NBII), U.S. Geological Survey.

Campbell, J.B. 1983. *Mapping the Land: Aerial Imagery for Land Use Information.* Washington, DC: Association of American Geographers.

Carstensen, L.W. 1999. "What Is GIS?" Training module for GIS Track of Faculty Development Institute, Virginia Tech. Blacksburg, VA.

Chattooga Conservancy. 1996. *Chattooga Watershed Conservation Plan.* Clayton, GA: Author. Retrieved June 28, 2003, from http://www.chattoogariver.org/ccp/ccp.htm.

Dale, V., and S. Beyeler. 2001. "Challenges in the Development and Use of Ecological Indicators." *Ecological Indicators* 1(1): 3–10.

Daratech, Inc. 2002. "GIS Software Growth a Dynamic 14.3%." Press Release. Cambridge, MA (November 6). Retrieved from http://www.gismonitor.com/news/pr/110702_Daratech.pdf.

Earth Science Research Institute (ESRI), Inc. *ESRI Map Book.* Various volumes. Accessed at http://www.esri.com/mapmuseum/index.html.

Earth Science Research Institute (ESRI), Inc. 2002. "What Is GIS?" Retrieved from ESRI website at http://www.gis.com/whatisgis/index.html.

Greene, R. 2000. *GIS in Public Policy: Using Geographic Information for More Effective Government.* Redlands, CA: ESRI Press.

Hart, M. 1999. *Guide to Sustainable Community Indicators* (2nd ed.). North Andover, MA: Sustainable Measures (http://www.sustainablemeasures.com/).

Hirschman, D., J. Randolph, and J. Flynn. 1992. "The Can-Do Book of Local Water Resources Management." Vol. C in *Sourcebook for Local Water Resources Management* (ten volumes), edited by J. Randolph. Blacksburg, VA: Virginia Water Resources Research Center and College of Architecture and Urban Studies, Virginia Tech.

Kent, R., and R. Klosterman. 2000. "GIS and Mapping: Pitfalls for Planners." *Journal of the American Planning Association* 66(2): 189–98.

Lillesand, T., and R. Kiefer. 2004. *Remote Sensing and Image Interpretation.* New York: John Wiley.

Muehrcke, P., and J. Muehrcke. 1998. *Map Use: Reading, Analysis and Interpretation.* Madison, WI: JP Publications.

National Research Council. 2000. *Ecological Indicators for the Nation.* Washington: National Academy Press.

O'Looney, J. 2000. *Beyond Maps: GIS and Decision Making in Local Government.* International City/County Management Association (ICMA). Redlands, CA: ESRI Press.

Randolph, J., and D. Zahm. 1998. "Information Technologies and Participation: Enhancing Communication and Interaction." In *Planning in Virginia,* pp. 26–28. Richmond: Virginia Chapter of the American Planning Association.

Sayre, R., E. Roca, G. Sedaghatkish, B. Youg, S. Keel, R. Roca, and S. Sheppard. 2000. *Nature in Focus: Rapid Ecological Assessment.* The Nature Conservancy. Washington, DC: Island Press.

Stone, B., and M. Rodgers. 2001. "Urban Form and Thermal Efficiency: How the Design of Cities Influences the Urban Heat Island Effect." *Journal of the American Planning Association* 67(2):186–98.

The Nature Conservancy. 1999. *Pathways: Building a Local Initiative for Compatible Economic Development.* Arlington, VA: Author.

Tomlin, C. 1983. *Digital Cartographic Modelling Techniques in Environmental Planning.* Unpublished doctoral dissertation, Yale University, New Haven, CT.

Chapter 12

Angoli, T. 2001. "Summary of the Status of On-site Wastewater Treatment Systems in the United States during 1998." In *On-site Wastewater Treatment: Proceedings of the 9th Symposium on Individual and Small Community Sewage Systems,* pp 316–22.

Brady, N., and R. Weil. 1999. *The Nature and Properties of Soils* (12th ed.). Upper Saddle River, NJ: Prentice Hall.

Coughlin, R., J. Pease, F. Steiner, J. Leach, A. Sussman, and J. A. Pressley. 1994. "Agricultural Land Evaluation and Site Assessment: Status of State and Local Programs." *Journal of Soil and Water Conservation* 49(1): 6–13.

Craul, P. 1999. *Urban Soils: Applications and Practices.* New York: John Wiley.

English, C., and T. Yeager. 2002. "Responsible Management Entities as a Method to Ensure Decentralized System Viability." *Small Flows Quarterly* 3(2): 25–29.

Gordon, S., and G. Gordon. 1981. "The Accuracy of Soil Survey Information for Urban Land Use Planning." *Journal of the American Planning Association* 47(3): 301–12.

Montgomery County (VA) Planning Department. 1984. *Land Evaluation and Site Assessment in Montgomery County, Virginia.* Christiansburg, VA: Author.

Toy, T., and G. Foster. 1998. *Guidelines for the Use of the Revised Universal Soil Loss Equation (RUSLE) Version 1.06 on Mined Lands, Construction Sites, and Reclaimed Lands.* Denver, CO: USDI-Office of Surface Mining.

USDA. Forest Service Southern Region. 2001. *Urban Forestry: A Manual for the State Forestry Agencies in the Southern Region.* Retrieved June 27, 2003, from http://www.urbanforestrysouth.usda.gov.

USDA. NRCS. 2000. "Erosion and Sedimentation on Construction Sites." Soil Quality—Urban Technical Note No. 1. Washington, DC: U.S. GPO.

USDA. NRCS. 2001a. *National Soil Survey Handbook.* Counties Soil Source (one example) http://www.statlab.iastate.edu/soils/nssh/.

USDA. NRCS. 2001b. *National Resources Inventory.* Washington, DC: U.S. GPO. http://www.nrcs.usda.gov/technical/NRI/.

USDA. SCS. 1983. *National Agricultural Land Evaluation and Site Assessment Handbook.* Washington, DC: U.S. GPO.

USDA. SCS. 1985. *Soil Survey of Montgomery County, Virginia.* Christiansburg, VA: Author.

U.S. EPA. 1993a. *Safer Disposal for Solid Waste: The Federal Regulations for Landfills.* EPA 530-SW-91–092. Solid Waste and Emergency Response. Washington, DC: Author.

U.S. EPA. 1993b. *Solid Waste Disposal Facility Criteria: Technical Manual.* EPA 530-R-93–017. Washington, DC: Author.

U.S. EPA. 1998. *A Citizen's Guide to Phytoremediation.* Retrieved from http://www.clu-in.org/products/citguide/phyto2.htm.

U.S. EPA. 2000. EPA Guidelines for Management of Onsite/Decentralized Wastewater Systems. EPA 832-F-00–012. Washington, DC: Author.

U.S. EPA. 2002a. *Municipal Solid Waste in the United States: 2000 Facts and Figures.* Retrieved from http://www.epa.gov/epaoswer/non-hw/muncpl/report-00/report 00.pdf.

U.S. EPA. 2002b. *Onsite Wastewater Treatment Systems Manual.* EPA 625-R-00–008. Office of Water. Retrieved from http://www.epa.gov/ORD/NRMRL/Pubs/625R00008/625R00008.htm.

Wischmeier W. H., and D. D. Smith. 1960. "A Universal Soil Loss Estimating Equation to Guide Conservation Farm Planning." *Proceedings of the 7th International Congress Soil Science Society* 1:418–25.

Chapter 13

Anderson, J. 2001. *Developing Digital Monitoring Protocols for Use in Volunteer Stream Assessment.* Major Paper. Master of Urban and Regional Planning. Blacksburg, VA: Virginia Tech.

California Department of Fish and Game. 1996. *California Stream Bioassessment Procedures.* Aquatic Bioassessment Lab. Sacramento: Author.

Chang, G., J. Parrish, and C. Souer. 1990. *The First Flush of Runoff and Its Effect on Control Structure Design.* Austin, TX: Environmental Resource Management Division. Department of Environmental and Conservation Services.

Claytor, R., and T. Schueler. 1996. *Design of Stormwater Filtering Systems.* Ellicott City, MD: Center for Watershed Protection.

Engman, E. T. 1986. "Roughness Coefficients for Routing Surface Runoff." *Journal of Irrigation and Drainage Engineering* 112(1): 39–53.

Dunne, T., and L. Leopold. 1978. *Water in Environmental Planning.* San Francisco: Freeman.

Federal Interagency Stream Restoration Working Group (FISRWG). 1998. *Stream Corridor Restoration: Principles, Processes, and Practices.* 15 Federal agencies. U.S. GPO 0120-A; Docs No. A 57.6/2:EN 3/PT.653. Retrieved from http://www.usda.gov/stream_restoration/.

Izaak Walton League of America. 1994. *Save Our Streams Stream Quality Survey.* Gaithersburg, MD: Author.

National Weather Service (NWS). 2002. Hydrologic Design Service Center. Retrieved June 23, 2003, from http://www.nws.noaa.gov/oh/hdsc/studies/prcpfreq.html.

Ohrel, R. 1996. "Simple and Complex Stormwater Pollutant Load Models Compared." Article 13 in *The Practice of Watershed Protection*. Ellicott City, MD: Center for Watershed Protection. Retrieved June 27, 2003, from http://www.stormwatercenter.net/Database_Files/Publications_Database_1Page470.html.

Prince George's County. 1999a. *Low-Impact Development: An Integrated Design Approach*. Largo, MD: Prince George's County, Maryland, Department of Environmental Resources.

Prince George's County. 1999b. *Low-Impact Development Hydrologic Analysis*. Largo, MD: Prince George's County, Maryland, Department of Environmental Resources.

Riley, A. 1998. *Restoring Streams in Cities: A Guide for Planners, Policy Makers and Citizens*. Washington, DC: Island Press.

Rosgen, D. 1994. "A Classification of Natural Rivers." *Catena* 22: 169–99.

Schueler, T. 1987. *Controlling Urban Runoff: A Practical Manual for Planning and Designing Urban BMPs*. Washington, DC: Metropolitan Washington Council of Governments.

Schueler, T. 1999. "Microbes and Urban Watersheds." *Watershed Protection Techniques* 3(1): 551–96.

Schueler, T. 2000. "Basic Concepts of Watershed Planning." In *The Practice of Watershed Protection*, edited by T. Schueler and H. Holland, pp. 145–61. Ellicott City, MD: Center for Watershed Protection.

Smullen, J., and K. Cave. 1998. *Updating the U.S. Nationwide Urban Runoff Quality Database*. 3rd International Conference on Diffuse Pollution. August 31–September 4, 1998. Scottish Environment Protection Agency, Edinburg, Scotland.

State of New York. 2001. *New York State Stormwater Management Design Manual*. Prepared by Center for Watershed Protection. Albany: NY Department of Environmental Conservation.

Steuer, J., W. Selbig, N. Hornewer, and J. Prey. 1997. *Sources of Contamination in an Urban Basin in Marquette, Michigan and an Analysis of Concentrations, Loads, and Data Quality*. U.S. Geological Survey, Water-Resources Investigations Report 97-4242.

USDA. National Resources Conservation Service. 1998. *Stream Visual Assessment Protocol*. Technical Note 99-1. Washington, DC: Author. Retrieved June 27, 2003, from http://www.nrcs.usda.gov/technical/ECS/aquatic/svapfnl.pdf.

USDA. Soil Conservation Service. 1986. *Urban Hydrology for Small Watersheds*. Conservation Engineering Division. Technical Release 55. Retrieved June 27, 2003, from ftp://ftp.wcc.nrcs.usda.gov/downloads/hydrology_hydraulics/tr55/tr55.pdf.

U.S. EPA. 1993. *Guidance Specifying Management Measures for Sources of Nonpoint Pollution in Coastal Waters*. EPA-840-B-93-001c. Washington, DC: Office of Water.

U.S. EPA. 1997. *Volunteer Stream Monitoring: A Methods Manual*. EPA-841-B-97-003. Office of Water (4503F). Washington, DC: Author. Retrieved June 27, 2003, from http://www.epa.gov/owow/monitoring/volunteer/stream/.

U.S. EPA. 1999. *Rapid Bioassessment Protocols for Use in Stream and Wadeable Rivers: Periphyton, Benthic Macroinvertebrates, and Fish*, 2d ed. EPA 841-B-99-002. Washington, DC: Office of Water. Retrieved from http//:www.epa.gov/owow/monitoring.rbp/download.html, September 11, 2003.

U.S. EPA. 2000a. *Liquid Assets 2000: America's Water Resources at a Turning Point*. EPA-840-B-00–001. Office of Water (4101). Washington, DC: Author.

U.S. EPA. 2000b. *The Quality of Our Nation's Waters: A Summary of the National Water Quality Inventory: 1998 Report to Congress.* EPA-841-S-00–001. Office of Water (4503F). Washington, DC: Author.

U.S. EPA. 2002. *Water Quality Conditions in the United States: A Profile from the 2000 National Water Quality Inventory.* EPA-841-F-02–003. Office of Water (4303F). Washington, DC: Author.

U.S. Weather Bureau. 1961. *Rainfall Frequency Atlas of the United States.* Technical Paper No. 40, Washington, DC: Author. Retrieved June 23, 2003, from http://www.erh.noaa.gov/er/hq/Tp40s.htm.

Virginia Department of Conservation and Recreation (VDCR). 1992. *Virginia Erosion and Sediment Control Handbook.* Richmond: Division of Soil and Water Conservation.

Washington State Code. 1997. *Water Quality Standards for Surface Waters of the State of Washington.* Chapter 173–201A WAC. Olympia, WA: State of Washington.

Chapter 14

Cappiella, K., and T. Schueler. 2001. "Crafting a Lake Protection Ordinance." *Watershed Protection Techniques* 3(4): 750–62.

Center for Sustainable Design, Mississippi State University. Undated. *Water Related Best Management Practices in the Landscape.* Prepared for USDA, NRCS. Water Runoff Management (http://www.abe.msstate.edu/csd/NRCS-BMPs/water.html); Stream System Protection, Restoration, and Resestablishment (http://www.abe.msstate.edu/csd/NRCS-BMPs/stream.html); Tree Protection and Restoration (http://www.abe.msstate.edu/csd/NRCS-BMPs/tree.html). All retrieved June 28, 2003.

Center for Watershed Protection. 1994. "Level Spreader/Filter Strip System Assessed in Virginia." *Watershed Protection Techniques* 1(1): 11–12.

Center for Watershed Protection. 2000. A Review of Stormwater Management Practices (slideshow). Retrieved June 28, 2003, from http://www.stormwatercenter.net/Slideshows/smps%20for%20smrc/sld001.htm.

Chang, G., J. Parrish, and C. Souer. 1990. *The First Flush of Runoff and Its Effect on Control Structure Design.* Austin, TX: Environmental Resource Management Division. Department of Environmental and Conservation Services.

Commonwealth of Virginia. 1999. *Virginia Stormwater Management Handbook.* Richmond: Department of Conservation and Recreation.

Commonwealth of Virginia. 2001. *Virginia Model Stormwater Ordinance.* Richmond: Department of Conservation and Recreation.

Federal Interagency Stream Restoration Working Group (FISRWG). 1998. *Stream Corridor Restoration: Principles, Processes, and Practices.* 15 Federal agencies. U.S. GPO 0120-A; Docs No. A 57.6/2:EN 3/PT.653. Retrieved from http://www.usda.gov/stream_restoration/.

Heraty, M. 1993. *Riparian Buffer Programs: A Guide to Developing and Implementing a Riparian Buffer Program as an Urban Stormwater Best Management Practice.* U.S. EPA Office of Oceans, Wetlands and Watersheds. Washington: Metropolitan Washington Council of Governments.

National Academy of Sciences. 2001. *Assessing the TMDL Approach to Water Quality Management. Commission on Geosciences, Environment and Resources.* Washington, DC: National Academy Press.

National Research Council (NRS). 1992. *Restoration of Aquatic Ecosystems: Science, Technology, and Public Policy.* Washington, DC: National Academy Press.

Prince George's County. 1999. *Low-Impact Development: An Integrated Design Approach.* Largo, MD: Prince George's County, Maryland, Department of Environmental Resources.

Prince George's County. 2002. *Low-Impact Development (LID): Integrated Management Practices Guidebook.* Largo, MD: Prince George's County, Maryland, Department of Environmental Resources.

Riley, A. 1998. *Restoring Streams in Cities: A Guide for Planners, Policy Makers and Citizens.* Washington: Island Press

Rogers, B., and A. Hazlett. 2001 "TMDLs: Are They Dead Letters?" *Agricultural Law Update* 4 (August): 4–5.

Schueler, T. 1994. "Invisibility of Steam/Wetland Buffers: Can Their Integrity Be Maintained?" *Watershed Protection Techniques* 1(1): 19–21.

Schueler, T. 1997. "Comparative Pollutant Removal Capability of Urban BMPs: A Reanalysis." *Watershed Protection Techniques* 2(4): 515–20.

Schueler, T. 2000. "Basic Concepts of Watershed Planning." In *The Practice of Watershed Protection,* edited by T. Schueler and H. Holland, pp. 145–61. Ellicott City, MD: Center for Watershed Protection.

State of New York. 2001. *New York State Stormwater Management Design Manual.* Prepared by Center for Watershed Protection. Albany: NY Department of Environmental Conservation.

USDA. NRCS. Undated. National Conservation Practices Standards website. Retrieved June 28, 2003, from http://www.ftw.nrcs.usda.gov/nhcp_2.html.

USDA. NRCS. 1999. CORE4 Conservation Practices Training Guide: Conservation Tillage, Nutrient Management, Pest Management, Buffers. Washington, DC: Author. Retrieved June 28, 2003, from http://www.ctic.purdue.edu/Core4/Core4TechnicalManual.pdf.

USDA. NRCS. 2002. Streambank and Shoreline Protection Manual. Lake County, IL. Retrieved June 28, 2003, from http://www.co.lake.il.us/planning/pdfs/Strm Manual.pdf.

USDA. Soil Conservation Service. 1986. *Urban Hydrology for Small Watersheds.* Conservation Engineering Division. Technical Release 55. Retrieved from http://www.wcc.nrcs.usda.gov/water/quality/common/tr55/tr55.pdf.

U.S. EPA. 1993. *Guidance Specifying Management Measures for Sources of Nonpoint Pollution in Coastal Waters.* EPA-840-B-93–001c. Office of Water. Washington, DC: Author.

U.S. EPA. 2000a. *Liquid Assets 2000: America's Water Resources at a Turning Point.* EPA-840-B-00–001. Office of Water (4101). Washington, DC: Author.

U.S. EPA. 2000b. *Low Impact Development (LID): A Literature Review.* EPA-841-B-00–005. Office of Water. Washington, DC: Author.

U.S. EPA. 2001. *The National Costs of the Total Maximum Daily Load Program* (Draft). EPA-841-D-01–003. Office of Water. Washington, DC: Author.

U.S. EPA. 2003. "Withdrawal of Revisions to the Water Quality Planning and Management Regulation and Revisions to the National Pollutant Discharge Elimination System Program in Support of Revisions to the Water Quality Planning and Management Regulation; Final Rule." *Federal Register.* March 19. 40 CFR Part 9, et al.:13608–14.

Winer, R. 2000. *National Pollutant Removal Database for Stormwater Treatment Practices* (2nd ed.). Center for Watershed Protection. Ellicott City.

Chapter 15

Aller, L., T. Bennett, J. Lehr, R. Petty, and G. Hackett. 1987. *DRASTIC: A standardized system for evaluating groundwater pollution potential using hydrogeologic settings.* EPA-600/2–87–035. Washington, DC: U.S EPA.

Breeder, N., and J. Dawson. 1976. *Roanoke County Groundwater: Present Conditions and Prospects.* Commonwealth of Virginia, State Water Control Board (SWCB). Bureau of Water Control Management. Planning Bulletin 301. Richmond: SWCB.

Crowley, J., and C. Tulloch. 2002. *Protocol Used to Identify High Risk UST Facilities in Santa Clara County (California).* Santa Clara, CA: Santa Clara Valley Water District.

Federal Interagency Stream Restoration Working Group (FISRWG). 1998. *Stream Corridor Restoration: Principles, Processes, and Practices.* GPO Item No. 0120-A; SuDocs No. A 57.6/2:EN 3/PT.653. ISBN-0–934213–59–3. Retrieved June 27, 2003, from http://www.usda.gov/stream_restoration/.

Fritch, T., C. McKnight, J. Yelderman, and J. Arnold. 2000. "An Aquifer Vulnerability Assessment of Paluxy Aquifer, Central Texas, USA, Using GIS and a Modified DRASTIC Approach." *Environmental Management* 25(3): 337–45.

Hamilton to New Baltimore (OH) Groundwater Consortium. 2003. Description of Programs. Retrieved June 28, 2003, from http://www.govconsortium.org.

Hayman, J. 1972. *The Significance of Some Geologic Factors in the Karst Development of the Mt. Tabor Area, Montgomery County, Virginia.* Master's thesis, Virginia Polytechnic Institute and State University, Blacksburg, Virginia.

Hirschman, D., J. Randolph, and J. Flynn. 1992. "The Can-Do Book of Local Water Resources Management." Vol. C in *Sourcebook for Local Water Resources Management* (ten volumes), edited by J. Randolph. Blacksburg, VA: Virginia Water Resources Research Center and College of Architecture and Urban Studies, Virginia Tech.

Osborn, N., E. Eckenstein, and K. Koon. 1998. *Vulnerability Assessment of Twelve Major Aquifers in Oklahoma.* Oklahoma Water Resources Board (OWRB). Technical Report 98–5. Oklahoma City: OWRB.

Santa Clara Valley Water District, California. 2001. *Santa Clara Valley Water District Groundwater Management Plan.* Santa Clara, CA: Author.

Tiemann, M. 2003. *Safe Drinking Water Act: Implementation and Issues.* Congressional Research Service. Library of Congress. Issue Brief for Congress. Order Code IB10118. Retrieved June 28, 2003, from http://www.ncseonline.org/nle/crs reports/03Jul/IB10118.pdf.

U.S. EPA. 1988. *Model Assessment for Developing Wellhead Protection Areas.* Washington, DC: Office of Groundwater Programs.

U.S. EPA. 2000. *Introduction to EPA's Drinking Water Source Protection Programs.* Washington, DC: Office of Water.

U.S. EPA. 2001. *Source Water Protection: Best Management Practices and Other Measures for Protecting Drinking Water Supplies.* Washington, DC: Office of Water.

U.S. Geological Survey. 1972. *Definitions of Selected Groundwater Terms.* USGS Water Supply Paper #1988. Washington, DC: Author.

U.S. Geological Survey. 1999. "Improvements to the DRASTIC Ground-Water Vulnerability Mapping Method." USGS Fact Sheet FS-066–99. Washington, DC.

Witten, J., and S. Horsley. 1995. *A Guide to Wellhead Protection.* Planning Advisory Service. U.S. EPA. PAS Report 457/458. Chicago: American Planning Association.

Chapter 16

American Forests. 1999. *Urban Ecosystem Analysis, Chattanooga, Tennessee, Metropolitan Region: Calculating the Value of Nature*. Washington, DC: Author. Retrieved June 28, 2003, from http://www.americanforests.org/resources/rea/.

American Forests. 2001a. *Gray to Green: Reversing the National Urban Tree Deficit*. Retrieved June 27, 2003, from http://www.americanforests.org.

American Forests. 2001b. *Urban Ecosystem Analysis, Atlanta Metro Area: Calculating the Value of Nature*. Washington, DC: Author. Retrieved June 28, 2003, from http://www.americanforests.org/resources/rea/.

American Forests. 2001c. *Urban Ecosystem Analysis, Willamette, Lower Columbia Region of Northwestern Oregon and Southwestern Washington State: Calculating the Value of Nature*. Washington, DC: Author. Retrieved June 28, 2003, from http://www.americanforests.org/resources/rea/.

American Forests. 2002a. *CITYgreen 5.0*. Washington, DC: Author.

American Forests. 2002b. *Urban Ecosystem Analysis for the Washington DC Metropolitan Area: An Assessment of Existing Conditions and a Resource for Local Action*. Washington, DC: Author. Retrieved June 28, 2003, from http://www.americanforests.org/resources/rea/.

Bernd-Cohen, T. and M. Gordon. 1998. *State Coastal Management Effectiveness in Protecting Beaches, Dunes, Bluffs, Rocky Shores: A National Overview* (Part of the Sea Grant National CZM Effectiveness Study for the Office of Ocean and Coastal Resource Management), National Ocean Service, NOAA, DOC. Washington, DC: NOAA.

Clark, J., J. Banta, and J. Zinn. 1980. *Coastal Environmental Management: Guidelines for Conservation of Resources and Protection against Storm Hazards*. The Conservation Foundation. Prepared for six federal agencies. Washington, DC: U.S. Government Printing Office.

Commission for Environmental Cooperation. 1997. *Ecological Regions of North America Toward a Common Perspective*. http://www.cec.org. Quebec, Ontario. Canada: Author. Retrieved June 28, 2003, from ftp://ftp.epa.gov/wed/ecoregions/na/CEC_NAeco.pdf.

Cowardin, L., Carter, and La Roe. 1979. *Classification of Wetlands and Deepwater Habitats of the United States*. FWS/OBS-79/31. Washington, DC: U.S. Department of Interior, Fish and Wildlife Service.

Federal Interagency Stream Restoration Working Group (FISRWG). 1998. *Stream Corridor Restoration: Principles, Processes, and Practices*. Washington, DC: Government Printing Office. Can be retrieved from http://www.usda.gov/stream_restoration/.

Grey, G., and F. Daneke. 1992. *Urban Forestry* (2nd ed.). Malabar, FL: Krieger Publishing.

Good, J., J. Weber, J. Charland, J. Olson, and K. Chapin. 1998. *Protecting Estuaries and Coastal Wetlands* (Part of the Sea Grant National Coastal Zone Management Effectiveness Study). Oregon Sea Grant Special Report PI-98–001. Corvallis: Oregon State University.

Goodwin, R., S. Hastings, and L. Ferguson. 1997. *Evaluation of Coastal Zone Management National Coastal Zone Management Effectiveness Study Programs in Redeveloping Deteriorating Urban Ports and Waterfronts*. Seattle: University of Washington.

Interagency Workgroup on Wetland Restoration (IWWR). 2002. *An Introduction and User's Guide to Wetland Restoration, Creation, and Enhancement*. NOAA, EPA,

Army Corps of Engineers, FWS, NRCS. Retrieved June 28, 2003, from http://www.epa.gov/owow/wetlands/finalinfo.html.

International Society of Arboriculture (ISA). 2001. *Guidelines for Developing and Evaluating Tree Ordinances.* Retrieved June 23, 2003, from http://www.isa-arbor.com/tree-ord/index.htm.

Keystone Center. 1991. Biological diversity on federal lands: Report of a keystone policy dialogue. The Keystone Center, Keystone, Colorado.

Landauer, R. 2001. "Exploring cities' leafy frontier." Retrieved June 28, 2003, from http://www.sactree.com/ruff/ufrf96/ Developed%20Areas%20as%20forests%20 article.doc.

Lewis, R. 1989. Wetland Restoration/Creation/Enhancement Terminology: Suggestions for Standardization. Wetland Creation and Restoration: The Status of the Science, vol. II. EPA 600/3/89/038B. Washington, DC: U.S. EPA.

Lewis, R. 1990. "Wetlands Restoration/Creation/Enhancement Terminology: Suggestions for Standardization." In *Wetland Creation and Restoration: The Status of the Science,* edited by J. A. Kusler and M. E. Kentula, pp. 417–22. Washington, DC: Island Press.

Marsh, W. 1978. *Environmental Analysis: For Land Use and Site Planning.* New York: McGraw-Hill.

McPherson, E. 2003. "Urban Forestry, The Final Frontier?" *Journal of Forestry* 101(3): 20–25.

McPherson, E. G., D. J. Nowak, and R. A. Rowntree. 1994. *Chicago's Urban Forest Ecosystem: Results of the Chicago Urban Forest Climate Project. Part 1.* NE GTR-186. Radnor, PA: USDA Forest Service, Northeastern Forest Experiment Station.

National Research Council. 1992. *Restoration of Aquatic Ecosystems: Science, Technology, and Public Policy.* Washington, DC: National Academy Press.

National Research Council. 1993. *Soil and Water Quality: an Agenda for Agriculture.* Washington, DC: National Academies Press.

National Research Council. 1995. *Wetlands: Characteristics and Boundaries.* Washington, DC: National Academies Press.

Odum, E. 1971. *Fundamentals of Ecology* (3rd ed.). Philadelphia: W.B. Saunders.

Salveson, D. 1994. *Wetlands: Mitigating and Regulating Development Impacts* (2nd ed.). Washington, DC: Urban Land Institute.

San Mateo County (CA). 1984. Overview and Resource Management, General Plan. San Mateo County: Department of Environmental Management.

Sayre, R., E. Roca, G. Sedaghatkish, B. Youg, S. Keel, R. Roca, and S. Sheppard. 2000. *Nature in Focus: Rapid Ecological Assessment.* The Nature Conservancy. Washington, DC: Island Press.

Somers, A., K. Bridle, D. Herman, and A. B. Nelson. 2000. *The Restoration and Management of Small Wetlands of the Mountains and Piedmont in the Southeast: A Manual Emphasizing Endangered and Threatened Species Habitat with a Focus on Bog Turtles.* Washington, DC: USDA. Retrieved June 28, 2003, from http://www.wcc.nrcs.usda.gov/watershed/piedmont/piedmont.html.

The Nature Conservancy. 1997. *Evaluacion Ecologica Integral: Parque Nacional del Este, Republica Dominicana Tomo 1: Recursos Terrestres.* Arlington, VA: Author.

U.S. Army Corps of Engineers. 1976. *Water Resources Development Plan, Charles River Watershed, Massachusetts.* Waltham, MA: Corps, New England Division.

USDA. Forest Service. 1990. *Urban and Community Forestry: A Guide for the Interior Western United States.* Ogden, UT: Forest Service, Intermountain Region.

USDA. Forest Service. 2001. *A Collaborative Approach for Reducing Wildland Fire Risks to Communities & the Environment: A 10-year Strategy.* Retrieved June 27, 2003, from http://www.fireplan.gov/FIRE.REPORT.1.pdf.

USDA. Forest Service. 2003. Forest Health Protection website. Retrieved June 28, 2003, from http://www.fs.fed.us/foresthealth/.

USDA. Forest Service, Southern Region. 2001. *Urban Forestry: A Manual for the State Forestry Agencies in the Southern Region.* Retrieved June 27, 2003, from http://www.urbanforestrysouth.usda.gov.

USDA. NRCS. 1998. *Riparian Forest Buffer.* Conservation Practice Job Sheet 391. Reprinted in USDA, NRCS. 1999. CORE4 Conservation Practices Training Guide. Washington, DC: Author. Retrieved June 28, 2003, from http://www.ctic.purdue.edu/Core4/Core4TechnicalManual.pdf.

USDA. NRCS. 1999. *Conservation Corridor Planning at the Landscape Level.* C. Johnson, Principal Investigator. Washington, DC: Watershed Science Institute, Wildlife Habitat Management Institute. Retrieved June 27, 2003, from http://www.wcc.nrcs.usda.gov/watershed/wssi-products.html.

USDA. NRCS. 2001. *National Resources Inventory.* Washington: USGPO. Retrieved June 28, 2003, from www.nrcs.usda.gov/technical/NRI.

USDA. Soil Conservation Service. 1986. *Urban Hydrology for Small Watersheds.* Conservation Engineering Division. Technical Release 55. Retrieved June 23, 2003, from http://www.wcc.nrcs.usda.gov/water/quality/common/tr55/tr55.pdf/.

U.S. Department of Interior, Fish and Wildlife Service. 2000. *Status and Trends of Wetlands in the Coterminous United States, 1986 to 1997.* Washington, DC: Author. Retrieved June 13, 2003, from http://wetlands.fws.gov/bha/SandT/SandT Report.html.

Wilson, E., ed. 1988. *Biodiversity.* Washington, DC: National Academy Press.

Wilson, E. 2002. *The Future of Life.* New York: Alfred A. Knopf.

Zinn, J. 1997. *Wetlands Mitigation Banking: Status and Prospects.* Congressional Research Service. Library of Congress. Issue Brief for Congress. Order Code IB16991. Retrieved June 28, 2003, from http://www.ncseonline.org/NLE/CRS/abstract.cfm?NLEid=16298.

Zinn, J., and C. Copeland. 2003. *Wetland Issues.* Congressional Research Service. Library of Congress. Issue Brief for Congress. Order Code IB16991. Retrieved June 28, 2003, from http://www.ncseonline.org/NLE/CRS/abstract.cfm?NLEid=16991.

Chapter 17

Adams, L., and L. E. Dove. 1989. *Wildlife Reserves and Corridors in the Urban Environment: A Guide to Ecological Landscape Planning and Resource Conservation.* Columbia, MD: National Institute for Urban Wildlife.

Barnes, T. G. 1999. *A Guide to Urban Habitat Conservation Planning,* Pub. 74. Lexington, KY: University of Kentucky Extension Service.

Beatley, T. 1994. *Habitat Conservation Planning: Endangered Species and Urban Growth.* Austin: University of Texas Press.

Beier, P., and S. Loe. 1992. "A Checklist for Evaluating Impacts to Wildlife Movement Corridors." *Wildlife Society Bulletin* 20:434–40.

Bradshaw, A. D. 1999. Natural ecosystems in cities—A model for cities as ecosystems. Plenary Session II. Cary Conference VIII, in *Urban Ecosystem Education: Its*

Importance, Foundations and Frontiers. Institute for Ecosystem Studies. Retrieved June 21, 2003, from http://www.ecostudies.org/cary8/plenary2.pdf.

Bryant, M., B. Smith, J. Randolph, M. Jeong, and M. Lipscomb. 2003. Urban Biodiversity in the Holmes Run/Cameron Run Watershed. Urban Biodiversity Information Node (UrBIN) Pilot. National Biological Information Infrastructure (NBII), U.S. Geological Survey.

Chicago Region Biodiversity Council. (undated). *Chicago Wilderness: An Atlas of Biodiversity.* Retrieved June 13, 2003, from http://www.epa.gov/glnpo/chiwild/. Chicago: Author.

Chicago Wilderness. 1999. *Biodiversity Recovery Plan.* Chicago: Author.

Diamond, J. 1975. "The Island Dilemma: Lessons of Modern Biogeographic Studies for the Design of Nature Preserves." *Biological Conservation* 7:129–46.

Federal Interagency Stream Restoration Working Group (FISRWG). 1998. *Stream Corridor Restoration: Principles, Processes, and Practices.* Washington, DC: Government Printing Office. Retrieved June 28, 2003, from http://www.usda.gov/stream_restoration/.

Fisher, E. 1996. "Habitat Conservation Planning under the Endangered Species Act: "No Surprises" & the Quest for Certainty." *Colorado Law Review* 67:371.

Forman, R., and M. Godron. 1986. *Landscape Ecology.* New York: John Wiley.

General Accounting Office (GAO). 1994. Endangered Species Act: Information on Species Protection on Nonfederal Lands. GAO/RCED-95–16.

Interagency Workgroup on Wetland Restoration (IWWR). 2002. *An Introduction to Wetland Restoration, Creation, and Enhancement.* Review draft.

International Association of Fish and Wildlife Agencies. 2001. *State Conservation Agreements: Creating Local and Regional Partnerships for Proactive Conservation.* Prepared by Mette Brogden. Washington, DC: Author.

James, F. C. 1999. "Lessons Learned from a Study of Habitat Conservation Planning." *BioScience* 49(11): 871–74.

Kareiva, P., S. Andelman, D. Doak, B. Elderd, M. Groom, J. Hoekstra, L. Hood, F. James, J. Lamoreux, G. LeBuhn, C. McCulloch, J. Regetz, L. Savage, M. Ruckelshaus, D. Skelly, H. Wilbur, and K. Zamudio. 1999. *Using Science in Habitat Conservation Plans.* Washington, DC: National Center for Ecological Analysis and Synthesis and American Institute for Biological Sciences.

Keystone Center. 1991. *Biological Diversity on Federal Lands: Report of a Keystone Policy Dialogue.* Keystone, CO: Author.

Leedy, D., R. Maestro, and T. Franklin. 1978. *Planning for Wildlife in Cities and Suburbs.* Planning Advisory Service 331. Chicago: American Planning Association

MacArthur, R. H., and E. O. Wilson. 1967. "The Theory of Island Biogeography." *Monographs in Population Biology* 1:1–203.

Noss, R. F., and A. Y. Cooperrider. 1994. *Saving Nature's Legacy: Protecting and Restoring Biodiversity.* Island Press, Washington, D.C.

Noss, R. F., and L. D. Harris. 1986. "Nodes, Networks, and MUMs: Preserving Diversity at All Scales." *Environmental Management* 10:299–309.

Noss, R. F., M. A. O'Connell, and D. D. Murphy. 1997. *The Science of Conservation Planning: Habitat Conservation under the Endangered Species Act.* Washington, DC: Island Press.

Pielou, E.C. 1975. *Ecological Diversity.* New York: John Wiley.

Pollak, D. 2001a. *Natural Community Conservation Planning (NCCP): The Origins of an Ambitious Experiment to Protect Ecosystems.* Sacramento: California Research Bureau, California State Library.

Pollak, D. 2001b. *The Future of Habitat Conservation: The NCCP Experience in California.* Sacramento: California Research Bureau, California State Library.

Randolph, J., and M. Bryant. 2002. "Urban Biodiversity Enhancing Data and Decision Tools for Urban Ecological Conservation." Paper presented at annual conference of the Association of Collegiate Schools of Planning, Baltimore, MD, November.

Scott, T. A., and M. Allen. (undated). "Functional Connectivity in Fragmented Landscapes." Working paper, Center for Conservation Biology, University of California, Riverside, CA.

Scott, T. A., and J. Sullivan. 2000. "Selection and Design of Multiple Species Preserves." *Environmental Management* 26(Supplement): S37–S53.

Scott, T. A., W. Wehtje, and M. Wehtje. 2001. "The Need for Strategic Planning in Passive Restoration of Wildlife Populations." *Restoration Ecology.* 9(3): 262–71.

Slingerland, G. 1999. *The Effect of the "No Surprises" Policy on Habitat Conservation Planning and the Endangered Species Act.* Master's thesis, Master of Urban and Regional Planning, Viginia Tech, Blacksburg, Virginia.

Smith, T. 1995. *Habitat Conservation Planning under the Endangered Species Act: Is It Ecosystem Management?* Masters Thesis, Urban and Regional Planning, Virginia Tech, Blacksburg, Virginia.

State of California, Department of Fish and Game. 2003a. Southern California Coastal Sage Scrub NCCP Region. Retrieved June 28, 2003, from http://www.dfg.ca.gov/nccp/cssreg.htm.

State of California, Department of Fish and Game. 2003b. San Diego Multiple Species Conservation Program. Retrieved June 28, 2003, from http://www.dfg.ca.gov/nccp/mscp/mscp_home.htm.

USDA. NRCS. 1999. *Conservation Corridor Planning at the Landscape Level.* C. Johnson, Principal Investigator. Washington, DC: Watershed Science Institute, Wildlife Habitat Management Institute. Retrieved June 28, 2003, from http://www.wcc.nrcs.usda.gov/watershed/wssi-products.html.

USDI. FWS. 2003. Conservation Plans and Agreements Database. Retrieved June 28, 2003, from https://ecos.fws.gov/conserv_plans/servlet/gov.doi.hcp.servlets.PlanReportSelect?region=9&type=HCP.

USDA. NRCS. 1999. *Conservation Corridor Planning at the Landscape Level.* C. Johnson, Principal Investigator. Washington, DC: Watershed Science Institute, Wildlife Habitat Management Institute.

USFWS/NMFS. 1996. *Habitat Conservation Planning Handbook.* Washington, DC: U.S. Department of the Interior.

Chapter 18

Anderson, L., W. D. Conn, C. D. Loeks, and J. Randolph. 1981. *Growth Management for Blacksburg's Environmentally Critical Areas.* Blacksburg, VA: Virginia Tech.

California Department of Housing and Community Development (CHCD). 2000. *Raising the Roof: California Housing Development Projections and Constraints, 1997–2020.* Sacramento: Author. Retrieved June 28, 2003, from http://www.hcd.ca.gov/hpd/hrc/rtr/.

Center for Compatible Economic Development (CCED). 1998. *Pathways: Compatible Economic Development.* Arlington, VA: The Nature Conservancy.

Clark, J. 1976. The Sanibel Report: Formulation of a Comprehensive Plan Based on Natural Systems. Washington, DC: The Conservation Foundation. Retrieved June 28, 2003, from http://www.worldpolicy.org/globalrights/environment/report/intro.html.

Commonwealth of Massachusetts. 2002. *Buildout Book. Where Do You Want to Be at Buildout?* Boston: Department of Environmental Affairs. Retrieved June 28, 2003, from http://commpres.env.state.ma.us/content/publications.asp#.

Commonwealth of Massachusetts. 2003. *Build Out Analyses and Maps.* Executive Office of Environmental Affairs. Retrieved June 28, 2003, from http://commpres.env.state.ma.us/content/buildout.asp.

Dasmann, R. 1964. *Wildlife Biology.* New York: John Wiley.

Hopkins, L. 1977. "Methods of Combination in Land Suitability." *Journal of the American Institute of Planners* 43(4): 386–400.

Lacy, J. 1990. *Manual of Build-Out Analysis.* Amherst, MA: Center for Rural Massachusetts.

McHarg, I. 1969. *Design with Nature.* Garden City, NJ: American Museum of Natural History.

National Park Service. 1997. *VERP: A Summary of the Visitor Experience and Resource Protection (VERP) Framework.* Denver, CO: U.S. Department of the Interior, National Park Service.

National Park Service. 2001. National Park Service Management Policies. Washington, D.C.: U.S. Department of the Interior, National Park Service.

Ortolano, L., and A. Shepherd. 1995. "Environmental Impact Assessment: Challenges and Opportunities." *Impact Assessment* 3(1): 3–30.

Phillips, C., and J. Randolph. 2000. "The Relationship of Ecosystem Management to NEPA and Its Goals." *Environmental Management* 26(1):1–12.

Randolph, J., and L. Ortolano. 1975. "Effect of NEPA on Corps of Engineers Planning for the Carmel River." *Environmental Affairs* 5(2): 213–53.

Raritan Basin Watershed Management Project (RBWMP). 2002. *Portrait of a Watershed.* Retrieved June 27, 2003, from http://www.raritanbasin.org.

Rees, W. 1996. "Revisiting Carrying Capacity: Area-Based Indicators of Sustainability." *Population and Environment* 17(2): 195–215.

Sayre, R., E. Roca, G. Sedaghatkish, B. Youg, S. Keel, R. Roca, and S. Sheppard. 2000. *Nature in Focus: Rapid Ecological Assessment.* The Nature Conservancy. Washington, DC: Island Press.

Stankey, G., D. Cole, R. Luca, M. Peterson, S. Frissell, and R. Washburn. 1985. *Limits of Acceptable Change (LAC) for Wilderness Planning.* General Technical Report INT-176. Washington, DC: USDA Forest Service.

State of Washington. 1998. *SEPA Handbook.* Olympia: Department of Ecology.

Tahoe Regional Planning Agency. 1982. *Environmental Threshold Study.* South Lake Tahoe, CA: Author.

Tahoe Regional Planning Agency. 1986. *Regional Plan for the Lake Tahoe Basin.* Stateline, NV: Author. Retrieved June 2003 from http://www.trpa.org/Goals/preface.html.

The Nature Conservancy. 1999. Pathways: Building a Local Initiative for Compatible Economic Development. Arlington, VA: Author.

Town of Blacksburg. 2001. Comprehensive Plan. Retreived June 28, 2003, from http://www.blacksburg.gov/comp_plan/.

Wackernagel, M., and W. Rees. 1995. *Our Ecological Footprint: Reducing Human Impact on the Earth.* Philadelphia: New Society Publishers.

Way, D. 1978. *Terrain Analysis* (2nd ed.). New York: McGraw-Hill.

Index

Page numbers followed by *f* indicate material in figures, those followed by *t* indicate material in tables, and those followed by *b* indicate material in boxes.

Island Press Board of Directors

Victor M. Sher, Esq., *Chair*
Environmental Lawyer, Sher & Leff

Dane A. Nichols, *Vice-Chair*
Environmentalist

Carolyn Peachey, *Secretary*
President, Campbell, Peachey & Associates

Drummond Pike, *Treasurer*
President, The Tides Foundation

Robert E. Baensch
Director, Center for Publishing
New York University

David C. Cole
President, Aquaterra, Inc.

Catherine M. Conover
Chair, Board of Directors
Quercus LLC

Henry Reath
President, Collectors Reprints Inc.

Will Rogers
President, Trust for Public Land

Charles C. Savitt
President, Center for Resource Economics/Island Press

Susan E. Sechler
Senior Advisor on Biotechnology Policy
The Rockefeller Foundation

Peter R. Stein
General Partner
The Lyme Timber Company

Diana Wall, Ph.D.
Director and Professor, Natural Resource Ecology Laboratory
Colorado State University

Wren Wirth
President, The Winslow Foundation